ASTROLOGY
AND THE POPULAR PRESS

ASTROLOGY AND THE POPULAR PRESS

English Almanacs 1500–1800

BERNARD CAPP

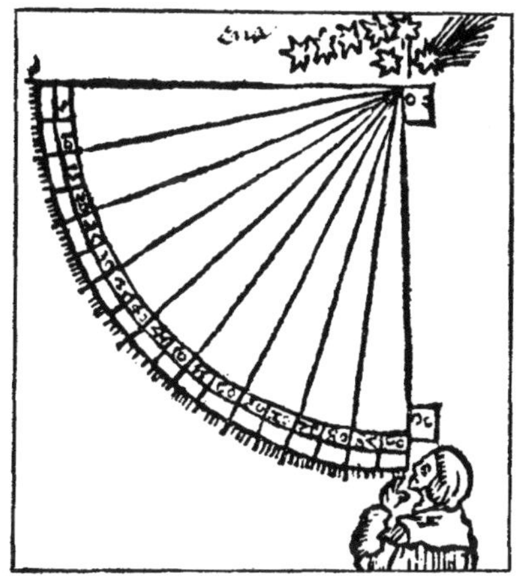

faber and faber

This edition first published in 2008
by Faber and Faber Ltd
3 Queen Square, London WC1N 3AU

Printed by CPI Antony Rowe, Eastbourne

A CIP record for this book is available from the British Library

ISBN 978-0-571-24191-0

Come, who buys my wares? Here's the
Sun, Moon and Stars all for sale!
from an American almanac for 1822

Contents

Illustrations

between pages 256 and 257

in the text

Preface

THE ALMANAC-MAKERS of early modern England boldly took as their subject the whole of Creation. I have tried to give here a general survey of their major interests and ideas, and I hope at least to persuade specialists that, in almost every field, almanacs constitute a neglected source well worth further investigation. My first intention was to take the story only to 1700. It gradually became apparent that this was impossible to justify, and the brief epilogue on the eighteenth century has grown into a full chapter. Even so the coverage of this later phase is less comprehensive than of the earlier centuries, and the bibliography of almanacs ends in 1700. I have incorporated details of the Hanoverian compilers and titles in Appendix I.

I owe much to the pioneering researches of E. F. Bosanquet, and to the bibliographical details given in the *Short-title Catalogue* and Wing. I am grateful to Miss Pantzer for permission to consult a draft of the forthcoming second edition of volume one of *S.T.C.* My great debt to Keith Thomas will be obvious in all that follows. I would also like to thank Margaret Spufford for some timely encouragement in the late stages of preparation. I have learned much from discussion following papers and lectures on this subject which I have given over the last few years.

I am very grateful to Mr. John Ehrman and Mrs. W. Potter for permission to use their private collections, and to the librarians and archivists of the British Library, Lambeth Palace, the Company of Stationers, the Guildhall, Westminster Abbey, Dr. Williams's Library, the Society of Antiquaries and the Society of Genealogists; the Bodleian Library, Oxford, and Balliol, Brasenose, Christ Church, Corpus Christi and Trinity Colleges; the University Library, Cambridge, and Emmanuel, St. John's and Trinity Colleges; the National Library of Scotland; Edinburgh, Glasgow, Lancaster, London and Newcastle University Libraries; the John Rylands Library, Manchester; Trinity College, Dublin; Canterbury, Lincoln and Salisbury Cathedral Libraries; and Shrewsbury School Library. I am also grateful to the archivists of all the County Record Offices who have been, almost without exception, immensely helpful in answering queries and supplying material. The librarians of Yale, Harvard, the Folger Shakespeare Library and the University of Illinois kindly supplied me with microfilms, and I would like to thank the University of Warwick for a grant towards the cost. The Library at Warwick has been most helpful in obtaining books and other materials.

Finally, I owe a lot to Helen and Michael, for their forbearance and for much besides.

University of Warwick September 1977

CHAPTER ONE

Introduction

THERE IS A certain irony in the modern fear that man's mastery over the environment will lead to its destruction. A far greater preoccupation for thousands of years was his inability either to understand or to control the world in which he lived. Until fairly recent developments in medicine and science, mankind was powerless to withstand natural disasters such as plague and famine. This situation produced, perhaps inevitably, both a sense of impotence and a belief in the existence of extraneous, supernatural forces. Early forms of religion and magic developed partly as attempts to explain the creation and operation of the world. Their function was also, very often, to strengthen man's position in his struggle against the environment. By prayers, sacrifices, charms and spells he sought to appease the gods and to harness supernatural powers to his own ends.

Among these early systems of explanation was the cult of the stars, which was to grow in the course of time into the complex science of astrology. The obvious link between the sun's movements and the changing rhythms of the seasons led very naturally to an interest in the heavens. The moon and the immensity of the stars must have made an equally powerful impact on the imagination, heightened by such dramatic phenomena as meteors, eclipses and comets. A sophisticated science of astrology evolved among the Babylonians, and was taken over and modified by the Greeks and Romans. In the second century A.D. the Egyptian astronomer, Ptolemy, reduced astrology to a clear set of laws which provided—with additions by early mediaeval Arab astronomers—the basis of European astrology for many centuries to come.

Astrology, it has been rightly said, was the most systematic attempt to explain natural phenomena according to rigorous scientific laws until the modern scientific revolution.[1] Whereas most early religions explained the vagaries of life on earth in terms of the erratic behaviour of quarrelsome gods, the astrologer set out to prove that all events were explicable by the rules of his science. The basis of astrological teaching in mediaeval and early modern Europe lay in the assumption of a close relationship between the planets and stars and all objects on earth, both living and inanimate. The planets possessed, in varying mixtures, the four qualities (heat, cold, dryness and moisture) which corresponded to the four elements of which all terrestrial things were made: fire, earth, air and water. Medical science taught that human physiology comprised four 'humours', corresponding with the elements: thus phlegm corresponded with water, melancholy with earth, blood with air and choler with fire. The astrologer observed the eclipses of the sun and moon, and the motions of the planets through the signs of the zodiac. He calculated the constantly-changing relationships of the planets to one another (in conjunction, opposition, trine and others). And from this material he was able to establish the nature of planetary influences reaching the earth at any given moment, and to predict their likely consequences for man and nature. Astronomy and astrology were thus complementary; in the words of a seventeenth-century almanac-maker, the study of the motions and effects of the stars were simply the 'theorical' and 'practick' parts of a single science. The commonplace analogies of the period between death and the Last Judgement, and between the 'little world of man' and the universe, were images which grew naturally out of the prevailing and orthodox belief in the intimate relationship between microcosm and macrocosm.[2] Astrology lay at the heart of mediaeval science, its ramifications leading to medicine, physiology, botany and metallurgy.

The science of astrology was divided into two parts, *natural* and *judicial*. Natural astrology was concerned with the general character of planetary influences in such fields as agriculture and medicine. Judicial astrology was the attempt to interpret these influences in order to make predictions and give advice. General predictions for a city or country showed the likelihood of war, disease or famine in the year or years ahead. The destiny of an individual could be predicted by drawing up the client's 'nativity', a calculation of the state of the heavens at his birth. 'Elections' denoted the process of choosing the most propitious moment, when the influence of the planets would be most favourable, for undertaking any action, ranging from matters of state to the weaning of an infant. Finally there were 'horary' questions, when the astrologer resolved personal problems (medical, moral and very often matrimonial) according to the state of the heavens when the question was posed. Not all branches of the subject enjoyed equal repute. Horary astrology, an Arab innovation, was especially controversial and lost ground during and after the Renaissance, when there was a tendency to reject mediaeval accretions and return to the purity of the Ptolemaic science.[3] Most attacks on astrology, however, were aimed only at particular aspects, and even in the sixteenth century an uncompromising rejection of its basic assumptions was very rare indeed.

Astrology was incorporated into the belief-system of mediaeval Christendom with little difficulty. Astrologers taught that God was the first cause, and defined the stars as secondary causes operating by divine permission. They argued that the stars inclined man's will without compelling it, and were therefore able to claim that their science did not destroy moral responsibility. With this accommodation, few people seem to have been conscious of any real conflict between the two systems of supernatural explanation. Very many of the greatest mediaeval astrologers were indeed churchmen, sometimes high in the ecclesiastical hierarchy, such as the fifteenth-century French cardinal, Pierre d'Ailly.[4] Even the blasphemous implications of calculating Christ's nativity, or seeking to explain the success of Christ and Mahomet according to a theory of history based on recurring major astrological conjunctions, produced no great outcry. The practice survived into the seventeenth century. The Restoration clergyman, John Butler, published a nativity of Christ in 1671, arguing that the reality of the incarnation was proved conclusively by the fact that Christ's body 'submitted unto the impression of the stars, as do other men's'.[5]

The close links between astrology and medicine made the astrologer-physician a respected figure at the courts of kings, princes and even popes. In 1437 the University of Paris decreed that every physician and surgeon should possess a copy of the current almanac, as a necessary aid to medical practice. Later in the same century the astrologer, Jean Avis, produced annual almanacs for almost forty years for the University's faculty of medicine, which was indeed known as '*facultas in medicina et astrologia*'.[6] Naturally, rulers also wished to exploit the prophetic powers of their astrologers. From the early fifteenth century annual prognostications were written by court astrologers for the rulers of many European countries.[7] Successive popes shared their interest. Sixtus IV (1471–84) had been noted for his astrological prowess. Pius II imprisoned a man for predicting his death (correctly, as it turned out), but his successor allegedly released and rewarded the captive. Paul of Middelburg, a noted astrologer of the late fifteenth century, was made a bishop and designated cardinal. In the early sixteenth century the court of Paul III became a centre of astrological learning; Lucar Gaurico, who had predicted Paul's accession, was rewarded with a bishopric. Gaurico was later invited to calculate the most propitious moment for work to begin on an important new building planned by the pope. On the day selected, Gaurico's assistant was present at the site and proclaimed the precise moment in a loud voice, whereupon a cardinal, in full robes, set the foundation stone in position.[8]

Throughout Europe monarchs, nobles and indeed city councils competed to secure the services of the best-known astrologers. Regiomontanus, one of the most famous in the late fifteenth century, was at the head of a cosmopolitan profession which had a wide choice of patrons in many countries. Royal patronage continued throughout the sixteenth century and much of the seventeenth. In France, the most celebrated practitioner was Nostradamus, who was influential at the court of Henry II's widow, Catherine de Medici, and was at the centre of a group of astrologers favoured by Catherine and her sons.[9] His influence has indeed lasted much longer, for admirers in every succeeding age have discovered references to contemporary events in his brilliantly delphic utterances. The Bourbon kings were rather more cautious. Nevertheless, Henry IV had an astrologer present at the birth of his son, the future Louis XIII; a generation later Louis in turn ordered the astrologer, Morin, to attend the birth of *his* son, the future Louis XIV. Later still, Morin was concealed in the royal bedroom to record the precise moment when the young Louis XIV and his bride consummated their marriage, in order to calculate the horoscope of the dauphin who would hopefully be conceived.[10] Court astrologers were also active in Spain. A counsellor advised Philip II not to visit Mary Tudor in England in 1556 because of astrological prophecies that there would be a conspiracy against him there. The Habsburg Emperor, Rudolf II, was well known as a devotee and patron of astrology and the occult.[11] In Italy the papal bull of 1631 against judicial astrology was prompted by recent subversive predictions rather than by a general disapproval of the art. Even towards the end of that century it was alleged that all the cardinals continued to maintain private astrologers.[12]

Late mediaeval England was an astrological backwater, but its kings shared the conventional beliefs of the age. One Master Welch calculated the most propitious time for the coronation of Henry VI. Richard de Vinderose, an Englishman trained in France, became prominent as an astrologer at Henry's court; he was succeeded under the Yorkist, Edward IV, by a Master Eustache.[13] The Italian astrologers, William Parron and Jerome Cardan, were attached on a semi-official basis to the courts of Henry VII and Edward VI respectively, as was Nicholas Kratzer, a German, to that of Henry VIII. Both Henry VIII and Mary patronized the English astrologer-priest, John Robins; Elizabeth favoured the astrologer and mathematician, John Dee. In the early seventeenth century the royal favourite, Buckingham, patronized Dr. John Lambe (apparently a fraud, rather fittingly, unlike his predecessors). During the interregnum William Lilly was seen as the 'State-Astrologer', and even after the Restoration there are some traces of the role of court astrologer in the position of Lilly's patron, Elias Ashmole.[14]

The extent of astrological practice in late mediaeval and early Tudor England is uncertain, but it was probably very limited. No major works on the subject were published during the first half of the sixteenth century, and there was no echo in England of the furore surrounding the great conjunction of Saturn and Jupiter in 1524, which some Continental scholars saw as a sign of the world's approaching end.[15] A nobleman might consult a foreign astrologer, but the dearth of simple vernacular guides to the subject makes it unlikely that there were many practitioners in the countryside to serve ordinary people. For most of the population, astrology was probably no more than a set of customs and beliefs based on moon-lore, eclipses, and phenomena such as the rising and setting of the Dog Star, handed down verbally from one generation to the next.

The revival of English astrology began in the second half of the sixteenth century. It was closely linked with the renaissance of mathematics; the leading mathematicians of the day, such as Dee, Allen and Leonard Digges, were also famed as astrologers. For John Dee, part of the explanation lies in his neo-platonic belief in an animistic universe, which led him to investigate the occult qualities of numbers and of stars, and into the higher reaches of alchemy.[16] More important, however, was the stimulus given by the development of applied mathematics. Digges, Dee, Recorde and others were concerned primarily with such topics as navigation, for which an accurate knowledge of astronomy was essential. The history of astronomy, astrology and applied mathematics in England shows repeatedly the close connections between the three fields.[17] Nevertheless, the bibliographies of leading astrological works of the seventeenth century, such as Sir Christopher Heydon's *Defence of Iudiciall Astrologie* (1603) and

William Lilly's *Christian Astrology* (1647), revea l the continuing debt of English writers to Continental authorities. Not until the middle of that century did English astrology reach its full maturity. By that time, paradoxically, it was already beginning to part company with astronomy, mathematics, medicine and the whole mainstream of scientific development.

The development of astrology at a popular level naturally owed much to the new intellectual vitality of the applied sciences. The foundations were also prepared by the circulation, in translation, of Continental prognostications and works such as the perpetual almanac, *The Kalender of Shepherdes*, translated from the French. It was only a matter of time before the English press developed sufficiently to set about exploiting the large popular market which clearly existed. This stage was reached in the mid-century; the rise of the cheap almanac coincided with the rise of the popular printed ballad. The circulation of almanacs helped—and in turn was helped by—the activities of astrological practitioners. Their roles were complementary. The almanac spoke in general terms of the harvest, disease and wars, while the consultant found solutions to individual problems and queries. No doubt the authority of the printed word, set out in weighty and portentous tones, gave an added depth to popular beliefs, and helped to enhance the status and respectability of the local practitioner.

The popularity of astrological practitioners, and later of printed guides, supports the suggestion that they were seen as supplying a need apparently ignored by the English Church after the Reformation: the harnessing of supernatural powers to help men avert danger and overcome obstacles in their daily lives.[18] The miraculous powers widely attributed to the sacraments, and the ability of a legion of saints to intervene on behalf of their votaries, were dismissed at the Reformation as papist superstitions, and swept away. The priest lost his magical aura. It was 'never a merry world since . . . the parson left conjuring', remarked the seventeenth-century lawyer, John Selden; his note of regret sprang from the belief that the magician-priest 'kept thieves in awe, and did as much good in a country as a justice of the peace'.[19] In fact, a considerable number of clergy preserved some kind of dual role as late as the seventeenth century by practising magic and astrology.[20] But most renounced the supernatural powers popularly attributed to them before the Reformation, and it was natural for many laymen to seek substitutes. The astrologer was a major beneficiary. Though he could not control the power of the stars directly, he could harness it through elections, and so enhance the prospects of success in any undertaking. One common indication of faith in astrology was the 'sigil', a charm thought to preserve favourable planetary influences, and to place them permanently at the disposal of the wearer. Magic here clearly fused with astrology.[21] Similarly, some astrologers taught that the stars offered a defence—sometimes, it was claimed, the only defence—against witchcraft and sorcery. It is likely that at the village level there was often little distinction between the astrologer and the magician or 'cunning man'.[22]

It may be the case, then, that we need separate causes to explain the new intellectual vigour of astrology in Elizabethan England and its simultaneous spread at a popular level. The science kept its academic respectability while gaining a new social dimension. The excitement generated by an important conjunction in 1583 and by a major eclipse in 1652 contrasts strikingly with the near silence of 1524.[23] Throughout the seventeenth century, a stream of clients poured into the astrologer's consulting room, from peers to serving-maids, and from Catholics to Levellers and Ranters. During the civil war Royalists and Parliamentarians alike exploited the propaganda value of astrological predictions.[24] In the field of medicine, very many reputable physicians and surgeons followed astrological precepts in the Tudor period, and a considerable (though smaller) number continued to do so in the Stuart age. In the mid-seventeenth century the village physician with a smattering of astrology culled from an almanac was said to be regarded by his neighbours as 'a little God-Almighty'.[25] We may doubt how far the patient understood the principles of the science, but as the phrase implies ignorance could be the 'mother of devotion' in astrology and medicine as well as religion.[26] Contemporaries noted that the physician (like his modern descendants) concealed prescriptions from the public gaze by a crabbed, abbreviated handwriting, which, one writer complained, 'seemeth rather to be Arabic'. Impostors claimed exotic titles and origins to impress the gullible. 'I believe I have seen twenty mountebanks that have given physic to the Czar of Muscovy', the editor of *The Tatler* remarked sardonically. 'The great Duke of Tuscany escapes no better.'[27]

Nevertheless, the seventeenth century did see a growing number of handbooks which set out the basic rules of astrology in a clear and simple manner. Popular knowledge of the science was probably greater in the late Tudor and the Stuart period than ever before or since. Astrological terms passed into common usage; a few echoes have survived down to the present day, in such words as jovial, lunatic, and mercurial. In the process by which simple moon-lore developed into a pattern of astrological beliefs more elaborate and of far wider application, nothing was to have so great a role as the annual almanac.

CHAPTER TWO

The Development of the Almanac: Astrology and the Popular Press

Wit, learning, order, elegance of phrase,
Health, and the art to lengthen out our days,
Philosophy, physic, and poesie,
All this, and more, is in this book to see,

declared Richard Allestree in modest praise of his almanac for the year 1622.[1] To any modern reader, such an assertion belongs to a world of fantasy. Yet, when Allestree wrote, the sale of annual almanacs had probably outstripped those of any other category of books. In the 1660s, for which detailed evidence survives, sales averaged about 400,000 copies annually, a figure which suggests that roughly one family in three bought an almanac each year.[2] The almanac-seller was a familiar figure in the streets of London and in the provinces—and even, according to a Restoration wit, in hell itself, where the Devil always possessed a copy for the current year.[3] The most successful compilers became household names. *When the King Enjoys His Own Again*, perhaps the most popular song of the mid-seventeenth century, contained puns on the names of six contemporary almanac-makers.[4] Bottom's almanac in *A Midsummer Night's Dream* remained anonymous, but Ben Jonson and other dramatists expected their audiences to be able to recognize allusions to Allestree, Bretnor and many other compilers.[5] From the middle of the century several almanacs began to include a portrait of the author. The features of William Lilly, circulated annually in thousands of copies for forty years, were probably the best known of anyone in England after the king.[6]

The appeal of the almanac did not lie in any literary value. A recent critic speaks sharply of the 'nasty lushness' of its prose, and the contemporary charge that many of the verses were the schoolboy exercises of the Elizabethan controversialist, Gabriel Harvey, was on the whole rather flattering.[7] The almanac was successful because it filled a wide variety of roles, cheaply and concisely. Whereas we think of the modern almanac as an extravagant prophecy, its predecessor had a largely utilitarian purpose. It contained valuable information on such matters as fairs, highways and later posts, and supplied medical and farming notes. In the dark nights before the arrival of artificial lighting, a table of the moon's phases had an obvious value quite apart from any astrological significance. 'What man nowadays, that hath any dealings in the world's affairs', asked the compiler, Joseph Chamberlaine, 'but hath need of a Kalendar, whereby he may know the day of the month, the moveable Feasts, the Lawdays, and the like?' One fierce critic of judicial astrology was willing to concede that 'if we had not almanacs, great losses, inconveniences and confusions in human affairs would immediately ensue.'[8] The almanac was thus in part a reference-book. Indeed several handbooks of the period adopted the name, though they contained nothing astrological. *The Attornies Almanack* (1627), for example, was a legal guide, and *The Money-Monger. Or the Usurer's Almanack* (1626) merely supplied tables of interest.[9]

The golden age of English almanacs, however, was the period from 1640 to 1700, when they plunged into political, social and religious controversies. Most successful of all was William Lilly, whose political predictions brought him overnight celebrity. His first edition, for 1644, was sold out within a week, and a few years later a preacher addressing the Society of Astrologers in London could pronounce him to be the undisputed head of the profession in England.[10] During this same period the almanac-makers supplied, more than ever before, the public appetite for sensationalism, violence and bawdiness. John Gadbury inserted scientific notes, but knew he would have pleased his readers more if he had 'told them a story of dragons seen in the air in Sussex, . . . some *ignis fatuus* haunting Clerkenwell, . . . killed a king or two, destroyed an army', and generally given free rein to his imagination.[11] Fortified with confident predictions of unnatural murders, rapes and piracies, the reader could wait with patience for the detailed accounts of these events which ballads and (later) newspapers would supply in due course. (One contemporary indeed defined the newspaper of the interregnum as a retrospective almanac.[12]) Henry Coley described prodigies such as battles in the sky between ships and armies, and promised his readers 'vast slaughter' and a 'deluge of blood'.[13] Another almanac reported the discovery of a race of South Sea Islanders, 'eleven foot high and all hairy', though even this could not rival the scoop of a Scottish almanac which printed a prophecy (in verse) 'uttered by a mermaid to a Dutch-skipper' on a voyage to Greenland.[14] Modern scandals pale beside John Booker's revelation in

1664 that at Rome there were '40,000 harlots, courtesans, &c, and maintained for the most part by the clergy there'.[15] There was further excitement in the scandalous abuse flung at each other by rival astrologers. Charges of plagiarism and incompetence were a regular feature during the reign of James I, and were revived and intensified in the 1640s when the political and religious issues of the civil war were disputed with unconstrained personal rancour.[16] Renewed political upheavals from the late 1670s brought an intensification of the personal feuds. John Gadbury, John Partridge, George Parker and their disciples denounced each other as traitors, impostors, papists or fanatics. At the level of personal scurrility, Partridge was easily victorious. His almanacs declared that Gadbury had debauched another man's wife, and had then contrived the murder of her husband. Parker, he alleged, had locked his wife in a garret for a week, whipped her, and later driven her out to make room for his mistress.[17] Partridge's personal and political virulence aroused a great deal of resentment and scorn. But it was only in the early years of the next century that an adequate assailant appeared, when Jonathan Swift, the satirist, produced a mock almanac for 1708 solemnly predicting the date of the astrologer's death. Swift and other wits subsequently asserted, with some success, that Partridge had indeed died, but their victim was by no means ruined: having begun life as a cobbler, he died in 1715 with pretensions to gentility, leaving an estate of over £2,000.[18]

The origins of the almanac were less sensational. An almanac was, technically, a table of the astronomical and astrological events of the coming year: the movements and conjunctions of the planets and stars in the zodiac, and details of eclipses. As such it can be traced back, like astrology, to antiquity. The manuscript almanacs of the Middle Ages often combined a kalendar, which supplied ecclesiastical information, notably the dates of the festivals of the Church. More common, till the sixteenth century, were the carved sticks or rods known as 'clog almanacs', made from wood, brass and probably horn. A series of notches and symbols provided a calendar showing the lunar cycle and the Christian feasts. Simple clog almanacs were small enough to fit into a pocket, while the larger were hung near the fireplace; they were still in use in northern England in the late seventeenth century.[19]

Following the invention of printing, almanacs (supplying astrological data) and prognostications (predictions derived thence) were among the earliest works to be published, at first separately. Gutenberg issued a printed almanac in 1448, and by the 1470s large numbers were being published.[20] The prognostication was also an established genre by that decade. Manfred of Boulogne, who settled in Italy, issued editions for thirty-five years in the late fifteenth century. The Laet family of Antwerp and Borchloen began a long tradition in 1469, with works which circulated widely in Flanders and, in translated editions, in France and later (by 1493) England.[21] The earliest surviving printed prognostication dates from about 1470, and many others appeared in the following years in Germany, France, Italy, Hungary, the Netherlands and Poland.[22] Probably the first to be published in England were by an Italian, William Parron, who published a series in both Latin and English in the period 1498–1503. Parron was linked for a time to the court of Henry VII, but disappeared abruptly—perhaps as a result of the embarrassing death of the queen at the age of thirty-seven after he had predicted that she would live to be eighty.[23]

The transition from manuscript to printed almanac was gradual. An intermediate stage was the xylograph (a form of wood engraving) produced on a long strip of vellum and designed to be updated each year by hand. One copy, beautifully illustrated, was still in use after much modification at the close of the sixteenth century.[24] Manuscript almanacs were still composed throughout the Tudor period and beyond. John Robins, formerly chaplain to Henry VIII, and prebendary of Windsor, compiled a perpetual calendar in 1549 for his friend, a Master Tildesley. Simon Forman and Sir Christopher Heydon, well-known astrologers, drew up almanacs with no apparent plans for publication. Another was compiled in 1644 by Thomas Lydiat, formerly tutor to Prince Henry.[25] In the 1580s Gabriel Frende circulated his almanacs in manuscript for some years before any were published, and a century later John Silvester of Bristol followed the same course.[26] Even in early printed editions, the astrologers' former links with aristocratic patrons were still sometimes apparent. William Parron sought to please the king as well as a wider public. Elis Bomelius, an astrologer and physician born in Bremen, declared that his almanac for 1567 was for the use of 'his singular good Lord, the Lord Lumley' (to whom a translation of a prognostication by Nostradamus was also dedicated); in later years Bomelius became court astrologer to the Czar Ivan IV.[27] Another Elizabethan compiler, George Hartgill, dedicated his works to his patron, the Marquis of Winchester.[28]

Following the disappearance of Parron, the only astrological works published in England for some time seem to have been small almanacs setting out astrological data for several years to come, and containing nothing prophetic. Prognostications, and later works containing both almanac and prognostication, were firmly in the hands of Continental astrologers. By far the most important was the Laet family, the dynasty of Flemish astrologers and physicians whose works appeared annually from 1469 to about 1550. Editions for the English market were at first translated abroad, printed in Antwerp and then shipped to England, but English printers soon became aware of the possibilities. Richard Pynson, the king's printer, organized the translation of Laet's prognostication for 1520, preferring Laet to other compilers because of the popularity of his earlier works and because he was known 'of old for an expert master in that science'.[29] Other printers were quick to imitate. The Continental origins of all the Laets' editions were always evident in the detailed predictions they gave for the provinces and towns of the Low Countries, and from the fact that the fortunes of Henry VIII were handled after those of the Pope, Emperor and King of France. Nevertheless, the series provided a firm, regular basis for later English developments, and explored all the forms subsequently used: the broadside 'sheet' almanac, designed to be hung on a wall, the quarto, octavo (destined to become the standard form) and the small pocket sextodecimo, the ancestor of the modern diary.

The Laets were only the most prominent of many Continental astrologers whose works were translated for the English market in the first half of the sixteenth century. Among others were Jean Thibault, who claimed to be astrologer to the Emperor Charles V, Master Salomon, a Jewish physician who also wrote 'to the laud and praise' of Charles, and Mathias Brothyel of Ravensburg, whose work was dedicated to Frederick, Count Palatine.[30] Most of the Continental works originated in Germany and the Netherlands, reflecting current commercial ties and the early development of printed almanacs in these areas. To attempt all, a weary translator remarked, would be 'a tedious business'.[31] The only Italian works were prophecies by the mediaeval astrologer, Montulmo, published in the 1550s. France was represented by the important *Kalender of Shepherdes*, a large perpetual calendar which contained religious, moral and astrological advice, and rules for preserving health. The first English translation appeared in 1503, and despite the work's Catholic flavour there were many further editions throughout the century and beyond. In the early seventeenth century Arthur Hopton expressed the hope that his *Concordancy of Years* (1612) would at last supplant it.[32]

The imported editions of the early sixteenth century contained a wide range of material: a calendar, weather forecasts, predictions of the harvest, lists of 'good' and 'evil' days, medical notes, and sometimes the Gospels laid down for church services.[33] Some compilers added further information. Achilles Gasser, for example, went beyond the usual discussion of dearth or plenty, and supplied a detailed breakdown of likely price levels for various cereals, fruit, dairy products and metals.[34]

A political section was a feature of almost all early prognostications. The authors attempted, prudently, to avoid provocation. Brothyel's list of expected plagues was an indirect appeal for social and political passivity. Diseases, he wrote, were divine vengeance on 'stiff-necked or inobedient persons, for God doth always punish the stubborn and unruly people, as we read in holy scripture'.[35] Laet's prediction for 1517 that Henry VIII would be inclined to 'pass the time in honour among fair ladies' was too early to have the barbed significance it would later acquire, and a forecast in the late 1530s that Henry would encounter matrimonial difficulties was by then platitudinous.[36] Nevertheless, the government looked with suspicion upon astrological predictions which it realized possessed, like other forms of prophecy, an obvious subversive potential. Fears of offending authority probably account for the absence of English writers in this field in the first half of the century, despite the buoyancy of the market.[37] The first apparently native product to include a prognostication was a small, sextodecimo edition published anonymously in 1539.[38] The first author to reveal his identity was Andrew Borde, a former Carthusian monk, who in 1545 announced proudly that he was 'an Englishman of the University of Oxford'. Although the prognostication no longer survives, Borde conceded on the title-page that to predict future events was to infringe God's sovereignty and the king's laws (presumably referring to the Witchcraft Act of 1542), so the predictions were probably couched in very general terms.[39] Borde was followed a few years later by Anthony Askham, priest, physician and brother of the better-known Roger, tutor to Queen Elizabeth. Askham published a series of almanacs and lively prognostications for the years 1548–57.[40]

At the mid-century, Continental astrologers were still dominant. There were regular editions by Sauvage of Antwerp in the 1540s and Hubrigh of Middelburg (in Zeeland) in the 1550s and 1560s. But the same period saw the rapid emergence of the English almanac. A series issued by Henry Low of Salisbury began in 1554, and was supplemented by the regular works of Cunningham and Williams (from 1558), Vaughan (1559), Hill (1560), Mounslow (1561) and Securis

(1562), and a number of occasional works by others. A timely handbook appeared in 1558 explaining how to use an annual almanac.[41] To some extent this development was a natural evolution, but it was probably related also to the incorporation of the Company of Stationers in 1557, which facilitated governmental supervision of the press, and may also have held out to printers and booksellers the prospect of an organized defence in case of trouble.[42] A further contributory cause was no doubt the popular excitement created by the publication in numerous editions of the cryptic but dramatic political predictions of the French astrologer, Nostradamus, in 1559 and subsequent years. A critic complained that he 'reigned here . . . like a tyrant with his sooth sayings', and his works probably served to stimulate the market for astrological prophecy.[43]

The government was still sensitive to the dangers of political prophecy, and the royal injunctions of 1559, which set up a system of licensing for the press, were applied to control prognostications. The editions of Nicolson for 1563 and Stephins for 1569, for example, both carried assurances that they had been 'perused and allowed' according to the injunctions.[44] In 1562 twenty booksellers were fined for selling a prognostication by Nostradamus, probably an unauthorized edition.[45] Elis Bomelius sought to avoid the repercussions that might follow a detailed political prophecy by listing the effects of a solar eclipse over twenty years earlier, and suggesting that similar events might follow a comparable eclipse in the coming year; even so, an overactive interest in matters of state landed him in prison.[46] A series of proclamations against seditious pamphlets in 1568–9, prompted by the troubled situation which culminated in the Northern Rebellion, heralded a further clamp-down by the government. The nineteen editions issued for 1567 shrank to a mere six for 1571, mostly (and perhaps all) licensed by the Archbishop of Canterbury or his chaplains.[47] Much stricter control for the future was guaranteed the same year by making almanac-publication a monopoly, granted to two stationers, Watkins and Roberts. This arrangement survived until the death of Watkins in 1599, after which almanacs were produced by the assigns of Roberts until 1603. James I issued a new monopoly to the Company of Stationers, in whose hands control remained until the late eighteenth century.[48] Political speculation did not disappear altogether, but after 1571 it was reduced to extremely vague and ambiguous generalizations, and this remained so until 1640.

During the Elizabethan period the almanac rapidly assumed its standard form. The first section contained a calendar and details of planetary motions and conjunctions, together with a table showing the legal terms, and the 'Anatomy' or 'zodiacal man' (a figure, unchanged since classical times, which showed the organs and parts of the body controlled by the various signs of the zodiac).[49] The prognostication usually had a separate title-page, and discussed the four quarters of the year, with the weather prospects and prevalent diseases, medical notes and data on farming and gardening. Other standard features were gradually added. A list of fairs was first included by Leonard Digges in 1556 and became common in the following decade, road directions appeared in Gossenne's edition for 1571, and a table giving the dates of kings since the Conquest was introduced at about the same time. The development of the almanac's secondary role as a diary seems to have begun with Hubrigh's edition for 1565, which contained a blank page facing the calendar for each month. *A Blancke and Perpetuall Almanack* (1566) was designed primarily for the reader to note debts, expenses and other 'things that passeth from time to time (worthy of memory to be registered)'.[50] The format was quickly imitated, by Bomelius in 1567, and Thomas Hill, who described his edition for 1571 as 'a book of memory, necessary for all such, as have occasion daily to note sundry affairs'. An almanac for 1582 by Evans Lloyd contained blank pages for accounts ready marked off in columns headed 'L.s.d.' Works of this kind became known in the trade as 'blanks', to distinguish them from the standard type, known as 'sorts'.

English compilers were predominant during Elizabeth's reign, and relatively few Continental predictions were translated. The prophecies of Rudolph Graphaeus of Deventer for 1598 probably attracted notice because they proclaimed the fall of the Ottoman Empire in 1610. The *Certaine Wonderfull Predictions* of the French astrologer, Himbert de Billy, published in 1604, offered gloomy vistas of wars, disasters, rebellions and royal mortalities, but contained on almost every page a reassurance that they might be averted by repentance and divine mercy, so that 'none shall feel these calamities, except barbarous and strange nations, which call not upon his holy name.'[51] In 1622 there appeared the prophecies of the Lombard mathematician, Magini. The work was essentially an anti-Spanish diatribe, in which Magini described the misery of the American Indians under Spanish rule. He called on all European states to resist the spread of Spanish power, and on all Italians to 'unite our selves together, and force the Spanish to leave our borders; our country is strong enough to defend itself.'[52]

In addition to almanacs proper, there was a category of cheap perpetual prognostications offering advice and rules of divination. Some claimed exotic origins. One was ascribed to Kinki Abenezrah, 'a wandering Jew'—an allusion to the ancient legend of the Jew condemned to roam the world for ever in atonement for his cruelty to Christ at the crucifixion.[53] The same legend was echoed in another title, *Erra Pater* (allegedly a 'Jew born in Jewry'), which was published at least a dozen times between the Reformation and the civil war, and occasionally thereafter. *Erra Pater* was the most successful of the handbooks aimed at the bottom end of the market for almanacs. Like the *Kalender of Shepherdes*, its primary function was to explain astrological medicine and inform the reader how to ensure that he 'shall never have infirmities of body'.[54] It added lists of lucky and unlucky days, and crude semi-astrological rules of prophesying by thunderstorms, the moon's changes, the day of the week on which 1 January fell, and so on. Later editions added lists of fairs, highways and other data from conventional almanacs. Astrologers were justifiably scornful of the whole compilation, and wits often mistranslated its title as 'erring father' or 'father of lies'. Booker and Wharton labelled each other 'Erra Pater' as a term of abuse.[55] But it is clear that Erra Pater and kindred works such as *Godfridus, Arcandam* and the *Compost of Ptolomeus* enjoyed widespread popularity.[56] Information of a similar kind appeared in *A Perfyte Pronostycacion Perpetuall* (c. 1555), which was aimed specifically at 'the ignorant' and 'them which knoweth not a letter on the book'. The compiler met the needs of the illiterate by adding crude illustrations of sickly cattle, sinking ships, and corpses.[57] *A Prognostication Everlasting* by Leonard Digges (first published in 1553) contained some comparable material but was a much more ambitious work, with serious astronomical and mathematical data, and it appeared in such respectable libraries as Sir Walter Ralegh's.[58]

The increasing popularity of almanacs provoked a series of works against them. Though belief in natural astrology was almost universal in Tudor England, there was considerable scepticism over the claims of judicial astrologers to be able to predict the future. Similar criticism had met the early Continental astrologers. Printed satires of German almanacs were circulating as early as the 1470s, and Rabelais's *Pantagrueline Prognostications* was only the most famous of several French equivalents. Laet's prognostication for 1520 contained a vindication of astrology against his detractors, and Cornelius Scute included a reply to a satirist who had criticized him.[59] The campaign against the English almanac followed three broad lines of attack. One was to condemn it for drawing men away from God, by offering information which was diabolical in origin. Another stressed its subversive and antisocial effects in producing panics and confusion. A third approach was to ridicule the whole subject as a mere fraud and confidence trick.

Many works were of course aimed at judicial astrology as a whole, but some were directed specifically at almanacs. One of the earliest was William Fulke's *Antiprognosticon* (1560), provoked by the recent spate of works by Nostradamus, and carrying the attack to the leading English compilers. *A Short Treatise* by Francis Coxe, himself an astrologer, was also concerned with Nostradamus.[60] As early as 1569 Nicholas Allen exploited the devastating method of printing data from rival almanacs side by side to illustrate their blunders and contradictions. The method was modern, but it failed to liberate even the author from the assumptions of the age; he merely concluded 'the fault to be in the artificer, not in the art', and recommended his readers to consult the almanacs of one (William) Johnson, who seemed a 'good, honest man and skilful'.[61] An Elizabethan surveyor, Edward Worsop, was more sweeping in rejecting the predictions of almanacs as no more than blind guesses,[62] but perhaps the most impressive work of the period was by the celebrated Puritan, William Perkins.[63] He denounced almanacs for producing 'distrust in God' and 'contempt of the providence of God', and tried to prove that it was unlawful to buy or use prognostications. They were, in any case, abject failures for their prophecies generally fell out 'flat otherwise than they say, to their perpetual shame'. 'Truly I am persuaded', he added, 'that it is the judgement of God upon them.' Perkins attacked the ambiguity of the predictions and their 'absurd, unknown' terminology, and demonstrated their contradictions by printing several weather-forecasts side by side. He ridiculed too the exotic authors, 'wondrous doctors having a great deal of small learning, and being far born in Chaldea, Persia, Arabia, Jewry'. The stars may be an instrument of divine intervention in human affairs, he conceded, but their significance was beyond human comprehension, and they were at most only one of several methods at God's disposal. Perkins was equally critical of the motives of the average reader. 'Thy whole desire is to fill thy coffers', he complained, 'and to heap up wealth' by exploiting possible shortages.

One of the most common forms of attack was the spurious prognostication. Some of these were serious works, informing the reader that astrology was unlawful and supplying a set of biblical precepts declared sufficient for all occasions.[64] But the majority were satirical. The first, *A Mery Prognostication* (1544) was a compound in verse of nonsense, mild social satire and ridicule of the almanac's empty but solemn predictions.

If the ninth day of November
Had fallen upon the tenth day of December,

the compiler wrote gravely,

It had been a real hot year for bees
For then would the Moon be like a green cheese.

In 1591 there appeared the first of a series of burlesque almanacs, in prose, which combined predictions of the obvious—'old women that can live no longer shall die for age'—with attacks on contemporary social habits. The mock almanac was to flourish throughout the Jacobean age.[65] The combined efforts of critics and satirists appear, however, to have made little impact on the public. A bookseller in Chester was supplied with nearly four hundred new almanacs in the autumn of 1650, but he thought it necessary to add to his stock only one copy of a single work against astrology.[66]

The almanac trade developed steadily in the seventeenth century under the control of the Stationers' Company. There was increasing specialization. *Perkins* provided a very full chronology (a table of historical events and dates), *Woodhouse* and *Dade* contained detailed lists of fairs and agricultural advice, Swan's *Ephemeris* supplied data on herbal medicine, and Rose and Fly provided specimen forms of bonds, bills of acquittance, apprenticeship indentures and even wills. Several compilers continued to discuss the probable price and availability of various goods. In 1585 Lloyd went beyond corn and cloth and included speculation about dates, sugar, rice and other commodities.[67]

Titles were varied to aim at particular occupational and other groups. The first in the field was John Tapp's *Seamans Kalendar* (first published 1602); later came *The City and Country Chapmans Almanac* and *The Weaver's Almanack*.[68] Others were still more specific. One set out excise rates for brewers; *The Constables Calendar* summarized the duties of that office; and *The Farriers Almanack* listed the diseases of cattle and horses, and prescribed remedies.[69] Editions by and for women first appeared in the interregnum, though they did not become common till the end of the century.[70] Sheet almanacs grew steadily in popularity. Even before the death of Elizabeth they were commonly seen on screens and doors, and posted up in chandlers' and barbers' shops. Their sales rose steeply from 28,000 in 1664 to about 100,000 in 1687. An edition for 1678, 'adorned with sculptures, lively representing the liberal arts and sciences', was advertised as 'an ornament for closets, chambers and shops'.[71]

From the 1640s different varieties of political beliefs were catered for by Lilly, Booker, Wharton and others. Religious rivalries appeared at the same time, ranging from the *Scripture Kalendar* by the Baptist, Henry Jessey, to the Catholic almanacs of the 1660s and 1680s. The Restoration *Protestant Almanack* 'set forth the ridiculousness' of Catholicism, while *The Episcopal Almanack* abused all nonconformists and *The Yea and Nay Almanack* concentrated on the Quakers.[72] Catchpenny titles were quick to exploit popular moods. During the panic over the alleged Popish Plot (to kill Charles II and re-establish Catholicism) there appeared *The Last Protestant Almanack*. Only when the agitated reader turned past the title-page did he discover the anticlimactic announcement that this was 'the last that has been, not that shall be published'.[73]

The seventeenth century also witnessed a rapid development in regional specialization. Although publishing was confined to London (and later, to a lesser extent, Cambridge and Oxford), the astronomical calculations were often for the meridian of the town or village where the compiler lived. The almanacs of Vincent Wing were thus composed for North Luffenham, Rutland, and those of John Vaux were for St. Helen Auckland, Durham, where he was curate. Lists of fairs often had a local emphasis. The first to appear, by Leonard Digges, contained only fairs in Kent; the edition for 1607 by Henry Alleyn for Petworth in Sussex (where he was born) listed 108 fairs in Surrey and Sussex. Similarly, John Tanner of Amersham, Bucks., announced in 1683 that the local lord of the manor was reviving the old market in the town, 'both for corn, and the women's market'.[74] Some of the 'chronologies' adopted a regional character, notably Vaux's almanacs stressing northern affairs, and Pigot's edition for 1630 which concentrated on Shropshire events. In a few cases this feature developed into a general survey of a county comparable in miniature to the popular works of contemporary local historians.[75]

Other authors chose different forms of specialization, by providing popularized accounts of scientific developments, for example, or an introduction to classical mythology.[76] Many, perhaps regrettably, yielded to a temptation to write poetry, usually pastoral verses on the changing seasons. The results ranged from competent to abysmal.[77]

Even medical advice, on blood-letting and emetics, was offered in verse:

> Now art thou bid by gentle May
> Purge, vomit, bath and bleed.

In *Hudibras*, the satirist Samuel Butler remarked justifiably that the almanac-maker could

> an elegy compose
> On maggots squeez'd out of his nose.

One astrologer, William Pool, indeed surpassed this by composing a doggerel verse to celebrate leaving excrement on the grave of a magistrate under whom he had formerly suffered.[78]

Political prophecies, vague and in decline during the first half of the century, once more became a common feature of the almanac from 1640. The most daring and successful compilers, such as Lilly, Wharton, Gadbury, and Partridge, committed themselves to a dangerously partisan position, and all risked imprisonment and even execution. Many other writers, however, preferred to shelter behind a screen of platitudes and cryptic ambiguity. Adam Fouleweather's burlesque prophecy that old men would die was not merely a caricature: the prophecy did appear regularly in serious works.[79] Lilly's platitudinous prediction of 'claps got by . . . polluted ladies' provoked a reader to query whether claps could be caught from any other source.[80] Ambiguity was an inevitable characteristic of astrology. Its rules were phrased in generalizations, and practitioners conceded that the stars could not be wholly binding, for men retained some degree of free will and God's power was sovereign.[81] Lilly's almanacs always contained the motto '*non cogunt*'—they (the stars) do not compel. 'Mention not a great evil to happen to any Prince,' he advised, 'but only some danger of such a thing.' William Andrews was a specialist in this technique. His cryptic hint in 1675, 'God bless the City of London from fire, and unruly actions', contained, typically, an in-built escape clause. John Wing was another master and surpassed even Nostradamus with such delphic remarks as 'Who lurks in a corner now, Ha?' The interrogatory form was a favourite device for hinting at future events without commitment. 'Why not an ecclesiastical person, or lawyer, promoted to great honour?' ran a typical entry in John Russell's almanac for 1661.[82]

Many predictions were of course more specific, and a certain number appeared to be fulfilled. As early as 1569 John Securis had printed the prophecy of Regiomontanus which was duly 'discovered' to refer to the Spanish Armada. John Booker achieved fame by his alleged prediction of the death of Gustavus Adolphus of Sweden in 1632. Richard Edlin correctly prophesied a great plague to afflict London in 1665.[83] With a little special pleading, the list could easily be extended. Vincent Wing's prediction of the death of a great man in August 1658 could be applied to Cromwell's death on 3 September. John Gadbury claimed in 1668 that his prophecy in the preceding year that many eminent people would die had been vindicated by the demise of the Pope, Bishop Wren, the Shah of Persia and the Queen of Poland. Andrews conceded that the Pope had not died in 1666, as he had expected, but he had at least been 'much indisposed'.[84] Critics complained that the people noted a few dramatic successes more than a multitude of total failures. Astrologers simply ascribed disastrous errors to God's unforeseeable intervention, or hinted that censorship had prevented them from revealing all they had known.[85] Lilly's career was not ended by his failure to predict the Scottish invasion of 1648, nor the upheavals of 1659–60. He explained the first omission with the casual remark that 'the wicked people of that nation deluded me'. The fall of Richard Cromwell and the other revolutions of 1659 what 'man or angel could predict?' The cause was the 'finger and hand of God: the actions themselves so miraculous . . . that they were not in any way demonstrable, or to be found out by the sharpest rule of Astrology'. The restoration of the king in 1660, another failure, was an act 'above nature'. When the second Anglo-Dutch war brought humiliating failures instead of the predicted triumphs, Lilly turned to divine intervention by a wrathful God, 'without doubt our heinous sins thereunto moving him'. 'It was our sins we feared all along', he added sententiously, 'and which we frequently mentioned.'[86] Similarly Gadbury replied to the widespread criticism that astrologers had failed to predict the Great Plague or Fire of London by claiming that he had been referring to these events in his prophecy that 'London now/ Some *petit* discontents begins to know.' 'I called them *petit*', he explained disingenuously, later, 'because I wished them so.' Persistent criticism, he thought, was merely an affliction predestined by the astrologer's nativity.[87] Other compilers resorted at times to the defence that their science was in its infancy, and necessarily imperfect, or conceded graciously that they too were human and fallible:

> Since Adam's Fall, we all transgress, alack;
> And thou amongst the rest, poor almanac. [88]

The primary objective of the Stationers' Company, or more accurately the smaller group of stationers who controlled the lucrative English Stock (which included almanacs), was to extract the maximum profit from their concession. They were energetic in resisting attempts to undermine or abolish the monopoly, and in waging war against those who flouted it. The government generally gave support, though it was not wholly consistent, and periodically renewed the Company's grant. There was one loophole by which it was possible to issue an annual prognostication, provided there was no almanac. Thus John Silvester, whose draft almanac was rejected by the Company, retaliated by issuing annual prognostications for several years in the 1690s. But popular taste demanded an almanac, and this device did not pose a serious threat.

The major challenge to the Company came from the two universities. Seeking a dependable foundation from which to launch more ambitious and academic projects, they regarded almanacs and schoolbooks as a valuable prize for the university presses. Cambridge made the first bid, and in 1623 persuaded the Privy Council to grant the university printer (Cantrell Legge) the right to share in printing certain privileged books, including any almanacs which might be offered first to the University, not the Company. Cambridge made good use of this concession, and the appearance of a number of almanacs by apparently fictitious authors (such as Lakes, Rivers and Waters, in obvious imitation of the well-known works by Edward Pond) suggests that it was sponsoring editions rather than waiting for them to be offered. In 1631 the privileges were reduced, and in 1639 the Cambridge authorities signed an agreement by which the university press undertook to print almanacs only with the written consent of the Company, in return for an annual payment of £200 and a guarantee that an adequate supply of work would be provided. Thus *Pond* for 1651, for example, comprised a first portion printed at London, and a second at Cambridge. Later agreements in 1655 and 1670 were similar in form, the generosity of the terms varying according to the energy with which the printers had challenged the Company's position.[89]

Oxford entered the struggle in 1632 as part of Archbishop Laud's efforts, as chancellor, to create a strong university press. Its threat of publishing almanacs became reality in 1637 when the university printer issued editions by Booker, Cowper and Wyberd. A prompt reaction by the Company led to a covenant of forbearance in the same year, by which the University was to be paid £200 a year to refrain from publishing further almanacs. With variations, this agreement lasted for twenty-five years until the ambition of Dr. Fell provoked a new dispute. In 1672 the Oxford press produced about 30,000 pocket almanacs by Maurice Wheeler, a minor canon of Christ Church. But with no organized channels of distribution, the University was forced to accept an agreement along fairly traditional lines: it was to publish only a sheet almanac (still appearing as *The Oxford Almanac*) in return for an annuity of £100 from the Company.[90] This agreement survived, broken only during the political turmoil of 1688 when the University seized its chance and published twenty-three illegal almanacs for 1689, blatantly designed to capture the traditional market.[91]

There were challenges too from hopeful individuals who urged the crown to revise the Company's grant in their favour. The most determined interloper was an old cavalier named John Seymour, who in 1669 received a grant entitling him to publish any almanac first offered to him. The Stationers found an excuse under the Printing Act of 1662 to raid Seymour's press at Westminster and smash the type, and they showed their anxiety by hiring the attorney-and solicitor-general to plead their case before the Privy Council. Despite further raids, Seymour remained steadfast. He achieved something of a *coup* by publishing the edition for 1676 by the eminent astrologer, John Gadbury, claiming to have royal authority; this development provoked a suit in the Court of Common Pleas. Seymour published two further almanacs in the following year, and only came to terms in 1678, when he accepted £200 yearly from the Company in return for surrendering his rights.[92] A lesser area of dispute, the publication of almanacs in Welsh, was resolved in 1679 when the Company fined one Thompson for illegal printing, and made an agreement with Thomas Jones, who compiled and published a series of Welsh almanacs from 1680.[93] A few years later William Lloyd, Bishop of St. Asaph, urged Fell to accept a draft sheet almanac in Welsh to provide profitable work for the Welsh press at Oxford.[94]

The Seymour episode showed the limits of the government's support for the Company. In this area, as in others, Charles II did not always abide by his own laws. In 1669 a printer, Peter Lillicrap, was questioned by the Company for printing a Catholic almanac which had been brought to him by one Father Basil, claiming to act on the orders of the king. Undeterred, the Company sent Lillicrap for trial.[95] A few years later, in 1674, William Godbid was asked about an almanac allegedly by Sir Jonas Moore, which he said he had printed at the king's 'special order'. Torn between offending the crown and conceding its claims to exclusive control, the Company compromised: Godbid made a submission, and paid a token fine of half a crown.[96]

The struggle against illegal and counterfeit almanacs was unending. The Company was vigilant in tracking down and fining printers who offended, confiscating their stocks and sometimes their printing presses.[97] Serious offenders were prosecuted. Roger Bradley, a frame-maker of Distaff Lane who was discovered printing an illegal almanac for 1697, was ordered to be proceeded against in Chancery.[98] The interlopers showed an impressive resourcefulness. A search of the King's Bench prison in 1685, following a tip-off, revealed copies of an almanac being produced by one of the prisoners.[99] Lack of astrological knowledge proved no obstacle. John Booker, whose almanacs were often counterfeited, complained that his edition for 1642 had been reprinted illegally and passed off as an almanac for 1643.[100] It was a common practice for interlopers to use the author's name, the title and format of an almanac already established. During the second half of the seventeenth century, the almanacs of Andrews, Gadbury, Partridge, Trigge and Vincent Wing all appeared with notices warning the reader against spurious imitations; Partridge complained that three or four fake editions of his almanac circulated each year.[101] In 1650 William Lilly had to compete with an imitator who stole his name and even his portrait.[102]

The breakdown of printing controls in the turbulent 1640s facilitated the work of the interloper, and also made possible a stream of burlesque almanacs. Probably because the authorized editions supported parliament or were non-political, the satirists were strongly royalist in sympathy. Jokes, and crude ribaldry against astrology, were mixed with a constant vendetta against the political, social and religious trends of the revolutionary period.[103] The genre continued for some years after the Restoration, becoming still more extreme in language and political sentiment. The Company searched for and seized copies whenever possible, with some success: *Tom a Bedlam's Almanac* and *Punchanella's Almanac* have survived in name alone.[104] Copies still exist of others, including *Montelion* which in 1662 contained a mildly obscene drawing and a picture of Hugh Peter, Cromwell's former chaplain, with his alleged mistress, a butcher's wife; the work was seized on the orders of the Secretary of State, on the grounds of 'the vile contents'.[105] Most successful of all was *Poor Robin's Almanac* by

William Winstanley, which first appeared in 1662 and was promptly suppressed as 'scandalous' (though only after 3,000 copies had been distributed). It is indicative of the Company's sound commercial instincts that the almanac appeared in later years under its own auspices, and continued throughout the century, selling about 7,000 copies a year and of course undermining the market for illicit satirical rivals. *Poor Robin*'s formula was to combine jokes and satire with much of the useful information to be found in the conventional works. It thus contained both a serious and a facetious chronology, and a calendar with saints' days as well as one with villains' days—the latter a wonderfully bizarre collection, including in a typical year (1666) the names of Cesare Borgia, Moll Cutpurse, Robin Hood, Empson and Dudley, Mother Shipton, Dr. Faustus, Caligula, John Lilburne, Richard III, Tom Thumb, Copernicus, Peter Quince and the Witch of Endor.[106]

The Stationers' campaign against the illegal production of almanacs was weakened by their own lax standards of professional morality, which left them open to the temptation of underhand dealing. Thus in 1686 Henry Hills the elder, a senior member, was found guilty of printing almanacs without authority 'for his own private lucre'. 'Deeply resenting' this affront, the Company seized his shares and stock—and then elected him as its Master in the following year.[107] Years after the event, it was found that the Treasurer had been selling almanacs printed at Cambridge on his own account, and thus defrauding the Company.[108]

Many illegal almanacs did slip past the Company's vigilance, and it was prepared to spend considerable sums to buy in stocks before they reached the public, and to advertise in the *London Gazette* and circularize provincial booksellers and chapmen. With the expiry of the Printing Act in 1695, it became almost impossible to track down the interloper in the provinces until damage had been done.[109] The danger had been illustrated by the case of a York bookseller, Francis Mawburne, who in 1666 distributed 4,000 illegal almanacs under twenty titles before he was checked. Threatened with prosecution, Mawburne submitted and paid to the Company a fine of £95, but the market was spoiled, and thousands of its almanacs remained unsold.[110] One response was to speed up the publishing process and distribute almanacs before the appearance of counterfeits which, the Master reported in October 1697, were already being offered for sale for the following year.[111] Some pears earlier, all authors had been ordered to send in their copy not later than 1 May, and probably most complied. Partridge, for example, completed his edition for 1680 in April 1679, and for 1681 on 28 February 1680.[112] Such an early deadline brought a danger of embarrassment by an unexpected turn of events. Thus Gadbury's edition for 1689, written in the middle of the previous year, informed the reader that 1688 had brought none of the expected upheavals, and that the birth of the Prince of Wales was a guarantee of future security. By the time it appeared, the regime had of course been swept away, and Gadbury conceded in his edition for 1690 that 'my muse hath of late been planet-struck, and I must waive predictions for a season.'[113]

To maximize profits, the Company sought not only to oust rivals, but to conduct its business with maximum efficiency and minimal costs. This was attempted in a number of ways. Almanacs appeared, for example, in a variety of forms and sizes to appeal to different sections of the market. A major objective was to keep prices low and stable. Naturally prices varied according to the size of the edition, and whether it was bound or interleaved (to supply extra space for memoranda); they may have been higher in the provinces to cover carriage charges, and were possibly reduced at the end of the season to clear stocks. In the sixteenth century the normal price appears to have been 1d for a sheet almanac, and 2d for one in book form. In the following century, the price of 'sorts' (the smaller and largely standardized book almanacs) crept up from 2d to 3d to 4d, with larger works by Lilly, Wharton and others costing 6d or more.[114] Prices thus did rise gradually, but the Company maintained some check by curtailing strictly the length of each item. An inflated almanac would simply price itself out of existence. Gadbury's edition for 1658 ended with a comment that the countryman would never pay more than 2d—

ask him more,
Uds' lid (saith he) chil en'e ha none avore:
Chave liv'd these vorty years, and nere did gee
A varthing more. . . . I vaith chill leese my eyes
Avore chil pay (vor Almanacks) Excise.[115]

At the end of the century George Parker admitted that by including details of planetary motions his almanacs had swollen to cost 6d, and that the public had preferred to buy rival works at 'half-price'.[116] Most astrologers accepted as a 'law' that 'an almanac is to three sheets confined'. Ferdinando Beridge embarked on an ambitious history of the world, but ended abruptly at 1315 having filled the third sheet. 'You may have too much for your money', he told his readers, 'and I nothing for my pains.'[117]

There were many possible economies of production to be exploited. Most copies were sold unbound, which reduced costs and allowed the almanac to be rolled up 'fit for one's pocket'.[118] The paper used was thin and cheap, and the printing was often blurred and smudged, despite attempts by the Company to impose some minimum standards.[119] The print for tables of fairs, highways, weights and measures was kept standing and used year after year in the cheap and stereotyped 'sorts' (though much of it was destroyed in the Great Fire). The compiler of *Pond* for 1659 apologized that readers might be 'cloyed for lack of variety'.[120] Working with haste and little care, printers naturally made frequent blunders. The wrong pictures appeared over the monthly calendars of an almanac by Securis for 1568. Under the heading of 'Fairs throughout England' the printer of Alleyn's edition for 1609 inserted a list of highways.[121] The northern history which first appeared in Vaux's almanacs reappeared in many other Stuart editions which had no northern connotations.[122] The practice whereby different printers took responsibility for the almanac and for the prognostication led to other confusions. *Perkins* for 1643, for example, appeared with a chronology in both sections.[123] The verses which appeared over each month in the calendar, often giving medical and dietary advice, were also plagiarized. Most popular was a set of doggerel rhymes beginning,

> If thou be sick and help would have,
> The counsel of the learned crave. . . .

which appeared in Buckminster's almanac for 1595, and reappeared in the editions of (among others) Frende (1616), Neve (1635), Dade (1642), Fowle (1687), Pearse (1741) and Season (1800), and even across the border in a number of Scottish almanacs.[124]

The market for almanacs was not infinitely expandable. The Company recognized that excessive expansion would result merely in more unsold copies at the end of the year, and accordingly restricted the number of titles and copies printed.[125] Aspirant authors sent their work to the Company which referred it to one of the established London astrologers with whom the Stationers had close links, such as Booker during the Revolution and Henry Coley from the later 1670s. The chances of acceptance were slight: Coley's commonplace book contains a list of ten manuscript almanacs sent to him from the country, of which only two or three appear to have been published.[126] Charles Atkinson compiled an almanac almost every year from 1660, but none were accepted until 1670; each year his contact in London was turned away with the remark that 'there were so many others to do'. Atkinson, a minister, consoled himself with the thought that such disappointments must be 'effectual to the salvation of my poor soul'.[127]

The criteria applied were partly those of quality. An almanac offered by James Baston for 1655 was rejected because it contained 'scarce a word true English'. Political considerations were also present, as when Booker deleted the more explosive parts of Lilly's first edition.[128] But undoubtedly the major criterion was profitability. The Company authorized an almanac for 1658 by a new compiler, Joseph Blagrave, only when the printer agreed to bear personally any loss incurred. Authors were sometimes paid no royalty the first year, and made liable for any losses, and unsuccessful authors were ruthlessly axed: John Coulton was dropped in 1656 with a consolatory payment of six shillings. The remarks of many new compilers that their works would reappear in later years if encouraged by the public referred not to their own morale but to hopes of a stay of execution by the Company.[129]

Rather than introduce new titles, the Stationers preferred to keep alive old favourites. Woodhouse and Pond both died long before the civil war, but almanacs continued to appear in their names into the eighteenth century. Francis Moore issued his first annual edition in 1699 and (as 'Old Moore') has done so ever since. A Victorian cynic explained the banal nature of his predictions by remarking that 'having reached the mellow age of three hundred years, he cannot read the stars as clearly as in his younger days.'[130] Sometimes a series was continued by relatives of the founder, as in the case of the Wing, Neve and Gadbury families. More often later editions were written by a small group of astrologers enjoying close ties with the Stationers, such as Gadbury, Leybourne and Coley. A note dating from 1691, probably by Gadbury, lists the titles of twelve separate almanacs 'I formerly wrote for the Company'. The Treasurer's books show that Leybourne was paid for compiling seven different editions for the year 1693.[131] This kind of arrangement had obvious advantages in terms of speed and simplicity of organization. The initiative lay clearly with the publishers (the Company and the universities). Cambridge issued and probably commissioned editions ascribed to fictitious authors, with names usually derived from birds (e.g. Swallow, Dove and Peregrine) or water (e.g. Rivers and Lakes, obviously suggested by Edward Pond).[132] Sometimes individual stationers issued their own works, such as those of the Elizabethan printer, Thomas Dawson (offered without charge, as a promotional device) and Thomas Dunster. The later London bookseller, Raven, published almanacs in his own name in the late seventeenth century, though he relinquished his copy and engraving to the Company in 1704. *Gallen* was produced by the 'broken-Bookseller', Thomas Langley.[133] In some other countries, notably Scotland and France, the publishers' control was even more complete.[134]

The Company of Stationers' monopoly over almanacs was highly profitable. As early as Elizabeth's reign Thomas Nashe had described them as 'readier money than ale and cakes'.[135] There are no official figures of sales for the early seventeenth century, though John Booker's edition for 1640 had a print-order of 12,000, which gives some indication of the scale. The civil war and interregnum led to a massive and almost certainly unprecedented expansion. Seth Partridge's almanac sold 18,500 copies in 1648, and sales of almanacs by Lilly climbed steadily until they reached (it was alleged in 1659) roughly 30,000 copies a year.[136] Both sales and profits were buoyant in the later part of the century. Total sales exceeded 400,000 a year in the 1660s, and held firm at about the same level in the 1680s. The most popular individual title, by Vincent Wing, sold over 50,000 copies annually at its peak. In the early Restoration period the Company made profits of between a thousand and fifteen hundred pounds each year for a few weeks' work. At the end of the century it could afford to pay £500 a year with equanimity to buy out competition from Cambridge.[137]

The astrologers were much less content with the system. They were at the mercy of the Stationers who, they realized, cared little about the fate of an individual title. A slow or negligent printer could ruin the prospects of a particular author by delaying the date of publication.[138] In addition, printers often flouted the wishes of the compiler. John Heyman, a new author, asked his printer to omit a chronology, but found that his request had been ignored. The printer added a further insult by removing Heyman's name from the title-page and substituting that of the better-known Vincent Wing.[139] A similarly frustrating experience befell John Silvester, a Bristol compiler. Not only did the Stationers block the publication of the draft almanac he submitted, but they also pirated much of the material and published it in an almanac under the name of Richard Saunders (who had been dead for some years).[140] Eminent astrologers suffered in the same way. Arthur Hopton attacked the printer of his edition for 1610 which had a 'paltry old rutter [a nautical chart] thrust into my book to stuff up the volume, which I much disdained should pass under my name'. Pond criticized his rivals' works, but conceded that the printers filled his own 'with naught but draff, which food for swine doth yield'. George Wharton wrote in his edition for 1642 that he would 'purposely omit' a chronology and 'such other trumperies': but a chronology was duly inserted by the printer. John Gadbury complained that one of his editions had been so altered by the printer that he had failed to recognize it.[141]

Those excluded by the Company's restrictive practices were naturally indignant. There were frequent complaints at the 'roguery' of publishing the purported works of authors long dead. Booker denounced the practice in 1640, and was himself criticized in later years for upholding it. Almanacs

from dead carcasses are raised like flies, . . .
Whose fathers thrice ten years were dead and rotten
Before their feigned offspring were begotten,

complained John Tanner in 1660.[142] The small fees and vast profits of the Company were a further source of grievance. The standard fee of forty shillings at the beginning of the seventeenth century was still paid to the compilers of 'sorts' at its close.[143] Edward Pond complained in 1612, in the decent obscurity of mathematical language, that for twelve annual editions he had received a total of 'only the cube of twelve third parts of twelve deniers', and demanded a 'just reward'; receiving no satisfaction, he withdrew from the field. The rewards were 'scarce porters' wages', Coley declared at the end of the century.[144] George Wharton was goaded into publishing an illegal almanac in 1655 to set out his quarrel with the 'crew of monopolizers', the 'few corrupted covetous members' who dominated the Company. In June 1652 he had reached an agreement with it for an almanac for 1653; he was paid a sum of money for the copy with the balance to be paid on publication. By November, however, the edition had been published and indeed was sold out, but the balance was not paid. Wharton retaliated by having his next almanac, for 1654, published independently; the Company countered by lodging a complaint that it was subversive (though previously the Stationers had encouraged Wharton's 'malignancy, as the only selling subject of an almanac'). Six thousand copies were seized, and the Company issued another compilation under Wharton's name and with his portrait, though apparently written by John Taylor, the 'Water-Poet'. The original unpaid balance was paid only when Wharton began legal proceedings in the Guildhall (though his case failed because he refused, on political grounds, to take the Engagement.)[145] At the Restoration the Stationers were prompt in reducing the fee paid to John Booker who, as a Parliamentarian, was no longer likely to be popular with the authorities. Booker however appealed directly to the king for permission to sell his copy privately 'to his best advantage and profit'. Charles, surprisingly, appears to have agreed: the edition for 1661 was not under the Company's imprint.[146]

The astrologer had few weapons at his disposal, except perseverance and the threat of publishing illegally (as Charles Atkinson did in 1666 after years of rejection by the Company).[147] More effective was the support of an influential patron. The young astrologer, Jeremy Shakerley, sent his draft almanac for 1650 to William Lilly for his approval and support. Lilly himself cultivated a patron in favour at the Restoration court, Elias Ashmole.[148] The career of the Dublin-based astrologer, John Whalley, illustrates the situation. In 1687 he made an agreement with a London bookseller, who was to leave copies of Whalley's almanac for the following year at Chester by 31 October. They failed to arrive, and the bookseller vanished after claiming that the edition had been seized in the press; Whalley, however, was convinced that he had been bought off by other London printers and booksellers. His next English edition, for 1690, contained an ostentatious dedication to the Secretary of State, Daniel Finch, stressing Whalley's close links with his patron.[149]

Most published almanacs were by authors living in London, the south-east and a belt of land extending towards the other centre of production at Cambridge, probably because the works of more distant astrologers stood little chance of acceptance without a patron or representative in the capital. Richard Allestree of Derby compiled editions for 1615 and 1616 which were rejected, partly through lack of an influential contact to plead their merits. Vaux's almanac for 1623 was refused by the printer on the grounds that the manuscript had arrived too late; Vaux had no friend in London to argue the case, but took care to remedy the situation the following year.[150] Other reasons no doubt contributed to the geographical basis of almanac production. The proximity of a noted astrologer could prompt other works in imitation or rivalry, as probably happened at Salisbury where Henry Low found a successor in John Securis. The small market town of Saffron Walden, in Essex, enjoyed remarkable eminence in this respect, with almanacs calculated for it by Searle, Pond, Kidman, Adkin and Andrews, perhaps reflecting a tradition derived from the three Harvey brothers, all astrologers, who belonged to the town in the Elizabethan period.[151]

For the Company the attraction of a monopoly was of course financial. For successive governments it was a convenient way of regulating a sensitive area of the press. The Elizabethan monopolists,

Watkins and Roberts, had exercised strict control over the contents of their pieces. Fearful of losing its privileges, the Company too operated an internal system of licensing in addition to that laid down by the state. Indeed, despite the theoretically comprehensive nature of state provision for censorship, the official licensers seem usually to have ignored ephemeral publications such as almanacs and ballads.[152] This relative freedom lasted until the growing controversies of the 1630s prompted stricter control. In 1631 there appeared an 'offensive' almanac under the name of William Beale, but possibly composed by his master, Henry Gellibrand, professor of mathematics at Gresham College, London. Instead of the usual saints, the calendar contained a list of Protestant martyrs drawn from Foxe's *Acts and Monuments*. Such a move was bound to offend the Arminian and Catholic interests at court, and the queen, Henrietta Maria, urged William Laud (then Bishop of London) to prosecute Gellibrand and Beale before the Court of High Commission; this was done, though the case surprisingly failed.[153] A further incident, in the autumn of 1634, was handled more firmly when John Booker was imprisoned for issuing an almanac which was deemed offensive and (like all others) had not been vetted by the state licensers. At the end of October, the High Commission ordered that no future almanacs should be published without a licence from the Archbishop of Canterbury or Bishop of London; the Company repeated the command to its members.[154] Though no details survive, a stricter control seems to have existed thereafter. Booker complained, years later, that he had almost abandoned his annual almanacs because much of the material was 'most maliciously expunged' by 'peevish episcopal chaplains'. One of Wharton's earliest editions suffered heavily at the hands of the chaplains who made 'an Index Expurgatorious thereof'.[155]

The system collapsed with the ruin of the Church in the early stages of the Revolution. Parliament, however, showed equal concern over sensitive areas of the press, and by a set of ordinances in 1643 John Booker was metamorphosized into licenser for mathematical books, which included almanacs.[156] His victims reacted much as he had done under his predecessors. George Wharton, indignant at seeing his royalist almanac at the mercy of a political rival, issued his own illegal and uncensored edition for 1648, and warned the public against any bowdlerized version that might be put out under his name by the Company. A York astrologer, Francis Metcalfe, complained at the confiscation of his books and at the ignorance of Booker, and demanded a new licenser.[157] At the Restoration, a royal proclamation ousted Booker and put Wharton in his place.[158] Wharton's task was at first not difficult. Booker and especially Lilly were fearful of prosecution over their role as propagandists for the republican regime, and were too grateful at being left untouched to risk any provocation. Lilly's rather obvious eulogy of 'King Charles the Merciful' and the 'darling Act of Indemnity' indicated the degree of his concern, though his edition for 1663 provoked cuts by the censor.[159] Wharton also banned notes of the anniversaries of civil war battles and executions which John Tanner's almanacs usually supplied. Tanner was a staunch republican, and the government did not welcome such reminders of political mutability.[160]

Wharton was succeeded as licenser by Roger L'Estrange, who became a highly controversial figure as the relative unity of the early Restoration period began to crumble.[161] A series of handwritten draft almanacs submitted to L'Estrange by William Lilly has survived, and provides a vivid glimpse of the licenser's activities in the 1660s and 1670s. Lilly's celebrity made L'Estrange doubly cautious, and several editions suffered heavily. The licenser deleted material which reflected adversely on the English government, and struck out prophecies of upheavals and of discord between crown and people. Thus the almanac for 1668 appeared without Lilly's intended allusions to the dishonour and blunders exposed by the humiliating Dutch attack on the Medway in 1667. Passages warning of the danger of fires in London, and hinting at arson, were thought too disturbing in the aftermath of the Great Fire of 1666. A reference to recent disorders in the realm caused by Venerious pastimes' was probably interpreted, perhaps rightly, as a veiled attack on the character of Charles II.[162]

Lilly's draft for 1670 suffered in the same way. L'Estrange removed a prediction of the fall of kings and tyrants, and a long section prophesying the death of the King of Spain and the outbreak of a war of Spanish Succession which would involve the whole of Europe.[163] Lilly announced that in future he would try not to give offence, and his next edition caused no problems. But by 1672 his good resolution was forgotten. He planned to insert a fierce attack on clerical greed, and a plea for religious toleration for 'tender consciences', which would at last create harmony between king and people; persecution bred resentment and was destroying the trade of the nation. Years earlier, in a passage also deleted, he had warned against rigid ecclesiastical policies of any kind, declaring that the English of all classes preferred liberty. In

1672 he also predicted disorder and disobedience, popular complaints of oppression, and exorbitant customs and impositions which were damaging trade. In a time of 'flames and fury', he hinted ominously, it was likely that kings would be refused their 'timely supplies'. England would also face insults from a threatening neighbour, and there was danger of war and invasion. All this material was removed by L'Estrange.[164] Lilly complained, with some justice, that his work was 'macerated, obliterated, sliced and quartered'; he urged Ashmole, his patron, to press for a better licenser than 'old Crackfart', but in vain.[165] The draft for 1674 was still more unacceptable. Fortunately Ashmole was able to get possession of the copy, and probably arranged the removal of the offensive material and the substitution of an innocuous mediaeval treatise on astrology; otherwise, Lilly reflected, 'perhaps I must have taken up my quarters in the Tower'.[166] As a skilled journalist, Lilly had no difficulty in extracting some benefits from these setbacks. Dramatic blank spaces and dashes in the printed almanacs showed where material had been removed, and invited the reader to speculate on what further secrets would have been revealed. Lilly encouraged such thoughts. In 1655 he had hinted darkly that he 'would tell more, but . . . loves not a prison'. Twenty years later he was making the same point, alluding to greater secrets, 'had we but liberty of emitting unto the world what we might very well predict'. In addition, censorship provided of course a convenient excuse for prophetic sins of omission. In 1673 he assured readers that many of his prophecies made the previous year, unfortunately expunged by the censor, had been triumphantly verified.[167]

By the late 1670s the political world was in a state of upheaval over the 'discovery' of a popish plot to kill the king, and over fears of a Catholic succession to the throne. The authorities were aware of the potential of almanacs to inflame the situation further, and watched carefully for any sign of deviation from orthodoxy. In 1679 John Gadbury, known as a Catholic sympathizer, was brought before the Privy Council and rebuked by the Bishop of London for failing to include the anniversary of Guy Fawkes' plot in his almanac.[168] Control was facilitated by the Company's practice of giving presentation copies of new almanacs each December to political and legal dignitaries, including the secretaries of state, lord chancellor and lord chief justice.[169]

By the time of the Popish Plot, Lilly was too old and infirm to exploit the situation. His position was taken by a newcomer, a violent

Whig named John Partridge, who demanded the exclusion of James from the throne and heaped abuse on the pope and Tories.[170] On the accession of James II in 1685, Partridge retired to the Netherlands, but the king decided to curb any danger from the almanac-makers. In August 1685 William Sancroft, Archbishop of Canterbury, refused to license any almanac which contained the prophetic section known as the prognostication. The Company considered legal action, but a compromise was achieved: the almanacs appeared in their usual form, but there were strict instructions to avoid anything contentious in the prognostication.[171] Most writers complied, though some (like Tanner) with obvious reluctance. Gadbury omitted political prophecies, being 'given to understand, it was the pleasure of our superiors that we forbear', though he made an exception to predict the birth of a Prince of Wales who would perpetuate the dynasty. One astrologer who chose not to comply, John Harrison, complained that 'what I inserted, others out did raze'. But he found a loophole which the censor failed to notice, by speculating on foreign affairs with an ingenuous explanation to the reader that 'what here I look for's put beyond the seas'.[172]

After the Glorious Revolution of 1688–9, responsibility for licensing almanacs remained at first with Robert Midgeley, first appointed by the archbishop in 1685.[173] Midgeley showed no difficulty in adapting to the new political requirements, but his scrutiny proved less than complete. The major embarrassment came not from a Jacobite but from the republican Whig, John Partridge, who waged a surreptitious campaign in the seemingly innocuous column of saints' days. January 30 was normally recorded in red letters to commemorate the 'martyrdom' of Charles I in 1649; in his edition for 1691, however, Partridge demoted the event by noting merely the death of the king, and the following year he omitted it altogether. This was noticed by Archbishop Tillotson, who sent a rebuke to the Company, and demanded that future almanacs be approved by one of his chaplains. Yet by 1694 Partridge was testing official vigilance once more by recording the martyrdom of Charles in ordinary black print, while the execution of a Whig plotter in 1682 was proclaimed in red as 'St. Col. M.' (Stephen College Martyr).[174] The expiry of the Printing Act in 1695 meant the end of the licensing system. Henceforth almanacs could be published with no external controls other than the threat of prosecution for any editions considered seditious, though in practice archiepiscopal chaplains continued to scrutinize and approve each year's productions.[175]

The motives which led astrologers to compile almanacs were more complex than those of the publishers. Indeed a Jacobean compiler, Daniel Browne, declared himself unable to comprehend his own motives, finding neither pleasure nor profit in the work.[176] The astrologers were a very heterogeneous body, and only a minority had no wider interests. Most combined astrology with the practice of astrological medicine or with branches of practical mathematics, such as teaching, surveying and instrument-making. In the seventeenth century, this second category seems to have expanded at the expense of the physicians. But some writers fitted into neither category. There was, for example, a group of clerical compilers from Anthony Askham to Restoration clergy such as Charles Atkinson.[177] The motives of this group were often largely evangelical: astrological predictions of doom were used to summon men to repentance and a return to Christian social values, as the only means of averting God's wrath. Some lay astrologers wrote in similar vein, notably Richard Allestree, and Vincent Wing, whose almanacs were said to be 'in a manner, sermons'.[178] A few compilers are best described as journalists, popular writers on a variety of subjects, such as Andrew Borde, who also published works on medicine and a jest-book, and Thomas Hill, who has been seen as an 'Elizabethan Huxley' for his work in popularizing scientific progress.[179]

Satirists had no doubt that the motivating force behind the astrologers was greed. The author of *Montelion* caricatured this by offering to include in his calendar of saints the name of anyone who would buy his book. *Poor Robin* told his readers bluntly that 'every word in this almanac was writ on purpose to get money'. Bucknall, a Restoration compiler, conceded the charge on behalf of the whole profession.[180] The lucrative investments of Henry Coley in the Company of Stationers were not missed by the satirists.[181] But the smear loses much of its force in view of the small fees actually paid by the Company to its compilers. An astrologer with the journalistic flair of William Lilly might receive as much as £70 a year for his almanac (plus entertainment), but the normal pattern was that of William Andrews, whose annual fee climbed laboriously over forty years from £2 to a princely £15.[182] But equally unconvincing are the assertions of altruism made by the compilers, often parading the motto '*Non nobis solus nati sumus*' and referring coyly to the duty of disseminating knowledge, and to the pressure of friends who had persuaded them into print.[183] The financial rewards of publishing were not great, but for many they would not have been negligible, and there were further indirect benefits.

Probably the most compelling financial inducement was not the fee but the role of the almanac as a free, indeed subsidized advertisement for its author. In the second half of the seventeenth century, vast numbers of printed advertisements by astrologers and astrological physicians were circulated in London and elsewhere. Some were visually dramatic—printed, for example, diagonally—and many were posted on walls, trees and other prominent places.[184] Almanacs reached a still wider audience, and compilers often filled a whole page with details of the services they provided. Edward Pond in 1612 offered tuition in arithmetic, geometry, cosmography, dialling and navigation. Charles Atkinson, the minister, informed the public that he was also a physician and astrologer, willing to calculate nativities, trace lost or stolen goods and solve horary questions. John Wing was available for laying out enclosures. John Keene combined erudition and optimism in offering to teach mathematics and science in Greek and Latin. He announced that vacancies existed at his grammar school in Tottenham.[185] Occasionally almanacs were used to declare that the author was still alive and in practice, denying reports of his death spread by rumour or malicious rivals.[186] William Davis informed his readers that he attended at the Red Lion in Broomham, Wilts., each Monday, Wednesday and Saturday to resolve astrological queries and dispense pills. The role of the inn in the social life of the district is also reflected in a later advertisement by Edmund Weaver, who attended at the Angel in Grantham during fairs and the fortnightly markets, and by appointment at other times, to offer his services as a physician.[187] Perhaps the most blatant self-advertisement was by William Salmon, whose first published almanac warned of an impending outbreak of plague and asserted that the medicines prepared by the author were by far the best antidote. Daniel Woodward showed similar enterprise in listing the names and addresses of retailers selling his patent medicines throughout the country. Self-advertisement was combined with regular and fierce condemnation of charlatans and quacks and their remedies.[188]

There seems little doubt that advertisements were successful. As the seventeenth century advanced, almanacs grew steadily in importance as a vehicle for advertisements of all kinds. Books and easy credit (with no questions asked) were the first subjects, but the range widened to include an extensive list of goods and services.[189] It is clear that many people were prepared to consult astrologers and physicians of repute living far from their own neighbourhood. Almanac-makers often 'deplored' the weight of postal enquiries they received. Gadbury warned that only prepaid correspondence would be answered, and at times was driven to urge provincial clients to find an intermediary in London. At the beginning of the eighteenth century, William Salmon was receiving over fifteen hundred postal enquiries each year.[190] Some astrological physicians advertised overnight accommodation in London for visiting clients. A letter or journey to the capital offered anonymity, as many advertisements pointed out, which may explain the heavy emphasis on venereal diseases in many advertisements. One physician, John Archer, underlined his irrefutable respectability by stating that he had been physician for venereal disease to King Charles II.[191] A modern touch is provided by the practice of some astrologers, as well-known 'personalities', of sponsoring products. Lilly, for example, recommended an elixir for 'gripes', smallpox and other diseases with the assurance that 'I make frequent use of it, and . . . with very good success.'[192]

Another major driving-force behind the almanac-maker seems to have been a concern with status. Ben Jonson noted the point in discussing attitudes to the astrologer who had achieved publication. 'You style him doctor,'cause he can compile/An almanac', complains a character in *The Staple of Newes*, and the vain astrologer is told that his conceit could be dated 'since your thumbs/Have greased an Ephemerides'.[193] A satirist remarked that the astrologer's 'mighty ambition is to write an almanac, which he doubts not but will make him more famous, than either Copernicus or Kepler'.[194] William Lilly remarks in his *Life and Times* that he had been struck, as a young man, by the description of an astrologer as 'a great scholar, nay, so learned that he could make an almanac'.[195] In later years Lilly was accused of harbouring grandiose aspirations, and certainly seems to have enjoyed his pre-eminence. He wrote with the royal 'we', and his private correspondence reveals a taste for inventing imposing (albeit humorous) titles for himself, such as 'the Mogul of Hersham' and 'William, Duke of Moab'. A surviving copy of one of Booker's almanacs contains comparable jottings, probably by the author, such as 'Right Worshipful John Booker', and the verse 'Booker is thy name/and all the world doth know the same.'[196]

Quite often a printed almanac represented a 'masterpiece' with which a novice astrologer hoped to win acceptance among the ranks of the learned. The compilers were frequently very young when their first work appeared. William Andrews compiled his first edition, for 1655, at nineteen; John Rowley completed his 'infant work' on the 7,394th day of his life (which makes him a little over twenty); it was, he added, less than a year since he had taken up the study of astrology. Shakerley confessed that he too was 'but newly crept out of the limits of childhood'. Wyberd and Kaye published works precociously before going up to university. Vincent Wing was twenty-two when his first edition appeared.[197] Like modern young academics, the more ambitious signalled their arrival with a blast at the errors and incompetence of the existing masters of the field. Gresham began by ridiculing the blunders of established compilers, while Keene denounced two of the leading figures, Pond and Bretnor, as mere charlatans, adding gratuitously that Pond was an ape-like or 'simeatical fellow'.[198] Similarly Booker heaped abuse on the 'illiterate hare-brains, that have scarce learned the ABC of astronomy', and Wing's first almanac spelt out lovingly the massive errors of the 'company of hare-brains, that abuse the art very much'.[199] Once the principle was established that good astrologers published almanacs, the practice was self-perpetuating. John Keene felt obliged to enter the field to prove his competence, 'that I might no longer be thought the blockish picture of Harpocrates the god of silence'.[200]

The concern with status reflected more than mere vanity and professional self-advertisement. Fame or respectability offered a degree of protection to the astrologer, whose position in the eyes of the law was highly ambiguous. While there was no law explicitly against astrology, there were many against witchcraft, sorcery and seditious prophecies, which gave ample scope to hostile magistrates who chose to believe that astrology fell into these categories. Astrologers naturally attempted to emphasize the distinctions between them, but their case was undermined by the activities of a number, including Lilly, who dabbled in magic and attempted to raise spirits.[201] Much therefore depended on the attitude of the magistrate; 'ignorant' justices were said in 1650 to be eager to bind over to the assizes astrologers accused of fraud, or of libel (the result sometimes of over-hasty identification of 'criminals' based on no more than the calculations and judgement of an astrologer).[202] To be known in print was a useful way of leaping the chasm that separated the quack from the 'professor of astronomy and astrology': the charge of being a cheat was less likely to stick, and there was a greater chance of finding a favourable magistrate or gentleman to intercede. Thus the Elizabethan astrologer, Evans Lloyd, dedicated an almanac to the stern Recorder of London, William Fleetwood, with an epistle listing eminent champions of astrology from Aristotle to Melancthon, while pledging full support for Fleetwood's campaign against impostors and quacks.[203] A little-known astrologer named William Hills, prosecuted in 1651, sought to establish his respectability by assuring the court that the celebrated Lilly was his mentor.[204] Lilly himself, though indicted for sorcery, was defended by an eminent lawyer, and the charge failed. He escaped from more serious trouble through the help of eminent politicians such as Lenthall and Strickland and, after the Restoration, by the intercession of Sir Edward Walker, clerk to the Privy Council, with Secretary Nicholas.[205] But of course the publication of an almanac was no guarantee of immunity, and could even invite trouble. Booker's almanac, regarded as offensive, brought him before the High Commission. George Wharton decided to publish under a pseudonym in order to prevent his name from coming to the notice of hostile magistrates.[206] Several compilers fell foul of the law. Francis Coxe was pilloried for sorcery, Bomelius imprisoned, and Simon Pembroke prosecuted before a church court as a conjuror, causing a sensation when he dropped dead as the judge entered. John Vaux was brought before the High Commission in Durham, and a pamphlet by John Evans, advertising his medical practice, led to a complaint by the College of Physicians, and to Evans' appearance before the High Commission in London.[207]

Ideally the almanac would bring the author both popular fame and the protection, and perhaps even the patronage, of the wealthy. But these objectives demanded different, even contradictory approaches. Compilers anxious to impress a large and unsophisticated audience stressed that the work was a 'Herculean task'. Thomas Jeffereys, while confident that he lived 'in a region beyond the vulgar's reach', reminded the 'common' reader that 'almanacs are not all men's acts, but the labour of the learned'.[208] Other compilers, especially the mathematicians of the Jacobean period, emphasized that their almanacs were trivial toys, and protested their indifference to public response. Gregory Burton explained that he had published only at the 'request of my good friends, whom I promised to spend some idle hours' at the task. Edward Gresham spurned 'popular applause' and declared that his almanacs were the 'fruits only of my idlest hours, and pauses from greater studies'.[209] Arthur Hopton stressed that his editions were designed not for the masses, but for lawyers, scholars and clerics; even so, they were only the products of his moments of relaxation, 'wandering for recreation in this lower region of invention'. 'I hold it no part of praise', he declared, 'to be praised of the multitude of mean mechanics'; Burton, too, scorned the approval of 'the badder sort'.[210] George Wharton's adoption of a pseudonym was partly to conceal his name from the common people. When rivals altered his anagram, Naworth, to No-worth, he was forced to drop the disguise but confessed that

> I can't but blush, for shame, when I do meet
> My name (like small coal) cried in ev'ry street.[211]

John Booker and a number of others contrived to establish genteel credentials at the same time as impressing the ordinary people who formed the majority of their readers by a liberal use of Latin quotations, which provoked criticism during the Revolution.[212]

The satirists and coffee-house wits of the seventeenth century were, of course, unimpressed by the astrologers' display of erudition. Instead, they mocked the 'science' and the integrity of its practitioners, whom they presented as plausible rogues gulling their clients.[213] The astrologers naturally defended themselves, though typically they often tried to exploit criticism by asserting their own integrity while conceding that many of their rivals were cheats and quacks. A contemporary satirist noted that the astrologer 'would willingly (like the grand seigneur) strangle all his brethren'.[214] Partridge's almanac for 1697 contained a list of the addresses of notorious cheats, which included some of the leading practitioners in London; they were not amused.[215] Even Booker and Lilly, close associates for many years, stooped occasionally to professional sniping at each other. Lilly felt that Booker's reputation was greater than he deserved, and Booker once confided that Lilly devised predictions to 'keep in with the times'.[216]

The stereotype of the astrologer—the ingenious cheat of Ben Jonson's plays—is, however, unconvincing. Given an intellectual climate in which astrology was widely accepted, it is absurd to imagine that all its practitioners were frauds, though a large number of ignorant charlatans certainly existed. While professional standards may often have fallen far short of the ideal, there is no reason to doubt the astrologers' belief in their science. Figures calculated by astrologers for themselves and their friends, and private correspondence, confirm this judgement. A graphic example is an agitated note sent by Booker in 1662, reporting that his son Samuel had absconded and begging Lilly's astrological help in tracking him down.[217] Commercial pressures sometimes obliged almanac-makers to insert material they despised, but the compilers generally made their scepticism explicit. Thus Richard

Allestree supplemented a list of astrological rules on farming and blood-letting with some biblical texts to show the ungodliness of such 'foolish fables'. *Winter* in 1633 reproduced the standard anatomical figure, but with a derisive comment that,

All Afric ne'er conceived so strange a son
As this, by Egypt's doting brains begun.[218]

Others pointedly omitted material of which they did not approve, often with a few words of explanation. Thus an edition might lack the anatomy, weather predictions, political prophecies ('gibberish, self-contradictory, and time-serving oracles'), the list of good and evil days (standard in Tudor editions, but often rejected later as 'heathenish' on the grounds that 'their Maker made them all alike'), or speculation on the world's end (an 'unsearchable mystery' which belonged to God alone).[219]

William Lilly was the most abused as well as the most celebrated astrologer of the seventeenth century, and deserves a closer scrutiny. He was certainly no simple impostor. The notebooks of his astrological apprenticeship, still extant, show his diligence in copying rules and key passages from the standard authorities, and in calculating practice figures. His textbook, *Christian Astrology* (1647), re veals his acquaintance with an impressive range of Continental and English writings, and there is at least some plausibility in his claim that he studied 'many times twelve, or fifteen, or eighteen hours, day and night'.[220] Yet there is also an obvious streak of opportunism. He had settled in London, he later recalled, 'perceiving there was money to be got'. Two marriages which brought him independence, leisure and a string of thirteen houses in the city bear witness to his skill in exploiting the possibilities.[221] He approached astrological journalism with something of the same spirit. 'I well know, how to humour the people', he remarked to his patron Ashmole, and the Latin motto which appeared in his almanac for 1682—'*Si populus vult decepi, decipiatur*'—was, to say the least, ambiguous.[222] His autobiography suggests a man of ingenuity but questionable ethics. He told with apparent pride of how he made an enemy drunk in order to steal papers from him. Examined by a parliamentary committee in 1652 after his almanac had attacked the Rump, he escaped by blatant perjury and the manufacture of false evidence, with the connivance of the Stationers. He explained his public support for Sweden in the 1650s by referring to a debt of gratitude to another patron, Whitelocke, who was ambassador to Sweden, and to the advantages a Swedish alliance might bring—without mentioning astrology.[223]

His favour with the Protectorate regime, followed by a timely submission and survival under Charles II proves his skill in political acrobatics. 'Obedience is better than sacrifice', he told his readers.[224]

Yet the charge of mere time-serving is not wholly conclusive. Though Lilly submitted in 1660 and thereafter stressed his loyalty, his later almanacs show little pretence of royalist enthusiasm. Several were censored heavily, and his private correspondence shows a growing revulsion towards the cavalier politics of 'feathers and Damn blades'.[225] He described the Act of 1670, which banned nonconformist conventicles, as 'the worst ever done in England'.[226] The fact that Lilly was arrested on nine separate occasions during his career suggests that he did not write merely to please the powers in being. His practice in the late 1640s and early 1650s was rather to support a particular faction in parliament and the army. Expediency as well as principle determined his allegiance, but he was certainly willing to take considerable risks. His almanac for 1652, for example, contained his provocative attack on the Rump Parliament, and the ingenuity with which he escaped from the consequences of his action does not detract from its courage.[227] Lilly's letters to his patron, Elias Ashmole, reveal a droll personality, with a taste for banter and facetious humour, but they also express disapproval of Ashmole's loose morals, Tory politics and High Church sympathies. 'I'll ha' you gelded', Lilly warned his patron jocularly on one occasion.[228]

The evidence suggests that other leading political astrologers possessed a genuine seriousness of purpose. Wharton suffered repeatedly for the royalist zeal of his almanacs. Booker was attracted to astrology from his childhood, was widely respected and, according to Lilly, 'abhorred any deceit in the art he studied'. Culpeper was addicted to the subject from the age of ten, and forfeited a considerable inheritance by persevering in it instead of entering the ministry, as his guardians wanted.[229]

The antithesis between the astrologer as ignorant rogue or scholar of integrity is however an artificial one. Lilly noted with righteous indignation that though his tutor, Evans, was a skilled practitioner, yet 'for money he would willingly give contrary judgements'.[230] Probably all astrologers were anxious to please their clients and to confirm their own preconceived opinions as far as their science permitted. The high degree of subjectivity in astrological judgements made this process all too easy. Ptolemy and later authorities had laid down complex laws, but these were couched in generalizations. Where the textbook stated that a particular conjunction foreshadowed the death of a ruler, or some upheaval in the church, the almanac-maker was willing to publish a specific and partisan judgement on an individual, party or sect. Though stretching rather than breaking astrological laws, the political astrologers were clearly manipulating the stars into a party allegiance. It is impossible now to discover how far this was a conscious process. Lilly's standards of professional ethics were by no means high. Men such as Wharton and Culpeper, however, displayed a passionate certainty concerning political issues or the nature of God's purposes on earth. They may well have believed that His message in the stars could be truthfully interpreted only in the way they described. Astrological prophecy was thus akin to divine providence (epitomized in Cromwell's conviction that his victories were proof of divine support), and the possession of grace. All were controversial. In each case claims were made which appeared grossly hypocritical to contemporary opponents, but which often seem to a modern reader to have developed from a combination of idealism and self-delusion. No real objectivity could—or can—exist in deciphering God's providence, or the meaning of the stars.

New almanacs were distributed in the last two or three months of the old year. In the later seventeenth century the Stationers' Company issued printed notices announcing which editions had been published—a precaution against interlopers—and when they could be collected by city and country chapmen.[231] Booksellers throughout the country laid in considerable stocks, especially no doubt of series known to be popular, and those designed for the locality. Wilkinson's *Apollo Northamptoniensis* was clearly aimed at a local market. An edition of *Fly* for 1666 was explicitly printed for a bookseller in King's Lynn.[232] Other shops were also used as retail outlets. Thomas Jones built up a network of mercers, grocers and others throughout Wales to sell his almanacs, and found that in addition London haberdashers were selling them without his permission.[233] Physicians often made arrangements for selling their pills and medicines in the shops of booksellers, tobacconists, coffee-house-keepers and many others. Daniel Woodward, physician and astrologer, had a wide network of this kind, which he extended through advertisements in his almanacs, and it seems likely that these links with grocers, mercers and many others were utilized to sell his prophecies as well as his pills.[234] Contemporary references to sheet almanacs in the shops of barbers, chandlers and grocers suggest that copies could be bought there.[235] Many more almanacs were sold by travelling pedlars in towns and villages and at fairs and markets up and down the country.[236] One compiler alleged that most new editions were mere 'cuckoo almanacs', as stale and repetitive as the bird's song, and suggested tartly that their only value was to provide work for pedlars.[237] The hawker was an important outlet, and 'Buy a new almanac' had become a familiar street-cry in London and no doubt elsewhere by the early seventeenth century. There is a longer version of the street-cry in a poem written on the eve of the civil war:

> Come buy my new almanacs every one,
> come pick over your choice before they be gone;
> One thousand six hundred forty and one,
> come buy my new almanacs buy.[238]

In County Durham the enterprising parson-astrologer, John Vaux, assisted the process of distribution by selling almanacs to the congregation from the altar of his church.[239]

The purchasers belonged to almost every social group. The collection bearing the autograph of the future Charles I, in 1624, would have been a presentation copy, but the king was said to follow Lilly's activities and he sponsored Wharton's rival productions.[240] Lord Burghley, Elizabeth's Treasurer, owned a series and in one edition (for 1594) marked such data as the sun's entrance into Aries. The Parliamentary general, Essex, possessed a copy of Lilly's current edition.[241] Bishop Wren of Norwich and the second Earl of Clarendon both owned and made notes in current almanacs during their respective sojourns in the Tower.[242] Among academics, copies are recorded in the libraries of the Oxford dons, Brian Twyne and John England, and of John Locke, which included editions by Lilly.[243] An Elizabethan mason of Coventry, named Captain Cox, was said in 1575 to possess a collection which included editions by Jasper Laet, Nostradamus and John Securis, as well as *The Kalender of Shepherdess.*[244] Lieutenant John Weale, who served under Admiral Blake, took as part of his necessary equipment on the voyage 'a bottle full of ink, a pocket almanac and a sheet almanac'.[245] At a much later date, Derbyshire Friends purchased an almanac (for 1½d) in December 1706 to add to their lending library.[246]

Most surviving copies originally belonged to the gentry or professional men; although the great majority of buyers were yeomen, husbandmen and artisans (like Bottom), their purchases have long since perished. At the lower levels of society, however, the annual almanac faced competition from cheap perpetual prognostications, such as *Erra Pater*, which combined crude astrology with elementary magic and bird-and animal-lore. At the very bottom, the illiterate were forced to rely on educated neighbours, and on traditional folk-beliefs and natural phenomena. A contemporary remarked that cock-crow was the 'clown's almanac', to mark the passage of time; another suggested 'the cow's tail', indicating the practice of divination by animal behaviour. A later poet found part of the swain's rustic innocence in his lack of an almanac to mark the passing seasons.[247]

One of the reasons for both the popularity and the survival of almanacs was their suitability as diaries. Many surviving copies contain memoranda, accounts or farming notes. Best known is the diary of the Oxford antiquarian, Anthony Wood. Others have been published, in part or fully, such as those of Adam Winthrop, John Greene, the Recorder of London, Walter Powell, Lady Twysden and Thomas Byng, Master of Clare College, Cambridge.[248] A lot more material remains in manuscript, such as the diaries of Sir Edward Nicholas (Secretary of State to Charles II) and his son, covering a period of forty years; the diary kept by a clergyman in England and when travelling abroad (probably Griffin Higgs, chaplain to Elizabeth, the 'Winter Queen'); shorter notes by Bishop Moore of Ely, Simon Patrick and Archdeacon Sellcock; and extensive notes and reflections by Anthony Hammond, a minor late-Stuart politician.[249] Prominent nonconformists who kept diaries include Henry Newcome, Samuel Angier, Philip Henry and Richard Steel. Newcome's notes include accounts, and the almanacs were sufficiently important to be mentioned in his will. Steel, like many Puritans, carefully recorded his sins, and also details of the prayer meetings he attended. When he was arrested in 1665, and his almanac seized, these notes were used to blacken his character and to bring charges against him under the Conventicle Act.[250] When the Ranter, Laurence Clarkson, was arrested, his almanac was found to contain a list of presumed associates. Gregory King, the demographer, crammed his almanac for 1696 with a diary, extracts from books, recipes, pedigrees and notes on military expenditure.[251] Sir Thomas Rokeby, Chief Justice of the Common Pleas, noted his incidental profits (from gratuities) during four terms in 1694–5, amounting to £629. James Yonge, the physician, listed his patients and the profits he derived from them.[252] An observer at court noted in 1672 that the queen was willing to consider a divorce so that Charles might remarry and produce an heir to the throne. Robert Pugh, less deferential, used his almanac to record the 'follies and vice' of the king; it was later seized, with his other books, and brought before the Privy Council.[253] An almanac for 1692 contains a handwritten division-list of the House of Lords.[254] But the memoranda are, of course, usually far more commonplace. They include accounts, travel notes, jokes and miscellaneous comments ranging from the mundane (for example, a neighbour's 'pigs in my oaks') to the delightfully banal ('this night one of my great teeth fell out by the fireside').[255] Indeed, personal and farming notes of this kind became so common that they attracted the notice of satirists. *Endymion* appeared in 1663 with a 'diary' already printed, with entries such as 'The red cow took bull', 'My son John born' and 'The black cat caught a mouse in the barn.'[256]

Almanacs sought to fill many roles, and it is difficult to determine which section the average buyer felt to be most important. They had an obvious utilitarian role in providing data on fairs, weights and measures, postal services and the like. The table of the kings was designed to help in dating leases and deeds which often used the regnal year.[257] Similarly the kalendar of saints was included because saints' days were often used to date fairs, law days and legal documents. Astrologers sensitive to the charge that they were thereby perpetuating popish superstitions urged their critics to 'desire reformation at their hands in whom the power to reform doth consist'.[258]

Much of the astrological data of the almanac was itself utilitarian, notably the weather forecasts. This was a controversial area, and compilers were aware that their frequent failures and contradictions exposed them to ridicule (though fortunately no contemporaries seemed to notice that the London and Cambridge editions of *Fly* for 1687 contradicted each other). They were naturally on the defensive against 'wily weather watchers', and stressed local variations and the complexity of the subject. Gilden thought it 'lost labour' and wisely printed merely the rules of weather forecasting, leaving the reader to work out the prediction for himself. William Davis complained that people still complained even though a majority of the prophecies were fulfilled, so that ''tis as possible to cut out a coat fit for the moon as to write an almanac to please every man'. Gabriel Frende offered detailed forecasts, but cautiously called them his 'guess' and declined to pin his reputation on the results.[259] The Master of Clare was pleased to note that where *Frende* forecast prolonged rain, there had been a 'great and continual drought', but he continued to buy subsequent editions.[260]

Despite the satirists, it is clear that the public demanded weather predictions. The husbandman regarded an almanac without them, a contemporary remarked, as 'like a pudding without suet'.[261] From literary evidence at least, it seems that some notice was taken of the pronouncements. Ben Jonson's Sordido based his assessment of the coming harvest and grain prices on the almanac's predictions of the weather, and as late as 1708 Jonathan Swift asserted that it was common for country gentlemen to consult the almanac for a fine day before arranging a hunting expedition. Charles I was reported in 1648 scrutinizing a (royalist) almanac to find the weather.[262] There is similar literary evidence that readers took note of the lists of good and evil days, and the mottoes which supplemented them. 'What's the word? What says Bretnor?' asks a perplexed character in Middleton's *A Fair Quarrel*. 'The word is, sir, *There's a hole in her coat*.' 'I thought so,' he concludes, 'the physician agrees with him; I'll not marry today.' In one of his masques, Middleton asserted that

> The farmer will not cast his seed i' the ground
> Before he looks in Bretnor; there he finds
> Some word which he hugs happily, as, *Ply the Box*,
> *Make hay betimes*, . . .[263]

Most almanacs contained similar astrological information relating to farming, with the best times to plough, sow, geld animals or fell timber. Both astrologers and their critics believed that these guidelines were widely followed. 'Every husbandman or peasant' declared the astrologer, William Ramesey, knew the value of the right astrological moment for gelding livestock and breeding cattle. It was said to be the custom in the north to choose the appropriate time to set hens to brood, kill pigs for the longest preservation of the bacon, and fell timber when the wood would last longest. Land should be manured during the wane of the moon, said an Elizabethan astrologer, for during its increase the manure would merely stimulate weeds. Similarly, pease set when the moon was waxing would bloom indefinitely but produce no fruit. Swallow's almanac for 1640 noted that 'many country people use to take observation of the Prime in covering and weaning of cattle', and explained the rationale for this. All these practices, declared Ramesey, were 'so common, that to spend more time hereunto, were to no purpose'.[264] A mid-eighteenth-century compiler was confident that the 'industrious' farmer still adhered to the astrological rules.[265]

Most of the countrymen who bought almanacs would not of course have been able to grasp and apply complex astrological data. It demanded no special skill, however, to observe the phases of the moon. Henry Coley believed that the sole interest of country readers in the 'language of the stars' was to be told the stages of the moon, and the sign. Authors who provided more comprehensive information found that they were likely to confuse and alienate their readers.[266] Many purchasers probably supplemented lunar data with the lists of good and evil days and the semi-proverbial hints supplied by Bretnor and others, as Thomas Middleton alleged.[267] Many contemporary guides to farming and gardening also contained astrological rules and advice. Firsthand accounts of the use of such rules are scarce, but enough survive to suggest that these practices were not uncommon.[268]

As William Perkins and other critics pointed out, predictions of the weather and of harvest had a further practical application, in enabling profiteering farmers to exploit an anticipated shortage of grain. Contemporaries realized that such prophecies could be self-fulfilling, as farmers hoarded supplies and waited for prices to rise. Some almanac-makers conceded the point; Henry Rogeford suppressed details of the coming harvest to frustrate hoarders and prevent the 'impoverishment of the poor common people': 'through my pen I should not be the occasion of their malice.'[269]

The astrological data supplied on medical problems was equally utilitarian. Belief in the importance of astrology in determining the proper times for surgery, letting blood or taking medicine was widespread in the sixteenth century and still common, though declining, in the seventeenth. At the village level, its authority almost certainly lasted far longer. The Anatomy or 'zodiacal man' was probably the only work of reference available to a vast number of unqualified physicians, and the rules supplied were said to be followed widely and scrupulously.[270] There was equally little provision for the unqualified surgeon. Aware of the unintentional mayhem which the ignorant surgeon was capable of inflicting on his patients, the Elizabethan astrologer Gabriel Frende modified the usual Anatomy and included a figure showing the veins of the arms and lower legs most suitable for blood-letting. He added a note to the surgeon explaining that it was intended, 'thy hand to guide' aright.[271] A number of Stuart compilers derided the Anatomy, claiming rather disingenuously to be baffled by its significance; but they generally inserted the figure, conceding its popularity with the ordinary buyer, who without it 'with contempt would straight refuse to buy/the book, and 'tis no almanac contend'.[272] Almanacs also provided the dates of the dog days, in high summer, when it was widely believed that to take any medicine would be highly dangerous. James Primrose, a respected mid-Stuart physician who scorned most astrological medicine, accepted this belief, and a physician at the end of the century alleged that large numbers of people died needlessly each summer by refusing to take medicine during this period.[273]

There is no reason to doubt that many people bought almanacs for these strictly practical purposes. But the most popular editions, by men such as Lilly, Wing, Partridge and later Moore, were those which contained also social comment, political speculation, or cheap sensationalism. John Gadbury had nothing but scorn for those who attracted buyers with extravagant prophecies, but he conceded that 'an almanac without them (like a gentleman money-less) is not regarded.[274]

Where a series of almanacs bought by a single person has survived, there seems usually to have been some degree of selection between the rival editions, but rarely complete consistency. An owner who was loyal to Wing's productions from 1657 to 1672 was exceptional.[275] Another buyer fluctuated between the works of Bretnor, Allestree and Browne in the years 1615–24, apparently indifferent to the mutual recriminations of the first two. Adam Winthrop noted that Allestree was by far the best compiler, but bought and used editions by several others.[276] Lady Twysden, wife of a prominent cavalier, bought the parliamentary almanacs of John Booker in 1647 and 1649, before switching to the royalist, Wharton.[277] There is a certain pattern visible in the progression of John Greene, a moderate parliamentary lawyer, from the devout Allestree to the Puritan and parliamentary Booker and thence (perhaps in protest at republican extremism) to the non-political *Gallen*.[278] There may well have been many readers, though, who were intrigued by works offering a rare glimpse into the exclusive world of high politics, without having any particular affiliation to a party or cause. An order by the Stationers' Company in December 1672, that Lilly's edition should not be distributed until Gadbury's was ready, suggests that, despite their differences in outlook, they were rivals for the same 'political' readership.[279]

There is some evidence of choice too at a more mundane level, Thomas Fowle's almanac for 1693 is made to bewail its future fate: lying on the market stall

to make up the dirty heap
Of penny-ware; where the disdainful eye
Pores on me two long hours before he buy.

Fowle complained that men were 'as curious in the choice of books (amongst which I may include almanacs) as that of women'.[280] John Booker lamented the impossibility of satisfying the public's varied and contradictory demands: 'This man will have the fairs, another the highways. . . . some care for nothing but the days of the month; others will have no Latin in an almanac. . . . This man will know nothing but when to sow, set, plant, plough etc. Another man would know other things in Church, state, commonwealth.'[281] No doubt the husbandman had to ponder the relative advantages of a list of fairs or a table of expenses. The Company's policy of preserving the names of compilers long dead suggests that he was also strongly influenced by a famous or familiar name. (The fiction was strengthened in the case of Vaux's editions by adding the purported age of the author on the title-page, until his 'eighty-fourth' year in 1659. Vaux had in fact died in 1651.) Authors were aware that the average buyer had certain other criteria and demands: cheapness, a weather forecast, the saints' days marked in red, and the medical Anatomy.[282] They did their best to comply.

Of the millions of almanacs printed, only a few thousand copies survive, mostly those collected by bibliophiles such as Ashmole, Wood and Rawlinson, or preserved for the sake of the memoranda or accounts they contained. The majority perished when the year ended, and the word 'almanac' became a synonym for transitoriness. They were utilitarian even as they passed into oblivion, used as lavatory paper, for putting under pies, lighting tobacco or 'stopping of mustard pots.'[283] But enough survive to make possible an assessment of their contribution to the culture of the period, and it is to this that we should now turn.

CHAPTER THREE

Almanacs and Politics

THE MOST FAMOUS mediaeval astrologers were drawn towards the courts of kings and princes. Their patrons valued their medical skills, and perhaps still more their ability to predict the outcome of wars and rebellions. It was natural that early printed prognostications should contain much material of this kind. Governments soon came to believe, however, that what was suitable for the eyes of the king was best concealed from his subjects. Speculation of upheavals in the state had an unsettling effect, and could easily give encouragement to potential rebels. The sixteenth century witnessed the gradual suppression of dangerous political material in almanacs through a combination of censorship, licensing and the self-restraint of timid compilers.[1] Political prophecies were extremely vague in most Elizabethan almanacs, and they were often wholly absent from early Stuart editions. But this trend was reversed by the outbreak of civil war in 1642. Astrologers were able to give free rein to speculation and controversy, which quickly reached unprecedented levels. Though a degree of governmental control was gradually restored, political speculation remained an important feature in the more popular almanacs throughout their later history.

The earliest surviving English prognostications were by the Italian astrologer, William Parron, as we have seen, and were composed primarily for the use of Henry VII. Not surprisingly, the political commentary was sycophantic in tone: Henry would 'overcome his enemies', reign with wealth and splendour, and be 'exalted and fortunate with his children'. Parron was cautious in discussing other European kings, and reserved his prophecies of disaster for the remote and infidel Ottoman Empire.[2] The translations of Continental editions, which were imported into England, usually contained a section on the fortunes of European rulers. For foreign compilers, English affairs were not of primary importance, and other countries were discussed first. Henry VIII was probably not pleased to find an edition for 1534 which began with the affairs of 'Clement, our holy father the pope'. Flattery played a lesser role than in Parron's works, and there were sometimes predictions of popular disturbances, misfortunes for London and 'murmuring' against the government. But there was nothing really offensive, and the translator of Laet's edition for 1516 was confident that his work would be 'to the glory' of King Henry. The Laets listed their successful prophecies, and English readers may have been impressed by the prediction of the fall of a bishop or nobleman in 1529, which could easily be applied to Wolsey.[3] It is possible that the government saw a potential value in astrological prophecy, properly controlled. The Council suppressed a Flemish prognostication for 1535, which was deemed subversive. But it tolerated an edition for 1544 by Cornelius Scute of Bruges, who predicted success for the Emperor Charles and Henry VIII and misfortune for Francis I. The French king would be deserted by his supporters and would have 'great loss in his dominions and . . . little luck in the seat of war'.[4] Such a prospect suited perfectly the anti-French direction of English policy at that time.

In the second half of the century political speculation diminished considerably. English compilers now held sway and were no doubt aware of their precarious legal status.[5] Many in effect renounced political prophecy. In the early seventeenth century the heading *Prognostication* on the second title-page was often replaced by one more neutral, such as *The Latter Part*, offering no prophetic material.[6] Such political predictions as remained were expressed in safe generalizations. For 1560 Henry Rogeford prophesied that there would be some princes 'given to great excess of war', but he hastened to add the likelihood of 'some other princes desirous of peace'. 'If they fail we are like to have great war', he ventured to predict, 'except God of his goodness remedy it.' Vague predictions of wars and disasters remained common throughout Elizabeth's reign, but the authors were careful to avoid precision.[7] Rather than spell out the detailed effects of a major conjunction, Thomas Stephins merely listed the effects of an important eclipse many years before, leaving the reader to draw any conclusions. A writer in 1568 spoke of 'many heinous and lamentable things' arising from an eclipse, but resolved not to 'meddle' with them for fear of displeasing the authorities. Similarly James Carre declined to discuss the likelihood of war as a subject 'offensive to the humour of my reverent superiors'.[8]

It is not difficult to see why monarchs found political speculation offensive. A Scottish astrologer named Bruce was expelled for predicting the imminent death of James I's son and heir, Prince Henry, and his chief minister, Salisbury. Bruce was lucky to escape so lightly; and doubly lucky in that both predictions were fulfilled.[9] Speculation in print was far more guarded, but still dangerous. There was a risk that it might encourage rebellion and subversion by appearing to legitimize them. It was plausible to see a rising which had been foretold by an astrologer or in an ancient prophecy as the fulfilment of an inevitable destiny, perhaps God's own purpose, and thus no longer treasonable. Such an interpretation offered both a justification and a guarantee of success. One peasant rising in early seventeenth-century France was indeed led by an astrologer. The important role of prophecies in early modern English rebellions is well known.[10] Royal fears were thus not misplaced. Chapuys, imperial ambassador to Henry VIII, was visited by the agent of a disaffected peer who wished to seek the subversive Flemish prognostication for 1535 which the government had banned.[11] Even vague speculation might appear dangerous in times of crisis, as when Woodhouse's almanac for 1601 (predicting upheavals) was suppressed by the government in the aftermath of the Essex rising. A few years later some loose talk of plots was found to have been suggested by passages in Gresham's almanac. Astrology and conspiracy continued to be linked throughout the seventeenth century.[12]

The most dangerous astrological prophecies of the sixteenth century were by the French astrologer, Nostradamus, many of whose prognostications were circulating in the early years of Elizabeth's reign. Nostradamus was a master of dramatic ambiguity, which has kept his prophecies alive down to the present age. It was clear, though, that he was guaranteeing the glory of the King of France and the Catholic Church, and the ruin of the enemies of both. 'To France supreme victory, *salve* king Emperor, build a new city in the north, Henripolis. *Et salve victor*', ran a passage in his prognostication for 1559, shortly before the sadly unexpected death of the French king, Henry II. Most of the predictions foretold, in obscure but dramatic language, a series of upheavals, wars, plagues, seas red with blood, and catastrophes greater than any known since the age of the Vandals. Predictions of the 'death, ruin, affliction and banishment of the enemies of Christ's church', scheduled for April 1559, and later of the flight of bishops, must have been unsettling for the newly-established Protestant Church of England.[13] Matthew Parker, Elizabeth's first Archbishop of Canterbury, scornfully rejected the suggestion that he had hesitated over accepting the post because of Nostradamus's dire warnings.

Though we may accept his denial, it remains of interest that an eminent politician (Sir Nicholas Bacon) should have harboured the idea. Belief in the predictions of Nostradamus and other astrologers was widespread in the Elizabethan court, and a Puritan complained that the nobility put more trust in the astrologer than in God.[14]

For most of Elizabeth's reign there was fairly tight supervision over the contents of prognostications. English compilers appear to have submitted to this without complaint, and the only two other highly dramatic predictions of the period (apart from those of Nostradamus) both had Continental origins. Philip Moore's large work, *A Fourtie Yeres Almanacke, with a Prognostication* (1567, and several later editions), prophesied wars, aristocratic treachery, major rebellions which would overthrow kings, and the ruin of a queen. Moore was careful to explain that the predictions were drawn from the works of the Bohemian astrologer, Cyprian Leowitz, and to add marginal notes at the more sensitive points, indicating that the anticipated disasters would probably occur in Continental countries.[15]

There were few such restraints in *A Most Strange and Wonderfull Prophesie* (1595) ascribed to one John Cypriano, allegedly translated from Italian and derived from two German astrologers and the magical studies of 'Tarquatus Vandermer'. Within a year, it asserted, massive wars, famines and plagues would sweep through the earth, and all the biblical signs of the world's dissolution would become apparent. The prophecy of Cypriano was part of an old tradition linking astrological and apocalyptic speculation, a combination familiar in mediaeval predictions. On the last page the compiler remarked that England, though wrapped in a 'cloak of sin', might be spared from the general disasters as God's 'new Jerusalem'. The authorities were not mollified, and were perhaps provoked by the prediction that an unnamed island was to be engulfed in a second deluge 'because the sins of the prince is (*sic*) so heinous before the majesty of God'. The Company of Stationers seized the press and equipment of the printer, Abel Jeffes, and imposed a ban on him which was never lifted.[16]

By the early seventeenth century, many almanac-makers were omitting political speculations altogether, from principle as well as prudence. Jacobean compilers were often professional mathematicians, interested less in politics than in advances in instrument-making or astronomy. William Bourne, an Elizabethan expert in gunnery and navigation, observed in an almanac that the widespread belief in the dramatic prophecies generally contained in such works was 'most vain and foolish'. Several compilers argued on scientific and religious grounds that political speculation was beyond the proper scope of astrology. A compound of scepticism and indifference was characteristic of the authors of the period.[17] Astrologers such as Gresham tried to satisfy all readers by including dramatic prophecies but adding a rider that they were based on 'old and vulgar astrology', and far from reliable.[18] In an 'Almanack against Almanackes', Gervase Dauncy denounced such 'pagan trumpery', and asserted that 'to commit odd presages and riddles of feigned signs and sorceries to the multitude' was 'to give a sword into a mad-man's hand'.[19]

During the reign of Charles I, the only practitioner of the traditional type was John Booker, whose political speculations won him both popular renown and official displeasure. His comments on corruption in government and the law would have found little favour at court. 'When bribes dare not be took, and none dare give', he remarked, then plagues—the consequence of sin—would cease. He found few grounds for hope: 'If I say the plague shall visit us, it is answered, when is it not? . . . If bribery, oppression, extortion etc shall reign among us, it is demanded, who seeks to reform it?[20]

The majority of Elizabethan and early Stuart almanacs, however, were deferential in tone. Many contained exhortations to obedience and gratitude, and thus provided a useful additional prop to royal authority. In 1589 John Harvey urged his readers to offer hearty prayers for the queen, privy council and nobility. Buckminster composed loyal anthems:

O Lord, preserve our gracious Queen,
Defend her from all foes;
Thy favour still on her be seen
Whersever her Majesty goes.

The commons and the people, Lord,
Subjected to her grace,
Maintain in wealth and one accord
Obedience to embrace. Amen.[21]

A few years later Robert Watson called for thanks to God for the unexpectedly peaceful accession of James I, and for national repentance so that He might prolong the blessings. The duty of subjects was clear: they must 'reverence give, unto the higher power'. Compilers expounded the horrors of the Gowry conspiracy (1600) and the Gunpowder Plot (1605) against King James, with suitable warnings:

Come traitors all, behold the fall
Of Gowrie, that traitor he:
Who wrongs the Lord's annointed shall
Receive such meed [sc. recompense] and misery.[22]

The same sentiments appeared in the next reign. 'Long live King Charles, triumphantly to reign', prayed *Pond*, 'God give him sons.' 'Long live King Charles, else we are undone', Hewlett agreed. Sin might provoke God to take away this blessing, but 'If people turn their lives to mend/Then King and realm God will defend.'[23] John White published the birthdays of members of the royal family for the benefit of loyal readers.[24]

The political quiescence of almanacs, almost complete by 1640, was shattered by the revolution—though many of the standard editions, the 'sorts', chose to ignore its existence for the next twenty years. At first the astrologers were cautious, with a spate of pseudo-almanacs and similar works, some published, offering more direct comment.[25] Booker's edition for 1643, written early in the previous year, denounced the Irish Rebellion, and feared the possible approach of war.

Once fighting began, the tone of commentaries changed noticeably. Booker's almanac for 1644, the first to be written after the outbreak of war, prayed for peace but threatened the 'Romish rout' with destruction. Most of his political predictions were in Latin, taken directly (and prudently) from classical and Arab astrologers, but the phrase '*Cave ab homine trium literarum*', with a reference to his impending ruin, provoked a violent reaction from a rival astrologer, George Wharton. Wharton had sold his estates to raise a troop of horse for the king, and became one of the best known and most committed propagandists for Charles. His earlier almanacs had been moderate in tone, but his edition for 1644, written at the king's command, took an openly partisan course. He denounced Booker, and complained that Booker's friends were interpreting the 'man of three letters' as a reference to '*rex*', King Charles; Wharton countered that they should stand rather for Pym or Lord Say, whose imminent fall he predicted. He supplied a highly slanted account of the battle of Edgehill, contrasting the courage of the king with the cowardice of leading Parliamentarians who were said to have been found 'skulking in . . . holes and saw-pits'. The war, he alleged, was caused not by the stars but by the malice of Parliament. The stars, however, heralded the triumph of the king, the suppression of the sects and the hanging of the rebel leaders.[26] Wharton's onslaught provoked a fierce controversy. Booker replied in

January 1644, defending the parliamentary cause and his own writings, and denouncing the professional incompetence of his rival. Wharton retaliated in kind, and others entered the fray, Silvanus Morgan in defence of Booker, and John Taylor the 'Water-Poet' in support of Wharton.[27]

To harness fully the propaganda value of the stars, it was necessary to discredit claims by opponents that there could be any different interpretation. Astrologers accordingly heaped abuse on the political beliefs, professional competence and personal morality of their rivals, and for good measure predicted their early and ignominious death. Wharton's pseudonym, 'Naworth' was amended to 'No-worth', sparking off a war of abusive anagrams. George Wharton's name, for example, was remoulded as 'A huge rot'n rogue' and 'Hang, O true rogue'. Victory went to John Taylor who claimed that he had studied Assyrian manuscripts in the Bodleian, and could now reveal—using much fake etymology in many archaic tongues—that 'Booker' was 'a Syriac word', meaning 'a ranting rebel, who . . . deserves to be hanged'. Booker denounced him as a 'pagan villain', and was goaded by Wharton into an outburst of wild and almost meaningless rage: 'You puppy, you *hic, haec, hoc, you qui, quae, quod*, you neuter, you commune. . . .'[28]

It was in this heated atmosphere that the first almanac by William Lilly appeared, in April 1644, under the title *Merlinus Anglicus Junior.* Lilly's journalistic flair brought him instant celebrity as the leading political astrologer. He had composed a manuscript prognostication for 1642, and his prophecy for 1644, originally compiled in January, had circulated for some months in manuscript form. It contained a brief statement of the author's position. Lilly described himself as a 'friend to monarchy: to the Parliament of England. I am enemy to Independency. I wish the Church reformed, and all sectaries at Amsterdam.' The predictions attracted the notice of a number of M.P.s, and the printed edition was sold out within a few days; a larger, unexpurgated edition followed in July.[29] The same month (July) saw the publication of *A Prognosticall Prediction*, denouncing the 'Spanish Protestants' who surrounded the king. The author admitted his ignorance of astrology, but utilized its popularity to predict Charles's conversion to the parliamentary cause.[30]

Lilly's almanac provoked the anger of Wharton, who denounced him in his own next edition. Lilly claimed later that it was this attack which had driven him into the parliamentary camp, but this was less than the truth. His manuscript predictions for 1644 had contained criticism of the queen and abuse of the 'rascal Irish' who would come to fight for Charles against the 'Protestant cause'; some of his other publications in 1644 gave a clear endorsement of the parliamentary position.[31] But the attack probably hardened his attitude, and the edition for 1645 was more outspoken. In it, he set out his views, supporting moderate church reform in a Puritan direction, but opposing Presbyterianism. 'Wholly monarchical', he nevertheless blamed the war on the king's evil councillors, and thought that a royalist victory would mean 'we are slaves'.[32] The endorsement of Parliament, though clear, was qualified. Lilly was sensitive to the public mood, and reflected discontents which were widespread. He feared that the weight of taxation would reduce all 'to beggary', attacked the corruption of the 'new lords, called Committee-men,' and suggested that prominent officers on both sides were prolonging the war deliberately for their private ends. He hoped however for a speedy peace based on compromise not total victory, and called for the suppression of the Independents, both as a religious group and a political faction: 'He that would have no peace is no Christian, though he be an Independent.'[33] In subsequent years Lilly adopted a still more committed position. In 1646 he predicted total victory for Parliament and included the horoscope of the royalist commander, Prince Rupert, for whom he forecast a series of blunders, scandals, a sordid disease and early death. He turned towards the Independents and the army, expressing disillusion with the Presbyterians, under whose religious settlement 'our slavery would have exceeded that of the worst of times preceding'. In 1648 he championed the army as 'God's Instruments' in its quarrel with Parliament. In the following edition (dated by him 4 December 1648) he predicted a purge of Parliament, which took place two days later and cleared the path for the execution of the king, already prophesied by Lilly 'with a mournful quill'.[34]

Other astrologers also published almanacs in defence of Parliament. Booker was less outspoken than Lilly, but there was no ambiguity in his comment that the stars promised 'joy to our friends, disaster to our foe'. Vincent Wing gave guarded support. Nathaniel Nye's almanac for 1645 contained a detailed and highly partisan account of events from the meeting of the Long Parliament, hailing Pym as a 'worthy patriot' and denouncing the queen. Nye mentioned the capture of some royalist colours bearing the motto '*spero meliora*', and the tone of the work is indicated by his very free rendering of the Latin words as 'I hope to see popery up again'.[35]

George Wharton continued to defend the royalist cause in his almanacs and newspaper, *Mercurius Elencticus*. When the king's armies collapsed, Wharton looked towards Ireland and declared resolutely that the wars 'ended not with the surrender of Oxon'. But there was nothing to substantiate his dreams that 'the people's eyes are opened' and that the rebels would be brought to account. His newspaper turned in desperation to scandalous stories about Lilly's professional misconduct and amours. Lilly, he said, looked 'like a pig, over-roasted'. (In similar vein, a later critic alleged that Booker's hairy face would 'fright a razor' and that Culpeper, another parliamentary astrologer, resembled an ape.[36]) Wharton's position was precarious after the defeat of the king, and he was indeed arrested and imprisoned for six months in 1648. He managed to escape, however, and published a defiant new almanac composed in his cell.[37] Similar adventures befell another royalist astrologer, one Humphreys, who attacked his former tutor, Lilly, in a pamphlet entitled *Anti-Merlinus*. He predicted the triumph of King Charles and the ruin of the Independents; the devil, he suggested, was 'the first Independent that ever was'. Humphreys acted as astrologer to the royalist garrison in Colchester during its siege in 1648, while Lilly and Booker 'encouraged the soldiers' of the attacking parliamentary force. He survived the anger of the garrison when his prophecies failed, and escaped to lead a hectic life until his death on the way to a safer refuge in Barbados.[38]

Lilly and Booker emerged from the war supreme as the doyens, the 'Castor and Pollux', of English astrologers.[39] Skilful propagandists, they were always ready to give timely support to Parliament's cause. Within a few hours of seeing a pamphlet by Wharton, claiming that the king's march in spring 1645 was destined to lead to victory, Lilly had compiled a refutation guaranteeing a parliamentary triumph, which duly occurred at Naseby on the very day of publication. As already mentioned, Lilly and Booker were invited to join the troops at the siege of Colchester in 1648, and passages from Lilly's almanac were read to encourage the English soldiers invading Scotland a little later.[40] Booker's outlook was symbolized in 1644 when he christened his daughter Victoria in celebration of a parliamentary victory.[41] Lilly gave more direct assistance to the cause by supplying information on French affairs, which was derived from his many Continental contacts, among them the confessor to one of the French secretaries of state; his usefulness was recognized by a state pension paid between 1648 and 1650. Lilly's claim to have known the entire spy network in the royalist garrison in Oxford in the later stages of the civil war suggests that he may also have been engaged in domestic intelligence. The wide circle of his professional clients, crossing political and religious divisions, would have provided many opportunities.[42] Walter Frost, a former almanac-maker who became secretary to the Council of State, was certainly active in collecting intelligence, and indeed clashed with Lilly in this field. Frost gave one of his agents the pseudonym 'Mrs. Strof', the anagram under which he had issued some of his pre-war editions.[43] Another parliamentarian compiler, Henry Harflete, wrote in support of Lilly, and was active in the county administration of his native Kent. Culpeper and Coelson, later well-known astrologers, were both wounded while fighting with the parliamentary armies.[44]

The success of astrological propaganda is well attested. Though the sales-figures of Lilly's earlier almanacs are not recorded, his first passed quickly through two editions; 13,500 copies were printed of the 1646 almanac, and sales were more than double that figure by 1659. Moreover his monthly predictions were reprinted from 1648 as 'circulation-builders' in the popular newspapers of Daniel Border, Henry Walker and others. Enterprising publishers lifted prophecies from the almanacs of Lilly and Booker and republished them in their own compilations.[45] A number of prominent Parliamentarians encouraged and protected Lilly, and one testified that Lilly's predictions had boosted their own morale as well as that of the army and general public.[46] The violence of royalist abuse indicated Lilly's popularity, as did the contrasting practice of issuing royalist propaganda under the names of Lilly and Booker. A cavalier lamented that the two astrologers 'led the commons of this kingdom, as bears . . . are led by the nose with bagpipes before them'.[47] A pamphlet, ostensibly written by a royalist colonel, which remarked on Lilly's integrity and European fame and wished 'he were ours', thus had at least a shadow of plausibility. An intercepted letter written in 1645 to the royalist courtier, Lord Digby, showed cavalier susceptibility: the author said that he was 'deeply struck' by Lilly's prediction of disasters awaiting the nobility. Lilly claimed that even King Charles accepted his astrological skill, though there is nothing to corroborate this.[48]

Lilly's practice of first setting out his beliefs and then giving an 'objective' account of the stars probably strengthened his credibility. His protestations of affection for the monarchy and regret at the execution of Charles I were probably genuine and certainly more likely than crude vindictiveness to convince his stunned readers that the regicide was ordained by God and the stars.[49] His reputation however rested on more than technique alone. Lilly adjusted constantly to shifts in the political balance, but retained a degree of independence. His support for Parliament in the 1640s was combined with attacks on taxation and excise, and the corruption of county committee-men. This was no doubt popular with the readers, but it provoked the wrath of such powerful politicians as Sir Arthur Haselrig and Miles Corbet.[50] In 1647 General Fairfax had Lilly and Booker brought by coach to army headquarters, apparently seeking to persuade rather than direct them into taking the army's part in its developing quarrel with Parliament. The astrologers were treated courteously, and Fairfax supplied an account of the army's viewpoint and objectives. The tactic was successful, partly no doubt because Lilly was already growing suspicious of those he labelled Presbyterians. He pinned his hopes on a treaty between the army leaders and the king, warned London and the Presbyterians against challenging the army's authority, and combined a concern with the soldiers' arrears of pay with (later) a condemnation of the Levellers.[51]

Conventional political argument had only a secondary role in almanacs, the main purpose of which was to prove 'scientifically' that the stars guaranteed the success of the cause and the ruin of the enemy. Lilly and Booker both subscribed to a commonplace belief in a balanced polity of king and parliament. Up to 1648 Booker included each year the phrase '*Vivat Rex et Floreat Parliamentum*'. More explicitly, Lilly observed in 1648 that 'Some are for anarchy, others for democracy: *Anglicus* is yet for monarchy', with Charles 'enjoying his due regality, and we our native birth-rights'.[52] They blamed the war on the king's evil counsellors, and called for them to be brought to justice.[53] Lilly shared the fear that the Leveller appeal to the people represented a leap towards anarchy, and responded with an extravagant declaration of respect for properly constituted institutions: 'Let the people of England elect . . . a Parliament of dead men', he declared, 'I would . . . perform my ultimate service for that authority, so elected.'[54]

One of the most pronounced features of astrological propaganda was the blending of political and religious issues with racial hatred. This was most evident in the discussion of Irish affairs, reflecting a common English tendency to dismiss the Irish as a barbarous race. 'What shall we think of that king', asked Booker in 1644, who 'spoke friendly to those which have cut the throats of 200,000 Israelites, I mean Protestants in Ireland?' A reference to a lunar eclipse explained that the moon was 'ashamed/to view the Irish', who were labelled variously 'the nasty wild Irish', the 'stinking Irish', and the 'Irish mut', whose 'fertile fields' would be seized for ever by the invading English army.[55] Lilly promised success and lasting prosperity to the English who settled on expropriated Irish lands during the Protectorate.[56]

Hostility towards the Scots developed rapidly with their support for Charles in the second civil war in 1648 and their acceptance of his son as king after the establishment of a republic in England. The attempt to link the Stuart cause with foreign, Scottish oppression was an adroit move. Lilly compared the forty years of 'servitude' under two Scottish kings with the years spent in the wilderness by the children of Israel. King 'Jemmy the 6', that 'perfidious Scot', had been able to plant the Stuart dynasty to practise its 'treacheries and beggaries' in England only through the fully of the 'cowardly, ignoble nobility' of this country.[57] Now that the 'Scottish Yoke' had been thrown off, the astrologers looked for vengeance and heaped scorn on the Scots as a poverty-stricken, priest-ridden and treacherous nation. For any reasonable sum, it was alleged, the Scots would sell their new king to the English, as they had sold his father, so that 'to be an high constable in England is in effect to live a more comfortable life, and to have as much power and monies, as a king of Scotland.'[58] Cromwell's expedition in 1650 against Scotland was guaranteed success by the stars and was hailed as the instrument of God to punish a 'perfidious nation' and root out its 'Turkish clergy'.[59] The diatribes against the Scots were given still wider currency by being reproduced in the 'Black' and 'Bloody' almanacs compiled out of the works of Lilly, Booker and other astrologers by Henry Walker and other journalists.[60]

The concept of an alien Scottish tyranny was linked closely with the familiar contemporary belief that a 'Norman Yoke' had been imposed on England ever since the Conquest, when an earlier Saxon world of liberty and justice had perished. Lilly shared this doctrine, and described the execution of Charles as the recovery of 'our native rights' from the successors of the 'Bastard Norman' kings, who had ruled by the right of the sword alone. 'Be not sad', he urged the common people, for providence had 'well-provided for thy ease: the foundation of thy freedom is now laid'. The stars foretold that monarchy would never be restored in England.[61]

As in other later Revolutions, radical writers during the interregnum were confident that the establishment of liberty would have repercussions far beyond the national boundaries.[62] Others would follow the

English lead. Monarchy had at last been exposed as tyranny, for 'how can Charles the Gracious be better drawn to the life, than by the description of Tarquin the Proud?' One author declared that 'liberty and principality are incompatible, they meet not together', and many looked hopefully for the return of an age of freedom which had existed before the invention of kings, in a bygone state of nature or in the Garden of Eden. It was asserted roundly that 'liberty is natural, servitude violent', and the old question was posed once more, in slightly amended form,

> When Adam digg'd, and Eve did spin,
> Who was then to reign as king?[63]

The imminent downfall of all monarchs became a regular, almost standard prediction. 'All monarchs begin to look scurvily', reported the *Levellers Almanack* in 1652. Nicholas Culpeper, a prominent astrological writer in the early 1650s, assured his readers still more bluntly that, 'Monarchy begins to stink in the nostrils of the commonalty, as bad as a jakes.' Surveying the nations of Europe he predicted cheerfully the death and destruction of all the ruling heads, including ungallantly that 'crooked piece of flesh', Queen Christina of Sweden.[64] Before long, Booker agreed, 'there will be scarce a king in Christendom'. The French people would imitate the English, and a great wave of rebellions and wars would sweep monarchs aside. 'A sword and a gun are two prevailing arguments', Culpeper observed, with scorn at the academic as well as political establishments, 'there is none to be found like them in Keckerman's *Logick* nor Ramus's *Dialecks*'.[65]

The exuberant confidence with which astrologers anticipated the fall of kings was strengthened in many cases by an apocalyptic interpretation of contemporary politics, shared with many radicals. They believed that the revolution heralded the approaching end of the world, or the dawn of a new golden age, the reign of Christ in person or spirit.[66] The furore over the solar eclipse of 29 March 1652, known as 'Black Monday', revealed the potency of a combination of astrology and apocalypse. Culpeper's contribution was entitled starkly *Catastrophe Magnatum: or the Fall of Monarchy*, and heralded the incursion of the Turks, fall of kings and popes and establishment of a golden age. Lilly predicted the ruin of the clergy, a curb on lawyers and the approach of an age of peace, with 'a cessation of all taxes and all things governed by love'.[67] A mass of pamphlets speculated on the likely effects of the eclipse, and many people awaited an instant disaster. There are reports of the rich fleeing from London, farmers driving livestock under cover, people laying in supplies of drinking water before it could be contaminated, sealing their windows with pitch and cowering in bed. Other accounts speak of deserted streets and abandoned markets, and even of breakdowns and suicides.[68] Opponents of astrology were appalled that the public 'put more confidence in Lilly, than they did in God', and when the eclipse proved to be a tame anticlimax, preachers and wits exacted retribution by heaping abuse and scorn on that 'incarnate devil' and his colleagues.[69]

The combination of apocalyptic with astrological themes helps to explain the extravagant nationalism and xenophobia of the almanac-makers. Their jingoism reflected a belief in England as God's holy and elect nation, chosen to fulfil divine plans and execute divine vengeance on His enemies.[70] Foreigners could thus have at best only a secondary place in God's purposes, and enemies could be brushed aside. Lilly dismissed fears of invasion in the 1640s with the rejoinder, 'Tell me not of fiddle faddling French, or Danes, or Irish, or their invading us; when such a thing is, let's make store of graves to bury the foreigners in.'[71] It was reassuring propaganda in a time of anxiety, and was buttressed by the claim that 'the God of Battle is for the English nation', so that 'he fights against providence who draws his sword against the commonwealth.' A minor compiler, John Smith, declared that the stars showed that 'no weapon formed against the English will prosper', so that other powers had no choice but to submit to English terms. God had done wonderful things 'by a hand-full' in England, said John Booker, but 'the sword is not sheathed; other nations must drink of this cup: the vial of wrath is pouring out.'[72]

This outlook produced a militant attitude in most almanacs towards the Dutch before and during the Anglo-Dutch war of 1652–4. The fact that the Dutch were Protestant and republican was outweighed (as for many contemporaries) by an awareness of commercial rivalry and a sense of ingratitude on the part of the Dutch, and irritation at their failure to accept their proper subordination.[73] Lilly argued that the English had rescued them from Spanish 'slavery' in the reign of Elizabeth, since when 'they have lorded it unthankfully over the English. Witness their barbarous butchery' of English merchants at Amboyna, in the East Indies, in 1622. The stars indicated that the English and Spanish would combine to force satisfaction from the Dutch, and the Old Testament appeared to corroborate them; 'O thou that dwellest upon many waters, abundant in treasures', the prophet Jeremiah had warned, 'thine end is come. . . .' The Dutch

JUNES *Observations.*

IF there be a Town, Castle or City in *Scotland* worthy our taking, or if that Nation produce any considerable thing, let our *Army* by Land or Sea expect it; yea, though the *Tory Irish* doe seeme to send them some Rennagadoes for assistance. Some fight at Sea or such like Rumors. The Stars portend victory unto us as well at Sea (against the *Hollander* if they provoke vs) as by Land, both in *Scotland*, *Ireland* or where else our Forces shall arrive. But this Months actions have most relation to the Northerne *Scott*; the Sword enforces those poore wretches unto the barren Mountaines, Famine drives them from thence unto the desolate Vallies, Death carries them unto their wretched graves. Let thy wrath, O Lord, be powred upon the *Antichristian Priesthood* both of *Scotland* and *England*, for they onely, & not we the People have occasioned these bitter Wars, even these breaches betwixt both Nations. There are many hot encounters in or neer this Month; some set Field, or aboundance of Blood-shed where Armies are neer each other: Oh that the good Angels of our God may guard our Armies from Treason or sudden Trechery, and then we are very neer two or three Victories: and surely I feare we loose some gallant Men: I am fully assured God will protect our Forces, and as certain I am that they will not credit *Scottish* Faith. Wicked men do not relate our Army worsted, nor detract from their valour. I heare a noyse of much action, and towards the Months end, it thunders, lightens, or some sudden showres annoy the ripening Corne; but the storm is prepared for cutting downe of Man, and men. Disturbed Councels at *Westminster*, and our Grandees even wearied with expectation to heare from our Northern friends, who faile us not, as the next Messenger will relate:

July.

A prediction for June 1651 from Lilly's almanac, guaranteeing English triumphs against the Scots, Irish and Dutch ambassador was provoked into lodging a formal complaint against Lilly before the Council of State, but to no avail.[74] Commercial tensions were reflected in a campaign for the establishment of an English herring fleet, to reduce economic dependence on the Dutch.[75] The *Black Dutch Almanack* and *Dutch Bloody Almanack* offered a strong diet of hatred, scorn and ridicule, and Culpeper added a prophecy of doom.[76]

A similarly hard fate awaited France. The English had discovered the 'sweetness' of liberty, and the oppressed French people would be anxious to follow in their path. 'The vial of wrath is preparing for that kingdom', wrote Lilly in 1649, adding with reference to the contemporary upheavals, the Frondes, that 'some drops fell casually in Paris last year'. Much worse was to follow: 'France must fall to pieces.' The people would recover their liberties, but 'farewell thy monarchy of France to eternity'.[77] Spain was handled with, greater moderation, partly perhaps because of economic considerations, partly because it was cast as the joint agent of God's wrath against the Dutch and against Portugal, which would lose its king and its new independence as the price of giving shelter to the naval forces of Prince Rupert.[78]

The themes of the elect nation and millennium occurred throughout the rest of the interregnum and indeed the century. But the republican regime of the Rump Parliament, which for a time provided an important focus for them, soon lost its appeal. Lilly at first performed notable feats in its defence, arguing that the king's death was caused by 'providence only, and the inevitable decrees of heaven', foretold centuries before in the prophecy of the White King, which Lilly had published in 1644 and now confirmed was applicable to Charles. To resist the new government was thus to resist God, whose will was written clearly in the stars. Divine retribution would fall on Royalists, Presbyterians or Levellers who failed to submit. The Scots ignored the message of God and the stars and were duly crushed, as Lilly predicted, by Cromwell's army in 1650.[79] More positively, his almanacs held out hopes of relief from the weight of taxes and tithes, and indicated that holders of debentures (government bonds) would be paid in full. He assured readers that it was safe, legal and morally right to purchase lands confiscated by the state from the crown, church and delinquents. Such sales were compared to the dispersal of monastic lands by Henry VIII, and no king would ever reign again in England to challenge the transactions.[80] Another astrologer, Thomas Herbert, spoke warmly of the contented happiness of the English people under a just and powerful government.[81] But

Lilly's support gradually eroded into hostility towards the 'rabble of dunces' who ran affairs for their private ends, neglecting the army, burdening the people and scorning the city of London. His tract on the great eclipse of 1652 anticipated a new representative, and his almanac for that year contained a boldly premature vote of thanks to the Rump in expectation of its impending departure, coupled with references to the declining standards of many members and public demands for a new parliament. There was also a 'warning' on the precarious nature of political power, addressed to all,'whether soldiers or magistrates, who lord it over their fellow creatures'. Lilly recalled later that by the time his next edition appeared, at the end of 1652, his 'soul began to loath the very name of Parliament'. The almanac described the Rump as 'tottering', and predicted that the army and people would rise against it if any further taxes were levied, and would then investigate the widespread belief in its financial corruption.[82] Not surprisingly, Lilly was arrested over these remarks and held prisoner for almost a fortnight. His release came through some skilful perjury and the backing of prominent Independent politicians, including Speaker Lenthall, Haselrig and possibly Cromwell.[83] His almanac for 1654, compiled in September 1653, defended Cromwell's dissolution of the Rump in April 1653 an d hailed the convening of the Nominated or Barebones Parliament (July) as marking 'our redemption from Norman conquest in England'.[84]

Barebones lasted only a few months, too short a period to make much impact on the annual prognostications, and was succeeded by a more conservative regime under Cromwell as Protector. Most of the parliamentary astrologers had little hesitation in adapting to the new situation. The new government offered law and order, and the astrologers' exuberance at the fall of tyranny had stopped far short of social revolution. It was still possible to hope for mild reforms and further curbs on the traditional ogres, the lawyers and clergy, without fear of chaos caused by political radicals or sectarians. Lilly took the lead in championing the new government. His enemies alleged that he hoped for financial reward and official recognition from the state. Certainly he regarded Cromwell as sympathetic, and had a close link with the Protector through the latter's son-in-law, Claypole, though he denied receiving money from the regime. Its outlook was fairly close to his own, and Cromwell answered his taste for the heroic.[85] He and his protégés, Gadbury and Saunders, stressed the themes of order and settlement. Lilly condemned the disruptive Fifth Monarchists and predicted their total failure, while Saunders delivered strictures against

> Fantastic frantics, that would innovate
> and every moment change your form of state.[86]

John Gadbury, later notorious as a popish Tory and Jacobite, gave his support to the system of major-generals, designed to curb the cavaliers by military repression and introduced after Penruddock's rising in 1655, which Gadbury ridiculed as 'childish and effeminate'.[87] Several reacted favourably to the proposal to make Cromwell king. Lilly was hampered by his earlier prophecy that monarchy would never be restored in England, though he recalled his respect for the institution, and Booker prevaricated with the remark that on such a great issue 'I would write high, but dare not trust my wings'. Saunders however elaborated on the several forms of government and criticized both aristocracy and democracy as

> People-sway (like a tossed ship,
> Void both of pole and pilot in the deep).

He concluded that monarchy was the best form of government, referred to Cromwell as 'Royal Protector' and 'Royal Highness', and allegedly speculated that the Protector's younger surviving son, Henry, would one day become King Henry IX. Gadbury added Cromwell's name to his table of English kings and Vincent Wing, nostalgic for settled times, reflected that 'the old way is best, when all's done'.[88]

Attitudes towards Cromwell, and especially his foreign policies, were coloured by the mood of millennial jingoism.[89] Comments on the war against Spain, however, which broke out in 1656, showed also a variety of other considerations. To William Andrews it was a religious crusade:

> Forbear proud Spain against the Cross to fight,
> Think on't i'the cloud, remember Eighty Eight . . .
> O England, England, *sub hoc signo vinces.*[90]

Henry Phillippes saw the war primarily as 'one of the chiefest means of the overthrow of Antichrist' in Spain and its colonies, but recognized the secular objectives of establishing free trade and protecting Protestant merchants. Similarly Saunders placed the war in the context of the overthrow of the Habsburgs by the Northern Lion, while stressing also the benefits that would follow from the acquisition of colonies in the West Indies.[91] Lilly supported the government and pinned the blame on the Spaniards for refusing Cromwell's wish to 'have the English traffic freely with all the habitable parts of the world, there being no divine precept against it'. But he was far from enthusiastic about the breach and, with many of the merchant community, was anxious for a speedy settlement.[92]

The idealization of Sweden showed a similar mixture of motives. Since the age of Gustavus Adolphus, Sweden had been seen as the Protestant champion, and in 1659 Lilly emphasized the benefits that Swedish protection would bring to the Protestants of Europe.[93] But he was aware too of the advantages to be derived from control of the Baltic Sound by the Swedes in alliance with England: guaranteed supply of naval stores and the chance to exclude the Dutch (allied to Sweden's enemy, Denmark) from a profitable area of commerce. Lilly had accepted Cromwell's peace with the Dutch in 1654 but his hostility to them was deep-rooted, apocalyptic in language though largely commercial in essence. During the Anglo-Dutch war he had declared there was a 'vial of wrath brim-full to be poured against them, which will not leave them until most of that nation are massacred' and their shipping lost—'except they comply with England'. He was grieved that the Dutch should prosper through English preoccupation with the war against Spain, and saw in a Swedish alliance both the basis of national prosperity and the means to a full if vicarious revenge against the Dutch.[94] The King of Sweden, duly grateful for such support, sent Lilly a present, and had his almanacs translated into Swedish and German for local distribution.[95] In his autobiography, Lilly later discussed ingenuously the 'occasion' of his support for the Swedes. He stressed hopes of gaining an English foothold at Elsinore and excluding the Dutch from the Baltic, and a wish to help his patron, Whitelocke, who had been sent as ambassador to Sweden.[96] Critics ridiculed his extravagant prophecies of Swedish success, which events did little to justify. John Gadbury championed the Danish cause, largely it would seem from personal rivalry towards his former teacher. The Danish ambassador supplied him with details of his king's birth, in the (justified) hope that Gadbury would be able to proclaim a 'mighty geniture'.[97]

With tighter censorship during the Protectorate, relatively few almanacs ventured to support the royalist cause. As in the 1640s, the most conspicuous defender of the Stuarts was George Wharton. Undeterred by the execution of the king and by his own imprisonment, he issued an almanac for 1650 hailing the future Charles II as 'monarch of my heart', and vowing to 'serve no mortal, but the cavalier'. The pamphlet contained a splendidly ferocious denunciation of the leaders of the Rump as 'the most prodigious monsters that ever the earth groaned under: in whose proditorious breasts, the spirits of all expired traitors, by a kind of Pythagorical transmigration, are entered'. He was rearrested and in some danger of hanging until his release through the unexpected intervention of Lilly and Whitelocke, on a promise to act no more against the government.[98] Wharton was not over-scrupulous in keeping his promise. The edition for 1652 hinted darkly at an approaching upheaval, and the one for 1653 declared bluntly that the 'republic is sick and like to die'.[99] The following edition was suppressed as subversive, on the orders of the Council of State.[100] Unabashed, Wharton responded in 1655 by marshalling astrological and other supernatural evidence to prove that the days of tyranny were numbered: a shower of blood at Poole, an apparition of Christ in the sky (albeit a century earlier, and in distant Transylvania!), armies seen fighting in the air, and even a portentous swarm of bees, '(those monarchical creatures), that came murmuring through the air, (as if offended at all governments but their own)'. His conclusion was that the 'time is at hand . . . for every one to have his right', doubtless with the right of Charles Stuart uppermost in his mind. Wharton's obduracy brought a further spell of imprisonment, but his later almanacs showed little sign of submissiveness. When the edition for 1660 appeared, his long-awaited 'sovereign remedy' was at last becoming a possibility. Cromwell was dead, and Wharton bid the Grandees begone:

> Lay 'side your purple, and your robes off cast,
> Play'rs are but princes while the play doth last.[101]

No other royalist astrologer possessed Wharton's endurance or journalistic skill. One Richard Fitzsmith aroused official anger in the autumn of 1653 by defending the Anglican Church, and suggesting that Black Monday heralded the re-establishment of church and crown.[102] Sir Edward Dering boosted the morale of Royalists in exile by astrological calculations proving that a restoration was inevitable. Exiled cavaliers turned also to Continental almanacs which could make predictions for Charles with greater freedom and security.[103] Another astrologer, John Heydon, was imprisoned for plotting against Cromwell, perhaps in connection with the 'conspiracy' of Dr. Hewit, with whom he was gaoled.[104] Printed propaganda of a different kind was supplied by a journalist, Samuel Sheppard, who issued a series of almanacs 'between jest and earnest', defending the cavaliers, abusing the 'Lord Plebs' and ridiculing astrology.[105] In addition there were occasional pseudo-almanacs, such as Prynne's *An Old Parliamentary Prognostication* (for 1655) which listed passages from the Bible and mediaeval statutes describing the terrible fate of rebels and traitors, and

The Roy all Merlin (1655) which contained a portrait of Charles Stuart and an attack on Cromwell.

There was no republican astrologer to fill a role equivalent to that of Wharton. Most compilers accepted the Protectorate, and were even able to accommodate their millennial dreams within it. The most likely potential exception was Nicholas Culpeper, whose career was cut short by his early death in January 1654. His millenarian hopes had tended not towards a heroic conqueror but the withering away of states and rulers. Culpeper predicted English victory in the first Anglo-Dutch war but added barbed comments on the character of rulers which could apply to both governments involved: 'for an idle piece of a thing called Honour, as striking sail, or the like, what care princes how many thousands of Christians' lives they throw away?' Almanacs for subsequent years were published from his notes, and included the subversive remark that the common people had merely 'leapt out of the frying-pan into the fire' without regaining their liberties. Culpeper also looked forward to losses by Spain in the American colonies, and explained them as a punishment for its 'cruelty and oppression' towards the native Indians.[106]

The only other critic to appear was Sarah Jinner, a hitherto apparently unnoticed female radical. She published several almanacs from 1658, combining a spirited defence of women with medical notes, social comment and a vigorous political commentary. Her outlook was anti-authoritarian, summed up in the prediction that the 'eminent contend about dividing the spoil of the inferior'. She was determined to avoid the charge of sedition, but her position was made clear in a string of observations scattered through her writings. Thus she observed that government 'hath no other foundation than the humour of the people', and that in submitting to the domination of the 'great', the people were showing merely 'the virtue of an ass'. She concluded that the people are 'not bound to obey well, when governors do not govern well'. The misrule of governments was of course her basic theme, and she looked forward to a time when 'the people may have some eminent champion to assert their liberties'.[107]

Oliver Cromwell died in September 1658, and the authority of the Protectorate crumbled quickly. Events made mockery of Blagrave's prediction for 1659, that 'our heroic governor and prudent council seem united, and our nation in a great measure settled'.[108] Instead the year was marked by political confusion, a major rebellion by Sir George Booth in favour of monarchy, and anxiety over rumoured plots by

Jesuits, Royalists and sectarians. Booker clung to the hope that Booth's rising represented the 'gripings and wringings' of a dying Antichrist, but others were less confident.[109] Writing in November 1658, Lilly gave his support to the new Protector, Richard, but anticipated upheavals in the army and the resurgence of radical sectarianism. He was careful to cover every eventuality by heaping praise on all the rulers of England, 'especially the king, prince, protector or governors thereof. The dramatic reversals of 1659 far surpassed anything he had foreseen. Prudently he abandoned the Cromwellian cause and gave his approval to the junta of army officers ('heroes') who were in power when he was compiling his next edition in the autumn of 1659.[110] Their tenure of power, however, was to prove equally short-lived. The fragmentation of the parliamentary cause benefitted only the Royalists. Though a restoration remained uncertain well into 1660, the changed political situation was evident to all. The journalist, George Horton, ventured in September 1659 to publish a tract entitled *Now or Never: or, The Princely Calendar. Being a Bloudy Almanack* in which he promised the end of taxes and the return of the king.[111] All the major astrologers failed to anticipate the Restoration, except, one could argue, George Wharton, who had been predicting it throughout the previous decade.

In May 1660 Charles II returned to England as king. There dawned a new age of extravagant royalism. Wharton understandably gave vent to old hostilities against the Presbyterians, whose

prodigious ears,
Short hair and hatchet faces . . . delude
A monster-headed, giddy multitude.[112]

The Rebels Almanack, another of the tracts issued by Horton, demanded the execution of the regicides and other grandees. There were demands that all those active in the late regimes should be brought to trial. This category might have included Lilly, and extracts from his writings against monarchy were reprinted to prove that he was guilty of treason. It was a token of the moderation which prevailed, and of their own dexterity, that both Lilly and Booker were unharmed, and were indeed allowed to continue publishing.[113]

Having failed completely to predict the events which led to the Restoration, Lilly had to fall back on the plea that they were 'acts above nature', as we have seen. 'However, God is just, and we must acknowledge so much', he added, stressing that the people should remember 'how happy' they were under the new king. He declared his acquiescence in the regime, and promised to write nothing against it. His new caution and his dismal record as a prophet in the late 1650s led to a slump in the sales of his almanacs: from an estimated 30,000 on the eve of the Restoration, they fell to below 8,000 by 1664. In subsequent almanacs Lilly revealed an awareness of the narrowness of his escape in 1660 by ostentatious references to 'King Charles the Merciful' and 'his darling Act of Indemnity'.[114] Booker wrote in similar terms of the king, whose

> Birthday, and return to us, let not
> (Or his *amnesty*) ever be forgot.

He was accused later of still 'fishing in troubled waters', but there seems to have been little substance to the charge.[115] John Tanner, another republican astrologer, reacted to the Restoration by reflecting on the mutability of political affairs, with the slightly ambiguous wish that all could see

> what's our best
> Estate, and all subscribe *quietus est*.

Some of the material in his next almanac was deleted by the censor, and later editions contained no more than questionable prayers for 'better times than heretofore'.[116]

Through a combination of censorship and self-restraint by the astrologers, the government suffered little embarrassment from them. Tanner was reported as a plotter in 1665, but was not arrested. It was alleged in 1663 that Lilly was composing a prognostication to assist a group of plotters led by the Fifth Monarchist, Colonel Danvers. Three years later a number of ex-soldiers, planning to fire London and kill the king, appear to have chosen a date for their attempt after studying Lilly's almanac.[117] Another astrologer, John Heydon, dabbled in political speculation which led him to the Tower.[118]

Many of the Restoration almanacs reflected the mood of the period by fervent expressions of loyalty and devotion to the crown. The standard table of kings often appeared with an extravagant verse commending monarchy. Gadbury, for example, added the blunt assertion that 'kings are Gods below', and that anyone who dares resist them 'runs the road to hell'.

> Let traitors' plots, like wand'ring atoms, fly
> And on their heads pay tenfold usury,

exclaimed another writer, continuing with a four-page rhapsody on the restoration of Charles.[119]

The compilers set out a variety of arguments to prove the divine foundation of the monarchy, and to encourage obedience. God had thrown down each succeeding regime 'until he came whose right it was', and the stars decreed that 'whosoever doth act any thing against him will but bring ruin to themselves'.[120] Even an eclipse of the sun was held to signify 'tranquillity, peace and happiness' to both church and state, in marked contrast to normal interpretations.[121] Some astrologers elaborated these remarks into an entire section on 'the duty of subjects'. *Vaux* assured its readers that according to the Bible they owed total obedience 'even to wicked princes, not only for fear, but for conscience towards God, who counts himself neglected, resisted and opposed' by any opposition towards His deputies on earth. Subjects must therefore 'pay all subsidies, taxes, customs &c.' promptly. Another author asked the sectarians how they came 'to forget this scripture, to fear God and honour the king'. 'Perhaps this is left out of their bibles', he noted sarcastically. Making a direct appeal to self-interest, the author of a slightly later sheet almanac equated stability with prosperity, and declared that

> Our loyalty is the high-road
> To a full trade at home, abroad.[122]

John Gadbury developed the same point, arguing that obedience 'adds to the advantage of the commonalty in general'. Monarchy was surely better than the anarchy of 1659, when 'every one had a snap at the government, as dogs at the nose of a bear'. History showed 'what virtuous things have free-quarter, public-faith, excise, decimation, and 120,000 *l. per mensem* been to England, in comparison of a trivial story of ship-money'. It was thus proven that 'unlimited monarchy is far better for England than the most moderated democracy can be', for monarchy was 'naturally agreeable' to England, laid down by 'God and Nature'. Gadbury cited with approval the dictum of Wharton that 'the body's monstrous [that] hath more heads than one'. Vaux too used an image of physical deformity in observing that 'a commonwealth without a king is like great *Polyphemus* without an eye; then there is nothing but *Cyclopian* cruelty and oppression: great men feeding on the flesh of the poor.' Others repeated the conclusion that a republic meant tyranny:

> Hence anti-monarchists, from you there springs
> Slavery; but freedom is from heaven and kings.[123]

Strident support for England against all foreign powers was as marked after the Restoration as before. Astrologers provided confident predictions of victory during the renewed Dutch wars of 1664–7 and 1672–4. The English, wrote Thomas Trigge in 1667, were 'a people from the beginning ordained for victory!' 'The stars have designed . . . them never to take the foil . . . from any people in the whole world'; the 'ravenous' Dutch must thus submit, and the French take heed. England would 'terrify and vanquish' all its 'perfidious, self-centered and unconstant neighbours', and the Dutch would have to 'stoop, and (with reverence) lick our English dust'. Two collections of extracts in this jingoistic vein were published, in 1667 and 1673, as contributions to national propaganda.[124] Though the wars were at heart commercial, pamphleteers exploited other grievances. In particular, the republican status of the Dutch offended royalist sentiment. Trigge thought it 'scandalous, that so small a democracy should out-nose so many glorious princes round about them', which must 'render monarchy cheap and contemptible, which is in itself the very best government in the world'. Another astrologer argued that the title 'High and Mighty', used by the Dutch government, was blasphemous.[125]

The relative domestic harmony of Charles II's reign was shattered in the late 1670s by a growing anxiety over the open Catholicism of the heir apparent, the king's brother, James, Duke of York. Fears that popery and tyranny would follow his accession were inflamed by the exposure (or rather invention) of a massive popish plot to kill the king and subvert the government. A wave of hysteria swept through the country, and a number of innocent Catholics and others were judicially murdered on the perjured evidence of Titus Oates, William Bedloe and other adventurers. There was a determined attempt to exclude James from the succession, and the collapse of monarchy and even a new civil war seemed possible.[126]

The crisis was naturally reflected in the popular press and in almanacs. The oracles of Nostradamus, expounded by one J.B., a 'faithful Protestant of the first and best rank', held out the reassurance that Charles would produce a son, 'lawfully begotten' for once, who would reign as Charles III, leaving James to find honours elsewhere.[127] Most of the astrological combatants of the Revolution were no longer active. Booker was dead, Wharton had retired from the field; Lilly was old and infirm, and his amanuensis, Henry Coley, was of 'a quiet and peacable disposition', frightened more of mobs than of James.[128] Most almanacs were in fact restrained in their handling of the crisis, but two revived the partisan violence of the 1640s: John

Gadbury, in defence of the monarchy, and John Partridge, a newcomer, against it. Partridge's almanac for 1679 alluded to the impeachment of the chief minister, Danby, and to the discovery of seditious letters by Coleman, formerly secretary to James, and predicted further 'villainies' to be unearthed 'among the servants of princes', and more attempts to subvert the government. In a pamphlet entitled *Prodromus*, Partridge launched a fierce attack on Catholic plotters and declared that it was an article of faith for every 'true-bred' Englishman to believe in the Popish Plot.[129] His almanac for 1682 made no concessions to the growing doubts over the plot's authenticity, and indeed contained a denunciation of 'rascals' who

believ'd it not,
And by their unbelief helped on the Plot.

Even the standard table of kings ended with an Exclusionist prayer:

let us pray
No popish heir may England's sceptre sway.

Partridge developed a conspiracy theory according to which the pope was seeking to 'build his Babel over all'. 'King-killing doctrines never came to light', he asserted, 'Till Hell had spawn'd the pope and Jesuit,' Rule by 'fagot and dagger' would ensue. He recalled the 'martyrdom' of Sir Edmund Berry Godfrey, the magistrate before whom the first allegations of the plot had been laid. Godfrey's death symbolized the fate awaiting the English: 'We may well thy death remind', he remarked, for 'thy throat was cut, and ours all design'd.' The Tories, as those supporting the court were becoming known, were lumped with the papists in doing 'all they can/By plots to undermine both God and man.' In his edition for 1683 Partridge surveyed the history of popish subversion from the reign of King John to the present. He went on to predict further plots and to denounce Rome for having 'filled the earth with blood, the Church with heresy, and the world with sedition'.[130]

Gadbury was naturally on the defensive in the early stages of the popish scare. Events mocked his hopeful prophecy that in 1679 'kings and governors shall be willingly and without grumbling honoured and obeyed', and there was little chance of success in his attempts, with Trigge, to divert popular anger from papists to Dissenters, whom he saw as 'pious frauds, godly cheats', 'squirting out their filth against authority'.[131] Suspected to be a papist himself, and labelled the 'Pope's astrologer', Gadbury was soon caught up in the furore over the plot. He was accused of calculating the best time for an attempt on the king's life, and admitted being asked to discover whether Charles was shortly to die and whether there would be a Catholic succession. He was arrested in November 1679 and examined by the Privy Council in the presence of the king, who inquired sardonically whether he could prophesy to which prison he would be sent. The questions concerned Gadbury's contacts with Mrs. Cellier, Sir Robert Peyton, a renegade Whig, George Dangerfield, and other suspected conspirators. Dangerfield accused him of complicity in the 'Meal Tub' plot, an alleged scheme of several Catholic peers and others to murder the king. Gadbury composed a defence while in prison, pleading his loyalty to the crown and devotion to the Church. Some observers expected him to be put on trial and executed, but instead he was released after fifteen weeks. Rumour ascribed this to bribery, and there was talk of a sum of £200 paid to Gadbury by Catholic plotters grateful for his discreet silence. It is likely, though, that he earned his release. The only witness against him was Dangerfield, whose credibility was destroyed at the trial of Mrs. Cellier. Gadbury did useful service by testifying that Sir Robert Peyton had claimed to be ready with forty thousand men to seize the Tower as soon as he heard the king was dead. Peyton denied this charge, but confessed enough to be expelled from the House of Commons, which cited his links with 'the devil Gadbury' and other alleged conspirators. Gadbury's release may also have owed something to his friend and champion, George Wharton, who was now a baronet and in the king's service, and to his other contacts among the bishops and peers.[132]

John Gadbury had become notorious. He had the honour of being 'twice burnt with the pope' in effigy, in the monster processions through the streets of London. (Cats were trapped inside the burning figures, and their screams provided a lurid touch of verisimilitude.[133]) On his release from prison he took a more aggressive political line. Even during his examination by the council he had argued that the really dangerous plotters were the Dissenters, and in his almanac for 1681 he launched a fierce attack on Whigs, Dissenters and 'madmen' who sought to divide the king from his brother. In private he predicted that Charles II would remarry and produce an heir, and that the Whig leader, Shaftesbury, would be tried and executed. Gadbury's edition for the following year saw a defence of James and of the queen (a Catholic, and a popular target for attack), ridicule of the 'sham-plot', and an attempt to discredit the Whigs by recalling the 'wickedness and barbarities' of the radicals during the Revolution. In 1683 he included a perfunctory condemnation of the Popish Plot, but his emphasis was on the need to suppress 'Jesuitical Dissenters', 'bred up in rebellion and schism'. The acquittal of Shaftesbury by a London jury brought a sharp rebuke:

What boots it monarchs to be styled Gods,
If they are subject to the subject's rods?
People are arbitrary, not their prince,
When *Ignoramus* quits the high'st offence.
Who votes against his king on earth would (even)
Vote against God too! and exile him Heaven.[134]

The last years of Charles's reign saw a massive Tory reaction, with the Whigs broken and discredited by the discovery of a Whig conspiracy, the Rye House Plot. Gadbury and other Tory astrologers rejoiced at the restoration of monarchy to its 'pristine glory' and the downfall of 'exclusion-mongers' and 'trimming-dissenters'. They heaped abuse on the 'raving multitude', 'giddy-headed' rabble who 'would be masters'.[135] The crown strengthened its position by seizing town charters and remodelling urban corporations into narrower oligarchies amenable to royal control. Gadbury was exultant when London, the centre of resistance to the crown, forfeited its charter:

'Tis proved a legal maxim (just and strong)
Cities may err, but kings can do no wrong.[136]

It was now the Whig astrologers who found themselves on the defensive. John Hol well, who had published a tract in 1682 predicting that kings, magistrates and J. P. s would be destroyed by rebellions which their tyranny had provoked, was indicted and convicted of seditious libel.[137] Partridge was accused of complicity in the Rye House affair. It was alleged that he had agreed to join in the assassination of the king, and had prophesied the approaching death of both Charles and James and the victory of the common people. Other accounts spoke of his contacts with the king's illegitimate son, the Duke of Monmouth, for whom Partridge was said to have drawn up a nativity predicting great triumphs.[138] Though these charges were not pressed, Partridge decided wisely to avoid provocation, and in his almanac for 1685 indicated that the reader would find 'not a word of the popish crew this year'.[139]

The death of Charles in 1685 revealed the extent of the crown's recovery: James succeeded to the throne totally undisturbed. The new government banned political speculation in almanacs, and the most violent Whig astrologer, Partridge, fled abroad, finding'England was grown too hot for him'.[140] The remaining compilers prudently offered hymns of loyalty and gratitude to 'Great James', epitome of all that was best in every English king:

Obedient loving subjects may he find,
As He to them is always just and kind.

Had he not 'overlooked our . . . monstrous provocations' (notably Monmouth's rebellion in 1685)? 'He spares our purses, and takes care of our souls.'[141] William Davis, a Wiltshire astrologer, attempted a paean of praise of monarchy based on natural and metaphysical arguments:

The rational soul performs a prince's part,
She rules the body by monarchic art.
Poor cranes, and silly bees (with shivering wings)
Observe their leaders, and obey their kings.[142]

Richard Saunder of Leicestershire imitated Dryden in comparing the upheavals and plots of late years with the biblical episode of Absalom and Achitophel, and wished a similar fate on all future plotters.[143]

John Gadbury was naturally prominent among the champions of the new regime. 'Thrice welcome is that happy year', he declared, 'wherein no bold excluders dare appear.' King James far surpassed even St. George, for whereas the saint had slain only one dragon, the king had dispatched a 'million' Whig plotters. Gadbury predicted the birth of a Prince of Wales to perpetuate the new order, and three years later proudly announced the fulfilment of his prophecy.[144] His almanacs glorified the controversial policies of the reign. He heaped praise on the hated Tyrconnel, Lord-Lieutenant of Ireland, and on the Declaration of Indulgence, which gave religious freedom to Catholics (and, incidentally for Gadbury, to Dissenters). He acclaimed Castlemaine's 'splendid' embassy to Rome, the first official mission from England to the papacy since the Reformation. The Reformation itself he described as an 'unhappy schism'. He hailed as martyrs the Catholics put to death during the Popish Plot, and sought to rehabilitate even Mary, Queen of Scots, 'most barbarously murthered' by Elizabeth Tudor. Describing the recent Whig conspiracy in loving detail, Gadbury dismissed the Popish Plot as a mere sham, and issued a special 'plot almanac', with royal privilege, to provide a high Tory interpretation of it.[145]

Most Whig astrologers hastened to assure the crown of their loyalty, for, as the Irish Whig John Whalley remarked ingenuously, 'kings have long arms, and . . . strike severely.' The compilers avoided political comment.

My wary Genius, the heavens contemplate,
Glance not thy eye o'er th'intrigues of state,

wrote John Tanner:

beware
How thou dost meddle: 'tis not safe to say
Who 'tis shall win, or who shall lose the day.[146]

A satirical ballad, entitled *The States-Mans Almanack*, helped to fill the vacuum. The author mocked the loose morals of James, the 'fumbler royal', and derided his apparent inability to pack a parliament sufficiently to establish popery by law.[147]

The only major opposition to the royal cause came from John Partridge, living in exile in the Netherlands. His almanacs for 1687 and 1688, printed abroad, contained ferocious attacks on the regime, especially on the clergy who had 'pulled in popery by preaching that cursed slavish doctrine of passive obedience'. James II, the 'worst of men', was even appointing popish bishops (an allusion to Cartwright and Parker; neither in fact openly Catholic, but both certainly compliant). 'Now hangs your freedom on each villain's sword', Partridge wrote. With a little 'dragooning' in the French style, the king would pack parliament and use it to destroy all the legal rights of Englishmen. But Partridge expressed confidence that the English would recognize their mistake and drive out popery together with the king. The stars indicated that James might die by October 1688, and the almanacs spelled out the superior benefits of a republic: 'a commonwealth's the thing that kingdoms want.' In republics there were no spurious Whig plots, 'little tricks of state that monarchs use', 'no burning cities to promote the cause', no charters forfeited and rogues made judges.[148]

In August 1687 Gadbury published *A Reply to That Pernicious and Scandalous Libel*, namely, Partridge's almanac. He blamed the Fire of London not on papists but on nonconformists. Republics he condemned as 'uncouth' and 'disgustful', and notorious for the heavy taxation which had certainly marked the Commonwealth and Protectorate. Holland too was 'a hell to the subject, where he cannot so much as wear a pair of shoes, or eat a herring, before they be nine times excised'. Descending to a personal level, Gadbury revived the charge that Partridge had been connected with the Rye House Plot and with Monmouth.[149] Partridge retaliated with a damning biography of his rival, whom he portrayed with gusto as a Ranter turned papist, pimp, plotter and philanderer. He added later that Gadbury had helped to poison Charles II, and had murdered his mistress's husband. In private as in political life, Partridge fought with no holds barred.[150]

In 1688 William of Orange invaded England, and King James fled abroad. Partridge was vindicated, and extracts from his fugitive almanacs for 1687–8 were reprinted as propaganda for the new regime. He did not issue an almanac for 1689, but his *Mene Mene, Tekel Upharsin*, published in the spring of that year, gave an astrological guarantee that the 'Glorious Revolution' would be permanent. Though King James had not died as predicted, Partridge observed, his flight was clearly 'a civil death'.[151]

The Revolution came as a totally unexpected blow to Gadbury. He had already compiled an almanac for 1689 which duly appeared, asserting that James would triumph over all his enemies. On the eve of the invasion Gadbury allegedly circulated a paper in which he proved from the stars that it must fail, and that William would be beheaded on Tower Hill.[152] In his next almanac he prudently declared that 'to be passive is the only province of a subject'. Nevertheless, the government carefully watched his visits to prominent Jacobite prisoners in the Tower, such as the Earls of Castlemaine and Peterborough, and he was soon arrested on a charge of sending Jacobite letters and papers through the post—an incident which Partridge naturally exploited.[153]

William of Orange, who became king as William III, was greeted with a chorus of joy by the astrologers. He was 'William the Great', 'that Darling of Renown', 'Good', 'Mighty' and 'Great, beyond the sphere of men', king 'by miracle', outshining all his predecessors. Partridge changed the title of his almanac to *Merlinus Liberatus*, and the title-page commemorated England's deliverance from 'popery and arbitrary government'. John Whalley observed wittily that William's triumph over a Catholic regime proved that 'one drop of Orange juice works greater effects than a whole barrel of holy-water'.[154]

The previous regime was now portrayed in a vastly different light. King James, surrounded with 'ruffian guards', 'base Machiavellian slaves' and 'priestcraft arts', had reduced England to a 'miserable sea of disorder and confusion'. Partridge told his readers, more bluntly, that William had

> Saved your babes, your lands, estates and wives,
> And your throats too from dispensing knives.

The law courts were returned once more to honourable judges instead of the sycophantic creatures of James, 'their hearts for Rome, their hands for bribes and blood'.[155] The Bloody Assizes (after Monmouth's rebellion of 1685), the birth of a 'spurious' Prince of Wales, and the army's camps on Hounslow Heath to intimidate London were all cited to discredit the late government.[156] Even George Parker, known later as a Jacobite, conceded that James had lost the affections of his people, being misled by 'Jesuitical, pernicious counsel', and he felt constrained to honour the seven bishops gaoled in the Tower in 1688 'for withstanding popery and arbitrary power'.[157]

A 'true blue Protestant', such as Partridge or Whalley, was prepared to go much further. Whalley charged James and his supporters with inventing the Rye House Plot, importing a bogus Prince of Wales, and murdering Charles II, the Earl of Essex (a Whig peer who had died in the Tower) and the Whig 'martyrs', Russell, College, Argyll and Monmouth.[158] Partridge set out a comprehensive indictment of the Stuart monarchy from 1660, in the form of a 'chronology'

> Since Charles the merciful came to the crown
> Whose virtue and piety none can disown.
> Since Dunkirk was sold to our brethren the French,
> And paid for in gold, instruction, and wench,
> Resolved to destroy us and ruin the nation,
> And bring our religion and laws to their fashion.

He honoured the Whig martyrs and even attempted to rehabilitate Titus Oates. And, to the horror of Gadbury, he adopted an openly parliamentarian position in describing the civil wars, praising Cromwell as a 'great man' and 'true Englishman' and dismissing the cavaliers as Tories and papists.[159] John Tanner condemned James II in a passage describing all kings as potential tyrants:

> Caesar or Nothing's writ in all they do
> For monarchs know no medium twixt these two.[160]

Opposition to the regime was naturally muted. Gadbury prayed only for the 'present' king and queen without giving their names. Partridge denounced this as veiled Jacobitism, especially as Gadbury no longer included a table of kings which would have made him clarify his position.[161] Tory astrologers could vent their feelings only in violent abuse of their tormentor, Partridge. They recalled his seditious past and his membership of the radical Whig 'Calves Head Club', and they spread scandalous stories about his private life, to which he naturally replied in kind. These attacks served only to increase his notoriety, and he emerged as the foremost astrological writer of the 1690s. Each year several fake almanacs and other pamphlets were published in his name, and he was even thought sufficiently important to be threatened with assassination, a fact of which he was rather proud.[162]

The Whig astrologers showed no restraint in their attacks on Tories and Jacobites. They greeted plots against William with ironic references to the old Tory doctrine of non-resistance.[163] Two lines of argument were presented. The first was the charge that supporting James meant accepting the tyranny which he had sought to impose, and would seek again if circumstances permitted. The Jacobites must like oppression, Partridge remarked. They

would be slaves,
Wear chains, and wooden shoes, and dwell in caves.

'Rags and chains', John Tanner warned them, would be the 'fruit and just rewards of all your pains'. Whig astrologers professed bewilderment at the blindness of popish Jacobites who, though 'dull, deluded, few,/ Still toil to ruin their posterity.'[164]

James II had found protection and support in France, a country at war with England during most of the 1690s. This situation prompted the Whigs' second line of attack: that the Jacobites were treacherously assisting the national enemy. The return of James would let in the 'French dragoons, that impious scum of hell'.[165] For a number of years astrologers had been reflecting the growing belief that it was the French, rather than the Dutch, who posed the greatest threat to England. Commercial rivalry was linked with fears of French absolutism, characterized by its large standing army, religious persecution and heavy taxation. James, an admirer of French values, aroused similar fears. One of Partridge's early almanacs deplored the encroachment of French cultural values: 'A p— on all French modes, we're English still.' In the early 1680s both Partridge and Holwell published predictions of Louis XIV's imminent death.[166] The 1690s saw a wave of bitter attacks on the French king, intensified by the war, the suppression of the Huguenots and French support for James II in Ireland. Louis was the Christian Turk, 'Christian Nero', 'French Ruffian', the 'Grand Robber of Europe' and 'Murderer in Chief.' 'His will's his justice', it was alleged, 'and his lust his God.' The astrologers proclaimed his approaching death, ruin or expulsion, and offered a variety of dates. (A sceptical reader noted dryly how Partridge 'hath been constantly killing' Louis for years, without effect.[167]) The public need not be shocked by the destruction of a king, said Richard Kirby, for such a fate was written in the stars. Men gave undue reverence to monarchy, but 'God regards bad kings no more than silly shepherds; for are they not cast in the same common mould, as we are?'[168] Other compilers guaranteed that English armies would penetrate to the very heart of France, where William would 'smite' the 'vile Lewis'. The French navy had already been crushed ('eighty-eighted') at the Battle of La Hogue, wrote Matthew Hobbs in 1693. 'Defend thy shores if thou canst,' he told the French, 'the brave English, thy old masters, are coming. Alas, poor slaves of France! William, the king of gentlemen, is coming.[169] As in the mid-century, there was a clearly apocalyptic streak in this outburst of national euphoria.[170]

Political controversy, which became an established tradition during the 1640s, thus survived throughout the century. Only compilers who favoured the government of the day were allowed free expression, but through innuendo and illicit publication the opposite viewpoint was generally available. Moreover the frequent political reversals of the period gave Parliamentarian, Cavalier, Tory and Whig each a turn as the representatives of orthodoxy.

The effectiveness of astrological propaganda is impossible to measure. It is certain that the public welcomed such material, and there can be little doubt that it was important in boosting or undermining morale. The efforts of successive governments to suppress or harness political prophecy show that they regarded it very seriously. The virulence of attacks on William Lilly showed the measure of royalist concern. Similarly Presbyterian M.P.s raised the contents of one of his almanacs 'for a whole week every day in the Parliament house'. A few years earlier, in 1647, members had debated the equally subversive contents of Wharton's almanac.[171] The Swedish king's pleasure and the Dutch ambassador's anger over comments by Lilly demonstrated that even foreign governments took careful note of the prophecies. Many of the politicians who defended Lilly may have been merely exploiting his fame and the public's credulity. But it is unlikely that all were cynical. Walter Strickland, ambassador to Holland and a member of the Council of State, is said to have declared that Lilly's predictions had 'kept up the spirits' of 'many of us Parliament-men'. Lilly was consulted by clients from every part of the political spectrum, from cavaliers to Major-General Lambert and Richard Overton, the Leveller.[172] When prominent men of affairs believed, or half-believed, in astrological predictions on political matters, there seems no reason to doubt that many of the almanacs' ordinary readers would have been deeply impressed. Belief in astrology was declining among the educated in the second half of the century, but there were still politicians towards its close who were willing to take note of what the stars decreed. The success of John Partridge suggests that the average buyer devoured political prophecy as avidly as in the golden days of Lilly.[173]

Yet perhaps still more important than the direct effects of astrological propaganda was the almanacs' role in fostering political awareness among the reading public. Even before the civil war a number of almanacs provided factual information such as lists of boroughs returning members to parliament. Some later series, notably Lilly's, contained an annual survey of the political situation throughout Europe and further afield.[174] Though censorship of newspapers and the press after 1660 stemmed the flood of pamphlets, almanacs preserved a public awareness of political events and issues. Their partisan violence helped to sustain party loyalties and divisions. In publicizing threats to liberty or religion they helped also to establish the idea that political issues were of vital importance to all; to that extent they reduced the likelihood of royal absolutism. During the Whig era of the 1690s, the Tory astrologer Gadbury reflected that he might have weakened the monarchical cause, for which he stood, by his career of political speculation. Good things, he reflected, 'may be abused, and ignorant, or malicious people are apt to take things by the left handle'. Perhaps, after all, astrology was suitable only for kings and gentlemen. He had sinned in 'divulging so many of Urania's secrets to common eyes. But what is done is past retrieve.'[175]

CHAPTER FOUR

Society

ALMANAC-MAKERS DEVOTED as much space to the condition of society as to the fate of kings and princes. Each year they listed impending social disasters: pestilence, harvest failure, crime, and disputes between ruler and ruled, rich and poor, and husband and wife. They declared that man's sinfulness had provoked these calamities, and that through repentance they might be averted. In calling for amendment of life, compilers often felt an obligation to describe proper social behaviour. Frequently they abandoned their prophetic role, and wrote simply as commentators and critics of English society.

Though attitudes naturally varied over two centuries, the great majority of almanac-makers throughout the period displayed an outlook of conservative paternalism. They upheld the distinctions of birth and wealth, while arguing that privilege carried responsibilities, in providing charity, protection and example. This formula was admirably suited to the astrologers' twin objectives, of attracting a mass readership and winning approval and perhaps patronage from the wealthy.

In the Garden of Eden, wrote John Gadbury, 'all men were Levellers'. Since the Fall of Adam, however, social and economic distinctions were a natural and inevitable characteristic of human society, and must be recognized and respected. Several compilers set out, with due reverence, a comprehensive list of the English nobility.[1] Each level of the social hierarchy possessed rights and obligations. The poor owed deference and obedience to the rich, but the rich had a duty to supply them with food, clothing and medicine, and to lend them money. The gleaning after harvest was the moral right of the poor. Wealthy millers should grind their corn without charge.[2] In almost every calendar the notes for the last month reminded readers that

> cold December is come in,
> The poor man's back is clothed thin,
> Then feed and clothe him as you may,
> The Lord will it three fold repay.[3]

And at Christmas the rich should feast their poorer neighbours and tenants.[4] The higher a man's status, the greater was his obligation to set a good example to the neighbourhood, for

Each man's offence so much the greater is
By how much great he is that doth amiss.
For every one a spot will know
Sooner upon a swan than crow.[5]

The astrologers used a combination of promises and threats to encourage virtue among the rich. John Wing, a late seventeenth-century astrologer and surveyor, warned that ownership did not confer unlimited rights: 'no man must do that in his own property', he argued, which 'may hurt another man'.[6] Those who practised charity were promised prosperity in this life and the next, and told that their good works would bring the land peace, affluence and freedom from plague. Those who did not, however, provoked divine wrath against the earth and risked damnation. Adam Martindale declared that the Lord would blast those who gamed away money at Christmas which should have been used to relieve the poor.[7]

The poor were reminded that the social hierarchy was ordained by God. Just as 'kings are our nursing fathers', the rich were set over the commons with an authority asserted in scripture and quoted frequently in the almanacs of George Wharton: 'Curse not the king, no not in thy thoughts, and curse not the rich in thy bed chamber.'[8] 'God keep us this year, and for ever, in due obedience to our superiors', prayed George Parker, and many warned of the heavy burden of divine anger awaiting the disobedient.[9] The poor must accept their station in life and be grateful for any favours they are shown. 'If thou be poor and canst not feast at all/Thank God for such as thee to feasting call', advised a Restoration compiler. If the poor would cease 'murmuring' at the wealth of the rich, and if they

could pray while rich men feast,
England would see a joyful day,
A time of plenty at the least,

thought Robert Watson in 1604.[10] The husbandman had an honourable and indispensable position in society, even if it was not always recognized. 'What should we do', asked Hewit, 'Wert not for th' husbandman? Yet slighted too.'[11] Lest he resent these slights, he was assured that he was 'the only happy man', free from the cares of wealth and of city life. 'The obtaining of riches', he learned, was 'not the end, but the change of misery.' John Securis claimed to know from direct experience that 'superfluity' of wealth brought rich men 'great care, sorrow and pensiveness' and often 'the shortening of their life'.[12] Lancelot Coelson argued, in a vigorous *memento mori*, that social ambition was ultimately futile, for

The poor, the rich, noble and mean shall have
E're long one common lodging in the grave;
Then all our feuds and all our wants shall cease,
The conquering worms reduce us all to peace.

It was therefore better to 'secure an interest in the other world,/And let this as it list be tossed and hurled.'[13]

The almanac-makers frequently predicted that the age of social harmony, for which they longed, was about to dawn. John Gadbury thought in 1665 that the stars showed that landlords would be 'more kind and less cruel to their poorer tenants than formerly'. *Vaux* prayed for a bold, resolute nobility and gentry, and a loyal, peaceable commonalty. Thomas Strutt indulged his dreams in a prediction that 1690 would be a year when 'judges and noblemen are had in estimation, the people prosper and flourish, and receive immunities from the king, . . . lawyers will prove just and honest, . . . the people shall be pleasant, . . . (and) shall delight in acts of charity and alms-deeds.' Others nourished similar visions.[14] But there was a general recognition that this ordered world, a hierarchical, moral and contented society, bore very little resemblance to the reality of Tudor and Stuart England. Compilers often lamented how Christian charity had decayed. 'The world is strangely changed', wrote John Booker. 'When I was young,/Houses were open, poor to rich did throng,/And fared well'—but no longer.[15] Instead greed was now the driving force of social behaviour. 'We now cry, Every man for himself, and God for us all', said John Wing, 'but as one well inverted it, where every man is for himself, *Non Deus sed Diabolus*, the devil is for all.' John Securis denounced extortion by the rich. He wished the poor an increase of wealth—'but of the increase', he added sadly, 'I can find nothing by my calculation.' Only in the millennium did Nicholas Culpeper expect to see the rich helping the poor.[16]

A few compilers reacted to the gulf between ideal and reality by urging those in authority to take action. Henry Harflete called on the local magistrates of Sandwich to relieve the poor, prosecute oppressors and deal justly. Gadbury wished the government to take measures to prevent the hoarding of grain and its export to the Continent, which drove up prices beyond the reach of the poor. Richard Saunder devised a comprehensive programme which he presented as a means of ending poverty and securing harmony. The government should foster trade and manufactures, regulate prices, reduce taxes, improve the soil, curb idleness, enforce the sumptuary laws and (rather vaguely) prevent an imbalance between the nobility and people. It was only during the Revolution in the mid-seventeenth century that any of the compilers considered major changes in the structure of society.[17]

The great majority of astrologers responded to the evils around them in two ways. They exhorted their readers to carry out traditional social duties, and they pilloried the groups which appeared responsible for contemporary abuses. The most common targets were oppressive landlords and covetous corn merchants. Like most social critics of the time, astrologers placed the blame for high food prices on grasping dealers who hoarded grain to push up prices. They would 'sooner fill their wide barns for a dearth, than their narrow pinching hearts with enough', complained Edward Pond. 'But I would wish such to remember, how hard it is for them to enter into the kingdom of heaven. And how grievous are the pains of hell.' Victuals would be both plentiful and expensive in the coming year, James Carre predicted for 1593: 'rather covetousness than scarcity will make them dear'.[18] The point was still made frequently in the late seventeenth century that, even after a good harvest, the export and hoarding of grain would make prices high. In 1682 Thomas Trigge declared it was 'most excellent justice done upon the hoarders of corn (as I have read it in our English chronicles) to hang them up as enemies to the country'.[19]

Compilers condemned many of the practices of modernizing or oppressive landlords, notably rack-renting, high entry-fines, and engrossing (turning two or more holdings into one, a process which sometimes involved eviction and depopulation). Such practices, Securis complained, brought 'great misery and poverty'. The attitude of the compilers was not simply reactionary. Vincent Wing and his nephew John, who were among the most vocal critics, indeed advertised their services in laying out enclosures. But they argued that land, like rank, carried social responsibilities. Vincent Wing told how farmers asked him, 'Is it not reason that I should make as much of my own as I can? Aye,' he would answer, 'but not to oppressing poor tenants, by racking their rents, as is too common. I tell thee, thy riches are not thy own, thou hast only a share of them for a short time.' He recognized that this principle was widely disregarded. 'How many houses, yea whole towns (that I know) are depopulated, ruined, and consumed of late years.' The laws against squatters were enforced rigorously, 'but where is there any that strives or endeavours to hinder depopulation? Not one.' Landlords without a qualm 'grind their poor tenants to powder, to maintain their pride and wickedness'. Finding the magistrates inactive, the Wings looked for the vengeance of God: 'Woe to you depopulators, that join house to house, and land to land, until there be no place left for the poor.'[20]

The usurer was an equally traditional figure of obloquy, and appeared regularly in the almanacs. 'The biting frosts that will this month abound', wrote Ranger in a verse for January 1628, 'Hurt not so much as usury shall wound.' Buckminster left no doubt that usurers would go straight to hell. Gresham hoped, in vain, that the stars foreshowed the imminent ruin of them all.[21] Most writers, however, accepted a distinction between usury and the lending of money at reasonable rates of interest as permitted by law. Many printed tables of interest at the standard rate, often coupled with biblical quotations condemning usury; the tactlessly-named *Usurer's Almanack* had indeed no other function. John Vaux provided details of the legislation of 1624 which reduced the maximum rate of interest to eight per cent. A growing awareness of the widespread use of credit at most levels is evident in a Restoration almanac which noted that

> Some rigid spirits cry down usury,
> And against interest as extortion cry.
> But let those peevish dons forbear their rants;
> For how shall poor men else supply their wants?[22]

The reality of usury may often, however, have been far removed from the system envisaged by the law. Henry Harflete denounced the money-lenders of Sandwich who demanded pawns worth five or six times as much as the money advanced, and charged interest at the rate of twenty per cent. At that time (1656) the legal maximum was six per cent, but the usurers, he explained, simply refused to allow witnesses to be present at their transactions.[23]

The law was another major target for criticism throughout the period. At one level this was directed at a moral abuse—the litigiousness of the age, and the greed and quarrelsomeness which lay behind it. Astrologers set down the dates of the legal terms, but added stern advice to their readers to shun the courts, which would reduce them to beggary. 'Who speeds to law, shall slowly thrive,/And soon a beggar's paths discern', commented Walter Gray. A popular verse told how

> Goose goes to law for Cousin Gander's land,
> And Fox the lawyer takes the cause in hand:

Who (for his counsel) takes fees of either,
And in the end leaves neither worth a feather . . .
Fools they fell out, and beggars they agreed.[24]

A similar anecdote related how two rustics went to law over a rake worth 4d, and both spent £8 in fees. Edward Pond made the same point with added visual impact:

Short Lines Term's commence and end
be the of ing
Long times cares, turmoils, spend

adding the query, 'is there not a wise man amongst you?'[25]

The failings of the law were seen as springing from the corruption of the lawyers. Bretnor in 1617 predicted 'terrible abusion of the laws by some double-feeing attornies'. The law 'with tricks of knaves is so beset', it was alleged, that 'the suit proves worse than losing of the debt', and lawyers with

crafty practices, poor clients squeeze,
By fraud, delay, tricks and excessive fees.[26]

The point was made repeatedly. Greedy lawyers, seeking to 'undo the poor, and cheat the rich', took bribes shamelessly and turned the law into a mere 'lottery'. Money was essential to speed a suit ('slow who sues in *forma pauperis*') and to secure a favourable result, for the 'judge is made by friends, bribes, &c like a nose of wax'.[27]

In the years of upheaval in the mid-seventeenth century a number of astrologers prophesied hopefully the reform of the law and the curbing of lawyers. The stars, said Nicholas Culpeper, indicated struggles between the lawyers and clergy, adding dryly that 'when thieves fall out, honest men come by their goods again'.[28] Even royalist writers during those years called for reform. Fitzsmith appears to have welcomed the attack by Barebones on the 'execrable court of Chancery', and Samuel Sheppard cheerfully endorsed the wish that the 'Norman' laws 'be/Convict and banished for malignancy.' George Wharton, the most important royalist astrologer, defended the law (whilst expecting it to come under attack) but shared the common scorn for the lawyers —though largely perhaps because the key legal officials were men who had accepted the parliamentary regime.[29] Radical proposals for restructuring the law reached a peak in the years round 1650, and found expression in Barebones Parliament, in 1653. Writing in that year, Saunders anticipated with equanimity the possible disappearance of the lawyers before his next almanac appeared: 'I'll cease to wonder if they be no more,/Themselves having lost their principles before.' Culpeper advocated extreme measures in his usual vigorous style. Minor modifications to the law, he said, were 'to little purpose. If you would hinder the growing of crabs, the best way is to pluck up the tree by the roots'.[30] But such extreme demands merely hastened the inevitable reaction. Barebones was followed by the more conservative Protectorate, and most later almanacs discussed legal matters in far more cautious terms. Instead of denouncing the law as tyrannical, William Lilly defended the common law against the attacks of 'precious libertines who own no propriety'. Lilly and Gadbury expressed their satisfaction with the very modest legal innovations of the Protectorate, and their gratitude for Cromwell's preservation of the body of the law.[31] John Booker was exceptional in lamenting (though not in print) the premature death of the former Leveller, John Lilburne, in 1657,

too soon, because
He that himself could ope and plead his cause
Left us, fore he mended had the laws.[32]

After the Restoration, astrologers wrote more often in defence of the laws, which, very properly,

do men's unjust desires confine,
Maintain our peace, distinguish mine and thine.[33]

Some even championed the lawyers. Wharton naturally rejoiced at the return of the law to 'spotless hands' instead of the 'unhallowed Olivarian crew', and several former Parliamentarians deemed it tactful to retreat in the changed political climate. Saunders replaced his allusion to the law as a lottery by a respectful reference to the 'reverent and learned judges', whilst Gadbury dedicated his edition for 1661 to the attorney-general, Sir Jeffrey Palmer, combining a defence of judges and lawyers with an attack on corrupt juries.[34]

Most almanacs thus discussed the law in fairly elementary terms, stressing corruption and the folly of the public. A few showed a deeper awareness of the role of the law in upholding a particular form of government and society. The idea that the law was part of the Norman Yoke was widespread during the revolutionary period. On the eve of the Restoration, John Tanner of Amersham called for a radical reform of the law as the only means to provide a firmer foundation for the republic:

The people cry Reform, let us be free,
The long robe stinketh still of monarchy;
The regal title to the law's best known,
For liberty nor freedom it can own:

Give them th'old title, or give us new laws,
Or farewell our free-state and Good Old Cause.

He was not optimistic, despite the renewed talk of reform following Cromwell's death. 'Treachery' and 'underhand dealing', he commented, 'put the commonalty in doubt of non-performance'.[35] The legal reforms of the preceding years had not been sufficient to underpin the regime, nor to provide an equitable system of law. A bitter verse which appeared in the almanacs of Tanner and Sarah Jinner remarked that the lawyers, 'void o'the fears' of the early 1650s,

Have lined their gowns, and made them pistol-proof,
And Magna Charta clad in coat of buff.
And with a bolder confidence can take
A larger fee for Reformation sake.[36]

The law thus continued to serve the interests of a hierarchical, propertied society. Several astrologers complained that a society which ignored its destitute was prepared to hang them if they stole to keep alive. None seems to have been aware of Thomas More's discussion of the point in *Utopia*, and certainly none followed his line of reasoning to a communist society. What struck them, rather, was the visible contrast between the consequences of apparently similar actions by the rich and by the obscure. 'A poor man shall be hanged for stealing a sheep, when, it may be, compelled by necessity', remarked a royalist astrologer, William Ramesey, 'when as a great man in office may safely rob the whole nation, undo thousands'. ('Too true', a contemporary reader noted in the margin.[37]) *Poor Robin*, repeating an ancient analogy, likened the law to a cobweb in which 'small flies were hanged' whilst the great broke free.[38] The civil wars accentuated such contrasts. Taking the property of another is called theft when poor men do it, observed Culpeper, 'but when rich men do it, then 'tis pillaging, plundering, and seizing on malignants' goods'. Making a similar point, Lilly lamented that 'justice is gone to heaven. The little man dies for stealing a sheep; the great one steals ten oxen, and yet is pardoned. . . . Doth not God see this? and is he not angry at this partiality?'[39] In addition the civil wars disrupted the economic life of the nation. When the armies were eventually disbanded, it was by no means easy to reabsorb into society the thousands of former soldiers. Crime was for many of them a tempting solution: 'war makes thieves, and peace hangs them.'[40]

The most important of the remaining targets of criticism, the clergy, are discussed elsewhere.[41] The other groups regularly under attack were those who exploited rather than oppressed the people—the quack physicians and astrologers. Not all the criticism was high-minded. The astrologer was often prepared to libel his rivals as ignorant quacks. Thus the lugubrious remark of John Partridge that 'astrology is now like a dead carcass, to which every crow or rook resorts and takes a mouthful', was merely a prelude to a thinly veiled attack on the knavish 'Tr-ers' and 'Co-eys' who infested London, and he set out the addresses of some leading 'cheats'.[42] To attack illiterate practitioners was a conveniently simple way for the astrological physician, himself often denounced as a quack, to appear in public on the side of virtue. The almanacs (especially those by astrologer-physicians) thus contained repeated onslaughts against the 'barbers, tailors, tinkers, cobblers, weavers, women and witches' who took up medicine when 'they cannot think what to do', and with their universal medicine or 'hotch-potch' brought the soundest of men to an 'untimely grave'.[43] 'Quack-salving knaves, and silly women doctors' killed more than they cured, more indeed than died in most wars. John Gadbury reworked the biblical phrase describing the exploits of Saul and David, and declared that while poverty had slain its thousands, the 'practices of illiterate and impudent pretenders to physic have murdered their ten thousands'. The author of *Culpepper Revived* estimated, probably conservatively, that a quarter of the medicines used were useless and another quarter positively harmful, 'more fit for the dunghill than to come into the body of a man, and he that takes medicines of that sort needs no other disease'.[44] Warning readers to shun quacks and amateurs was of course a form of self-advertisement, but it was sometimes coupled with a genuine concern. Mary Holden, a midwife, naturally wanted to sell her concoction guaranteed to cure toothache, but we can accept her claim that she mentioned it partly 'because I see such great cruelty in them that cure by plucking out of teeth, and breaking of jaw-bones in young children, that they never have any teeth in their places'.[45] John Tanner told his readers that every universal medicine was bogus. The author of *Vaux*, recognizing that people resorted to 'witches, charmers and empirics' to save money, sought to help them by providing simple advice on herbal medicine by which any reader could become his own physician. Beridge provided similar cheap prescriptions.[46]

The advice was probably sound. The remedies of professional physicians were as lethal as those of the amateurs, and *Poor Robin* did not discriminate in his prediction that the physicians would all be busy 'killing sick people'.[47] Occasionally there were direct attacks on the medical élite, the College of Physicians in London. During the interregnum, Richard Saunders alleged that the College physicians and the clergy

> have both from God and nature vilely swarved,
> The body one, and the soul the other starved.

And the whole career of Nicholas Culpeper was a sustained attack on the privilege and exclusiveness of the College, which to some extent he was able to undermine through his writings.[48]

The almanac-makers thus used their position as publicists to condemn all who disturbed the balance of the social order. Social harmony, they recognized, could not coexist with exploitation and oppression. They denounced profiteers during the Revolution who rose suddenly in wealth or status, and who often acquired lands confiscated from the crown or church. The Independent politician, Gilbert Millington, fell under the lash of William Lilly who derided him as 'Abbot of Fell in Nottinghamshire, high priest of plundered ministers'. Lilly also prophesied the ruin of those who had 'Spencer-like enriched them-selves', a jibe at John Spencer, successively groom, preacher, army officer and land speculator.[49] John Tanner condemned those

> like a Courtier, or a new made Lord,
> With a compliment at every word
> Who visit rich friends, forget James and Tom.

William Ramesey wondered 'what greater madness' there could be 'than to see Lords no gentlemen, . . . serving-men able to buy out their masters'.[50]

Many astrologers were equally swift to denounce the potential danger of lower-class discontent. Like many Tudor and Stuart writers, they displayed an uneasy mixture of benevolent paternalism towards the poor, and fear and hatred of the mob. Such phrases as the 'perverse and giddy multitude', 'foul-mouthed multitude', 'rabble-rout of rural wretches', 'raving' and 'monster-headed multitude', 'rabble and giddy-headed multitude' were common currency, especially in the decades after 1640, and were used by both Royalist and Parliamentarian to describe the 'clowns or vulgar ordinary sort of people'.[51] 'The mobile would be masters', warned John Gadbury (once allegedly a Ranter) in 1684.[52] The fear and anticipation of popular violence runs throughout the period. Laet's prognostication for 1520 expected riots and popular discontent. Evans Lloyd in 1582 thought the common people would be 'factious . . . quarrelous, impatient, and outragious, one envying the estate and degree of another: as the poor the rich, the ploughman the gentleman, the private man the magistrate . . . each one seeking how to entrap and circumvent the other'. A prognostication by the French astrologer, Himbert de Billy, translated into English, spoke similarly of 'hate between the commons and the greater sort'.[53] The Revolution naturally strengthened these fears. The 'baser sort of people', thought William Ramesey in 1652, 'shall envy and raise themselves up against their superiors; such animals I must confess there are frequently to be found.' 'The common people will be still common people', Henry Coley predicted gloomily at the end of the century, 'they will sometime or other show what they are, and vent their unstable passions.'[54] Gadbury's hostility was such that he was able to regard the Great Plague as a disguised blessing, describing it as 'a broom in the hands of the almighty! with which he sweepeth the most nasty and uncomely corners of the universe, that the more noble parts of it may remain secure and safe'.[55]

Even more alarming was the prospect of rebellion in the very heart of the social order, the family. Almost every year it was predicted that wives would seek to challenge the subordinate position they held in a patriarchal society.[56] Servants and labourers also attracted attention. As early as 1498 William Parron feared that servants would be proud, disobedient and hard to keep, a view that in some quarters has remained remarkably constant. 'Why dost thou delve and drudge', another writer asked the reader, 'since servants spend all, and yet ever grudge?' An Elizabethan astrologer, John Securis, gave eloquent expression to the common view that servants 'shall be as they were wont to be of late years; that is, they shall be sick of the lourdain disease, they will be negligent, careless, somnolenti (that is, given to much sleep), going about their work and business like snails creeping, for fear of stumbling. And to be short, slack enough in all things, saving in their tongues.' Others similarly expected them to be 'untrusty and disobedient'. A Restoration satirist advised labourers solemnly to beware of killing themselves by overwork, lest they be treated as suicides and buried beneath the gallows.[57] In his almanac for 1666, Thomas Trigge struck a modern note with a prediction of student agitation—'young hot-headed scholars, who make it their business to libel their superiors, and for their pains are expelled', which, he added, would be 'their just merits'.[58]

Only a handful of astrologers during the Revolution were prepared to welcome social change and upheaval. Many people, however, were aware of the implications of the doctrine that 'as the grave equals all men, so do celestial influences.' An alarmist Restoration writer envisaged the poor asking 'why should any man be inferior, or subject, that may presume his stars have ordained him to superiority?' By contrast Culpeper remarked with equanimity that 'Jupiter delights in equality, and so do I.'[59] Much of the radicals' writing took the form of a generalized attack on the Norman Yoke of kings, priests, lawyers and such 'cattle'.[60] Magna Carta was said (as by some Levellers) to be no more than what 'this poor pitiful nation, when it was unluckily vanquished by a Bastard, by fair means obtained from the hands of a conqueror'. Parliament's view of liberty was merely freedom for the gentry, and former parliaments, which 'should have been enlarging the liberty of their subjects, spent their time and consultation how far the bounds of a forest must go, who must keep a park, and who must not, who must keep hounds . . . and who not . . . and thus they sweeped the liberty of the nation up and down, as the maid swept the surreverence about the house till at last she lost it.'[61] No longer would the common people be 'content with bread and water'; they would 'cry out for vengeance' upon the upper classes and would not 'be quiet, till they are all become kings'.[62] But the new order was discussed only in the haziest terms. Culpeper for example predicted that those the gentry 'call vile, plebeians, and evil men . . . will rise up'; 'kingdoms will be changed and beggars will get on horse-back.' Lilly anticipated the liberation of copyholders from 'insulting landlords', but the Levellers filled him with alarm, and even Culpeper stressed his opposition to any 'community' of property.[63] The radicals were content with an imprecise dream, until the Restoration shattered any such hopes.

Hopes or fears of upheaval were only one part of the almanacs' discussion of English society. Many compilers touched only briefly on these matters, and devoted more space to questions of personal and social behaviour, and to recording the changing seasons of the year, and the duties and pleasures associated with each.

The rhythm of the farming year, following the seasons, made it natural for the compilers to provide appropriate farming advice, often in short verses over the calendar, but sometimes in more extended form. While contemporary French almanacs seem not to have advanced beyond platitudinous advice on when to sow and reap, many English astrologers showed a more informed and progressive outlook. They provided information not only on common crops but on new and less frequently-grown ones, such as turnips (e.g. in 1598), beet, hemp, flax, cucumbers, melons, vines and hops, with advice on grafting, dunging land, gelding livestock, felling timber and making malt. Though some of the advice was aimed at the kitchen or herbal garden, the almanacs probably served a useful function in spreading elementary information and awareness about new and specialized crops.[64] Vincent and John Wing, among others, were professional surveyors and specialized in the laying out of enclosures, and Daniel Woodward gave advice on the drainage of water-meadows. James Ward, an engineer, advertised in Lilly's almanac his skills in cutting new river channels, constructing water-mills and repairing bridges.[65] A number of authors provided specialist advice on the diseases of livestock, and prescribed remedies; one, Robert Gardner, was indeed a farrier by profession. Some of the formulae, however, seem less than promising, such as Dade's method of curing an ailing cow by letting its blood and giving it to drink a pint of 'old urine, . . . with a good quantity of hen's dung steeped in'.[66] Perhaps the most important information was the detailed list of markets and fairs throughout the country which most almanacs carried, and which the Company of Stationers tried to keep up to date.[67] Equally important for the farmer were the forecasts of the weather and of the prospects for the coming harvest. Predictions of dearth or plenty were a basic part of the almanac's fare throughout the period, and compilers often went into considerable detail concerning different crops, even late in the seventeenth century. Thus a reader studying the prospects for 1678 learned that 'hops . . . will be a very ticklish commodity, promising a great price, but suddenly falling, even contrary to all expectations.'[68] In 1648 John Booker suggested that instead of merely listing fairs and predicting the state of the harvest, compilers ought each year to record details of recent trading at important regional centres such as London, Bristol and Exeter. Sadly, this promising idea was still-born.[69]

Both Tudor and Stuart almanacs reflected primarily the rural nature of society, emphasizing the duties of the farming year and the delights of the countryside. Farming was of course linked most clearly with the weather, the seasons and the influence of the sun and moon on growth. 'Let clowns and ploughboys . . . pray for brave days', cries a London journeyman portrayed by Dekker. 'We work in a dry shop; what care I if it rain?'[70] The astrologers continued, in a traditional manner, to see the farmer as the truly happy man, doing the work of greatest value.

Perse, go thou to plough, and take with thee thy wife,
Dig and delve, sow barley, wheat and rye,

said Frende in 1585;

Of one make ten, this is an honest life,
As Aristotle affirmeth in his Philosophy.[71]

Only London inspired a comparable enthusiasm for urban life among the astrologers. A Restoration series gave a glowing description of the capital, its size, antiquity and natural resources. Yet even some of London's virtues seem almost pastoral, as when the author boasted 'of the fat and sweet salmon, daily taken' with many other species from the Thames.[72]

The growing importance of trade and manufacture was however frequently evident. Before the civil war, Pigot supplied an account of the commodities of his native Shropshire, and Peregrine gave a brief résumé of the economic resources of the different English counties.[73] Some almanacs were designed specifically for dealers and artisans, such as the *City and Country Chapmans,* which provided tables of accounts, and specialized weights and measures for commodities such as coal, beer, iron and timber. *The Merchants Daily Companion* (1700), by John Axford, set out details of the carriers, wagons and stage-coaches leaving London each week, and the inns from which they commenced. The common practice in late Stuart almanacs of printing specimen bills of obligation, apprenticeship indentures, and letters of attorney reflected the increasingly formalized nature of transactions at every level.[74] Occasionally there were flattering remarks designed to please 'mechanics' among the readership. Thus, Tanner expected 'rare and admirable inventions' among them. 'Let none crush them under', Bucknall declared, 'If they hold on, they'll make the world to wonder.'[75] Occasionally too there were more circumstantial comments on various aspects of economic life. Henry Harflete of Sandwich, for example, predicted high tides and floods to follow the solar eclipse of 1652 (Black Monday). When they failed to materialize, he was unrepentant, and declared that the local commissioners for sewers should have heeded his warning and repaired the causeways leading to the town. Access by foot, he explained, was impossible each winter because of flooding. If the causeways and sluices were repaired, the local country people would use the market at Sandwich instead of travelling to Canterbury, and the townsmen would benefit.[76] A glimpse of the organization of retail trade is provided by Woodward's almanacs, in which he listed the outlets of his patent medicines. He supplied names and addresses throughout the south and west, and as far north as Derbyshire, and they form a reminder that individuals could pursue simultaneously a variety of occupations. Nurse Norbery of Deptford and a barber-surgeon were predictable figures, but the list also named a grocer, girt-web-maker, coach-harness-man, mealman, bookseller, schoolmaster and baker. Woodward offered to supply any shopkeeper who so wished, and to provide free supplies of printed labels and handbills.[77] The author of *Englands Almanack* (1700) used it to launch an attack on the East Indies trade which, he alleged, was bringing unemployment to English weavers, combers and other clothworkers as consumers switched to Eastern silks. The trade was doubly iniquitous in causing loss of life among sailors, documented by a list of ships recently lost, and among those who bought inflammable calicoes and muslins, proved by a list of people burnt to death, including a niece of Godolphin.[78] Both Lilly and Gadbury showed interest in the development of an English herring fishery in the North Sea, which would enrich the government and create employment.[79] Gadbury also publicized the colonization of the West Indies, following the capture of Jamaica during the Protectorate. He published a series of *Jamaica* almanacs, describing the natural resources of the island, and discussing with enthusiasm the history and prospects of the settlement. Two of these works were dedicated to Sir Thomas Modyford, late governor, and Henry Morgan, the former buccaneer and lieutenant-general of the island, whom Gadbury thanked for help and 'civilities received'. If he were a poor man in England, he told his readers, he 'would not tarry here to beg, steal or starve; when by going thither, I might live like a man, and happily'.[80]

Other nations figured in the almanacs almost invariably in a political context, often hailed as allies destined to glory or condemned as foes facing ruin. Comments on different racial and social characteristics were brief and crude. The Irish and Scots were barbarous and treacherous, the Welsh squalid and comical, the French slaves, the Venetians 'sodomitical' and the ungrateful, grasping Dutch the 'greatest drunkards of this world'.[81] *Poor Robin*'s interest in marital relationships prompted him to describe a Lapp custom whereby a girl and her suitor run a race to determine whether they shall be married. If the man wins, he can claim the girl; but she is given a lead so great that he can win only by her connivance. The same author's misogynist humour, however, led him to suggest that the Indian practice of suttee, by which the wife was put to death at the funeral of her husband, should be introduced into England![82] John Booker drew attention to the strict seclusion of married women in Rome, where they were allowed 'scarcely to peep out of a lattice-window, hence comes the proverb . . . In Rome the harlot hath a better life/Than she that is a Roman wife.' Booker saw this as additional proof of the depravity of the Roman Babylon.[83]

More fundamental questions of race received only cursory treatment. *Arcandam* had no doubt of negro inferiority, for 'naturally black men are fearful, as the Ethiopians be.' The eighteenth-century astrologer, Henry Season, was fond of comparing his enemies and critics to the Hottentots, for him the lowest form of human life. John Gadbury speculated briefly whether different skin colours were caused by differences in heat, in the colour of the seed, in the amount of sulphur in the body—a Paracelsian touch—or by the nature of the country. His contemporary, Richard Saunders, dreamed of improving the human race by scientific breeding. If people observed the stars in human reproduction, he suggested, as they did for their animals, the degeneration of mankind could be reversed and 'we might possibly find such heroic spirits and famous worthies of valour and learning in the world as past ages have produced'. It was a novel approach to the issue of human progress or decline, but Stuart canons of good taste prevented a full discussion, Saunders being fearful lest he 'offend the queasy stomachs of some, and gain an immodest repute with the weak'.[84]

Much of the standard almanac was concerned with the daily life of the ordinary countryman. At the heart of this discussion was the nature of the ideal regimen, the means to preserve perfect health. Good health was analysed in traditional terms as a balance between the four humours governing the body, and the ideal was thus a moderate pattern of life which would avoid imbalance. A mid-Tudor compiler, Anthony Askham, advised men to

Eat, drink and labour, sleep, rest and be merry
In due time and order, measure not exceeding.

Similarly, a typical Jacobean compiler exhorted the reader:

Neither in labour, meat, or drink,
In sleep or venery
Exceed: but keep the golden mean
To hold thy health thereby.[85]

Gabriel Frende taught that whoever kept his 'five points of moderation' (in work, food, drink, sleep and sex) 'shall not only in this world keep his body in good estate free from sickness, but shall preserve even his mind and soul also in a good case towards God and receive the final recompense of eternal bliss in the world to come'.[86]

Work was a virtue, idleness 'a deadly foe'.[87] The industrious reader should be ready, if necessary, to 'Drive idle poor out of the street,/To work at harvest or else glean', for 'idleness is the nurse of sin.'[88] Nevertheless, the general approach was far from mirroring the ascetic life-style associated by Max Weber with early Protestantism. Attacks on sloth were balanced by hearty endorsements of the traditional round of jollification at Christmas and at other festivals throughout the year. Askham, a Catholic priest, had prescribed 'mirth and pastime'; Buckminster, a Protestant minister, similarly advised his readers to be merry. 'Holla, holla joyfully', wrote John Harvey as his motto for May. Another compiler was confident that the 'best physic is . . . a merry honest heart'.[89] The injunction to work was to 'labour moderately', 'honest, moderate labour'. Readers among the gentry were allowed to believe that any mildly energetic pursuit constituted labour. Almanacs prescribed hunting, hawking and 'tracing hares'—'but be sure that the park or lordship be your own'. Gabriel Frende advocated a very pleasant regimen of 'walking, rowing in boats, swimming . . . soft riding, easy tennissing'.[90]

Food and drink also attracted comment. Gluttony was naturally condemned, but moderation could be relative, as was apparent in Allestree's advice to eat venison only at appropriate seasons and to drink only the best wine. Moderation was especially important during the dog days (in late July and August), which had been linked since antiquity with the prevalence of disease. The reader should

Eat salads fresh to cool the blood,
And bathe in rivers free from mud.[91]

Compilers also sometimes noted current dietary habits and prejudices, such as the marked preference for white rather than brown eggs and bread.[92] In 1581 John Securis listed the common drinks of his time as wine, ale, beer, cider, metheglin (a kind of mead), whey and water, remarking that the last four were less popular and that water was of doubtful merit. The introduction of coffee, compared by one author to the 'water of Styx', was duly noted.[93] In drink as in food moderation was the key, and compilers spelled out the consequences of excess. Monday was said to be noteworthy for the drunkenness of shoemakers, and for tailors suffering headaches provoked by the previous day's hard drinking.[94] *Vaux* disapproved of the effects of strong drink in arousing unseemly lust in the aged. Another compiler reflected that it was easy to predict that 'many ancient houses shall decay' when he saw 'prodigal young gallants dicing and revelling'. Vincent Wing saw drunkenness as leading to 'the utter destruction both of body and soul, and oftentimes to the ruin of . . . estates and families'. Nicholas Culpeper provided the most forceful attack, which was based on both moral and social considerations. He urged legislation to reduce the potency of beer, arguing that it was 'easy to be proved that there is more corn drunk down in strong liquor in one day in London, than would suffice the poor a week'. With weaker beer, no longer would the 'beastly sin of drunkenness rage in the nation'—a reform which would be more pleasing to God than seven years of fasting and praying.[95]

Sleep, linked with personal hygiene, also came within the astrologers' purview. Six hours of sleep in summer and eight in winter were declared adequate for the 'most drowsy drumbledozy', with an afternoon nap tolerated in the summer and for the aged. John Securis even provided detailed instructions on whether it was better to lie on one's right side or left, and when and how often to turn over. He added advice on bowel movements and what he politely termed 'other evacuations: as by the nose and mouth'.[96] In 1642 John Woodhouse provided a medley of good and bad advice on personal hygiene, reinforced by some dubious arguments: 'comb your head the hair backward, it purgeth rheum and cleareth the eyes, wash behind your ears with cold water, an enemy to toothache, wash hands often, feet more seldom, head not at all.'[97] Astrologers seemed slightly surprised that some people took baths 'only for cleanliness' sake', 'rather for pleasure than for profit'. The medical origins of bathing were still evident in the detailed instructions they provided: the bath should be taken at least an hour after rising, and be preceded by some exercise; the head should be kept covered, and if possible the moon should be in the sign of Libra or Pisces.[98] Householders were advised to smother the 'stinks' of summer by scattering rue, gall and wormwood, which would also destroy fleas, and to carry something to combat the smells of the street. In times of plague, the house and clothing should be fumigated with brimstone, and the bedroom with 'tar upon a chasing-dish of coal', with 'some zealous prayers' to appease the almighty.[99]

Despite their endless pleas for moderation, the astrologers were always aware that such rules were widely and flagrantly disregarded. Henry Coley, an astrological physician, counselled restraint but prudently made notes of an 'admirable pill after a debauch or hard drinking'.[100] 'What vicious lives many live', Vincent Wing lamented, 'how they drink, roar, swagger, domineer, revel and what not.' Greed and excess were ever-present, and sinful pride was visible in the dress of all those who preferred to look more like 'fiddlers and players, than good Christians'. 'We clothed our selves at first for shame, to cover our nakedness,' he added, 'but now we are so void of shame that we take pleasure in it.'[101] Moderation was advised in dress, as in all things, but the compilers were fully aware of the sudden and dramatic changes of fashion: Henry Harflete even ventured to predict in his almanac the following year's taste.[102] Edward Pond denounced as 'effeminate follies' the lapdogs which were in vogue from the early seventeenth century.[103]

Compilers lamented that still more depravity was apparent in sexual conduct, despite the fact that excess brought 'insatiable torment', 'decayeth the body or dulleth the mind', and led to early death. Booker recalled that even

Rome's great and potent state did never shrink
Till they began to wench, to coach, and drink.[104]

Whores were an 'intolerable liberty in a Christian commonwealth'. The young emptied a man's purse, said a mid-Tudor compiler, and the old should be burned alive 'if the law would suffer it'. Even during the 'Puritan Revolution' prostitutes were alleged to be infesting Covent Garden.[105] The reader should therefore 'refrain . . . from hateful stews', especially in the summer when the danger of infection was at its height. William Ramesey engagingly promised to set a good example: 'young men, be as resolute as my self, for I promise you, I will have nothing to do with them this summer quarter, they are too hot to meddle with. . . . stay but till autumn, and ye shall be rid of these beasts, death is coming for a great many of them.'[106]

Complaints of sexual licence were only part of a broader discussion of sexual relations, and indeed general relations between the husband and wife. Intercourse was always to be with moderation, and should be avoided totally during menstruation (when it would produce deformed children) and after blood-letting.[107] There were also astrological taboos, when the position of the stars made sex dangerous. The astrologers failed to agree on details, and the credulous reader who heeded every warning would in effect have taken a vow of chastity. But there was a rough consensus that the summer months were especially risky, and most of all the period known as the dog days in July and August.[108] It is difficult to establish whether contemporaries observed these taboos.

Satirists naturally pounced upon them. It 'seems astronomers do rule the earth', Gervase Dauncy complained, 'none without them might meddle with his wife.' A wit predicted for June 1662 'high dissatisfaction among women' on the grounds that 'men this month observe the rule of physic too much.' Others claimed that women were indeed unwilling to accept any period of restraint and turned to adultery during the summer, on the principle that 'if husband won't, another must.'[109] The evidence from parochial registers is far from straightforward. Assuming the lapse of only a few days between birth and baptism (apparently the most common situation), it is impossible to see any sign of sexual abstinence in June: March was a popular month for baptisms. But abstinence during August may help to explain the dramatic fall in baptisms in May and June. There is clearly a summer trough in the baptismal figures, usually ascribed (on no clear evidence) to abstinence during harvest. A seasonal taboo during the heat of summer, linked through the dog days with some kind of astrological rationale, may help explain the low figures for the early summer.[110]

By no means all the sexual advice was negative. 'Let Venus be embraced', Walter Gray recommended, rather primly, for May 1581. A coy but enthusiastic contemporary urged his readers to 'embrace Venus honestly' in May and 'entertain Venus daintily' in November.[111] A century later Dorothy Partridge showed much less restraint in prescribing 'a lusty squab fat bedfellow very good physic at this season' (January). Her endorsement of sex in December, January and February fits in well with the autumnal peak in baptisms, though we can hardly assume that this was cause and effect. Almanacs did set out astrological elections for sexual relations, among many other activities. It was widely recommended that the ideal time 'to be as a husband to thy wife' was when the moon was in Sagittarius. But it seems highly unlikely that these rules were followed except by the most faithful disciples.[112] Nicholas Culpeper found little to praise in the sexual act, observing that man was 'conceived between the places ordained to cast out excrements, . . . and in such a manner that his mother was ashamed to tell him how'. 'All men and women desire children', he thought, partly 'because they are pretty things to play withall', but he conceded that 'where the desire for children moves one to the act of copulation, the pleasure in the act moves a hundred.'[113]

Tudor and Stuart astrologers did more than merely give advice on times and seasons. They offered immediate solutions to the emotional and sexual problems of clients and readers. They made and sold astrological sigils (small tokens believed to contain occult powers) by which the buyer could capture the affection of the person desired, and they published herbal and other aphrodisiacs.[114] They also sold sigils to hinder conception, and supplied appropriate herbal prescriptions. Culpeper's edition of the College of Physicians's directory announced that honey suckle was able to 'procure barrenness, and hinder conception'. With greater detail, John Swan's almanacs explained that juice from honeysuckle, 'drunk of a man by the space of 37 days together, will make him that he shall never beget any more children'. Another contemporary herbal promised that mountain mint and water-lily each 'extinguisheth the generative faculty', as did lettuce and other specified herbs. Other astrologers prescribed herbal 'anti-aphrodisiacs'. Purslain and herb-agnus, or 'the chaste-tree', were said to 'restrain all venerious notions' and to 'dry up the natural seed'. Thomas Hill advised readers to take rue and herb-grace regularly as an anti-aphrodisiac during July, a period for which he urged sexual abstinence.[115] According to Sarah Jinner, rue made a man 'no better than a eunuch', though Swan warned of alarming properties in that it 'makes men chaste and women fills with lust'. Perhaps to atone, Jinner prescribed an anti-aphrodisiac specifically for women, a powder made from 'a red bull's pizzle'.[116] Whatever the effectiveness of these prescriptions, they suggest a widespread wish to be able to limit family size, and that such methods were perfectly acceptable.[117] A large number of almanacs also asserted that mere proximity to sowbread would cause instant abortion. This was phrased as a warning, though of course there was nothing to prevent its misuse as a prescription. There are numerous references from this period to attempts to induce abortion, some using herbal concoctions.[118] It seems true, however, that most couples wanted children, if not as many, perhaps, as they often produced. Sarah Jinner published aids to conception in her almanac, as did the compiler of the popular sex handbook, *Aristotle's Master-piece* (which included astrological advice on how to conceive sons rather than daughters).[119] One compiler alluded briefly to the practice of 'bundling', asking whether pre-marital sex was not 'a cunning trick to know whether the wives would be fruitful of no?'[120]

The almanacs assumed marriage to be the normal condition, but were almost without exception critical of women in general and wives in particular. The most extravagant views were in the satirical almanacs, the authors of which were reflecting contemporary fears of female insubordination but were also seeking to amuse their readers. The insults belong to an old tradition of crude misogynist humour found in ballads, jest-books and other chap-books. Extreme language was no doubt necessary to give bite to rather stale jibes. The burlesque almanacs are useful evidence for taste in popular humour, but much less reliable for charting the evolution of ideas and practice concerning the role of the wife within the family.

Among both the satirists and the genuine astrologers there was general agreement on the natural inferiority of women, and on the rebelliousness and ambition of many wives. 'I cannot but rejoice when I consider I am not married', declared William Ramesey, explaining the superiority of the single condition. However good the woman, said another compiler, it was almost impossible to turn her into a good wife.[121] One of the most common predictions throughout the period was of domestic brawls and unhappy marriages. 'Women will scold their husbands, a thing of no great moment', ran a weary prophecy for 1659. *Poor Robin* anticipated 'civil wars between drunken husbands and scolding wives, mother-in-laws and their daughters'. Quarrels, runaway wives and attempts to secure divorce were annual fare.[122] A Jacobean edition of *Erra Pater* printed a very long list of unlucky days, with a warning that a couple who married on any of them would 'soon be parted, or else they shall live together with much sorrow'.[123] Such gloomy prospects led to speculation on whether it was better to be hanged than marry a shrewish wife, and to the old cynical jest that the only two happy days of married life were the first and the day of the wife's funeral.[124]

Women were held to be guilty of all the deadly sins. To some extent the stars were responsible. *Arcandam* provided a pessimistic list of the fate of women according to the sign of the zodiac under which they were born: under Taurus they would be thieves, under Gemini liars, under Scorpio harlots and under Sagittarius witches—there seemed little prospect of safety anywhere in the zodiac![125] The pride and vanity of women were shameful. There was no sympathy for the use of cosmetics, which were denounced in vigorous terms, for

> To paint is nature's high disgrace
> And painted snouts are ladies' shames.[126]

In May, according to an acid note by *Poor Robin*, 'my Lady leaves off eating green pease and cherries as being so vulgar that the common people eat of them as well as she'. But the common people were no better. In the spring 'Joan shall jet it in finery with my Lady although if you search her pedigree, you shall find she comes of the family of the Fustylogs, the Dowdies, the Trollops, the Trugmouldies. . . . and the Bartholomew Fair Pig-dressers'.[127] Female garrulousness, a popular topic, was likened to a tide which flowed but never ebbed; women were silent only in the grave. 'Many ladies shall prove with egg, not with child,' predicted *Poor Robin*, 'and this may be made out by their extraordinary cackling.'[128] Women's promiscuity was regarded as beyond doubt, not only by the satirists.

Maids wanton, wives willing, widows wilful
Bring hope, horns and harm to the unskilful,

warned Arthur Hopton in 1613. Parents were advised to watch closely over their pretty daughters, for 'seldom beauty is with virtue matched'. Sarah Jinner prescribed an anti-aphrodisiac for women with the comment that 'this may be a good medicine for the preventing of young girls throwing themselves away upon madcap fellows.'[129] *Poor Robin* observed coarsely that in the spring

The blood beginneth now to rise,
Which makes some maids to scratch their thighs.

He thought there were few virgins left at eighteen, and was liberal with allusions to tumbles in the cart at haymaking. He regarded a faithful wife as equally rare, and in one edition listed nine distinct modes by which wives commonly cuckolded their husbands. The Rev. John Swan provided a herbal prescription to enable a widow to look suitably sad at her husband's burial.[130]

Worst of all, many wives failed to 'observe the principle of reason', and struggled to overthrow the husband's supremacy within the family. Predictions appeared each year that women would 'lord it over their husbands', and the compilers left no doubt of their strong disapproval.[131] Many women, it was alleged, preferred to marry weak and foolish husbands, whom they could dominate; most wives showed deference only as long as they were kept short of money.[132] The Revolution accentuated fears of upheaval within the family. An alarmist feared that women would soon be held in common. Samuel Thurston, one of the most radical astrologers, was nevertheless highly disturbed by the growing interest of women in politics. Turning these fears to ridicule, a wit declared that a parliament of women was impossible, for all the members would want to be Speaker.[133]

The subject of the shrewish wife raised the problem of how best to curb her (though she had, of course, the merit of reminding her husband of the torments of hell and so bringing him to repentance).[134]

The burlesque almanacs defended wife-beating and the use of the cucking stool, and jocularly advocated hanging scolds or cutting out their tongues. *Poor Robin* made a brief reference to skimmingtons, the raucous processions which ridiculed shrews, adulterous wives and (as his phrase, a 'skimmington cuckold', suggests) their weak or deceived husbands.[135] He also alluded to the semi-official sale of wives, a practice well known in the eighteenth and nineteenth centuries as a method of popular divorce by consent. Earlier examples are rare, but the edition for 1665 contained a mock indenture for such a sale, couched in formal terms, by which William Weakbody, scrivener, sold his wife Joan to John Lusty, gent., together with her virtues, the 'beauty of her mind, chastity, temperance', for a consideration of £20. Though obviously meant to amuse readers, the passage does provide some indication that wife-selling was well known and perhaps even formalized at an early date.[136]

The misogynist extremes of the burlesque almanacs should not obscure the fact that most serious writers, while suspicious of women, were more balanced in their comments and proposed remedies. Most recognized the wife's important role in the economic life of the household. They referred to women accompanying their husbands to ploughing and sowing, and to the female tasks of 'weeding of corn and shearing sheep', gelding cocks and managing the dairy. The task of supervising domestic servants made a conscientious wife essential. Where there was an 'evil wife and many hands' the husband faced disaster.[137] A mid-Tudor compiler thought that a bad wife could be reformed more effectively 'with smiling than with a staff'. A later writer advised

> With love and not with fury let her know
> Her error's ground, for thence amendments grow.

If this failed, total disregard was an alternative remedy, 'for silence cuts a shrew, worse than a sword'.[138] Even *Poor Robin*, rather inconsistently, showed occasional glimpses of enlightenment. In 1694 he advised the young to marry for love, for 'he who marries where he doth not love, will soon love where he doth not marry.' He once inserted a jest mocking the traditional double standard of morality. A wife, he wrote, one day 'found her husband kissing his maid in a dark hole behind the parlour-door; who asking her, how she spied him out in that place? She returned him answer, That formerly she had been kissed by several men in that place herself.' The earlier *Ravens Almanack*, which had advocated beating shrewish wives, offered also the story of a group of women who drugged and thrashed a man notorious as a violent and unfaithful husband. Other almanacs predicted with stern disapproval that husbands (as well as wives) would be unfaithful and desert their families.[139]

The earliest thorough-going defence of women appears, perhaps predictably, in the first almanac written for women by a woman, Sarah Jinner. More surprisingly, William Ramesey, a committed bachelor, wrote in their support in one of his non-astrological works. He asserted that women were as intelligent as men, and often more faithful. Reversing a common argument drawn from Genesis, he declared that while man had been made from dust at the Creation, woman had been made from man, 'a more noble matter'. But though nature taught the equality of the sexes, religion (reassuringly?) decreed otherwise, for 'were we not taught by an infallible spirit, that the man is the head of the woman?'[140] Sarah Jinner made a lively defence of the natural ability of women, 'although it is the policy of men, to keep us from education and schooling, wherein we might give testimony of our parts by improvement'. As proof she listed women poets, the Amazons, the achievements of Queen Elizabeth and the fact that 'we have had a Pope of our sex, named Pope Joan, which the best historians do not deny.' But she reassured readers that she had no wish 'to animate our sex, to . . . usurp the breeches', and like some of the other abler women of the period still accepted many traditional prejudices against women. They were garrulous, she conceded, and promiscuous: they were tempted to extra-marital sex and 'more maids, than do, would venture upon it, were it not for fear of the rising of the apron, which usually detects such actions.'[141]

The early modern period was more concerned with the rebelliousness of women than of youth, and almanacs had little to say about the position of children or adolescents. The child's duty was of course obedience, but parents were advised to combine discipline with affection.[142] Quite often almanacs printed the dates of school holidays—the only part of the book which interested the young, according to Gadbury—and sometimes there were vague predictions that children would be eager or slow to learn.[143] Scattered remarks provide a few further glimpses of the life of the very young: thus the almanac was said to be a useful source for a 'bug-bear name or two every month' to quieten crying children. There were references to nurses going out to buy plums to still the baby, and to tradesmen's wives buying their children farthing pies at the fair as a treat. *Poor Robin* ventured the prophecy that there would be less bed-wetting in summer—because the nights were shorter![144] Culpeper, a physician, had some discussion of child-care in his *Directory for Midwives*. He advised that babies should be weaned at a year, at an appropriate stage of the moon, though he noted cases where babies had not been weaned until the age of three or four. The lack of specialized infant foods and the problems of hygiene favoured long breast-feeding; a journalist at the end of the century referred to the practice of chewing food to soften it, and then transferring it to the child's mouth, 'as I have seen some nasty old sluts feed their own grandchildren'. Culpeper thought detailed advice on infant care was needed, believing that not one woman in twenty was competent to nurse her own child properly.[145] He also touched on the question of maturity, and mentioned the age of menarche for girls as being usually in the fourteenth year, rarely before the thirteenth and never before the twelfth—considerably earlier than modern estimates. Ramesey however seemed to expect that whilst some girls would have reached it by sixteen, it was not universal until twenty-one.[146]

Most almanacs stressed primarily the duties and obligations of their readers. Many however also discussed recreation which often, like farming, followed a seasonal pattern. References were particularly common in the burlesque almanacs. We hear of boys playing with whips and tops during Lent (originally, Gadbury said, in imitation of the sufferings of the early martyrs), and killing cocks in the spring by throwing cudgels at them, around 'St. Pancake Day' (Shrove Tuesday).[147] The *Owles Almanack* predicted that boys would break as many windows as in former years, and other children's games were mentioned, such as leap-frog, 'scotch-hoppes' (hopscotch) and 'spurn-point', said to be highly destructive of children's shoes.[148] At Easter and in the spring, apprentices, journeymen and artisans took their girls to Islington and made merry on cakes, custard, stewed prunes and bottled ale.[149] On May Day there was dancing round the Maypole, and women and girls appeared in their fine new clothes, or if they had none stayed indoors.[150] At the same time fashionable society repaired to Hyde Park, Tottenham Court and Spring Gardens to see and be seen, watch the races (both foot and horse) and be titillated as 'the Adamites run naked before the ladies'. The Revolution made a temporary break in this routine, but it revived in the 1650s. 'Haste to Hyde Park', said Andrews in his almanac for 1658,

> and tell who's the race,
> What fashion's Allamode, who's the best face.[151]

Easter was also apparently regarded as the start of the season for football matches and other games. *Poor Robin* referred to Londoners trooping to Moor fields for nine pins and pigeonholes; girls played at stoolball and barley-break, boys and young men at football and wrestling, and both enjoyed dancing.[152] August was the month of the celebrated Bartholomew Fair in London, with its stalls, treats (roasted pigs), puppet shows and pickpockets. An advertisement in 1688 offered the additional attraction of a display of 'monumental relics of Rumpish-antiquity', including Lord Hewson's shoehorn, Alderman Hoyle's rope, 'a ruby from Old Noll's nose', and a portrait of the celebrated 'hog-faced gentlewoman'.[153] In September there was the traditional nutting on Holy Rood Day, when one might chance to meet the Devil, according to legend, and October saw the shoemakers' festival of St. Crispin's Day, when all the shoemakers were said to go 'fox-catching'.[154] November the fifth was celebrated with bonfires, squibs and crackers, and was followed by the traditional merrymaking at Christmas.[155] Sport had, of course, other functions besides recreation. Gadbury noted that football and cudgel matches provided a means for settling village disputes, and both were suitably violent: football, ran a Jacobean prediction, would provide plenty of work for the surgeon. In former times, Gadbury remarked, disputes had been settled by the parties drinking together in the churchyard at the time of the patronal festival.[156]

Casual violence in sport did not disturb the villager, though it offended some contemporary moralists. There was far more to be feared from the hazards of nature, and from the deliberate malice of those on the fringe of society, such as criminals and witches. Violent crimes, such as murder, rape and highway robbery, appeared frequently among the listed disasters expected to follow an eclipse or major conjunction. The comments however were rarely specific. The ballad was better suited as a vehicle for exploiting the popular taste for details of horrific crimes, though occasionally a celebrated criminal was cited by name in an almanac, such as the bogus 'German Princess'. Compilers did not romanticize the robber or highwayman during this period, but there was an exception in an admiring reference to one Thomas Reynolds, a patriotic thief who chose to be hanged in his native land rather than be transported.[157]

The witch posed more of a problem to the astrologer, for many critics claimed that his own activities were no more than a form of witchcraft. The astrologers naturally disagreed, and many claimed that their art was valuable, even essential, in the diagnosis and cure of evils attributed to witches. Many of the best-known practitioners, such as Lilly, set figures for clients on cases of alleged witchcraft. Sarah Jinner published in one of her almanacs a remedy for impotence caused by a witch. Many almanacs predicted that witchcraft would be rife and that many witches would be discovered. Compilers cited the biblical denunciation of the crime, and urged magistrates to be severe, though attitudes changed as the seventeenth century passed.[158] Good or white witches (or 'cunning men') were sometimes held to be evil, but were often seen as quacks and impostors. Blagrave thought there was a sinister agreement between black and white witches to put on and take off *maleficium*, and to share the profits, paid in fees by the victim. But most believed that 'tricks' with 'sieve and shears, key and Bible' merely exploited the credulity of 'old doting' country folk, who should be protected by law.[159] Popular credulity meant of course that such devices could be effective in identifying a thief or restoring stolen goods. Pond explained in 1609 that the mistress of the house had only to tell the servants that she had consulted a cunning man who would soon reveal the thief's identity, and the person who has the stolen property '(through fear) is moved to convey it to some place where it may soon be found: and then floweth out a report, that such a cunning man hath caused it to be brought again'. At the end of the century another compiler set out a 'pleasant device' to determine which of the domestic servants had stolen a missing article. The servants are ushered into a darkened room, where they find a stranger suitably dressed as a cunning man, 'muttering hard words'. They walk round and round holding hands, in total darkness, and are then told suddenly to place their hands on a kettle, blackened with soot, on the table, and informed that a cock will crow as soon as the guilty person touches it. Naturally no cock performs, but the culprit—too frightened to move—can easily be identified as the only person with clean hands.[160]

Other categories on the fringe of society, and often mentioned among the impending calamities, were lunatics, suicides and vagrants. Nothing further was said about the insane, though towards the end of the period almanacs sometimes contained advertisements offering medical treatment.[161] The compilers displayed little of the horror traditionally associated with suicide. From the mid-seventeenth-century Wharton, Gadbury and others began to list prominent suicides in their calendars. But only in the burlesque series was there any discussion of the subject, which was treated there as a slightly macabre jest: ratsbane and hanging, for example, were solemnly prescribed as sound remedies for scurvy or the pains of love.[162] Discussion of beggars and vagrants followed the same pattern. Both were commonly predicted by Tudor astrologers among other afflictions, but the few seventeenth-century references reveal a neutral and sometimes even jocular attitude. *Poor Robin* indeed included a panegyric on the beggar's happy lot:

He's neither hated, nor doth hate,
None lives in a more happy state: . . .
He neither borrows, nor yet lends,
Nor by extortion gets or spends.
His heirs no wrangling nor debate
Have, when he dies, for his estate.
He never feareth quarter-day,
For why, he hath no rent to pay.
Then we may all conclude in this,
A beggar's state most happy is.[163]

Of course, this was meant to entertain the reader, but its tone was far removed from Tudor writings. It is perhaps a reflection that by the end of the period society was beginning to acquire the greater stability and security—if not the harmony—long desired by a multitude of almanac-makers.

CHAPTER FIVE

Almanacs and Religion

(i) The Controversy over Astrology

BY 1500 ASTROLOGY had already behind it a long and controversial history in Christian Europe. There was little opposition to the notion of planetary influences on the weather or physiology, but the belief that it was possible to predict human behaviour, whether individual or collective, raised profound moral and religious problems. The dispute reached a new intensity in the sixteenth and seventeenth centuries; by 1700, despite a vigorous defence, astrology was fast losing its religious as well as its scientific respectability.[1]

Objections to judicial astrology fell into two major categories. First, it was alleged that the stars supplanted God, undermining his power and distracting man's attention. Men looked to the stars, not to God's providential intervention, as the determining influence on human affairs. The excitement raised by the predictions of Nostradamus, the great conjunction of 1583 and later Black Monday in 1652 gave substance to the charge. Astrology thus appeared as the rival of Christianity, leading men away from God, and serving the Devil. There was a sustained attempt to link astrology with witchcraft, sorcery and demonism. One critic indeed likened the astrologer to a 'Doctor Faustus in swaddling clouts'. It was easy to explain the fulfilment of many of the prophecies, for successes showed merely 'how easy it is for the Devil to predict those things which he intends to act himself'.[2]

The second major anxiety concerned moral freedom. If the stars determined human behaviour, with

> but a twinkling of a star
> Between a man of peace and war,
> A thief and justice, fool and knave,

there could be no place for moral responsibility. 'How could I help it,' the criminal would plead, 'seeing I was born under such a star?'[3] This was clearly intolerable in a Christian or indeed any society. It was aggravated by the blasphemous claims of some earlier astrologers that the fortunes of Christianity and Islam could be explained by the nativities of Christ and Mahomet. Some contemporary practitioners, including Anglican clergy, continued to calculate the horoscope of Christ.[4] Critics recalled that earlier astrologers had guaranteed the salvation of all people born under certain conjunctions. Astrology and Calvinism could be seen as offering rival and irreconcilable brands of determinism. 'Shall we not then have predestination (in the acts of election and reprobation) urged to depend upon the destinating stars?' asked one opponent.[5] Protestantism, with its greater emphasis on the power of God, was thus likely to bring a new impetus to the attack on astrology. The English Reformer, Miles Coverdale, translated and published a German 'prognostication' which was, in fact, a Protestant denunciation of astrology. (Its prophetic scope was limited to guaranteeing all Catholics a 'very evil and unfruitful year'.[6]) The well-known importance of astrology in mediaeval times prompted a further Protestant charge that it was a relic of popery. But the fierce anti-Catholicism of most English practitioners made the charge implausible, and as propaganda it may even have been counter-productive, for belief in the prophetic and healing powers connected with Catholicism was still widespread long after the Reformation. Indeed as late as the 1690s a quack medical preparative, promised to cure every known disease, was being peddled as 'The Vatican Pill'.[7]

The major issues raised by astrology had been debated for centuries. The controversy itself has been traced in some detail elsewhere, primarily from the critics' perspective. This section therefore concentrates on the character and validity of the defence offered in almanacs and other astrological writings.

Much of the argument was conducted, predictably, at an elementary level. Astrologers and their opponents resorted to personal abuse, and often preferred a telling anecdote or a neat debating-point to a sustained argument. It was easy to score by declaring that critics who denied the influence of the stars must be lunatic or planet-struck, especially when an eminent minister endorsed the view.[8] The enmity of William Perkins, the celebrated Puritan, was brushed aside as 'that good man's error'.[9] Sir Christopher Heydon and many others thought that the enormous critical compilation of Pico della Mirandola had been disproved conclusively by the fact that three astrologers had predicted the exact day of Pico's death.[10] Similarly compilers recounted with relish the story of William Herbert, third Earl of Pembroke. Assured that he would not live to see his fifty-first year, the earl celebrated his fiftieth birthday in good health, mocked the astrologers, and promptly died.[11]

The most influential work in the field was Sir Christopher Heydon's *A Defence of Iudiciall Astrologie* (1603), which provided the arguments and texts for a host of later works, and was itself derived largely from earlier Continental authorities. Heydon paraded an imposing array of political figures, churchmen and scholars who had practised astrology, from the Roman Emperor Hadrian downwards, to prove its respectability and antiquity. Its antiquity was indeed offered as a proof of its validity.[12] Aware that the greatest hostility came from the clergy, defenders made much of the earlier role of churchmen as theorists and practitioners. Some clerics now wrote against it, Gadbury remarked sarcastically, but the reader should note that some modern clergymen also attacked the divinity of Christ.[13] The Bible provided ready ammunition for both sides. There were certainly hostile passages in the Old Testament, but also others which indicated the force of the stars and their place in the divine system. The most popular texts included Genesis, i:14. ('let them be for signs, and for seasons'), Judges, v:20 ('the stars in their courses fought against Sisera') and Job, xxxviii:31 ('Canst thou bind the sweet influences of Pleiades, or loose the bands of Orion?'). An eighteenth-century editor of 'Partridge' thought that Psalm cxxi:6 ('The sun shall not smite thee by day, nor the moon by night') was 'a singular evidence of lunar energy'.[14] Ingenuity added other texts to the list. Against those who denied the existence of the houses or mansions of the zodiac, John Vaux, curate and almanac-maker, retorted triumphantly in the words of Christ, 'In my Father's house are many mansions.'[15] The star which led the three Magi to Bethlehem was cited as proof of divine approval, and indicated that the Magi, the very first Christians, were no 'other than plain astrologers'.[16]

Some acquaintance with Jewish writings provided supplementary material. According to Josephus, Seth the son of Adam had mastered the science of astronomy (including astrology), and had inscribed its rules on pillars of brick and stone which survived the Flood. In later times Abraham passed on this knowledge to the Egyptians, and in due course it reached the Chaldeans and Greeks; classical astrology thus acquired a Jewish and indeed divine origin.[17] In apologetic writings Adam was presented as the first astrologer, succeeded by a line of astrologer-patriarchs which included Noah, Abraham, Moses, David (author of 'astrological hymns') and Solomon.[18] The mediaeval claim by Guido Bonatus that 'Christ himself was an astrologer, and made use of elections', was well known, though firmly denied. Sir Christopher Heydon, however, recalled that when Christ was prophesying the fall of Jerusalem he 'forwarned the Jews to lift up their heads to heaven and to behold the signs that should be in the sun, and in the moon, and in the stars before that day. Neither did the event fail', said Heydon, noting the dramatic portents described by Josephus.[19]

Many astrologers did set out to refute the major arguments against astrology, and to reconcile it with Christianity. Almanacs often began with a brief summary of the proffered synthesis, to reassure their readers. The compilers replied to the first charge, that the stars displaced God and undermined his power, by stressing that the stars were secondary causes, used by God (the primary cause) to bring about his purposes on earth. They were thus not the rivals but the instruments of God, his 'subordinate magistrates' and 'heavenly ministers'. Who could doubt 'God's government of the world by angels and stars', asked John Booker. 'The angels are his ministring spirits, and the stars his militia; the stars are the host of heaven, and God the Lord of Hosts.'[20] John Securis explained that God was indeed sovereign, but generally 'worketh by his instruments', such as angels, prophets, holy men and stars.[21] Reversing the critics' argument, the astrologers suggested that it was the denial of planetary influences which undermined belief in divine intervention on earth. A Jacobean compiler condemned those who 'out of their peevish holiness' seek 'to please Master Calvin' and thus 'take away all the influences of heaven'. Lilly claimed, with gross unfairness, that those who denied astrology must believe that 'all things happen casually', which he thought showed them to be 'not much better than beasts'.[22] As sovereign, God could intervene to remove the evils indicated by the stars. After cataloguing the disasters which they prefigured, most almanacs inserted a verse reminding the reader that, for example,

> So threat the stars, but One on high
> Above the stars, when his will's bent,
> Can stay their force, and put them by,
> They nought can do without's consent.[23]

An early Elizabethan compiler warned readers not to take his prophecies as implying 'fatal necessity, but that it shall chance if God do not forbid'.[24] Lilly and many others made it a principle to predict only the probability of events.[25] The astrologers thus devised a coherent system by which God used the stars as both signs of his wrath to warn men to repentance, and as instruments of vengeance if they proved obdurate. It was proof of God's mercy that he warned the world before punishing it, and the possibility of repentance and pardon disposed of the charge that astrologers merely increased human misery by predicting evils which could not be averted. The whole purpose of prognostication, John Vaux explained, was 'as a premonition to prevent the danger ensuing'.[26]

This formula raised the problem of whether the godly were punished for the sins of the reprobate. Thomas Buckminster side-stepped the difficulty by positing a merciful God who used the stars as a call to repentance but was likely to pardon men whatever their merits.[27] Blagrave believed that God sometimes spared the whole world for the sake of the elect. More often astrologers taught that evils would fall on the ungodly, but that God would preserve the elect; Gadbury observed that the Great Plague was destroying the dregs but sparing the more 'noble' part of the population.[28]

The defenders of astrology rejected entirely the charge that their science distracted mankind from God. They argued that, on the contrary, the heavens revealed the glory of God and thus served to strengthen faith, a principle used widely and successfully to defend scientific progress in this period.[29] Traditional views on cosmology placed the earth and mankind at the centre of the universe. To claim that the stars had no force was to leave them no role, and appeared as a derogation of God's power and purpose. Were they merely 'to be gazed upon as a sign at a door?' demanded Vaux incredulously. Even at the end of the seventeenth century such an assumption struck one compiler as 'a little unreasonable'.[30] Given the popular assumption that a purpose existed in the framing of the universe, this was probably an effective line of defence, and made the critics—including the clergy—appear in an irreligious light.

The second major charge against astrology was that it destroyed moral freedom and responsibility. The apparent irony of this allegation being made by Calvinist clergy was not lost on the astrologers, who countered that 'the great doctrine of election and reprobation' was equally determinist.[31] Nevertheless, a formula for reconciling astrology and moral responsibility had been handed down from the days of Ptolemy, and continued to serve: the stars were held to influence but not compel human actions. Men were thus the 'cause absolutely, and *Per se*, of their own wickedness and sin, and not the planets'. John Securis explained that God and his instruments could by definition only be good, and that planetary influences were not evil in'themselves, but that the wicked, in receiving them wickedly, turneth them into evil'.[32] The stars had dominion over the body, not the soul or will,[33] and astrologers taught that by 'sanctified reason', through grace, 'divine light' and education, the wise and godly were able to overcome the stars.[34] At the end of the seventeenth century Daniel Woodward injected a typically nationalist note by claiming that it was possible, 'as we are Englishmen and Christians', to withstand the strongest planetary influence.[35]

The doctrine that the stars were only secondary causes and exerted an influence which was strong but not binding had long provided an adequate formula for reconciling astrology and religion. The concept of secondary causes was also used, for example, in harmonizing medical or historical explanations with providence. But in the case of astrology the harmony often broke down, and the astrologers must take much of the blame. Frequently they listed impending disasters, with merely a comment that

Thus will the stars, if God assent,
Whose power alone can all prevent.

This appeared to leave nothing to human effort, and had overtones of a dualist system with the 'will' of the stars curbed only by the intervention of a benevolent but seemingly arbitrary God.[36] More important was the suspicion that the synthesis of astrology and Christianity was an artificial device, paraded in the preface to satisfy critics, and thereafter forgotten. Not all astrologers were as circumspect as Lilly, and some offered *pro certo* predictions in both private and political matters. Others modified, and undermined, the formula on which the synthesis rested. The astrologer, said Gadbury, must find 'a mean between chance and necessity'. No such ideal position existed. The more astrologers sought to reduce the workings of the universe to a pattern of fixed laws, the more they excluded divine intervention and the possible effects of repentance. But if they conceded the role of divine power and human free will, they faced the objection that astrology was insignificant and unscientific. John Partridge summed up the insoluble conundrum:

If Fate be not, then what can we foresee,
Or how can we avoid it, if it be?[37]

The attempts to improve the old synthesis were hardly acceptable to theologians. William Ramesey was willing to concede that God as sovereign could overrule the stars, but added that 'it followeth not that he doth, or that therefore the art is uncertain.' The only instances which occurred to him were the darkness at the crucifixion and the sun going backwards in the days of Joshua. Gadbury agreed that God could alter the action of the stars but in practice 'seldom doth'.[38] Some compilers discerned a threat to God's consistency and omniscience in the notion of sudden changes in divine policy as a result of human repentance. They therefore spoke in terms of absolute predestination through the stars. John Booker declared that

> God hath so ordered all things by his power
> Each year, month, week, day, minute of an hour
> Are in his hands; whatever comes to pass
> Was preordained, before time ever was.

Allestree agreed that 'all events be ordained of God from eternity.' Through God and the stars, taught Gresham, everyone 'hath his fate, I mean his time of coming into essence, his continuance, his accidents good or bad, his end and determination exactly measured, limited and prefigured before the event'. Ramesey thought it added to God's glory 'that when he made those heavenly bodies, the planets, to rule all sublunary things and times, that he fore-knew the events, dispositions of men, alterations of kingdoms' and indeed all things.[39] These comments were not intended to exclude free will or divine forgiveness. John Butler, the Restoration clergyman-astrologer, explained that there was 'a Fate in the frame of nature' and that God did not alter his purposes as a result of prayer. However, God 'foresaw all men, and all their cases, and their prayers, and thoughts, from the beginning; and laid his frame of nature so, as to answer all prayers, cases, and thoughts as was fit, all from the beginning'. God had thus devised a fixed order at the Creation which nevertheless took into account every prayer and every act of free will that could ever occur.[40] It was an intelligent and tenable argument, but hardly suited to mass consumption. The reader was likely to see only that his prayer and repentance could have no effect on God; the idea that they had been foreseen and allowed for aeons before his birth was probably beyond his mental grasp. The doctrine would thus appear as fatal necessity *tout court,* and the tone in many of the almanacs would have strengthened this probability.

Similar problems and inconsistencies surrounded the formula over free will. In theory 'the wise man rules the stars' but in practice 'there are very few so prudent either by force of nature or education, but most submit.' 'The effects of nature are commonly seen before the force of education', observed William Conyers;

> Saints over-rule the stars, but who are they
> That are not over-ruled? Most men obey.

Though it is possible to overcome the stars, George Atwell agreed, 'it be seldom done'.[41] Even the general view that the stars influenced the body, not the mind or soul, did not command total assent. Planetary influence inclines the mind, said John Smith, 'and we are so sensual as to be led by our inclinations'. The Laudian cleric and astrologer, John Swan, believed that the stars influenced even the soul indirectly, through their effects on the bodily humours, 'whereof the soul's operation dependeth'. Henry Coley thought the soul was affected by the stars while it was contained in the human body and thus 'submerged in elementary matters'.[42]

The issue of free will raised further problems. How were the wise and godly to be defined? Contemporaries had not forgotten the mediaeval claim that salvation depended on one's horoscope.[43] In the early Tudor period the perpetual prognostication, *Erra Pater,* told its readers that they would be either 'religious' or 'mischievous and untrue' according to the day of the month on which they were born. Moral and religious attributes were a standard part of the horoscope, signified by the ninth house of the zodiac. At the end of the period Henry Coley could still assert that the stars were in part 'the cause of depraved minds and vicious actions', which were likely if Mercury 'be not in good aspect with the moon and Saturn, by which means Reason gets the conquest of lust and passion'.[44] This was close to saying that the wise and godly could overrule the stars, but that only through the stars could one become wise and godly. Moreover to reserve moral freedom to the godly, however defined, was implicitly to deny it to the rest of the population, who were given a will theoretically free, but with no possibility of using it for good. 'He who lives a dissolute and sensual life,' said Thomas Fowle, 'here and upon him or such like persons the stars pour down their dire influences, and he is subject to their mal effects, and puts them into execution.' Where 'grace lacketh, the heavens enforceth', said Philip Moore; 'where grace is wanting, the will is captivated', agreed Tanner.[45] It was indeed possible to make specific and certain predictions, argued William Ramesey, when the astrologer could tell his client to be 'nowise either rational or religious'—the client presumably not being informed of this part of the calculation.[46]

The synthesis of astrology and Christianity was thus not above suspicion. Astrologers believed, rightly, that many people still thought they taught fatal necessity. Robert Gell was popularly held to have preached astrological determinism in a sermon to the Society of

Astrologers, though he complained that he had in fact argued the opposite.[47] Though they denied that astrology distracted men from God, some practitioners clearly feared it might be true. Coley, for example, thought it necessary to remind his readers not 'to be so intent upon this curious delightful study, as wholly to neglect those things which appertain to salvation'. There is a certain aptness in a laconic entry in one of Booker's notebooks: 'Memorandum. Our father which art in heaven.'[48] Moreover it is clear that many regarded astrologers as little different from wizards. The point was conceded frequently by the astrologers themselves, and seems to have been the result more of popular ignorance than clerical opposition. Blagrave's comment that many of his clients came secretly because they feared his art was 'diabolical' suggests an awareness of the church's disapproval, but more typical was the remark that the mere sight of a book of astrological symbols was, for countrymen, a proof of sorcery. Whenever 'the wind blows strongly', Culpeper complained, 'they say men are conjuring'.[49]

There is only a little evidence of the direct worship of the stars as gods in the early modern period.[50] But there are plentiful indications of an equally insidious development, the blurring and fusion of astrology and Christianity. Many clergy who might accept the stars as the passive instruments of God's will baulked at the suggestion of their animate nature. The stars were ascribed characters, of which faint echoes survive in the terms 'saturnine', 'mercurial,' 'martial' and so on. They had a sexual character, still utilized in the symbols for Mars and Venus (which in 1653 prompted the jest that the conjunction of the two planets rendered them liable to prosecution under the recent law against fornication).[51] During periods of crisis they took on political attributes. Mercury was 'like a bloody malicious Tory', and the reader learned of 'Tory Mars', the Whig 'Petitioning' comet, and the evil 'Whiggish-deep designs' of Saturn. The sun was alternatively a Tory absolute monarch of the sky or a Whig 'Stadholder of the heavens'.[52] Similarly, the planets possessed religious characteristics. Heydon thought that Jupiter was the protector of Christianity. In the 1640s Booker feared that godly Jupiter had become a sectarian, 'turned hypocrite, and given to factions'. A generation later John Case looked for an age of peace on earth, suggesting that Jupiter had 'convinced Saturn of his wicked designs', and thus reformed a malevolent planet. John Silvester thought that 'Jupiter is too virtuous a planet to own the pope. . . . It being more natural to him to own good Christians, he hath assigned the pope up to Saturn, the author of plots and mischief.'[53]

Edward Pond reported a widespread contemporary belief that the sun and moon felt great pain when they were eclipsed, 'as though the moon hath a reasonable soul, or a feeling body'.[54] There are many other examples of the invasion of astronomy by popular Christianity. The belief that the sun danced for joy on Easter morning lasted into the twentieth century. The Man in the Moon was widely held to have been banished thither for breaking the fourth commandment; in a rival French account he was identified as Judas Iscariot.[55] Heydon and Gadbury knew of the ancient belief that the signs of the zodiac represented the patriarchs. Almanacs reported the popular names of Orion's belt, 'our lady's elwande' (i.e. measure), and the Milky Way, 'our lady's way', and the belief that Saturn (or Mars) was Hell, and Jupiter the habitation of the elect.[56]

Astrologers and indeed religious writers often contributed to this blurring of astrology and Christianity. A literary figure such as James Howell might relish the conceit that 'the articles of the creed are as the twelve figures in the zodiac of faith, which make way for the sun of righteousness to pass through the centre of our hearts', but such language was likely to confuse ordinary people. There was a similar risk in the earlier spiritual almanac of Miles Coverdale, in which he presented a 'theological astronomy' with bold metaphors proclaiming the sun as Christ, and Mars as the Gospels. The image of Christ as the sun of righteousness dispelling the dark night of ignorance was used repeatedly by writers of all religious persuasions, including Fox, Winstanley, Saltmarsh, Milton and many Anglican divines. The solar eclipse of 1652 prompted a sermon entitled *Jesus Christ the Mysticall or Gospell Sun, Sometimes Seemingly Eclipsed, Yet Never Going Down from his People.*[57] The danger in this imagery was that God might be identified with his instruments, or that the stars might appear as deities themselves. The resulting confusion is apparent in the remarks of a late-Elizabethan parson-astrologer, James Carre, expressing the hope that 'the gods have so ordained, and the constellations of the stars are so well inclined, that neither God himself will be affected contrary to his preordinance, nor the planets otherwise disposed, than according to their prefixed inclination.' Both syntax and meaning are confused, but Carre appears to be implying that the stars could affect God's own actions.[58] Roger Crab, the sectarian, thought that if 'all men take Christ as their example, then Mars and Saturn, the two chief devils, will be trampled under feet'.[59]

Many astrological writers were drawing consciously on neoplatonist and Cabalistic traditions of an animistic universe and astral spirits. In a pre-war almanac, John Booker described the sun as '*oculus & anima mundi*' and 'cor coeli'.[60] The Elizabethan astrologer, John Harvey, endorsed the Cabalistic theories of the fifteenth-century Abbot Trithemius, and in 1647 Lilly published a tract by the same author, setting out the names of the planetary angels and the epochs over which they held sway in the history of the world.[61] George Wharton, Lilly's rival, published a treatise on the 'soul of the world' by the sixteenth-century German philosopher, Rothman, who had claimed that it would be 'absurd to deny a life and soul to be in the heaven and the stars'. The stars were rational and intelligent beings, with power not only to influence life on earth but to create it, as seen (he claimed) in the generation of animals without copulation and of plants on remote mountains 'without natural seed'.[62] Other annual writers, such as Andrews, Blagrave and Howell, incorporated similar ideas in their almanacs.[63] The theory of planetary angels offered a means of harmonizing stars and angels as instruments of God, but it gave greater substance to the clerical attack that the stars were akin to an array of rival gods, or that astrological science was in reality a cult of demons.[64] Most readers of almanacs would of course have been wholly innocent of Neoplatonism, but the ideas they found presented may have served to strengthen and make respectable notions of an animistic universe derived from the very different tradition of Christian folklore.

The synthesis of astrology and religion was thus by no means watertight. It proved sufficient, however, to dissuade the state from intervening to suppress the art altogether, as opponents demanded repeatedly. John Chamber, canon of Windsor, observed wryly that if astrologers possessed lands and endowments, as monks had done, the government would long since have recognized the need for their suppression.[65]

But it was not only the theoretical aspects of astrology which antagonized the clergy. As Mr. Thomas has suggested, the astrologer and cunning man emerged after the Reformation as rivals of the minister. Clients brought to the consulting room a wide range of personal problems which would earlier have formed part of the pastoral work of the priest. Moreover the astrologer, through the doctrine of elections, still possessed a capacity to harness supernatural powers which the Protestant minister had relinquished in the break from Rome.[66]

The professional rivalry of astrologer and cleric was as apparent in the almanac as in the consulting room. The annual almanac was used as a quasi-pulpit from which the compiler preached repentance, a sanctified life and the approach of death and Judgement, explained the rudiments of Christianity, and incidentally abused the clergy. Lilly drew attention to this element of professional rivalry, explaining that the clergy attacked astrology because they wished to preserve their monopoly in the teaching of religion. Bishop Hall aptly described almanac-makers as 'star-divines'. Not everyone was prepared to accept the implied—and not always justified—godliness of the astrologers. They were rather, a critic told them, sanctimonious hypocrites

who to the world declare
How great your own *Religiousnesses are,*
And are with Pharisean lips so free
To cry, Stand off, we're holier than ye.[67]

The astrologers naturally presented themselves as the partners, not the rivals of the clergy. They argued that God was to be understood through his works. 'In those mighty creatures', the stars, men 'behold the Almightiness of their Creator', so that astrology was 'a way . . . to know the most high God', a system of 'Natural Theology'.[68] 'Oh then what's nearer to theology/Than are the secrets of astrology?' exclaimed a Jacobean prognosticator.[69] The very regularity of planetary motions was a salutary lesson to wayward mankind:

The sun, the moon, and all the stars
To praise God do not let:
They keep their course and order full
Wherein he hath them set.
But man who is a living soul
And born for that intent,
Hath no regard to keep his law
Nor his commandment.[70]

Astrology was the 'alphabet of divinity', an essential part of clerical learning. Correspondingly, Lilly claimed that only a godly man could be a good astrologer.[71] 'Let the minister interpret the word of God, but the astrologer his works', said George Atwell, 'no question but God would have both interpreted.'[72] Some clergy, jealous of the divine prerogative, did of course question this assumption, arguing that 'Heaven is God's book, which we must leave to him.' But the metaphor belonged more naturally to the opposite camp, where it was very popular. Booker, for example, retorted that

The stars are letters and the Heaven's God's book
Which day and night we may at pleasure look,
And thereby learn uprightly how to live.[73]

A considerable number of Tudor and Stuart clergy believed, like their mediaeval predecessors, that astrology and Christianity were complementary. Some even compiled and published almanacs: in the Tudor period we find Andrew Borde and Edmund Harcock (ex-regulars), Anthony Askham, William Bulleine, Thomas Buckminster, George Hartgill and James Carre. They were followed in the next century by Jeffereys, Vaux, Evans, Eaton, Swan, Childrey, Atkinson, Martindale, Krabtree and others.[74] Many other clerics studied astrology, acted as astrological physicians or showed a sympathetic interest. Some consulted astrologers on their chances of preferment.[75] Richard Harvey's extravagant predictions for 1583 were able to appear in print despite having been submitted to the Bishops of London and Rochester, and scrutinized by Adam Squire, a former Master of Balliol College.[76]

Seventeenth-century defenders of astrology found an eminent sympathizer in Archbishop Laud, who noted astrological data in his diary, and cited the evils of a conjunction of Saturn and Mars in a sermon at the opening of parliament in 1628. He was indeed reported to have declared that 'God's aspect to the world is planetary.'[77] John Gadbury noted the interest of Bishop Sanderson, and the remark of Jeremy Taylor, Bishop of Connor and Down, that 'a fool and a wise man differ not . . . save only one hath a better star.' Gadbury was himself personally associated for many years with another bishop, Joseph Henshaw of Peterborough. [78] John Gregory, author of a nativity of Christ, was chaplain to the future Bishop Duppa and a protege of Laud, who admired his erudition.[79] Though there were few Puritan supporters, polemicists knew of the astrological learning of John Preston, and made the most of some apparently favourable remarks by Joseph Caryl and William Greenhill. On the whole, astrology seems to have been repugnant to Calvinism, with its stress on the majesty of God and the impotence of mankind.[80] Yet many of the fiercest 0clerical opponents of judicial astrology felt unable to condemn istrology altogether. This was especially true of the sixteenth century. William Perkins attacked almanacs, but conceded that God worked through the stars as well as his other instruments. Calvin refuted judicial astrology, but thought natural astrology an 'honorable' science, In the mid-seventeenth century John Vicars, one of the sternest critics of Lilly, nevertheless endorsed a more restrained almanac.[81] The force of clerical opposition was thus weakened by being framed in an intellectual climate still pervaded by astrological dogma. Only when critics were prepared to reject the entire system were their attacks likely to carry real conviction.[82]

In addition to the parson-astrologers, there were men of undoubted piety among the lay practitioners. Edward Gresham, for example, compiled works of devotion, Philip Kinder elaborated a religious creed in his notebook, and Parkhurst published a synopsis of the Bible. Allestree's almanacs were genuinely pious in tone, and those of Vincent Wing were justly described as 'sermons, or expositions'.[83] Though William Lilly was a figure of dubious morality, there is no reason to doubt his professed admiration for the Puritan, Arthur Hildersham, nor his regular attendance at lectures before the civil war.[84] Even Simon Forman, the notorious astrologer whose amorous pursuit of female clients has been traced by Dr. Rowse, revealed another aspect of his personality in his manuscript writings, which include prayers, psalms, and biblical exegesis by the author, with reflections on the restoration of the Jews, the coming of Antichrist and the end of the world.[85] There were certainly plenty of rogues and charlatans among astrological practitioners, but enough men of genuine religious interests and commitment to refute any simple equation of astrology with profanity.[86]

(ii) Religious Teaching

As partners of the clergy, the first task of the almanac-makers was to provide basic factual information. Many Tudor editions gave the gospels and epistles for church services on each Sunday of the year, and the dates of moveable festivals; in the next century Kidman's almanac collected such data on the last page, designed to be cut out and 'set up in any church'.[87] Einer, which was composed expressly 'for divines', took a modest view of their accomplishments and listed the twelve apostles and the major events of the Christian calendar.[88] Several almanacs printed a list of episcopal sees and even of their occupants.[89] At the invitation of Charles I, John Booker composed a treatise on the true date of Easter, and Gadbury wrote a similar piece later in the century.[90]

The tradition of providing religious teaching for the laity went back to the *Kalender of Shepherdes,* which first appeared in England in

1503. It printed the creed, pater noster and commandments, set out the seven virtues and the seven deadly sins, and added the ten commandments of the devil and a lively description of hell. Later editions included a discussion of the value of prayers for the dead.[91] In one of the earliest English advertisements in print, an almanac of 1522 informed readers about the 'Jesus fraternity' meeting under St. Paul's, which offered weekly masses for the souls of departed members, and special prayers for the brethren and sisters.[92] Some later almanacs met basic needs by printing the ten commandments in rhyming verse, 'fit for a weak memory', and explaining the festivals of the church. A Restoration almanac even contained a section proving the immortality of the soul.[93] Philip Ranger tried to summarize the essence of Christian doctrine in two lines of verse:

> Thy sin, thy death, the death of Christ, th'eternal pains of hell,
> The day of doom, the joys of heaven, these six remember well.

William Wroth, the pioneer Welsh Puritan, used this verse later as an elementary summary of faith when teaching the children of the Bristol separatists.[94] In *Writing Tables and a Kalendar*, a handbook issued several times in the late Tudor and early Stuart period, the reader found a number of prayers for household use.[95]

Many compilers also set out the dates of the 'forbidden times' when marriage was not permitted by the Church without special licence. There were three such periods of restraint: from Septuagesima to Low Sunday (covering Lent), Rogation to Trinity, and Advent to Hilary. Vaux explained that the first was a period of mourning for the fall of mankind, the second a time of fasting and prayer in preparation for Ascension, and the third a period of spiritual, not carnal joy. The first and third appear to have been widely observed. Edward Pond noted that the Council of Trent had prescribed two shorter periods only, Lent and Advent, but observed that he 'knew not why it should be received in England'.[96]

One of the needs of the sick and aged was met from the mid-seventeenth century, when Fly's almanac began printing a specimen of a will, which included a suitable religious preamble. The phraseology of wills sometimes reflected the religious outlook of the testators; more often, though, it followed the formula of the scribe responsible. The origins of the formulae used are unknown, but from 1658 one was readily available in a work which sold several thousand copies each year. From 1687 it was printed also in the almanacs of William Turner. The formula provided was already known before it appeared in these works, and was used in wills in Cambridgeshire and Warwickshire early in the century.[97]

The call to repentance dominated the religious teaching of the almanacs, and intruded into every part. Thus Thomas Wilkinson presented his name in the pious anagram 'Now-kil-sin' on the title-page of one of his editions. To John Booker, even the prediction of a spell of rainy weather had a religious dimension: 'The heavens themselves for us to tears do turn.' 'When sun doth rise, then mind thy rise from death,' advised Henry Harflete, 'when sun doth set, then mind thy setting breath.'[98] The calendar and changing seasons suggested obvious analogies. Each January prompted such appeals as:

Now as this new year doth begin,
So let us fly from wicked sin.

It was a time to 'put off the old man, abandon deadly sin'. Similarly the renewal of nature in spring suggested a fresh start to life, while the close of the old year was clearly a good time to 'forsake our old sins'.[99] Godly compilers such as Buckminster and Twyne ended their predictions for the four quarters of the year with short prayers. 'God the giver of health and life,' prayed Buckminster in 1589, 'turn from us all evil, and cause us with the spring to grow in virtue and all goodness, that we may be inheritors of the kingdom of Heaven. Amen.'[100] A century later Thomas Fowle warned that the harsh winter of 1683–4 was a special sign of God's anger. Far from repenting, the profane Londoners had erected booths on the frozen River Thames 'to drink and tipple in'; retribution would surely follow.[101] Most compilers similarly emphasized the certainty of punishment in this life and the next if their pleas for repentance were ignored. John Evans used more colourful language than most, but his argument was typical:

O wretched man enwrapped in crimson sin,
Repent with speed thy sinful life, Begin
Before the vial of God's wrath (whose wine is red)
Be fiercely poured down upon thy head.[102]

The message was clear and forceful: 'convert today', 'repent constantly', and thus escape the 'hellish lake'.[103]

Behind the repeated exhortations lay a conviction that by most people

The physic of our sacred soul
Is not thought on till bell doth toll.

The compilers therefore sought to increase their impact by varying their methods. One device was to weave the theme of sin and repentance into more sensational material, which was likely to have a greater popular appeal. Gabriel Frende was explicit about his design:

> Of strange events I know some love to hear,
> To whose desire I willingly consent:
> For why, I see a Monster will appear,
> Although he be full close in prison pent.
> And would you know what monster this should be:
> Tis Pride, O Man, that's closely pent in thee.[104]

Edward Gresham published a translation of a German tract, which described and speculated on a series of monstrous apparitions in the sky over Karlstadt. The verity of the account, Gresham added ingenuously in a preface, was 'a thing I greatly respect not'. But it was undoubtedly true that vengeance would follow unless men repented.[105]

Most astrologers intensified their call by stressing the nearness of death and—utilizing the apocalyptic mood of the age—the approach of the Last Judgement. *The Almanack for One Day* was for doomsday.[106] Even if the apocalypse failed to materialize, compilers reminded the reader that 'this may be dooms-day's final year with thee.' The purchase of each new edition marked the reader's passage through life towards the grave, for

> every year thy almanac thou buyest,
> Th'art one year nearer to the year thou diest.

A character in Beaumont and Fletcher's *The Woman Hater* indeed measured his age in such terms, remarking how

> Full eight and twenty several almanacs
> Have been compiled, all for several years,
> Since first I drew this breath.[107]

The *memento mori* was a standard feature of the almanac. 'Death's near'st at hand, when man least fears', ran a typical warning. An Elizabethan compiler told his reader that

> Thou wouldest weep, if well thou wist
> But one month here to bide:
> Yet dost thou laugh, and art not sure
> What may this day betide.

Philip Ranger began one of his many verses on the theme with the promising reflection that 'we subject are a thousand ways to grisly stroke of death', on which he proceeded to elaborate. Nature provided unlimited analogies:

> The grass that grows tomorrow is hay,
> And man that's now as soon is clay.[108]

Gadbury thought that in the death of Queen Mary and a number of peers in 1694 there was much 'true divinity and useful religion to be learned'. For if such great people succumbed, 'how much less shall those of more common blood and birth hope to shuffle off Death's black and fatal summons?'[109]

The astrologers were on safely uncontroversial ground in denouncing sin and urging repentance. Some went further and discussed the path to salvation. An early Elizabethan compiler, William Cunningham, declared that only through the grace of God could the reader hope for the gift of repentance, 'for thou art wholly sin and canst of thy self do nothing but sin . . . repent, repent, God grant us all to repent.' Thomas Bretnor agreed that man was not able to 'will any good thing at all, without the especial and prevailing grace of Almighty God'. John Evans, parson and astrologer, published a large volume of 'tears, meditations and prayers', and took from it for his almanac a brief summary of Calvinist doctrine:

> Corruption made us sons of wrath and fiery brands of hell.
> But grace in Christ made us thy sons and heirs to dwell
> In heaven where thy kingdom is, most glorious be thy name,
> Which hast in Christ elected us before all world's frame.[110]

But most often the term 'elect' was used loosely to mean merely the godly, forever tempted by sin and in danger of damnation. 'Saints turn sinners, sinners saints', observed Thomas Trigge, 'the holiest are subject to mutation like others.' 'Back-slide not', Evans warned.[111] John Gadbury denounced the Calvinist doctrine of predestination which had once, he said, brought him to despair. Few were so explicit, but many implied that all men were constantly in danger of hell, just as (if prayers were answered) God might 'make us all partakers of heaven'.[112]

Most of the emphasis was on the importance of a holy life, as a means to win divine favour and salvation. The Elizabethan, John Dade, explained that God had made a covenant

> With man if he live well
> And keep his promise and his word
> In heaven he shall dwell;
> But if he roll his years about,
> And run a sinful race,
> The hell for heaven shall be his lot,
> Because he slid from grace.

Thomas Balles summarized the doctrine in the promise:

Show forth your faith by works of charity
And you shall live with Christ eternally.[113]

Gabriel Frende believed that a 'virtuous life doth purchase grace'.[114] Most writers stressed that a virtuous life was indeed the essence of Christianity. Buckminster, like Vincent Wing, framed his calls for repentance in terms of behaviour: 'Let us depart from evil and do good. Let us cast off the cloaks of unhonesty, and unrighteous dealing. Let no man defraud or beguile his brother in any manner of thing.'[115] Each year saw renewed pleas for charity and hospitality.[116] Very many almanacs thus combined elements of Calvinist terminology with a general message suggesting that salvation depended on moral conduct, with no apparent awareness of the contradiction. Compilers found repugnant any attempt to separate faith and works, a feeling evident even in writers of a puritanical cast, such as Bretnor and Booker, who condemned roundly those who

under zealous habits' mask
Hunt after sermons, haunt each heavenly task,
But mark them well, their charity is small,
Their friendship less, their actions worst of all.

During the Revolution Culpeper denounced religious reformers who failed to appreciate that behaviour was the essence of Christianity, observing that 'the main way to judge between a saint and a sinner is not who professes most duties.'[117]

The link between virtue and salvation fitted neatly into the astrologers' treatment of the doctrine of providence, which was largely in accord with contemporary clerical thought.[118] God constantly intervened, it was believed, to reward virtue and punish sin, and the doctrine was used as both carrot and stick to strengthen moral exhortation. Plague, robbery and wars were all the result of human sinfulness; peace and tranquillity were the reward of godliness. Thomas Stephins left no room for doubt:

O wretched man, thou dung and dust,
Of this thing be thou sure,
Thy life long in loathsome lust
Doth all these griefs procure.[119]

The Spanish Armada was a clear example of God's anger, and its defeat showed his mercy when repentance followed; later generations were reminded of the need to repent lest still greater disasters ensued.[120] William Lilly offered an elaborate explanation of the new star of 1572 which he saw as a token of divine wrath and the'fore-runner of the downfall of all monarchical pomp' and 'pontifical pride'. The rulers of Europe remained unperturbed, so the comet of 1618 followed as a second warning, and when again 'not one prince amended, or a priest repented', it was allowed to work its dire effects, and resulted in the Thirty Years War. Blithely ignoring this example and a final warning (the conjunction of the two superior planets in 1642), the English provoked a civil war in their own land.[121] At a far more mundane level, the almanac-makers crudely offered virtue as a means to prosperity. 'Leave off to sin, your grass full well shall grow', John Smith promised the husbandman:

(in times of wet) if you will cease
To pour out sin, and with God make your peace,
The showers shall stay.

Or, as Frende claimed,

Repent thy sin, and do no more,
Then corn and cattle thou shalt have store.[122]

Joseph Blagrave left no doubt that 'riches are tokens of God's especial love and favour unto his chosen people', citing Psalm xci in support. Another compiler promised 'great riches to godly men'. The honest tradesman learned that he could expect reward, for 'God will surely bless the hand, that weighs and measures right.'[123] Those who showed charity at Christmas would themselves receive riches. 'Lend them that want, the Almighty favoureth such', William White advised, 'And in short time repays them twice as much.'[124] It was an attractive prospect, especially with the reminder that God would ruin those who spurned the poor. But a morality which placed such emphasis on material benefits as the reward of virtue came dangerously close to presenting gain as the very purpose of virtue. Some comments indeed passed over the line. *Vaux* advised its readers to be generous to the poor, adding

For why, the fervent prayers of the poor,
Will move the Lord thy charges to restore.[125]

The thought was natural enough, given the providential beliefs of the period, but it throws a rather cold light on contemporary concepts of godliness.

(iii) Religious Polemic

Almanacs in the seventeenth century devoted as much space to religious polemic as to the rudiments of faith. The dominant themes were anti-clericalism and attacks on Catholics, Puritans and later non-conformists. Each of these groups, however, found some champions when circumstances permitted.

The earliest and one of the most fiery English polemicists was Anthony Askham. His almanac for 1555 was a comprehensive indictment of Protestant innovations under Edward VI. It constitutes one of the few attempts during the brief Catholic reign of Mary Tudor to reinvigorate Catholicism by appealing to a large, popular readership. Askham was a Yorkshire priest, physician and astronomer, and brother of a well-known humanist; his own outlook, however, seems to have been wholly traditional. The Edwardian Reformers, he wrote, were a 'generation of vipers' worse than Judas; they had 'pulled down God's house over his head, for fear to rise again', in their pursuit of plunder. They had swept away the mass, holy water, crosses, Corpus Christi Day, the veneration of the Virgin and much else; 'such wonderful heresy was never seen before.' Their endorsement of clerical marriage was a surrender to 'carnal liberty'. Their heresies sprang from a monstrous pride in human reason. Askham saw transubstantiation and the Virgin birth as mysteries beyond 'foolish reason' and 'carnal fantasy'. The heavens displayed the glory and omnipotence of God, and taught the inadequacy of human reason.

> Works above reason, the which be miraculous,
> Will not be known by reason, but by faith only. . . .
> What can their wits and reason discern of God's might?
> Leave their senses and take to faith, if thou wilt judge aright.

The publication of the Bible in English seemed to Askham the source of much of the vain speculation, 'the spring and well of heresies a rout'. But now Queen Mary, 'our noble Judith', had rescued England from heresy, and her marriage to Philip of Spain heralded a new era of peace and godliness.[126]

In the later Elizabethan and early Stuart period, a number of compilers attacked the Puritan 'sect' as the author of schism. Arthur Hopton denounced the Puritan minister who hates the vestments,

> the reverent bishops scorn,
> Makes all days like, loves no array but that
> Which in a self-conceited fashion's worn.
> Though he seem pure, call Pope the Antichrist,
> Believe him not, 'tis a dissembling priest.

Hopton looked forward to an 'umpire' who would root out such divisive hypocrites. Thomas Jeffereys, a minister, inserted into his almanac for 1635 a section headed unambiguously 'The author's wishes': that the Puritans 'were all banished into New England without revocation', and for those who 'cannot without heart-burning suffer a superior, or endure an equal, that their heads were off'. His interest in clerical education reflected a Laudian concern for the status of the clergy rather than a wish for a preaching ministry. Clergy unable to speak and write fluent Latin should, he urged, be sent back to college, while recruits from the trades and of no university 'but only of the college of the collectors of sermon notes' should be driven out.[127] In the late 1630s John Swan, also a minister and later an almanac-maker, was attacking Puritans and propagating Laudian views on *iure divino* episcopacy and the right of clergy to hold civil office. But it was no longer possible to publish such ideas when his almanacs began to appear in the 1650s.[128]

Puritan objections to Christmas as a popish superstition also provoked criticism throughout the period. The Elizabethan, Walter Gray, was aware of its associations with the pagan Roman Saturnalia, but urged his readers:

Be not self-willed, newfangled, nor too nice,
Whereby to shun this solemn feast to keep.

A century later *Poor Robin* saw opposition to it as puritanical hypocrisy:

Old Christmas is turned out of door
By some who would not feast the poor,
Who for the same excuse can find
Good works are popishly inclined.[129]

The prohibition of festivities at Christmas during the Revolution was ignored by most compilers, who continued to urge on their readers a round of jollification. 'Tis Christmas time', remarked Wing in 1654, 'therefore be merry.' 'With mirth and music keep thy Christmas feast', another urged. [130] The revolutionary years did however make possible a clear statement of the opposite view. Humphrey Howell stressed the religious objections: a feast derived from the pagan Saturnalia was blasphemous towards Christ in its origin and its conduct, 'for when in all the year is he more dishonoured? What less pleasing to him than swearing, drunkenness, and all manner of villainy?' *The Scripture Almanack*, compiled by the Baptist, Henry Jessey, contained similar arguments.[131] Vaux printed a verse on the suppression of holy days, adding that the Gospels too should be purged 'of all suspected popery': 'Nor must we call th'Apostles saints,/Of popery it them attaints.'[132] The pagan associations of Christmas were a reminder that the whole of the traditional calendar had a non-Christian foundation. It is not surprising that during the Revolution many Protestant sectarians ceased to use it and called for its reform. *The Scripture Almanack* explained the Hebrew calendar and advocated reform along biblical lines, citing a number of Independent and Baptist ministers in support. The scheme won for its author the nickname 'Jessey the Jew'.[133] Another compiler, Richard Atlee, also denounced Christmas, Easter and other festivals as based on human tradition instead of scripture. But he added too an economic argument. The time devoted to religious festivals should properly be spent in work, for, he argued, God had ordained six days of labour each week and 'here is no room left for holy days.' An attack on holy days at the end of the century was couched in primarily secular terms, calling them a 'burden' which others across the seas 'still groan under'.[134]

Until the Revolution there was no explicit defence of the Puritans. The nearest approach was a passage in Lloyd's almanac for 1585 predicting that through the 'cruelty of magistrates' the laws would be 'wrested, perverted and misinterpreted, and the consciences of zealous and godly persons through restraint . . . injured and oppressed'.[135] A Puritan outlook was obvious in William Beale's almanac, where the traditional 'popish' saints of the calendar were replaced by Protestant martyrs from Foxe. In similar vein, the owner of a Jacobean almanac added 'Udall M (artyr)' to the calendar to commemorate the imprisonment and death of a celebrated Elizabethan Puritan.[136] The godly probably also found solace in the puritanical tone of Allestree and Booker. John Booker, who suffered under the Laudian authorities, optimistically predicted 'wonderful change in the church'. But, as a contemporary noted, he failed to foresee the hated *Et Cetera* Oath devised in 1640 to penalize the Puritans:

> O Booker, Booker, how cam'st thou to lack
> This fiend, in thy prophetic almanac?[137]

The wish for a learned, resident and preaching ministry, generally associated with the Puritans, was also apparent in a number of pre-war compilers who condemned Puritanism as schismatic. Hopton, for example, attacked the Puritans as trouble-makers but demanded that the clergy should earn their tithes by preaching more than the statutory quarterly sermon. As 'too much honey doth the mouth distaste', he observed, so a 'sweet . . . double benefice' had a cloying effect on a minister's zeal for preaching. Philip Ranger defended tithes, promising that God would reward those who paid willingly, but called on the clergy to devote more effort to saving the souls of the poor, and less to devising 'new-fangled conceits to raise schisms'.[138]

The changed situation in the years after 1640 made it possible for compilers to denounce the 'malice of the clergy' in unequivocal terms, not least for their part in suppressing astrological publication.[139] William Lilly indulged in a joyful tirade against 'those caterpillars, locusts, devouring wolves, the lazy humble-bee bishops, lubberdly canons, slovenly prebends, the sucking-venerian doctors and officials of the spiritual courts'. A few years later he justified the sale of bishops' and deans' lands on the grounds that 'the possessors were most part lubbers and drones, did God no service'.[140] It soon became clear, however, that the Presbyterians were even more hostile to astrological prophecy, and the astrologers' ferocious anti-clericalism was in part a defensive measure. Descending from generalization, the clergy attacked by name leading astrologers such as Lilly, Booker and Culpeper. Lilly recalled later that he had been denounced from thirty pulpits in London on the Sunday following the solar eclipse of 1652. The astrologers replied in kind, heaping abuse on prominent Presbyterians and hostile Independents.[141] Most notorious was the feud between Lilly and the veteran Puritan, Thomas Gataker, who had attacked him in a biblical commentary. Lilly retaliated with gusto, mortifying his opponent by his iconoclasm in 'baiting' Calvin like a 'hellhound'. He claimed a moral victory when John Gauden (subsequently a bishop) called to express the clergy's embarrassment over the controversy and begged him to desist. One polemicist hailed the death of Gataker in 1654 as the result of an eclipse and thus a vindication of astrology. We are more likely to agree with a sceptical reader who declined to see anything significant in a man being 'cut off at 80 years'.[142]

Any early hopes in the Presbyterians thus quickly soured. 'We do know the bishops were no saints, and we remain doubtful whether the Presbyter will prove an angel', remarked Lilly. John Booker declared roundly in 1651 that 'The three grand Ps, *Pap.*, *Prel.*, and *Pres.*, the pest and poison of the rest of the alphabet . . . must down.'[143] Presbyterian hostility to astrology explained much of this animosity.[144] But the astrologers were also reacting violently against the extent of clerical power in the projected Presbyterian church settlement. The clergy were 'rampant', said Culpeper, and sought like Cardinal Wolsey to be '*aut Caesar aut nihil*'; they would be '*nihil*', he assured worried readers.[145] Under the Presbyterian system, Lilly thought, 'our slavery would have exceeded that of the worst of times preceding', under clergy who sought to 'lord it and domineer like petty tyrants over commonalty and gentry'. The derisive comments in his autobiography on the 'three-penny Directory' and the 'pitiful idiots' who replaced ejected Anglicans were no doubt coloured by hindsight. He was probably sincere though in his judgement that the Presbyterians were good preachers, but 'more lordly than bishops, and usually in their parishes more tyrannical than the Great Turk'. To the end of his life he attacked the Presbyterian system whilst favouring the toleration of Dissenters.[146]

In the eyes of parliamentarian astrologers, Presbyterianism was damned still further by its association after 1648 with the Scots and cavaliers. For clergy to preach that 'it is lawful to destroy this army as rats and mice, and vermin' was 'Billingsgate divinity', Lilly asserted, and deserved Bridewell rather than tithes. The activities of Christopher Love, a Presbyterian minister executed for treason in 1651, prompted the reflection that 'Not a treason can be managed without a priest.' Rumours that the widespread thunderstorms on the day of Love's death were tokens of divine wrath were firmly discounted: these particular storms had a purely natural cause.[147] Lilly asserted that the principles of the Presbyterians were subversive, 'whether derived from John Calvin or the babbling of a silly Scottish Presbytery', and expressed feigned surprise that the Scottish clergy 'conjure not up the Picts and Redshanks, their bloody ancestors, to assist themselves'.[148]

Though the Presbyterians provoked the deepest odium, some astrologers—like other radicals during the Revolution—rejected a professional clergy of any denomination, and any established church. Culpeper in particular shared the bitterness and the barbed language of Winstanley and Walwyn. He denounced the 'monster called Religion', and refused 'to make a little God-almighty of the present clergy'. His writings are punctuated with aphorisms such as 'All men are liars, and clergymen are but men', and observations that the clergy 'eat and drink of the best, live idly and deceive their princes'. He was a warm advocate of civil marriage. 'We all know that marriage is a civil thing, therefore ought more properly to belong to the civil magistrate than the clergyman; but the clergy gets money by it, that's the key of the business.' The people, he hoped, were 'willing to be priest-ridden no longer'.[149] For sixteen hundred years, Lilly agreed, the clergy had 'abused us with forms and ceremonies, slobbering over their cheats with a pretended holiness'. He would pray for all manner of men, he remarked, but 'let ministers pray for themselves'.[150] The theme was echoed in other almanacs, anticipating the downfall of the 'domineering vicious priests'. Samuel Thurston noted caustically during a prolonged outbreak of plague that God appeared unmoved by their 'chattering'.[151]

Like the sectarians, Levellers and Diggers, the astrologers denounced the beneficed clergy for making a trade of the Gospel given freely by Christ: they 'prate for tithes', Culpeper complained. Surprisingly the, point was made most forcefully by the royalist astrologer, Wharton, attacking

> The snarling priest (who numbers never knew,
> More than to tithe his pigs, or whence they grew),
> But like the ale-wife chalks behind the door
> And sets even Christ and Moses on the score.[152]

The confiscation of tithes from the 'tottering time-serving Levite' was at hand.[153]

With the return of censorship after 1660 it was no longer possible to publish denigrations of the clergy in such terms. But the theme of anti-clericalism survived and flourished once more in the writings of Whig astrologers from the latter part of the reign of Charles II. Woodward packed scornful innuendo into his prediction that 'some of the clergy leave their hypocrisy and double-hand dealing'; Henry Hill in the same year (1684) sniped at the clergy from the safe cover of a Dutch proverb, that 'priests' covetousness, and God's goodness, are perpetual.'[154] Secure in exile during the reign of James II, Partridge felt free to denounce two new High Church bishops, Parker and Cartwright, as men 'of excellent parts and great proficients in atheism, Socinianism, and popery'. A few years later he recalled with pleasure Oliver Cromwell's victory at Worcester in 1651 when no less than 'NINE PARSONS' had been captured on the battlefield.[155]

The rhetorical violence of the anti-clerical abuse gives nevertheless a rather exaggerated impression of the astrologers' radicalism. Most in fact favoured an unobtrusive national church, calling for a body of learned, godly and above all submissive ministers. Tanner called for a new kind of clergy who would learn 'humility, meekness and lowliness' from Christ, and would be content to 'save souls'. Wing approved of 'pious and orthodox divines', and even Lilly declared his support for a preaching ministry in every parish, provided with a good stipend.[156] Probably others would have been willing, like Gadbury, to call off the attack on the clergy if the clergy had been prepared to cease abusing astrologers.[157] Almost certainly the majority of astrologers had no objection in principle to a mild low-church episcopal or Presbyterian system: their enemy was clerical power, in whatever form it manifested itself.

Understandably, there were few attempts to defend the episcopal church during the interregnum. George Wharton, the Royalist, proved a brave and determined exception, daring to justify Archbishop Laud and to denounce the sacrilege of the present age. Richard Fitzsmith published a solitary work defending the 'true sons of the Church of England', and promising that God would remain their champion.[158] In the years after the Restoration a much more vigorous defence of the Anglican Church and its clergy was possible. 'Let the clergy be honoured, and the service of the church be followed', Gadbury exhorted. Thomas Trigge wrote in similar vein, praising Laud and reviving the archbishop's campaign to beautify St. Paul's.[159] Much more outspoken propaganda was published in the *Episcopal Almanack* in the years 1674–8, eulogising the 'divine hierarchy' of bishops, cataloguing early episcopal martyrs and pouring a torrent of abuse on 'stinking elders', sectarians and tub-preachers.[160]

It was the Catholic Church which aroused the most vitriolic hostility of the astrologers. This sprang in part from the widespread identification of the pope as Antichrist and the apocalyptic excitement of the period, but much of the attack was in terms of alleged Catholic blasphemy, credulity, perversion and political subversiveness. The peak of the campaign was the half-century from 1640, but its roots went back much further. Thus Cunningham's almanac for 1564 anticipated a plague, sent by God as retribution for the burnings by Mary Tudor, which would 'like an insatiable monster . . . everywhere devour both man and beast. O the blood, the blood of God's martyrs shed in London and through England for the testimonies of Christ, crieth for vengeance.' A few years later another compiler denounced the Marian persecution 'of men, women and children, to the great sorrow of many that lived under that cruel government'.[161] The Massacre of St. Bartholomew in 1572 and the Gunpowder Plot of 1605 provided the classic proofs of papist cruelty and treachery, and were cited repeatedly with prayers to God to protect his people 'from Romanizing traitors all'.[162] During the Revolution, anti-Catholicism assumed a markedly political and apocalyptic character, and is discussed elsewhere. The 'powder-plotting, blood-thirsty papists' were indeed sometimes presented as the originators of the civil war, the result of a vast conspiracy for 'the abolishing of the Reformed Churches and the doctrine of the Gospel'.[163]

During the latter part of the century, the charge of blasphemy grew in importance in anti-Catholic polemic, linked with popular credulity and priestly cynicism and corruption. The most violent abuse is found in *The Protestant Almanack,* which indeed had no other purpose. Its methods were blunt and crude. The pope was Antichrist. The merits of individual popes were conveniently tabulated: fourteen were proclaimed guilty of incest or adultery, twenty-four were conjurers and sorcerers, nine practised simony, and so on. The pope was presented as a monstrous vampire, sustained only by the blood of the godly, for 'every drop of Protestant blood is a present and sovereign cordial to a sinking Antichrist'. Bestial cruelty was the very essence of Catholicism. The almanacs contained liberal extracts from Foxe and a regular section entitled 'A short Scheme of the varieties of popish tortures.' 'Hang, draw and quarter', it was suggested, 'is popery in the modern Irish dialect', and a fair definition of all Catholicism, whether 'silk-and-satin popery' or 'iron-and-steel popery'.[164] But the compilers sought to instil ridicule as well as fear, and turned to the legends of saints as the easiest method. With mock solemnity they told the story of St. Fingare, who sailed from Ireland to Cornwall on a cabbage leaf and who, after being beheaded, was able to wash his severed head in a well which appeared miraculously, and to bury it himself. *Dove* similarly mocked the legend of Henry the hermit, who lived on bread and water and accepted with equanimity the putrefied condition of his leg, which was alive with maggots. When some fell out, *Dove* narrated, 'the good man . . . was so kind as to put them in again, bidding them go to their inheritances where they were born and bred. . . . is not all this enough to make a great saint?'[165] The veneration of relics was ridiculed by spurious advertisements offering for sale the Virgin Mary's work-basket and scissors, Christ's slippers and Joseph's breeches. A spurious Table of Absolutions poked fun at the Church's venality: fornicating in church could be absolved for ten shillings, killing one's parents for ten and sixpence, and taking a potion to produce an abortion for a mere seven and sixpence. [166] In a more sadistic vein, there was an illustrated account of how to make an infallible sundial: the reader had merely to 'take a Jesuit, hang him on an approved gibbet', and see where the sun cast 'the shadow of his Roman nose'.[167] John Partridge was able to exceed this performance by his own virulence, denouncing the doctrine of transubstantiation as the invention of the devil, when

in revenge (with heaven being at odds)
He taught the papists how to eat their Gods.

'Priest!' he exclaimed, 'P—on the name, I loathe the very smell'—a view he later elaborated:

> A whoring nun, and bawdy buggering priest,
> A noble church! Daubed with religious paint,
> Each priest's a stallion, every rogue's a saint.

The 'little dough-baked God' could be only an object of scorn to true Christians, but 'what Satan preacheth, Belzebub believes.'[168] John Whalley's strictures were in the same vein, with a strong Irish flavour. The only good priest, he thought, was a dead one; there should be a price of £5 on the head of each. Catholics as a whole were 'God-eating monsters, cannibals most true'.[169] The tide of scurrility, of which these examples form only a tiny part, flowed strongly into the next century.[170]

Attempts by astrologers to defend Catholicism were, naturally, far fewer and generally restrained in tone. Perhaps the earliest and boldest was by George Wharton, who in 1654 condemned contemporaries for 'snarling against the Blessed Virgin, denouncing the Church for a whore, and the pope for Antichrist', when, as he justly argued, the Catholic Church was the most energetic evangelist in 'remote and barbarous countries' throughout the world. Samuel Sheppard used different tactics, ridiculing the exaggerated fears of the period by reporting with mock solemnity how the Presbyterian pamphleteer, 'Mr. Prynne sets up his beacons, to give warning of many thousand men of China; armed with copes and mitres they intend to introduce popery.'[171] In 1663 there appeared a surreptitious almanac by Thomas Blount providing a calendar of Catholic festivals and defending the English Catholic community by stressing its loyalty and sufferings during the civil wars. Similar works appeared in the following year and, with royal approval, during the reign of James II.[172] In the late 1660s William Andrews was one of several compilers who adopted a more restrained position towards Catholicism. Criticizing the common belief that the pope was Antichrist, Andrews was willing to accept that Clement IX, the reigning pontiff, was a man 'of great abilities, integrity and moderation', and he described the next pope (Clement X) as 'most eminent and learned'.[173] The most vigorous champion of Catholicism was, however, John Gadbury, at the end of his evolution from Ranter to crypto-Catholic. Replying to Partridge's verbal assaults, Gadbury deplored the 'pretended Reformation' of the sixteenth century and declared that

To Rome none need be slaves! 'Tis heresy
Engulfs our souls! The true Church sets us free.[174]

In 1644 William Lilly posed the question of whether the Jesuit or sectarian was the 'more knave and most destructive'. Many astrologers, like other contemporaries, regarded the two as linked: sectarianism was often seen as a Jesuit trick to undermine the unity of Protestantism.[175] John Booker's 'wished for Reformation' in 1646 had no place for sects, Independents or even 'formalists' (by which he presumably meant Presbyterians). He was pained by the quarrel between Independent and Presbyterian, and critical of both:

There's but one truth, good God discover that,
Lest we contend about we know not what.

But he found no such discovery and a dozen years later, at the very end of the revolutionary era, denounced all the contending churches as 'but sects, every man striving to maintain their several opiniative interests; the Presbyter against the Anabaptists, Libertines and other sort of sects, and this against that, when as neither for aught they have yet set forth are in the right way, for if they were, whence came these sad differences and quotidian contests?'[176] Vincent Wing prayed 'that religion may be settled in its purity, and all sects and schisms be extirpated', denouncing Anabaptists, Brownists, Seekers and all such 'Pharasaical hypocrites'.[177] Lilly's almanac for 1645 called on the army to set about 'heading or hanging' the 'tub-men, Anabaptist and Independent'. His opinion of the Independents improved dramatically in subsequent years, but he remained an implacable enemy of 'that monstrous people called Ranters' and of the seditious, 'besotted' Fifth Monarchy Men. [178] It is no surprise to find the Royalist, Wharton, mocking the 'croaking' of 'epileptic prophets and other religious lunatics', but even Sarah Jinner, one of the most radical astrologers, had similar scorn for the 'audacious public babblings' of 'novice-lay pulpiteers'.[179] The most dramatic testimony against the sects was provided by a renegade Ranter named Thomas Webb, who in 1659 launched a one-man campaign against the Quakers and Fifth Monarchists. He began by disrupting a large Quaker meeting in Kingston (Surrey), dressed bizarrely with 'an ugly, hideous, grisly vizard' (visor), surmounted by a red cap with 'two horns sticking up at my ears', and calling on the Devil to appear in the midst of his disciples. But making similar appearances in St. Paul's and two other London churches in November, he was severely beaten and ejected by the congregations, and wisely decided to continue his campaign in the safety of print. The result was an 'almanac' in which he reported, with engaging candour, that it was only two or three days since he had taken up astrology, twenty-four since his escapade in St. Paul's, and twenty-three 'since my resolve never to act madness more'.[180] After 1660 attacks naturally redoubled on the 'giddy zealots' and 'illiterate asses', and for the remainder of the century *Poor Robin* ridiculed the beliefs and damned the politics of the Dissenters.[181]

Nevertheless, during the Revolution a number of astrologers did come gradually to sympathize with sectarian ideals, partly because they shared a keen millennial vision, but partly also because they found in the sects a religious zeal untainted by clerical power. Culpeper was no sectarian, but shared a doubt of seeing religion 'ever flourish by public authority'. He defined his own faith by declaring that 'all the religion I know, is Jesus Christ and him crucified, and the indwelling of the spirit of God in me.'[182] By 1651 Lilly had come to believe that those 'we vulgarly call sectaries' would find a 'new higher light' in 'seeking God after a new way'. He was drawn to the mystical writings of the German philosopher, Jacob Boehme, whose blend of astrological and millennial beliefs did something to shape Lilly's own. Lilly reacted violently to Gataker's sneer that Boehme was 'a Dutch wizard', and retorted that he was on the contrary a major instrument of religious enlightenment.[183] There was a link between some of the astrologers of the mid-century and what a contemporary described as the 'Familistical-Levelling-Magical temper'. It was apparent also, for example, in John Heydon, an astrologer who professed Rosicrucian beliefs, and whose works appeared with admiring tributes from Gadbury and Booker.[184]

For a variety of reasons most astrologers were content to see the return of episcopacy after 1660. Not all, however, wished it to be exclusive. Lilly, for example, had protected some episcopalian clergy, including Oughtred, during the interregnum and had no difficulty in deciding after the Restoration 'to build our tabernacle upon the 39 Articles of the Church of England'; he even became a churchwarden. But he ventured to hope for an accommodation between the bishops and the 'more moderate divines of contrary judgement', criticized the Anglican zeal for monopoly and criticized the Conventicle Act of 1670 as a disaster.[185] Later in the century attitudes were shaped by the rise of the 'popish t hreat'. Daniel Woodward was concerned primarily with the creation of Protestant solidarity in the face of Catholic dangers. The Anglican Church 'in its purity is the best-constituted church in the world', he conceded, but that gave it no right of

The PROTESTANT

ALMANACK,

For the Year 1690.

Since	The Creation of the World	5696
	The Incarnation of Jeſus Chriſt	1690
	England received the Chriſtian Faith	1500
	Martin Luther wrote againſt the Pope	174
	Our deliverance from Popery by Queen *Elizabeth*	131
	The horrid deſign of the Gun-Powder Plot	85
	The Burning of the City of *London*	24
	Our miraculous Deliverance from Popery, by K. *William*	2

Being the Second after

BISSEXTILE or LEAP-YEAR.

WHEREIN

The Bloody Aſpects, Fatal Oppoſitions, Diabolical Conjuncti-ons, and Pernicious Revolutions of the Papacy againſt the Lord and his Anointed, are deſcribed.

With the Change of the Moon, the Riſing and Setting of the Sun, ſome obſervable Fairs, and the Eclipſes, together with the moons place in the Zodiac throughout each month of the year.

Calculated according to Art, for the Meridian of *Babylon*, where the Pope is elevated an hundred and fifty degrees above all Reaſon, Right and Religion; above Kings, Canons, Coun-cels, Conſcience, and every thing therein called God. 2 *Theſſ.* 2. And may without ſenſible Errour, indifferently ſerve the whole Papacy.

By *Philoprotest*, a well-willer to the *Mathematicks*.

Licenſed, Auguſt 3. 1689. *Rob. Midgley*.

London, Printed by *John Richardſon* for the Company of STATIONERS. 1690.

The Protestant Almanacr, a long-running annual onslaught on Catholicism, closely followed the style of conventional editions exclusiveness. He had made a study of Independent, Baptist and Presbyterian writings and reported blandly that he had found no significant differences: Protestants should therefore tolerate one another.[186] From an opposite viewpoint, Gadbury and Trigge welcomed the declarations of Indulgence by James II as measures of relief for Catholics; it was 'better all religions be indulged', they argued, 'than the one Ancient Faith excluded, persecuted, harrassed'.[187]

These concepts of toleration were obviously limited and partisan. During the reign of James II Woodward defended toleration on more general principles, demanding

Why should a man be beaten black and blue,
Because he cannot think as I or you?

Faith was not to be 'kept by knocks, or learned by blows', and the 'best divinity is all for love'. But his virulent attacks on Catholicism during the preceding and succeeding reigns hardly correspond with these enlightened views and indicate the limits of his toleration.[188]

Perhaps of more significance than the calls for toleration were the occasional attempts to investigate religion from a secular angle, and seek explanations in social and environmental terms. Thus, Wharton observed in 1653 that

the Turks are very holy in their way;
They preach, give alms and most devoutly pray,

and argued that

Had we been born in Turkey, we should set
As great a rate the rascal Mahomet
As Turks themselves.

He ended with the challenging conclusion that

'Tis birth and education, which doth make
Religion; and which seals it is the stake.[189]

Similarly, at the end of the century Richard Saunder attempted to create an elementary sociology of religion. For a movement to flourish, he considered, two things were needed: 'the opposing of authority established: for nothing is more popular than that. The other is the giving licence to pleasure and voluptuousness.' Miracles, evangelism and force would all help its subsequent propagation.[190] The wish to reduce even religious phenomena to a code of fixed laws was typical of the age, and ultimately as inimical to Christianity as earlier attempts at explanation in terms of astrological determinism.

(iv) The Apocalypse

A close connection between astrology and the apocalypse seems at first sight improbable. There was, as we have seen, considerable friction between astrologers and the church. Moreover the revolution of the stars suggests a cyclical view of the world, whilst the Judaeo-Christian tradition sees an inexorably linear course from Creation to Last Judgement. The contrast is however less stark than appears. The origins of eschatology lay in the concept of a regeneration of time, in which the changing cycles of the moon and the seasons were basic.[191] Even within the Christian tradition, cyclical elements of return and renewal were not wholly lost: the Protestant Reformers consciously sought to return to the pure church of the Apostles, and some of their successors in the seventeenth century aimed to revive the government and institutions of Old Testament Israel.[192] The ancient and widespread belief that the world would last only seven thousand years stemmed from Chaldean astrology, and was linked with the seven planets. A Jewish version, ascribed to Rabbi Elias, taught that it would endure for six thousand years followed by a seventh 'sabbatical' era, and had immense influence in Europe down to the end of the seventeenth century.[193] In mediaeval Europe attempts to date the second coming commonly used astrological as well as biblical data.[194]

The Bible itself contained material which encouraged attempts to find a synthesis. St. Matthew's Gospel spoke of dramatic portents in the heavens which would signal the world's approaching end. The otherwise inexplicable 'new star', discovered in 1572, appeared to many to be a clear fulfilment.[195] Similarly the biblical passage affirming that 'as the days of Noah were, so shall also the coming of the Son of man be' was taken as an endorsement of the Renaissance search for correspondences. Following the clue, scholars calculated that the Flood had occurred in the year of the world 1656 and deduced that the second coming, or some other great upheaval, was probable in A. D. 1656.[196] A comparable train of thought suggested to the German astrologer, Mussemius, that as Christ had been born following a conjunction of Saturn and Jupiter in Virgo, the appearance of Antichrist would be when they met in the opposite part of the zodiac, which would occur in the ensuing year, 1544.[197]

The Reformation shattered mediaeval eschatology.[198] Protestants took a far more literal approach to the prophecies which they saw being fulfilled in the upheavals of the age. The papacy stood revealed as Antichrist, and its fall and the end of the world must be at hand. This theme was developed by theologians on the Continent and in England, and found echoes among the prognostications translated into English in the first half of the sixteenth century. Mussemius declared that the end of the world was approaching, and the English edition of his tract carried a sensational illustration of a sun-king, with a Latin caption hailing Henry VIII as Defender of the Faith.[199] Master Salomon, a Jewish physician of Ghent, drew on biblical and astrological evidence to predict that Charles V was about to overthrow the Turks, followed by the conversion of the Jews and return of Christ. A similar motif appeared in the prognostication of Otto Brufelsius, published in 1536 and dedicated to the Privy Council; it attacked the 'papists' and stressed that the biblical tokens of the world's end were already apparent.[200]

From early in the reign of Elizabeth there appeared a steady stream of commentaries, sermons and popular tracts declaring the imminent end of the world. Almanacs gave still further publicity to the idea, and stressed that the six thousand years of Elias were almost expired.[201] The uncertainty of the first years of the queen's reign, the precarious nature of European Protestantism and the alarms raised by Nostradamus heightened the tension. A prophecy of the apocalypse by the fifteenth-century German astrologer, Johannes Lichtenberger, was still in vogue, and pointed to dramatic events in 1567.[202] A flood of pamphlets and ballads describing prodigies, monstrous births and apparitions met the popular taste for sensation, often explaining them as signs of the deformity of nature which must surely indicate the dissolution of the world. They were indeed the popular manifestation of a very widespread belief in universal degeneration which stemmed from classical theories of rise and decline.[203] Almanacs and other pamphlets grafted the theme of decay on to the body of apocalyptic speculation. 'Come are the days that Chaucer erst foretold', lamented Bretnor,

> Religion's now a cloak to cover sin,
> O would to God these days had never been.

John Booker agreed that

> The world itself is dying and decaying,
> The earth more sterile, heavenly stars more straying.

He had no doubt that it was an age of depravity, 'the latest times'.

Other compilers felt that the biblical tokens were unmistakable, and heralded a new 'barbarism' and the Last Judgement.[204]

These comments differed little from those in a host of other popular tracts. More specific and far more significant was the almanac for 1569 by John Securis. Christ had said that no man could know the hour of his coming, he observed, 'yet it is possible . . . to give a guess'. He suggested several possibilities, drawing on Continental speculation about Noah's Flood, and the mediaeval prophecies of Joachim, Bridget, Lichtenberger and others. Most important, he introduced into England the prophecies of the Bohemian astrologer, Cyprian Leowitz, concerning the end of the world and based on the conjunction of Saturn and Jupiter in 1583 and an old prediction, fathered on Regiomontanus, of a *mirabilis annus* in 1588.[205] Leowitz's text was republished in London in 1573 and popularized in a series of pamphlets which added sensational detail to the original: at twelve noon on 28 April 1583, Richard Harvey predicted, a great wind would spring up which would mark the onset of calamities leading to the end of the world. There was considerable excitement, and the months preceding April saw a fierce pamphlet war over the conjunction, with the Bishop of London preaching at Paul's Cross against the astrologers. A modern commentator has observed that 'astrology never recovered from its success' in arousing alarm in 1583, for the conjunction passed without incident. Fear turned to scorn; Richard Harvey and his brother and fellow-prophet John were openly mocked. John indeed abandoned his apocalyptic faith, and in his almanac and subsequent pamphlet repudiated Regiomontanus, Elias, the Sibyls and the whole army of prophets.[206]

The year 1588, 'so notoriously famous' a little earlier, thus approached with less excitement than had seemed likely. An almanac by William Farmer cited floods and other evils in a rather lame effort to prove that 1583 had indeed been as calamitous as predicted. More dramatically an Italian, John Doleta, catalogued ten major disasters which he promised for 1587. There were still some people, said the almanac-maker Gabriel Frende, who expected that in 1588 the 'world should take the last gasp and final overthrow', but he scorned to discuss such vanities and doubted whether he 'would ever repent me hereof'.[207] Unexpectedly, Philip II of Spain came to the rescue of astrology. The Invincible Armada was hardly what the prophets had anticipated but it certainly made 1588 *mirabilis*. The astrologers thought themselves vindicated.[208]

The Doomsday scare of 1583 was remarkable in having an exact date when upheavals were to begin, but its eschatology was wholly orthodox: a series of calamities leading to Christ's return and the world's destruction. The almanacs of the Elizabethan and early Stuart period remained firmly within this tradition, anticipating the speedy end of the world and warning the reader that 'it behoves us to expect the end every day and hour.'[209] Around the turn of the century, however, some astrological writings began to anticipate a future age of bliss on earth to come before the Last Judgement.[210] Though Protestant exegesis centred on Daniel and Revelations, mediaeval commentators had speculated as much on the classical Age of Gold, the messianic Last Emperor, Elias and the sabbatical era, and the prophecies linked with Abbot Joachim, heralding a third age or *status* of spiritual enlightenment and peace.[211] These themes were enmeshed in astrological prophecy, which was much less disrupted by the Reformation, and it was through astrology that they came to infiltrate English Protestant eschatology. The most dramatic illustration was *A Most Strange and Wonderfull Prophesie,* an unauthorized pamphlet of 1595 based on the prophecies of 'John Cypriano' and 'Tarquatus Vandermer'. It foretold that, within the year, the seas would turn to blood, and there would be terrible wars, famines and plagues. But in November a great conqueror would arise, who 'takes a truce unto all the earth', and by the end of the year 'all wars shall end, religion preached truly through the world, all things united up in peace'. The sources, only thinly disguised, were the predictions of Cyprian Leowitz and the Italian astrologer Antonius Torquatus, whose *Prognosticon* was first published in 1534 and enjoyed great popularity. Like many mediaeval prophets, Torquatus did little more than collect earlier predictions. His messianic conqueror had a long pedigree stretching back through the Second Charlemagne foretold by Telesphorus in the fourteenth century to the fourth-century Last Emperor prophesied by Sibyl Tiburtina. The age of peace which would follow probably derived originally from the third age of Joachim.[212] The well-known English astrologer, Simon Forman, copied into his notebook a rather similar prophecy, translated from Portuguese. The events now stretched over ten years, from 1591 to 1600, but the content was much the same: the great man would arise in 1597, the infidels' conversion would follow in 1599, leading to the world's end and the pacification of mankind, 'all sheep under one pastor'. A generation later this prophecy appeared in print, now allegedly referring to the years 1621–30 and with the claim that it had been found under the church of St. Denis in Paris; it ended again with a vision of unity, 'one shepherd and one sheepfold'. Other versions circulated in manuscript.[213] There were echoes too in the prophecy of Edward Gresham that the Kings of the Islands would join to overthrow Gog and Magog, leading once more to unity, '*unus pastor, and unum ovile*'. This last phrase, from St. John's Gospel, had been part of eschatological hopes for centuries. It took on a new force in the divided Europe of the sixteenth century, and was to grow steadily in importance in English prophecy in the Stuart period.[214]

The motif of the Last Emperor was reinforced by Tycho Brahe's discovery of a new star in 1572, which he interpreted as a herald of the second coming. King James I of England endorsed this view. Calvin's successor at Geneva, Beza, hailed the return of the star which had guided the Magi. A generation later, John Bainbridge, professor of astronomy at Oxford, linked the new star with the comet of 1618 as tokens of the downfall of Catholicism (and the 'foggy mists' of Arminianism) leading to the second coming of Christ. Tycho Brahe also linked the new star to the ancient prophecy of a great northern ruler (or lion, or star, or hero) destined to perform wondrous deeds towards the end of the world. Derived from various parts of the Bible (for example Esdras, Jeremiah and Daniel) and the messianic tradition, the prophecy was reinforced by the 'discovery' in 1520 of a prediction by Sibyl Tiburtina of a great northern light, and again by the prophecy of Paracelsus of a future conqueror and last golden age. The triumphant conquests of King Gustavus Adolphus of Sweden in the Thirty Years War appeared to fulfil these predictions. Both in Sweden and Germany, Gustavus was seen as the messianic northern conqueror, and over twenty editions of Paracelsus's prophecy appeared in Germany in 1631–2.[215] A version of the prophecy reached England in 1582 in the manuscript of Paul Grebner, whose northern conqueror was to be named Charles, son of Charles, and was clearly a descendant of the Second Charlemagne. After the death of Elizabeth the manuscript passed to Trinity College, Cambridge, but was not forgotten, and in 1632 the predictions of Sibyl Tiburtina, Tycho Brahe and Grebner were all discussed in print in England and applied to Gustavus. The Swedish king died that year in battle, a perverse disaster which one English disciple refused to believe. But the northern star was to rise again many times in the years that followed.[216]

The new star of 1572 also played a part in the millenarian speculations of Sir Christopher Heydon, composed in 1618–19. Heydon saw in the seventh return of Saturn and Jupiter to the fiery trigon 'a secret mystery of sabbatism', foreshadowing the collapse of the Habsburgs, the destruction of the papacy (about 1646), the fall of the Turks (in the 1680s or 1690s), the calling of the Jews and at last an era of peace and happiness throughout the earth 'which I confidently affirm . . . shall be the kingdom of Christ'. Heydon was once a follower of Elizabeth's rebellious favourite, the Earl of Essex, and his politics remained far from conformist. God, he predicted, 'is about to restrain monarchical pomp, and to reduce all to an aristocratical mediocrity both in government of the common wealth and also the church'. Early modern kings were flattered by hints of a possible messianic role, but were hardly likely to welcome a millennial version of aristocratic constitutionalism. Not surprisingly, the tract remained unpublished.[217]

During the 1640s the civil wars in England gave a massive new impetus to apocalyptic interest. At last there were universal upheavals to match the prophecies and portents, which many now believed heralded the reign of Christ instead of the approach of doomsday. Traditional Elizabethan eschatology had been challenged by a succession of later interpreters, notably John Napier, Thomas Brightman, the German Johannes Alsted, and Joseph Mede. They turned increasingly to the idea of further reformation in the church, and a final age of godliness and glory still to dawn. Alsted and Mede saw the Reformation as merely the prologue to a thousand-year reign of the saints, still wholly in the future.

The development of millenarianism owed much to Puritan, Calvinist and sectarian dreams of purifying the church: a truly pure church would be, in a real sense, the kingdom of Christ on earth. Millennial ideas were linked too with the growing belief in the possibility of progress, challenging traditional notions of universal decay. In a celebrated defence of progress, George Hakewill quoted Alsted and his authorities as evidence for future advance in religion. The English editor of Alsted's work on the millennium in turn proved the respectability of the doctrine by citing Hakewill's endorsement.[218] Alsted's millenarianism also drew heavily on the astrological speculations of Tycho Brahe, Kepler and others. A favourite source for later English writers was Alsted's *'Speculum Mundi'*, a large table in which he synchronized the three eras and seven ages of Elias, the revolutions of Saturn and Jupiter, the four monarchies of Daniel, and other data, all pointing towards a future golden age.[219] There is no such clear testimony that the major English theorists were influenced by astrological prophecies, but they were probably aware of them, and a subconscious influence is at least possible. John Napier, the Scottish commentator, was 'a great lover of astrology' and a distant cousin of the famous English parson-astrologer, Richard Napier.[220] The latter was a fairly close neighbour of Thomas Brightman, and indeed he taught astrology to Brightman's successor as minister of Haynes, the Rev. Wilson. Brightman was alleged later to have drawn on the prophecies of Grebner.[221] Joseph Mede was familiar with Grebner's writings for most of his adult life, and as a young man he was an enthusiastic practitioner of astrology. But his opinion of Grebner was low, and his interest in astrology waned with the passing years.[222]

Millenarian theories were spread widely during the civil wars by preachers and pamphleteers who explained that the revolution heralded the reign of the saints. With almost no restrictions on the press, pamphleteers blended biblical analysis with the messianic, sabbatical and astrological traditions. A series of *Bloody Almanacks* summarized Napier's eschatology with an endorsement from John Booker, pirated from his almanac. For good measure the *New Bloody Almanack* for 1645 added the prophecy allegedly found in the Parisian church of St. Denis, now ascribed to 'Caleb Shilock' and applying the massive upheavals to 1645 and the years following.[223] William Lilly saw in Brightman's interpretation of Daniel the fulfilment of Grebner's prophecy that a great scholar would arise to unravel the mysteries of the Bible.[224] The collected works of Brightman appeared in 1644 with an appendix discussing the prophecies of Grebner, Nostradamus, Savonarola and James Maxwell, a Jacobean scholar of mediaeval prophecy who had dreamed of a messianic monarch to arise in England.[225] Similarly the millenarian pamphlet *Nuncius Propheticus* (1642) drew on Alsted, Tycho Brahe, Kepler and the Sibylline prediction found in 1520.[226] Thus Protestant eschatology lost its religious purity in the process of popularization, and became an amalgam of Christian and astrological speculation.

Many saw in the civil war the beginnings of an upheaval that would sweep through Europe, leading to the destruction of all its kings and (as the fateful year 1656 approached) the downfall of Rome itself.[227] Even the royalist compiler, Fitzsmith, accepted that the pope was an Antichrist (if not *the* Antichrist), and that his fall was imminent, along with the ruin of the Turks.[228] Despite this confidence, one almanac-maker argued that it was nevertheless 'no golden but an iron age . . . a wicked, perverse and crooked generation', which clearly indicated the world's end, not its rebirth as some 'have foolishly held forth'.[229] Many compilers indeed seemed unsure whether the world's end or renewal was to follow the upheavals around them. Thus Vaux bemoaned the wickedness of the age and declared each year that the end was nigh, but in the edition for 1654 he noted that 'many of our divines do believe, that the world shall be rather renewed than annihilated.'[230] Probably most held a rather hazy mid-way position, believing that the end of the world was approaching, but that a period of glory or tranquillity would come between the fall of Antichrist and the Last Judgement. This view was implicit in the writings of Vincent Wing. His almanacs stressed repeatedly the approach of Judgement, but also occasionally predicted a 'golden age' in which 'the divers forms of religion and politic government shall be changed and made conformable to the will of God.' He reconciled these differences by explaining that though 'undoubtedly the night of this evil world is far spent, there would follow' before its consummation 'a more peacable and quiet age'.[231] Within this framework it was possible for Richard Saunders to combine a traditional view of decay—

> This may indeed be called the Age of Gold,
> For honour, love and all for it are sold,—

with speculation on a messianic emperor.[232] Henry Phillippes was more explicit in describing his position. After reviewing the biblical evidence, the views of the Early Fathers, of Napier, Brightman and Alsted, and of contemporary Catholic scholars, he rejected the notion of a millennium. But between the fall of Antichrist and the end of the world he anticipated that all nations would submit to the 'spiritual sceptre of Jesus Christ', with a godly ministry and magistracy. This could not last, however, for a thousand years: the godly would long for heaven, the worldly would relapse into sin, and Christ would soon return to Judgement.[233]

There were however a number of almanacs during the Revolution which adopted an openly millenarian position. Henry Jessey's *Scripture-Calenders* replaced the traditional anatomical figure with that of Daniel's image (Dan. ii), promising that the four world-empires it signified were about to be followed by the kingdom of God, the Fifth Monarchy. Worldly governments would perish till Christ came. In the edition for 1661 Jessey computed that since the upheavals began in 1640 there had been forty-seven changes in the government of England, a clear fulfilment (he thought) of God's promise to 'overturn, overturn,

overturn'.[234] A prognostication by the Flemish astrologer, Paul Felgenhauer, was published in England, predicting a seventh sabbatical age of peace.[235] The almanac of John Coulton quoted from the Fifth Monarchist writer, John Canne, and looked for the kingdom of Christ and downfall of tyranny, whilst *Dove* drew on the calculations of Mede.[236] Nicholas Culpeper, a more important compiler, anticipated the fall of the Rump, upheavals throughout Europe, and the conversion and restoration of the 'beloved Jews', 'which people I love', whom God would 'speedily make . . . the glory of all the world'. Though Christ might not appear in person, there would be more than a mere 'hideous coming of Christ in your minds', as falsely taught by many clergy. '(If we trust to a piece of art Cabalistic)', he argued, in April 1655 'Rome falleth and Jesus Christ, the Prince of Peace, may reign among us.'[237]

William Lilly, too, acknowledged his debt to Napier, Brightman and Alsted, but his writings showed still more strongly the influence of mediaeval prophecies of a last emperor or a final era of peace and enlightenment.[238] His role as controversialist would in any case have brought him to these themes, for royalist pamphleteers discovered excellent propaganda material in the predictions of Grebner and Sibyl Tiburtina. Might not Charles Stuart, son of the king executed in 1649, be the Charles, son of Charles, spoken of in the messianic prophecies? In a flurry of pamphlets around 1650 royalist writers claimed that Charles Stuart was destined to recover England, conquer most of Europe and destroy the pope, founding a messianic fifth monarchy in the Stuart line.[239] Lilly riposted by proving that the Stuart dynasty had fallen for ever, and giving the authentic version of Grebner's prophecy. The northern lion, he argued, was not yet born, and would probably be a future king of Sweden.[240]

Lilly's interest in a messianic monarchy was evident some years before this controversy. In a collection of prophecies published in 1644 he spoke of 'the mightiest actions Europe ever beheld since the birth of our saviour', about to be performed by some 'northern people'. In other pamphlets he drew on Sibyl Tiburtina and Tycho Brahe to predict the rise of a northern star, great upheavals culminating in 1666, the fall of Rome and an age of peace and reformation. His collection entitled *The World's Catastrophe* (1647) contained a translation by Elias Ashmole of a tract by the Italian astrologer, Spineus, relating the new stars and the conjunction of 1583 to the mediaeval prophecy of the King-Chastiser (one of the variants of the last emperor) destined to punish and purify a corrupted Christendom. Spineus predicted the fall of Islam and the overthrow of all the monarchs of Europe at the hands of the Chastiser, whose great eyes, broad forehead and aquiline nose preserved even the physical features of his mediaeval origins.[241] Lilly also republished the sensational predictions of a messianic conqueror which had appeared sixty years earlier under the name of Cypriano. [242] In the 1650s he developed these themes in his annual almanacs. He stressed the significance of 1666, claimed that the effects of the new star of 1572 would not be fully evident until a whole century after its discovery, and prophesied that a great conqueror would dominate Europe by 1692, only to die at the moment of triumph (the predicted fate of the original, fourth-century Sibylline emperor.[243] Lilly saw Cromwell as the fulfilment of prophecies, but the northern lion would be among the successors of Charles X of Sweden. England should therefore join the Swedes in a great alliance which would prepare the way for the conquest of Europe.[244] He speculated also on the significance of 1656, a date paralleling the days of Noah, and looked for the calling of the Jews.[245]

A number of other almanacs contained discussions of a similar kind. Richard Saunders, an associate of Lilly, argued that 1656 would mark the beginning of a 'sabbatical revolution' leading to the conversion of the Jews and, in about 1694, to the 'wonderful birth of the fifth monarchy, the foundation of which must be laid by a northern lion'.[246] According to Joseph Blagrave, a great monarch from the north was to destroy Antichrist—the pope and Turk—by the year 1666. Using Cabbalistic theories of the rule of planetary angels over different epochs, Blagrave calculated that a great world-empire would arise in the early eighteenth century. His edition for 1660, when the return of Charles Stuart was becoming a possibility, identified Charles as the northern conqueror destined to crush the pope and establish the 'greatest and last' monarchy on earth.[247]

The return of the king in 1660, and of bishops soon afterwards, dealt a calamitous blow to the ultra-Protestant millenarian hopes aroused by the Revolution. One by one the great changes in church and state, which had provided proof that the predictions were true, were reversed by the new regime. A few authors looked hopefully to the conjunction of all the planets in Sagittarius in 1662, and many more expected great events in 1666, which echoed the Number of the Beast in Revelations (666).[248] But the attempt to fit Charles II into the role of messianic monarch died away as time revealed its absurdity.[249]

ALMANACS AND RELIGION

Several Restoration compilers, among them William Lilly, turned away from political upheavals towards a different prophetic tradition, which was derived ultimately from Joachim's concept of a third era of enlightenment and peace. The vision appealed to the divided Europe of the sixteenth century, and found a place in the mystical-astrological dreams of Jacob Boehme, whom Lilly admired.[250] The theme was already present in Lilly's almanacs during the interregnum, when he had looked forward to an age of peace to dawn around 1663, with 'all things governed by love'. By 1666, he believed, 'a very child' would understand the scriptures more clearly than any of the contemporary 'envious rabbies'. In the era of enlightenment, religious scholars would be men of learning and modesty, revealing the true nature of the deity and Trinity, instead of wrangling over whether the pope was Antichrist. Though the pope would continue 'to fleece his flock', he wrote, he was not Antichrist.[251] Richard Saunders held a similar hope that after 1663 'such glorious light will break forth, that will make us (by looking back) admire at this Egyptian darkness'.[252]

The theme of peace, unity and spirituality was all the more congenial after 1660. Lilly's almanac for 1664 looked to an age of enlightenment fostered by learned clergy, both Protestant and Catholic, and denounced sectarian zealots who might hinder it.[253] He now played down the significance of 1666, regarding predictions about it as merely 'an opinion or guess'. Though 666 (the Beast's Number) could be construed as the pope, an equally plausible case could be made for Luther, Laud, Cromwell, Mahomet and many others. Antichrist was yet to appear. Not all popes had been evil, and the current one (in 1667) was seeking reconciliation and a deeper religious understanding. The 'quiet age' still beckoned.[254] The almanacs of William Andrews, ridiculing 1666 and defending the pope, had a similar foundation of hope. It was still more explicit in the case of John Gadbury, who saw in the heavens signs of a General Council which would reconcile all religious differences.[255]

The approach of the *mirabilis annus* 1666 thus brought a varied response from the almanacs. While Lilly was dismissive, his old colleague, John Booker, remained faithful to the older tradition, pouring abuse on the pope and promising his downfall in 1666. Thomas Nunnes predicted the fall of Turk and pope, and the calling of the Jews. John Tanner expected the return of the Ten Lost Tribes of Israel, and the ruin of the Turks, the pope and (for good measure) the Dutch.[256] Vincent Wing foresaw the gradual fading of papal power with the emergence of a messianic conqueror 'out of these northern islands of Great Britain' who would establish a universal but short age of peace before the world's end.[257] Another patriotic writer calculated that the Number of the Beast referred to Louis XIV and that his fall was imminent, accompanied by the destruction of the Dutch at the hands of Charles II.[258]

The religious sympathies of the Restoration court made it possible, however, for other astrologers to mock the anti-Catholicism behind these predictions. Gadbury dismissed such 'foolish oracles', with the remark that 'astrology hath its heretics as well as religion'. Trigge observed that Rome 'stands yet where it did'.[259] In *Dies Novissimus* Gadbury set out to prove *Dooms-Day Not so Near as Dreaded.* Biblical talk of wars to precede the end could be applied to every age of history as convincingly as to the present. In any case, he suggested, it was unnecessary to go to Rome in search of Antichrist 'when we may find him at home in the conventicles of our Dippers' (the Baptists). In similar vein, *Poor Robin* revived cavalier propaganda that the Solemn League and Covenant of 1643 contained 666 words and was thus clearly the Beast of Revelation.[260] George Wharton turned the whole furore into a jest:

> Here's seven years' purchase offered for their land
> Who thinks the Dreadful Day so nigh at hand;
> And (if his Holiness suspect his chair)
> I'll take't my self . . .[261]

There were miseries enough in 1666, but none to foster apocalyptic excitement, which sank to a low ebb in the years following.[262] Its revival came towards the close of the 1670s, inaugurating a new period of anticipation which lasted to the end of the century. The eschatological schemes of Napier, Alsted and others had pointed to the fulfilment of prophecies in the 1680s and 1690s; comets in 1677, 1680 and 1682, and the triple conjunction of Saturn and Jupiter in 1682–3 provided astrological corroboration. Political events once more fanned the speculation. The fierce rivalry of Whigs and Tories was sharpened by the great Popish Plot and the struggle to prevent a popish succession. On the Continent, the rise of an aggressively Catholic France under Louis XIV aroused more fears, heightened by the invasion of the Turks, culminating in the siege of Vienna in 1683. The combination of prophecy and political and religious tensions thus in some ways recreated the situation in the 1640s. It is arguable that where biblical prophecy was dominant in the earlier period, astrological and mediaeval predictions were the more pervasive in this later popular millenarianism.

The onslaught of the Turks created great and genuine fears. Gadbury announced in 1678 that it meant that 'the Ark of God, even Christianity itself, was about to be destroyed (basing this on an old prophecy of Albumazar that Christianity would last only 1,460 years from its establishment). Added to his accounts of apparitions and armies seen fighting in the sky, this served only to stir up fears, which he later attempted to quell.[263] The sensational *Catastrophe Mundi* (1682) by the Whig, John Holwell, sought rather to fan the flames, describing how the Turks would sweep through France, Germany and the Netherlands and threaten England; *Ambras Merlin* spoke even of a Turkish invasion of Cornwall.[264] An Anglican minister, Henry Krabtree, published an almanac proving that the Turks were destined to overthrow the fourth and last monarchy of the world, signalling the approach of Judgement Day.[265] The meeting of Saturn and Jupiter confirmed that upheavals were at hand. Lilly's posthumous almanac for 1683 recalled that the conjunctions of 1603 and 1623 had led to the death of the sovereign and to plague, in 1643 to civil war and d revolution, in 1663 to the Great Plague and Fire of London: who could doubt that similar catastrophes were at hand? The more sensational sections of his and other almanacs were collected and republished as pamphlets.[266] Very many almanacs saw in these signs clear evidence of the fall of Rome, and apocalyptic upheavals.[267] The *Catastrophe Mundi* of 1683 attacked Hol well's work bearing the same title, but offered an equally sensational prospect of wars and disasters leading to the rise of a great conqueror and a last age of peace, drawing on Tycho Brahe, Alsted, Elias and the Sibyls, and printing once more the apocalyptic schema which Lilly had taken from 'Cypriano'.[268]

There were differing opinions on what would follow the upheavals, but most anticipated an age of tranquillity or a messianic conqueror rather than the biblical reign of the saints. In the 1670s Lilly had continued to speak of a general peace, 'a peaceful and quiet age' of happiness, and his comments were given wide circulation.[269] Thomas Fowle observed in 1684 that the fall of Antichrist was at hand, 'after which times (and before the consummation of the world) shall be a more peaceful and quiet age'. Christopher Nesse, a nonconformist, drew on Alsted's synchronization of the seven ages of the world with the seven revolutions of Saturn and Jupiter, and looked to an imminent sabbatical age; John Case, a prominent London astrologer, predicted a similar sabbatical era to last until the next revolution of the two planets and the world's end, eight hundred years hence.[270] Others laid stress on the theme of a last emperor. Israel (or Ezreel) Tongue, a minister who had played a squalid role in making false allegations about the mythical Popish Plot, claimed to see in the comet of 1680 a 'northern star' which he collated with the prophecies of Tycho Brahe, Grebner and others, and concluded with the prophecy of a series of messianic monarchs in the Stuart line.[271] The most sensational prophecies were offered by the rival Whig astrologers, Kirby and Holwell. Using the hieroglyphs printed in Lilly's *Monarchy or No Monarchy* (1651), Kirby predicted the death of the king of France, and the destruction of Italy, Spain, France, the Netherlands and the papacy, to be followed by the rise of a great conqueror in 1699 who would 'give peace to the whole earth'.[272] (The year 1699 was, as Partridge and others pointed out, the sum of 1666 and 33—the years of Christ's life—and also figured prominently in the prophecies of Holwell and many more.) Holwell anticipated the death of Louis XIV within two years, and thought it likely that the Emperor Leopold would be captured by the Turks, who would then break into Italy and overthrow the pope. But in 1699 a great conqueror would arise, followed by the conversion of Turks and Jews, and a last age of peace.[273]

The Turks in fact failed to take Vienna, and the excitement gradually subsided. Moreover the royalist reaction in the last years of Charles, and the accession of his Catholic brother James in 1685 made impossible the publication of the anti-Catholic apocalyptic diatribes of recent years. During the reign of James speculation was muted. One notable exception was John Gadbury, who devised an ultra-royalist thesis, suggesting that the conjunction of 1682 was similar to that of 1066 which had preceded the establishment of a strong monarchy under William the Conqueror, and thus signified the strengthening of royal authority. The next conjunction, in 1702, he expected to herald a great monarch who would establish order, peace and godliness.[274]

The Glorious Revolution of 1688–9, which expelled James, was hailed as the vindication of apocalyptic prophecies. Years before, Partridge had calmed agitated readers with the remark

Tush, for by and by,
After these things, comes the Fifth Monarchy.

Whilst in exile during James's reign, Partridge had foretold the king's downfall with hints of an apocalyptic nature. Later, with James himself safely in exile, Partridge was far more specific in speculating how the king's reign fitted the Old Testament prophecies of Daniel. It had been calculated, he reported in an almanac, that the 1290 days of abomination (Dan. xii:11) matched exactly the time from James's coronation to the landing of William of Orange at Torbay, while the further forty-five days to the time of bliss (Dan. xii:12) pointed precisely to the day when William entered St. James's Palace.[275] A pamphlet by the Whig lawyer William Atwood illustrated graphically the mood of the time. In a long preface the author discussed the revolution with reference to Hobbes, Filmer and other political theorists, but in the body of the work he printed the prophecies of Nostradamus, Grebner, Torquatus and David Pareus, pointing to the apocalyptic nature of the event.[276] There was a marked messianic element in the jingoism with which astrologers greeted the victories of William in the 1690s. William was to be the conqueror and the 'umpire' of Europe, destroying the pope and his champion, Louis XIV. The title of the French king could be calculated as 666, and a prophecy ascribed to William Lilly, foretelling the destruction of a great family in '90' was probably applied to the Bourbons.[277] Henry Coley recalled an old prediction by Lilly that a conqueror would dominate Europe by 1692, leading to the conversion of Jews and Turks and an age of peace.[278] Others looked forward to a 'golden age', in which, said Richard Kirby, adding a Whig gloss, 'every man is master of his own, and lives at peace in a free patent government'.[279] A lively apocalyptic interest survived to the end of the century, and even far beyond.

The role of astrology thus adds a new dimension to the millenarian enthusiasm of seventeenth-century England. Continental sources, especially Alsted, were the channels through which this influence flowed. There is evidence that almanacs and other popular astrological works on the Continent showed a similar combination of astrological and Protestant millennial speculation, for example in the 1650s and even as late as 1680.[280] In England astrologers did much to keep alive a popular millenarian faith after the collapse of the hopes aroused by the civil war. It is becoming apparent now that the millenarianism of the late seventeenth century was not after all a mere delusion held by a few eccentrics. On the contrary, millenarian beliefs, shorn of the political and social radicalism and the enthusiasm of the mid-century, were held by a considerable number of eminent Anglican churchmen, scientists and philosophers.[281] This school of thought was largely separate from the popular tradition, which was maintained primarily by astrological and sectarian pamphleteers. Occasionally the two streams converged.

Thus Partridge in 1701 included in his almanac a millenarian treatise by the mathematician and diplomat, Dr. John Pell. But the popular tradition possessed a viable separate existence, which enabled it to outlive academic interest and survive into the nineteenth century.[282]

CHAPTER SIX

Astrology, Science and Medicine

(i) The Reform of Astrology

ALMANACS WERE CHEAP, popular annuals, and so by their very nature unsuited for an extended investigation of scientific problems. They contained, however, far more than the mere repetition of traditional ideas which might be expected. Many compilers showed a marked awareness of scientific advances, and were active in reporting them. The almanacs had an important role, especially in the seventeenth century, in the popularization of the new science.[1]

To modern eyes, this progressive role seems at variance with the defence of astrology, which naturally remained of central importance. The compilers saw no such incongruity. Aware of defects in their subject, they were confident that by applying modern techniques they could remould it in a pure and systematic form. Though the scientific respectability of astrology was certainly far lower in 1700 than in 1500, the process of decline was by no means simple or continuous. The practitioners made a serious effort to reform their science, impressive despite its eventful failure.[2]

In the sixteenth century, astrology was part of the scientific mainstream. It was accepted by all the great Elizabethan scientists. The Earl of Leicester's sphere of patronage included Richard Forster, his astrological physician, Thomas Allen, Cunningham, Thomas Digges, Hill and Gale, all of whom (except Allen) issued almanacs.[3] The most important scientists of the period, however, made their major contributions in other fields, notably in mathematics, astronomy and navigation. England remained an astrological backwater, and efforts to create a reformed astrology were small by Continental standards until the middle of the following century. Astrologers were certainly aware that they needed accurate astronomical data, and that the mediaeval Alfonsine tables were wholly inadequate. As early as 1558 William Cunningham used his almanac to denounce the 'blind' Alfonsine tables and assert the superiority of those by Copernicus and Reinhold.

Compilers using the old data, he remarked, 'did rather dream than truly find the situation' of the planets.[4] English compilers did turn to these newer tables, and to those of Stadius, Tycho Brahe and other modern astronomers. English *Ephemerides* based on the new calculations appeared steadily throughout the period, by Field (1557), Hartgill (1594), Searle (1609) and Lilly's tutor, John Evans, who in 1633 published tables based on those of David Origanus, whom he thought superior even to Tycho.[5] The writings of Continental reformers found some echo in England. There was a Latin edition of a work by Leowitz on nativities, and an English translation of a treatise on the same subject by the French astrologer, Ogier Ferrier. Elizabeth's reign also saw two English editions of a guide to astrology by the French Calvinist, Claude Dariot, which contained a treatise on elections.[6] English writers published relatively little original material. John Dee, a major exception, set out his theories on astrological reform early in Elizabeth's reign. Allen and Forster composed treatises on Ptolemy which remained in manuscript. Robert Fludd, Nathaniel Torperley and John Bainbridge declared their interest in reform, which was shared by Sir Christopher Heydon. Heydon corresponded with Kepler and Magini, and compiled a major work in around 1606; however, it was to remain in manuscript until 1650, and he was thus known to contemporaries as a polemicist, not theorist.[7]

Nicholas Fiske later explained the dearth of important English writings in this period by citing the 'malice of the clergy', who 'wilfully refused' to allow their publication, and the 'servile fear' of astrologers uncertain about their legal status.[8] The paucity of material also reflects the undeveloped character of astrological thought in England, which is often evident in the almanacs. Many of the early Stuart compilers were capable mathematicians, sceptical of the claims of traditional astrology. Walter Frost, for example, while accepting that the planets might influence the earth, thought the existing state of astrology, 'standing all upon conjecture', could offer no basis for a rational understanding. Prophecies rested on the 'uncertain conjectures' of the nature of the stars, 'which natures are guessed at by the effects, the effects supposed to have their causes in the irradiations and aspects; which aspects being calculated from erronious tables, have bred false and erronious aphorisms, which yet are the rules whereby all prediction is regulated'.[9] But apart from calling for better astronomical tables, these writers did little to provide the new astrology. They met criticism by asserting the general validity of astrological influences while disavowing the more controversial parts which had been added since the time of Ptolemy. Thus Frost denounced elections and horary astrology (the resolution of questions by the state of the heavens at the time of the query) as invented by 'the Arabians and Indians, long ago rejected, and unanimously condemned as an unlawful sortilege'. Edward Gresham supplied sensational prophecies but added the rider that they were based on traditional 'vulgar' astrology, to which he clearly attached little weight. Allestree claimed to have practised traditional astrology for twenty years until 'God opening mine eyes' had shown it to be full of 'deceits, frauds and lies'. He provided details of elections in his almanacs, but ridiculed them as 'foolish fables'.[10]

The flood of astrological publications in the 1640s and later represented more than a merely quantitative increase. The dramatic success of Lilly and other political prophets brought greater vigour, confidence and assertiveness, and (paradoxically) a new respectability. A more general movement developed towards the revitalization and reform of astrology as a whole. The starting point was the publication in 1647 of Lilly's *Christian Astrology,* the first comprehensive guide to its theory and practice, and a work 'very much wanting and as earnestly longed for'. It was based on a wide reading of Continental authorities, and Lilly aspired to correct the rules of the science which he claimed to have found 'for the most part defective'. The book was well received, and Lilly gave public readings from it to young disciples in 1648–9. The choice of timing was influenced by his knowledge of support from among the rising political forces of the army and the Independents, contrasted with Presbyterian hostility.[11] Heydon's *Discourse* appeared in 1650, and in the decades that followed many of the major astrological texts were translated and published. Two collections of aphorisms, ascribed to Ptolemy and Hermes Trismegistus and each entitled *Centiloquium,* appeared regularly in almanacs.[12] There was far more widespread interest in Continental writings on reform. Dariot's rules on elections were summarized frequently, and there were a number of references to the attempted systematization of astrology by the celebrated French practitioner, J.-B. Morin. Morin's posthumous *Astrologia Gallica* (1661), which has been seen as the last great attempt to rehabilitate judicial astrology, impressed Booker as 'the most rational and exquisite piece' ever written. George Wharton published Morin's 'Cabal of the 12 Houses Astrological' in his almanac for 1659, with a commendatory note from the mathematician, William Oughtred, who did 'very much applaud and admire it'.[13]

Later in the century a group of astrologers, including John Partridge, championed the reformed system of the Italian monk, Placidus de Titis (d. 1668). Partridge learned it from his tutor, Dr. Francis Wright, and found fellow-enthusiasts in Kirby and Whalley. Earlier practitioners, such as Lilly and Gadbury, had allegedly dismissed Wright as 'crazy' and 'brain sick'. Placidus, like other reformers, stressed that astrology was a natural science, operating through the effects of light. The essence of his reform was to return to the purity of Ptolemy, sweeping away later accretions. He therefore rejected elections, horary astrology and the houses of the zodiac, all unknown to Ptolemy. Partridge complained that modern practitioners knew only the name of Ptolemy, not his system; hence their calculations were erroneous, as Partridge explained at length in his *Defectto Geniturarum.* The obvious remedy was to publish Ptolemy's major work, *Quadrapartite,* in English. This was done by John Whalley in 1701, and the work was dedicated to Partridge. Whalley added a commentary, an appendix drawn from Placidus, and a fiery introduction denouncing the 'scandalous, ridiculous falsehoods' imposed on the world by Gadbury, Coley and others. Not surprisingly, the Placidian theory aroused controversy. Gadbury called it 'pale and sickly', and Parker joined in the abuse. The dispute seems to have run along party lines, of Whig against Tory. Richard Gibson, another critic, pointed out the irony of Whig astrologers annually denouncing 'monkish religion' and yet being 'sticklers for monkish astrology'. He attacked Partridge's outmoded assumption that there had been no progress since classical times. A more mundane but crucial objection was that the abolition of horary astrology would bar most of the population from the services of the professional astrologer, 'for to one that can procure his nativity, there are twenty-one that cannot obtain it.'[14]

The appeal of Morin in the mid-seventeenth century lay largely in his belief that the reform of astrology must rest on the systematic collation of meteorological, political and religious change with astrological data. The similarity to Baconianism is clear. Bacon himself had urged the reconstitution of astrology, not its abolition; Reynold Smith, who described himself as a servant of Bacon, issued almanacs in the 1620s.[15] During the interregnum Joshua Childrey urged a thorough reform of astrology along Baconian lines. Jeremy Shakerley complained that 'astrology consists of too much uncertainty, to inform us of anything', and promised that he would 'from philosophical principles seek a foundation for a more refined astrology'.[16] Astrology like other sciences ought 'to be founded on experiments', thought Henry Coley, and the scholar who wished to study it 'scientifically' must 'observe what rational experience affords concerning it'.[17] John Gadbury argued that 'one real experiment is of greater worth and more to be valued than one hundred pompous predictions.' His claim that Ptolemy was 'as certain as Euclid' was at least a clear indication of his aspirations. 'My inclinations aim at a certainty in science', he explained, adding less plausibly that 'I can truly say that I have found more in astrology than in all others put together.' To the taunt that marine insurance would be unnecessary if astrologers could really predict whether a ship would be lost at sea, Gadbury retorted by telling sceptics that 'a little astrology (would you take pains in it) may prove more advantageous to you than your insurance-office.'[18] Gadbury was assiduous in the prolonged campaign to distinguish astrology from visions, omens and the whole area of the magical and miraculous. The clergyman who told his flock in 1652 that Black Monday could produce no terrible effects because eclipses had a natural cause was thus missing the point that most astrologers regarded their subject as a natural not occult science. 'God help his calf's head', exclaimed Culpeper. 'Is not meat and drink natural, and yet doth it not nourish? Is not poison natural, and yet doth it not destroy?'[19]

Unfortunately astrology posed special problems to the scientific method, in that there was no apparent way to measure or even to identify planetary influence. There was plenty of speculation in the later seventeenth century. The stars, it was said, must operate 'by some invisible wires, some unknown magnetisms'; or by 'balsamic atoms emitted from the stars, as well as corroding ones'. All terrestrial phenomena, claimed 'J. H.' (probably John Heydon), could be explained by 'the motions of corpuscles (viz. small bodies, viz. atoms) *(vide* Boyle, Dr. Charles &c). These have no first mover but stars.'[20] Others offered explanations in terms of heat or light. Saunders explained that comets caused wars and the death of princes by scorching the air, which disturbed the blood, causing choler and hence the risk of war, and sometimes bringing death to great persons who lived 'more delicately' than the common sort and were thus more susceptible to changes in the atmosphere.[21]

The most promising course appeared to lie not in attempts to identify the nature of stellar influence but in the accumulation of data about its effects, with a systematic comparison of known events with the astrological circumstances. The most vigorous English exponent of this approach was John Gadbury, building consciously on the ideas of Morin, Bacon and Childrey. His introductory *The Doctrine of Nativities* (1658) was followed by a discussion of a large collection of specific cases (*Collectio Geniturarum,* 1662). In his almanac for 1665 he appealed to the public to send in the times of birth and chief 'accidents' of all boys born in 1657–9 and on 4–5 September 1664, to form the basis for a 'body of astrology'. The response was apparently good; some years later Gadbury indeed reported that he had compiled an 'army' of ten thousand genitures.[22] Others showed some interest in collections of this sort. Neve compiled several hundred astrological figures, carefully worked out, and Lilly promised a comprehensive work based on the collections of Cunningham, Bredon and other eminent predecessors. (It never materialized, and Gadbury complained that it was merely a device to spoil his sales; as he pointed out, Lilly showed little interest in experiments.[23]) No others however shared the assiduity of Gadbury, who combined sound scientific instincts with an awareness of the wider implications of his work. He held that a thorough knowledge of the genitures of people born in 1599 and 1600 (which would include Charles I, Pym and Cromwell) would have been of great value: 'I am not so great a fatist but that I believe much of the misery this nation (during its civil wars) underwent, might (by such a knowledge) have been prevented.'[24] Many of his almanacs in the 1670s contained 'experiments', usually detailed analyses of particular horary problems.[25] He was equally interested in the field of weather forecasting, a subject dominated by his friend, the schoolmaster-astrologer, John Goad. For thirty years Goad carefully recorded and compared data on the stars and the weather; he sent regular reports to Elias Ashmole, and discussed his findings with Charles II.[26] Similar efforts to detect a pattern were made by the Scottish astrologer, William Cock, and records were also kept by Richard Napier and Joshua Childrey.[27] Gadbury published in one of his almanacs a table showing the weather following every new and full moon over a thirty-year period. He welcomed the barometer but affirmed that in time astrology would make predictions possible far longer in advance.[28] A possible key lay in the belief held in the Netherlands and reported by Bacon that the weather moved in cycles of about thirty-five years, an idea frequently discussed by Gadbury and other compilers. But at the end of his life he reported that he had made a daily study of the weather for thirty-five years, as Bacon indicated, without having yet reduced it to a clear system.[29]

Many astrologers shared Gadbury's aspirations. The mood is evident from titles such as Ramesey's *Astrologia Restaurata* (1653), Partridge's *Opus Reformatum* (1693) or Godson's *Astrologia Reformata* (1696). Following the maxim that experience alone was 'the astrologers' oracle', they tabulated major comets and conjunctions since the creation and investigated the historical 'results'. Wharton derived from William Camden the suggestion that London was liable to outbreaks of plague when Saturn was in a fiery triplicity, and documented the theory with examples from history since the fourteenth century.[30] Records of comets existed covering many centuries, but most other phenomena lacked comparable documentation. 'Astrology wanteth its history', Gadbury lamented. Astrology taught that the fortunes of buildings, cities and even countries were influenced by their nativities. The University of Wittenberg had accordingly been founded at a propitious astrological moment. Such data was rarely available, but Francis Bernard devised a method of reconstructing London's nativity by treating fires in the city as its 'accidents'. Gadbury published the nativity of Chelsea College, founded in 1609, and referred to a nativity calculated for the warden's window in Merton College, Oxford (adding a defensive note rebutting the ridicule he anticipated). The capture of Jamaica in 1655, leading to the establishment of an English settlement, provided a rare opportunity to draw up the horoscope of a colony, later published by Gadbury with predictions of future prosperity for the settlers.[31]

The reformation of astrology was a massive undertaking. Recognizing that it was beyond the capacity of any one individual, Gadbury suggested that the subject be divided into six major areas, each to be allocated to a different expert, and called also for the free exchange of astrological information.[32] The corporate idea was widespread in seventeenth-century science, and culminated in the foundation of the Royal Society. Before that event, a formal Society of Astrologers was established during the interregnum, with almost fifty members, regular meetings in London, and annual sermons. It was supported by Lilly's influential friend, Bulstrode Whitelocke; an official letter from the Society to Whitelocke in 1650 referred to his great love of astrology, his patronage of Lilly, and the encouragement he had given to all astrologers. The Society failed to survive the Restoration, probably because of its republican associations, but was re-established for a time in 1682–3 under the leadership of Joseph Moxon, F.R.S.[33]

There is a considerable amount of evidence to document the increasing neglect and indeed disparagement of astrology at Oxford and Cambridge as the seventeenth century advanced.[34] The picture is modified by Lilly's claim that his *Christian Astrology*, the work which inaugurated the English astrological renaissance, was well received in both universities. No doubt he was exaggerating greatly, but his surviving correspondence and other sources show beyond doubt that there were still many enthusiasts in the universities in the middle of the century. Thus Abraham Whelock, professor of Arabic and university librarian at Cambridge, hailed Lilly as raised by God to be 'the promoter of these admired studies in the universities', and declared himself a belated but enthusiastic disciple. He believed optimistically that even the Presbyterian academics at Cambridge were impressed.[35] The astrologer-mathematician, George Atwell, taught at Cambridge and was linked with Trinity College; his friend Walter Frost, son of the almanac-maker, was manciple of Emmanuel College.[36] Several members of the University wrote to Lilly seeking advice or tuition. Joshua Barnes (d. 1712), later professor of Greek and F.R.S., was a friend of Gadbury.[37] At Oxford Sir Richard Napier, Fellow of All Souls, wrote to Booker for advice in a land transaction, with the assurance that his 'judgement is to me like the oracle of Apollo'. Dr. Clayton, professor of medicine and Master of Pembroke College, Oxford, contributed an epistle to Neve's manuscript 'Vindication of judiciarie Astrologie'.[38] The *Ephemerides* published by Wing and Gadbury appeared with tributes from members of both universities (though the authors belonged to neither).[39]

The universities were of course notorious for their reluctance to incorporate the new science into the teaching syllabus. It is perhaps greater testimony to the vitality of astrology that despite its political extravagances it was not rejected by many of the leading scientists of the day. During the second half of the century the social circles of leading scientists and astrologers overlapped constantly. The expertise of the best astrologers in the fields of astronomy or mathematics partly explains this acceptability, but it is clear that a surprisingly high number of the foremost scientists retained a degree of belief or at least interest in astrology itself. William Oughtred accepted astrology, commended Wharton's work and wrote in highly respectful terms to Lilly.[40] The young astronomer Shakerley, formerly a member of the Towneley circle, sought out the friendship and patronage of Lilly after the civil war.[41] Jonas Moore, the astronomer and mathematician (later Sir Jonas, F.R.S.), was on friendly terms with Lilly, Wharton and

Gadbury. Wharton indeed appealed to Moore, Scarburgh (later Sir Charles, F.R.S., physician to Charles II) and Richard Holland of Hart Hall, Oxford, as skilled astrologers able to settle the disputes between Lilly and himself.[42] Wharton was also the friend of Richard Rawlinson, fellow of Queen's College, Oxford, a member of thc Oxford group of scientists, assistant to John Wallis, and Petty's nominee for the Gresham chair of astronomy.[43]

The Royal Society, founded shortly after the Restoration, showed as an institution a sceptical attitude towards astrology. Its secretary, Oldenburg, mocked Gadbury's analysis of the Plague and dismissed the views of Sir Christopher Heydon as 'not likely to be received' in the modern age. Gadbury expressed the hope in an almanac that the Society would one day adopt a more favourable attitude. He pointed out that he shared the members' zeal for the 'promotion of experimental philosophy', so 'why should not experiments in astrology be . . . patronized by them?'[44] But the gulf was by no means wide. During the Restoration period John Aubrey and Elias Ashmole played an important role in linking the astrological and scientific worlds. Both were friends of leading astrologers, both were active members of the Royal Society, mixing socially with its leading figures. Both provided contacts and brought respectability. In addition Ashmole gave financial support and had useful links with the royal court; he was indeed complimented as the man who 'first gave a public credit to astrology'.[45] There were other links between the two worlds, provided notably by Jonas Moore and George Wharton, who both resided in the Tower in the 1670s, making it a centre of scientific observation, discussion and patronage. It was said that John Flamsteed, the future Astronomer Royal, first attracted notice by sending astronomical data to Lilly, who arranged with Moore and Wharton to meet him. Flamsteed had an early interest in astrology, though it faded in later years. Moore's friend Sir Edward Sherburne, well known as a poet and amateur astronomer, and the son of Bacon's secretary, was also a friend of Gadbury.[46] Joshua Childrey, advocate of astrological reform, was a respected correspondent of the Royal Society. Thomas Streete, the author of a number of almanacs, was possibly an early Fellow of the Society, and certainly enjoyed a high reputation within it as an astronomer and mathematician.[47] Data and calculations compiled by the almanac-makers, Martindale, Henry Phillippes and Stynred, were presented to the Society, and Flamsteed praised highly the work on tidal predictions done by Booker and Phillippes.[48] The network of friendship, patronage and sympathetic interest extended much further. Henry Coley was a friend of Sir John Hoskins, F.R.S. Gadbury was a friend of John Collins, mathematician and Fellow.[49] Other early Fellows who gave support were George Ent, Edmund Wylde (an early president) and Sir Frescheville Holles, a client of Gadbury.[50] Sir John Robartes (later Earl of Truro and Lord President of the Council) was very interested in Ashmole's collection of the manuscripts of John Dee; his chaplain, Robert Sterrell, was an old associate and would-be pupil of Lilly.[51] The first president, Viscount Brouncker, was able to draw up an astrological figure. John Evelyn showed a sympathetic interest.[52] Sir William Petty was a 'lover of astrology', according to Gadbury, though he 'abhorred the frauds practised under pretence thereof. He was said to believe that the influence of the stars was clearly demonstrable in growing crops. As a young man, Petty had indeed proposed a teaching and research hospital, to be directed by a master 'skilled in the best rules of judicial astrology, which he may apply to calculate the events of diseases, and prognosticate the weather; to the end that by his judicious and careful experiments, the wheat may be separated from the chaff in that faculty'. He was to keep and correlate data of weather, crop fertility and animal and human diseases with the astrological conditions.[53]

Other Fellows combined scepticism with a residual belief in a potential astrological science. Thus Robert Boyle, who was claimed as a patron by the astrologer, John Bishop, certainly believed that the sun, moon and stars had an influence on earth distinct from heat and light, some kind of 'subtle but corporeal emanations', which he was anxious to identify. Sunspots, lunar phases and major conjunctions were all legitimate data to be used in seeking to explain earthly phenomena.[54] In 1664 the Society circulated an official questionnaire on agriculture seeking *inter alia* information on the phase of the moon in which crops were normally sown.[55] Edmond Halley had no particular interest in astrology, but was nevertheless the 'very loving friend' of John Holwell, one of the most sensational political astrologers of the period, and his library contained Lilly's *Monarchy or No Monarchy* and other works of prophecy.[56] Dr. John Beale remarked on the potential value of almanacs in publishing data of the weather as a means of understanding meteorological change, if only astrologers would include 'fewer false predictions, and more faithful registers', a call which Gadbury endorsed. (Some eighteenth-century compilers heeded the call and inserted details of the previous year's weather in place of the usual predictions.[57]) Robert Hooke, the eminent professor of geometry at

Gresham College, thought Gadbury was 'mad' and astrology 'vain'. But even he was far removed from modern indifference. A close friend of Hoskins and Aubrey, Hooke and his circle made astrology a staple topic of discussion at thecoffee-houses they frequented. He called to see Gadbury, Lilly and Goad, regularly bought or borrowed astrological books, and during the critical winter of 1688–9 looked over the prophecies of Merlin, Lilly and the Sibylline oracles.[58]

None of this evidence refutes the fact that the intellectual status of astrology gradually declined (for reasons discussed later). But the decline was slow, and scientists were not the most prominent critics. Mr. Thomas has observed that 'the clergy and the satirists chased it into its grave, but the scientists were unrepresented at the funeral.' Many indeed seemed hesitant to certify its death. Their outlook was ambivalent, sceptical of contemporary astrology but sympathetic to the idea of some kind of astral influence.[59]

Given the notorious interest of Charles II, it is not surprising that astrology was well represented at the royal court. Forman, Napier, Lilly and Booker had counted many noble and gentle families among their clients. In the later period, Lord Treasurer Clifford resorted to Ashmole, and Sir Robert Peyton and the Earl of Peterborough were linked with Gadbury.[60] The Duke of Buckingham, a patron of John Heydon, declared his nativity to have been verified. Rochester, poet and rake, sent details of his birth to Gadbury and requested a nativity. The Earl of Bristol 'excelled in . . . astrology', and frequently summoned Gadbury for discussion of abstruse problems. William Hunt's treatise on astrology 'founded upon the Copernican hypothesis' (1696) was dedicated to the Earl of Manchester, with thanks for his favours to the author.[61] The collections of Partridge and of Francis and Charles Bernard contain the genitures of many of the leading politicians and courtiers of the period.[62] Probably most were sceptical as well as curious, but scepticism had not yet developed into indifference. Dedications in almanacs show that patrons were still plentiful among the country gentry, merchants and officials; they included two ill-fated members of parliament, Sir John Coventry (mutilated after criticizing the morals of Charles II) and Sir John Friend (executed for treason as a Jacobite in 1693).[63]

(ii) Astronomy and Applied Science

The eventual death of astrology has naturally diverted attention from the reforming efforts of its practitioners. A better-known and more enduring claim to scientific respectability lies in the pioneering role of almanacs in accepting and popularizing the new astronomy, especially Copernicanism.[64] One of the earliest English references to the Copernican theory was made by John Dee in an introduction he provided to Field's *Ephemerides* in 1557. In 1576 Thomas Digges provided a large-scale exposition and defence, in English, of Copernicanism in a new edition of his father's *Prognostication.* The Jacobean almanacs of Bretnor and Gresham endorsed the Copernican system, as Gresham had done earlier in an unpublished but widely-known tract written in 1603.[65]

The connection between astrology and the new astronomy is only superficially surprising. Astrology was by tradition applied astronomy, and its practitioners were fully aware that in figures erected from false planetary tables 'errors must needs follow'.[66] The celebrated astronomers Tycho Brahe and Kepler were themselves interested in the astrological implications of their discoveries. Very many of the Stuart almanac-makers were also practising astronomers. Gresham referred to personal observations extending over fourteen years, and the list includes (besides Sir Christopher Heydon) Wyberd, Wing, Childrey (who designed several telescopes), Nye, Streete, Leybourne, Shakerley, Colson and, in a much more amateur way, Lilly.[67] Shakerley was the second man ever to observe the transit of Mercury, and provided a full discussion of the method, and of the planet itself, in his almanac for 1651.[68] Vincent Wing's *Urania Practica* was 'the first substantial English compendium of astronomy', and was well received. His planetary tables and those of Thomas Streete were standard works, and were widely admired. Neither author had been to university, but Wing became the friend of 'nearly every notable mathematical practitioner of the day', including Scarburgh, Pell, Wingate and Wallis, while Streete conducted observations with Halley, an admirer, and Hooke.[69] The library of John Flamsteed, the Astronomer Royal, contained Wing's *Ephemerides* and his other astronomical works.[70] George Parker published tables in his almanac for 1690 with a letter of commendation from Edmond Halley praising their accuracy. Flamsteed was said to have provided astronomical data for the almanac-maker, John Wing.[71]

A number of compilers in the seventeenth century published in their almanacs summaries of recent astronomical discoveries. John Rudston in 1624 set out a list of 'new discoveries in the celestial regions', ascribed largely to Galileo, 'a principal furtherer of the perspective glasses'. It included Jupiter's moons, the luminosity of the fixed stars, and the 'mountains, vallies, seas and rivers' of the moon. He referred also to Tycho's proof that there were no solid orbs, Kepler's work on sunspots, and various theories on the nature of comets.[72] Similar lists were provided by clarke, Nye, Shakerley and John Wing.[73]

The advocates of Copernicanism were confident that astrology, calculated for centuries on the Ptolemaic assumption of the earth's fixed and central position, could be adapted to the new theory. John Partridge asserted flippantly that it was 'not a rush matter which your principles are, whether geocentric, heliocentric, or selenocentric'.[74] Many other compilers, who were better scientists, took the matter more seriously. The pioneering support of Copernicanism by Digges, Gresham and Bretnor has already been mentioned. Bretnor's friend, Arthur Hopton, wavered between Ptolemy and Tycho, discussing also the theories of Copernicus and his reasons for rejecting them. In the 1620s Abraham Grammar set out both the Tychonic and Copernican systems, without choosing between them. Ranger did likewise, heaping praise on both while indicating a tentative preference for Tycho.[75] Before the civil war, committed Copernicans were thus very few. But the Ptolemaic system was already crumbling rapidly. From the second decade of the seventeenth century there were few compilers showing any real interest in astronomy who remained faithful to Ptolemy.[76] Instead they turned increasingly to the theories of Tycho Brahe and Argol, by which Mercury and Venus circled the sun which, with the outer planets, revolved round the earth. This had the psychological advantage of adapting rather than destroying tradition, and the Tychonic thesis was buttressed by a mass of careful and detailed planetary observations which Copernicus had neglected to provide. Their excellence was stressed by most Stuart astrologers, who rarely referred to Tycho without the laudatory epithet 'tres-noble'. Before 1640 the Tychonic system had been adopted by Booker, Ranger, Rivers, Rudston, Sofford, Dove and Strof (a pseudonym used by Walter Frost).[77] The spread of support for the Tychonic system was reinforced by its endorsement in a popular astronomical handbook, *Speculum Mundi,* published in 1635 by John Swan, later to become a well-known almanac-maker.[78]

From roughly the middle of the century the Copernican system gained steadily in appeal at the expense of the Tychonic. The publication of a number of highly competent astronomical works in English during the revolutionary period was probably the major cause, prominent among them being the works of Vincent Wing. During the 1640s Wing had endorsed Tycho's system in his almanacs, but in the 1651 edition and subsequently he expressed strongly Copernican views and expounded the system repeatedly in almanacs and his substantial works on astronomy.[79] Tycho retained supporters even in the Restoration period, and his scheme was championed consistently by John Swan. But they slowly dwindled in number and impressiveness. In 1656 Seth Partridge thought that most people, 'right or wrong', still adhered to Ptolemy. But by 1683 Coley could claim that the Copernican system was now generally accepted. After half a century of support for Tycho, *Dove* fell into line at about this time. Even the most stereotyped productions, such as *Dade* and *Swallow,* switched their allegiance before the end of the century. In 1689 Mary Holden, a midwife, was still advocating Tycho's theory, and a few years later *Poor Robin* sought to prove the earth's stability with the venerable argument of the arrow which, fired vertically into the air, falls to the ground at the same place.[80] But these were by now archaic survivals. By the end of the century, the 'tres-noble' Tycho had become in the eyes of Henry Coley 'vicious and absurd'.[81]

Progressive astrologers at the end of the period were explaining to their readers some elements of the gravitational theories of Kepler and Newton. Tycho's destruction of the solid orbs had produced a disquieting lacuna in failing to give any alternative solution to the problem of how and why the planets moved in their courses. *Dove*, which adopted Tycho's system, did face the problem but could offer no more than a vague Aristotelian assertion that 'the aptness and readiness of motion in the planets was essentially in themselves, or given them by God, whereby they are compelled to keep their constant and regular course in the heavens.'[82] Gravitational pull offered a more demonstrable solution, which simultaneously showed how the moon influenced the tides. John Wing expounded the point. The fact that tidal movement or 'flux' was not intrinsic but 'depends on an extrinsical agent, which impels only the superficies of the sea is most evident', he argued, 'by the experiment of a late diver, that discovers there is no flux in the bottom of the sea'.[83]

It has been suggested that a link existed between progressive beliefs in politics and astronomy, and that the civil war was fought between royalist Ptolemaics and parliamentarian heliocentrists.[84] The evidence from almanacs does not bear out this intriguing hypothesis. The real struggle by the mid-century was between Tycho and Copernicus, and allegiance does not seem to have been tied closely to political beliefs. William Lilly, the foremost Parliamentarian, was a lukewarm Copernican, and Nye, Culpeper and (by the 1650s) Wing were committed advocates.[85] But John Booker, the earliest and one of the most important astrologers to support parliament, was a fierce critic of Copernicanism, which he attacked year after year. 'I am as fixed as I conceive the earth to be', he declared in 1657, and d know no motion of the earth, but the commotion thereupon in this Iron Age'. His almanac for 1661 contained verses (by Sir Robert Heath) suggesting that Copernicus must have framed his theory of the earth's motion when drunk or on board ship.[86] By contrast George Wharton, the leading royalist compiler, was a staunch Copernican and was ridiculed as such by one of the parliamentarian astrologers.[87] Joshua Childrey, another royalist astrologer, was noted as an advocate of the heliocentric system.[88] In the corresponding pamphlet war between Whig and Tory astrologers a generation later, John Partridge poked fun at the Copernican beliefs of his rival, mocked as a rogue who beat his wife and 'whipped her too the heliocentric way'.[89]

Religious principles seem to have been more decisive than political. Devout believers found it difficult to reconcile Copernicanism with the account in Genesis, whereas the Ptolemaic system, with the earth at the centre, matched traditional Christian teaching about man's place in the creation. Religious considerations were at the heart of the conservatism of Allestree, who denounced the 'vain deceits' of Copernicus and invited Tycho Brahe to abandon astronomy and 'learn some handy trade'.[90] Daniel Browne cited his patron's assertion that 'the Holy Scripture did manifestly affirm the earth's stability.' Browne added scientific arguments in favour of Ptolemy, reasoning that the earth, as a heavy body, could only be moved by a violent force; but the earth 'is not moved violently: therefore not moved at all'. Retaining traditional beliefs about the total contrast between the earth and the heavens, he argued that the earth must be static 'for circular motion is proper to the heavens. And as the earth differeth from them in nature: so likewise in moving.'[91] Tycho's system, retaining the earth's central position, posed fewer religious problems. Walter Frost, a supporter of Tycho, objected that the Copernican system necessitated a vast distance between the outer planets and the fixed stars, taking away 'that proportion, which God the creator hath observed in all things'.[92] James Bowker, who developed an extended critique of Copernicanism in his almanacs for 1678–80, reiterated the point, and argued that the idea of life on other planets contradicted biblical teaching.[93] At the beginning of the century Edward Gresham had met the problem by claiming to be able to reconcile Copernicanism and the Bible. By its close heliocentric writers asserted boldly that biblical language was often metaphorical, and that in all matters not essential to salvation scripture must be 'subject to the jurisdiction of other arts and sciences'.[94]

The dispute over heliocentrism was only one aspect of the new astronomy. Tycho Brahe's discovery of a nova or new star in 1572 (newly visible through its sudden expansion and brightening) had an equally shattering implication for traditional belief in the immutable perfection of the heavens. At first most almanacs referred to the apparition as a 'blazing star' or comet, but by the 1630s it was being described correctly as a new star by compilers who realized and accepted the implications this had for traditional cosmology.[95] Tycho's observations of the comet of 1577 had a still greater significance. Proving that the comet passed between the paths of the planets, Tycho was forced to the conclusion that the solid orbs in which the planets moved, an accepted feature of the cosmological system for many centuries, could not exist. Rudston's almanac for 1624 discussed the problem and claimed that Tycho's conclusion was 'infallibly proved'. Sofford discussed the point in the same year, and a few years later Rudston's judgement was endorsed by Strof and Nye.[96]

Though comets continued to arouse interest primarily for their prophetic significance, there was a steady growth of interest among compilers in their physical characteristics and composition. Thus Rudston, in the edition cited above, discussed the theories of Snellius and Kepler but inclined to Tycho's belief that comets originated in the Milky Way. In the latter part of his life William Lilly, in outlook one of the least scientific compilers, provided detailed descriptions and diagrams of comets, which he based on his own observations, letters from friends and correspondents in England and abroad, reports in the *London Gazette* and the *Philosophical Transactions* of the Royal Society, and the observations made by Flamsteed at Greenwich, passed on by their mutual friend, Ashmole.[97] William Andrews, also one of the least scientific in attitude, inserted notes on the nature of comets drawn from Tycho, Paracelsus and Campanella as well as Aristotle. By the end of the period some astrologers were supplying their readers with brief accounts of Halley's work on the periodicity of comets.[98]

Astrologers were thus bringing to a wide public the ideas of the most advanced modern astronomers, in a popular and elementary form. But perhaps equally significant was the contribution to astronomy made by the almanacs at a far humbler level. With their roots in the modest social strata from which they drew many of their clients, the astrologers could realize that at the popular level the crucial struggle was not between the Copernican and Ptolemaic systems, but between *any* form of scientific astronomy and crude notions based on magic and the evidence of the senses. As Wharton remarked of the common people, 'Ptolemy may be something to eat for aught they know.'[99] Even some of the abler compilers failed to free themselves wholly from the influence of sense-perception. Nathaniel Nye, a champion of Copernicanism, believed that the moon was larger than the planets. Henry Phillippes, an authority on tidal predictions, thought it was 'manifest by daily experience (by Copernicus his leave) that the sun and moon have a daily motion round about the earth'. James Bowker, a generation later, taught that the moon was made of the same substance as the clouds and had retained its shape for so long 'by God's appointment' alone.[100] Many less critical people accepted the evidence of their eyes and concluded that the sun and moon were about the size of a football or cartwheel, and about as far distant as the clouds. John Reeve, the co-founder of the Muggletonians, believed that heaven itself was only six miles distant. Throughout the period astrologers played a valuable role, which has been little recognized, in supplying simple proofs that the earth was round, and that it was separated from the other planets and stars by immense distances. The 'vulgar', they conceded, were likely to regard these facts as 'incredible' and 'mere fictions'.[101] The ignorant, said Evans Lloyd in 1582, refused to believe that the planets could be larger than the earth because it was easy to see that 'a millstone is far greater than the greatest of them', and were sceptical of attempts to measure their distances on the grounds that it was impossible to go there. The proposition that the earth was round and that the sun was always shining on some part of its surface was 'to the common sort thought an impossibility', said Walter Gray in 1604.[102] From the time of Leonard Digges many almanacs therefore set out figures giving the sizes and distances of the heavenly bodies. Digges's figures, stating that the earth was 15,750 miles from the moon, and 280,734 miles from the firmament, were probably as staggering to the 'common sort' as he supposed. As the mediaeval tables of Alfraganus (on which these figures were based) were replaced in almanacs by those of Tycho and other modern astronomers, the size of the universe expanded rapidly. The sun, according to Ranger in 1631, was about 3.8 million miles away. In order to circle the earth, its speed thus had to increase from the leisurely nine hundred miles an hour, computed by Hopton for a smaller universe, a generation earlier, to 1,094,300 miles an hour, a figure *Strof* thought 'too swift even for our conceit to bear company'.[103] The traditional Christian universe was in ruins. Instead of being the greatest body, set in its midst, the earth was shown to be merely one peripheral planet, 'of a most contemptible smallness'. But most compilers were sure that the new astronomy was to the greater glory of God. The immense sizes and distances involved, said Saunders in 1675, 'cannot but infinitely amaze our understandings, and possess us with dread and unspeakable wonder of the power, might and majesty of that great God . . . which is the reason I here fall upon this subject'.[104]

In a similar way, astrologers throughout the period inserted simple explanations and diagrams to prove that eclipses were natural, not magical occurrences. A solar eclipse, wrote Rogeford in 1560, 'doth terribly amaze and fear them which have no knowledge in astronomy, considering the marvellous sudden dark coming thereof'.[105] Some compilers were willing to conclude that eclipses had no prophetic significance. 'It is said that eclipses through all ages have had evil events' remarked William Hewlett in 1628, 'yet their true use (as I suppose) is not so much for predictions as for other purposes. As thereby to know the true longitude of any place.' At the end of the century Thomas Fowle listed ten points of scientific value which an eclipse possessed before mentioning an eleventh, prophetic role.[106] The majority of astrologers continued to find a prognosticatory character in each eclipse, but the natural explanations they provided did take the phenomena out of the sphere of the occult and miraculous. Arthur Hopton also refuted as 'absurd' the popular notion that there were more eclipses than in the days of Ptolemy, and that this was a sign of the universal degeneration of nature.[107] Similarly throughout the period almanacs provided simple scientific explanations of phenomena such as mock-suns (*parelii*), meteors, the twinkling of the stars, thunder and lightning. Much was inevitably highly repetitive, but the process of popular enlightenment was doubtless slow. As late as 1763 the astrologer Henry Season reported his Wiltshire neighbours describing a violent thunderstorm as 'conjuring weather'.[108] It is impossible to measure the effects of this long and patient labour, but they should not be disregarded. The almanac was a valuable educational medium whatever the reader's level of astronomical knowledge or ignorance.

Many of the compilers were conscious of the wider implications of the new astronomy they taught. The realization that the earth was merely one of several planets, and that the moon apparently shared many of its features, led to speculation in almanacs as elsewhere that life might exist in space.[109] As early as 1603 Gresham declared that the moon was habitable.[110] At the end of the century John Wing cited Wilkins's *Discovery of a New World* (1638) and thought that every fixed star might have its own planetary system, perhaps inhabited.[111] William Andrews took the Copernican (and hermeticist) belief in the pre-eminence of the sun to its logical conclusion and suggested that the sun itself might be inhabited by a race more 'advanced' than on earth, 'by as much as the lustre and brightness of the one surmounts the shadows and darkness of the other'. This belief was shared by James Howell, discussed by Hooke and Halley, and championed as late as the 1790s by the eminent astronomer, Sir William Herschel.[112] But such hypotheses were of course incapable of proof, and there was no answer to the scornful comments in Thomas Nunnes's almanac, which warned aspiring astronauts that a journey to the moon at the reasonable rate of twenty miles a day would take twenty-seven years, with 'few inns on the way' and no guarantee of 'any civil entertainment' on arrival.[113]

The idea of the infinity of the universe posed problems to astrology. An unlimited number of stars would make their influence, even if demonstrable, of infinite complexity. An understandable but hardly scientific solution was provided by the astrologer, George Hawkins, who declared plaintively that science would recognize '1,025 stars and no more', on the grounds that no astronomer could be expected to take notice of 'every little star'.[114] Nevertheless, the astrologers felt themselves to be on the side of the Moderns in the struggle against the Ancients. In the lists of recent astronomical discoveries they put into their almanacs there was an implicit concept of progress, which as time passed often became explicit. It can be found in the writings of Lilly and of his assistant, Henry Coley, who thought that the telescope and microscope had led to discoveries such as 'no age, I believe, could ever boast of before'. Modern Europe, Coley claimed, was recognized as being without parallel 'for empire, religion and learning, arts and sciences'.[115] The authors of antiquity, thought Richard Edlin, were 'rather to be pitied than cavilled at', and were worth a little respect for their 'willing endeavour'. Young and brash writers, such as Shakerley, dismissed classical astronomy as 'equally deserving laughter and pity'. He and others expressed a boundless sense of optimism concerning the future. Gadbury was sure 'the one half of the power of nature is not yet discovered.' Nathaniel Culpepper expected truth unfolding over the centuries, for 'an age is not sufficient for so many discoveries. . . . it must be the work of successions and posterities, and the time will come when we shall wonder that mankind should be so long ignorant of things that lay so open.' Shakerley was still more forthright. 'Why then shall we subject our selves to the authority of the Ancients,' he demanded, 'when our own experience can inform us better?' 'And indeed what shall we mortals now despair of? Within what bounds shall our wits be contained?'[116] Almanacs were thus supplying both the facts and the theory of scientific progress—while within the universities, paradoxically, the ancient Ptolemaic universe lived on in the undergraduate syllabus.[117]

Astronomy, like astrology, had strongly utilitarian connotations, notably in navigation. Utilitarianism was indeed the thread connecting the various branches of science in which Digges and many of the Jacobean and later compilers were interested. There was in particular a close link between astrology and mathematics, especially practical mathematics. It is apparent in the interests of the greatest Elizabethan mathematicians, Dee, Thomas Digges and Hariot. Very many seventeenth-century compilers labelled themselves mathematicians and used their almanacs to advertise the fields in which they practised and taught. Most offered an ambitiously long list, including arithmetic, accounting, geometry, land-and quantity-surveying, navigation and the use of instruments. Many were respected and progressive practitioners, linked (especially in the first half of the century) with the greatest mathematicians of the time.[118] The valuable role of the London almanac-makers in the pioneering days of English mathematics was recognized later by John Wallis, one of the founding members of the Royal Society.[119] During the reign of James I, Bretnor and Gilden (among others) were close friends of the celebrated mathematician, Edmund Gunter, a professor at Gresham College (who himself cast astrological figures), and of the leading contemporary instrument-makers, Elias

Allen and John Thomson. Bretnor and John Johnson, almanac-maker and author of a standard textbook on arithmetic, were friends of William Pratt, famous as the inventor of a calculator known as the 'Arithmetical Jewel'. Arthur Hopton was a friend of the well-known mathematicians Edward Wright and Mark Ridley, the latter also working with Sir Christopher Heydon. Edward Pond was bequeathed the papers and instruments of the prominent mathematician and surveyor, John Blagrave. George Atwell, another contemporary astrologer and surveyor, was the friend of Edmund Wingate, as well as of Allen and Thomson.[120] The list could be extended, but it is clear that the almanac-makers were established at the very heart of the mathematical circles of early Stuart London. Surveying and the use of instruments were, with astronomy, important areas of common interest. From William Cunningham in the mid-sixteenth century, through Arthur Hopton (noted for his use of triangulation in surveying) to Vincent Wing and William Leybourne, the almanac-makers included many of the most eminent surveyors of the period. Edward Pond, for example, took over the surveying of Middleton's 'New River', a major piece of construction which on completion in 1613 carried drinking-water forty miles from Amwell, near Ware, to London. Leybourne was one of the six men who surveyed the capital following the Great Fire of 1666, prior to its rebuilding.[121] Other compilers developed the military applications of mathematics. Thomas Digges was an important pioneer in this field. William Bourne, a self-taught Elizabethan, composed an early work on gunnery; he found a successor in Nathaniel Nye, astrologer and master-gunner in the parliamentary army, who wrote a book utilizing his practical experiences. Philip Stynred, a contemporary of Nye, was the author of a tract on fortification. Still later, William Walgrave, astrologer and surveyor, taught gunnery to members of the king's forces, and published a work on the subject.[122]

The nature of almanacs made them unsuitable for discussions of abstruse mathematical problems. But they could play a valuable role, as in astronomy, in publicizing innovations. Thus Gilden and other Jacobean astrologers gave prompt notice of Napier's work on logarithms, and described the latest scientific instruments and the London craftsmen who supplied them.[123] Like many contemporary mathematicians, the astrologers sometimes devised and made their own instruments. Seth Partridge was indeed possibly the inventor of the slide rule.[124] Provincial readers had of course little chance of obtaining the expensive instruments of the kind made in London. To a limited extent, however, their needs were met by almanacs which provided cut-out figures of quadrants and astrolabes, needing only to be threaded and pasted to a board, and accompanied by detailed instructions on their use. Leonard Digges's *Prognostication* contained descriptions of how to make and use a simple dial, quadrant and square. Askham devoted much of his edition for 1556 to 'the declaration of the horse rod, the shadow and parts of the horse rod or staff, whereby is known all times of day and also the height of castles, towers, trees and steeples', with pages of tables collating the time with the length of the shadows. A number of Stuart compilers gave advice on instruments and dials, *White* adding for variety instructions on how to set up a ceiling dial.[125]

As in the case of astronomy, almanacs contained too a great quantity of much more mundane information on mathematics. Lists of weights and measures, ready reckoners and tables of simple interest were probably far closer to the needs of most readers than the tables of square and cube roots provided by Humphrey Daniel. An early Elizabethan almanac set out data in tabulated form, recognizing that 'every man is not skilful to multiply and divide'.[126] Daniel Browne offered tuition in geometry and higher arithmetic but also in the prosaic arts of 'keeping of a shop-book, by debtor and creditor'. Accounts and indeed any elementary calculations were a formidable problem for most people at a time when Roman numerals were still in general use. Often they would be tackled with an abacus rather than pen and paper, a point echoed in Chamberlain's almanac for 1631, which offered tuition in accounting, 'either with pen or counters'. Vaux offered rules for calculating expenses 'without either pen or counters'.[127] Several early Stuart almanacs set out the Arabic and Roman numerals side by side, and this, with the compilers' own use of the Arabic system, must have done something to assist a change at the popular level, without which mass numeracy was impossible.[128] The material contained in the almanacs, and the services they advertised, are a striking indication of the expansion of elementary mathematical teaching in both London and the provinces in the seventeenth century, outside the framework of the formal educational system. By the eighteenth century the almanacs of John Tipper and others were setting out mathematical problems at a far more advanced level for their readers, with solutions provided in the following edition.[129]

From an early date the astronomical and mathematical data provided in almanacs were linked with the problems of navigation. The pioneering role of almanacs in this field has long been recognized, and has been explored in some detail. As early as 1541 the English edition of Laet's almanac contained tide-tables for London, Sandwich and Bristol. Leonard and Thomas Digges were in the vanguard of the movement to harness mathematics to navigation. By the late 1560s almanacs regularly supplied information on tides. Thus a perpetual almanac published in 1566 gave tables for the tides in over thirty harbours throughout the British Isles and the Channel. Hubrigh's edition for 1569 supplied notes to assist coastal navigation from Portland Bill to Berwick, giving notable landmarks, locations of dangerous shoals and so on. Tide-tables became a standard feature, mostly for the Thames but quite often for other areas; George Osborne of Hull set out tables for the Humber.[130] The most important contribution was by the Elizabethan, William Bourne, who in a series of almanacs and related works, beginning in 1567, provided the first English guide to ocean-going navigation, explaining tides, the use of the compass, longitude, soundings, and navigation by the stars.[131] After his death similar information was published in John Tapp's *The Seamans Kalender*, which first appeared in 1602 and was continued for many years under the editorship of Henry Bond and Henry Phillippes. Both Bond and Phillippes were experts on the problems of compass-variation and tidal prediction, and their papers and studies were followed closely by the Royal Society.[132] The heavy and continuing demand for nautical almanacs is indicated by the publication of a number of similar works, by Timothy Gadbury, Colson, and the pseudonymous 'Seaman' and 'Waterman'.[133]

The compilers of nautical almanacs were in general little interested in astrological prophecies; Bourne was indeed openly sceptical.[134] Among the compilers of more conventional almanacs, John Gadbury showed the greatest interest in nautical affairs, and compiled a monograph indicating the value of astrology to them. The celebrated captains, Owen Cox and Sir Frescheville Holles, were among his clients.[135] Gadbury was a champion of English settlement in the West Indies, and had also a strong interest in attempts to find a northern route to the Far East. In his edition for 1703 he reviewed the history of northern exploration, drawing on the writings of Dee and Edward Gresham, among others, and on a paper presented to the Royal Society by Joseph Moxon a generation earlier. A northern passage was perfectly feasible, he argued, claiming the support of John Goad, but only at the right astrological moment. When all the planets were united in a northern sign, there would be open water at the Pole. Thus, if a voyage had been attempted in 1686, Goad had reasoned, it would have been successful.[136] Gadbury returned to the theme two years later, noting evidence from a French voyage in 1703, and listing as his heroes Columbus, Dee, Campanella and Goad, for their practical and theoretical contributions.[137]

Gadbury's interest was exceptional, but most Stuart almanacs had a few geographical notes. Some, aimed at the general reader, listed the continents and the major countries in each, or the seven climates into which the world was, rather arbitrarily, divided. More enterprisingly, Anthony Askham in 1555 gave a detailed account of the sun's position, month by month, throughout the year. Thus 'in January the sun riseth over the east coast of Africa, over a place called Rio de Saint Vincent, and at noon the sun goeth over the Indish Ocean sea, near vii isles called Formosa, and setteth at the coast of America in Brazil, and at midnight the sun goeth over the Moluccas Islands.' Other authors looked towards seamen, more or less seriously, and gave the bearing and distance of leading cities and other places throughout the world. Dade's edition for 1589 mentioned Brazil and Calcutta, and Bretnor included Bermuda, Virginia and Greenland.[138] For many years, however, new discoveries jostled uneasily with ancient learning, and Moscow and Calcutta appeared alongside Babylon and the Lakes of Sodom. The Chinese city, Quinzay (Hangchow), described by Marco Polo, was generally noted as 'the greatest city in the world', though with differences of almost two thousand miles on the question of its location.[139] In the second half of the seventeenth century *White* provided its readers each year with a crude map of England, showing the county boundaries.

Of all the utilitarian aspects of astrology covered by the almanac, weather predictions probably aroused the widest and most immediate interest, despite a long history of ridicule. Attempts to reform this branch of the subject have already been mentioned, and it remained a standard feature into the eighteenth century. The author of *The Royal Almanack* remarked loftily in 1676 that 'instead of giving foolish guesses of the weather hap-hazard, I shall acquaint you with that excellent instrument the Baroscope, long since known to the Royal Society.' Most astrologers, however, did not regard the barometer and meteorological astrology as incompatible.[140] Some compilers supplemented astrological rules with others derived from animal-and bird-behaviour, or the shape of clouds and similar phenomena.[141] Others also inserted traditional lore based on saints' and other significant days, of which the popular belief concerning St. Swithin's Day is a survivor. 'If it be fair three Sundays before S. James's day' (25th July), reported John Wyberd, 'some say . . . corn will be good; but being wet, corn withereth.' Similarly, if leaves were still on the trees in late October, 'some say, it portends a cold winter, or many caterpillars'.[142] Much of this lore sprang from folk tradition, but some was drawn from classical antiquity, and compilers cited Pliny, Vergil and others to prove its respectability.[143] To a godly mind, all such beliefs were pagan falsehoods, blaspheming God who had made all days equally good. Allestree offered instead a list of maxims on the weather based on the appearance of the sky and drawn from the Bible.[144] Many later compilers were sceptical of day-lore as merely an ignorant superstition, but a few attempted valiantly to adapt such concepts to meet the more rigorous demands of the age by supplying a scientific defence. Thus *Dove* in 1653 listed a number of omens, including the fact that oak-apples full of worms, flies or spiders signified respectively dearth, wars and plague. 'Some perhaps may think this to be but a superstitious observation', remarked the compiler. But he believed such critics to be '. . . simple and foolish not to know that this proceedeth from the constitution of the air; which (whether wholesome or unwholesome) appeareth more subtly in such things as these, than to the sense of man it either doth or can. And if the air be corrupted, putrefaction abounds, things growing are blasted, the humours altered, blood corrupted, and diseases equivalent produced, as also the mind of man inclined to such and such actions as agree thereunto.' *Dove* was seeking to convince by reason rather than experiment, but given his traditional premiss, the argument was by no means absurd.[145]

(iii) Medicine and Magic

The last and perhaps the most important application of astrology lay in the field of medicine.[146] Traditional medical theory and practice depended heavily on astrological assumptions, especially the belief that the four humours of the body corresponded to, and were influenced by, the qualities of the planets and the signs of the zodiac. Different parts of the body were governed by particular signs, explained in most Tudor and Stuart almanacs by an illustration of the 'zodiacal man'. Illness was seen as a disturbance of the humoral balance, to be cured by restoring the equilibrium, which naturally required a close study of the state of the heavens. Most leading Tudor physicians accepted the importance of astrology, whatever their practical knowledge. Richard Forster, almanac-maker, was president of the Royal College of Physicians in the early seventeenth century. A few years previously, the notorious astrologer, Simon Forman, had been condemned as an impostor by the College, not for practising astrological medicine, but because the Queen's physician found him ignorant of its rules.[147]

Throughout the period, most almanacs provided detailed advice on the best times ('elections') for a physician to bleed or operate on his patient, or administer a purge or vomit. Gabriel Frende provided an unusual anatomical figure, showing the veins commonly used in phlebotomy, with a note to inform the surgeon that 'this figure is prefixed, thy hand to guide.' Astrologers regularly stressed the need to adhere to the rules. Astrology was essential for the physician, said Pond, adding the testimony of the influential Tudor physician (and almanac-maker) William Bulleine. Adding further force to the warning, Bretnor and later Gadbury declared that to give the right medicine at the wrong time would kill the patient. Blagrave agreed: a purge administered at the wrong astrological time would act instead as a vomit, and vice versa.[148] In setting out these rules, almanacs were supplying a large number of provincial and amateur physicians with the rudiments of astrological medicine, to which they had earlier probably paid little more than lip-service. A prominent critic in the mid-seventeenth century complained that the reader, armed with the rules by an almanac, was all too scrupulous in observing them.[149]

A considerable proportion of Tudor and Stuart almanac-makers were themselves practising astrological physicians. Their almanacs and medical tracts were an important form of self-advertisement. Many, such as John Partridge, Woodward and especially Salmon, took the opportunity to praise their patent medicines and pills. Almanacs were also used to advertise the standard proprietary remedies of the time, notably Buckworth's lozenges and Bateman's 'famous' spirit of scurvy-grass. The medical notes contained in almanacs amounted also to a sustained attack on the monopoly of the élitist College of Physicians and on the secrecy and exclusiveness of the medical profession. This aim was often explicit. Nicholas Culpeper was indeed the standard-bearer of the campaign to throw open all medical secrets. His celebrated herbal, *The English Physician* (1652), was 'an astrologo-physical discourse', designed as 'a complete method of physic, whereby a man may preserve his body in health, or cure himself, being sick, for three pence charge, with such things only as grow in England.'[150] Lilly's *Christian Astrology*, published a few years earlier, had already provided a detailed account of the principles of astrological medicine, and there followed a stream of popular handbooks, including works by the almanac-makers, Andrews, Coelson, Blagrave, Saunders and Tanner. The enterprising William Salmon issued an encyclopaedic herbal in twice-weekly instalments, amounting to seven hundred and fifty pages. [151]

The limited space of the almanac made it difficult to do much more than tabulate rules on when to administer medicines, but some compilers included also a brief section on the medicines themselves. The pioneering *Kalender of Shepherdes* had contained information on things good and bad for various parts of the body, a feature continued in several later series.[152] The Elizabethan astrologer, John Securis, listed a number of safe herbs in his almanac, and John Vaux assured readers that

> No metal, shrub, nor simple is
> On earth, but used may be.

John Swan's *Speculum Mundi* (1635) contained a long medico-herbal section, drawn from Galen, Pliny and other classical authors, much of which was summarized in his later almanacs.[153] Gadbury's medical interests led him to write a tract on the astrological causes and character of the Great Plague of 1665. He assured readers that it was not infectious, though his assertion that no plague could last more than four years must have been a doubtful solace.[154] Brief herbal sections became a common feature of Stuart almanacs. The information was obviously derivative, and not always of practical value. Thus Allestree's prescription of camel's milk to cure consumption was hardly more realistic for most readers than the contemporary medicine which required the yolk of a phoenix's egg.[155] But many compilers did show a keen awareness of their readers' situation. Beridge, for example, listed only cheap and plentiful herbs, which he described as freely available to those who could not afford medical fees. (The patient might be obliged, however, to live with unwanted side-effects. The boiled leaves of the blackberry cured the itch, *Pond* reported, but dyed the hair black.[156])

Throughout the seventeenth century almanacs ensured that knowledge of astrological medicine was more widely accessible than ever before, ironically at a time when it was already declining in respectability at the higher levels of the profession. Culpeper's delight at finding some residual traces of astrological practices in the official

Pharmacopeia of the College of Physicians—' who dares affirm that our Collegiates are no astrologers?'—was a tacit admission of their obsolescence.[157] But at a popular level it is likely that the sheer volume of propaganda in almanacs, manuals and handbills outweighed the effects of criticism. Even at the higher levels the decline was neither rapid nor complete. Traces survived in the practice of William Harvey, who prescribed a mixture to be taken 'every new and full moon'.[158] Gadbury pointed out that the standard Continental authorities, Sennertius and Riverius, supported astrological medicine.[159] English astrological physicians were by no means confined to the back alleys, nor despised by all members of the medical élite. William Ramesey was for a time a physician to Charles II. Gadbury and Partridge obtained the title (though perhaps nothing more) of physician to Queen Katherine and Queen Mary II respectively.[160] Sir Thomas Browne admired Lilly, and was himself said to be skilful in the theory and practice of astrological medicine. Robert Wittie, a noted medical reformer, praised Lilly as above 'all others whatsoever, ancient or modern'.[161] Gadbury's friend Sir Richard Barker, physician to Charles II, by whom he was knighted, was hailed as one who had done much to revive astrological medicine. Scarburgh, another royal physician, had astrological interests, as mentioned above. Sir Francis Prujean, president of the College, was noted as an admirer of the Italian astrologer, Cardan.[162] John Brown, surgeon to Charles II, was a patron of Henry Coley, and Thomas Gardiner, surgeon to the household of William III, was a patron of John Partridge.[163] Many more prominent physicians and surgeons, among them several Fellows of the College, practised astrological medicine or were friends of astrologers. Dr. Thomas Wharton requested an astrological calculation to assess his chances of election to the College.[164] Francis Bernard, physician to James II, calculated many nativities and was earlier an enthusiastic disciple of William Lilly, who he thought 'gave the first life to astrology in this nation'.[165] The application of astrology to medicine was rooted in tradition and in humoral pathology. It escaped much of the obloquy heaped on judicial astrology. The idea of some kind of astral influence, especially that of the moon, proved tenacious. When Robert Hooke informed the Royal Society of a man with a hole in his head, whose brain visibly grew turgid at a full moon and flaccid at a new, the Society responded by ordering a detailed investigation. Similar beliefs were held by Richard Mead, an eminent physician in early eighteenth-century London. At a humbler level, it remained possible for astrological physicians to obtain licences to practise throughout the eighteenth century, and a popular belief in the influence of the moon on the human body survived down to the twentieth century.[166]

Traditional medicine was itself under attack in this period from the disciples of Paracelsus, the sixteenth-century German chemist and physician who (to over-simplify) replaced the four humours with the three 'principles' of sulphur, mercury and salt. He argued that illness sprang from the disorder of particular organs, to be remedied by specific, chemically-based medicines. This doctrine of therapy was part of a vaster concept of chemical transformation involving the regeneration of mankind and the 'divine alchemy' of the creation.[167] Paracelsian ideas were given a cool reception by the English medical establishment. 'I am sure', remarked a prominent Caroline physician, that 'no learned and honest man will approve of such an illiterate man as Paracelsus was', a 'conjuror' and 'magician'.[168] Modern writers, more sympathetic, have found value in the new therapeutic teachings and in the attack on the Galenic tradition.

From an early date a number of almanac-makers showed interest in at least the therapeutic aspects of Paracelsian thought. William Bulleine in 1562 made one of the first English references to it. Thomas Hill, Bretnor and Parkhurst translated or published works on chemical medicine; that by Parkhurst contained a complimentary poem from his friend, Lilly.[169] John Evans, who was Lilly's tutor, practised the new medicine and published an account of his wonder-working distillation from gold, *aurum potabile,* and the antimonial cup in which it was produced. He offered a month's free trial to prospective patients, and became sufficiently notorious to arouse the hostility of Archbishop Laud and the College of Physicians.[170] Both Lilly and Booker were friends of the Hungarian alchemist, Hunniades, who distilled antimonial medicines. Booker was said to be skilled in the use of the antimonial cup, though he did not practise publicly.[171] Nicholas Culpeper was a well-known advocate and practitioner who produced his own *aurum potabile* and was dubbed, after his death, 'our British Paracelsus'.[172] He had many successors: Gadbury, for example, championed both Paracelsian and traditional methods, while Baston and Coelson used their almanacs to advertise their practice of Paracelsian techniques.[173]

Astrological medicine was a natural corollary of traditional views of the cosmos. Man was thought to be placed on earth at the centre of God's universe, and the various parts of his body corresponded with the greater world and were subject to its influence.[174] As scientific practitioners, many astrologers were drawn to the new mechanical world-picture gradually emerging. But the old cosmology, with its relationship between the universe or macrocosm and the microcosm of man, was at the very heart of astrology, and proved inevitably tenacious. There were frequent echoes of the old order, as in John Booker's prophecy for 1637, that the stars would 'alterations cause i'the microcosm, as likewise wonders in the macrocosm'. Similar ideas appeared throughout the century. Thus for 1684 Henry Hill offered the gloomy prospect of 'storms in the Archetype, between Jesus Christ and Belial; in the Intelligible world, between good and bad angels; storms in the Elementary world: unheard of winds and floods; in the Microcosm, the heart and brains being at odds; and in the habitable world, between good and bad men'.[175] Several authors attempted to harness the new science to defend older assumptions. Coelson argued plausibly that gravity was a conclusive proof of the influence of the macrocosm on the microcosm. *Swallow* used a biological analogy to illustrate how the sun's heat and moon's coolness kept the earth in a temperate balance, claiming that similarly the human body would 'wither and languish away by the excessive heat of the heart', the bodily sun, but for the refreshing effect of the 'pericardium and refocillation of the lights which are next to it'.[176]

The mechanical philosophy made steady progress in seventeenth-century almanacs, but a certain ambivalence is apparent: writers endorsed the new science, but clung to some aspects of the older cosmology. Their comments sometimes reflected too the Renaissance world of natural magic and occult forces. John Dee, the most important English representative of that world, provided a link to the world of practical mathematics. Edward Gresham, an admirer of Dee, compiled a *'canon horarum magicarum'*. John Harvey distinguished between necromancy and natural magic (the magical properties inherent in all matter), and criticized those who confused 'the black arts of the devil, and the fair gifts of God'. A similar distinction was perhaps implicit in Arthur Hopton's promise that

> Of pyromancy I not speak,
> Ne geomantic spells,
> As do adjure such demons up
> As in our centre dwells.[177]

William Lilly showed less restraint. His attempt to find buried treasure beneath Westminster Abbey was interrupted, he tells us, by demons who stirred up a wind so 'fierce . . . that we verily believed the west-end of the church would have fallen upon us', till Lilly 'gave directions and command to dismiss the demons'.[178] Several astrologers showed interest in the sympathetic powder of Sir Kenelm Digby (allegedly able to cure at a distance), and Neve and Blagrave provided formulae for its preparation.[179] Nathaniel Nye's expertise in optics included the ability 'to represent the faces of several persons in a glass, they not being present'. Saunders and Wharton published works on palmistry, Gadbury quoted with approval from the Hermetic 'divine Pimander', and Booker and Tanner were (among others) adepts in the occult significance of numbers. Blagrave explained that 'every planet doth own certain numbers', a doctrine he had adopted from Cornelius Agrippa.[180] At the very end of the period, the surveyor John Wing noted that the heliocentric universe had been known to Pythagoras, and felt it was Very probable that Pythagoras . . . had the whole philosophic cabala of the creation communicated to him by some knowing priest or philosopher in the oriental part'. [181]

At a lower level, other almanacs set out doctrines which owed less to Renaissance magic than to popular superstition, or to magical systems long forgotten. For example, divination by the day of the week on which it thundered or on which New Year's Day fell was quite common, and the rules were set out in Digges's prestigious *Prognostication* (though with the author's rider that the 'ground I see not'). Lore of this kind formed the basis of such compilations as *Erra Pater*.[182] The common lists of good and evil days also fall into this category. Their ancient origins had long since been forgotten. Some astrologers created a new rationale, explaining them as days propitious or otherwise for such activities as phlebotomy, according to astrological science. The French astrologer, Himbert de Billy, claimed that they had been told by an angel to Joseph or Job. Usually they were listed without any explanation, and at the popular level they were simply a part of the superstition of luck. The nadir is reached in John Wilson's play, *The Cheats,* where a character is informed that, 'your good days are Monday, Wednesday and Friday—your evil, Tuesday, Thursday and Saturday.'[183] The editor of *Allestree* supplied a worthless formula for telling the time, by picking up objects from the ground at random. If the object was vegetable, the time was one, four, seven or ten o'clock; if mineral, two, five, eight or eleven; if animate but dead, for example a stick, three, six, nine or twelve. Langley provided rules for judging personality from the colour of finger-nails.[184] Classical and popular traditions were mixed in recommendations that, for example, owls, bats or cats should be fastened to stakes in the corners of a field as a protection against hail or storms. A buried toad, or sprigs of holly and ivy, would protect crops against lightning. A magpie, dissected alive, was good for gout if applied to the affected part of the body. Some of these beliefs rested on a concept of correspondence, obvious in the idea that wolves' teeth strung round a child's neck were 'good against frightening', and that bat's blood would enable a person to see as well by night as by day (which, commented a sceptical compiler, 'may well be true with them that cannot see at all').[185] One compiler described astrological sigils which would give protection against fleas, ghosts, robbers and witches.[186]

This material is a reminder that the mental climate of at least some of the almanacs contained elements which now appear crude and primitive. The credulity is put into perspective by the fact that the official handbook of the College of Physicians accepted the healing properties of the head of a black cat, well-baked, and of a powdered human skull, taken from a fresh corpse. Mrs. Tillotson, wife of the future archbishop, told Hooke that 'the moss of a man's skull' was 'a sovereign remedy for the falling sickness'. Sir Christopher Wren was proud of having cured his unfortunate wife of thrush 'by hanging a bag of live boglice about her neck'.[187] Much of the traditional lore was, moreover, denounced by the more reputable astrologers. Others, as in the examples cited above, made their scepticism clear. Many ridiculed weather forecasts based on saints' days, and the belief in good and evil days.[188] John Gadbury was anxious to protect scientific astrology by distinguishing it from all other forms of prophecy and divination with which it was popularly associated. 'It is by reason of the apocryphal part of astrology', he declared, 'that the sound part so extremely suffers.' Thus, astrological sigils were a mere cheat. Blagrave was a fraud in claiming that astrology provided a cure for witchcraft and in prescribing a weapon-salve, the existence of which Gadbury denied. Similarly Lilly had done a disservice to astrology by publishing the prophecies of Mother Shipton, Merlin, the Dreadful Dead-man and the 'crack-brained Sibyls', all of which Gadbury thought 'fit only for laughter'.[189] Quite often the astrologers published popular beliefs merely as curiosities, or in order to ridicule them. Thus Vaux reported the belief that will o'the wisps were 'souls tormented in the fire of purgatory'. Blagrave noted a popular delusion that scrofula was called the 'King's Evil' not with reference to royal powers of healing, but because the king was thought to cause the disease.[190] 'Bickerstaff's' almanac for 1710 developed Jonathan Swift's mockery of astrology into a general assault on popular superstitions of all kinds. The Welsh still 'put live coals in a sieve when they brew,' the author claimed, 'to keep the witch out of the drink'. And, in every English county, people put 'a platter in the kettle when they boil hog's puddings, to preserve them against enchantment'.[191]

The growth of a critical, scientific attitude was naturally gradual. Even Gadbury published a work, admittedly early and obviously propagandist, on the subject of omens and prodigies, which included an account of the king's headless body hovering in the air at Whitehall in 1649.[192] Almanacs thus reflected both the new, mechanical view and older views of the world, in varying proportions. William Lilly tried to raise spirits but also read the *Transactions* of the Royal Society. Nathaniel Culpepper set scientific explanations of storms alongside the opinion that they might be caused by 'wicked, condemned spirits'. Accounts of apparitions, battles of birds or armies in the sky remained quite common to the end of the period.[193] Compilers often seemed reluctant to admit that natural and supernatural explanations were incompatible. William Andrews conceded that thunderclaps generally had a natural cause, but claimed that sometimes they 'proceed from supernatural causes', when God wishes 'to let us know that he is angry'.[194] Arthur Hopton, who belonged to the most distinguished group of Jacobean mathematicians, described the apparition of a fiery dragon seen in the sky in Shropshire in May 1609. He was sure that it had a natural cause, in vapours drawn up from the earth, and thought the possibility of such a precise shape was proved by a German precedent when an image had appeared of the Emperor Charles V, so realistic'that the beholders put off their hats, thinking it was the emperor himself. As a champion of the new science, Hopton thought it might be possible to produce such apparitions 'artificially . . . by certain glasses and instruments according to the art *Catoprice,* of which a little credit may be won by these homely perspectives, commonly to be sold in London'. But equally he had no doubt that the dragon was an omen sent by God to warn men of divine vengeance, if they failed to repent.[195] This overlapping of two essentially contradictory intellectual worlds is also evident in the almanacs of Thomas Langley. He described at length the dire significance of a rain of wheat, blood or frogs, but was anxious to provide some kind of natural explanation. The eggs of frogs, worms and fish, he concluded, were sometimes drawn up into the clouds in a hot exhalation, and there 'being in the clouds brought to form, fall down among the rain'.[196]

The ambivalence of attitudes and the direction of intellectual change are most apparent in the treatment of witchcraft. Before the civil war astrologers generally accepted its reality, and some set out rules for its diagnosis, and appropriate remedies. Blagrave and Saunders claimed that the astrologer was the only person able to relieve the victim and undo the witch's spell.[197] In refuting assertions that astrology was itself a form of witchcraft, it was customary to stress the distinctions between them, but not to deny the existence of the witch.[198]

The almanacs of the later Stuart period show however a wide range of opinions. Gadbury became more critical as time passed. He felt that astrology could be reconciled with the new science, but that witchcraft and the occult could not. Astrology was part of 'natural philosophy, and meddleth not with things preternatural, as witchcraft must needs be'. While it might be 'against reason and religion' to deny witchcraft absolutely, he thought that commonly 'lewd physicians . . . term those diseases witchcraft that they cannot have the success and honour of a speedy cure by.' Indeed he claimed never to have encountered a case of suspected witchcraft 'whose original I could not reduce to a natural astrological cause'.[199] Henry Coley argued similarly that the effects popularly ascribed to a witch were really produced by the planets, acting 'by a magnetical sympathy or antipathy in the actives and passives of nature'.[200] These explanations may seem as benighted as the ones they sought to replace; but there is a crucial difference, in the astrologers' determination to prove that the phenomenon had purely natural causes. William Ramesey displayed a far more uncertain attitude. He was adamant that witches existed. This was proved, he claimed, by the Bible, by the hundreds of convictions in the English courts, and by his first-hand experience, when he had heard nine Scottish witches confess their guilt before they were burned together in 1644. Yet he was willing to concede the near-impossibility of establishing certainty in any particular case: 'swimming' a witch was mere superstition, confessions under torture were untrustworthy, and even voluntary confessions were often prompted by melancholy or delusions. Ramesey thus accepted the arguments being used to question traditional beliefs, but felt unable to adopt the conclusion towards which they pointed.[201]

Discussion of the issue in early eighteenth-century almanacs showed still more clearly the direction in which opinion was moving. John Partridge, citing the critical works of Weyer and Webster, argued that most witches were 'notorious impostors, or else poor deluded creatures'. Moore's almanac, hardly in the vanguard of intellectual progress, carried an 'Essay towards proving that old women are no witches'. The compiler argued that the whole concept of witchcraft was 'a barbarous conceit', and that the alleged proofs contained in *Malleus Maleficarum* were 'false and fabulous'.[202]

Joseph Glanvill, the Cambridge Platonist, defended belief in witches partly through fear that the current of scepticism would go on, after dismissing witchcraft, to erode all belief in the supernatural and would eventually destroy Christianity itself.[203] By contrast, Gadbury and other leading astrologers joined in the work of destroying other branches of supernatural explanation and divination, in order to create a pure astrology, freed from superstition. Their efforts did much to popularize and publicize the new science, but also, by a fatal irony, helped to destroy the assumptions on which astrology itself was based.

CHAPTER SEVEN

History and Literature

(i) History

One of the most common features of the Stuart almanac was the 'chronology' or brief history of the world. Notes of this kind had occasionally appeared in mediaeval almanacs, but Tudor compilers generally provided no more than the number of years which had elapsed since the Creation and the birth of Christ. A precursor of later developments was Thomas Porter, whose edition for 1585 listed the dates of the invasions of England from the legendary Brute (or Brutus) to the Normans, and of the foundation of several cities.[1] The chronological section appeared in the first years of the seventeenth century, and rapidly became an almost universal feature.[2] The standard format was a list of major events, with the number of years to have elapsed; for example, 'Since the Great Armada . . . 70.' The list commonly ran to one or two sides, but in some more ambitious works, such as *Perkins,* it extended to eight, and formed the major part of the prognostication.

The modern reader may be shocked—or perhaps reassured—at the idea of reducing the whole of the world's history to one page of compressed plagiarism. Nevertheless, for many readers the almanac was probably their only source of instruction. It would be supplemented, of course, by oral tradition, and by ballads; John Aubrey recalled that in his childhood his 'nurse had the history from the Conquest down to Charles I in ballad'.[3] For all its obvious limitations, the history provided by almanacs was better than this. It was not dominated, as were ballads, by kings, knights and battles. Moreover it was linked, however tenuously, to the work of professional historians. The compiler, regarding history as both 'delightful and profitable', set out to summarize a mass of chronicles 'into this portable volume, for the advantage of such as cannot purchase great books'. Historical works, written in English, had been very popular with the Elizabethan book-buying public. The astrologers continued the tradition and extended it to reach a far wider audience.[4] Some listed their sources, which included most of the standard sixteenth-century chronicles, by Lanquet, Grafton, Holinshed, Stow (and his continuator, Howes), and the prolific German compiler, Seth Calvisius. The names of Plutarch, Geoffrey of Monmouth, Polydore Vergil, Sleidan and Scaliger appeared also, though less often. It must be admitted, however, that often the most important source was the chronology contained in some earlier edition. Indeed printers often used old copy year after year, a device which became transparent when the list of events ended twenty years or more before the date of the almanac. *Neve* for 1666, for example, recorded no events after 1648; *Pond* for 1667 ended with the Spanish Armada.

With a total of many hundred chronologies, the range of topics covered was naturally enormous. The overall shape of the section, however, remained broadly constant. The chronology almost always began with the date of the creation, and often a short list of biblical events taken from the Old Testament. This was interspersed with events from the legendary history of pre-Roman Britain, derived indirectly from the imaginative history of Geoffrey of Monmouth. Christ and Caesar were generally mentioned, and William the Conqueror almost invariably—the Norman Conquest was, then as now, the best-known event in English history. Mediaeval references usually included the invention of guns and printing, and quite often famous victories, such as Agincourt. In more recent times, the Northern Rising of 1569, the Spanish Armada and the Gunpowder Plot were the favourite topics, accompanied by the most important plagues, comets and the nova of 1572. As the seventeenth century progressed, the civil war, Great Plague and Fire, Popish Plot and Glorious Revolution were added to the list.

Though it was naturally impossible to develop a general philosophy of history within the format of a list of dates, the selection of items did reflect a number of clear and enduring themes. One of the most prominent was the assertion of the antiquity and pre-eminence of England. Compilers did indeed record many events from classical history and myth, from the slaying of the Minotaur and the rape of Lucrece to the exploits of Alexander and Caesar. But they were concerned primarily with the attempt to graft British antiquity on to this body of history. The key method was through the legend of Brute, believed to have led a band of refugees from the fallen city of Troy and to have founded a new civilization in Britain. Similar theories had emerged to provide desirably ancient pedigrees for most of the states of

Europe; it was a natural consequence of growing national consciousness and self-assertiveness. The story of Brute owed most to Geoffrey of Monmouth, and some of Geoffrey's wealth of circumstantial detail survived in the almanacs. Most compilers mentioned the fall of Troy, Brute's arrival in England (c. 1100 B.C.), and the foundation of London in the same year.[5] Many recorded the names of his more eminent successors, such as Bladud, Memprick and King Lear; a few listed all the legendary kings of England from Brute to the Saxons.[6] England was thus provided with a history stretching back far beyond the foundation of the Roman Empire. The dates when Rome and London were founded often appeared side by side to stress the centuries of seniority enjoyed by the Londoners.[7] Similarly fanciful dates were given for the foundation of many other English towns, taken from Stow or one of the other chroniclers, and ultimately from Geoffrey. Hence it appeared that York, Canterbury, Leicester, Bath and many more were also founded long before Rome.[8] King Alfred, the reader learned, had merely restored the University of Oxford; its foundation was the work of King Memprick, two and a half thousand years past.[9] A parvenu status was conceded for Cambridge, but even so its origin was ascribed to Sigisbert, a king of the East Angles who flourished, precociously, about 300 B.C.[10] With local pride, Vincent Wing asserted that his local market town, Stamford, was the site of an ancient university, founded by Bladud and flourishing until the arrival of St. Augustine.[11] A number of heroes from other traditional legends appeared also, boosting the general aura of heroic antiquity; King Arthur and Guy of Warwick were by far the most popular.[12]

The Brute legend was necessary to disguise the insignificance and barbarity of England in antiquity. The same problem applied to its religious origins. Once again later historians, patriotic and credulous, provided a more edifying account, which duly appeared in a multitude of almanacs: the story of the visit of Joseph of Arimathea to England in A.D. 63, and the account of King Lucius, reputed to have reigned about A.D. 180, and to have been the first Christian king in Europe.[13] A perpetual calendar issued in 1577 pushed the story back still further. The author alleged, drawing indirectly on the work of Bishop Bale, that England had first been inhabited by Samothes, grandson of Noah, two hundred years after the Flood. 'Their religion was good', the compiler noted, 'for they learned it of Noah.' In his eyes, the later conquests by Albion and Brute were regrettable descents into paganism.[14]

The patriotic strain was equally apparent in the treatment of later events. Almost every almanac mentioned the defeat of the Spanish Armada, and Elizabeth's rousing speech at Tilbury; the story was embellished by Pigot, who supplied detailed information on the strength of the Armada and the number of guns carried.[15] The importance of the Armada arguably justified the degree of attention given to it. But the current of patriotism was equally evident in the treatment of the reign of Henry VIII, with much less rationale. References to Wolsey or Thomas Cromwell were rare: the event which captured the imagination was Henry's seizure of Boulogne from the French in 1544, an incident which was given the same degree of prominence as the Norman Conquest or the Armada campaign. Some compilers indeed regarded the capture of Boulogne as the first event worth recording after the arrival of the Normans.[16] (The Jacobean poet, Samuel Rowlands, incidentally noted the popular belief that the 'good old days' referred to the time before Henry's expedition to Boulogne.[17]) Similarly many almanacs stressed the victories of the English over their neighbours: Athelstan's victories against the Scots and Welsh, the conquest of Ireland by Henry II, the triumphs of Edward III and Henry V against the French, and Drake's exploits at Cadiz.[18] After the Restoration, compilers denounced Oliver Cromwell but recalled with pride his victories over the Dutch (avenging the massacre at Amboyna) and the Spanish.[19] References to major rebellions and plots served as a reminder of the defeat of the king's enemies at home as well as abroad. Wat Tyler, Robert Kett, the northern earls and the Gunpowder plotters appeared regularly. The London riots against German merchants on 'Evil May-Day' in 1517 were also frequently mentioned, and the career of the self-appointed Elizabethan Messiah, William Hacket, was still being cited in the early eighteenth century.[20]

From the time of the civil wars, history became far more partisan in tone. John Heyman, a Parliamentarian, included references to the 'wretched' Duke of Buckingham, the abolition of the House of Lords as 'out of date', and the creation of a 'Free State' in England.[21] From the opposite camp, George Wharton commemorated 'brave' Buckingham, 'learned' Strafford and the day when 'Reverend Laud triumphed o'er the axe'. During the 1650s he recorded each year the anniversaries of Royalists killed and executed during and after the wars. There was, he claimed,'a pleasure in misery itself, but the purpose was clearly to dissuade Royalists from coming to terms with the new government by making them 'reflect on the exquisite cruelties, unheard of rapine and bloodshed' committed by their enemies in bygone years.[22] But there were also non-political compilers who surpassed the achievements of any modern 'official' historians by failing to mention Charles I or Cromwell, in some cases omitting any reference to the civil wars whatsoever.[23]

Radicals during the English Revolution found a valuable propaganda tool in the theory of the Norman Yoke, the idea that an egalitarian order in Saxon England had been crushed by the Normans. The idea appeared in a number of parliamentarian almanacs and other astrological writings.[24] A successful foreign invasion raised the question of the legitimacy of the political order descended from it, and was an obvious affront to the Brute legend, and to national pride. The Elizabethan, Thomas Porter, listed the conquests from Brute to the Normans and remarked that they had all 'prevailed by treason, or else if this country had joined together, they might have shaken their ears'.[25] Compilers explored several ways of circumventing the harsh implications of the Conquest. Most commonly they cited the marriage of Henry I to Matilda, of the Saxon royal house, and claimed that the succession in 1154 of their grandson, Henry II, marked the restoration of the Saxon line. 'Maud [Matilda] the English-Saxon blood restored', claimed Wharton. In the second half of the century, the tables of kings usually had a break at 1154, with the heading 'Saxon line restored'. Continuity was thus achieved.[26] This formula offered one argument to critics of the Norman Yoke theory. Another was implicit in Porter's earlier denunciation of all the ancient conquests, as bringing successive tyrannies. The idea was kept alive by Saunders, who lamented the 'Roman, Saxon, Dane and Norman Yoke'.[27] Another refutation was provided by *White*, which annually (from before the civil war) published a verse praising the Normans and reducing the Saxons to merely one of a long stream of earlier invaders. Only the 'noble Normans' had been able to hold on to their conquests, and pass them down in unbroken succession, 'such stout victorious kings of them have reigned'.[28] After the Revolution, Trigge made a direct onslaught on the myth of a golden age of Saxon equality, carefully tabulating the sharp divisions in pre-Conquest society. He cast the Normans in the novel role of liberators, rescuing the English from the 'Danish tyranny' which had '400 years miserably wasted the English nation'. Robin Hood, by tradition a popular champion against Norman oppression, now appeared as a mere renegade who 'greatly molested the highways'.[29]

The events of the Revolution provided a rich mine of propaganda material for later partisan astrologers. Partridge, a Whig, offered a heavily-slanted chronology commemorating Charles I, who levied ship-money and gaoled gentlemen for not paying forced loans, Laud, executed for 'bringing in popery', and the great victory of Naseby which had been 'fatal to the then Tories and Papists'. By contrast, George Parker venerated the memory of 'pious' Laud, and deplored the execution of Strafford merely 'to please the people'.[30] In due course the dramatic events from the Popish Plot to the victory of William of Orange were fitted into similarly partisan accounts.

Politics formed by no means the only major theme. Religious history, in a variety of aspects, was equally prominent. The date of the world's creation, with which almost every list began, was calculated from biblical chronology. Scholars differed over the precise year, but most of the dates offered by the almanacs fell within the traditional range, mostly between 3900 B.C. and 4030 B.C., the most popular being 3949 and around 4000. It was one of the few occasions when compilers needed to exercise some historical judgement. John Rudston boldly declared his preference for the calculations of Calvisius, who, 'as he is the last, so he hath come nearer the truth than those before him; confirming it as well by celestial observations'.[31] But many contrived to avoid a decision by providing, without comment, a number of dates, with the sponsors of each.[32] Once past the Creation, the chronologies launched into Old Testament history. *Perkins* began purposefully with the creation of Adam in *Anno Mundl* 0001, and moved on to the stories of Abraham, David, Sodom and Gomorrah and much else.[33]

In the seventeenth century, the power of the Ottoman Empire was still a stark reminder of the strength of Islam. Turks and Muslims were regarded as virtually synonymous. Many compilers recorded the date when 'the grand Impostor Mahomet' 'reared up Turkism'.[34] Others listed the Saracen campaigns against Jerusalem, the temporary successes of the Crusaders, and its final capture by Selim the Grim in 1517, 'whereupon the Turk calleth himself the Keeper of the Christian God'.[35] There were occasional references to the Jews' expulsion from England by Edward I and, later, to their bid for readmission under Cromwell.[36] The most prominent theme in more recent religious history was naturally the Reformation. Luther's detection of 'popish falsehoods' was a standard item, and there were also numerous references to the Anabaptists and Familists.[37] But the compilers were interested primarily in English affairs, and Continental developments were mentioned usually only when there was a political aspect or a propaganda point to be made. Thus the Massacre of St. Bartholomew in 1572 appeared regularly, as did the foundation of the Jesuits' 'sect', and the 'butchery' of the Protestants of Magdeburg during the Thirty Years War. Later the massacre of Protestants in Piedmont 'by bloody tyrants' (commemorated in Milton's sonnet) joined the canon. [38] God's espousal of Protestantism was proved by what the almanacs called the 'fall of Blackfriars', the collapse of a building in which a secret Catholic service was taking place, with many casualties, in the year 1623.[39] National pride was also again clearly evident. Ranger recorded how Henry VIII had 'crushed the pope's power'. Henry Jessey urged his readers to 'honour the excellency of this island', and to consider its godly pedigree: Lucius, the first Christian king; Constantine (born in England), the first Christian emperor; Wycliffe, harbinger of the Reformation; Henry VIII, first monarch to overthrow papal power; Edward VI, the 'young Josiah' who established the true faith; and the Long Parliament, which had 'rooted up expiring prelacy'.[40] The patriotic, strongly Protestant approach remained dominant throughout the period. Towards its end, however, a minor counter-current is apparent in some high Tory and Catholic almanacs, Wharton, the cavalier, had only scorn for what he called 'Geneva trash'. Later Catholic almanacs pointed out that Henry VIII's title, 'Defender of the Faith', had been given for his defence of Catholicism against that 'apostate friar', Luther. They lamented the death of the 'excellent' Mary, Queen of Scots, and dared to allege that the Gunpowder Plot had been 'politickly contrived by Cecil'.[41]

A final major theme implicit in the chronologies (as in other parts of the almanacs) was the concept of progress and innovation. This was clearest in the history of London. Compilers regularly listed the foundation of Westminster Hall, the first Lord Mayor of London, and the first wooden and stone bridges over the Thames. In more modern times they noted the foundation of Gresham College, Sutton's Hospital, the Globe playhouse, the New River from Amwell (bringing drinking-water to the capital), the paving of Smith field, foundation of Chelsea College, and development of Moorfields.[42] In part this reflected the influence of the traditional urban chronicle, evident in much Tudor historical writing: it was natural for the city chronicler to reflect civic pride. But more was involved. No local pride explains the frequency with which such events as the development of glazing, tiling and dialling were recorded, or the introduction of parish registers or of coaches.[43]

Two of the most common entries of all were the invention of guns (often dated 1380) and of printing (usually ascribed to Gutenberg or Fust, though *Bell* remarked that printing had been known to the Chinese far earlier.)[44] The growth of English interests overseas was charted by references to the voyages of Drake and Frobisher, the settlements in Virginia and New England, the introduction of tobacco and the foundation of the East India Company.[45] A mere list of dates precludes the exposition of any specific philosophy, but the strong impression gained from scanning the lists of events is of the long and steady march of progress.[46]

Naturally, not all the events recorded fell neatly into the categories discussed above. There were many miscellaneous items, such as plagues and other diseases, comets and 'blazing stars', and human oddities such as Haddock, the 'sleeping preacher', and 'Old Parr', who died in 1635, a national celebrity, at the reputed age of 152.[47] Trigge unearthed an earlier patriarch, one Johann de Temporibus, said to have flourished in the time of King Stephen and to have reached the age of 360. His nativity, Trigge conceded, 'would puzzle a good astrologer'.[48]

There were several departures from the standard format of the chronology. One was to take a shorter period of time and cover it in greater depth. This was foreshadowed in Hopton's *Concordancy* (1614) where the author began more modestly in 1066, and provided a far more comprehensive list of events. Winter's almanacs from 1634 began the chronology in 1485 and tried to give one event for each year.[49] Towards the end of the interregnum George Wharton added a greatly expanded chronology, labelled '*Gesta Brittanorum*', covering the years since 1600 and treating the 1640s and 1650s in detail, based partly on firsthand information. This became an annual feature in his editions, and after his retirement was continued and revised for several years by his friend, Richard Saunders.[50] Later in the century, *Swan* and *Dove* provided histories from the accession of Elizabeth or from 1640 to the present.[51] The most detailed account of all was in Gadbury's 'Plot Almanac', a comprehensive survey of the upheavals following the Popish Plot. This, and the biographical data which Gadbury inserted into his later editions, made his almanacs a useful historical source, recognized and used by the antiquarian, Thomas Hearne. (Gadbury himself was a friend of the historian, Sir William Dugdale.[52]) Wharton's *Gesta* was a major source of *A Chronological History of England*, published in 1714 by John Pointer, fellow of Merton College,

Oxford.[53] Detailed histories also tended naturally to be more partisan. This was evident in the case of Wharton, and still more so near the end of the century in Partridge's almanacs for 1694–7, in which he provided a history in four instalments from the interregnum to the Glorious Revolution, contrasting the national triumphs achieved under Cromwell with the national humiliation suffered under Charles II.

Another method of presenting historical facts was to intersperse the months of the calendar with anniversaries (a method still used in Whitaker's *Almanack*). This was developed during the interregnum by Saunders, Wharton and Tanner, and was used later in the semi-official *The Royal Almanack*, by the Venetian historian Coronelli, which traced the career of William III by recording month by month anniversaries of his exploits.[54] One final variant was the regional history, stressing events in the area for which the almanac was primarily designed. Thus Vaux for many years offered a chronology of events in the north, especially Durham, Pigot did the same for Shropshire, and Balles for Norfolk.[55]

A few compilers did indicate some overall framework of history. The most common, and traditional, was the division of the past into four great world-empires (based on Daniel), with the present age identified as the last phase of the fourth, Roman Empire.[56] A division of the world into seven ages, again derived from antiquity, was also used.[57] Both implied that the world was in its last phase, a widespread belief, linked with the eschatological preoccupations discussed elsewhere.[58] Other classical concepts, such as the world's eternity or the Platonic idea of the world renewing itself and repeating its history after a grand cycle of 36,000 years, were mentioned but condemned.[59] Nevertheless, some writers were attracted to the idea of a constant flux in earthly affairs, or to the turn of Fortune's wheel. 'If we examine history and chronology,' said Henry Coley, 'we may behold the microcosm of mankind for many 100 years acting over and over again the same tragi-comedies.' He enshrined the point on the title-page of a subsequent edition: 'what is, was before us, and will be when we are no more; war follows peace, as summer follows winter, for Fortune's wheel is constantly turning, and all mankind ceases not to act the same things over and over again, which must be expected to the end.'[60] A similarly cyclical view, with a suitable moral gloss, was contained in a broadsheet almanac issued in the name of Vincent Wing in the late seventeenth century. A verse declared that

War begets poverty,
Poverty, peace.
Peace maketh riches flow
(Fate ne'er doth cease).
Riches produce pride,
Pride is war's ground,
War begets poverty, &c,
(The world goes round).

This idea had also been a commonplace in antiquity, and was still widely held. A number of very similar verses circulated in England, the Continent and even North America between the fifteenth and the end of the seventeenth centuries.[61] Other astrologers were drawn towards cyclical theories of widely differing kinds. Lilly was interested in the world's government by planetary angels in rotation, while Wharton discerned periods of change every thirty years, corresponding to the succession of generations, and an overall cycle of empires, each lasting five to seven hundred years.[62] Several compilers noted a possible correlation between conjunctions of Saturn and Jupiter, every twenty years, and outbreaks of plague. Observing that plagues had followed the conjunctions of 1603 and 1623, Richard Edlin correctly predicted the Great Plague of 1665, as an effect of the conjunction of 1663.[63] The two earlier outbreaks had followed the accession of James I and Charles I, and suggested a possible non-astrological correlation between a new monarch and plague. Lilly commented on this belief, but refuted the suggestion that Cromwell's elevation as Lord Protector would provoke an outbreak: Cromwell, he claimed, had 'more propitious stars, besides, he is of English blood, they not so'.[64] Gadbury and others took up a Dutch belief, mentioned by Bacon, that the weather followed a cycle of about thirty-five years, and suggested that this might relate to the revolution of Saturn through the zodiac roughly every thirty years. Gadbury went on to elaborate a general cyclical theory based on this hypothesis: the return of Saturn might be the cause of periodic outbreaks of plague, that of Jupiter might produce periods of peace and plenty, and so on. It was, he conceded, no more at present than an interesting possibility.[65] Even so, his speculations reflect, once again, the confidence that astrology, properly studied, could provide the key to universal understanding. History itself might become a branch of astrological science.

(ii) Language and Literature

The literary merits of almanacs were far more modest than their authors believed. Allestree's claim to be offering 'elegance of phrase' was hardly truthful, and it certainly failed to convince contemporaries.[66] Compilers who sought to rise above a merely functional style generally became florid and verbose. Instead of predicting an eclipse of the moon, John White thought it better to describe how

Bright, silver Cynthia's fair rotundeous face
Is masked, and eclipsed in disgrace
By melancholy *Terra,* for a while,
But she will soon unveil, and at earth smile.[67]

The countryside in its changing seasons provided the most common theme for literary flights. Winter, when 'the bald-pate woods are periwig'd with snow', suggested a popular metaphor (and one of the best.)[68] In spring, the reader learned, 'the tatling, twatling, pratling birds do sing.' 'Gardens prank them with their flow'ry buds,' sang *Dove,* 'The meads with grass, with leaves the naked woods.' The 'earth begins to smile, and to exchange her weather-worn weeds for the delectable livery of fresh Flora'.[69] Elizabethan compilers were fond of alliterative language, typified in Buckminster's forceful warning to sinners that 'flaying fire your woful flesh shall fret.'[70] One of the more memorable images was John Keene's description of the rain pouring into 'earth's vast urinal'.[71]

The badness of almanac-verse was, literally, proverbial: a Restoration writer quoted 'our proverb: as bad a rhymer as an almanac-maker'.[72] Contemporaries compared the flow of the verse unfavourably with the 'hobbling' gait of a hackney carriage. The most unkind comparison which occurred to an enemy of Ben Jonson was to tell the poet that Allestree was 'like Homer unto thee for poetry'. A later wit mocked Lilly and his 'fellow poet, Homer'.[73] The astrologers themselves sometimes seem to have conceded the charge. Coelson's invocation of his genius, 'jog on, dull muse', was hardly stirring; a successor, William Cookson, referred to his own 'insipid rhyme'. George Parker, recognizing the limitations of his talent, was said to buy ready-made verses from a professional versifier.[74] John Peter, astrologer and journalist, claimed that science had rendered the muse obsolete. He had developed a system of 'artificial versifying' by which 'any one that only knows the ABC, and can count to 9, is now immediately taught as well to make hundreds of pentameters as hexameters, which shall be true Latin, true verse, and good sense.' *The Spectator* remarked later that most almanac-verse was so appalling that it must have been composed by using such 'poetical logarithms'.[75]

The literary deficiencies of the astrologers can, however, be exaggerated. A modern critic has judged that the verse of Pond, for example, was no worse (if no better) than that of a recognized poet, John Davies of Hereford. Indeed he suggests that the satirists' venom against astrologers was directed more at their literary pretensions than at their astrology. As in the case of clerical opposition, there was an element of professional rivalry.[76] It is striking that the flow of burlesque almanacs dries up in the 1620s and 1630s, a period when the almanacs reflect scientific rather than literary or political interests. Some contemporaries thought less badly of the verses offered, and even copied them out. An Elizabethan student at Gray's Inn entitled his own verses 'English epigrams much like Buckminster's almanac'.[77] William Winstanley included the almanac-maker, George Wharton, among the subjects of his *Lives of the Most Famous Poets* (1687). Wharton's verses were collected and published as a separate volume, and have an undoubted vigour, though their success no doubt reflected political as much as poetical qualities: in the turbulent years at the close of Charles II's reign they were thought 'fit to be revived in this plotting age'.[78]

It was in polemical writings, rather than consciously literary efforts, that the astrologers were at their best. The torrent of abuse poured by Wharton, Partridge and many others on their rivals and political or religious enemies, illustrated in earlier chapters, was often forceful and vivid. Gadbury had a similar talent, and seems to have pursued a secondary career as a maker of political ballads. (Wharton was a successful journalist.[79]) William Lilly had no talent for verse, but did inspire a fiery polemic on his behalf by the Whig pamphleteer, Henry Care, who bade one of Lilly's critics to go and

With nappy-ale inspire thy muddy brain
To write some Tyburn-tragedy. In vain
To scratch thy noddle, anagrams to frame
On thy sweet miss, Madam Van Harlot's name;
Steal nonsense from some farce to make fools laugh,
Or scribble some dead monkey's epitaph.

Care, like Lilly, was out of sympathy with the mood of the Restoration:

Unhappy Age! Too witty to be wise,
Where learning's huffed, and droll's ye only prize.[80]

Contemporary literature did not receive the detailed and informed attention given to scientific developments. Burlesque almanacs show far greater familiarity with modern writers than the genuine works; it was a mock prognosticator who complained during the Revolution that

Poetry, indeed, be such a sin
As I think brings the plague and the Dutch in.

(A verse of that calibre might well be deemed sinful.) [81] The astrologers had some literary interests and connections, though strikingly few when contrasted with their scientific links. Thus Culpeper was a friend of the repulican poet, Tom May. Gadbury was a friend of two minor poets, and devoted one edition of his almanac to biographical and critical notes on famous poets. Milton's poems he preferred, predictably, to 'his unhappy *Iconoclastes;* wherein he traduced his lawful sovereign. . . . For which God struck him with blindness.'[82] The most widely quoted literary source was the poetry of the French Protestant, Du Bartas, in the immensely popular English translation by Silvester. The moral tone and astrological themes fitted ideally the almanac's purpose. Large extracts from the work appeared (without acknowledgement) in one of Evans's editions.[83] Francis Quarles, similarly pious in tone, was also popular, but Restoration compilers drew on very different authors such as Cowley, and on Butler's 'incomparable *Hudibras*' (despite its attack on astrology), and Dryden's *Absalom and Achitophel,* which was echoed and imitated.[84] A few compilers showed wider interests. Ferdinando Parkhurst translated literary as well as scientific works. During the Revolution two other minor compilers, Henry Harflete and Philip Kinder, published collections of their essays. Kinder's *The Surfeit to ABC* (1656) was a good-humoured attack on the immense quantity of classical and modern literature of all kinds, and on the unwarranted reverence given to it. Though he was critical of modern authors, the two clearest threads running through the work are scorn of the classics and of scholasticism. He thought Homer preferable to Cervantes only as 'the more exquisite piece of drollery'; Holinshed was as good a historian as Livy, who had belonged to that 'uncivilized' race, the 'beggarly, rude, barbarous' Romans. Kinder mocked the inflated claims made for Aristotle, Cicero and Ramus, and showed no mercy to scholastics. 'Voluminous men farced up with authorities' enjoyed a wholly undeserved respect, and stripped of their dry erudition would 'appear but poor naked skeletons'.[85] Richard Saunder thought more highly of the classics, and in the 1680s and 1690s his almanacs contained summaries of the most famous classical myths.[86]

References in almanacs to music and the other arts are scarce and of little significance. Walter Gray's advice to his readers at Christmas is typical of the few that do exist:

> Clap your hands, set harp and lute in tune,
> On shawms sound out new ditties to the Lord.

By contrast a later puritanical compiler of *Vaux* was deeply suspicious of 'time-betraying music', and of 'odious fiddlers with their smooth-faced boys'.[87] Music was still however a basic part of polite education, and several of the more versatile compilers, such as Nye, Coley and John Wing, offered tuition in it. Nye also taught pupils how to construct musical instruments. Pont's *Register* supplied the esoteric information that sheep were very fond of music, a fact listed among similar 'useful observations'.[88] In 1581 John Securis condemned all 'foolish plays, songs, idle pastimes', and a stern Restoration compiler used theatrical terms to denounce the debauched people of England, 'acting obscene scenes on her drunken stage'.[89]

The almanacs contained surprisingly few illustrations, presumably on the grounds of cost. Several Tudor sheet editions carried simple woodcuts, depicting seasonal pursuits for each month of the year, but the practice died out before the end of the century. There was a far more ambitious visual element in the late Stuart *Raven's* and especially the *Oxford* almanacs, which were dominated by engravings on mythological and allegorical themes. [90] The only visual material in the standard octavo almanacs was the Anatomy and sometimes diagrams of comets and eclipses.

It was only in Wales that the literary role of the almanac assumed major importance. The Welsh editions written and published annually by Thomas Jones for over a generation from 1680 provided a point of contact for Welsh authors, and a forum for their works. Jones was an important champion of the language, in which he claimed 'God himself spoke to Adam and others' for two thousand years after the Creation. He used his works to advertise eisteddfods, and used his press at Shrewsbury to build up a wide range of popular works in the vernacular, for which almanacs provided the financial basis.[91]

Almanacs are far more rewarding as a rich source of archaic words, and of proverbs and aphorisms. They show, for example, the common use of the expressive adjective 'slabby' (used to describe wet, dirty weather), 'cray' (white, used of the ripe harvest), 'lobcock' (bumpkin), 'lollard' (idler), 'lerry' (i.e. 'lurry', cant, babel) and 'vafrous' (sly, cunning).[92] Some terms are rarities. Porter's use in 1585 of 'kickish' (to mean 'slippery or dangerous') was earlier than any recorded in the *Oxford English Dictionary* and different in meaning. 'Groll' (a foolish, superficial person), used by Pearse in 1758, appeared over a century later than in the one author to whom the word has hitherto been attributed. 'Scommas' (jeers or flouts) appears to be unknown in this form.[93] Colloquial phrases are also common, such as 'a pin and web' (a bloodshot eye), 'ear-finger' (little finger) and the well-known 'Gaffer Grey-beard' (winter). The month of March, Hewlett reported,

> the country folks call Lyde,
> Which at some house each day will dine
> And as he fares, where he doth ride,
> So (say they) the weather storms or shine [*sic*].[94]

Poor Robin, retaining a traditional interest in roguery, supplied a list of common slang words for stealing: padding, cloving, milking, filching and nabbing.[95]

Proverbs appeared in vast numbers. Most are familiar, but a number are uncommon or appear in variant forms, for example: 'Bad was the old, but worser is the new' (1631);[96] 'God sends a cursed cow short horns' (1648); [97] 'When the lion's skin will not serve thy turn, then take the fox's' (1653);[98] 'Hungry dogs will eat dirty puddings' (1710).[99] Others appear to be unknown, for example Pond's advice:

> When year doth leap, beware women and sheep
> (The proverb saith) the shrew and rot will catch them,

though this is clearly related to a woman's right to propose marriage in a leap year and demand payment if refused, and to the proverb, 'A leap year is never a good sheep year.'[100] The expressions, 'Hunger digs through a cave' (1654) and 'to look upon it as a cow on a new gate' (1656)—i.e. with surprise and mistrust—do not appear in the standard collections, though there are related proverbs with similar meanings.[101] A few other proverbs were of local significance.[102] In addition many almanacs contained semi-proverbial aphorisms which were used most often to indicate astrological elections and good or bad days. Those by Thomas Bretnor were the best known. 'What's the word? What says Bretnor?' asks a character in one of Middleton's plays. The calendar of his edition for 1616 had days with the cryptic notes, 'catch at the moon', 'it falls out pat', 'strike while 'tis hot', 'not one hair to choose.'

Gresham had begun the practice some years previously. His first edition, for 1603, contained comments of a similar kind, for example, 'beware the thief, 'he cannot deny', 'words are but wind.' Many other compilers throughout the century followed suit, among them Booker, Vincent Wing (who included the motto, *'Moustarde apres disner',* for his readers to contemplate), and Saunders.[103]

Perhaps the most important literary role of the almanac was indirect. Terms relating to almanacs, as well as to astrology in general, pervade Elizabethan and early Stuart literature.[104] Ben Jonson introduced a character named Almanac in *his The Staple of News*. Middleton's *No Wit, No Help like a Woman's* contains a character, Weatherwise, who regulates his whole life, including his courtship, by the almanac's rules and aphorisms. Middleton went still further in his *Inner-Temple Masque* (1619), where he presents a Dr. Almanac as the central figure, attended by a supporting cast of 'Three Good Days, Three Bad Days, and Three Indifferent Days'. The word passed into proverbial lore, as in the saying that 'The court has no almanac' (i.e. is not bound by times and seasons), and the widely-used phrase that 'old men carry an almanac in their bones.' A contemporary explained that 'decrepit men are said to carry a prognostic in their bones, with pains and aches' by which the weather may be foretold—as in the surviving popular belief about corns.[105]

The various qualities associated with the almanac made the term attractive to authors. A writer referring to 'an almanac of your diseases' meant a comprehensive list. James Howell, admittedly striving for effect, told an acquaintance that 'in the large register or almanac of my friends . . . you are one of the chiefest red letters.' Shakespeare's Rosaline calls Katherine 'my red dominical, my golden letter'. An out-of-date almanac was an obvious and popular simile for something utterly worthless.[106] Several writers harnessed the ephemeral quality of the almanac to the misogynist humour of the period, and dreamed of a golden age in which, 'when wives are like almanacs, we may have every year a new one.'[107] The idea was developed in a later chap-book entitled *An Almanack-Husband,* a humorous tale recounting the hero's acquisition of twelve wives at monthly intervals in the year 1706. (The author gave some plausibility to his tale by admitting that the women were not attractive. The hero was unperturbed, believing in the old proverb, that 'dirty water quenches the fire best.'[108]) The different sections as well as the qualities of the almanac attracted notice. The allusion to the red print used in the calendar for festival days has already been mentioned. A moralist attacking the desire for fame echoed the style of the chronology by telling his readers that 'the most famous of thy exploits will not be enough to make an almanac's *Since*.'[109] Best known of all was the anatomical figure, the 'man i'th'almanac', the subject of repeated allusions and jests from Dekker, who compared it to a corpse used for an anatomical dissection, to Robert Southey, who likened it (rather similarly) to a disembowelled traitor.[110]

The ubiquity of the almanac stimulated the development of a distinct and popular sub-literary genre of satirical works in burlesque form.[111] There was a spate of them around the turn of the seventeenth century, and they were revived successfully during the Revolution. Their primary purpose was, obviously, to ridicule astrology and almanacs; Adam Fouleweather, a pseudonymous compiler, styled himself 'student in ass-tronomy'. The earlier burlesque works sought also to pillory social vices, such as drunkenness and debauchery, and expose sharp practices, for example the brewers' custom of diluting their beer with Thames water.[112] But they aimed in addition to entertain the reader as an end in itself. Dekker, for example, devoted more space in his *Raven's Almanacke* to humorous short stories than to satire of astrology. The later generation of mock almanacs evolved as a branch of royalist journalism; Samuel Sheppard was active in both fields. As royalist fortunes waned, it was natural for propagandists to turn to satire and ridicule, and the link between astrology and parliament symbolized by the careers of Lilly, Booker and Culpeper made almanacs an obvious target. The translation of Rabelais's *Pantagrueline Prognostication* into English in 1653 no doubt encouraged the revival of the burlesque. The blend of royalist politics, anti-Puritanism and earthy humour was typical of the cavalier newspapers of the period, and the formula remained popular after the Restoration. In its most skilful and successful form, the almanacs of 'Poor Robin', it survived down to the nineteenth century.

The earliest and most popular form of ridicule was to parody the platitudinous nature of much astrological prediction. It was unlikely, 'Rabelais' prophesied, that the blind would see clearly, or the deaf hear well. The very aged might die, Fouleweather suggested, and the very poor would go hungry. Few paupers would be chosen High Sheriff. A great person was likely to die somewhere in Europe, America, Africa or Asia.[113] The same method was applied to weather forecasts: 'No hot, sultry weather', *Poor Robin* assured his readers for the first of January.[114] Carried to extreme lengths, the banal merged with the absurd. *Poor Robin*, for example, listed things good and bad for various parts of the body, in imitation of *White* and others. It was rather bad, he noted solemnly, 'to have a cannon bullet shot in at one ear, and out the other'.[115] Medical and domestic advice in the same vein was common. 'Dr. Tyburn' offered a good remedy for a sore throat, ratsbane was a guaranteed cure for the lovesick, and a bed could be rid of fleas by pushing it into a field and setting fire to it.[116]

The more skilful productions followed closely the format of the works they mocked. *The Owles Almanack* of 1618 was a pioneer in this field, with sections parodying the chronology, law terms, tide-tables, feast days, fairs and highways. Under the heading of elections, the author advised that the best time to fell timber was when one needed a good fire, and to cut hair, when 'it be too long, or . . . the head is lousy, or when you are to go before a starving Justice, lest he cut it for you'.[117] Others developed this approach, providing sinners' days as well as saints' days, and facetious chronologies commemorating, for example, the farmer who tried to teach his cow rope-dancing, and the gentleman who bought a periwig for his magpie.[118] The solemn language in which compilers weighed the fate of nations offered an obvious target. Comets 'have ever been attended with change of government', Sheppard observed gravely in 1654; in '1630 there was a comet, and Russell the bargeman of Brainford died; 1633 there was a comet, and Hobson the carrier died.'[119] He was aiming, successfully, at both the self-importance of the almanac-makers and the banality of much of their material.

Every feature of the almanac was open to parody. Even the notes which private owners jotted in the blank pages opposite the calendar were imitated in the satirical versions, which often carried a pseudo-diary: 'lost my best shirt off the hedge', for example, and 'rainy weather and yet the almanac said it would be fair!'[120] The impression of scientific omniscience given by many compilers irritated a number of contemporaries and was lampooned by Jack Adams, who asserted definitively that there were 13,060,519 stars in the sky, 'not one more, nor one less'.[121] The common instructions on how to make simple scientific instruments were paralleled by *Montelion*'s picture of a sundial, which consisted of a stick protruding from the rear of a bending rustic, with instructions advising how to calculate the time from the shadow cast.[122] Even the specimen forms of bills and bonds did not escape. *Poor Robin* supplied his own example of a bill of obligation, with a typical political twist: 'I, Hugh Peters of Westminster, jester

Obſervations on May.

Sweet *May* the Glory of our Kalendar,
In which there ſhone that Bright Auſpicious Star,
That freed our galled backs from Rebels whips,
And cured Monarchy of her Ecclips.

1 Catesby
2 Squire Dun
3 Moth. Shipton
4 Col. *Okey*
5 Tyrone
6 Vulcan & Venus
7 Miſo & Mopſa
8 Jack-a-Leyden
9 *Salmon*
10 Cap. *Manning*
11 Van Trump
12 Marriot
13 Card. Richelieu
14 *Rainsborough*
15 Jack Pudding
16 Tho. Wiat
17 Juſt. Nineholes
18 S. Stall
19 Gowrey
20 Dr. Parrey
21 7 Champions
22 Hercules
23 Wil. Low.
24 *Edw. Harvey*
25 *Fennor*
26 Garagantua
27 Lucian
28 Queen of Spades
29 Icarus
30 Edm. Campion
31 Martin Parker

The firſt day of this month I believe will be *May-day*. The graſs being ſlippery, we ſhall have many Ladies in *Hide-park* turn'd topſy-turvy. Now the Lady *Aurora* hath clothed the earth with her chiefeſt Ornaments, if I miſtake me not, the Laſſes ſhall have many a Green-grown. He that cannot get remedy to aſſwage Love, let him drown'd himſelf, for that's a wound paſt my skill to cure. We are like to have a good Summer, but a wet Winter, he that wiſheth he may never live to ſee it, let him take a knife and hang himſelf, or a rope and cut his throat. If any one want work, let him build Caſtles in the air. The days are now grown to a pretty length, therefore its no wonder if you ſee a man twice drunk in a day. He that ſleeps with his mouth open, may chance to have a Flea drop into it. The Sun ſhall ſhine bright all this month, if no clouds appear; and a blinde man ſhall ſee as well at midnight, as at noon-day.

B

From *Poor Robin* for 1665, a mock almanac which replaced saints' days with sinners', and offered a blend of humour and strong royalism and chaplain in ordinary to Oliver Cromwell, brewer and Protector, do acknowledge myself to owe and be indebted to London Bridge, my head. . . .'[123]

Not all the humour was based on parody. *Poor Robin,* and others, had a taste for verbal humour, puns and conceits. 'The grocers' trade will be *current* this year', he predicted, 'a. *fig* for care, their calling will never be out of *date.*' More striking was his description of the gallows ('a great eye-sore' for highwaymen) in heraldic terms:

Three Trees, two Rampant, and the other Cressant,
One Halter Pendant, and a Ladder Passant.[124]

Another edition contained an elaborate love-letter in the language of bell-ringing; the lover declared that 'if the rope of my capacity could reach the belfry of your beauty, these words of mine, like silver bells, might be worthy to hang in the ears of your favour; but the ladder of my invention is too low to climb up the steeple of your understanding; if it was not, I would ring out my mind to you in a sweet peal of most savoury conceits.'[125]

Much of the humour was in fact less than savoury in character, and was based on racial, religious and sexual prejudices. The abuse of the Scots, Irish and other nations was linked to political issues, but the mockery of the Welsh appears to have been purely racial. The Welsh were cowardly, ignorant, spoke in a ridiculous manner and were, of course, besotted with leeks. The *Prognostication* of Shinkin-ap-Shone graciously rejected the hypothesis that the race was descended from the droppings of Alexander the Great's horse, only to assert that it sprang from eight ship-loads of French whores, deported by a king of France in antiquity, who 'since by procreation,/A re now become a nasty nation.'[126] Many of the genuine almanacs indulged in religious polemic, directed at both Catholics and nonconformists. The *Yea and Nay Almanack* was a vehicle for abuse of the Quakers, late in the reign of Charles II. It accused the Friends of debauchery and hypocrisy, recalled the excesses of the early days of the 1650s, and presented a vivid (if implausible) pedigree showing the Quaker descent from Mahomet, the Whore of Babylon and John of Leyden. The venom was strong, though it was mixed with lesser pin-pricks: many women 'follow the Light', readers were told, 'because they are commonly light women'. Quaker women were held to say that 'whereas others wear store of ribbons to show their pride outwardly, we will wear none of them, but carry our pride inwardly.'[127]

It was commonplace in this period, like most others, to accuse religious nonconformists of sexual deviation. Almanacs and especially mock-almanacs freely levelled charges of immorality and perversion against Catholics and Dissenters. *Montelion* proved its soundness by attacking both at once, predicting that the pope would exchange one of his boys for one of the whores of the regicide, Henry Marten. It also published a compromising picture of Hugh Peter, the Cromwellian preacher, with the butcher's wife to whom he was linked by rumour.[128] One of the most popular 'jests', on a different theme but showing equal lack of taste, was the story of how a pile of excrement was left on Lilly's doorstep as a challenge to his powers of astrological detection.[129] The satirists might aspire to 'savoury conceits', but they had few qualms in descending to the cruder depths.

The astrologers' limited interest in literature and the other arts reflects partly the fact that the majority were self-taught men. Many of the Elizabethan compilers were graduates, but the numbers fell steadily in the following century. Most Stuart almanac-makers had no formal education beyond a grammar school, and many probably less even than that. They accordingly lacked the veneer of polite culture acquired (then) at the universities, and their interests tended to be scientific or political rather than literary. There were some exceptions, especially in the Jacobean period. John Keene discussed Greek and Latin prophecies which he claimed had been fulfilled. He was able to demonstrate both the truth of prophecy and his own erudition, and took the opportunity to mention the excellence of his grammar school at Tottenham. Thomas Bretnor offered tuition in French, Spanish and Latin. John Evans claimed to teach Latin, Greek and Hebrew (though Lilly, one of his pupils, found him totally ignorant of Greek).[130] Most of the standard astrological texts remained in Latin throughout the century, and any self-respecting practitioner felt it necessary to be able to use them, whatever his lack of interest in the rest of the classics. Booker, Lilly and Partridge, among others, reached a competent level of Latin and a smattering of Greek (both self-taught in Partridge's case), and they quoted freely from classical and mediaeval sources.[131] John Booker used Latin for many of his political prophecies, perhaps in part to hide them from the eyes of the 'common sort'. If prosecuted, he could also claim in defence that an offending passage was merely a quotation from some classical source. He had no sympathy for the 'blockish stupidity' of those who objected to the practice. The ignorant, he thought, could 'thank their covetous or careless friends who have brought them up better fed than taught. . . . I know not why we should humour every man.'[132] Some of the compilers were defensive, and even apologetic, about their lack of higher education. Gabriel Frende admitted modestly that he was 'but a simple man, in respect of many in both the universities'. Gadbury tried to show that his lack of a university education was foreshadowed in his nativity, so that 'my education having been below my birth hath proved astrology true.' Richard Kirby similarly confessed his 'meanness' in having attended neither university. William Lilly was proud of his skill in Latin, as a schoolboy. His fellow scholars, less talented, went on to Cambridge; 'only poor I, William Lilly, was not so happy.' His father's debts made it necessary for him, like many another, to walk the hundred miles to London in search of a livelihood.[133] Vincent Wing, who lived near Stamford, was proud that this had once been a university town.[134] Lilly and others predicted a glorious future for the universities, invoked a divine blessing upon them, and set out details of their history.[135]

There was, nevertheless, a marked ambivalence in the astrologers' attitudes to the universities and to academic learning. On a different occasion Gadbury defiantly proclaimed his lack of degrees or other 'rattles to his name', and asserted that 'the stars speak English as well as Latin.' Culpeper mocked the university syllabus, and all learning based on Aristotle 'and his followers in folly'. [136] This attitude no doubt owed much to the growing hostility of the universities towards astrology, leading to John Butler's fear, in 1680, that 'all astrology must be banished' thence.[137] But it reflected also a criticism of the university syllabus, highly conservative in outlook, and unwilling to find room for scientific or utilitarian subjects. The leading astrologers were far more closely linked to Gresham College and later the Royal Society than to the universities. The *Musaeum Minervae,* a short-lived college founded on utilitarian principles in the mid-1630s, also found place for an astrologer, Nicholas Fiske, among its professors.[138]

Several educational reformers during the interregnum, including Winstanley, urged that astrology be made a standard part of the curriculum. One of them, John Webster, wished it to be taught at Oxford and Cambridge. His proposals were derided on behalf of Oxford by Seth Ward, who mocked astrology as 'a ridiculous cheat' and challenged its advocates to provide experimental proof of its validity.[139] This was, of course, what a number of reformers were attempting to do, though in vain. The universities and grammar schools, having defeated the pressure for change in the mid-century, saw no reason to amend the methods and content of their teaching. At the end of the seventeenth century, the astrologer, Robert Godson, wrote scathingly about the 'modern unhappy method of education' by which the young were kept so long in 'learning a parcel of silly miscalled Arts and foreign tongues' that they never reached subjects of real value, of which he listed medicine, astronomy and divinity as examples. Oxford appeared to the Whig astrologer, John Partridge, as no more than a den of political and religious vice, where a young man went 'to be poisoned in his principles by that horrid brew of—',[140] His hostility was largely political, but it underlines a growing cultural divide. Partridge, the foremost almanac-maker of his generation, was a cobbler by trade, and his knowledge of Latin, medicine and astrology was self-taught. The graduate compilers of the Tudor and early Stuart age belonged firmly to the past.

CHAPTER EIGHT

The Eighteenth Century

THE YEAR 1700 is an artificial point at which to break off a history of almanacs. Any date must be artificial, for their publication has continued without a break to the present. Nevertheless, the eighteenth-century edition did differ noticeably from its predecessors, not in format but in character and often purpose. The change took place gradually during the first twenty years of the century. The Hanoverian almanac lacked the vitality and individuality of many of its Tudor and Stuart forbears. At the root of the decline lay the reduced intellectual and thence social standing of astrology.[1] John Partridge, John Gadbury and Francis Moore, the greatest names in the world of popular astrology at the opening of the century, were all dead by 1720 and found no successors of comparable stature. The fact that almanacs continued in Partridge's name for another century, and that *Old Moore* lives on still, owes something to the journalistic skill of the founders but more to the absence of younger astrologers with the ability and drive to establish themselves as Partridge and Moore, and many before them, had done. Eighteenth-century London seems to have lacked the famous or notorious practitioners who had flourished from the time of Forman to that of Moore. Their successors were less educated (or rather, less self-educated). They were regarded as quacks, and cut off from the scientific and genteel society which earlier men, most notably Gadbury, had enjoyed. The movement for the reform of astrology petered out quickly in the new century.[2] Most almanacs henceforth offered only a cursory and stereotyped justification of astrology, and some (as will be seen) openly denounced it. Astrology no longer drew fiery denunciations from the clergy. Having lost its intellectual vitality and respectability, it was left to fade away, a subject for wit not controversy.

The titles and authors of the late seventeenth century therefore lived on, compiled by successive editors appointed by the Stationers' Company. Thomas Sparrow, introducing his first edition in 1726, told his readers that the work was genuinely composed by the author named on the title-page, and claimed that this was a rare distinction.[3]

The attitude of many of the compilers was casual, sometimes almost derisory. Charles Leadbetter, who edited Partridge's almanac for many years after the founder's death, provides a particularly flagrant example. Though he included some scientific material, Leadbetter filled his almanacs with material plundered without acknowledgement from the original Partridge and other Stuart compilers. He used his anonymity to glorify the immense skill of his 'close friend' Mr. Leadbetter, and the excellent value of his mathematical textbooks. He even, tastelessly, reprinted Swift's mocking epitaph on John Partridge:

Here, five feet deep, lies on his back
A cobbler, starmonger, and quack.

Leadbetter's rivals soon discovered his identity, and very justly condemned his practices.[4]

The predictions offered by the pseudo-Partridge were vague and repetitive compared with those of the original. Many of the new series of the early eighteenth century contained no prophecies at all, and some compilers explicitly repudiated judicial astrology. Richard Saunder pioneered this development in the editions he published annually for half a century from 1684. His was the first major series openly hostile to astrology since that of Richard Allestree before the civil war. Whereas Allestree had condemned the science as blasphemous, Saunder derided its falsity and total lack of scientific foundation. He ridiculed Lilly, Gadbury and Whalley, attacked the 'impudence, absurdity and falsehood' of John Holwell, and mocked the 'frightful stuff' written by Partridge. One edition supplied the reader with 'A Discourse on the Invalidity of Astrology'. Saunder did not deny that planets and comets might have some effect on mankind, but thought that their influence was largely unknown and probably unknowable.[5] The influential *Ladies' Diary*, founded in 1704, gave no space to astrology and told its readers bluntly that 'there's no such thing as foretelling events.' A later compiler, Robert White, poured abuse on 'fallacious' prophecies and the whole 'nonsense of judicial astrology'.[6]

There is a further contrast between the Stuart and Hanoverian periods in the very different pattern of sales, which became ever more marked as the new century advanced. Though the Stationers continuad to issue a variety of titles, one series—Moore's *Vox Stellarum*—left its rivals further and further behind. By 1761 Moore was selling 82,000 copies a year, ten times as many as the next almanac which contained prophecies (Partridge's).[7] Within a few years it was selling more copies than all its rivals added together. The story of the almanac was becoming little more than the triumphs of one title. Its immense popularity makes it a historical source of some importance, though one that has apparently been overlooked. But its pre-eminence signalled the end of the traditional pattern, in which twenty or thirty titles complemented and competed with each other, which had characterized most of the Stuart period.

For most of the century almanacs continued to be published under a monopoly held by the Company of Stationers. As before, the Company submitted its editions each year for episcopal approval, long after the expiry of the licensing laws. During the reign of Anne approval was by no means automatic, and editions by both Partridge and Richard Gibson appeared with blank spaces where material had been deleted.[8] In some respects monopolistic control was strengthened, for after the death (in 1705) of John Hayes, printer to the University of Cambridge, the Company obtained an agreement by which it paid the University £210 each year in return for an undertaking not to print almanacs or similar works. The annual sum was later increased to £500. Similar arrangements existed with Oxford, and the large sums involved reflect the continuing profitability of the trade.[9]

The trade was indeed too profitable for the Company to enjoy its monopoly undisturbed. Some authors and publishers evaded it by producing works which were technically outside the terms of the patent but aimed at almost the same market. George Parker, whose almanacs the Company refused to print for most of Anne's reign, produced his own annual *Ephemeris* which aimed at the same market but tried not to infringe the monopoly. The edition for 1705 had a calendar printed by the Stationers attached to the main body of the work, which was by Parker. But, as he complained later, the Company was determined to suppress anything which even remotely resembled an almanac, and hired the best lawyers to ensure the success of a weak case. 'Should they but see a two-foot rule in my hand', he declared bitterly, 'they'd be ready to seize it for a calendar, because it has the figures 1,2,3, &c thereon.'[10] But he persevered and used his liberty to denounce the 'antiquated' monopoly which the Stationers abused by their 'false and abominable stuff'. He estimated that only a third of their compilers were 'in the land of the living'; some had indeed never existed. Instead the Company employed hack writers at cheap rates: 'Coley' for example was now written by a night watchman—'a paltry nocturnal guardian to a deal-yard' (an unflattering allusion to Francis Moore). Its living authors, such as Wing and Partridge, he denounced at great length as rogues and charlatans. This publicity was highly unwelcome to the Company, which eventually reached an agreement with Parker. From 1716 it once more published his *Ephemeris*, though Parker continued to print it and retained his freedom to denounce the Whigs, which seems to have been at the heart of the dispute.[11] In the middle of the century a number of *Diaries, Journals, Memorandum Books* and others trespassed on the Company's property. *The Gentleman's and Lady's Palladium* imitated *The Ladies' Diary*, and was indeed written by its editor, Robert Heath, who was predictably dismissed by the Company for thus undermining its position. In 1774 this encroachment developed into a successful frontal assault by the publisher, Thomas Carnan, though the Company's prosperity continued for a further half century.[12]

The expiry of the licensing laws at the close of the seventeenth century brought further problems to the Company. It was very difficult to control the activities of the new provincial presses, and to suppress pirate editions of almanacs before they harmed the market.[13] The London printers were themselves not above suspicion. Benjamin Harris and his sons were a constant irritation. Harris was undeterred at being cited in Chancery, where he admitted disposing of several thousand illegal almanacs under the name of Vincent Wing. He proceeded to make unauthorized additions to the almanacs of Partridge, and to issue spurious works in the name of 'John Patridge' and 'Dorothy Partridge', allegedly John's wife.[14] The problem was perennial. Several of the editions for 1752, for example, carried stern warnings from the Company, threatening counterfeiters with prosecution, and constant vigilance was needed.[15]

Harris's exploits were facilitated by the absence of any authorized editions by Partridge in the years 1710–13, an irresistible invitation to dishonest publishers. The hiatus followed a dispute between the Company and the astrologer over the size of his fee. Partridge, dissatisfied with the figure offered, sold his copy for 1710 to another printer; the Company promptly obtained an injunction from Chancery to restrain publication. Partridge appealed to parliament, and the issue was referred for an opinion to Queen's Bench from which (to date) no final judgement has been delivered. Both parties were losing by the dispute; Partridge's almanac had indeed been the best-selling title in the first years of the century. In 1713 they accordingly reached a compromise, by which he was to be paid £100 a year, instead of the £150 he claimed.[16]

John Partridge was far from typical in being able to challenge the Company and extract concessions. On the whole the Stationers were even more dominant than in the seventeenth century. Their supremacy was illustrated and reinforced by the practice, already mentioned, of hiring compilers to write anonymously using the format and title of a long-established series. Thus Partridge was edited by Charles Leadbetter. John Gadbury's series was continued by his cousin, Job, and then by the Company's nominees.[17] Many of the almanacs were written by the members and connections of the Wing family of Rutland, an influential and pervasive astrological dynasty. Vincent Wing senior, born in 1587, was an amateur astronomer. His son, also Vincent, founded in 1641 a popular almanac which survived into the nineteenth century. For a hundred and fifty years the family produced a succession of respected surveyors, mathematicians, astrologers, astronomers and almanac-makers. They made the East Midlands a centre for all these activities in the eighteenth century, and the production of almanacs was dominated for many years by members of their circle. A number published almanacs in their own names: Richard Saunder, who lived near Melton Mowbray, and was a friend of John Wing, Joseph Pepper of Stamford, Thomas Sparrow of Hose, near Melton, Robert White of Grantham and Edmund Weaver of Frieston, near Grantham. Others edited established titles, such as Edward Sharpe of Stamford, and William Harvey of Knipton (near Grantham), who edited Moore for some years. In 1730 Tycho Wing compiled the almanacs of Coley, Moore and Andrews, as well as his own. In the 1760s and 1770s Thomas Wright of Eaton (also near Melton Mowbray) wrote Wing, Moore, Partridge, Andrews, Saunders and (from 1775) Season, in collaboration with Henry Andrews and probably Vincent Wing. Henry Andrews, born in Frieston, was a self-taught and respected astronomer who supplied the astronomical data for most of the Company's editions. After Wright's death he turned his hand to predictions, and compiled Moore's *Vox Stellarum* with immense success until his death in 1820.[18]

Another local tradition existed in the Coventry area, and owed its existence to John Tipper, founder of *The Ladies' Diary*. After his death, the *Diary* was continued by Henry Beighton of Griff, near Coventry, later by Thomas Simpson, born at Nuneaton, and later still by Olinthus Gregory, who was born at Coventry and was editor until 1840. Two other early eighteenth-century compilers may have been connected with Tipper: John Chattock of Castle Bromwich, and

William Sharpe of Hinckley, on the Warwickshire border of Leicestershire.[19]

As in earlier periods most compilers made relatively little money from their work. John Tipper was paid nothing for the first edition of his *Diary*, and indeed thought the Company was being unusually generous in not demanding that he should indemnify it against loss. Half-way through the century the editor of the *Diary* was paid ten guineas a year; the compiler of Moore, which sold better but was less respectable, was paid only five.[20] Thomas Lane launched a series in his own name, only to abandon it in disgust at the lack of rewards. It was taken over by his friend, Henry Season, who made clear his own disgust that he and his colleagues in the 'noblest branches of the mathematics' should be less well rewarded than 'a French cook, Italian songster, or even an English dapper-witted dancing-master'. In 1759 he told readers that the Company had now increased his fee, but took the opportunity to stress how abysmally low it had been.[21] Robert Heath, who compiled *The Ladies' Diary* for some years in the mid-century, was bitterly resentful of the Company's meanness, and longed for the destruction of its monopoly. At the end of the century Henry Andrews was paid no more than £25 a year, though his skill as editor of Moore brought the Company an annual profit which reached several thousand pounds.[22]

For those who compiled editions under their own name, the almanac still provided a means of self-advertisement. Thus, Edmund Weaver, a licensed astrological physician, used his series to set out in detail his professional arrangements. George Parker became sufficiently well known through his publications to be troubled by at least two impostors, one operating near Croydon, and one or more further a field.[23] In addition astrologers, as always, were drawn irresistibly by the opportunity for public combat. Professional rivalry, political differences and the smell of blood seem to have been the dominant motives. In the early 1700s Partridge and Parker denounced each other and almost all their contemporaries; Cookson, Wing, Coley and others joined in the fray.[24] Little had changed a generation later: a new feud smouldered between Weaver and his neighbour, Tycho Wing, while Wing and Leadbetter abused one another as conjuror and fraud.[25]

There is no evidence that disputes harmed sales, and accordingly the Company saw no reason to intervene. Its continuation of *Poor Robin* is an indication that the Company always placed profit above the defence of astrology and astrologers. The editor for 1741 was allowed to pour abuse on all the serious compilers, whose names were thinly disguised. He ridiculed

> cuckolding S(easo)n,
> Fluttering W(in)g, and trifling P(ears)e;
> For true sons of darkness, there's P (artridge) and M(oo)r,
> Ever clawing the papist and Babylon's whore.
> With Leadawry [LeadbetterJ too, who incog.' makes great pothers
> Himself to advance by bespotting others.[26]

The Company's attitude, and commercial instincts, were best illustrated by their response to the Bickerstaff episode. In *Predictions for the Year* 1708, issued under the pseudonym of Isaac Bickerstaff, Jonathan Swift lampooned mercilessly the claims and methods of the almanac-makers. He exposed their platitudinous ambiguity and denounced their groundless and partisan political predictions. Swift made his chief target John Partridge, the most popular and most quarrelsome of contemporary compilers, and the most violent Whig among them. Unlike earlier satirists, Swift kept up the pretence that the *Predictions* was a work of genuine astrological prophecy. 'Bickerstaff' repeated earnestly that his quarrel was with the cheats who abused the public, not with the art itself. As proof of his own skill he solemnly predicted that Partridge would die of a fever at 11 p.m. on 29 March 1708, and added with equal assurance that Louis XIV would expire at 6 p.m. on 29 July, followed by the pope on 11 September. The jest was hugely successful. Neither Partridge nor the pope was amused—the French king was presumably used to being killed off each year in this way. In due course a highly circumstantial account appeared of Partridge's death in fulfilment of the prophecy. The astrologer attempted, indignantly and ineptly, to prove his continued existence, only to find his arguments carefully refuted by the wits. At the same time he became involved in a dispute with the Company of Stationers, as mentioned above, and no further editions of his almanac appeared for several years. Deprived of its profits from Partridge's works, the Company decided to exploit the profitability of works ridiculing him, which might in addition prove a useful bargaining counter. Accordingly there appeared in 1710 a new edition of Bickerstaff's almanac, openly ridiculing Partridge and other astrologers, but not written by Swift, and now appearing under the Company's imprint. It did not however become a regular series, partly because it overlapped with

Poor Robin and because Partridge commanded a far greater market than Bickerstaff could ever hope to capture.[27]

More commonly the Company sought to maintain profits by cutting costs. The standard of printing was as bad as earlier. A new device for reducing expenses was found by omitting punctuation and capital letters in the lists of fairs and markets.[28] Henry Season once had to apologize for a blundering printer who had set down 'Onions for Orion'.[29] Critics used such gaffes, with other material, to persuade the House of Commons in 1779 not to restore the Company's monopoly. Did a body deserve so great a privilege when it could publish a calendar showing Plough Monday as falling on a Saturday? Time did not bring amends. Victorian readers of *Notes and Queries* were entertained with an account of printing errors in a contemporary almanac, from which it appeared that St. Thomas Becket died in 1863, and King James II in 1801.[30]

The story of the eighteenth-century almanac is, nevertheless, one of evolution as well as stagnation and decay. The editions of Moore and Partridge changed little in form, offering an endlessly popular diet of jingoism, abuse of Catholics and predictions of the downfall of the pope and the French. The 'sorts' also changed little, on the whole surviving less well. *Riders*, however, which was small and often interleaved to make it suitable as a pocket-diary, continued well into the nineteenth century. In the 1730s there appeared *The Court Kalendar*, setting out the birthdays of English and foreign royalty, a list of the privy council, and the names of English and foreign ambassadors. It was designed to be bound with a list of members of parliament and with *Riders*, at a total price of two shillings. The composite work resembled a modern *Whitaker* in miniature.[31] Poor Robin flourished throughout the century, offering such new material as a serialized burlesque romance, 'The Witch of the Woodlands', and musical catches.[32]

The most important new development was the emergence of almanacs which provided a blend of instruction and amusement in place of astrology. An early series by Richard Saunder, already mentioned, supplied brief accounts of classical mythology, natural theology and scientific subjects, such as astronomy, the tides and extraterrestrial life. *The Ladies' Diary*, founded in 1704 by a Coventry schoolmaster, John Tipper, was the best known and most successful series. It aimed primarily at the new market of educated, leisured, middle-class women, and in many ways resembled a modern women's periodical. The contents of early editions included essays on female virtues, the nature of love and the history of famous women (among them Lady Godiva), a short story and culinary recipes.[33] The most successful feature was an annual section of riddles or 'enigmas' in verse, which were to be widely imitated. Readers sent in their solutions, also in verse, and were no doubt gratified to see their names and addresses in print and to win one of the prizes (which were—a modern entrepreneurial touch—further free copies of the *Diary*). In later years readers also devised many of the enigmas, and indulged themselves by inventing fanciful pseudonyms such as 'Xantippe' of Helmsley, 'Druselinda' and the like.[34] The flavour of middle-class politeness was impeccable. The editor in 1731 added the conventional preface, explaining that it was proper to do so, but admitted lamely that 'after so many prefaces already, 'tis not easy for to know what to say.'[35]

Tipper possessed real journalistic flair, though of a kind very different from that of Partridge or Lilly. In 1711 he decided that the interest generated by the Diary justified a monthly magazine in the same style; this duly appeared, but fell victim to the stamp tax in less than a year. Tipper also launched a second series, entitled *Great Britain's Diary*, which aimed at the upper end of the market for 'sorts'. 'The design of this little book being chiefly to promote trade and business,' he wrote, 'I have inserted little else but what tends to that end', and the work consisted largely of detailed weights and measures used for various commodities, and notes on excise duties.[36]

The Ladies' Diary was not, however, merely light entertainment. Tipper was a mathematician, and his avowed purpose was 'to introduce our fair sex to the study of mathmatics'. The path was smoothed as far as possible: a later editor reassured ladies that mathematical problems were only another form of enigma or riddle, and so not at all formidable. Every year the *Diary* thus carried a set of arithmetical problems of considerable complexity, offering readers the chance of modest fame and a prize. It attracted many male readers, both amateur and professional mathematicians, and in time there appeared a more sober male companion, *The Gentleman's Diary, or the Mathematical Repository*.[37] In addition Tipper supplied data of modern astronomy: the size of the universe, distance of the fixed stars and Halley's work on the periodicity of comets. The *Diary* also provided meteorological data of the preceding year, in place of the traditional predictions.[38] *The Ladies' Diary* built up a wide circulation, and a sound reputation. Around 1750 it was selling about thirty thousand copies a year.[39] Its reputation rested securely on the eminence of the compilers. Following Tipper's death, the *Diary* was edited by Henry Beighton, a noted engineer who played a part in developing the steam engine; he was a Fellow of the Royal Society, an eminent surveyor, and a friend of Desaguliers. His successors included Thomas Simpson and Charles Hutton, both respected mathematicians and Fellows of the Royal Society. The claim made in 1759 that the *Diary* contributed more to the advancement of mathematics in England 'than half the books professedly wrote on the subject' was well founded. In the early nineteenth century the *Ladies'* and *Gentleman's* diaries were still respected as having 'exerted a great and beneficial influence upon the state of mathematical science in this country for near a century and a half'. 'More than one gentleman who now ranks high in the scientific world', observed another commentator, 'owes his first impulse to the study of these works.'[40]

Even so, the success of *The Ladies' Diary* is overshadowed by the triumph of Moore, and the tradition of sensationalism and polemic for which it stood. Figures of copies printed for 1761 show Moore at eighty-two thousand far ahead of its nearest rival, the modest Riders (twenty-four thousand); *The Ladies' Diary*, now declining somewhat, stood next at fifteen thousand. There were eight thousand copies of Partridge, seven of Wing, and only two and a half to three thousand of such old-established titles as Andrews, Coley, Gadbury and Saunders—far behind *Poor Robin*, still retailing its old jokes at the level of over eleven thousand copies a year.[41]

Many of the themes of late Stuart almanacs continued into the new century. In particular the almanacs reflected the stormy politics of the reign of Anne. The preponderance was Whig; a group led by Partridge, Salmon, Moore and John Wing was opposed only by the veteran George Parker and his friend William Cookson. John Gadbury, another high Tory, drew back from political comment, conscious of 'the brink of the grave being become the desk we write on'. Following his death in 1704 his series was continued by Job Gadbury, whose politics were closer to the Whig group.[42] The prevailing tone was thus extravagant praise of 'our glorious Queen', with euphoric prophecies of great victories and European domination, coupled with abuse of the French and of the Jacobite Tories. Moore's edition for 1705 began with a vigorous 'Introduction: being a modest curse against the enemies of our peace', those 'damned rebellious vipers', the Jacobites.[43]

The War of Spanish Succession (1701–13) encouraged the partisan nationalism which had characterized the previous reign. Louis XIV, still the enemy, was as before 'the Bully King', 'the Wicked', 'the Christian Turk', 'King of Wooden Shoes'. Madame de Maintenon, his queen, was a witch.[44] The stars, ancient prophecies and symbolic pictures or 'hieroglyphs' (published regularly by Salmon and Moore) all foreshadowed victories by Marlborough and the defeat of the French and their allies, the Bavarians and 'Frenchified Spanish'.[45] Job Gadbury thanked the Almighty who had 'been pleased to put a hook into the jaw of that Leviathan', France.[46] England's allies were glorified correspondingly—the Habsburgs, Eugene of Savoy, and Charles XII of Sweden, 'the greatest prince in Europe at present'.[47] Even the Tory rivals of the Whig group sustained the war propaganda for many years. In 1711 Gibson proclaimed the imminent death of Louis XIV, and Cookson quoted from Nostradamus and Lilly the prophecy of a French king to be driven out of his realm. George Parker, who by then was in favour of peace, was conveniently excluded by the Company of Stationers.[48]

The chorus of patriotism was not enough, however, to disguise the political and religious frictions within England. They focussed on the succession, and on the position of the Dissenters. The High Church preacher and polemicist, Dr. Sacheverell, played an important role in exacerbating the controversies. His agitation was in part responsible for the attempt to push through legislation to drive Dissenters from office by outlawing the practice of occasional conformity to the worship of the Church of England, a device by which many evaded the provisions of the penal laws. Three bills to this effect were introduced between 1702 and 1704. Partridge made his reaction to the proposals clear beyond doubt:

> 'Tis only Pop'ry by another name.
> The shortest way, blood, ruin and excess,
> Sa—ll's brimstone church is nothing less.[49]

All the bills failed. The rejection of the third by the small Whig majority in the Lords was greeted by Partridge with a poem entitled 'The true Englishman's thanks to the Noble Peers of England for sinking the bill', which he alleged to have been spawned by Versailles, nursed at Oxford, and calculated to hand over England to Jacobites, foreigners and a 'whipping Church'. John Tanner, a veteran of the Cromwellian era, wrote in similar terms, thanking the peers, condemning Sacheverell and recalling that the High Churchmen in Laud's days had led the monarchy to destruction.[50]

The union of England and Scotland in 1707 was hailed as a triumph which 'confounds the Christian Turks' and would 'end our quarrels and enrich our trade'. Moore indeed voiced the opinion that party differences owed more to greed than to principle:

> No High or Low Church, Whig nor Tory, more
> Be ever named within Great Britain's shore.
> Could we but love God more, and money less
> These marks of knave and fool would quickly cease.

In similar vein Tipper condemned the strife and drunkenness which accompanied disputed parliamentary elections.[51] But it comes as no surprise that Moore's advice was not followed, least of all by the astrologers. Partridge offered in 1709 a ferocious debate between a 'red-hot Jereboam Tory and a Jerusalem Whig', in which the Tory stood for popery, tyranny and idolatry, worshipping not true religion but the golden calf of the Book of Daniel. In a mocking imitation of James I's tag, Partridge supplied a new maxim for the Tories: 'No Calves, No King.'[52]

Support for the Hanoverian succession was clear. *Dove* set out the family's genealogy to show its descent from James I. Partridge, more coarsely, mocked the 'Old Pretender' who aspired to be 'King James the T—rd'. Moore claimed that his partisan efforts were favourably received at the Hanoverian court, as well they might be.[53] But the compilers left no doubt that they were concerned above all with liberty and the subject's rights: the Hanoverians stood for Protestant freedom against Jacobite popish tyranny. Similarly enthusiasm for William III and Anne was linked with the proud defence of the liberties gained as a result of the Glorious Revolution. Tanner, for example, set out the conventional table of kings, but ended with the query,

> 'Tis said you're Gods! What glory is't to be
> Accounted Gods, if Gods of tyranny?

Moore included a confrontation between a British cock and a French monkey—typically partisan emblems—in which the cock gloried as much in its freedom as in its martial exploits. Frenchmen were 'born with saddles on their backs, and willing to be slaves', said Partridge, echoing a Leveller phrase.[54]

High Tory views found open expression almost only in the editions of George Parker, which the Stationers refused to handle, largely on political grounds. Parker, who was accused of Jacobitism, asserted his loyalty to Anne but did not attempt to hide his High Tory position. Indeed he published the text of an offer he made to the Stationers in 1706, giving them a large share of the profits from his future almanacs in return for the liberty to drop the conventional references in the calendar to Guy Fawkes, the Popish Plot and so on, and replace them with notes on the Rye House plotters and other Whig villains. The Company rejected the offer. Parker filled his *Ephemeris* with material of this kind, hailing 'fam'd Sacheverell', the saviour of the church, and denouncing the 'holy cheats', 'pale, fanatic Whigs' who sought to destroy church and crown. Charles I, he reminded readers, had been 'beheaded by the Dissenters'. The Tory ministry of 1710 brought new hopes that the church would be defended, and the war concluded.[55] Cookson and Gibson published slightly more restrained Tory views, though some of Gibson's remarks in his edition for 1712, in which he welcomed the Tory ministry and reviled the Whigs, were cut by the censors.[56] *The Oxford Almanack* also sometimes gave support by publishing engravings clearly Jacobite in sympathy. The edition for 1706 showed the Jacobite oak overshadowing an orange tree, with the figure of a disconsolate queen, and Godolphin playing dice. It aroused considerable attention, and was indeed discussed in the House of Lords. The figure of Britannia trampling on a monster (1712) has been seen to allude to the Tory triumph in 1710 and in the subsequent general election.[57]

Tory hopes, however, were rapidly overtaken by events. Anne died in 1714, and George of Hanover succeeded peacefully. Parker made his feelings clear by heaping praise on the dead queen and referring to her successor as merely the 'present possessor of the crown', whose Stuart descent appeared to be his only virtue.[58] The Whig astrologers savoured the joys of victory. Partridge made 1 August (the day of the king's accession) a red-letter day of thanksgiving for deliverance from 'popery, French slavery and English traitors', reminding readers of the villainy of the 'Queen-killers'.[59] He derided the Tories' discontent by recalling their earlier devotion to Romans, xiii, the gospel of non-resistance ('Let every soul be subject unto the higher powers.'). Perhaps the text had been lost; 'about three or four years since, it was of mighty use', he remarked. 'Then they were all damned that did not believe it, and now those that do.'[60] Moore proclaimed George the 'Darling of Mankind', a title once bestowed on William, and thanked the new king for having

saved us from the jaws
Of Tories' folly, and Rome's destroying paws.[61]

Popular hatred of the French and the Jacobites owed much to religious sentiment. Memories of the Popish Plot and of the persecution of the Huguenots ensured that the name of popery stirred up deep and real fears of bloodshed and oppression. In the almanacs of Anne's reign, denunciations of the French and Jacobites went hand in hand with anti-Catholicism, the specialty of Partridge and Moore. For several decades Partridge's series contained a section entitled 'The Protestant Remembrancer', holding up Catholic practices and beliefs to fear and ridicule. The Inquisition, Irish Massacre and Gunpowder Plot were standard items, coupled with mockery of Catholic beliefs as blasphemous and superstitious. The style and contents were similar to the Restoration *Protestant Almanacks* and to earlier editions of Partridge, and much of the material was taken directly from them. Later almanacs in Moore's name stressed the political implications of Catholicism. The editor illustrated 'the miseries of popish government' with an account of Mary Tudor, Louis XIV, James II and Judge Jefferies, warning that the Jacobite Pretender was 'a pupil of the Jesuits, and tool of Rome'. His restoration would mean persecution and heavy taxation.[62] All ecclesiastical lands expropriated after the Reformation would be handed back to the church. These had at present an annual rental value of £3,277,282 19s 6d, the editor asserted with impressive assurance, plus the value of fines, heriots and the like. The church had once owned seventy per cent of landed wealth, and would do so once more.[63]

Anti-popery was linked, almost inevitably, with millenarian excitement. Millennial ideas revived during the troubled 1680s and remained at a high level for a further generation. Many of the most eminent figures within the Anglican Church shared these hopes, including Archbishop Sancroft and Bishop Lloyd. But on the whole the Anglicans reserved their opinions for private discussion among themselves, and for the ears of post-Revolution monarchs. The capacity of the masses for transforming the millennial victory of Protestantism into a creed of social revolution was a lesson unlikely to be quickly forgotten.[64] It was thus left to Baptists and other sectarians, and perhaps more significantly to the astrologers, to bring millenarianism before the wider public. The prolonged warfare against the popish French, the computations of Alsted and others which had pointed to stirring events at the close of the seventeenth century, and a timely conjunction of Saturn and Jupiter in 1702 kept excitement high throughout the reign of Anne. It remained an article of faith in the almanacs that the pope was Antichrist, and that his fall was at hand.[65] Many compilers offered a glorious millenarian future. Moore drew on the Sibylline oracles, the prophecy of the Northern Lion, Joachim and Nostradamus. He envisaged a messianic English conqueror sweeping through Europe to destroy the pope and Turk, and recall the Jews. At other times he echoed the equally mediaeval belief in an angelic pastor who would renew the church and purify its faith, or developed a more astrological concept based on the succession of planetary angels.[66] Similarly, Partridge in 1702 spoke of the millennium due to dawn in the following year and to reach perfection in 1778; his definition of Antichrist widened generously to embrace almost all 'priests of all persuasions'.[67] Many others shared the vision. Tanner anticipated a glorious age of sabbatism, Kendal, a 'peaceable and happy time'. Salmon looked for a messianic *Pax Brittanica.* James Corderoy, writing in 1705, expected cataclysmic upheavals during the next year, culminating in a universal peace and the establishment of Christianity throughout the entire world.[68] Andrews, not wholly convinced, repeatedly expressed the confidence of many in the dawning millennium, and hoped that they were right. Coley was less confident, but included prophecies proclaiming an age of peace, tranquillity and perfection.[69] The hopes were shared by John Wing and his successor, Tycho, which guaranteed that millennial prophecies would appear in almanacs for decades to come. In the 1730s, 1740s and 1750s editors still regularly discussed Lilly, Alsted, the Northern Lion and other traditional sources, now supplemented by later commentators such as William Whiston and Sir John Floyer. The fall of Rome and the Turk were still at hand, and the descent of the New Jerusalem must surely follow.[70] In the 1750s the editor of Moore cited the great earthquake at Lisbon as marking the beginning of the fall of Antichrist (for the city had been inhabited by 'most bigoted' papists), and mentioned a triumphant piece of Whig theology, by which the Young Pretender, Charles Edward, was unveiled as the little horn of the beast of Daniel. It may be that these last comments were disingenuous, a sop to please the readers. Modern credulity is certainly strained by the interpretation of the 'remarkable prediction' of the prophet Ezekiel: 'Thou shalt be desolate, O Mount-seir' (Ezek. xxxv: 15). 'The Mount-seir', explained the editor, 'correspondeth with Monsieur the Frenchman', and thus indicated the ruin of France in the Seven Years War.[71] But whatever the real beliefs of the compiler, it is clear that the attempt to fit contemporary events into a millennial pattern was popular with the vast readership. The edition for 1761 discussed the key prophetic texts of the Bible, and two years later the author returned to the subject and set out his interpretation of them, in response, he claimed, to demands from his readers.[72]

As the eighteenth century advanced, the Whig domination had a tranquillizing effect on the almanacs, as on society at large. This process was naturally gradual, however, and the early Hanoverian years witnessed further vitriolic attacks on the alleged Jacobite sympathies of the Tories. Partridge's edition for 1730 contained the description of a voyage to 'Tory Land' (perhaps in imitation of Swift's *Gulliver*) where

> Whipping posts like elms are set in rows,
> And at each cottage door, a gallows grows. . . .
> Free quarter is the word, for meat and drink,
> And men are hanged if they but dare to think.[73]

The expressions of loyalty to the Hanoverians were by no means unconditional. Early in the reign of George II, the editor of Moore spelt out the merits of a mixed constitution, where

> In equal distance from extremes we move,
> No tyranny nor commonwealth approve,

and where monarchy

> Is mixed and qualified with such allay
> That free-born subjects willingly obey.[74]

In the mid-century, suspicions of royal ambition grew, fed by resentment at the expensive Continental entanglements of the 1740s and 1750s, which appeared to serve only the king's private interests in Hanover. One result was a remarkable and ferocious attack in *The Coelestial Diary*, published under the name of Salem Pearse. Between 1756 and 1759 it carried long, successive instalments of an angry poem denouncing the king as a traitor and all politicians as factious and corrupt. The first section was taken *verbatim* (though unacknowledged) from Defoe's poem, *The True-born Englishman* (1701), a savage indictment of the politicians of William's reign. In the following years, the editor proclaimed the political degeneracy of his own age, and the consequences it would bring. The king, he warned, was hastening to his own destruction, and that of the nation. In pressing his private interests (however just) to the point where the people suffered hardship, the king was betraying his trust, and could rightfully be brought to account, and even laid aside. Politicians of every group were ignoring their duty in their lust for office. 'Tis a symptom of a sottish nation/To grow respectless of self-preservation', the editor lamented, complaining (in Defoe's words) that

> Statesmen are always sick of one disease;
> And a sound pension gives them present ease.
> That's the specific makes them all content
> With any king, and any government.

The monarch was surrounded by 'ear-bor'd slaves' who 'idolize and deify their king', recalling a bygone tyranny (of James II?) produced

> By parasites and priests, who, that a king
> Might make them something, made him any thing
> Which he desired to be.

Even the 'patriots' had deserted their beliefs in return for office (an allusion to Chatham and his friends, who had once shared the author's suspicions, but were now directing the war against France). The compiler sought peace and the liberty of the subject; both required a willingness to curb the crown. Kings, he thought, must be closely guarded at all times, like lions: both had aggressive and tyrannical natures which could never be wholly eradicated. Councillors must see their duty before it was too late, for the king would soon become able to dictate what terms he thought fit. The poet claimed to prefer a regulated monarchy to a republic. Even so, the poem is an undisguised and bitter condemnation of George II, his ministers and contemporary politicians, and it is astonishing that it continued to appear, apparently without interruption, in a series published under a royal patent.[75] Many of its themes were developed in the almanacs of Henry Season (discussed below), who proclaimed himself a champion of the subject's rights.

These fiery denunciations were far from typical, however, of the great mass of eighteenth-century almanacs. The first edition of Moore's almanac to appear after the founder's death contained, in place of the usual vitriolic introduction, a poem extolling the joys of a quiet life and peaceful end. The editor of Gadbury's almanac for 1736 enjoined his work

> To promote true loyalty where'er thou art
> But never act the Jesuit part;
> Never concern thyself with Whig and Tory
> Nor tell them of a court and country story.[76]

A later edition of Partridge contained a treatise on the 'folly of factions and divisions in contested elections', stressing the corruption they bred, and urging upon its readers a mood of apolitical resignation, for

Our rulers even what they think fit will do,
And care not how tis thought by me nor you.

The author implored his muse to 'inspire each pen to write sedition down' and 'unite each heart' to king and church.[77] On the whole, the muse obliged. Most compilers were content to heap praise on George I, George II and even Frederick, Prince of Wales ('Poor Fred'), who was led to believe that 'half the virtues your few years enfold/Have deified a hundred kings of old.'[78] After its few years of political fervour, Pearse sank back into docility; the edition for 1770 was a tame affair, containing a long and respectful account of George III's coronation (nine years earlier!), taken from the *London Gazette*.[79]

Political agitation thus disappeared from the majority of editions. Even religious polemic, though it survived, declined in violence.[80] Much of the religious material throughout the century followed the Tudor and Stuart pattern, preoccupied with repentance, moral reformation and the approach of death. The *memento mori* was unchanged in purpose, and often in language. Each new edition, warned Coley in a time-worn phrase, marked one year's approach nearer death. Pearse observed gravely that

The age of man's but threescore years and ten,
Scarce in a hundred two arrive to then.

Seventy years, he computed, were merely 613,620 hours, which would soon tick away. Another writer concluded with the memorable advice:

Then use thy time, and always bear in mind,
Time's forehead hairy is, but bald behind.[81]

The editor of Moore devised in 1775 a striking and novel method of expressing the old call for reformation, by printing a diagram of a pair of spectacles with the words (in the left lens), 'perspective spectacles of especial use', (on the bridge) 'new, new polished', (in the right lens) 'to discern the world's vanity, levity & brevity'.[82]

The astrologers did not follow the eighteenth-century drift towards deism or atheism. They offered instead a staunch defence of traditional Christian teaching. William Andrews denounced the profane wits who 'deny even the Godhead, and burlesque the glorious Trinity'; such people must be the false prophets predicted by the Bible as one of the signs of the world's approaching end. Much later in the century Season devoted two editions to proving the existence of God.[83] Compilers argued, as before, that God was the first cause of all things, able if he wished to overrule the stars. But the emphasis was now far more on the contribution of astronomy and astrology to the strengthening of religious faith. They explained, as their predecessors had done, that the contemplation of the universe led mankind to the worship of its maker—an argument now used widely by the school of 'natural theologians' within the church. The motions and influence of the heavenly bodies, and the atomic structure of matter, pointed equally to the unimaginable skill of God the creator.[84] There was, of course, no endorsement of the materialist atomism of Epicurus, which dispensed with divine providence. The universe could not have been created by a chance fusion of atoms, declared Job Gadbury emphatically, for 'though the air we breathe in be full of them, yet they tend to nothing but to make us wink', and in the 5,657 years since the Creation, 'they have not produced the least trifle in nature.'[85] Richard Saunder, though more sympathetic towards the new science, similarly had no doubt that the hand of God alone had shaped the universe. Having demonstrated that the moon had an atmosphere, he thought 'there will be no grounds left for the doubt or hesitations, namely, whether it be inhabited or no.' For just as 'the earth itself was made for the use of its inhabitants, chiefly for man', so the moon must likewise have been created 'certainly for the use, convenience and benefit' of some advanced form of life, probably human.[86] On a much lower plane, readers were advised to show respect to God's ministers on earth, and to pay their tithes without demur:

> Though vicar be bad, or the parson evil,
> Go not for thy tithing thyself to the devil.[87]

One clear sign of the times, however, was the appearance in 1775 of *The Free-Mason's Calendar*. It set out in detail a list of the society's officials, notes on its constitution, and the addresses of lodges throughout the country. It provided too a fanciful history of the movement in England, claiming a continuous development from the period of Roman Britain and asserting that St. Alban, Archbishop Chichele, Wolsey, Thomas Cromwell and William III had at various times been imong its distinguished members.[88]

Many of the other standard features of the Stuart almanac remained unchanged. Compilers continued to provide weather forecasts, tables of kings, chronologies and notes on the law terms (including the perennial denunciation of the lawyer, that 'Monster in a tufted gown').[89] They supplied medical notes, and criticized the addiction of decadent contemporaries to alcohol, tea, coffee, snuff and tobacco—the last being,

May hath xxxj. daies.

Be bold to vse such physicall intentions
as are prescrib'd by Artists true inuentions:
But loath Impostors and Quacksaluing knaues,
that bring the soundest men t'vntimely graues.

Malicious Saturne playes his wonted prankes,
with Mars, with Venus, Mercury, and Sol:
If May proue ill, wee'l con-him little thankes,
sith his coniunction bodes no danger small
to earths increase, to Cattle, fruite, and all.
Hee's Nature's foe, and he is no mans frend,
That all would haue, and nothing freely spend.

The calendar for May, from Thomas Bretnor's almanac for 1618, showing the saints' days, lunar signs, and memoranda by the original owner (see page 30).

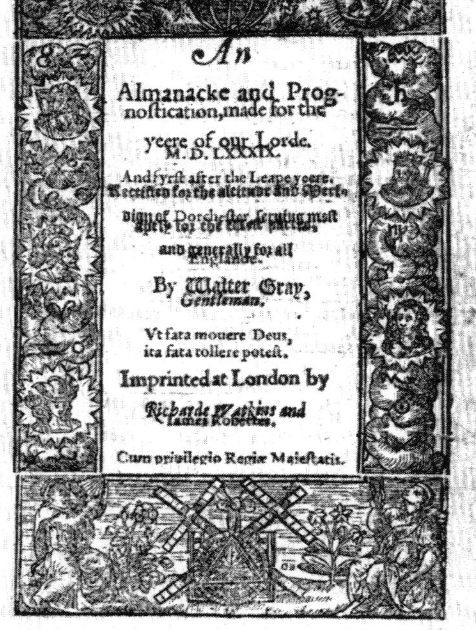

The pronostication calculed by mayster Jaspar Laet of Andwarpe / vpon the merydian of the sayd towne / for the yere of our lorde god. M. D. xxxiij.

An Almanacke and Prognostication, made for the yeere of our Lorde. M. D. LXXXIX.

And fyrst after the Leape yeere. Rectified for the altitude and Meridian of Dorchester, seruing most aptly for the [illegible] and generally for all Englande.

By Walter Gray, Gentleman.

Vt fata mouere Deus, ita fata tollere potest.

Imprinted at London by Richarde Watkins and James Robertes.

Cum priuilegio Regiæ Maiestatis.

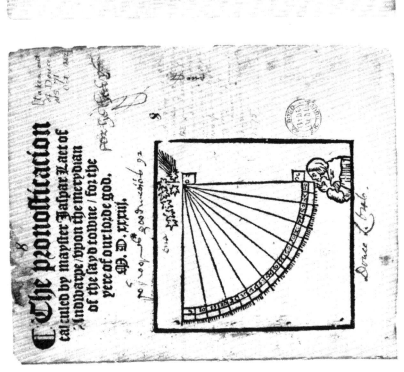

Left: An early Flemish prognostication by Jasper Laet, reissued in an English edition (see pages 27–8).
Right: Title-page of a typical Elizabethan almanac, by Walter Gray.

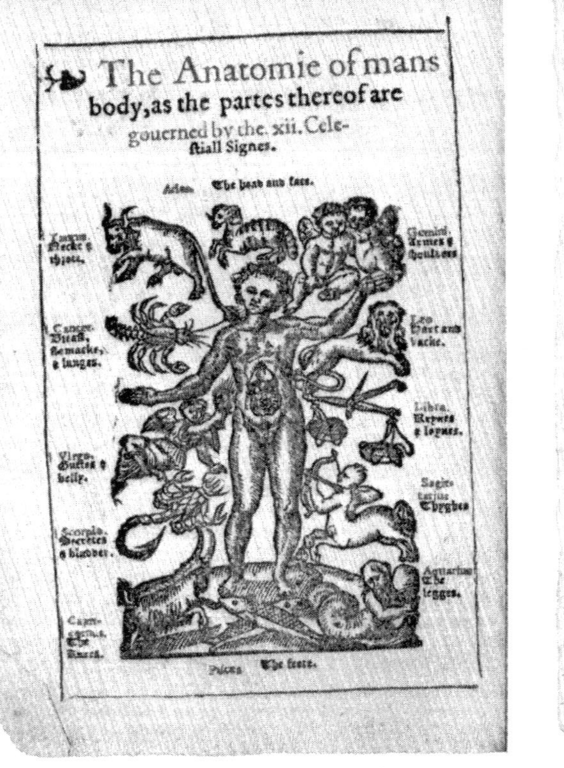

A Compendious Chronologie or Computation of Yeeres.

Since the Creation of the world 5577
Since the Floud of Noah. 3921
Since Israels departure out of Egypt. 3555
Since Salomon built the Temple at Jerusalem. 2645
Since London was built. 2736
Since Yorke was built. 2594
Since the building of Yorke Minster. 909
Since King William conquered England. 560
Since Paul Church in London was built. 542
Since Westminster Hall was built by W. Rufus. 529
Since London Bridge was built of stone. 452
Since the first inuention of Gunnes 248
Since the first inuention of Printing. 168
Since D. Luther detected Popish falshoods. 111
Since K. H.8. crushed the Popes power in Engl. 94
Since the Rebellion in Yorkshire by Aske. 91
Since Register Bookes began in euery Parish. 90
Since the beginning of bles. Q. Elizabeths raigne. 70
Since Ouse Bridge at Yorke was broken downe 64
Since the Rebellion of the 2. Northerne Earles. 59
Since the dolefull Massacre in France by Papists. 56
Since the first deepe Snow. 49
Since the generall Earthquake. 48
Since Tilbury Campe. 40
Since the damnable Powder Treason, Nouem. 5. 23
Since the birth of our Soueraigne King Charles, 26
Since the last great Frost 20
Since the last great Snow. 13
Since the beginning of King Charles raigne, March the 27. 3

Left: The Anatomy, from Walter Gray's almanac for 1589. Such figures appeared in most almanacs, showing the influence of the zodiac on the human body (see pages 204–5). *Right:* A Chronology, or brief history from the creation to the present, from Philip Ranger's edition for 1618. Ranger's works, calculated for York, had a northern emphasis (see pages 215–24).

Left: William Lilly, the celebrated Parliamentarian astrologer. He holds a paper bearing the motto 'Non cogunt' (the stars do not compel), and draws attention to the violent controversy surrounding his works (see pages 73ff).
Right: George Wharton, Lilly's cavalier rival; from Wharton's almanac for 1665 (see pages 72ff).

AN
ALMANACK
OR
PROGNOSTICATION for the year of our LORD 1658, Being the second after Bissextile or Leap year. Calculated for the Meridian of London, and may indifferently serve for England, Scotland, and Ireland.

By SARAH JINNER Student in Astrology.

London, Printed by J. Streater for the Company of Stationers.

To the Reader.

My Friend!

If thou beest *Loyal*, Rejoice with Mee! The *Black* and *Dismal Clouds* which of *late* surrounded us, are *Dissipated*; and the *Angry Genius* of 1678 &c is *retired*, or with its insatiate violence *wearied*, and (I hope for ever) *laid to sleep*. Our *Church* and *State* grows tranquile, and *flourishes* agen: The *English Monarchy*, (but lately bearded, not to say despited) hath recovered its *Pristine Glory*; and looks like *Heaven* it self, *Awful* and *Majestick*: The *Republican Interest* runs Retrograde: *Exclusion-mongers* are wholly *out of fashion*; and even the *Trimming-Dissenter* is unwilling to have it believ'd he ever design'd to *Rob the Heir of his Birth-right*; and would make himself *Loyal* again by a *Kiss*.

The *Salamanca Seer* hath Discover'd, and Talk'd himself *out of his Liberty*; and taken up his *Rest* in a *Prison*.

The late *busie Knight* who was wont to *disturb* his *Quiet Neighbours* at *Midnight*, to search for *Priests* in *Pepper-Boxes*, and to mistake *Jewels*, *Broad-Pieces*, &c. for *Popish Reliques*, now finds *English Air* disagreeable to him.

The *Colonel* of the *Meal-Tub Plot* hath time to study better upon that *villanous cheating Contrivance*, (which for a while dazled the Eyes of the Nation) and may probably be willing, for his *own safety*, to discover the *Nonconformist Parson*, *that wrote the Lying-Knavish Narrative thereof for him*, to which he *impudently* set his *Doughty Name*, and took *Twenty five Pounds for the Copy*.

Dangerfield, like a *Duck*, is *Div'd* into the *Dark*, even beyond all present Industry to discover; and his *fellow-Witness*, *Elizabeth Jenkinson*, not easie to be heard of.

Dugdale found a *Prison* too *hot* for him, and wanting a *Lord* or *Master* to *swear against* for purchase of his Liberty, hath broke *Stone-Walls*, and is *Run* for it.

Prance

Left: Sarah Jinner pioneered almanacs for women in the late 1650s, championing her sex and offering lively political comment (see page 87). *Right:* The author's epistle often grew into an editorial. Gadbury in 1685 celebrates the ruin of the Whigs and the discrediting of the Popish Plot (see page 94).

Aſtrological Obſervations, 1679.

THE Horoſcope of the Vernal Ingreſs being a ſign Bi-corporeal, ſome Aſtrologers will allow that the figure thereof ſhall laſt but one half of the year; and they appoint us to erect another for the remaining part. I have diſcourſed a little of this matter in my *Diary* for 1677, and given my Reaſon too, why I conceive that it ought not to laſt longer than a quarter: and that therefore the good or ill thereby ſignified cannot continue longer than ſuch a time.

[Note, that herein I do not include the effects of Eclipſes, they, I know, will take up longer time to breath in, and diſcover themſelves.] Howbeit, for want of room, am conſtrain'd to omit and wave my own, & follow their Hypotheſis, who allow a Solar Ingreſs of a By-corporeal Horoſcope, half a years Regency.

Under this Revolution, there will ariſe mighty diſcontents and troubles to mankind in general; poſſibly, ſome famous Battail, or Naval conflicts near at hand Northward, or North-eaſt. Great ſuſpitions and jealouſies between men and their Wives working a ſeparation of many of them. Much quarrelling and falſhood in, and among friends; ſundry Robberies at Land, the High-ways infeſted with Tories and Padders: many Piracies at Sea, ſudden Shipwracks, *&c.*——Many Abortions among Women with Child; and great frauds and treacheries diſcovered among perſons pretending piety; divers wicked and profane wretches will be very active to caſt dirt upon the Clergy, and upon the Lawyers and on the whole Eccleſiaſtical and civil functions together.——All theſe things, and more, are (or may be) collected from the great ☍ of ☽. ♃ ☍ and ♀ from the third and ninth Angles, and ☋ in ♈ on the ninth; together, with ♀ his caſting an oppoſition thither.

But, there is that which is ſomewhat more eminent and remarkable, *viz.* the ☍ ♃ ♂ and □ of ☉ and ♄, the latter of which is from Cardinal ſigns: and intimate many attempts, of notable import, near our grand Havens or Sea-ports, by Pirates and Forraigners. They alſo portend unquietneſſes at home, with many informations againſt ſundry in great places, (the ☉ ♄ ♃ ♂ are of ſuperiour rule in the Heavens) with a fear of impriſonments, arraignments, and death, we hope, of the King and Kingdoms enemies. One, or more very great perſon, or perſons dies ſuddenly, either by Poyſon, or Apoplexy, *&c.*

In this part of the year, *viz.* on *September* the 24*th*, about 6 h. P. M

Aſtrological Obſervations, 1679.

P.M. the Sun ſuffers an Eclipſe, juſt falling into the ſixth Angle, a place of ſervitude and bondage; and at the ſame time, ♃ ♂ and ♀ are in an ☍ from Angles, and ♄ caſts an envious Quadrate to both the Luminaries. This *Eclipſe* is celebrated in 11 ♎ and the benevolent Planet ♀ is Governeſs thereof. I ſhall not pourtray out its portents in this place, my colours are too weak, and my cloth too narrow, wherewith, or whereon to expreſs them. But let it ſignifie what it will, it doth not directly concern *England*; for ♎ is in ☍ of ♈, and I am glad I have that good news to befriend it withal. Only, I remember a Quadrin in *Noſtredame*, which after a myſtical manner ſeems to import its ſignifications.

Le Regne & Roy ſoubs Venus eſleve,
Saturne aura ſur Jupiter Empire,
La Loy & Regne par Jupiter leve,
Par Saturnins endurera le pire.

I render it briefly in this courſe *Engliſh.*
When *Venus* ſhall a Prince and Empire raiſe,
And *Jove* conſtrain'd to yield dal *Saturn* praiſe;
Then ſhall the Law and Power *Jove* did erect,
Strike ſayl, and bow, to a Saturnine Sect.

Before this Revolution be ended, there will happen a Lunar Eclipſe in ♈, *viz* on *Octob.* 9. about 11 a Clock before Noon; but it is inviſible as to us, or elſe it might have moſt unhappily aggravated the effects of the Solar Eclipſe in *March*; of which I ſpoke ſomewhat before. As it is, it menaces the Female Sex chiefly, and that with untimely births, and ſundry other inconveniences, *&c.* & ſo you ſee it accords with the Autumnal figure.

To conclude, The judgments of this year, have relation, Aſtrologically, to 17 figures of Heaven. In 14, whereof you will find ♄ or ♂ in an Angle: and ♃ or ♀ will not be Angular in more than 8 of them.—*Ergo*, the evil of the year is much greater, and more powerful than the good thereof. But had the Arguments been equal in number, ſtill there had been a diſproportion in Power, and mankind would ſo have found it. For, *ad Deſtruendum, unam ſufficit, ad conſtruendum, multum.* God ſend peace and plenty to ſurround this Nation, and bleſs the King, Nobles, Clergy, Gentry, and Commonalty thereof. *Amen.*

An

Astrological predictions for 1679, from John Gadbury's almanac for that year (see page 35).

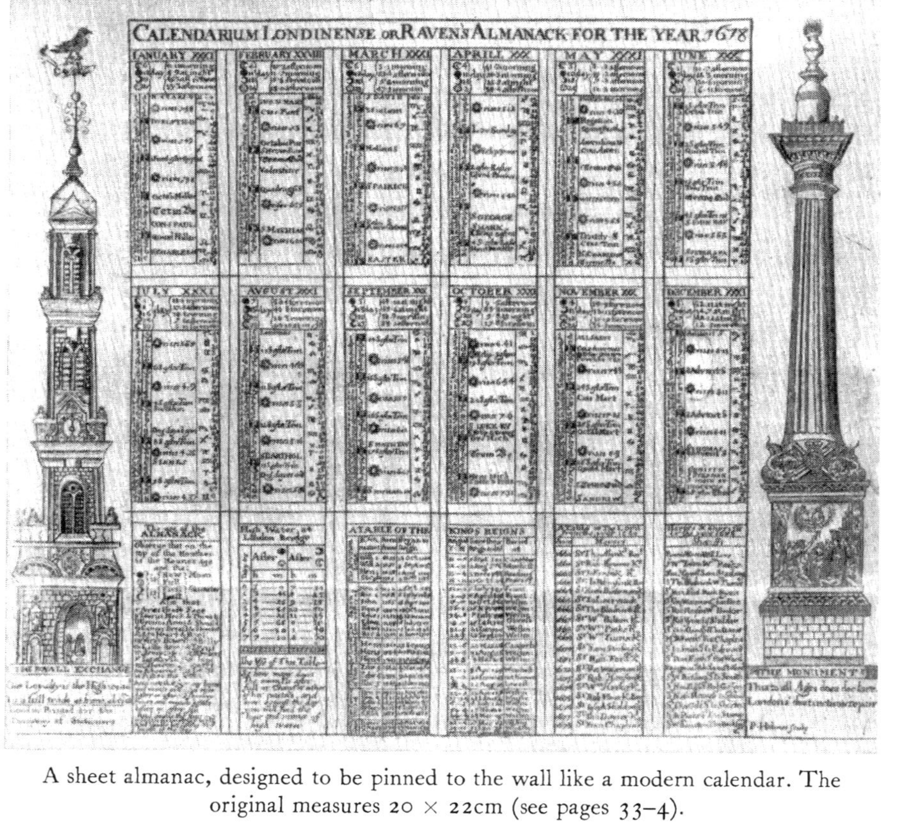

A sheet almanac, designed to be pinned to the wall like a modern calendar. The original measures 20 × 22cm (see pages 33–4).

18 *New Questions.*

Was to the Arch CE as ten to four;
From whence the unknown Side he may explore.

(2.) Question 206. *By* Merones.

If a *Cannon Ball* be projected upwards in a Direction perpendicular to the Horizon, Half a Mile high, and in the Latitude of 53 Degrees; where will it fall?

(3.) Question 207. *By Mr.* John May *Jun.*

There came three *Dutchmen* of my Acquaintance to see me, being lately married; they brought their Wives with them. The Men's Names were *Hendrick*, *Claas*, and *Cornelius*, the Women's *Geertruij*, *Catrijn*, and *Anna*: But I forgot the Name of each Man's Wife. They told me they had been at Market to buy Hogs; each Person bought as many Hogs as they gave Shillings for each Hog; *Hendrick* bought 23 Hogs more than *Catrijn*; and *Claas* bought 11 more than *Geertruij*; likewise, each Man laid out 3 Guineas more than his Wife. I desire to know the Names of each Man's Wife.

(4.) Question 208. *By Mr.* Hen. Travis.

Given this Equation, *viz.* $Axy + Bx + Z - C = 0$;
Expressing the Relation of the Sides of a *Trapezium* inscrib'd in a *Circle*, whose Diam. is known to be 75 Feet (or *d*). Requir'd the Sides separately, and Area, by a general Method that will resolve all such Problems?
N. B. A=100; B=5; C=432246.

(5.) Question 209. *By Mr.* Rob. Heath.

Ingenious Ladies of the *British* Isle,
Whose Minds are fraught with scientifick Arts;
Renown'd for *Virtue*, *Wit*, and *Excellence*;
The Admiration of the learned World:
Whose bright Reflections, swift, like Light'ning, pierce
The secret Pow'r, and hidden Depth of Things:
Disclose to Light * this dark mysterious Truth,
And distant Nations shall your Praise resound.

* $\overline{\frac{1}{x^{\frac{1}{2}}}}\Big|^{x^{\frac{2}{3}}}$ a *Minimum.* *Quære* x^2.

(6.) Question 210. *By Mr.* Ric. Dunthorne.

Suppose a *Cask* in Form of the *middle Frustrum* of an *Hyperbolick Spindle*, whose Length is 24 Inches, Bung Diameter 30, Head Diam. 20, and *Transverse Axis* of the generating *Hyperbola* 100 Inches. Required its *Content* in *Ale Gallons*?

(7.) Question 211. *By Mr.* Ri. Lovatt.

Suppose that in the *Spherical Triangle* ABD, there is given AB=80°:3'; AD=60:10; AC=40:21; the Angle BAD=73:04, and DCA equal to BCA: What are the Sides DC and BC?

A
D
C
B

(8.) Question 212. *By Mr.* Christo. Mason.

There is a *Triangular* Piece of Ground, whose *Center of Gravity* is distant

44 MOORE, 1794.

January, 1793, I erected a Scheme of the Heavens at that Time, and was not disappointed in my Expectation of the Figure being an admirable Picture of that memorable Transaction. And here I shall note, that those who doubt of the Verity of Astrology, if they understand its first Principles, and will be at the Trouble to take a retrospective View of the Position of the Heavens at that awful Moment, and think of the corresponding Event, will surely doubt no more. Here follows

The Scheme or Figure of the Heavens at the Death of the unfortunate Louis XVI. *late King of the French.*

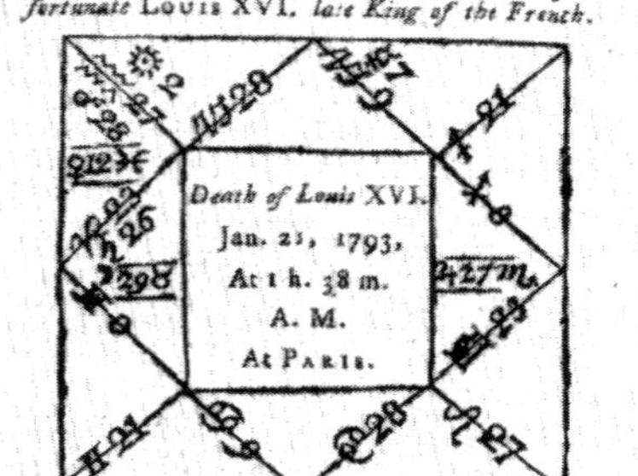

Here we see 9 Degrees of *Capricorn* culminated, and 23 Degrees of *Aries* were on the Ascendant; the Sign *Taurus* was intercepted therein, and the Planets as in the above Figure. The Planet *Saturn* (the great Infortune) in *Aries*, his Fall! and Lord of the 10th House, his Honour or Station he held here upon Earth; and Lord of the 11th House, denoting his Hopes and Friends; and also of the 12th House, denoting his Captivity and Undoing; *Saturn* is also located in the Ascendant, in reception with *Mars*, who is in the 12th in □ of the Planet *Jupiter* and the *Moon*; the latter Planet, namely the *Moon*, is posited in *Taurus* (which governs the *Neck*), *Venus* her Dispositor located

Left: The Ladies' Diary abandoned astrology and set out to educate and amuse its readers. In this edition (for 1739) a mathematical problem is introduced in verse (see pages 245–7). *Right:* For Francis Moore's editor, by contrast, the stars explained the execution of Louis XVI (see pages (265–6).

allegedly, a cause of scurvy.[90] A fierce denunciation of enclosures and depopulation, certainly relevant to the contemporary situation when it was published in 1768, was no more than a direct (though unacknowledged) quotation from Wing's diatribes over a century before.[91]

The tradition of scientific popularization also survived. The most important series in this respect were Saunder's, the *Ladies'* and the *Gentleman's*, but other, more conventional almanacs carried similar information. Thus *Culpepper*, one of the most traditional and stereotyped series, contained in 1702 a fairly elaborate explanation of the Copernican system. John Wing a few years later discussed Newton's gravitational theories, and the periodicity of comets. Andrews explained the significance of stellar parallax in proving the immense distances separating the earth from the stars, and cited Newton, Huygens, Hooke and Flamsteed.[92] Several compilers throughout the century discussed the high probability of life on the moon.[93]

As in the seventeenth century, many of the scientific notes display elements of tradition as well as innovation. Thus William Andrews set out several natural explanations of lightning, for example by Pliny and Bacon, but asserted that it could also be a direct act of God, and accepted this divine interpretation in discussing a dramatic stroke of lightning in his native village of Radwinter in September 1703. John Partridge used a contemporary mechanical idiom in speaking of 'the clock-work of nature', but went on to explain that angels had prior knowledge of its operation and likely effects, which they sometimes revealed to mankind. Fifty years later, Moore referred to the impending return of a comet according to Halley's theory of periodicity, but was confident that it would produce dramatic upheavals, including the fall of France. Still later, the physician Henry Season, a man of advanced political views, wrote in wholly traditional terms of the macrocosm and microcosm. The sun, he explained, had a comparable role in each sphere: it warmed the earth, making life possible, and warmed the body, producing perspiration and thus assisting the circulation of blood freed from impurities.[94] These remarks strike us as an uneasy juxtaposition of traditional and modern explanations of nature, but the writers themselves showed no signs of unease. They either felt that they had successfully synthesized these different modes of interpretation, or they were able—consciously or unconsciously—to believe in both at once. These characteristics were shared by many other more eminent contemporaries. The latitudinarians accepted natural explanations of earthquakes and similar phenomena, but were willing to accept some as caused directly by God. The astronomer, William Whiston, believed that the great world-empires of the past had collapsed after the occurrence of major eclipses, which were possibly the causes. Newton saw the universe in largely mechanical terms, but felt that it would decay, like all machines, with the passage of time, and required the divine hand of providence to refine and reshape it. Comets were a likely agency: Halley, Whiston and Newton indeed shared a belief in comets as instruments of divine intervention.[95]

Though traditional assumptions thus clearly survived in eighteenth-century almanacs, the attitude of the later compilers towards astrology itself contrasts sharply with the earlier period. As mentioned already, writers such as Richard Saunder and John Tipper openly denounced astrology. Saunder declared that it was based on ancient and erroneous tables, that the signs of the zodiac existed in the imagination alone, and that the influence of the fixed stars, 'hundreds of thousands of millions of miles' away, was beyond the wit of man to decipher. He welcomed Jonathan Swift's squib against the astrologers, noting urbanely that 'Bickerstaff' had killed Partridge at the first attempt, whereas Partridge and his friends had been trying to kill Louis XIV for twenty years, to no avail.[96] Many compilers did, however, remain loyal to their science. Tycho Wing asserted defiantly that 'astrology is my Diana', 'the most sublime and excellent of all sciences, and next to theology . . . the most valuable of all human learning'. Edlin's successful prediction of the Great Fire was a vindication beyond question.[97] John Hartley and George Parker made similar defences.[98] There was some attempt to secure scientific respectability by quoting Robert Boyle's belief that each planet emitted a different light which affected the air, which in turn (through 'some peculiar tincture, virtue or power') influenced 'the spirits or subtler parts of all bodies'. Whiston's interest in astrology was also noted.[99] But generally the defence offered was little more than a token recitation of traditional biblical texts and hallowed names, from Ptolemy to Heydon, and sometimes no more than flat assertion. The attempt to prove and study astrology experimentally died away early in the new century. John Gadbury, the most ambitious of the reformers, came close to admitting his failure. He wrote shortly before his death that he could not 'wholly renounce or bid Good-night to astrology', but no longer felt able to defend many of its doctrines and claims which he had once accepted.[100] Many later compilers admitted the disregard and derision with which their science was viewed.[101] The editor of 'Coley' inserted a stern rebuke to those who consulted astrologers in search of fun, not instruction. The client, he stressed, should prepare himself by prayer and approach the astrologer 'with a serious intent of being satisfied'. Facetious questions 'may cause a wise respondent to err, which brings a scandal upon art'—a novel, and doubtless welcome escape-clause. The astrologer, Samuel Penseyre, advised the young practitioner that it was often possible to expose frivolous clients by openly challenging their motives and, more prosaically, by demanding prepayment before casting a figure.[102] Job Gadbury confessed that though astrology was 'most indubitably true', 'there are few that practise it who rightly understand it.' William Andrews's assertion in 1712 that the effects of the new star of 1572 had still yet to appear fully seems to symbolize the intellectual exhaustion of the subject.[103] Astrology, it was said, needed its Newton to revive and restore it, but few even aspired to the role. Henry Season was unique among the almanac-makers in declaring his resolve to purify the science. He published almanacs for a further forty years, but appears to have achieved little. In 1769 he told his readers, rather lamely, that 'though the art is excellent and much truth is in it, yet much difficulty attends it, for want of just principles to proceed by.' Many of the rules seemed to be arbitrary. He could find no basis for the doctrine of elections, nor for the rule of certain signs of the zodiac over particular countries, and rejected all Arab innovations and any 'rattle-brained whim . . . brought in by Placidus, and other monks, Jesuits &c.' By the end of his life he had, like Gadbury, renounced many of his earlier astrological beliefs; any prediction claiming exactness must be 'perfect heresy', based on 'crude principles', and utterly worthless.[104]

Though Henry Season failed to revitalize astrology, his *Speculum Anni* stands out from the stereotyped almanacs of the mid-eighteenth century and displays the lively individualism of the best Elizabethan and Stuart editions. Season was born in the small Wiltshire village of Broomham in 1693 and brought up by his grandmother, his mother having died at his birth. He tells us that he could read the Bible at five, but his education was slight and spasmodic, its longest unbroken period being a mere six weeks. In 1710 he went to London to join his father, and worked as an assistant to a funeral undertaker. Returning to Broomham (where he settled, appropriately, in Bones Lane), he taught himself astrology and medicine with the encouragement of a local squire, John Nicholson. From about 1723 he set up as a practising astrologer and astrological physician, calculating elections, preparing Sloane's powder, tinctures for the eyes and teeth, and medicaments for rickets. In due course he became a licensed physician and surgeon.[105]

Season published an almanac in his own name from 1733 till his death in 1775. Its sales were modest, about three thousand copies a year. Though some reached London and further afield, most were clearly sold in and around Wiltshire. The enigmas, which he included in imitation of *The Ladies 'Diary*, drew replies from local readers, some from his own parish (among them his friend, the rector). The author did however acquire fame enough to be attacked by many of the rival compilers, and to be mocked by *Poor Robin* as 'Nostradamus Season'.[106] He was conscious of his special position among almanac-makers: unlike many, he wrote under his own name; unlike some, he firmly believed in astrology; and he disdained the practice of filling his works with pirated extracts from seventeenth-century almanacs, commenting that 'such practices I detest.'[107]

Season's almanac was traditional in form. It contained a lively chronology which began with the Trojan wars and ended with the author's fall when his horse stumbled while crossing a river. The chronology, and the entire work, contained a mass of tendentious comment on modern politics and society.[108] Season believed, conventionally enough, in the total superiority of England and the English in every respect. He denounced papists, atheists, and Jews. Sir James Dashwood, who in 1753 moved the repeal of a recent measure for the naturalization of foreign Jews, earned by his action an honourable place in the chronology:

> Since right'ous Dashwood did repeal the bill,
> For which God bless'd him, and will bless him still.[109]

Season combined national pride with a gloomy conviction of the moral degeneracy of his age. Discussing the probability of life on the moon, he rejoiced that man could never travel there, 'for we should use such treachery' towards the lunar inhabitants that 'we should ruin them, or teach them our vices, and so they would ruin themselves ('tis scarce to be thought they are so base as we).'[110] A major cause of this baseness, he thought, was the availability of cheap liquor; he returned frequently to the evils of drunkenness, and spoke dramatically of 'whole families swept away by an inundation of strong liquors'. He added denunciations of tobacco, gambling, and the new fashion of taking snuff (when 'nastiness sprang up'). Similarly, stage-plays 'enervate all true religion', bred effeminacy and bound people 'in firmer league with their passions and lusts'.[111] With these vices went an unprecedented profanation of the sabbath. 'In my parish we have a great increase of inhabitants, but a vast decrease found at church; not a third part to what was formerly; few women after marriage.'[112] He attempted to remedy this lack of interest by providing some basic religious teaching, while dismissing the popular preoccupation with the apocalypse. One edition contained a defence of the Trinity, which Season found proved and paralleled by the threefold division of God's Creation into the elementary, celestial and intellectual heavens, animal, vegetable and mineral matter, and the three (Paracelsian) elements of salt, mercury and sulphur.[113]

Season's preoccupation with popular vices was matched by his hostility to the values and policies of the government. He held that the chief cause of famine was the transportation of corn and cattle out of the country, a practice so iniquitous that it made lawyers seem almost harmless. He urged parliament also to suppress quack physicians, another major cause of popular hardship, but had little hope of any response: members of parliament, he thought, 'are generally more solicitous about hares and wagon-wheels than about the health or lives' of the poor.[114]

The most distinctive feature of the almanacs was political. Season adopted a radical stance, and had personal links with the Earl of Shelburne, leader of a group of the more radical Whigs, and a future prime minister. He described the earl as his friend and benefactor, and reported that Shelburne had sent him the (naturally correct) solution to one of the annual enigmas. Sir Edward Rolt, M.P. for Chippenham, was another friend and correspondent.[115] The link with Shelburne clearly influenced Season's political outlook. His almanacs defended Pitt, Shelburne, Beckford and Wilkes. The dominant issues were patriotism and the defence of liberty against unscrupulous politicians willing to connive at royal tyranny in return for office. In an early edition he offered the barbed prayer, 'God bless the Commons of the land,/And God bless some o'th'peers'. A later edition commemorated Pitt's arrival in office in1756, when

> Patr'otism reviv'd, when nearly dead
> By Pitt the Just, who's justly honoured.[116]

The death of William Beckford, the London alderman who was Pitt's ally and the champion of the small merchants against oligarchic power, was recorded with an elegy mourning Liberty's champion,

> For who, like him, 'midst the degenerate race,
> Will brave the truth before the monarch's face?

He asked the Lord to preserve King George

From the bane of princes, fawning flattery;
And banish from him all those scurvy elves,
That rob the land to enrich themselves.[117]

A new champion of the people against the royal prerogative was in fact already to hand, in the person of John Wilkes, repeatedly expelled from parliament in the 1760s for allegedly libelling the crown. In 1769 Wilkes became an alderman of London, and in 1771 he was chosen sheriff. Season was delighted, celebrating in his almanac the fact that from

vast malignant foes
Wilkes has emerg'd, and now to Honour rose;
Go on, great hero, for our rights engage,
Fetch Astraea down, to reform this age.

In the last edition he ever compiled, Season was still denouncing the 'bribery and corruption' endemic in public life.[118]

Season's almanacs contained also a wealth of lively comment on contemporary practices and attitudes, often with a local bearing. For example, at the request of some neighbouring gentlemen he published in 1763 a denunciation of the country people who refused to accept the new Gregorian calendar introduced in 1752, which advanced the date by twelve days. 'Some such apes we have in my own parish', he remarked. Several years later the village was apparently still celebrating both Old and New Christmas.[119] He was equally scathing about some of the local people who called him a conjuror: such people he thought 'not an ace above a Hottentot', for they 'just know how to labour, eat and produce their own species and that is all'.[120] The deep-rooted ignorance and suspicion of the illiterate was another of his targets. He held simple-minded mothers to blame, for believing that any 'learning' would damage their children's brains. Season used both sarcasm and abuse to combat this attitude. He told the story of a rich tenant farmer, invited to bring his accounts to his landlord's feast, who was unable to tackle the most simple sums and had to trudge a mile and a half carrying a door on which the figures had been chalked. He concluded uncharitably that there was more difference between ignorant and idle rustics and men like 'Sir Isaac Newton and Mr. Locke . . . than between some men and monkeys'.[121] Season had a genuine concern for the rural poor, but a total lack of respect for them. After his death the series was continued by Thomas Wright, but almost immediately lost its flavour of individuality.

The monopoly held by the Company of Stationers ended abruptly in 1775 when Chancery ruled in favour of a London publisher named Thomas Carnan. He had defied the Stationers 'exclusive rights, and after his legal victory showed himself to be an entrepreneur of genius. Issuing almanacs under the popular, traditional names of Moore, Wing, Andrews and others, he built up annual sales of a hundred thousand copies. Other, lesser publishers entered the field, and as a result the Company's sales slumped dramatically: the number of almanacs it printed had to be cut by half in two years.[122] The Prime Minister, Lord North, introduced a bill into parliament to restore the Stationers' monopoly, but it was rejected in the Commons: Erskine, the lawyer, railed against the 'senseless absurdities' of the Company's works, and made good use of the crude humour found in *Poor Robin*. 'I know of no house but a brothel', he claimed, which could endure to hear quotations from it; Rochester's verse was by comparison a model of chaste restraint. Parliament did however agree to raise the stamp duty yet again, putting the cost of production beyond the reach of the small publisher. The field was thus narrowed to Carnan and the Company, and when Carnan died in 1788, the Stationers bought out his interests. The Company's sales promptly leapt back to over half a million copies annually, and it enjoyed an Indian summer of prosperity.[123]

This final golden age was based almost entirely on the success of one title, Moore's *Vox Stellarum*. The number of copies printed rose steeply: 107,000 in 1768, 230,000 in 1789, 365,000 in 1802 and a peak of 560,000 in 1839. Profits from Moore were over £560 in 1789; those from Season, another long-established title, were a mere £7. In 1802 the profit from Moore was almost £3,000, a better revenue, as a contemporary remarked, than was enjoyed by many a German principality.[124]

The success of *Fox Stellarum* was deserved. It was vastly superior to its rivals. Partridge offered predictions, but was vague and dull. Pearse had become nondescript, and Season declined sharply after the founder's death. The highlight of its edition for 1787 was an essay on man's faithful friend, the dog, followed improbably the next year by a discourse on crocodiles. In 1789 the editor merely reprinted some hymns by Isaac Watts. He conceded that some of his readers preferred prophecies and offered some in a very perfunctory way, remarking disdainfully that 'in my line of writing many different tastes are to be pleased.' If any readers wanted predictions, he wrote derisively in the edition for 1789, he begged leave to 'tell them that the papers of the year 1789 will inform them of several things which in 1788 they never expected'—a prophecy which the outbreak of the French Revolution amply fulfilled.[125]

Under the editorship of Henry Andrews, 'Moore' offered far superior fare. As a good astronomer, Andrews was able to provide full explanations and descriptions of eclipses, comets and similar data, including accounts of the newly-discovered planet, Uranus, and the transit of Mercury in 1799. Like the best Stuart compilers, he read the *Transactions* of the Royal Society while writing for the masses. He supplied astrological predictions of the weather, but also explained in detail how barometers worked, urged their value, and offered to supply readers with sound instruments. In each month of the calendar he set down precise readings of the rainfall measured in the corresponding month of the previous year.[126]

Public taste demanded prophecy and sensationalism which Andrews also provided in good measure. A contemporary described a rustic couple, Griffin and Grace, looking through the new almanacs on market-day. They are baffled by the 'poems and pot-hooks' (incomprehensible astrological symbols) which most editions contain, but Grace has no hesitation in making a choice:

> Take Moore (says Grace), I tell you Moore's the thing,
> Of fall of kingdoms, Lord, it talks so finely,
> And Oh it curses papists most divinely.
> I know that Moore will suit you to a minute;
> Then look you, Griffin—here's a picture in it.[127]

Each edition did indeed contain a hieroglyph, a symbolic picture suggesting war, peace, the fall of empires or some other upheaval. Andrews also usually printed an extract from the prophecies of Nostradamus, which he applied to the present. It was said after his death that his predictions were 'as much laughed at by himself, as by the worshipful company of Stationers for whom he annually manufactured them, in order to render their almanacs saleable among the ignorant'. This was probably true of the hieroglyphs, which often appeared without any provenance or explanation. The figure in 1793, showing a smiling Britannia playing the cello while her spear leans against a tree, symbolized harmony and peace, but is hard to take seriously. Another edition depicted warriors, and was allegedly copied from an ancient Egyptian engraving and sent from Grand Cairo to the editor by his purported friend and tutor in Hebrew, Nathan ben Shaddai; it was surely meant to amuse less credulous readers.[128] But it is not clear that Andrews rejected astrology outright. He received large numbers of queries from would-be clients, and died leaving a large collection of astrological writings in manuscript. He returned frequently to the defence of astrology in his almanacs. He told readers how Halley had shown that comets travel on a regular orbit, but declared that this need not invalidate a belief in their influence. Was there not a cyclical pattern in human history? Might not like causes produce like effects? These apologias may have been disingenuous, but it is by no means certain.[129]

Much of Moore's appeal came probably from the section entitled the 'Astrological Judgement', an annual review of English and foreign affairs which was in effect a synthesis of the author's personal convictions, biblical prophecy, and astrological predictions. There is no reason to question its sincerity. Sometimes Andrews abandoned prophecy and printed blunt editorial comments on current issues. Thus in one edition he turned against enclosers. 'Remember, in the rage of enclosing, the labourers you employ: hard is it for them to be robbed of a common, which with the utmost industry they have raised a cow to graze upon.' Enclosure could be beneficial, for waste was an evil; but 'I insist upon it, that the cottagers ought to have in lieu of their rights certain quantities of land granted them', to supply their personal needs and a modest surplus.[130]

The editor's outlook was that of the more radical Whigs. After the end of the War of American Independence he rejoiced that the struggle, though disruptive for the English, had 'paved the way for freedom'. Before long, other enslaved peoples would 'with a noble and manly daring, assert their liberties, and break off the shackles which have so long oppressed them'. Liberty would spread to Africa and India and throughout the world. The slave trade he denounced as a 'diabolical business'. At home he found grounds for optimism in the construction of hospitals for the poor, the establishment of Sunday schools and the spread of a spirit of 'universal philanthropy'. All pointed to the approach of the millennial day 'when religion, philosophy and the glorious love of liberty shall banish false enthusiasm, gloomy superstition, barbarous ignorance, and most barbarous tyranny from the face of the earth'.[131]

Andrews's deepest beliefs were in the triumph of liberty and Protestantism over royal and popish tyranny. Accordingly he welcomed the French Revolution, in which he saw 'the glorious and happy spirit of liberty'. Its principles would spread to the other states of Europe: 'Despotism, bigotry, and the Inquisition . . . must be, ere long, annihilated both in Spain and Portugal. The prevalence of reason, of truth and of knowledge in France must illuminate all around.'[132] By 1794 the editor was regretting the excesses which accompanied the Revolution, and the execution of the French king. But his sympathies were clearly still with the revolutionaries. Louis XVI was a 'treacherous' and despotic king who had shared the fate of 'his equally insincere prototype, Charles I'. The moral to be drawn was not the evil of revolution but the inevitable downfall of tyrannical monarchs.[133] 'Moore' was of course far less radical than Tom Paine, and carefully refrained from hinting at the need for sweeping changes at home. Nevertheless, its comments must have been an important formative influence in the growth of English radicalism in the early 1790s; even Paine's *The Rights of Man* reached only a fraction of the homes which possessed an annual copy of the almanac. 'Moore' left its readers in no doubt that the French Revolution was the decisive turning-point in the struggle for popular freedom against civil and ecclesiastical tyranny.[134]

From 1793 England was at war with France. The editor proved his loyalty and calmed popular fears by giving an unconditional guarantee that any nation which sought to invade England would fail and be annihilated.[135] His sympathies however continued to lie with the Revolution. The French monarchy, he claimed, had been one of the two beasts of the Book of Revelation. The other was the papacy; both were doomed to destruction before the end of the century. Almanacs had been one of the key vehicles for the preservation of millennial hopes in the eighteenth century. Andrews was familiar with a wide range of writings on the subject, and he shared and no doubt helped to extend the widespread upsurge of millenarian dreams prompted by events in France. He admitted, after the Terror, that the revolutionaries were by no means unspotted champions of the Protestant truth, but argued that God made use of instruments of all kinds to serve his purpose. After all, 'what was Henry VIII who began our reformation from Popery? Was he not a Monster of Iniquity?' Andrews was reassured by the establishment of the Directory in France, which he believed would guarantee a settlement 'on a firm, broad and extensive basis, both of civil and religious liberty'. Year after year he set down his confident expectation of a new age about to dawn.[136] His dream was finally shattered by the rise of Napoleon and the renewal of warfare. The issue now at stake was French imperialism, not liberty. 'Europe by French tyranny's oppressed', he told his readers. England had a divine duty to bring peace and freedom to the Continent by destroying French power; but the millennium had faded.[137]

The popularity of *Vox Stellarum* continued to grow during the first thirty years of the nineteenth century. The day of its publication, said a contemporary, 'is an epoch in the history of the year. . . . with what eagerness are the political prognostications devoured. Even the weather, the alpha and omega of the countryman, is on this occasion a secondary consideration.' At least a proportion of readers continued to believe the prophecies they devoured. During the brieflull in the Anglo-French wars, in 1802–3, 'a man high in office in the City of London' told his friend,'"By God, sir, there will be no war! Moore's almanac predicts a year of prosperity, and at this time speaks only of peace; and I would sooner believe in Moore than in Bonaparte, or Mr. Addington"' (the Prime Minister). In her novel, *Adam Bede*, set around 1800, George Eliot created the character of a prosperous, God-fearing and sensible yeoman, who shows a faith in astrological predictions unchanged since the age of William Lilly. The yeoman studies the hieroglyph in his almanac (clearly based on Moore) and, 'speaking in rather a subdued reverential tone', demands '"What could be truer nor that pictur' o'the cock wi'the big spurs, as has got its head knocked down wi'th'anchor, an'th'firin', an' the ships behind? Why, th'cock's France, an'th'anchor's Nelson—an'they told us that beforehand."'[138]

Henry Andrews died in 1820, but the almanac lost nothing of its vigour or bluntness. A few years later, the editor reviewed the wars and upheavals of recent decades, and asked what results they had brought. 'Why! at home an enormous debt, and on the Continent of Europe the restoration of the ancient governments, with all their monkish absurdities, tyranny, and blasting influence—standing monuments of disgrace to the age we live in.' He believed, like the embittered Levellers after the civil war, that the ordinary people had gained nothing:

> What is it after all the people get?
> Why, taxes, widows, wooden legs and debt.[139]

Material of this kind guaranteed high sales but provoked sharp criticism. Respectable opinion was outraged by such radical and sensational 'clap-trap', which must appeal only to the worst and lowest of mankind: 'how this disgusting medley of faith and absurdity should have found purchasers, even amongst the most besotted slaves of superstition, is utterly incomprehensible.' Similarly, the crude humour still purveyed by *Poor Robin* was seen as 'one of the most gross libels on public taste we ever knew'. The Stationers, decent men as individuals, grew rich collectively by cheating the gullible and through 'the circulation of obscenity'.[140]

Reformers hoped that the spread of education would undermine the hold of astrology. A journalist declared that 'for twenty years education has been marching onward with a sure step. The people have learned not only to read and write, but to think', and were growing ashamed of their former credulity. The appearance in 1828 of *The British Almanac*, published by the Society for the Diffusion of Useful Knowledge, was seen as a major breakthrough. The new almanac provided a wealth of factual information, uncontaminated by astrology or prediction. An optimist declared that 'from that hour the empire of astrology was at an end.'[141] The verdict proved highly premature, but the Society's challenge was real. The Stationers responded by dropping *Poor Robin* and slightly moderating Moore and Partridge. They were embarrassed by their financial dependence on crude sensationalism. In the edition of Moore for 1830 they inserted an apologetic, and disingenuous, statement that prophecies were included only 'from a persuasion that they delude nobody, and because many thousand readers are amused by tracing the coincidences which often occur'. A few years later they launched the *Evangelical* and *Family and Parochial* almanacs, as tokens of their respectability.[142]

The changes proved to be insufficient. In 1834, when the Stationers pressed for a further increase in the stamp tax (already is 3d a copy) to squeeze out rivals, parliament decided that the privilege was outmoded and had been ill-requited and abolished the tax altogether. This move had a far greater impact than the formal abolition of the Stationers monopoly in the previous century. Costs fell dramatically. The Company was able to reduce the price of Moore's edition for 1835 to sixpence, and sales allegedly doubled. But the field was now open to a host of small, mostly provincial publishers. The Stationers, in their best tradition, took over publication of the rival *British Almanac*, but they failed to meet the wider challenge. Sales and revenues dwindled steadily. Even Moore fell away to 50,000 copies in 1895, and a mere 16,000 by the 1920s. The Company handed over production to Letts and then Cassell's and finally, in 1927, severed all connection with almanacs, deciding (rather tardily) that they were beneath its dignity.[143]

The decline of the Company's almanacs was a commercial failure, not the result of the triumph of rationalism. The Victorian period saw the proliferation of cheaper almanacs, mostly produced in the provinces for a local market. *Old Moore's Penny Almanack*, founded in 1842, soon outstripped the Company's more expensive version. Over a million copies of its edition for 1898 were printed, and all were sold by the preceding November. The more elaborate almanacs founded by 'Zadkiel' and 'Raphael' sold together roughly 300,000 copies each year by 1900.[144] Half-way through Victoria's reign, Charles Knight, the publisher, complained that 'the power of imposture has increased, is increasing, and ought to be diminished . . . . The people of England are essentially as ignorant now as they were in the palmy days of Francis Moore. Undoubtedly a large number can read and write; but this is not education.' There was virtually no house in southern England, he thought, without an almanac. 'There was scarcely a farmer who would cut his grass if the almanac predicted rain. No cattle-doctor would give a drench to a cow unless he consulted the table in the almanac showing what sign the moon is in, and what part of the body it governs'. The country people believed implicitly in the dramatic and ominous predictions of '"Master Moore", as the good folk called him', set out under 'the awful heading of "*Vox Coelorum, Fox Dei*, the voice of the Heavens is the voice of God". How small sounded the mundane reasonings of the newspaper writers', by comparison.[145] Moore's appeal may indeed have been wider. In Mrs. Gaskell's *Cranford* the eminently respectable Miss Matty Jenkyns 'read, and was slightly alarmed at Francis Moore's astrological predictions;' 'as to astronomy,' however, 'in a private and confidential conversation, she had told me she never could believe that the earth was moving constantly.'[146]

The later nineteenth century saw a modest revival of astrology at a more respectable level, and this has continued in the present century with the rapid expansion of the subject in newspapers and magazines since the 1930s, and the growth since the 1960s of fashionable and even scientific interest in the occult. Sales of *Old Moore* have soared again. In 1975 its print-order ran to one and three quarter millions. In an uncertain world, the survival of *Old Moore's Almanac* seems one of the safer predictions.[147]

CHAPTER NINE

Conclusion

MEDIAEVAL ASTROLOGY DEVELOPED with little regard to national boundaries, and the history of almanacs too has international ramifications. They evolved in England from foreign, usually Flemish editions, which were imported into this country and eventually imitated by native compilers. It was not until the early Elizabethan period that English astrologers became predominant, and Continental influence survived on a lesser scale for several decades beyond.

Almanacs flourished throughout Europe during the early modern period.[1] They developed precociously in Italy in the fifteenth century, and the *genre* also took root in Spain. (The chair in judicial astrology at the University of Salamanca was to remain occupied until the 1770s. *Don Quixote* contains the story of a diligent student of the University, whose family and friends, 'being ruled by him, grew extremely rich in a short time' by applying astrology to their farming.[2]) It was in Germany and the Netherlands that printed almanacs first flourished in northern Europe, creating a tradition which lasted until the end of the seventeenth century. Some of the German compilers of the late seventeenth century paralleled the English fusion of astrology and millenarianism.[3] French almanacs, which have been studied most thoroughly, formed a prominent element in popular literature down to the nineteenth century. They offered many of the features found in the English editions: religious and moral advice, sensationalism (*étranges merveilles*), tips on medicine and farming, notes on fairs and historical data. Despite the lack of a monopoly comparable to the Stationers', control lay firmly with the French publishers, not the compilers. Production was centred in Normandy and in Troyes, where a handful of publishers held sway for generations. In 1672 the publisher, Oudot, issued thirteen almanacs; in 1696 Blanchard issued twenty-six. Most of the purported authors were mere pseudonyms concealing hack writers who neither understood nor believed in astrological science.[4]

A closer investigation of French almanacs reveals, however, as many contrasts as similarities. In the sixteenth century they were not cheap works aimed at a mass market, but relatively expensive quartos. Though there was no monopoly, it was necessary for astrological works to be approved by a bishop. There were very few provincial booksellers, and distribution in the provinces was in the hands of haberdashers and, in the countryside, of travelling pedlars, the *colporteurs*. In 1611 only forty-six *colporteurs* were licensed for the whole of France, and though there was doubtless some illicit circulation, the narrow channels of distribution must have retarded the development of the almanac. Its metamorphosis into a cheap, mass-produced work was gradual, and only completed in the eighteenth century (helped by the growth of the colporteurs to over five hundred in 1740 and 3,500 by 1848.[5])

By the time the French almanac reached a mass audience, astrology in France was moribund. There was nothing in the late seventeenth-century almanacs to revitalize it; there was no reforming figure like Gadbury among the compilers. The almanac belonged rather to the category of popular literature known as the *bibliothèque bleue*, simple, derivative and largely unchanging. The type was based on the adaptation of other forms of literature—the romance, the occult, religion and history—simplified to match the tastes and capacity of a barely literate readership. Its chief characteristic has been described as 'a steadfast rejection of originality'. Instead it offered useful and entertaining information in an undemanding format. The pseudonymous compilers claimed in their titles to be providing an epitome, digest or summary of wisdom for the countryman. Shunning political, religious or social problems, they taught the reader that by virtue, moderation, wisdom and piety he would find health, prosperity, peace of mind and at the last salvation. The archetypal French almanac, *Le Grand Calendrier Compost des Bergers* (first edition, 1491), matched this pattern admirably. It contained a calendar which linked useful seasonal information with the unfolding stages of human life, and stressed the related themes of moral and physical well-being. This indeed became the core of the French almanac:

Le plus grand secret de ce Livre
Est pour bien mourir de bien vivre.[6]

The English almanac shared many of these features, but others predominated. In England the almanac was characterized by political, religious and social speculation, and by an awareness of change and progress. Thus the chronology often developed into a partisan history or a list of inventions and discoveries, while in France it became merely a recital of the triumphs of the reigning king and his predecessors.[7]

Whereas the French almanac was usually anonymous, the English served often as a means of self-advertisement for the compiler.[8] There was overall a degree of diversity and individuality lacking in the French works. The English almanac does not belong to the *bibliothèque bleue* (or its nearest English equivalent, the chap-book).[9] The most closely related forms in England would be *Erra Pater, The Compost of Ptolomeus Godfridus, Arcandam* and *Aristotle's Master-piece*, which contained astrological rules and predictions and other secret lore, and passed through frequent editions. They were not classified as almanacs, did not come under the Stationers 'monopoly, and were regarded with contempt by more sophisticated astrologers, for whom 'Erra Pater' was indeed a term of abuse.

It is less easy to explain why English and French almanacs developed in these different ways, especially as judicial astrology was extremely influential in sixteenth-century France. Nostradamus, who had considerable sway over Catherine de Medici, the Queen Mother and Regent, was only the most famous of a group of astrologers and magicians patronized by the court.[10] The key lies probably in the fact that in France the almanac and the prognostication developed as two largely separate genres. The reason for that may lie, paradoxically, in the greater status of j udicial astrology in France. The political astrologer was, or aspired to be, a court astrologer rather than a pamphleteer. Nostradamus won lasting fame through his delphic predictions, but his influence rested on his personal connection with Catherine. The pattern survived into the next century, ending with J. B. Morin who owed his chair at the University of Paris to the Queen Mother, Marie de Medici, and who was patronized by both Richelieu and Mazarin.[11] Aspiring astrologers therefore dedicated their predictions to the reigning king. Henry IV was assured that Nostradamus was only the last of a long line of seers who had predicted his reign. Louis XIII learned from the astrologer, Jean Belot, that he was ordained by God and the stars to establish order and root out heresy.[12] To attract the king's attention, something more than mere flattery was required, but the dividing line between attracting and alarming the monarch was narrow and uncertain. Himbet de Billy was less obsequious than some and predicted a series of disasters, but he stressed that he had merely followed the rules of an ancient authority and, to indicate his lack of malice, implored 'Almighty God to make that prognosticator a liar'.[13] Less successful was Noel Morgard, whose vague predictions were deemed subversive in 1614, and who was thereupon sentenced to nine years in the galleys. Any astrologer close to the court was inevitably the object of close and sometimes justified scrutiny. Ruggieri, an Italian astrologer favoured by Catherine de Medici, was twice arrested on suspicion of sorcery. In 1631 a royal astrologer and physician, Senelles, was condemned to the galleys for predicting the death of Louis XIII on the basis of the king's horoscope. The papal bull of the same year against judicial astrology was prompted by a similar prediction of the death of the pope, not by the spread of scientific rationalism. Royal and papal fears were however balanced throughout the sixteenth and early seventeenth centuries by continuing faith in the validity of astrology, and consequently the bulls and edicts were only rarely enforced.[14]

The French prognostication was perhaps too ambitious a work to fit easily with the humble almanac and calendar. When the tide of educated opinion in France turned against astrology, apparently in the 1650s, the prognostication (and the court astrologer) perished, and only the simple almanac survived, by its very nature largely repetitive and stereotyped.[15] The fusion of the almanac with the prognostication in England was thus of great importance. It was in the prognosticatory section that the author displayed his political, religious or scientific interests. It was indeed quite common for the compiler to place his epistle to the reader at the beginning of the second, prognosticatory section, which indicated clearly that the almanac itself could be wholly stereotyped. The more complex and individual characteristics of the English almanac grew out of its fusion with the prognostication, a development which failed to take root in France.

There are two further reasons which help to explain the character of the English almanac and its differences from the French. One is the role of the civil war. There was little sign in the English almanacs of the 1630s of the vitality and variety of the following decades. Through censorship, the role of political prophecy and other discussion of current issues had shrunk steadily from the Elizabethan period. Many of the leading Jacobean and Caroline compilers were more interested in scientific developments; John Booker, the popular representative of the older style, was harassed and imprisoned. It was the prolonged crisis of the 1640s and 1650s, when compilers were encouraged to become polemicists, which ensured that the English almanac was henceforth to be a forum for the discussion of major contemporary issues. Restoration governments were naturally uneasy at this situation, but it probably seemed better to exercise a degree of control through the Stationers' monopoly and by censorship than to provoke a direct confrontation. The Stationers were a powerful vested interest, and even if the government succeeded in suppressing prediction, it might then face a greater danger from a proliferation of unauthorized and uncensored almanacs filling the vacuum.

The vitality of the English almanac owed something also to the timing of intellectual change. In France, astrology appears to have been at its peak in the fifteenth and sixteenth centuries, and to have perished in the seventeenth under attack from newer philosophical and scientific ideas. In England, by contrast, astrology developed more slowly, and its growth coincided with the beginnings of scientific advance. The astrologers believed themselves (and to a considerable extent, were believed) to be on the side of progress, modernity and scientific rationalism. Sixteenth-century French astrologers, like their contemporaries and predecessors throughout Europe, were mostly physicians and sometimes clerics. The seventeenth-century English compiler was just as likely to be an applied mathematician, or a scientific teacher. The popularization of scientific changes in England thus influenced the English almanac, which in turn became an important instrument for their further dissemination. The connection with modern science helped to prolong the intellectual and hence social respectability of both almanacs and astrology throughout the seventeenth century.

During the Stuart period, English almanacs appear to have advanced beyond their European progenitors. There were few translations of Continental predictions into English, unlike the previous century. Indeed the direction of influence was to some extent reversed. Lilly's almanac for 1653 was republished in the Netherlands in two separate Dutch editions, and there were other translations into German and Swedish. Somewhat later, John Partridge's *Mene Tekel* was translated into French, no doubt to reassure the Huguenots or undermine French morale.[16]

English astrology had, naturally, a strong influence on other parts of the British Isles. The printing of almanacs at Edinburgh is first recorded in 1603, but the Scottish almanac developed slowly.[17] The first edition known in any detail dates from 1619, and there was only one regular series, printed at Aberdeen, until after the civil war. Early titles such as *Gabriel Friends Prognostication* and *Whyte* show clearly the debt to the English almanac. From the 1660s regular publication also began in Edinburgh and Glasgow. Some of the works became more lively, with the compilers quarrelling in print in the manner familiar south of the border. But on the whole the printer remained the dominant figure, and in the Aberdeen series the only hint of an author was the presence of two initials on the title-page, apparently fictitious and chosen at random from the alphabet. By the 1680s, 50,000 copies of the 'Aberdeen Almanack' (as it was generally known) were issued annually. Nevertheless, the Scottish almanacs remained rather colourless. Most were of only eight leaves (sixteen pages), and after the calendar, fairs, chronology and weather forecast there was almost no scope for the prophecies or other material which characterized the English works. The Scottish almanac was an almanac only, without a true prognostication. In the 1690s prophecies from John Partridge's almanacs were reprinted in Scotland to help fill the vacuum.[18] In Ireland, a pioneering almanac was published for 1587, but regular production began only in the mid-seventeenth century. From 1609 the King's printer-general in Ireland held a total monopoly over the production of books, including almanacs, which was enforced with a fair degree of success. At the close of the century the most prominent compiler was the English Whig settler, John Whalley, though he faced vigorous competition from Andrew Cumpsty, John McComb and others, and a lively tradition developed in the eighteenth century.[19] An almanac was the very first book to be printed in North America, in 1639, but again the development was slow.[20] Until the last decades of the century, almanacs were written by young Harvard graduates (some aged no more than sixteen), for whom the work was a test of their mathematical and versifying powers. The calendar filled most of the eight leaves, with a chronology, moral exhortation in verse, and sometimes notes on Copernican astronomy; there was no place for astrology, even for weather-forecasts. From the 1680s almanacs developed a more popular style, offering more varied material in a far less serious manner. The typical eighteenth-century edition contained farming tips, recipes, essays, verse, humorous stories and sensational, often illustrated accounts of murders, monsters and prodigies of all kinds. Astrology now found some place, with weather forecasts, the anatomical figure and at times prophecies of war or upheaval. But the predictions were often lighthearted. Only a minority of compilers seem to have believed seriously in judicial astrology, and the predictions they offered were of unexceptionable vagueness.

The English origins of the American almanac were clear. Many contained verses plagiarized from seventeenth-century English editions, as well as material borrowed from English poets from Shakespeare to Pope. There were even aphorisms of the kind pioneered by Bretnor. Jonathan Swift's assault on Partridge was imitated in detail by Benjamin Franklin in the 1730s. Franklin, like 'Bickerstaff' predicted and then announced the death of a prominent almanac-maker, Titan Leeds, and carefully refuted the victim's attempts to prove that he was still alive. The American almanac possessed a real vitality, but different in kind from that of its progenitor. Its basic qualities were utility and wit. It lacked the astrological depth of the English works, and never achieved their political, polemical or scientific significance. Developing fully only when astrology was in the final stages of decay, the American almanac naturally evolved in a different direction.[21]

Almanacs, like astrology itself, were at their peak in England in the Elizabethan and Stuart period. Decay in their standing and vitality is evident by the eighteenth century. A current of scepticism was always present, and by 1700 had become dominant among the educated classes. It is less clear precisely when this change occurred. The shift was gradual. Peaks in the satires or polemics against astrology, in the late sixteenth century and in the 1650s and 1660s, reflected high points in the impact of astrological writings rather than advances in rationalism. There was a lively debate on the validity of astrology in the mid-century. A similar debate in France, occasioned by a major eclipse in 1654, proved to be the decisive turning-point for astrology in the intellectual history of that nation.[22] The English episode was less decisive. In the second half of the century no major scientist devoted his efforts to astrology. The Royal Society, the universities and the College of Physicians displayed a common hostility to it. Yet from the 1640s interest in a reformed astrology widened dramatically. The freedom of the press is one part of the explanation. Another is that the Baconian scientists of the mid-century sought consciously to control nature by unravelling the forces of natural magic, alchemy and astrology.[23] Men like Childrey bridged the gap between the scientists and the almanac-makers and other practitioners such as Gadbury who made a vigorous effort to place their subject on a sound scientific basis. Disinclined to accept extravagant claims, many scientists were willing to believe that a core of truth lay buried among the superstition. It is this which helps to explain why many prominent scientists and physicians retained an interest and a degree of faith in the subject, and close links with its practitioners, throughout the century.

The status of astrology in the eighteenth century has yet to be explored. Belief was never wholly extinguished even in the upper levels of society. A critic complained in 1710 that the gentry were as besotted as the common people with astrology and other superstitions. Edward Thwaites, a noted Anglo-Saxon scholar and professor of Greek and moral philosophy at Oxford under Queen Anne, learned astrology towards the end of his life from George Parker, and later boarded Parker in his rooms at Queen's for several weeks.[24] The members of the Zodiac Club, founded at St. John's College, Cambridge, in 1725, may not have believed in astrology, but the fact that its constitution was based on astrological rules presupposes at least a certain amount of knowledge.[25] Richard Mead, a prominent physician 'at the head of his profession' for almost half a century, and vice-president of the Royal Society, defended the influence of the sun and moon on the human body. William Whiston argued, as already mentioned, that the downfall of the empires of antiquity had been 'ushered in, and sometimes in part occasioned' by 'eclipses immediately beforehand: sometimes in a natural, and sometimes in a supernatural way'. (Both testimonies were cited in Hanoverian almanacs as proofs of the validity of astrology.[26]) Tycho Wing was a respected mathematician, and Henry Season had connections—however tenuous—with the highest levels of society. Still later in the century, the astrologer Ebenezer Sibly described how a group of naval officers, about to sail to the West Indies with Admiral Rodney in 1779, consulted him for information on the likely success of the expedition. His friend, George Witchell, Master of the Royal Naval Academy at Portsmouth and F.R.S., was a lover of astrology and able to cast his own horoscope. Sibly also described the conversion of the young poet, Thomas Chatterton, to belief in the subject.[27] Other instances may well come to light. But it seems highly unlikely that astrology formed more than a very minor undercurrent in educated Hanoverian society.

We can point to no new compelling argument or discovery to explain why astrology lost its hold over the educated classes.[28] For several centuries sceptics had pointed out that the zodiac had no objective existence, and that predictions differed from each other and were usually wrong. The objections were traditional, and yet only now proved effective. Like witchcraft, astrology seems to have been destroyed not by new arguments but by a new view of the universe which eroded traditional beliefs. The role of the new astronomy and mechanical science was crucial. Copernicus and his successors did not disprove astrology. Tycho Brahe and Kepler were themselves practitioners. But cumulatively the effect of their work was to undermine the old cosmology in which astrology had taken root. Traditional cosmology stressed the relationship between the macro-and microcosm, between the perfect, unchanging heavens and mankind on earth at their centre. This pattern of beliefs became more and more implausible as astronomers revealed that the heavens were neither perfect nor unchanging, and that the earth was merely one, insignificant planet in an infinite universe. The likelihood of life in space weakened still further the idea of man's central position. Though knowledge of the periodicity of comets did not in itself disprove their influence, it was possible after the work of Halley and Newton to explain as well as predict their return. Their doom-laden significance diminished with their mysteriousness. Moreover, the immense distances involved in the new astronomical theories made astrological influence less credible. Henry Season accepted that 'the nearer we are to a planet, the greater effect it must show, witness the moon.'[29] But what force could travel the huge distances from the fixed stars? For two centuries almanac-makers had been popularizing new theories on the size of the universe, translating the huge and incomprehensible figures into more concrete images. Thus, Wing in 1732 was continuing a long tradition when he explained that a cannon ball flung into space and travelling at its maximum velocity would take 700,000 years to reach the nearest of the fixed stars.[30] The prognosticators were undermining their own credibility.

During the course of the seventeenth century, scientists increasingly turned away from astrology. Yet even in the later years they made no systematic attempt to destroy it. They may have felt that its influence in educated society was crumbling, and that no frontal assault was needed. We have seen, though, that a substantial residuum of belief survived in the Restoration period. The scientists' restraint probably owed as much to a lingering belief that the pseudo-science contained an element of truth, as discussed earlier. If that were so, then their task was not its destruction but the separation of truth from mere tradition, and the extension of the scientific revolution into a new sphere.[31] Why scientists eventually lost hope or interest in a reformed astrology is difficult to explain. They were slowly convinced, perhaps, that experiments and observations were failing to produce satisfactory results, and that it was impossible to apply modern methods in this field. Perhaps too as the generation of Baconian scientists died away the impetus behind the search was lost.

It is probable that other, non-scientific reasons contributed to the decline. Mr. Thomas has pointed to the social role of astrology, showing how it offered (like magic and religion itself) a hope of supernatural help and protection in a period when life was extremely precarious. In the later seventeenth century, he suggests, changing circumstances made the need less urgent; a more stable population, steadier grain prices and the rapid development of banking and insurance brought a greater degree of security.[32] Medical science, however, brought no new protection against the greatest threat of all, disease and premature death. It may be more important that, although life was still precarious, people were ceasing to look for supernatural aid in solving their problems. One reason for this was the steady rise of the concept of progress, which made the conquest of all problems through human effort seem a real possibility. Another cause lay in the changing attitude of the church. Before the Reformation it was possible to see the church as a 'vast reservoir of magical power', official and unofficial, from which the faithful could benefit. After it, the Protestant and later the Catholic Church turned to more spiritual forms of religion, emphasizing faith, piety and work instead of the propitiation of God and the saints in pursuit of immediate rewards.[33] No doubt this new approach seemed unappealing to the masses. Sancho Panza remarked how the curate taught that 'we ought to love our Maker for His own sake, without either hope of good, or fear of pain: though, for my part', he added, in traditional vein, 'I would love and serve Him for what I could get.'[34] But it is likely that the new religious teaching had an impact on the educated classes, gradually filtering downwards. It would create in time an outlook which had no place for the performance of rituals (whether religious or astrological) designed to secure immediate personal benefits.

The changing character of the church also played a more direct part in the decline of astrology. In 1500, as earlier, leading astrologers were often clerics, and for long afterwards astrologers were able to refute hostile ministers by citing eminent champions within the church. Moreover, even critics generally conceded the value of natural astrology, which obviously weakened the force of their attacks. If it was agreed that the stars did have some influence, why not all that the astrologers claimed? Calvin accepted natural astrology, and Perkins conceded that the stars were one of God's instruments (though he denied that they could be used to predict the future).[35] For long the debate was thus about the extent rather than the existence of astrology. In 1700, by contrast, the church was willing to sweep aside the entire edifice. A wide gulf opened between Christianity and astrology, which could only be damaging to the latter. Joseph Blagrave's admission in 1673 that many of his clients came to him secretly, fearing that his art was diabolical, illustrates one of the effects of the church's now almost universally hostile attitude.[36]

These developments within the church were part of a European phenomenon, but they were accelerated in England by the lessons of the civil war. Radical astrologers such as Lilly and Culpeper had proclaimed the stars as the instruments by which God was destroying monarchy and the established church. Conservative opinion, during and especially after the Revolution, reacted naturally by viewing astrology with a mixture of mockery, fear and suspicion. There was similar hostility to the old Puritan belief that God intervened constantly in human affairs; the sectarians 'conviction that the saints must advance divine providence by turning the world upside down aroused particular indignation. The need to formulate a safer religion, purged of enthusiasm, was widely recognized. It was met, perhaps surprisingly, by a group of scientists. Robert Boyle and others were convinced that science could strengthen Christianity. From the harmony and splendour of the universe they felt able to prove the existence of a divine Creator. They depicted a universe which was regular and ordered, shaped by the hand of God but run according to the constant laws he had created. Latitudinarian clergy welcomed this 'natural theology', in which they found support for moderation, comprehension and stability.[37] In this current of religious thought, which by 1700 represented the orthodox view, there was no place for a God repeatedly interfering in his own laws. Nor, by extension, could there be room for the stars as the instruments of such intervention, and still less for astrologers as the self-appointed interpreters of God's will.

It was not the scientists or clergy, however, who led the attack on astrology in late Stuart England, but the satirists. They were certainly influenced by recent developments in scientific and religious thought, and behind their wit lay the new concept of rationalism. Astrology as a superstition and sham was an obvious target for ridicule. The attack reached its apotheosis in a forceful treatise by Pierre Bayle, republished in England in 1708, which combined wit with philosophical and scientific arguments. In large part Bayle's method was mockery, and his purpose was to present astrology as a creed of ignorant, ancient and barbarous peoples, unbecoming an educated, rational, modern man. It was a 'most ridiculous' subject, he remarked, and unworthy of serious consideration. 'I shan't amuse myself with formal proofs', he told his readers.[38] This attitude is apparent also in Swift, who chose to ridicule astrology rather than refute it. From the mid-seventeenth century there was also a strong element of political animosity in many of the English satires. It can be traced, once again, to the lessons of the civil war. The writings of Lilly and his circle led political opponents to the belief that astrology was a pseudo-science blatantly misinterpreting the heavens in the cause of fanaticism.[39] Radical Whig astrologers later in the century served to strengthen and perpetuate this belief. Jonathan Swift chose as his target John Partridge, notorious as an extreme Whig and indeed a former republican. James Younge, another critic at the turn of the century, was explicit in linking astrology with fanaticism. Lilly and Culpeper 'poisoned the people formerly', he argued, and their 'successors carry on the same design now', namely the ruin of 'monarchy, episcopacy and nobility, and setting up democracy in these kingdoms'. Younge pointed out that Partridge's fame rested on his successful prophecy of the fall of James II, in *Mene Tekel*, which 'not only gave the author a great name, but patched up the decayed credit of astrology among the populace'.[40] Partridge's success probably did little to help the standing of astrology in the longer term. After the conservative settlement of 1689, the propertied classes had little further use for a science which flourished, as Swift took care to emphasize, on predictions of upheaval and the ruin of kings.[41] The fear that astrology was a threat to the political and social order was almost certainly groundless by 1700. It seems more likely that the opposite was true: that a general wish to preserve stability led to a further decline in the respectability of astrology.

It is far less clear that astrology had lost its appeal to the lower classes by the eighteenth century. The various reasons for its decline, discussed above, apply with much less force, if at all, further down the social scale. The buoyant sales of Moore's almanac suggest that the public remained faithful longer indeed than many of the compilers. In the mid-eighteenth century Henry Season bade his almanac farewell with the confident reflection that

> Thy character will bandied be about
> More than a hundred sermons, there's no doubt.[42]

But the level of astrological knowledge in the countryside in the eighteenth century was probably far more elementary than in the seventeenth. Astrology had lost its upper and middle echelons. In consequence there were almost none of the clear, simple guides to astrological methods common in the Stuart period (and common once more in the 1970s). Most of the 'students in astrology and physick' were succeeded by simple cunning men, with few books and little social or intellectual respectability. In Farquhar's *The Recruiting Officer* (acted 1706), the conjuror is given scant respect even by a rustic client who declares, 'Look'e Doctor, let me have something that's good for my shilling, or I'll have my money again.'[43] Thomas Hardy's discussion of the status of the astrologer and cunning man in *The Mayor of Casterbridge* (set in the early nineteenth century) is more subtle. The 'weather-prophet' lives in a mud cottage outside a lonely hamlet, isolated geographically as well as socially and intellectually, and outwardly despised by the local community. Yet few were 'unbelievers in their secret hearts', and Mayor Henchard himself pays a clandestine visit to learn the prospects for the coming harvest, as several neighbouring farmers had already done. He declines to enter the house, and tries to retain dignity by telling the prophet of his scepticism; yet he trusts, or partly trusts, the prediction he receives.[44]

Hanoverian almanacs give the impression that the common attitude towards astrology was of faith tempered by massive ignorance. Partridge declared in 1755 that the industrious farmer dunged his land and gathered corn during the wane of the moon, sowed during its increase and covered roots at the full. Season provided tables of the moon's southing for the benefit of farmers wishing to know when to geld livestock.[45] Another of Hardy's novels, *The Return of the Native* (set in the 1840s), contains a suggestive passage. A group of villagers discuss the saying, '"No moon, no man." . . . The boy never comes to anything that's born at new moon.' The feeble-witted Christian Cantle, seen as living proof that the dictum is true, recalls that when his mother gave birth she always asked for a neighbour's almanac to check the moon's phase.[46] But Culpepper pointed out that most readers could not comprehend the astrological 'jargon' which the almanacs contained: not one person in a thousand 'understands an ephemeris, and not one in ten thousand that has occasion to make use of one'. A hawker peddling almanacs in the London streets is made to say, in *Old Poor Robin*, that the *Ephemerides* of Parker and White are 'all made up of hooks and crooks and figures', and totally incomprehensible. Season accepted that while many farmers believed in the importance of the moon's position, they were often unable to understand the sign of the zodiac printed in the table, and did not know which part of the body it governed. He resolved to simplify the data by omitting the sign and writing 'head', 'reins', and so on, as appropriate.[47] Astrology survived in the eighteenth century and beyond, but in a crude form, as a subculture, cut off from the intellectual mainstream of the period, and based primarily on oral tradition and the almanac.

In assessing the rôle of the almanac in Tudor and Stuart England, we must recall that astrology in this earlier period was far more than a subculture. It formed a part of the dominant pattern of beliefs, though one which slowly declined and which coexisted very uneasily with other hostile elements. With sales that passed a third of a million copies a year, almanacs clearly did belong to the popular culture of the age. Yet that conclusion needs to be qualified, for their contents were far from a simple reflection of traditional beliefs. Folkloristic elements were few (outside related works such as *Erra Pater*), and were usually mentioned only to be condemned. Like the works which formed the 'middle-class culture' discussed by Professor Wright, almanacs drew ideas and assumptions from higher intellectual levels, and presented them in a cheap and digestible form to a far wider readership.[48] Though there was a long tradition of popular lore based on the moon, planets and eclipses, astrology as a coherent system was highly esoteric until the advent of printing. The development of almanacs and of simple guides brought a far greater awareness and understanding of the subject than had ever previously existed, both in England and Europe.[49] In addition to its direct effect, this growth made possible the dramatic expansion of self-taught and yet often well-informed practitioners, able to meet a rising public demand in Elizabethan and Stuart England.

The basic function of the almanac was to serve as a calendar. In the early modern period, awareness of the passage of time still came primarily from nature. The changing seasons marked the course of the year, and the progression of the months was visible in the phases of the moon. Except for the minority who owned clocks and watches, the passage of the day and night depended on the movements of the sun and moon and the shadows on the sundial. Dialling was indeed one of the skills most commonly advertised by almanac-makers, some of whom advised readers on how to make cheap substitutes. No one could fail to be conscious of time in these terms, which find reflection in the literature of the period.[50]

The almanac, on the wall or in the pocket, spelled out the divisions of the year. Those in book form laid down the characteristics, duties, pleasures and dangers of the rotating seasons. They indicated the Christian festivals, saints 'days,' good' and 'evil' days, and (especially in the Tudor period) days when it was safe or unsafe to let blood, take medicine and so on. Holy days often had a wider significance, in marking the date when a fair was held, a lease expired or rent was due. They often provided the basis for the farming calendar, reminding the countryman when ploughing or some other task should be begun or ended. They could also serve as a more personal reminder. 'I looked in the almanac,' wrote the Rev. Oliver Heywood in 1673, 'and there it's called St. Mark's day, April 25, the day of my first marriage eighteen years ago.' The almanac was thus a necessary reminder of the significance of times.[51] The owner did not necessarily possess any faith in astrology. But he was inevitably aware that time was uneven in quality, in the agrarian and ecclesiastical year, and in the fluctuating cycles of day-length and of the moon. A society forced to recognize that certain times did have especial significance was all the more likely to be susceptible to astrology. Urban life, the electric light bulb and effective street lighting have destroyed the rhythms which first gave rise to astrological beliefs. Only in the countryside can the moon and stars still strike the senses and imagination in a way that must have been almost universal for our ancestors.

The almanac served also as an accurate record of time past, emphasized by its increasing use as a diary. Hence there arose the notion of 'trial by almanac': the testing in court of an indictment or defence by its evidence of dates and conditions. Thus George Fox, the Quaker, confounded a court at Lancaster in 1664 by proving mistakes in the indictment against him.'"All people," I said, "take your almanacs and see whether any oath was tendered to George Fox the eleventh of January, and whether the sessions were not upon the twelfth." And the clerks and people looked at their almanacs and saw it was the twelfth.' Fox then alleged another mistake, in the number of the regnal year; again 'they looked at the indictment and their almanacs and saw that they had sworn a whole year false, . . . they were in a rage again and stamped', and the indictment was quashed.[52] Henry Fielding used almanacs in this way as a magistrate, in testing the veracity of witnesses; he used them too (like later novelists) in creating a detailed and accurate time-plan in his novels.[53] The almanac-maker thus became an authority on time. Booker's views on the correct calculation of Easter were sought by Charles I, and those of Season were requested a century later by an 'eminent lord'.[54] Many compilers supplied notes in their almanacs on the English and other calendar systems, and on the time and season of the world's creation. Their highly developed consciousness of time and its significance helps to explain the links between astrology and eschatology. It may explain, too, John Rowley's odd impulse to tell the reader that he had completed his new edition on the 7,394th day of his life, and Henry Season's similar declaration that it was 12,675 days since he had begun compiling almanacs.[55] The almanac itself became a symbol of time, with each succeeding edition providing, by its mere publication, a *memento mori*, reminding the reader of another step towards the grave. In creating a character who counted his age by the number of almanacs he had lived through, Beaumont and Fletcher were only developing an idea which was expressed regularly over two centuries.[56]

The prominent place of sensationalism is a reminder of another role of the almanac throughout the period, as escapist literature. Monstrous births, the fall of kings and seas red with blood were an important element in the public's appetite for entertainment and excitement. Gadbury was horrified by William Lilly's brusque treatment of royal fortunes. 'Kings and princes are his tennis-balls', he complained, 'and must be tossed and struck up and down as he is pleased to bandy them with his black and envious racket.' Gadbury's distaste sprang from his view of politics, not from a sense of the limitations of astrology. In private he was willing to stake its reputation on assuring a sceptical minister, whose nativity he calculated, that Charles II would remarry and produce a son, that Louis XIV would die in 1682 and that Shaftesbury would be executed. The minister went home and very properly threw the nativity into the fire.[57] But Lilly's popularity, and later that of Moore, proves that the public welcomed exciting speculation concerning the great.

In terms of historical significance, however, the major role of the almanac was not sensationalism but, perhaps paradoxically, education in the broadest sense. At the most humble level, the almanac was valuable as a cheap handbook supplying a wide range of miscellaneous information available elsewhere only in specialized works far beyond the price-range of most of its readers. Even critics conceded its usefulness as 'a dumb Mercury to point out highways, and a bailiff of all marts and fairs in England'. Compilers frequently asserted that it was thus ' of universal use, and indispensably necessary from the mechanic to his Majesty'.[58] There is pleasant corroboration of this latter claim in the account of the young George III calling for the *Berlin* almanac, a work at least distantly related, to scan through the list of eligible German princesses in his search for a suitable wife.[59] It remained common in the eighteenth century for noblemen to keep almanacs as diaries and pocket-books.[60] In the Tudor and Stuart period the widespread sale of almanacs in the countryside was a reflection of growing rural literacy, and a further stimulus to it; the countryman could see the value of a printed work which was cheap, useful and entertaining. Over the period compilers steadily expanded the range of subjects covered, to include specimen indentures, excise rates, postal information and the weights and measures used in various trades. Most of the discussions of diet, medicine, crops, history, geography and science were of course elementary, but they filled a vacuum which was largely ignored by contemporary schools. In science, especially astronomy, the information went far beyond the commonplace, and the almanac had a major role in the dissemination of the new discoveries. The compiler was often aware of a double task. He had to wean the reader away from belief in a huge, perhaps flat earth, dominating the universe and warmed by the sun, which appeared as some kind of luminous football beyond the clouds, and introduce him to the complexities of the Ptolemaic universe; and then, almost simultaneously, to hurry him forward into the new cosmology of Copernicus, Galileo and Newton. It was an ambitious programme, and no doubt required the constant repetition of elementary points.[61]

In politics and religion, a number of themes stand out prominently in the almanacs: their use, for example, as printed pulpits from which compilers preached repentance, anti-Catholicism and often anti-clericalism. A mood of extreme nationalism was apparent throughout the seventeenth century and beyond. From the 1640s there was a preoccupation with liberty which was never lost, though at times it could find expression only in polemical attacks on the 'French tyrant' or popery. Linking the two areas was a millennial thread which continued in the eighteenth century and brought an awareness of the doctrine to thousands who would never have seen specialized millenarian writings. Though these predictions and discussions no doubt had a direct effect, it may be that once again the almanac's primary role was as an educative force. Its success is evidence of a growing popular awareness of political matters, and a curiosity which the astrologer both satisfied and stimulated. It is now clear that before the civil war the size of the rural and urban electorate, for parliamentary elections, was far greater than has been assumed.[62] The popularity of almanacs and of ballads—there is evidence that ballads commenting on political issues were especially in demand at fairs—suggests that a considerable part of the population had an interest, however crude, in contemporary politics.[63] The almanac helped to keep alive an awareness of diversity in political and ecclesiastical affairs. From the 1640s to the early eighteenth century there was continuous controversy between royalist and parliamentarian compilers, crypto-Catholic and anti-Catholic, and Tory and Whig. Despite censorship it was always visible, discreetly or openly; even the blank spaces, where censors had deleted passages, proclaimed dissent. At the very least we can be sure that the fact of political and ecclesiastical dispute, the slogans and some of the principles were proclaimed year by year in the homes of tens of thousands of wholly ordinary families.

The extent of the almanac's direct effect on the reader is much more difficult to answer with confidence. It is clear from the pattern of sales that he wanted commentary and prophecy as well as utilitarian information. But how seriously did he take the advice and predictions he read? Did he act on them? On political issues the second question is wrongly formulated. A judicial astrologer such as Lilly was not directing his readers to specific actions, but was seeking to build up or undermine morale, or to secure a resigned compliance with what he claimed the stars decreed. His task was eased by the still widespread belief that comets and other celestial wonders had a political significance. The comet of 1618, for example, was reported by an observer at court to be 'the only subject almost of our discourse', commonly assumed to portend the death of the queen. (King James, unlikely to be disturbed at this prospect, commented coarsely that the comet was 'nothing else but Venus with a firebrand in her—'.)[64] When King Charles moved north against the Scots in 1639, an eclipse of the sun was widely thought to be 'an ominous presage of bad success to the king's affairs'.[65] For many readers the astrologer thus did not have to prove that the stars had a political significance; he had merely to provide a plausible interpretation. It is impossible to measure the success of such propaganda, but the attitudes of English and Continental governments leave no doubt that they thought it effective. This conviction lay behind Lilly's summons to the siege of Colchester in 1648, where he assured the troops of a speedy victory. A soldier read out predictions of victory from Lilly's almanac to English troops going into battle during Cromwell's invasion of Scotland. It is clear moreover that at least some of Lilly's protectors in parliament believed in his prophetic powers. After the Restoration, the parliamentary committee investigating the causes of the Great Fire summoned him to see what light his skills could throw on the matter.[66] Evidence of this kind is indirect but suggestive. So is the fact that Lilly was consulted confidentially on political matters by people spanning the political spectrum from cavalier to Ranter. His fame was founded on his almanacs and other printed prophecies, and these visits are a testimony to the impact of the works and the conviction they carried.[67]

Instances of people specifically declaring their faith in the almanac's prophecies are rare. From his diary, though, it is clear that Ralph Josselin, vicar of Earl's Colne, Essex, was swayed by the 'amazing particulars' he found in his almanacs and other collections of old prophecies concerning the White King, Grebner's predictions and so on.[68] (He also believed that his dreams on political and other subjects had prophetic value, and noted a friend's admiring remark that 'Josselin should write almanacs' himself.)[69] Another minister noted the report that the almanac-makers had predicted the Great Fire of London, but that this had been deleted by the licenser.[70] In 1672 the Earl of Northampton wrote to Secretary Williamson of his fears prompted by warlike preparations in France and by the 'terrors of Lilly's almanac'.[71] The most dramatic example of the power of astrological prophecy was of course the alarm over the solar eclipse of 1652. Critics writing after the event were as horrified by the extent of public credulity as by the sins of the astrologers.[72] A lesser scare in Wales in 1687 was produced by the prediction of an eclipse of the sun in the Welsh almanac of Thomas Jones. Farmers drove their livestock under cover, and fairs and markets were postponed. In the event, not merely the threatened disasters but the eclipse itself failed to materialize.[73] Similar panics are reported at various times in Germany and France. The people of Aix were said to have walled up the entrances of their houses to protect them from a predicted flood.[74]

Much of the almanacs' material was of course far more closely related to everyday activities, especially in such matters as farming, medical and personal advice. There is again a dearth of firsthand accounts confirming the use of these rules. The silence is ambiguous: were such actions too commonplace to be worth recording, or did they not occur? Though it is difficult to prove, contemporary evidence of a more generalized kind points strongly in the former direction. Naturally the astrologers declared repeatedly that the rules were observed by a multitude of countrymen and were validated by experience. More significantly, critics and satirists conceded the first half of this claim: scandalized ministers, progressive physicians, poets and wits agreed on the huge scale of the practices they condemned.[75] The moon's proven effect on the tides made its influence on terrestrial life a far less controversial doctrine than judicial astrology. For if the moon controlled moisture, it was obviously linked to growth and thus to farming, and equally to bodily health, which was governed by the fluctuating balance between the humours. There were many farming manuals and popular medical directories throughout the period which endorsed and amplified the almanacs' notes on these subjects.[76]

A number of firsthand testimonies do exist to confirm that the rules were followed. A letter from the young Lady Arabella Stuart in 1587 shows that she observed the proper lunar phase in cutting her hair. There is a striking illustration of the hold of astrological medicine in the rebuke which John Symcotts, a sceptical physician, had to give to a patient who had ignored the prescribed treatment on finding that the sign in his almanac was inauspicious. Some years later the patient did take physick during the dog days, against his better judgement, but he noted subsequently: 'I was not well all this summer, the sign in Virgo.'[77] Still more dramatic is the story of a Warwickshire man, a Mr. Erly. Finding his wife in childbirth and the midwives in attendance, Erly 'consulted his books' to discover 'the aspect of the stars' for the infant, 'and finding it bad, he bid them hold their hands'.[78] Josselin's *Diary* shows frequently his belief that the moon influenced the atmosphere and the weather, and thus affected both his health and his farming. He often noted the moon's change and its apparent consequences, and chose the appropriate phase for grafting his fruit trees. Referring to his suppurating leg, he noted on 6 October 1678: 'my leg in a hopeful way, though rain and new moon.' He described 21 March 1661 as 'a wonderful wet day, being the next to the change of the moon, which is sad; all the last moon very wet, few lands can be fallowed, not a plough stirred.' Heavy rain, he noted on another occasion, prevented the sowing of barley; 'the moon changed 6 in the morning, about 3 hours later it began to fog and about 4 rained so hard that this morning the flood high. . . .' Josselin believed that comets, too, affected the weather.[79] There is some direct evidence of the use of astrological rules in gardening and farming. Thomas Byng, an Elizabethan academic, noted in his almanac the best time to gather his grapes ('in the wane between 15 and 24 of Febr. this year'). Richard Shanne, a Jacobean yeoman, copied astrological rules on farming from an almanac into his memorandum book, no doubt with a practical purpose in mind.[80] John Evelyn, though sceptical about judicial astrology, observed the correct moment for planting trees, and he noted that the Earl of Essex's head gardener at Cassiobury Park (one Moses Cooke) was an astrological enthusiast.[81] Henry Best, a capable and methodical farmer of the mid-century, always chose a time when the moon was slightly past the full to geld his lambs.[82] There is also some evidence of astrological farming in eighteenth-century America, most notably in the works of Dr. Samuel Deane, minister and agricultural writer, who was himself careful to observe the lunar phases.[83]

Belief in the influence of the moon, and in natural astrology, need not imply acceptance of judicial astrology. Many authorities, from Calvin in the sixteenth century to the physician, Richard Mead, in the eighteenth, accepted the first while rejecting the second. It seems likely, though, that the general belief in lunar influence would make the claims of the astrologers more plausible. The impact of the almanac was strengthened also by the prevalence of other, related forms of supernatural belief and practice. Astrologers, cunning men and wise women were familiar and often respected figures in the community. It has been calculated that no village in Elizabethan Essex was more than ten miles from a known cunning man. Witchcraft was the second most commonly indicted offence in that county in the 1580s, and the web of suspicions of witchcraft extended still further.[84] Since far earlier times villagers had used religious and magical formulae for protecting the harvest, destroying pests and curing sickness. Charms, amulets and astrological sigils, thought to harness supernatural forces for the benefit of their owners, were in widespread use. Belief and practice thus went hand in hand. Mr. Thomas writes that the most common question put to the astrological practitioner was, in Lilly's phrase, '*Quid agendum*?—'What is to be done?'[85] Buying an almanac was in some ways comparable to visiting a practitioner, for the compiler supplied advice on many of the most common and general problems, in his lists of good and bad days, predictions of health and harvest, and rules on elections. These last could be quite precise, as in the Rev. John Evans' advice on how to wean infants according to the personal traits the parents wished to foster—including, rather improperly, how to ensure 'that they may be covetous'.[86] The almanac, like astrology as a whole, was designed to serve mankind in a highly utilitarian way from the cradle to the grave.

There is a relative abundance of information on popular belief in astrology or a simpler moon-lore in the nineteenth century, by when sceptics had won over educated opinion almost entirely. 'Many consult their almanacs more than their Bibles', it was reported, 'and follow the lunar phases as their sole interpretation of the will of God.'[87] In the nineteenth and even twentieth century there is evidence, from folklorists and others, of farmers applying astrological rules (mainly concerning the moon's phases and position in the zodiac) in felling timber, killing pigs, breeding horses, sowing peas and beans and cutting corn.[88] Almost certainly these practices represent a far older pattern of behaviour which was now attracting attention because of the widening gulf between educated and popular culture, and because the practices themselves were probably becoming rarer.

It remains to ask how great was the role of almanacs, and of astrology in general, in relation to other elements in the heterogeneous culture of early modern England. Mr. Thomas has shown that Christianity did not possess a complete hold over the beliefs and practices of the English, either before or after the Reformation. The power of the church was limited by scepticism and indifference, and by other forms of supernatural explanation. Astrology was perhaps the most important of these, through its antiquity and the universality of its claims. Yet we should not fly to the opposite extreme of exaggerating the role of the occult. Throughout the period there was clearly also a current of scepticism aimed at astrology, increasing as time passed. Almanac-makers claimed that the countryman observed their rules, but they complained almost as often of the mockery or suspicion of the 'common', 'vulgar' and 'ignorant sort'. Christianity had a stronger hold and deeper roots. There was no institutional equivalent to the church, with its enormous role in the social life of the community. Though the almanac-maker could attack the clergy, he had always to defend and promote the Christian faith. By contrast there was nothing to prevent the clergy from denouncing astrology as false, blasphemous and atheistical, and condemning its practitioners as conjurors. Even during their golden age, the astrologers were thus on the defensive. Conceding that many 'ignorant' justices regarded them as conjurors, they and their clients felt themselves to be in an ambiguous position on the fringes of the law.

Astrology thus also fell far short of universal acceptance. It is likely that its position varied considerably even from parish to parish. The attitude of the local justice, squire and minister, the views of the more substantial farmers and of those who frequented the village alehouse would each play a part in shaping belief and behaviour. So would the presence or absence, and the character, of a local astrological practitioner or cunning man. And so would, finally, the temperament of the individual.

The almanac itself clearly cannot provide a full answer. Its sales do prove, though, that it was one element both shaping and reflecting the beliefs and practices of the period. It has left its mark in the literature, the controversies and even the language of the time. In the history of publishing it is a unique story of success and survival. Centuries later, the almanac as reference-book has found its apotheosis in *Whitaker*. At the same time, *Old Moore* is able to compete triumphantly with the worst that Fleet Street can produce. In the early modern period costs were low and profits high. No prolonged demands were made on the time of the compiler. On 17 June 1693 Henry Coley began ruling the paper for the almanacs he was to compile for the next year. Despite his many other activities they were completed and delivered to the Stationers by 5 August.[89] And yet, despite all the repetition and crude sensationalism, the almanac played a valuable role. It was distinctive in its ability to span the intellectual and social horizons. Compilers familiar with Fellows of the Royal Society wrote on an immense range of subjects for the benefit of a mass readership. In the form it had already evolved by the Elizabethan period, the almanac was the greatest triumph of journalism until modern times.

APPENDIX ONE

Biographical Notes

I HAVE TRIED to identify the dates, occupations and places of residence of all the compilers, not to summarize their lives. Only brief notes are given for persons described in *D.N.B.* or by Taylor. A date given in italics as a source denotes the almanac for that year issued by the subject of the entry; a name in italics indicates the subject of a separate entry. I have retained the vague term 'philomath' used by many compilers to describe themselves. 'Gentleman' denotes a status claimed by the compiler, not necessarily with any formal recognition. I have included pseudonyms, such as the Cambridge series based on water (e.g. Lakes, Rivers) and birds (e.g. Swallow), but not the large number invented by the Oxford press for 1689, except Ben. Pond, the sole survivor; for the others see pages 38, above, and 396, note 91, below.

ABENDANO, ISAAC (c. 1640–c. 1710)
A Jew of Marrano origin, trained as a physician, who settled in England about 1662, living at Cambridge where he translated the Mishnah into Latin. In 1689 he moved to Oxford as Hebrew lecturer, and published a series of almanacs there for 1692–9.

Encyc. Judaica, ii, p. 66; I. Abrahams, in *Trans. Jewish Hist. Soc. of England*, 8 (1915–17), pp. 98–121.

ADAMS, JACK (fl. 1664)
Author of a burlesque almanac for 1664. Perhaps the Jack Adams, 'fatuus', born at Clerkenwell, 1 December 1624 (Ms Sloane 1683, f. 131v; ibid., 1684, f. 7).

ADKIN, M.
Compiler of an almanac for 1640, for Saffron Walden. Probably a pseudonym of *Kidman*.

ALLESTREE, RICHARD (before 1581–c. 1643)
Mathematician and astrologer, who claimed in *1618* to have been practising for twenty years, but had come to reject the claims of judicial astrology. Younger son of Wm. Allestree of Alvaston, Derbyshire, M.P. (d. 1581), and uncle of the well-known divine, Richard Allestree. Published almanacs 1617–43 for Derby and Coventry. An edition for 1651 appears not to be by him.

Taylor, p. 225; *The Genealogist*, N.S., 32 (1915–16), p. 164; *Familiae Minorum Gentium*, ed. J. W. Clay (Harleian Soc., 1894–6), iii, p. 1038; Wood, *Ath. Oxon.*, iii, col. 1272.

ALLEYN, HENRY (fl. 1606–d. 1614)
Physician, surgeon and student in astronomy. Compiled almanacs for 1606–12 for Petworth, Sussex, and Horsham, where he was born. Will proved, as of Petworth, 1614 (*Chichester Wills 1482–1800*, ed. Fry, Index Library, xlix, p. 4).

ANDREWS, HENRY (1744–1820)
Born at Friestone, near Grantham, of poor parents, and began astronomical observations at the age of ten. Bookseller and schoolmaster at Royston, Herts., where he taught maths, book-keeping, grammar, measuring etc., and made and supplied barometers and thermometers (advertisements in Partridge, 1773, sig. C5v; Saunders, 1779, sig. C4). Supplied astronomical data for *The Nautical Almanack* for forty years, and for other almanacs including Moore, which he compiled for many years, perhaps from 1783. His skill was respected by ***Hutton*** and Dr. Maskelyne, the astronomer-royal.

D.N.B.; *Gent. Mag.* (1820), pp. 639–40; *Monthly Mag.* (1820), pp. 484–5; Hone, *Year Book*, p. 59; *N. and Q.*, iv, 1851, p. 74.

ANDREWS, WILLIAM (c. 1635–1713)
Student of mathematics, astrology and physic, which he studied from 1652 (*1679*), living at Ashdown (*1658*), Saffron Walden (*1661*) and from 1668 at nearby Radwinter, all in Essex. *Aetat.* twenty-seven in August 1662. Will proved 1713, as schoolmaster of Radwinter. Published almanacs from 1655 for London and Saffron Walden, a work on astrological physic in 1656, and a lost school textbook on mathematics (mentioned *1679*).

D.N.B.; *Wills at Chelmsford, 1620–1720*, ed. Emmison, Index Library, lxxix, p. 9.

APIAN, PETER (1495–1552)
Professor of mathematics at Ingolstadt, and astrologer to the Emperor Charles V. Published a number of almanacs in the period 1524–44, including a lost English edition for 1541.

A.D.B., i, p. 505–6; Hellmann, *Versuch*, p. 26; Thorndike, *Magic*, v, pp. 246, 421.

ASHWELL, SAMUEL (fl. 1640)
Published almanacs for Ongar, Essex, 1640–3; not mentioned in Ongar parish register.

ASKHAM, ANTHONY (fl. 1532–d. 1559)
Minister and physician; M.B., Cambridge, 1540. Rector of Methley and vicar of Burneston, both Yorks., 1552–9; presented by Edward VI, but took a strongly Catholic line under Mary. Published almanacs for 1548–58, and works on herbal medicine and astronomy. Brother of Roger Ascham. Dead by December 1559.

D.N.B.; Venn, i, p. 43; L. V. Ryan, *Roger Ascham* (1963), pp. 11, 297; *Cal. Pat. Rolls, 1558–60*, p. 255; Dickens, in *T.R.H.S.* (1963), p. 65; Borthwick Inst., Institution Act Book 1, f. 57v (information from Director).

ATKINSON, CHARLES (fl. 1639–77)
Son of Henry, merchant of Richmond, Yorks. Minister of Kirkhammerton,

Yorks., from c. 1654 (paid £16 p.a. by the impropriator), and also practised physic and all branches of astrology, taught writing, Latin, Greek and Hebrew. Ordained deacon 1639, priest 1642, but fought with Rupert in the civil war, at Marston Moor and elsewhere, and was taken prisoner. Compiled almanacs from 1660, but they were only published, for York, for 1670–4. Last recorded at Kirkhammerton in 1677.

Account of life and family in *1670*; Venn, i, p. 53 (brother Francis); Cheshire R.O., EDV 2/8, 9 (information from Archivist).

ATLEE, RICHARD (fl. 1647)

Physician, published almanac for 1647.

AXFORD, JOHN (fl. 1660–1700)

Student in physic and astrology 'for these forty years', apparently in London. Published almanac for 1700, and (in 1693) an astrological herbal.

BALLES, THOMAS (fl. 1617–31)

Mathematician and licensed physician. Educated Cambridge (admitted 1617, B.A. 1621, M.A. 1625), of Cambridgeshire. Published almanac for Norwich, where he lived, for 1631.

Raach, *Directory*, p. 25; Venn, i, p. 77.

BARHAM, WILLIAM (before 1583–1643)

Physician, licensed at Eastbourne, Sussex; published almanac for Wadhurst, 1639. Probably fifth son of John B. of Wadhurst (d. 1583), yeoman, from whom he inherited £300. Living at E. Hoathly 1642; will proved 1643.

R. G. Fitzgerald-Uniacke, 'The Barhams of Wadhurst', *Sussex Arch. Coll.*, lvi (1914), p. 144; Raach, *Directory*, p. 26; see *Visit. of Sussex*, ed. Hughes Clark, Harl. Soc. (1937) for the senior branch of the family.

BARNARDYN, MASTER (fl. 1564)

Published almanac for 1564, now lost; unidentified. Possibly the name was corrupted from Barnaby *Gaynsforth*: both were licensed to Hacket.

BASTON, JAMES (1633–63)

Practitioner in 'spagyrical' physic and astrology. Born at Silverstone, Northants., 29 October 1633 (Ms Ash. 385, p. 7), educated at Inner Temple, taught himself medicine and astrology. Admired by *Gadbury*, who reports that he was subject to many legal and other troubles. Died suddenly in May 1663, 'some think by poison' (Gadbury, *Collectio*, p. 139 and Ms note in Bodl. copy, Ash. 1081).

BEALE, WILLIAM (fl. 1631)

Philomath, gentleman. Published almanac for 1631, for Oxford. Servant of Henry Gellibrand, who was held to be responsible for the work (above, p. 47). Possibly the friend of *Nicholas Culpeper* (Appendix II).

BEDWELL, WILLIAM (1561/2–1632)

Minister of Tottenham High Cross, mathematician, Arabic scholar and student of astrology. Educated at Cambridge. His *Kalendarium* (1614), designed for travellers abroad, was not a typical almanac, but was covered by the Company's patent. His astrological library was purchased by *Lilly*.

D.N.B.; Taylor, p. 194.

BEIGHTON, HENRY (1687–1743)
A noted engineer and surveyor of Griff, near Coventry. F.R.S., and compiler of the *Ladies' Diary* after *Tipper*'s death.

D.N.B.; Taylor, *HP*, p. 110.

BELL, GEORGE (fl. 1622)
Mathematician and physician, who published an almanac for Norwich for 1622.

BELLERSON, PHILIP (fl. 1624)
Gentleman; published an almanac for 1624 for London.

BERIDGE, FERDINANDO (1609–c. 93)
Gentleman and physician; published almanac for Leicester for 1654. Presumably the F.B., third son of John, rector of Kibworth Beauchamp, baptized 26 September 1609. F.B., clerk, of Wartnaby, Leics., had a son Charles born there in 1655 and another son, Basil, born about 1663 when Ferdinando was rector of Gt. Paxton, Hunts. Both sons were educated at Cambridge; their father was apparently still alive in 1693.

S. A. Beveridge, *The Story of the Beveridge Family* (1923), esp. p. 81; *Lincolnshire Pedigrees*, ed. Maddison (Harleian Soc., 1902), pp. 124–5; Venn, i, p. 139; Bishop's transcripts of Kibworth reg., f. 182; J. Nichols, *The History and Antiquities of the County of Leicestershire* (1795–1811), iii, p. 109.

BEVERIDGE, WILLIAM (1637–1708)
Minister, son of a Leicestershire minister, and nephew of *Ferdinando Beridge*. Educated at Cambridge, and became Bishop of St. Asaph. Published a non-astrological calendar for 1666.

D.N.B.; Venn, i, p. 139; *Beveridge Family*, pp. 85–91.

BILLINGSLEY, ROBERT (fl. 1646–d. 1675)
Born at Glaston, Rutland, educated at Cambridge (admitted 1646, B.A. 1651, M.A. 1654). Schoolmaster at Thurlow, Suffolk, and rector of Bradley Magna, Suffolk, 1662–75 (d.). A friend of *Vincent Wing* and *Lilly*, and published an almanac for 1650, now lost.

Taylor, p. 235; Venn, i, p. 151; Ms Ash. 423, f. 152.

BILLY, HIMBERT DE (c. 1544–c. 1630)
Published a series of prognostications in the period 1577–1630, including two English editions for 1604. Lived at Lons-le-Saulnier, in Burgundy. The edition for 1596, published at Rouen, gives the author's portrait, *aetat.* fifty-one.

J. Grand-Carteret, *Les Almanachs Francais* (Geneva, 1968; first publ. Paris, 1896) p. 1; *Cat. of Bibl. Nationale.*

BIRD, THOMAS (fl. 1661)
Mathematician, published almanacs for London for 1661–2; his portrait appears in the second. A contemporary namesake was a physician, and died of plague in 1665 (Munk, *Physicians*, i, p. 210; Smyth, *Obituary*, p. 68: possibly two separate individuals).

BLAGRAVE, JOSEPH (1610–82)
Gentleman, astrologer and physician of Reading, and belonged to a well-known family of mathematicians; also a surveyor (E. Phillipps, *The New World* (1658), sig. a2v). A friend of Ashmole. Published almanacs for 1658–62, and a work on astrological physic.
D.N.B.

BLOUNT, THOMAS (1618–79)
Catholic gentleman and landowner, born at Orleton, Herefordshire, and educated at Cambridge. Published Catholic almanacs for 1661 and 1663, and other works, including *Boscobel*.
D.N.B.

BLUNT, GABRIEL (fl. 1656)
'Well-willer to mathematics', and physician; published almanacs for London for 1656–7.

BOGARDE, ARNOLD (fl. 1552)
A physician, living in Brussels. There was an English edition in 1553 of a prognostication by him, possibly a translation of his large *Prognosticum futurorum temporum* (Antwerp, 1552).

BOGARDE, LODOWICK (fl. 1551)
Doctor of astronomy and physic; a prognostication by him was published in England with an almanac by *Heuring* for 1551.

BOMELIUS, ELIS (fl. 1560–d.c. 1574)
Physician and astrologer. Son of a Dutch Lutheran pastor, born in Germany, and educated at Cambridge, where he became M.D. Had a flourishing practice in London, but gaoled 1567–70 at the suit of the College of Physicians. Moved to Moscow as astrologer to Ivan IV, but suspected of plotting and died in prison. Published an almanac for 1567.
D.N.B.; J. Strype, *The Life and Acts of Matthew Parker* (1711), pp. 294–5.

BOND, HENRY (1588–1678)
Teacher of navigation, surveying and mathematics at the Royal Dockyard at Chatham. Edited *Tapp*'s *Seaman's Kalendar* for about twenty years.
Taylor, pp. 207–8; date of birth in Gadbury, 1699, sig. B5.

BOOKER, JOHN (1602–67)
Astrologer and physician (*1634*, *1652*, etc.), though according to Lilly he did not practise as a physician. Born in Manchester, apprenticed to a London haberdasher, later a writing-master and clerk to two magistrates. Appointed

licenser of mathematical books by the Long Parliament. Had a large astrological practice, and published almanacs from 1631 till his death.

D.N.B. (gives wrong date of birth; for the correct date, 23 March 1601/2, see Ms Ash. 225, fos. 3–4; Ms Aubrey 23, f. 121; Gadbury, *Collectio*, p. 181).

BORDE, ANDREW (c. 1490–1549)

Educated at Oxford and abroad, a Carthusian who was released from his vows and became a noted physician and traveller. Published a prognostication for 1545, and works on herbal medicine, astronomy et. al.

Emden, *Register*, p. 59; *D.N.B.*

BOURNE, WILLIAM (c. 1535–82)

A prosperous inn-keeper of Gravesend, where he served as jurat and port-reeve (mayor); he inherited a share in the river-traffic to London. Taught and practised mathematics, notably surveying, gunnery, navigation and the use of instruments; he published nautical almanacs and a textbook for seamen. The first of the self-taught mathematicians, he knew John Dee, and was patronized and consulted by Lord Admiral Clinton, Sir William Winter (Master of the Ordnance), and Lord Burghley.

Bourne, *A Regiment for the Sea*, ed. E. G. R. Taylor (Cambridge, 1963), introduction; Taylor, p. 176.

BOWKER, JAMES (fl. 1668–84)

Mathematician; published almanacs for London 1668–84. Chose not to publish earlier because his name resembled *Booker*, 'whose resplendency would have dazzled the light of my slender taper' (*1668*, sig. Av). Apparently not related.

BRECKNOCK, —

Apparently issued an almanac for 1618, for England and Ireland (Jackson, *Records of the Stationers' Company, 1602–40*, p. 100). A Roger Brecknock, surgeon, flourished 1605 (J. Young, *Annals of the Barber-Surgeons* (1890), p. 200), but the entry may well refer to an unauthorized impression of *Bretnor*.

BRETNOR, EZEKIEL (fl. 1629)

Mathematician; published almanacs for 1629–30 for Colchester. Probably a pseudonym derived from the next.

BRETNOR, THOMAS (fl. 1607–18)

Teacher of mathematics, astronomy and surveying, and a physician, living near Holborn Conduit, later at Cow Lane, London; claimed skill also in Latin, French and Spanish. Published almanacs for 1607 and from 1609, for London (edn. for 1618 was written at Cranbrook, Kent, where he then lived.) Also published on surveying and on the medical value of opium. A friend of Gunter, Elias Allen and their circle. Died 1618, in the parish of St. Sepulchre, London (admin., Guildhall Ms 9168/16, p. 313: 17 November 1618).

D.N.B.; Taylor, pp. 197–8.

Briscoe, John (fl. 1695)
Financial writer; published a series of pamphlets in 1694–8 on public credit, advocating a National Land Bank and criticizing the Whig Bank of England. Issued a brief almanac for 1695/6, which contained tables for the purchase of annuities.

J. E. T. Rogers, *The First Nine Years of the Bank of England* (Oxford, 1887), pp. 17, 50–1.

Brothyel (Brothbeihel), Matthias (fl. 1533–53)
'Magister' of Kaufbeuren, in Swabia. Published a number of prognostications in the period 1533–53, including an English edition for 1545 originally compiled at Ravensburg for Frederick, Duke of Bavaria. Also composed popular drama.

A.D.B., iii, p. 365; Hellmann, *Versuch*, pp. 11, 26.

Browne, Daniel (fl. 1614–31)
Teacher and practitioner of mathematics and astrology, and made instruments in brass (*1624*, sig. C2v). Educated at Christ's Hospital, London. Published almanacs for 1614–31 for London, Cirencester (*1615*), Calcot near Cricklade, Wilts., where he lived (*1616, 1619, 1626*) and Chester (*1620*). Living in Hosier Lane, London, in 1631.

Taylor, p. 203.

Brunfels, Otto (d. 1534)
A minister and early Protestant; later schoolmaster and town physician of Berne, where he died. Published astrological and medical works; an English edition of his prognostication for 1526 was prepared by John Ryckes, priest.

A.D.B., iii, p. 441; Thorndike, *Magic*, v, pp. 316–18.

Buckminster (Buckmaster), Thomas (c. 1532–99)
Minister, physician, astrologer. Published almanacs for London 1567–99; gives his age, *aetat.* sixty-six, in *1598*. Vicar of Twickenham, 1562–3, rector of All Hallows the Great, 1564–72, rector of St. Mary Woolnoth, 1572–99 (died). Perhaps related to William B., vice-chancellor of Cambridge, d. 1545.

D.N.B.; G. Hennessy, *Novum Repert. Ecclesiasticum* (1898), pp. 83, 315, 431, notes p. lviii.

Bucknall, John (fl. 1675–8)
Astrologer, shepherd ('I really am what I profess': *1676*, sig. Av), and physician (1678), living at Weston-on-Trent and then Stanton, both Derbyshire. Published serious almanacs for Ghotom (i.e. Gotham), Notts. ('where the Wise Men lived'), 1675–6, and Derby, 1677–8. Verses addressed to him by John Yarwood of Shepshed, Leics., teacher of writing and mathematics, and James Wright, philomath, and a reference to his friend, the farming author, John Claridge.

Bulleine, William (fl. 1550–d. 1576)
A prominent physician, born near Ely, a minister c. 1550, then studied

medicine and took an M.D. abroad, practising in Durham and London. Author of medical works and an almanac, now lost, for 1564.

D.N.B.; Wood, *Ath. Oxon.*, i, cols. 538–40.

BURTON, GREGORY (fl. 1613–21)
Astrologer and physician of Wymondham, Norfolk, who published almanacs for 1613–14 and 1616–21, mostly for Norwich.

BURTON, WILLIAM (fl. 1652)
Published several sheet almanacs for Oxford, 1652–5. Not the famous antiquarian of those names, for whom see *D.N.B.*; see also Wood, *Ath. Oxon.*, iii, col. 440.

BUTLER, ROBERT (fl. 1629)
Published almanacs for 1629–32, for Leicester. Probably the Robert Butler who published *The Scale of Interest* (1633), then living off Golding Lane, London.

BUTZLIN, VALENTINE (fl. 1552)
Doctor of astronomy and physick of Wangen (in Württemberg); an English edition of his sheet almanac was published for 1552.

CARRE, JAMES (fl. 1580–d. 1593)
Minister of Alnwick, Northumb., 1590–3. Educated Cambridge, M.A. 1586. Published almanac for 1593, dated from Giggleswick, Craven.

The Library (1927–8), p. 459; Venn, i, p. 295.

CATLETT, JOHN (fl. 1656)
Mathematician, of Sittingbourne, Kent. Published as a young man an almanac for seamen and travellers in 1656, with commendatory verses by Th. Catlett and Jo. Hurt of Sittingbourne, and one G.I. For Thos. Catlett of Sittingbourne, gent., see *Visit. of Kent* 1663–8, ed. Armytage, Harleian Soc. (1906), p. 33.

CHAMBERLAINE, JOSEPH (fl. 1627–49)
Gentleman, mathematician, of Stratford, Suffolk, who taught dialling, surveying, logarithms, navigation etc. Published almanacs for 1627–31 for Stratford and Bury St. Edmunds. Probably identical with the J.C., licensed physician of Gt. Finborough, near Bury, at this time (Raach, *Directory*, p. 35), and with the J.C., surgeon and student in mathematics, who issued almanacs for Bury St. Edmunds for 1647–9.

Taylor, p. 211.

CHATTOCK, JOHN (fl. 1708)
Of Castle Bromwich. Published *Coelestial Observations* for 1708, for Coventry, and *Telescopium Anglicanum* for 1710, for Birmingham.

CHERRY, THOMAS (fl. 1699)
Philomath; published almanac for Bedford for 1699.

CHESICK, WILLIAM (fl. 1661)
Published an almanac for that year, which gave no biographical information.

CHILDREY, JOSHUA (1625–70)
Minister, mathematician, and Baconian astrologer. Born at Rochester, educated at Oxford (B.A. 1646, D.D. 1661). Schoolmaster at Faversham 1652–8, chaplain to Lord Herbert; archdeacon of Salisbury 1664. Regular correspondent of the Royal Society, and friend of *Gadbury* and other contemporary astrologers. Published almanac for London for 1653.

D.N.B.; Taylor, pp. 226–7 (both give date of birth as 1623, but the correct date appears to be 20 October 1625: Ms Sloane 1683, f. 176v; Gadbury, 1695, sig. B4; idem, *Collectio*, p. 114); Foster, *Al. Oxon.*, i, p. 272.

CLARK, —
Published almanacs for Ipswich for 1633–7.

CLARKE, EUSTACE (fl. 1628)
Of Sandridge, near St. Albans. Published almanacs for 1628–31. Not recorded in Sandridge parish register.

CLARKE, WILLIAM (1668)
Mathematician and compiler of an almanac for 1668.

CLIFFORD, ABRAHAM (fl. 1642)
Gentleman, published almanac for Gloucester for 1642. Probably related to the Cliffords of Frampton-on-Severn, Gloucs., and thus to Abraham Clifford, physician and nonconformist minister (c. 1628–75) who belonged to that family (pedigree in Gloucs. R.O., D149; A. Clifford, *Methodus Evangelicus* (1676), sig. A3, 7; Venn, i, p. 355; Matthews, *Calamy Revised*, p. 122).

COELSON, LANCELOT (1627–c. 87)
Physician, surgeon and astrologer, living by the Royal Oak, Still Yard, Gt. Tower Hill. Born at Colchester (*1672*, sig. A2) on 25 March 1627, married 1645, wounded fighting in the Scottish campaign of 1650 (Ms Ash. 426, f. 295v). Practised medicine and astrology from about 1655 (*1685*), specializing in V.D., deafness and scrofula, and favouring Paracelsian methods. A friend of *Lilly*, *Saunders* and Sir John Friend, M.P., with whom he served in the Tower Trained Bands (*1686*, sig. Av). Published almanacs for 1671–87.

COLE, THOMAS (fl. 1704–d. 1720)
Physician, surgeon and astrologer of Haw, near Tirley, Gloucs. Advertised in *Cookson*'s almanac for 1704, and published his own *Ephemeris* for 1705, dedicated to Sir Wm. Lane, a local J.P. His will, as of Tirley, was proved in 1720 (*Gloucs. Wills*, ed. Fry and Phillimore, Index Library (1907), ii, p. 145).

COLEY, HENRY (1633–1707)
Mathematician and astrologer. Born at Oxford, the son of a joiner, he came to

London, worked as a tailor and took up mathematics and astrology, which he taught and practised for thirty years, boarding pupils at his house at Baldwin's Court, near Gray's Inn Road. Became *Lilly*'s assistant, and a friend of Ashmole, Henry Care, *Salmon* and many others. Published an almanac from 1672 (following the success of his astrological guide) till his death. Portrait appears in *Merlinus Anglicus Junior* for 1686.

D.N.B.; Taylor, p. 241; Aubrey, *Brief Lives*, i, pp. 181–2.

Colson, Nathaniel (fl. 1674)
Mathematician, published a nautical almanac in 1675, with several later editions.

Taylor, p. 268.

Conyers, William (fl. 1664)
Mathematician, published an almanac for 1664 which was commended by John Vicars. A friend of *Gadbury*. Perhaps the Conyers of Northants., born 15 August 1634, who was acquainted with Edlin (Ms Ash. 428, f. 272). Another Wm. Conyers was a physician, b. 1622, D. Med., Oxon., 1653, died in London during the Great Plague (Foster, *Al. Oxon.*, i, p. 318).

Cookson, William (fl. 1699–1711)
Astrologer and physician, living at the Beehive and Globe in Gunyard, Houndsditch, who published almanacs for 1699–1711. Friend of *Parker*, but denounced by *John Partridge* as a Scottish alehouse-keeper who merely plagiarized the ephemerides of Merrifield (Partridge, 1701, sig. Av: 1703, sig. C8).

Cornelius, Gilbert (fl. 1647)
Compiler of an almanac for 1647.

Coronelli, Vincenzo Maria (1650–1718)
'Cosmographer to the Republic of Venice.' Compiler of encyclopaedic works, esp. on astronomy and geography, and a *Royal Almanack* (2nd edn., 1696) recording the anniversaries of major events in the life of William III; it was not astrological in any way.

Coulton, John (1631–fl. 1655)
Philomath; born and lived at Cobham, Surrey, and published almanacs for 1653–5 for Guildford. Born 20 January 1631: Ms Ash. 183, p. 374.

Taylor, p. 240.

Cowper, Thomas (fl. 1637)
Compiler of an almanac for Oxford for that year.

Coxe, Francis (fl. 1560–75)
Physician; examined by the Privy Council and pilloried for sorcery in 1561. Published several almanacs in the period 1562–7.

Crawford, Henry (fl. 1676)
Practitioner in physic and astrology, living in Brickington Court, Coleman St.

Published almanacs for 1676–7. Friend of *Booker*, *Coley*, *Salmon* and Daniel de Bourcke.

CROOKE, WILLIAM (fl. 1652)
Student in mathematics; published almanacs for Oxford for 1652–3.

CULPEPER, NICHOLAS (1616–54)
Gentleman, astrologer and physician, who lived next to the Red Lion in Spittlefields where he had a large practice. Son of a clergyman, educated briefly at Cambridge, then apprenticed to a London apothecary. Fought for Parliament in the civil war. A popular translator and compiler of medical works, and critic of the College of Physicians' monopoly. Published almanacs for 1651–6, the last published from his notes by his friend Dr. Thomas Harrington. The 1653 edition is dated from his house at Chesham, Bucks.

D.N.B.; Poynter in *Journ. of Hist. of Medicine* (1962), pp. 152–7.

CULPEPPER, NATHANIEL (fl. 1679)
'Student in physic and celestial science.' Claimed to be a friend and relation of the preceding, and published almanacs from 1680 which continued till 1737. They were highly stereotyped, and the name is probably merely a pseudonym; *Coley* compiled the edition for 1694 (S.C., Journal Bk., f. 157).

CUNNINGHAM (KENINGHAM), WILLIAM (c. 1531–86)
Physician, astrologer, surveyor. Educated at Cambridge (M.B., 1557) and Heidelberg, where he probably took a doctorate. Practised at Norwich, and later in Coleman St., London. Published almanacs for 1558–64; portrait in *1558*.

D.N.B.; Venn, iii, p. 7.

DACQUETUS, PETRUS (fl. 1556)
Doctor of medicine (Bologna). Fellow of R.C.P., 1556, its Censor 1562–3. Published a Latin perpetual almanac in 1556 (Munk, *Physicians*, i, p. 56), and a commentary on the medical writings of Celsus. Born at Furnes, near Nieuport (*Biog. Nat. de Belgique*, iv, p. 616).

DADE, JOHN (fl. 1589–1614)
Gentleman, physician; published almanacs for 1589–1614.

DADE, WILLIAM (fl. 1615)
Gentleman, physician; perhaps son of last. Published almanacs from 1615 which continued into the next century, though Dade was said in 1655 to have been dead for many years (Wharton, 1655, sig. B3).

DANIEL, HUMPHREY (fl. 1651)
Student of mathematics in London; published almanacs for 1651–6.

DAUNCY, GERVASE (fl. 1609–15)
'Scientist.' Matriculated, sizar, at Trinity College, Cambridge, 1609 (Venn,

ii, 12). Published almanacs for Hereford for 1614–15, attacking judicial astrology.

DAVIS, WILLIAM (fl. 1687–92)
'Practical guager' and teacher of mathematics and surveying, astrology and handwriting (including shorthand) at Ludgershall, Wilts., for which he issued almanacs for 1687–8. There were later editions for Broomham, Wilts. (1689), and Clandfield, Wayvill, near Andover, Hants. (1692). Also advertised his pills for scurvy and dropsy and a balsam, and no doubt practised physic (*1692*, sig. C4v).

Taylor, p. 283.

DAWSON, THOMAS (fl. 1559–d. 1620)
A London printer, living at the Three Cranes in the Vintry; Master of the Stationers' Company in 1603 and 1615. Published a small sheet almanac in 1577 as a promotional device, with the legend:

> Take this in remembrance, and for no other no cause:
> Esteem not the gift, but the goodwill of Dawse.

McKerrow, *Dictionary, 1556–1640*, p. 86.

DERNYL, J. (fl. 1567)
Compiler of a mock almanac, now lost.

DESMUS, RAPHAEL
Pseudonym of *Sam. Sheppard*

DIGGES, LEONARD (1510–58)
Landed gentleman of Barham, Kent. A well-known mathematician and surveyor, also skilled in navigation; friend of John Dee. Involved in Wyatt's rebellion. Published annual and perpetual almanacs.

D.N.B.; Taylor, pp. 166–7; Emden, *Register*, p. 169.

DIGGES, THOMAS (fl. 1543–d. 1595)
Son of the last. Educated at Cambridge, and a pupil of John Dee. Practitioner in mathematics, military science, astronomy and surveying. M.P.; Muster-Master General in the Netherlands in 1586. Published revised editions of his father's everlasting prognostication.

D.N.B.; Taylor, p. 175.

DOVE, JONATHAN
Published almanacs for Cambridge, where they were printed, and later for London from 1627. The Christian name appeared only on the first edition, and Dove was no doubt one of the names invented by the Cambridge press.

DREKIN, PHILIP
Pseudonym of *Philip Kinder.*

DUNSTER, T(HOMAS) (fl. 1642–52)
Published a broadside almanac for 1652–3. No doubt Thomas Dunster, bookseller and printer, of the Red Lion, Grub St.

Plomer, *Dictionary, 1641–67*, pp. 68–9; Morrison, *Index, 1641–1700*, p. 74.

EATON, NATHANIEL (1609–74)
Doctor of Philosophy and Medicine (Padua, 1647). Educated at Cambridge, later at Leyden and Franeker. Went to New England in 1637, and became master of Harvard College, till dismissed in 1639. Returned to England; published an almanac for 1657. Vicar of Bishop's Castle, Salop, 1661, rector of Bideford, Devon, 1668, but died in prison for debt.
D.N.B.

EDWARDS, CHARLES (1628–c. 91)
Welsh Puritan, educated at Oxford; ejected in 1660. Published works on religion and education, and Welsh almanacs for 1683–5.
Dict. of Welsh Biography, p. 184; Jenkins, 'Welsh Books', pp. 529, 577.

EINER, N. (fl. 1620–6)
Practitioner in mathematics and astronomy; published almanacs for London for 1620–6.

ELAND, WILLIAM (1636–fl. 1656)
Philomath; published almanac for 1656 and a guide to astrology the next year. Born on 13 October 1636 (Ms Ash. 428, f. 272v).

ELLIS, JOHN (fl. 1608)
Published an almanac for 1608 for 'Cripplesham' (?Crimplesham, Norfolk).

EVANS, JOHN (fl. 1613–59)
Minister, physician and mathematician. M.A. (*Ephemerides*, 1633, t.p.); presumably the J.E. of Balliol, M.A. 1594, or of Jesus, M.A. 1595 (Foster, *Al. Oxon*, i. p. 470). Published almanacs for Worcester for 1613, and for 1625/9–31 for Shrewsbury. Occurs as curate of Enfield (i.e. Enville), Staffs., 1620 (W. N. Lander, in *Coll. for the Hist. of Staffs.* (1915), p. 99; Thomas, p. 378n), and in *1625* gives his address as Four Ashes, Enfield, offering tuition in Latin, Greek, Hebrew, handwriting and mathematics. Later practised medicine in Gunpowder Alley, London, in the 1630s, advertising his *aurum potabile*. He also published *The Palace of Profitable Pleasure* (1621), a dictionary with arithmetical and other tables, and *The Sacrifice of a Contrite Heart* (1630), a book of prayers and meditations. Taught astrology to *Lilly*. Evans reappeared in 1659 as rector of Little-on-Severn, Gloucs., announcing in the press that his antimonial cup was still much in demand and could be obtained through a relation in London (*Loyall Scout*, 23–30 September 1659, p. 182).

F., M.
Compiler of a sheet almanac published at and for Cambridge from 1660 which continued into the next century.

FAITHORNE, WILLIAM (1616–91)
Engraver and portrait-painter; published a perpetual almanac in 1678.
D.N.B.

Fallowes, Edward (fl. 1636–40)
Mathematician; published almanacs for 1636–40 for Nottingham, Coventry and Derby.

Farmer, William (fl. 1587–1614)
Surgeon. Published almanacs for Dublin, serving also for England, in 1587 and 1614, and one now lost for 1593. 1614 written from Gt. Warborough St., Dublin.

Felgenhauer, Paul (1593–c. 1677)
Born in Bohemia, the son of a Lutheran pastor. Lived mostly in Amsterdam, writing copiously on religious themes and becoming well known throughout North Germany. One of his prognostications was published in an English edition in 1655.

Neue Deutsche Biographie, v, p. 69.

Field, John (c. 1520–87)
'Farmer, sometime student in the mathematical sciences.' Published an ephemeris for 1557 with a pioneer preface by John Dee on Copernicanism. Thereafter lived on his estates at East Ardsley, Yorks.

D.N.B.; Dickens, in *T.R.H.S.*, 1963, p. 65; Wood, *Ath. Oxon.*, i, cols. 300–1; Emden, *Register*, p. 204.

Fisher, John (fl. 1680–1704)
Astrologer, surveyor, teacher of mathematics in London. Published *Stella Nova* for 1704, offering tuition in astronomy, mathematics and navigation.

Taylor, p. 276.

Fitzsmith, Richard (fl. 1654)
Philomath; friend of *Childrey* and of *Gadbury* (Gadbury, *Britain's Royal Star* (1661), p. 20). Published an almanac for 1654 for London, when he was living in Thames St. Nicolson (*Annals of Science*, 1939, pp. 4, 5n) regards him as a pseudonym of Childrey.

Flatman, Thomas (1636/7–88)
Poet, pamphleteer and miniaturist. Educated at Oxford and the Inner Temple; F.R.S. Author of the burlesque almanac *Montelion* for 1661–2, according to Wood, and perhaps *Gusmans Ephemeris*. Born 20 February 1635/6 according to Charles Bernard: Ms Sloane 1684, f. 9v.

D.N.B.

Fly, —
Published almanacs for King's Lynn from 1657 into the eighteenth century. A stereotyped work, and the name was probably pseudonymous. Variant London and Cambridge versions appeared simultaneously.

Forster, Richard (c. 1546–1616)
Physician, educated at Oxford, and rising to become president of the Royal College of Physicians in 1601–4 and 1615–16. Physician to Robert Dudley,

Earl of Leicester. Taught astrology to Sir Christopher Heydon (Heydon, *An Astrological Discourse* (1650), sig. A3–4). Published an ephemeris for 1575.

D.N.B.; Munk, *Physicians*, i, p. 69; Foster, *Al. Oxon.*, ii, p. 517.

FOSTER, WILLIAM (fl. 1662)

Philomath; published almanac for Lancaster for 1662. Probably identical with Wm. Forster, mathematician and surveyor (fl. 1630–74), who was a friend of Oughtred and *Leybourne* (Taylor, p. 212).

FOWLE, THOMAS (1631–1713)

Mathematician and astrologer, and published almanacs for London for 1680–1703. Lived at Ticehurst, Sussex. In June 1701 (*1702*) says he has now completed his seventieth year. Buried at Ticehurst 11 December 1713 (par. reg., Soc. Gen., p. 139).

FRENDE, GABRIEL (fl. 1584–99)

Astrologer and physician, who published almanacs for Canterbury for 1584–99, and had compiled earlier ones which were not printed. Not educated at university (*1585*). Almanacs were also issued in his name for 1614–23, but do not appear to be by the same author. There is no evidence to support the suggestion by Nashe that the real author was Gabriel Harvey (Nashe, *Works*, ed. McKerrow (1958), iii, pp. 70–1). Frende presumably belonged to the well-known Kent family of that name.

FROST, WALTER (fl. 1619–d. 1652)

Came from a Suffolk family; published Cambridge almanacs for 1626–7 and probably others up to the civil war. Then compiled newspapers, and served parliament, rising to become Secretary to the Council of State. His son entered Emmanuel in 1637 and became Manciple.

Aylmer, *The State's Servants* (1973), p. 256; J. B. Williams, *History of English Journalism* (1908), pp. 121–2, 124; *C.S.P.D., 1651–2*, pp. 198, 152; Taylor, p. 364.

FULKE, WILLIAM (1538–89)

Theologian, Master of Pembroke Hall, Cambridge. Published an attack on almanacs in 1560 but apparently issued almanacs himself in 1560/1 and 1562/3. If so, they were probably non-astrological, scriptural almanacs, though Richard Harvey later claimed Fulke as an astrologer (*Astrological Discourse* (1583), sig. iii).

D.N.B.; Venn, ii, p. 183; Bosanquet, pp. 194–5.

G., R. (fl. 1666)

Compiler of an English/Latin prognostication for 1666 which was eschatological, not astrological.

GADBURY, JOB (d. 1715)

Student in physic and astrology: a cousin of *John Gadbury* (*1706*, sig. Av; *1716*, sig. C3v), whose series he continued till his death in 1715 (*The Tatler*, ed. Aitken, ii, p. 54n). Ms notes by Job on his children Sarah and Judah are in Rawl. Alm. 112, 114. The series continued under the name of J. Gadbury (from 1718), Job (1723), J. (*1731*) and John (*1750*), all apparently pseudonymous.

GADBURY, JOHN (1627–1704)
Astrologer and physician. Born at Wheatley, Oxon., apprenticed to an Oxford tailor and later servant to a London merchant adventurer. Studied astrology under Fiske, and was probably a protégé of *Lilly*. Graduated in politics from Parliamentarian to crypto-Jacobite, and in religion from Ranter to crypto-Catholic. Lived for many years by Brick Court, near Deans Yard, Westminster. Published almanacs from 1656; his protrait is in the editions for 1673–5.
D.N.B.

GADBURY, TIMOTHY (1624–fl. 1661)
Teacher of navigation at Ratcliff, London, and compiled nautical almanacs. Born near Oxford, 18 July 1624; uncle of *John G.* (Ms Ash. 426, f. 291; J. Gadbury, *Britain's Royal Star*, p. 30), with whom he collaborated in a new editions of *Hartgill*'s tables in 1656.
Taylor, p. 243.

GALE, THOMAS (1507–87)
A prominent surgeon, born in London, who served as surgeon with Henry VIII's army in France in 1544, and later with Philip II; later practised in London. Master of the Barber-Surgeons' Company in 1561. Published an almanac for 1567, now lost.
D.N.B.

GALLEN, THOMAS
Mathematician. Published almanacs for London from 1639 to 1685. 'Gallen' was a pseudonym of the bookseller, *Thomas Langley*, who was known to be the true compiler (Wharton, 1645, sig. C6v).

GARDNER, ROBERT (fl. 1698)
Astrologer and farrier ('physical, chirurgical, and astrological') of Marden, Kent. Published almanacs for 1697–9.

GASSER, ACHILLES PIRMIN (1505–77)
Doctor in physic and astronomy; town physician of Feldkirch, and later Augsburg. A Lutheran apologist, and urban chronicler. Published several almanacs in the 1540s, including an English edition for 1546.
A.D.B., viii, pp. 396–7; *Neue Deutsche Biographie*, v, 79–80; Hellmann, *Versuch*, p. 27.

GAYNSFORTH, BARNABY (fl. 1567)
Published an almanac, now lost, for that year.

GESNER, JACOB (fl. 1555)
Doctor of physic; an English edition of an almanac by him was published for 1555. Not identified; there is nothing to identify him with the important Zurich printer of these names (*A.D.B.*, ix, pp. 95–6).

GIBBONS, WILLIAM (fl. 1655)
Issued an almanac for 1655, now lost. No doubt Wm. Gibbons of Market Harborough, Leics., a friend of *Lilly* to whom he wrote in 1655 describing lunar phenomena (Ms Ash. 423, fos. 225, 226v). A Wm. Gibbons of Hallaton (eight miles from Harborough) died 1660 (will in Leics. R.O.).

GIBSON, RICHARD (fl. 1707–23)
Astrologer of Bishop's Waltham, Hants. Published *Astrologia Britannica* for 1707–12. Described as schoolmaster there in a marriage licence, 1720 (information from Hants. R.O.).

GILBERT, SAMUEL (fl. 1655–d.c. 1692)
Minister and well-known botanist, married to the daughter of John Ray. Philomath, and perhaps also a physician. Publish an almanac for 1683 (with his portrait) and *The Florist's Vade-Mecum and Gardener's Almanack* (1683 and many later editions).
D.N.B.

GILDEN, G. (fl. 1615–32)
Mathematician. Published almanacs for 1615–32 for London and Shipston-on-Stour, Worcs. A friend of Gunter, Elias Allen and other instrument-makers. A George Gilden of London was arrested in 1642 by order of the Commons for refusing to pay war taxation (H.M.C., xxxi. Loder-Symonds, p. 385).
Taylor, p. 203.

GOLDISBOROUGH, JOHN (1632–1712)
Gentleman, student in astrology and physic; published an almanac for 1662 for London. Belonged to a family of small gentry at East Knoyle, Wilts., where he lived. His brother and son became ministers.
A. Goldsbrough, *Memorials of the Goldesborough Family* (1930), pp. 159, 206–9.

GOLDSMITH, JOHN (fl. 1656)
Published a pocket almanac of which editions survive from 1656 into the eighteenth century. *Endymion*, 1663, refers to Goldsmith as already a leading compiler, and a Mr. Goldsmith was paid £3 for his copy by the Company in June 1652 (S.C., Journal Bk, f. 10). *Gadbury* called him a skilled astrologer (Gadbury, 1698, p. 13), but the almanac was always a stereotyped production.

GOSSENNE, GERARD (fl. 1571–86)
Doctor of physic, poet and religious controversialist. A native of Brabant, he sought refuge in England as a Protestant, and published an almanac here for 1571. Possibly the unnamed Brabant physician prosecuted slightly earlier by the College of Physicians.
J. Aengelrammus, *Pseudoxia G. Gossennii* (1587); Goodall, p. 314.

GRAMMAR, ABRAHAM (fl. 1627)
Mathematician; published almanacs for 1627–8 for London. Perhaps Abraham Grame, admitted sizar at Emmanuel College, Cambridge, 1624, M.A. 1632;

an Abraham Grame, clerk, of St. Olave's Southwark, died 1636 (Venn, ii, p. 247).

GRAPHAEUS, RUDOLPH (fl. 1586–1618)
Doctor of physic, of Deventer. Published about thirty Flemish almanacs in the period 1586–1618, and an English edition for 1598: Hellmann, *Versuch*, p. 31.

GRAY, WALTER (fl. 1588–d. 1613)
Gentleman and physician, of the Gray family of Askerswell, Bridport, Dorset. 'A little desperate doctor, commonly wearing a pistol round his neck', and attended by the livelier young gentlemen of the district. Published almanacs for 1588–98 for Dorchester, and 1604–5 for Byport (Bridport). Buried at Swyre, near Bridport, 1613. A friend of *Hartgill*.

N. and Q., 1st ser, xi (1855), p. 260; J. Hutchins, *History of Dorset* (1863), ii, pp. 785–6; Morgan in *Annals of Science* (1968), p. 299.

GREEN, CHRISTOPHER (fl. 1691)
Philomath. Published a circular perpetual almanac, beginning 1691, printed for the author.

GREENWOOD, NICHOLAS (fl. 1689)
Worked for the Excise, but studied astronomy and practised physic and astrology as a secondary occupation (his *Astronomia Anglicana* (1689), sig. A2v). Published almanac for 1689.

Taylor, p. 405.

GRESHAM, EDWARD (1565–1613)
Physician, mathematician and astronomer. Born 14 April 1565 (Ms Sloane 1683, f. 176; Gadbury, *Collectio*, p. 180); of Stainford, Yorks. Later lodged in Thames St., London. Master of Arts (1606), and probably the E.G. who matriculated at Trinity, Cambridge, in 1584 (Venn, ii, p. 264). An early Copernican. Published almanacs for York for 1603–7. Buried 14 January 1613 at All Saints the Less, London (Ms Ash. 242, f. 200; will, Guildhall Ms 9050/5, f. 22v).

GUMDANTE, EDWIN (fl. 1621)
Mathematician; published almanac for London for 1621.

H., G. i.e. GEORGE HORTON, q.v.

HALLEY, EDMUND (1656–1742)
The celebrated astronomer and mathematician; compiled ephemerides for the Royal Society for 1686–8; a note on the Bodleian copy for 1688 runs 'Jo. Aubrey Ex Dono Edmundi Halley Auctor' (Bodleian shelfmark, Wood 498). They are not astrological. Halley also helped *Parker* with the astronomical tables of his almanacs.

HARFLETE, HENRY (1608–56)
Belonged to a family of gentry of Ash, near Sandwich, Kent. Born there in

1608 (Ms Ash. 387, f. 241), son of another Henry; educated at Cambridge and Gray's Inn. Essayist, astronomer and mathematician. A Parliamentarian, but also a friend of *Wharton* and *Childrey* (*1653*, sig. C2v, A4). Published almanacs for 1651–6 for Sandwich and Dover.

D.N.B. (confuses father and son); Taylor, p. 195 (gives date of birth as 1580—the father's); J. R. Planché, *A Corner of Kent* (1864), pp. 347–8 disentangles four generations of Henries; Venn, ii, p. 306.

HARRISON, JOHN (fl. 1689)
Student in astrology and physic; published almanac for 1689. Another of these names was M.D., Cambridge, 1682, Fellow of R.C.P., 1687: Venn, ii, p. 316.

HARTGILL, GEORGE (fl. 1555–d.c. 1597)
From a Somerset gentle family. Minister of Steeple Iwerne and West Chickerell, both Dorset; patronized by the Paulet family. Published almanac for 1581, and astronomical tables in 1594.

D.N.B.; Morgan in *Annals of Science* (1968) gives a full account.

HARTLEY, JOHN (fl. 1733)
Of Burholm, Bowland, Yorks. Published *Angelus Sideralis* for 1733–4, calculated for Lancaster.

HARVEY, JOHN (1564–92)
Physician, born at Saffron Walden (brother of Gabriel), educated at Cambridge; licensed physician at King's Lynn. Published almanacs in 1580s, and other prophetic works.

D.N.B.; Venn, ii, p. 323.

HARVEY, WILLIAM (fl. 1750)
Of Knipton, Leics., near Grantham. Said to have compiled *Wing* for some years after the death of *Tycho Wing* in 1750 (Hone, *Year Book*, p. 685). Perhaps Wm. Harvey of Knipton who married in 1709 (*Leics. Par. Reg., Marriages*, ed. Phillimore and Blagg, iv, p. 30), or a son.

HARYCOCK, DR. (i.e. HARCOCK, EDMUND) (fl. 1535–d. 1562)
'Prior of St. Augustine's fryery in Norwich' (Arber, *Transcripts*, i, p. 87b). B.D., but not in Venn, Foster or Emden. Prior of Norwich Dominicans, 1535, fellow of Wingfield College, 1541; paid a pension of £5 p.a. Later rector of St. Michael Coslaney, Norwich, 1556–61. Published almanac, now lost, for 1563.

E.H.R., xlviii (1933), p. 219.

HAWKINS, GEORGE (fl. 1624–7)
'Servant to Sir Neville Poole, of Woksey, Wilts, Kt.' Published almanacs for Cirencester for 1624–7.

HEALY, RICHARD (1634–fl. 1658)
Mathematician and astrologer. Published almanacs for Aylesbury, Bucks., and Buckingham for 1655 and 1658. Date of birth, May 1634, in Ms Ash. 183, p. 372.

HEATH, ROBERT (fl. 1737–79)
Military engineer and mathematician. Lived at Upnor Castle, Kent, and later London. Assisted *Beighton* with *The Ladies' Diary*, and succeeded him as its editor until dismissed in 1753. A fierce critic of the Stationers' penury, and of their monopoly, which he undermined by publishing quasi-almanacs.
D.N.B.; Taylor, *HP*, pp. 180–1; *N. and Q.*, (1855) p. 441; Ellis, *Orig. Letters*, p. 304.

HEATHCOTT, WILLIAM (1633–fl. 1664)
Lived at Cowdale, Derbys., and issued almanacs for 1664–5. Wrote to *Lilly*, giving his birth as 10 September 1633 (Ms Ash. 423, p. 160). No doubt belonged to a junior branch of the Heathcote family of Derbyshire, which had an offshoot in Cowdale (E. D. Heathcote, *The Families of Heathcote* (1899), p. 193 and *passim*).

HEATLEY, —
Author of an almanac for 1665, now lost; unidentified, unless *Healy* was meant.

HERBERT, THOMAS (fl. 1650–d. 1668)
Philomath, living at Eaton Bray, near Dunstable, Beds. (*1652*, sig. C4v). Published almanacs for 1651–3 for London and Leighton Buzzard. His will, 1668, describes him as schoolmaster of Eaton Bray (Beds. R.O., ABP/W 1668/162).

HEURING, SIMON (fl. 1545–82)
Doctor of physic and astronomy of Hagenau. Town physician at Speyer in 1554. Published German almanacs for thirty years, and two English editions for 1551 (Hellmann, *Versuch*, pp. 12–13, 24).

HEWIT, THOMAS (fl. 1653–6)
Philomath, living at Ansley in N. E. Warwicks. (*1654*, sig. C8v). Published almanacs for Coventry for 1654–5. A friend of *Vincent Wing* (Wing, *Astronomia Instaurata* (1656), sig. B2).

HEWLETT, WILLIAM (fl. 1625–30)
Published almanacs for Heytesbury, Wilts., 1625–9, and Devizes for 1630. Perhaps the Wm. Hewlett of Knook, near Heytesbury, whose will (1639) is in the Wilts. R.O.

HEYMAN, JOHN (fl. 1660)
Published an almanac for 1660 for Maidstone, Kent.

HILL, HENRY (d.c. 1608)
Mathematician; published almanacs for Tiverton for 1603 and 1609. From the t.p. of the latter he appears to have died before publication.

HILL, HENRY (fl. 1683)
Philomath; published an almanac for 1684. Also compiled one for 1683, which was not published; he was then living in Birmingham (Ms Sloane 2281, f. 57).

HILL, THOMAS (fl. 1553–75)
Mathematician, translator and compiler of popular scientific works. Educated at Cambridge, and lived at London. Published several almanacs for London and Oxford, 1560–72.

D.N.B.; Taylor, p. 172; Johnson in *H.L.Q.*, vii (1943–4).

HOBBS, MATTHEW (1662–fl. 1700)
Student in physic and astrology; taught mathematics, surveying and music at Swanbourn, near Winslow, Bucks. Baptized there 29 December 1662, and his children baptized 1696–1701. Published almanacs for London for 1693–6, and advertised in *Coley*'s almanac for 1691.

Taylor, p. 287; *Parish Reg. of Swanbourn*, ed. Ussher (1915), pp. 38, 51, 53, 54 (the register lacks entries for the period 1707–12).

HODGSON, MARMADUKE (fl. 1754)
Apparently the compiler of *The Ladies' Diary* for 1754, 1755 and 1759, but according to Ellis, *Orig. Letters*, p. 304, the name was merely one of the pseudonyms of *T. Simpson*; cf. Taylor, *HP*, p. 234.

HOLDEN, MARY (fl. 1688)
Midwife, astrologer, and physician for women's diseases, living at Sudbury, Suffolk. Published almanacs for 1688–9; 1688 contains her portrait.

HOLMES, WALTER, 'SENIOR' (1596–fl. 1649)
Published almanac for 1649 which was merely a daily guide to Bible-reading throughout the year. Perhaps Walter Holmes of Trinity College, Cambridge, M.A. 1622, ordained priest 1621 aged twenty-five, schoolmaster in London, and later minister in Kent and Essex.

Venn, ii, p. 399.

HONIWAX, I. (fl. 1629)
Mathematician, who published almanacs for Newcastle-on-Tyne for 1629–30.

HOOKER, RICHARD (fl. 1668)
Gentleman; published almanac for 1668.

HOPKINS, THOMAS (fl. 1569)
Published almanac for that year, now lost.

HOPTON, ARTHUR (c. 1588–1614)
Mathematical practitioner and surveyor, belonging to a family of Shropshire gentry; probably Arthur, fourth son of Richard Hopton of Hopton, Salop. Member of Clement's Inn; possibly educated at Oxford. A friend of John Selden, *Bretnor* and Edward Wright. Published almanacs for 1605–14 for Shrewsbury (which suggests he was born earlier than 1588).

D.N.B.; Taylor, p. 200; *Visitation of Shropshire, 1623*, ed. Grazebrook and Rylands, Harleian Soc., xxviii, pp. 257–8.

HORTON, GEORGE (fl. 1647–65)
Bookseller, printer and newspaper proprietor. As 'G.H.' compiled the *Bloody*

Almanack for 1652 and *Merlinus Anglicanus* for 1653, both concocted from other almanacs. Horton published and perhaps compiled many other plagiaristic almanacs in the 1650s, including *The Levellers*, those by 'Lele' and 'Liby' and other *Bloody Almanacks*. Imprisoned in 1653–4.

Williams, *English Journalism*, p. 172; Frank, *English Newspaper*, pp. 235, 247–8 etc.; Plomer, *Dictionary, 1641–67*, p. 101; Morrison, *Index, 1641–1700*, p. 107.

HOWELL, HUMPHREY (fl. 1655)
'Friend of science.' Published Puritan almanacs for 1655–7. Matriculated at St. John's Oxford, 1653, and became under-butler there (Foster, *Al. Oxon.*, ii, p. 755).

HUBRIGH, JOACHIM (1553–82)
Doctor in physic and astronomy of Middelburg, Zeeland (*1569*, t.p.) and Bieselinghe. Published English almanacs for 1553–69, and Flemish editions up to 1582.

Hellmann, *Versuch*, p. 31.

HUMPHREYS, THOMAS
Author of a late Elizabethan perpetual almanac, now lost.

HUTTON, CHARLES (1737–1823)
Mathematician, professor at the Woolwich Military Academy, Fellow and Secretary of the Royal Society. Edited *Ladies' Diary* 1773–1818, for which his fee in 1802 was £189.

D.N.B.; Taylor, *HP*, p. 235; Ellis, *Orig. Letters*, p. 304; Blagden, 'Thomas Carnan', p. 42.

JACKSON, THOMAS (fl. 1653)
Practitioner and teacher of mathematics, navigation, surveying and astrology at Winchester Yard, by St. Mary's in Southwark. Published almanacs for London for 1653–5. Probably born at Lutterworth, Leics., which was mentioned on the title-page of 1653.

JAMES, JOHN (fl. 1739)
Mathematician; published *Hemerologium* for 1739, for Winchester, with *Thos. White*.

JEFFEREYS, THOMAS (c. 1583–fl. 1635)
Minister, physician and mathematician, of Cornish origin. No doubt the T.J. of Cornwall who matriculated at Exeter College, Oxford, in 1597, aged fourteen; B.A. 1601. Published almanacs for Cardiff for 1623, and, after ten years abroad, for Dorchester, Dorset, for 1635. One of these names, 'stranger', buried 7 July 1658 at Holy Trinity, Dorchester, but there is no known connection (par. reg., Soc. Gen., p. 280).

Foster, *Al. Oxon.*, ii, p. 805.

JENKYNSON, THOMAS (fl. 1568)
Published almanac for 1568, now lost.

JESSEY, HENRY (1601–63)
Prominent Baptist minister, educated at Cambridge, who published a series of *Scripture Almanacks* for 1645–62.
D.N.B.; Venn, ii, p. 460; Matthews, *Calamy Revised*, p. 298.

JINNER, SARAH (fl. 1659)
Student in astrology; published almanacs for 1658–64. There are portraits in 1659 and 1664, but no biographical details.

JOHNSON, G. (fl. 1659)
'Physiol.' Compiled almanacs for 1659–60, with many meteorological details, admired by *John Gadbury* (Gadbury, 1674). It is possible that 'Johnson' *was* Gadbury.

JOHNSON, JOHN (fl. 1602–57)
Mathematician, physician, astrologer and surveyor. Of Thorp-le-Soken, Essex, later of Colchester and London. Published almanacs for Colchester and London for 1611–24, and author of a popular textbook on arithmetic.
Taylor, p. 196.

JOHNSON, R. (fl. 1683)
'Well-willer to science.' Published almanac for 1683, which was commended by *Salmon*.

JOHNSON, THOMAS (fl. 1598–1604)
Compiled several almanacs for these years, some for Loughborough, Leics. Perhaps the surveyor of these names (Taylor, p. 197). A member of the London Company of Salters, to which *1598* was dedicated.

JOHNSON, MASTER WILLIAM (fl. 1568)
Published almanacs for 1568–70; *1569* was praised by N. Allen, *The Astronomer's Game* (1569), sig. *4. Perhaps Wm. Johnson of Oxford, B.A. 1543, M.A. 1547, Fellow of All Souls (Foster, *Al. Oxon.*, ii, p. 816)

JONES, THOMAS (1648–1713)
Printer, bookseller and publisher. Born at Corwen, N. Wales, and had bookshops in Paul's Alley and elsewhere in London. Published the first Welsh-language almanacs, in a series from 1680 to 1712, and Welsh newspapers, textbooks for schools etc.
Dict. Welsh Biography; *Journ. of Welsh Bibliographical Soc.* (1915), pp. 239–45 and (1917), pp. 97–104; Jenkins, 'Welsh Books', chs. 8, 9.

JONES (JOANES), WILLIAM (fl. 1626)
Well-willer to mathematics; published almanacs for Chester for 1626–7.

KAYE, RICHARD (fl. 1608–d. 1632)
Practitioner in astronomy, living at Colthorpe (Cowthorpe), Yorks.; published almanacs for York for 1608–9. Rector of Cowthorpe 1615–32, succeeding Robt. Jackson, perhaps father of Kaye's wife, Grace Jackson. Kaye's children

appear in the register 1608–29; he was buried 16 December 1632. Probably same as Rd. Kaye of Yorks., pleb., matriculated at Oxford 1611, aged twenty-three, B.A. 1614.

Register of Cowthorpe, ed. Slingsby (1910), p. 32 and *passim*; Foster, *Al. Oxon.*, ii, p. 837.

KEENE, JOHN (fl. 1612–17)
Student in mathematics and physic; published almanacs for London for 1612–17. Gave private tuition and kept boarding school at Tottenham High Cross and then Shoreditch, where he taught Greek, Latin, arithmetic, geography etc.

Taylor, p. 204.

KENDAL, ROGER (fl. 1700)
Astrologer and physician of Froom (Frome), Somerset. Published almanacs for 1700–1. A friend of *John Partridge*.

KEPAR, GREGOR
Anagram and pseudonym of George Parker, which he used in *The Gardener's Almanack* for 1702–3 for Winchester. *John Wing*, who was attacked in the 1703 edition, exposed Parker's authorship in Wing, 1704, sig. C5ff.

KIDMAN, THOMAS (fl. 1631–8)
Compiled almanac for Saffron Walden, Essex; probably lived in a neighbouring village, for the name is not recorded in the Walden register until the eighteenth century.

KINDE, JOHN (fl. 1625)
Published an almanac for York for this year.

KINDER, PHILIP (1597–c. 1665)
Physician, licensed to practise at Leicester. Educated at Cambridge, and wrote widely on local history, geography, genealogy and religion. Published almanacs for 1619–20 under the anagram *Drekin*. Collections of his Mss are in Ms Ash. 429 and 788.

Raach, *Directory*, p. 61; Venn, iii, p. 17.

KINGSLEY, GEORGE (fl. 1715–23)
Gentleman; published *Ephemeris Britannica* for 1715–17 and 1721–3. He advertised tuition in all branches of mathematics at his house in Piccadilly, by Dover St.

Taylor, p. 305.

KIRBY, RICHARD (1649–fl. 1690)
Whig astrologer and physician. Born 13 July 1649 (Ms Ash. 421, f. 117), lived at Fulham and later in King St., Soho (his *Marrow of Astrology* (1687), preface). He had a joint astrological practice in Fetter Lane with his friend Philip Mayle, each attending for half the week (*1684*, sig. D5). Published almanacs for 1681–4, and other astrological works. Portrait in his *Vates Astrologicus* (1683).

KNIGHT, RICHARD (fl. 1638)
Published almanac for that year, printed at Cambridge.

KNIGHT, WILLIAM (fl. 1652)
Gentleman, student in mathematics; published a small almanac for seven years in 1652.

KRABTREE, HENRY (c. 1642–fl. 1686)
Curate of Todmorden, Lancs.; published an almanac for 1685. Born at Sowerby, near Halifax, and entered Christ's, Cambridge, early in 1664, aged twenty-one. Ordained deacon 1664, and licensed to Todmorden in 1665; last recorded there in 1686. The living was worth only £12 p.a.; he supplemented this by practising physic, and marrying a rich widow. Also noted as a persecutor of local Quakers.

J. Holden, 'Todmorden Antiquities', *Halifax Antiq. Soc.* (1907), pp. 203–11; information supplied by Cheshire and Lancs. R.O.s; Venn, i, p. 410; *D.N.B.* (as Crabtree).

KYNNET,—
Published almanacs, now lost, for 1581 and 1582.

L., T.
Published a sheet almanac for 1700, attacking the East India trade.

LAET, ALPHONSE (fl. 1548–57)
Doctor of physic and astronomy, and brother of *Jasper Jr.* An English prognostication for 1548 survives, and several French and Latin editions for 1551–7.

Hellmann, *Versuch*, pp. 16, 31.

LAET, JASPER, SR. (fl. 1485–d.c. 1532)
Doctor of physic and astronomy, of Borchloen and Antwerp. His prognostications appeared in Latin, Flemish, French, German and (from 1516) English. In 1533 he was said by his son Jasper to have published annually for forty-four years. He corresponded with James IV of Scotland, and was patronized by the Prince-Bishop of Liège.

Hellmann, *Versuch*, p. 31; Bosanquet, pp. 18–19; Zech-du Biez, *Almanachs*, p. 9n; *A.D.B.*, xvii, pp. 510–11.

LAET, JASPER, JR. (fl. 1512–67)
Son of the above; doctor of physic and astronomy (M.D., Louvain, 1512), living at Antwerp. Published prognostications from 1524, with English edition from 1530 to 1546.

References as for last.

LAKES, THOMAS (fl. 1627)
'Lover of mathematics'; published almanacs for Lincoln for 1627–8. A pseudonym.

LANE, THOMAS (fl. 1730)
'Student in celestial science', living at Quomerford (Comerford), Wilts. Published *Speculum Anni* from 1730. *Henry Season* compiled part of the 1733

edition, and thereafter took over the series. Lane's brother William advertised in the 1731 edition his skill in mending clocks and watches, and his clockwork model showing planetary motions.

LANGLEY, THOMAS (fl. 1611–d. 1646)
Published almanacs in his own name for 1635–48 for London and Shrewsbury (where he was born), and under the pseudonym *Gallen*. A London bookseller, 1611–35, when he broke. He was paid poor relief by the Stationers 1635–46, when he died; his widow, Mary, received relief, 1646–75.

McKerrow, *Dictionary, 1557–1640*, p. 168; P. G. Morrison, *Index of Printers, Publishers and Booksellers . . . 1475–1640* (2nd edn., Charlottesville, Va., 1961), p. 44; Wharton, 1645, sig. C6v; Ferguson, in *The Library*, 5th ser., xxxi (1976), p. 46.

LEA, PHILIP (fl. 1666–d. 1700)
Cartographer and instrument-maker, who sold maps, globes, books and instruments at his shop in London. Published an almanac covering thirty years, probably in 1680.

Taylor, p. 253.

LEADBETTER, CHARLES (fl. 1715–d. 1744)
A well-known teacher and writer on mathematical subjects in London, and gauger to the Royal Excise. Born at Cronton, Lancs. Compiled *Partridge*'s almanac in the 1730s and early 1740s, which he used for self-publicity. Died November 1744 (Armytage, *Obituary*, Harleian Soc., xliv–ix, vol. iv, p. 31; will proved Dec. 1744: P.C.C., Anstis, 288). *D.N.B.*, followed by Taylor, suggested that he survived till c. 1769.

D.N.B.; Taylor, *HP*, pp. 132–3.

LEYBOURNE, WILLIAM (1626–1716)
Initially a printer with his brother, Leybourne became a teacher of mathematics and a surveyor; one of the surveyors of London after the Great Fire. Published almanacs in his own name for 1648–51 and for years compiled many of the 'sorts' for the Company (S.C., Journal Bk, e.g. f. 89). Author of successful mathematical textbooks.

D.N.B.; Taylor, pp. 230–1; C. Kenney in *The Library* (1950–1).

LIGHTERFOOT, RICHARD (fl. 1607)
Gentleman; student in astronomy and astrology, living in London near Gray's Inn. Published an almanac for 1607.

LILLY, WILLIAM (1602–81)
Astrologer, political prophet and, later, a licensed physician. Born at Diseworth, Leics., son of a yeoman; moved to London and lived in the Strand as servant to Gilbert Wright, whose widow he married. Took up the study of astrology in 1632/3 and built up a large practice. Published almanacs from 1644. From 1664 he lived at Hersham, near Walton-on-Thames.

D.N.B.; Lilly, *Life and Times* (latest edn., ed. Briggs, 1974); D. Parker, *Familiar to All* (1975).

LIVIE, J. (fl. 1659)
Author of an almanac for 1659, where the author claims to have been abroad for some years. Two almanacs for 1654–5 seem to be in the same series; they are largely plagiarisms, published by *Horton*, and it is likely that Livie is only a pseudonym.

LLOYD, EVANS (fl. 1576–85)
Student in astronomy. Scholar of Oriel College, Oxford, B.A. 1576. Published almanacs for 1582 for London, and 1585 for Shrewsbury and the west.
Wood, *Ath. Oxon.*, i, col. 459; Foster, *Al. Oxon.*, iii, p. 923.

LLWYD, HUMPHREY (1527–68)
Physician and antiquarian. Educated at Oxford, and became physician to Lord Denbigh. M.P. in 1559 and 1563. Published a perpetual almanac, now lost.
D.N.B.; Foster *Al. Oxon.*, iii, p. 925; Taylor, p. 319 (describes the almanac).

LORD, JOHN, JR. (fl. 1678)
'Lover of celestial science.' Published almanac for 1678 for the Midlands, following *V. Wing*'s methods.

LOVE, GEORGE (fl. 1625)
Published almanac for London for 1625. It advertised a market at Stevenage, Herts., where the author perhaps lived.

LOW, HENRY (fl. 1554–74)
Doctor in astrology and physic, living by the Close Gate in Salisbury. Published almanacs there for 1554–74.

MAGINI, ANTONIO (1555–1617)
Professor of mathematics at Bologna, chosen in preference to Galileo. Noted as a cartographer, and published several prognostications, including English editions for 1622/4.
Thorndike, *Magic*, v, p. 250–1; vi, p. 164–5; *Dict. of Scientific Biography*, ed. G. C. Gillispie, ix (1969), pp. 12–13.

MARKHAM, GEORGE (fl. 1656)
Physician; published almanacs for 1656–7.

MARTIN, —(d. 1780)
Compiler of *Poor Robin* for some years; succeeded by *Pearson* (*Old Poor Robin*, 1795, p. 15)

MARTIN, HENRY (fl. 1662)
Author of a satirical almanac for 1662; perhaps pseudonymous.

MARTINDALE, ADAM (1623–86)
Presbyterian minister ejected in 1662; thereafter lived, mostly in Lancashire and Cheshire, by teaching mathematics, navigation etc., and practising as a surveyor. Published almanacs for 1675–7 under the initials A.M.; for identification see Ms Sloane 2285, f. 98v; *Life of Adam Martindale*, ed. Parkinson, Chetham Soc. (1845), p. 210.
Taylor, p. 227; Matthews, *Calamy Revised*, p. 343.

MATTHEW, WILLIAM (fl. 1602–14)
Physician and astrologer. Lived at Reigate, Surrey, for which he published almanacs for 1602–14.

METCALFE, FRANCIS (fl. 1654–d. 1658)
Physician; published almanac for Leeds for 1654, with verses by his brother St(ephen). Wrote the next year from Doncaster to *Lilly*, attacking the Stationers (Ms Ash. 423, f. 222). Probably the F.M. of Upper Headrow, Leeds, buried 17 March 1658 (*Reg. of the Parish Church of Leeds 1639–67*, ed. Lumb, Thoresby Soc., 7 (1895–7), p. 402).

MISSONNE, FR.
Published a prognostication for 1660. A pseudonym of *J. Gadbury*, which he revealed in his almanac for 1673.

MONIPENNIE, JOHN (fl. 1597–1612)
Published in 1612 a new edition of a Tudor scripture almanac. Issued editions of Scottish chronicles and other works in the reign of James.

MONTULMO (MOTULIND), ANTONIUS DE (fl. 1384–96)
Doctor of physic and astrology at Bologna, where he compiled works on various branches of the occult. A treatise on nativities was published in Germany in 1540, and his name was borrowed for two English almanacs for 1554–5.
Thorndike, *Magic*, iii. ch. xxxv; v, p. 363.

MOORE, FRANCIS (1657–1714)
Astrologer, licensed physician, and Whig partisan. Born at Bridgenorth, Salop., and had an astrological practice in Lambeth, and later Southwark. Published almanac from 1699 till his death. Buried at Christ Church, Southwark, 20 July 1714, ten days after completing his next edition (Gter. London R.O., P92/CTC/55/2, p. 237).
D.N.B.

MOORE, PHILIP (fl. 1564–80)
Practitioner in physic and surgery. Published a medical treatise, translated a work on 'Morbus Gallicus' (Ms Rawl. C724), and was a friend of *Wm. Bulleine*. Published an almanac covering forty years in 1567, several times reissued.

MOORE, ROBERT (fl. 1570)
Author of an almanac for 1570 (for identification see Bosanquet in *The Library* (1927–8), pp. 467–8).

MORGAN, EINON (fl. 1693)
Compiler of a Welsh almanac for 1693.

MORTON, ROBERT (fl. 1662)
Mathematician; published an almanac for 1662, when he was living in Pannier Alley, London. It was dedicated to the Barber-Surgeons and the Excise

officials, and contained much data on medicine and surgery, which Morton perhaps practised.

MOUNSLOW, ALEXANDER (fl. 1561–81)
Published almanacs for Oxford (*1561*) and Chester (*1579*, *1581*), and others now lost. Lodged at Smithfield near the sign of the Catherine Wheel.

MUSSEMIUS, JOHANNES (fl. 1544)
A German astrologer, whose Latin prognostication for 1544 was published in England. Perhaps Jean van Mussem, a Flemish writer of Wormhout near Dunkirk, who published a work on rhetoric (Middelburg, 1553): *Biog. Nat. de Belgique*, xv, p. 382.

N., H.
These initials appeared on the title-page of an anti-Quaker almanac for 1678; in 1679–80 the initials I.N., J.N., and M.Y. appear. The 1677 edition had 'Poor Robin' in the title, and the series was probably written by *Winstanley*, with the initials chosen at random.

NAPIER, JOHN (1550–1617)
Several 'Bloody Almanacks' in the 1640s purported to be summaries of the work of John Napier, the Scottish theologian and mathematician (for whom see *D.N.B.*). They were based in part, and very loosely, on his commentary on Revelations.

NEVE, JEFFREY (1579–1653)
Gentleman, from a Norfolk family. A merchant, alderman and port official at Gt. Yarmouth, until his business and civic career collapsed. He switched to medicine, acquired an M.D. in the Netherlands, and practised in physic, surgery, astrology and mathematics. Supported the king in the civil war, and fled to Oxford. Published almanacs for Yarmouth for 1604–25. Died in London 2 September 1653.

D.N.B.; Gadbury, *Collectio*, pp. 178–9; *Visit. of London, 1633–5*, ed. Howard (Harleian Soc., xvii), ii, p. 62; Smyth, *Obituary*, p. 35.

NEVE, JOHN (fl. 1626)
Gentleman. Published almanacs for Norwich for 1626–61. There were two Johns in the Norfolk branches of the Neves; a John died at Hammersmith in 1654 (see *Visitation*, cited above, and *D.N.B.*). John may have been a relative who took over the series, or Jeffrey may have adopted a pseudonym, perhaps because of his unpopularity at Yarmouth.

NEVE, ROBERT (fl. 1662–72)
Gentleman; continued the series for Norwich for 1662–72. In 1662 (t.p.) he says that he and his father have published the almanac since 1600, which suggests that 'John' was a pseudonym. A Robert, son of Jeffrey, was licensed as a physician in 1662 after ten years' practical experience.

J. H. Bloom and R. R. James, *Medical Practitioners in the Diocese of London . . . 1529–1725* (Cambridge, 1935), p. 59.

NICOLSON, JAMES (fl. 1563)
Physician; published prognostication for 1563.

NIGHTINGALE, ROBERT (fl. 1653)
Gentleman; published almanac for 1563 for Cambridge.

NORTON, HUMFREY (fl. 1581)
Student in astronomy. Published almanacs for Winchester, where he lived, for 1579 and 1581.

NOSTRADAMUS (MICHEL DE NOTREDAME) (1503–66)
Studied philosophy at Avignon and Montpellier, where he graduated in 1529. Practised physic and compiled prophecies from the late 1540s. His *Centuries* secured royal patronage, and he became physician to Charles IX. There were a number of English editions of his almanacs in the period 1559–68.

NUNNES, THOMAS (1630–fl. 1676)
Surveyor and mathematician, who published almanacs for Northampton for 1661–6. Baptized at Rushton, Northants., 29 June 1630. Did a survey for Sir Justinian Isham in 1671 which still survives. A friend of *V. Wing* (Wing, 1668, sig. C8v).

Taylor, p. 254; *Parish Registers of Rushton*, ed. P. A. F. Stephenson (1929), p. 44; *Diary of Thomas Isham*, ed. Isham (1971), pp. 63, 65; survey in Northants. R.O.

NYE, NATHANIEL (1624–fl. 1670)
Mathematician and astrologer. Taught all branches of mathematics, including surveying, the design of instruments, navigation (*1643*) and also music. Issued almanacs for 1642–8 for Birmingham; *1642* is dated from Arnhem, January 1640/1. Later a master gunner at Worcester, and wrote a treatise on gunnery.

D.N.B.; Taylor, pp. 221–2.

OSBORNE, GEORGE (fl. 1622–8; perhaps c. 1587–1661)
Taught mathematics, writing (in six styles), and navigation at Hull, for which he published almanacs for 1622–8. He may well be the George Osborne who occurs as perpetual curate of Marfleet, Hull, 1636–40; entered Oxford, aged twenty, in 1607, B.A., 1611, M.A. 1617; rector of Middleton-on-the-Wolds, Yorks., 1647–61 (d.).

Taylor, pp. 209–10; *V.C.H., County of York, East Riding*, i, pp. 300–1; Marchant, *Puritans and the Church Courts*, p. 267.

P., C.
Compiler of the *Shepherds New Kalendar* in 1700, purporting to be the result of thirty years' experience as a shepherd in the west of England.

PARKER, GEORGE (1654–1743)
Astrologer and physician, who made and sold his own medicines (*1695*) and was later also active as a printer; in *1727* he advertised tradesmen's bills, tax receipts, blank schemes for nativities, logarithms and tide-tables. Born 9

August 1654 at Shipston-on-Stour, Worcs. (Partridge, *Flagitiosus* (1697), p. 12; *D.N.B.* gives 1651, but the later year is confirmed by Parker, 1729, sig. B). Brought up among Quakers, and married one. Was at first a cutler in Newgate St., but lived for many years at the Blue Ball in Salisbury Court, off Fleet St. Taught astrology by *Streete*. Published almanacs from 1690, and later also separate ephemerides. A friend of Halley and Flamsteed (1692, sig. A3v). Banned from publishing almanacs in the early eighteenth century for listing the Old Pretender among European sovereigns.

D.N.B.; Taylor, p. 265 (gives wrong Christian name); Parker, 1698 and 1699 contain brief autobiographies.

PARKHURST, FERDINANDO (fl. 1648–62)

Philomath. Published a scriptural commentary and an almanac for 1648, and translations of dramatic and medical works. A friend of *Lilly*. Perhaps related to John Parkhurst (1564–1639), sometime Master of Balliol.

PARRON, WILLIAM (fl. 1497–1503)

An Italian astrologer, born c. 1460, who was attached to the court of Henry VII, and issued English and Latin prognostications for 1496 or 7 to 1503.

Armstrong in *Italian Renaissance Studies*, ed. E. F. Jacob (1960), pp. 433–54.

PARROT, JOHN (fl. 1702)

Gentleman; published *De Motu Stellarum* for 1702–3. From internal evidence, it seems likely that Parrot was a pseudonym of *John Partridge*.

PARTRIDGE, DOROTHY (fl. 1694)

Midwife, student in astrology; published almanac for 1694, with a portrait. Possibly a pseudonym; after the turn of the century Benjamin Harris issued almanacs under the name, claiming falsely that she was the wife of the celebrated John.

PARTRIDGE, JOHN (1644–1715)

Astrologer and physician, who lived in Henrietta St., off Covent Garden, and later in Salisbury St., off the Strand. Born in E. Sheen, son of John P. of Putney (1686, sig. A3v). Worked as a cobbler, but taught himself Latin, medicine and some Greek and Hebrew, and learned astrology from Dr. Francis Wright. Fled abroad under James II. A notorious Whig, though *Gadbury* alleged that he was a Tory and defected only through lack of patronage (Gadbury, *A Reply*). A physician in ordinary to Mary II. Died leaving £2,000. Published almanacs from 1678 till his death, except in 1710–13.

D.N.B.; Mayhew in *Studies in English Literature* (1961); Aubrey, *Brief Lives*, ed. Clark, ii, pp. 119–20.

PARTRIDGE, SETH (1603–86)

Surveyor and mathematician. Taught mathematics and the use of instruments, and mathematical works. Died at Hemel Hempstead in February 1686.

D.N.B.; Taylor, p. 209.

PEARSE, SALEM (fl. 1719)
Mathematician and physician; published *The Coelestial Diary* from 1719 (referring to his infancy in the art of astrology). The series continued till 1773, but contains no further details of his identity.

PEARSON, JOHN (c. 1729–91)
For several years compiled *Poor Robin*, Moore, Wing, Season and Partridge for the Stationers; introduced short stories and even music to *Poor Robin*. Lived at Nottingham, where he died 26 November 1791, aged sixty-two.
Armytage, *Obituary*, v, p. 4; Heywood, *Three Papers*, iii, p. 17.

PEAT, THOMAS (1708–80)
Writing-master, mathematics teacher and surveyor, who lived mostly in Nottingham, where he taught school at the Middle Gate; lived for some years at Thringston, Leics. Founded *The Gentleman's Diary* in 1740, and edited it for the rest of his life; his chief associates in the project were John Badder (d. 1756), Geo. Ingman, A. Thacker, Wm. Whitehead, Wm. Butcher, Thos. Mather and Jo. Granger (*Gentleman's Diary*, 1781, p. 2; for the first two see Taylor, *HP*, pp. 197, 209).
D.N.B.; Taylor, *HP*, p. 164.

PEMBROKE, SIMON (d. 1577)
Published an almanac for 1568. Lived in Southwark. Died suddenly during his trial for conjuring in 1577 (*A most strange and rare example* . . ., 1577).

PEPPER, JOSEPH (fl. 1701–d. 1740)
Of Stamford, Lincs. Published *Almanack* for 1703–5, advertising tuition in mathematics, surveying and writing, and offering to board gentlemen. In later years advertised frequently in other almanacs, e.g. Moore, Coley, Saunder. Subscribed as schoolmaster, 1701 (Diocesan records, Subs. V/6/68); will, 1740 (Lincs. Consistory Court) (these refs. kindly supplied by Dep. County Archivist).

PEREGRINE, AN(THONY) (fl. 1636)
'Astronomer.' Published almanacs for Newcastle-on-Tyne for 1636–7; no doubt another of the Cambridge 'bird' pseudonyms.

PERKINS, FR. (fl. 1655)
'Well-willer to mathematics.' Published almanacs for London from 1655; the series, which was stereotyped in character, continued into the eighteenth century.

PERKINS, SAMUEL (fl. 1625–43)
Gentleman, well-willer to mathematics; published almanacs for London for 1625–43.

PETER, JOHN (fl. 1667–84)
Physician and miscellaneous writer, who published works on topography, current affairs, a school text on Latin verse and an almanac for 1678.

PETER OF MOORBECK (fl. 1550–9)
A physician of Antwerp, who published a series of almanacs in Flemish and French, and an English edition for 1550.
Hellmann, *Versuch*, p. 31; Zech-du Biez, *Almanachs*, pp. 39, 40, 44, 45, 49.

PHILLIPPES, HENRY (1617–fl. 1677)
Teacher of mathematics and especially navigation, and a surveyor. Born on London Bridge, 27 October 1617 (Ms Ash. 225, fos. 87, 88), and lived there. Published almanacs for 1654–8, edited *The Seaman's Kalendar*, and published mathematical textbooks.
Taylor, p. 234.

PHILLIPS, JOHN (1631–1706)
Journalist and translator; Milton's nephew. According to Wood, he wrote *Montelion* for 1660, but not subsequent almanacs with that title.
D.N.B.

PIERCE (PIERS), MATTHEW (fl. 1634–41)
Student of mathematics; published almanacs for Durham for 1634–41.

PIGOT, FRANCIS (fl. 1619–d. 1666)
Mathematician, who practised and taught surveying, dialling and the use of instruments (*1630*), and lived at Cleobury Mortimer, Salop. (*1662*). Invented a ring dial about 1619 (*1659*). Died at Cleobury, buried 23 April 1666 (*Register*, ed. Childe (1909), p. 110); described in the register as minister, but it is not known of where. He also held some land, and was assessed for tithe in 1657 on some sheep and cattle, hemp, flax, and seven tons of hay; also connected with bulb-growing (I owe this information to K. W. Goodman's Keele Ph.D. thesis, in progress, 'Clee Hills Agriculture in the 16th and 17th Centuries'). Published a number of almanacs between 1630 and 1662 for Shrewsbury, Ludlow and Cleobury. He may be Francis, younger son of Walter Pigott of Chetwynd, Sheriff of Shropshire in 1624 (Fletcher, in *Shropshire Arch. Soc.*, 3rd ser., vi, pp. 67, 78, 90).
Taylor, p. 240.

POND, BEN(JAMIN)
Pseudonymous compiler of an almanac for 1689, published at Oxford; one of a large number concocted by giving new Christian names to established compilers.

POND, EDWARD (fl. 1601–d. 1629)
Mathematician, physician, and surveyor. Born and educated near Ingatestone, Essex (1602, sig. Bv), perhaps at Fryerning, where an Edward Pond was recorded in 1572 (*Elizabethan Life: Home, Work and Land*, ed. Emmison (1976), p. 211). Lived at Chelmsford (*1609*) and Billericay (*1610*); in 1611 had a shop at the Globe outside Temple Bar in London, where he gave tuition, and made and sold clocks, watches and mathematical instruments (*1612*, sig. A2). Published almanacs from 1601–12, and the series was revived

from 1625; they were for London, Chelmsford, Stamford and (*1630*) Peterborough.

D.N.B.; Taylor, pp. 198–9.

PONT, J. (fl. 1646)

Author of a perpetual almanac which was also a guide to the use of almanacs.

POOL(E), JOHN (1610–fl. 1656)

Gentleman, student in 'Theo-Philosophy' and physic. Born 19 December 1610 in Gloucester (Ms Ash. 426, f. 292). Published almanacs for 1642 and 1655–7 (might be two separate compilers); published also *Country Astrology* (1650), a manual.

PORTER, THOMAS (fl. 1585)

Surgeon of Bury (not identified), who published an almanac for 1585.

D.N.B.

POWELL, THOMAS (c. 1572–c. 1635)

Attorney of Gray's Inn, and author of several professional handbooks. His *Attornies Almanack* was a legal guide, not a true almanac.

D.N.B.

PRICE, LAWRENCE (fl. 1628–80)

Balladeer and journalist; author of *The Shepherd's Prognostication*.

D.N.B.

PRINCE, VINCENT (fl. 1660)

'Student in mathematics and the common law of England.' Published an almanac for 1660 setting out the duties of parish constables, and another for 1664, now lost.

RAMESEY, WILLIAM (1627–75/6)

Gentleman, physician and astrologer. Son of a Scottish clockmaker, educated at Montpellier (M.D. 1652), extra-licentiate of the R.C.P., and a physician to Charles II. Published a prognostication for 1652, and medical works. Settled in Plymouth in 1668, and died in 1676 (Ms Sloane 1683, f. 39) or in 1675, in prison for debt (Gadbury, 1699, sig. B5).

D.N.B.; Munk, *Physicians*, pp. 285–6; Venn, iii, p. 417.

RANGER, PHILIP (fl. 1615–31)

Gentleman, student in mathematics and astronomy; published almanacs for York, 1615–31.

RAVEN, — (?JOSEPH) (fl. 1676–1704)

A London bookseller who published a sheet almanac (*Calendarium . . . or Raven's almanac*) from 1676. *Gadbury* wrote the almanac for 1688 (S.C., Court Bk. F, f. 94v) and Raven probably supplied nothing but his name. In 1704 he made over all his rights to the Company.

H. R. Plomer, *A Dictionary of Booksellers and Printers . . . 1668–1725* (Oxford, 1922), p. 248; Morrison, *Index 1641–1700*, p. 163; S.C., Court Bk. G, f. 163v–4; Journal Bk., f. 115; English Stock Bk. 1663–1723, f. 100.

RAYNOLDS (REYNOLDS), RICHARD (fl. 1567)
Published an almanac, now lost, for 1567. Perhaps he was Richard Reynolds (fl. 1546–d. 1606), minister, physician and author of works on rhetoric and classical history; educated at Cambridge, rector of Stapleford Abbot, Essex, 1568–1606. A Richard Reynold was found 'ignorant and unlearned' by the College of Physicians in 13 Eliz. I, and was fined for unauthorized practice.
D.N.B.; Venn, iii, p. 445; Goodall, p. 315.

READMAN, WILLIAM (fl. 1680)
'Lover of mathematics and astronomy'; published almanac for Stamford.

RED (REDE, READE), WILLIAM (fl. 1337–d. 1385)
Bishop of Chichester, and a prominent member of the celebrated Merton School of mathematicians and astrologers at Oxford. His planetary tables provided the data for an almanac published in his name in 1507.
D.N.B.

REDMAN, WILLIAM (fl. 1704–d. 1719)
Of Longstanton, Cambridgeshire; published *The Country Man's Pocket Companion* for 1704. He was parish clerk of Longstanton, where he was buried 14 January 1719 (par. reg., information from Cambridgeshire R.O.).

RIDERS, SCHARDANUS (CARDANUS)
Pseudonymous author of a pocket almanac, founded about 1652 and surviving into the next century. The name was an anagram of *Richard Saunders*, its compiler (S.C., Journal Bk., fos. 23v, 30v etc.), and was perhaps suggested by Bishop Riders' well-known *Dictionary*.

RIDERS, THOMAS (fl. 1661)
Student in mathematics; published a sheet almanac for 1661.

RIVERS, PEREGRINE
Student in mathematics; published almanacs for Cambridge for 1625–40. It was no doubt pseudonymous, belonging to both the 'water' and 'bird' series.

RIVERS, WILLIAM
Well-willer to mathematics, and author of an almanac for Warwick for 1628. Probably pseudonymous, borrowed from the preceding.

ROBERTS, — (fl. 1639)
Published an almanac for London for 1639.

ROGEFORD (ROCHEFORTH), HENRY (fl. 1560–8)
Published almanac for 1560–8. Perhaps a London bookseller (McKerrow, *Dictionary 1557–1640*, p. 231).

ROLLINSON, EDWARD (d. 1773)
Contributed to *Ladies' Diary* in the later 1750s, and edited it from 1761 till his death (Ellis, *Orig. Letters*, p. 304).

ROSE, GEORGE (fl. 1656)
Mathematician. Published almanac for London from 1656; they continued into the next century, always stereotyped in form.

ROWLEY, JOHN (1630–88)
A student of astrology and astronomy, and lived at Luton. Produced almanacs for Luton (1651) and Cambridge (1652). His father, John, knew *Lilly* and the younger John was connected with the London Society of Astrologers. He was baptized at Luton 3 January 1629/30, and buried there 31 January 1687/8 (par. reg., information from Bedfordshire R.O.). A John Rowley of Luton, son of John, was educated at Cambridge and became a minister in Hunts., dying in 1688; he may well be identical with the astrologer, though he is recorded in Venn as being only eighteen in 1651.

Taylor, p. 238; Ms Ash. 423, fos. 185v, 187; Venn, iii, p. 494.

RUDSTON, JOHN (fl. 1615–28)
Mathematician, who published almanacs for London for 1615–28, and compiled a treatise on the conjunction of 1623 (Ms Harl. 5211). It is just possible that he was the John Rudston, cutler, of St. Katherine by the Tower, who died August 1625 (*Register*, Harleian Soc., lxxv, pt. i, p. 177).

RUDSTON, THOMAS (fl. 1606–13)
'Physiomathem.' Published almanacs for 1606–13 for Cambridge. Possibly Thomas R. of the Isle of Ely, married at Ely 1587 (information from Cambridgeshire R.O.; *Visitation of Cambridgeshire, 1575 and 1619*, ed. Clay, Harleian Soc., xli, p. 100). A friend of *John Searle* (*1609*, sig. A2).

RUSSE, WALTER (fl. 1560)
Published an almanac, now lost, for 1560. Unidentified, unless the name was a corruption of *Walter Ryff*.

RUSSELL, JOHN (fl. 1660)
An astrologer living in King St., Westminster. Published almanacs for 1659–61. One of these names was a physician and oculist living in Holborn about 1670 (Thompson, *Quacks of Old London*, p. 220; his advertisements are in B.L. C. 112 f. 9).

RY., H. (i.e. WALTER HERMANN RYFF) (fl. 1541–9)
An English almanac for 1544 was attributed to M. Walter and H. Ry, physicians and astrologers of Strassburg. This seems to be a corruption of Walter Hermann Ryff, a physician who lived in Strassburg and Frankfurt in the 1540s, published almanacs in 1544–5 and wrote a number of plagiarized medical works.

Hellmann, *Versuch*, p. 29; Thorndike, *Magic*, v, pp. 442–3; vi, p. 272.

S., J. (fl. 1668)
Probably a nonconformist minister; revived *Jessey*'s *Scripture-Kalendar* in 1668–9.

SALMON, WILLIAM (1644–1713)
A Whig astrologer and physician; claimed the degree of M.D. (*1700*), and lived at the sign of the Blue Ball in Thames St., later by Holborn Bridge and near Blackfriars Stairs. Born 7 June 1644 near Cambridge; compiled an almanac for 1665 which was not published (Ms Ash. 428, f. 270v), and published almanacs for 1684, and from 1691. In the intervening years he travelled abroad, including to the West Indies, partly to escape from James II (1694, sig. A2v). Wrote widely on medical topics, in part to advertise his pills and medicines.
D.N.B.

SALOMON (fl. 1528–60)
A Jewish physician who practised at Roermund (in Limburg, Netherlands). An English edition of his prog. for Ghent for 1531 and subsequent years was published in 1543. He issued many other Continental prognostications.
Hellmann, *Versuch*, p. 29; Zech-du Biez, *Almanachs*, pp. 24, 26.

SAUNDER, RICHARD (fl. 1681–d. 1735/6)
A 'student in physical and mathematical sciences' who lived at Ouston, Leics., 1683–94, Leesthorp, near Melton Mowbray, 1694–1717, and then moved between several villages in the area: Burton St. Lazars, Thorp Satchville, Brook, near Oakham, and Stapleford. He practised land- and quantity-surveying, and dialling, and taught writing, mathematics and navigation. Published almanacs for Leicester from 1684 until his death; the edition for 1736 appears to be the last composed by him. His wife and son were buried at Stapleford in 1730 and 1734. A friend of *John Wing* (*1715*, sig. C3).
Taylor, p. 277; Stapleford par. reg., information from Leics. R.O.

SAUNDERS, RICHARD (1613–75)
Astrologer and physician. Born in Warwickshire (date and portrait in his *Physiognomy*) and lived at the Three Cranes in Chancery Lane. He was a protégé of *Lilly*, and originally, according to a critic, a baker in Grub St. (*William Lilly, Student in Astronomy*). Published almanacs from 1654 till his death, and works on chiromancy and other forms of divination. Died 23 December 1675 (Wood, *Life and Times*, ii, p. 331; Josten, *Ashmole*, iv, p. 1442). Sent his son to Oxford (Foster, *Al. Oxon.*, iv, p. 1316).
D.N.B. (wrong on date of death).

SAUVAGE, JAMES (fl. 1547–52)
Doctor of physic and astronomy at Antwerp. English editions of his prognostications exist for the years 1547–50 (Hellmann, *Versuch*, p. 31).

SAVAGE, WILLIAM (fl. 1610)
Gentleman, of York, for which he published almanacs for 1610–11.

SCOURFYLDE, VICTORIUS (i.e. SCHÖNFELD, VICTORIN) (1525–91)
A mathematician and physician, born at Bautzen, Lusatia, who became professor of Mathematics at Marburg. He published a work on epilepsy, and

over thirty almanacs, of which English editions for 1564–5 appeared under the name of Scourfylde.

A.D.B., xxxii, p. 303; Hellmann, *Versuch*, p. 29.

SCUTE, CORNELIUS (fl. 1535–61)

Doctor in physic and astronomy at Bruges, and later Anvers and La Haye; he published almanacs for 1535–61; there was an English edition for 1544.

Hellmann, *Versuch*, pp. 27, 29; Zech-du Biez, *Almanachs*, pp. 28, 30 etc.; *Biog. Nat. de Belgique*, xxii, pp. 76–7 (s.v. Schuytt).

SEAMAN, HENRY (fl. 1675)

'Mariner', no doubt pseudonymous, who published a nautical almanac for 1675–7.

SEARLE, JOHN (fl. 1599–d. 1617)

Master of surgery, of Saffron Walden. Admitted to Emmanuel College, Cambridge, 1599, licensed to practise surgery 1607 (Venn, iv, 38). Published an ephemeris in 1609. Buried at Saffron Walden 27 October 1617 (Walden par. reg., Soc. Gen., ii, p. 67); will proved 1619 (*P.C.C. 1605–19*, p. 397).

SEASON, HENRY (1693–1775)

A licensed physician and surgeon of Broomham, Wilts. Took over *Lane*'s almanac in 1734. See further above, pp. 259ff.

SECURIS (i.e. HATCHETT), JOHN (fl. 1540–82)

A licensed physician of New St., Salisbury. Educated at Paris and Oxford, of which he was M.A. (not in Foster or Emden). Published almanacs for 1562–82, and other works on astrological medicine. On the title-page of *1569* he mentions entering Oxford over twenty-eight years previously.

D.N.B.; Wood, *Ath. Oxon.*, i, col. 458.

SELLER, JOHN, SR. (fl. 1658–d. 1697)

A compass- and instrument-maker who kept a shop at Wapping, where he also taught and wrote on navigation and gunnery. Royal hydrographer during three reigns. Compiled a sheet almanac, and several perpetual ones. Presumably the John Seller, Sr., who died at Wapping in 1697 (*P.C.C.*, *1694–1700*, p. 368), though he is described in his will as citizen and merchant-tailor.

D.N.B.; Taylor, pp. 244–5.

SEYFRIDT, G. (fl. 1537)

Doctor of physic of Sultzfelde (in either Bavaria or Baden); there is an English edition of an almanac for 1537 by him (see Bosanquet in *The Library* (1937–8), pp. 40–1).

SHAKERLEY, JEREMY (JEREMIAH) (fl. 1640–54)

Mathematician and astronomer. Born at Carre, near Colne, Lancs., and belonged to the Towneley circle, later seeking the patronage of *Lilly*. Published almanac for 1651, and perhaps also 1649–50. Visited Surat, whence he wrote in 1654 (Ms Ash. 242, f. 94v), and died in the East Indies (Sherburn, *Sphere of M. Manilius*, p. 93).

D.N.B.; Taylor, p. 235.

SHARP, JOHN (fl. 1739–d. 1757)
'Student in celestial sciences', living at West Wycombe, Bucks. Published *The British Diary* for 1740–6 (an earlier edition for 1739 was not published because of his illness: *1740*, sig. C7v–8). Apparently occupied Butchers Close cottage in the village; buried at W. Wycombe 8 October 1757 (conditional surrenders and par. reg., information from Bucks. R.O.).

SHARPE, EDWARD (fl. 1730–73)
A physician living on St. Peter's Hill, Stamford, Lincs.; he advertised judgements from the patient's urine or from his date of birth without any direct contact (Andrews, 1769, sig. C2v). Advertised widely in almanacs, and probably compiled several in the 1760s and later: Saunders and Pearse for 1766 contain overlapping material, are calculated for Stamford, and carry his advertisements; Andrews in the late 1760s contained treatises on scurvy, hypochondria etc. In 1770 he mentioned his forty years' medical practice. Last recorded advertisement in Saunders, 1773. A friend of *Henry Season* (Season, 1771, sig. C2v).

SHARPE, WILLIAM (fl. 1724)
Student in astrology, of Hinckley, Leics. Published *Panterpe* for 1724.

SHEPPARD, SAMUEL (fl. 1606–55)
Journalist. Son of a physician, he was once an amanuensis for Ben Jonson, and was in holy orders. Compiled royalist newspapers and published burlesque almanacs under the pseudonym Raphael Desmus.

D.N.B.; Williams, *English Journalism*, pp. 83, 85, 86, 114; Frank, *English Newspaper*, p. 234.

SILVESTER, JOHN (1635–fl. 1700)
Astrologer. Lived at the Market House on Aldons Key, Bristol (*1700*). Born 9 August 1635 at Burford (Bodl. Ms Add. B8, f. 97v). Published almanacs for 1681–1700.

SIMPSON, THOMAS (1710–61)
Born Market Bosworth, Leics., the son of a weaver. Taught himself mathematics and became a noted teacher and writer on the subject. Professor at Woolwich Military Academy, and F.R.S. Edited *Ladies' Diary* 1754–60.

D.N.B.; Taylor, *HP*, pp. 191–2.

SLITER, ROBERT (fl. 1652–d. 1695)
Student in astronomy and mathematics, who published an almanac for Rochester, Kent, in 1652. A master ropemaker employed at Chatham Dockyard, where he sought an official post as lecturer in navigation and mapping. Described as gentleman, of Chatham, in his will.

Taylor, pp. 239–40; *P.C.C. 1694–1700*, p. 377.

SMITH, EDWARD (fl. 1739)
Teacher of mathematics, mapping and surveying at Shrivenham, Wilts. Published *The Annual Advertiser* for 1739–40.

SMITH, JOHN (fl. 1631)
'Well-willer to mathematics'; published almanac for Evesham for 1631.

SMITH, JOHN (fl. 1652)
Philomath; published almanacs for London for 1652–6.

SMITH, JOHN (fl. 1673)
Philomath; published almanacs for 1673–5. Possibly John Smith, the clock-maker and instrument-maker, fl. 1678–94 (Taylor, p. 276).

SMITH, REYNOLD (fl. 1620–5)
Practitioner in mathematics. Published several almanacs for London, 1620–5, in one of which he calls himself servant to Francis Bacon. A Renoulde Smith matriculated at Oxford 1588, aged twenty, B.A. 1592 (Foster, *Al. Oxon.*, iv, p. 1378).

SOFFORD, ARTHUR (fl. 1618–41)
Mathematician; published almanacs for London for 1618–41.

SOLEMNE, ANTHONY DE (fl. 1568–79)
A Dutch refugee who settled in Norwich, and practised as a printer and publisher. Issued an almanac in his native tongue for 1570 for the refugee community.

SPARKE, MICHAEL (fl. 1610–d. 1653)
A London bookseller, and author of a number of controversial pamphlets. His *Usurer's Almanack* was merely a collection of tables of interest.
Plomer, *Dictionary 1641–67*, p. 169.

SPARROW, THOMAS (fl. 1726–37)
Published *The Celestial Journal* for 1726, for Nottingham, offering tuition in mathematics and surveying at his home in Hose, N. Leics. He made occasional contributions to *The Ladies' Diary*, and his astronomical observations are mentioned in the 1737 edition, p. 1. Not recorded in the Hose parish register.

STARTOPP, THOMAS (fl. 1568)
Published an almanac for 1568, now lost. Allegedly the pseudonym of another compiler, perhaps *Securis* (N. Allen, *The Astronomers Game*, sig. *3v).

STATHNNINGS, CHRISTOPHER (i.e. STATHMION, CHRISTOPH) (fl. 1543–85)
Town physician of Coburg. Published over forty prognostications in the period 1543–85, including an English edition for 1563.
Hellmann, *Versuch*, p. 30; Thorndike, *Magic*, v, pp. 654–5.

STAYNRED, PHILIP (fl. 1621–69)
Mathematician and surveyor of Bristol, who made and sold instruments.

Wrote on fortification, studied compass variation and published almanacs for Bristol for 1635 and 1648 (Taylor, p. 208).

STEPHENSON, NICHOLAS (fl. 1674–80)
One of H.M. Gunners at the Tower. Published the *Royal Almanack* for 1675–7 at the command of Charles II. Many of the tables were derived from Jonas Moore, and the work was known in the trade as 'Sir Jonas Moore's Almanack' (S.C., Journal Bk., f. 57v). Stephenson devised his own mathematical instruments.

Taylor, p. 269.

STEPHINS, THOMAS (fl. 1569)
Gentleman; published an almanac for Oxford for 1560.

STREETE, THOMAS (1621–89)
Mathematician and astronomer of London. Born 5 March 1620/1 in Cork (Ms Ash. 183, p. 367; 426, f. 292); later an ensign in Col. Kingsmill's regiment under Inchiquin, against parliament, fighting at Tredagh and Dublin and twice captured (Ash. 423, f. 237). According to *Partridge* he worked as a tapster in Dublin, and was 'poor, illnatured, morose, peevish, conceited, knavish and a good astronomer' (*Flagitiosus*, p. 9). After the Restoration he worked in the Excise Office, lectured at Gresham College, published the influential *Astronomia Carolina* (1661), and issued several almanacs. Died 17 August 1689, and was buried in Westminster New Chapel (Parker, *Mercurius Anglicanus*, 1691, sig. E).

Taylor, pp. 225–6.

STROF, WALTER
Published almanacs for 1626–7 for Cambridge; a pseudonym of *Walter Frost*.

STRUT(T), THOMAS (fl. 1688)
Student of astrology, living at Sudbury, Suffolk. Published almanacs for 1688–90. Probably belonged to the Suffolk/Essex family of Strutts (see Venn, iv, p. 177).

SWALLOW, THOMAS
Pseudonymous author of almanacs from 1628; one of the Cambridge 'bird' series.

SWAN, JOHN (fl. 1622–d. 1671)
An Anglican minister of Laudian views. Matriculated at Trinity College, Cambridge, in 1622, M.A. 1629; minister of Duxford, 1630, vicar of Whittlesford 1647–69 and rector of Sawston, 1641–60, 1664–9 (all in Cambridgeshire). Wrote on Laudian themes before the civil war, and in defence of astrology in the 1640s. Published a popular encyclopaedia, *Speculum Mundi* (1635 and many later editions), material from which appeared in his almanacs. Published almanac for Ickleton, Cambs. (close to all three of his livings) from 1657; the series continued till 1684.

Venn, iv, p. 190.

TANNER, JOHN (c. 1636–1715)
Astrologer and physician of Amersham, Bucks. Published a work on astrological medicine, and almanacs for London from 1657 to 1715 (*1657* contains his portrait; *1659* is dated from his lodgings in King St., Westminster). In *1705* (written 1704) he says he is in his sixty-ninth year. His will was proved 3 December 1715 (information from Bucks. R.O.).

TAPP, JOHN (fl. 1596–1631)
A London bookseller who wrote on and taught navigation, and founded the pioneering *Seamans Kalendar* in 1601.
D.N.B.; Taylor, p. 193.

TAYLOR, JOHN (fl. 1650–1701)
Gentleman, student in mathematics and astrology, living at the Market Place in Norwich. Published a mathematical textbook in 1686, and an almanac for Norwich for 1696.
Taylor, pp. 237–8.

TEMPLE, CHARLES (fl. 1656)
Well-willer to mathematics; published almanac for London for 1656–7.

THIBAULT, JOHANNES (fl. 1519–36)
A printer of Antwerp who became a physician and astrologer and published several almanacs for Antwerp between 1529 and 1533, denounced by *Laet*; English editions exist for 1530 and 1533. He claimed to be astrologer to Charles V. Gaoled by the University of Paris in 1536 for practising medicine; his claim to be a royal physician was rejected.
Hellmann, *Versuch*, p. 16; Thorndike, *Magic*, v, p. 286.

THOMAS, JOHN (fl. 1612)
Judicial astrologer and physician, who published an almanac for Bridgewater, Somerset.

THURSTON, SAMUEL (fl. 1652)
Well-willer to astrology, who published a prognostication for 1652. Possibly the Samuel Thurston, clerk of the check in the *Kentish* and *Sussex* frigates, 1652–3 (*C.S.P.D.*, *1652–3*, pp. 35, 606). A Samuel Thurston the elder, of Eye, Suffolk, died 1656 (*P.C.C.*, *Admin.*, *1655–60*, ii, p. 73).

TIPPER, JOHN (fl. 1699–d. 1713)
Master of Bablake School, Coventry, from 1699, where he taught mathematics, writing, surveying and music. Founded *The Ladies' Diary*, which he edited till his death, and *Great Britain's Diary*.
D.N.B.; Taylor, pp. 295–6; F. L. Colville, *The Worthies of Warwickshire* (1869), pp. 755–6.

TRIGGE, THOMAS (fl. 1659)
Gentleman, student in physic and astrology. Published almanac from 1659, and contributed verses to *Partridge*'s *Astrological Vade Mecum* (1679).

According to Partridge, *Gadbury* was the true compiler: the almanacs show his style, and contain many advertisements for his works. Gadbury was paid for the copy for 1669, *Coley* for 1674 (S.C. Journal Bk., fos. 49, 57v). Trigge was probably a fiction, designed to capitalize on the fame of the quack physician, Dr. Trigge, who died in 1665 (Smyth, *Obituary*, p. 62); he claimed to be an M.A. of Cambridge, and F.R.C.P., but was really an ex-shoemaker (T. Brian, *Pisse-prophet* (1637), pp. 103–4).

Turner, Thomas (fl. 1633)
Mathematician, published almanac for 1633–4.

Turner, William (fl. 1687–1701)
Gentleman; published almanacs for York for 1687–1701.

Twells, William (fl. 1637)
Published almanacs for Cambridge for 1637–9. A William Twells, gent., of Wisbech, sent his sons to Cambridge in 1647/50 (Venn, iv, p. 280).

Twyne, Thomas (1543–1613)
Physician, of Lewes, Sussex. Educated at Oxford, M.A. 1568, M.D. 1593, licentiate of the R.C.P. Published several almanacs for Oxford 1579–87, and a translation of the *Aeneid*.

D.N.B.; Foster, *Al. Oxon.*, iv, p. 1525; Munk, *Physicians*, pp. 103–5.

Upcote, Augustine (fl. 1614–19)
Gentleman, practitioner in mathematics and physic; published almanacs for 1614–19.

Vaughan, Lewis (fl. 1559)
Published almanacs for Gloucester, where he lived, for 1559–61.

Vaux, John (c. 1575–1651)
Minister; curate of St. Helen's, Auckland, 1616–50 (ejected), of Monkwearmouth, 1609–37, and St. Hild's, S. Shields, 1610–37; buried at St. Helen's Auckland, 15 May 1651 (information from Mr. C. R. Hudleston). Probably the John Vaux, B.A. of St. John's, Cambridge, 1605 (Venn, iv, p. 296). Suspended in 1633 for his astrological activities (Longstaffe, *High Commission*, pp. 34–42); gave his age that year as fifty-eight (ibid., p. 46). Published almanac for Durham from 1621.

(Velthoven), Master Adrian (fl. 1515–24)
Doctor 'of Art and Medicine'; published several almanacs for Antwerp, 1515–24, with an English edition for 1520. For identification see Bosanquet in *The Library* (1937–8), p. 42.

Vopelius, Kaspar (1511–61)
Doctor of physic and astronomy of Medebagh, in the Saar, and a noted carto-

grapher and mathematician. There is an English sheet almanac by him for 1549.

A.D.B., xl, p. 299.

WALTER, M.
A corruption of *Walter Ryff*, q.v.

WATERMAN, ANDREW (fl. 1655)
'Mariner', but no doubt pseudonymous; published a nautical almanac for 1655.

WATERS, FR. (fl. 1624)
Mathematician; probably pseudonymous, one of the Cambridge 'water' series. Published almanac for Bristol.

WATSON, ROBERT (fl. 1581–1611)
Licensed physician, practising at Braintree, Essex. Educated at Cambridge (B.A., 1585: Venn, iv, p. 350). Living at Coggeshall 1600, Braintree 1605; published almanacs for Braintree for 1595–1605. Presented at quarter sessions in 1611 for a breach of the peace, in rescuing offenders from the custody of the constable (Essex R.O., Q/SR 193/38, 39; also 151/54 and 173/38: information from Archivist).

WEAVER, EDMUND (fl. 1723–d. 1748)
A licensed physician of Frieston, near Caythorpe, Grantham. Published *The British Telescope* for 1723–49, advertising his medical and astrological services, and his barometers. He was also a surveyor, and in the 1740s repeatedly invited subscriptions for a projected map of Lincolnshire, but by 1748 had received only £48 instead of the £700 he had hoped for (*1747*). Admitted to teach an English school at Caythorpe in 1737 (Subs. VIII/49); will, Lincs. Consistory Court, 1748 (refs. supplied by Deputy Archivist, Lincs. R.O.).

WEBB, THOMAS (fl. 1650–60)
Rector of Langley Burrell, Wilts., but had Ranter views, and was ejected and tried for adultery in 1650. Published a non-astrological sheet almanac in 1660 (Hill, *World Turned Upside Down*, 1975 edn., pp. 226–7).

WEDHOUSE (WYDOWAS, WOODHOUSE), JOHN (fl. 1619)
Published an almanac for Britain and especially Ireland in 1619; it contained a description of Ireland by one I.B., practitioner in geometry. Introducing an English edition of Scribonius's *Naturall Philosophy* (1621), Wedhouse mentions having spent most of the preceding thirty years in Ireland, active 'with pike and pen' in surveying the country (sig. A2v).

WESTHAWE, ROBERT (fl. 1577–95)
Gentleman, student in astrology. Educated Trinity Coll., Cambridge, B.A. 1581: Venn, iv, 372). Published almanacs for Norwich for 1594–5.

WESTLEY, JAMES (fl. 1669)
Student in astrology and physic; published almanac for London for 1669.

WHALLEY, JOHN (1653–1724)
Astrologer and physician. Born in England, the son of a Cromwellian adventurer in Ireland, where he settled in 1682. Lived as a shoemaker in Dublin, and issued Irish almanacs. A prominent Whig, and friend of *Partridge*. Fled to England in April 1689, and published English almanacs for 1690–1 (*1688* was for England and Ireland). Back in Ireland he also published newspapers.
D.N.B.; Evans, *Historical Account of Almanacks in Ireland* (1897), pp. 20–34.

WHARTON, SIR GEORGE (1617–81)
A mathematician, born in Westmorland, son of a blacksmith. Raised a troop and fought for the king in the civil war; later became a royalist propagandist writing pamphlets, newspapers and almanacs for 1641–66 (for Durham 1641–3, Oxford, 1644, York 1647 and Kirkby Kendall 1648–53). A friend of Ashmole, Moore and Sherburne. Treasurer of the Royal Ordnance under Charles II, and made baronet 1677.
D.N.B.; Taylor, p. 221.

WHEELER, MAURICE (c. 1648–1727)
Minister, educated at Oxford (matriculated 1664, aged sixteen; M.A. 1670), rector of St. Ebbe's, Oxford, later held livings in Northants., and a canon of Lincoln. Published *The Oxford Almanack* for 1673 and subsequent sheet almanacs.
D.N.B.; Foster, *Al. Oxon.*, iv, p. 1609.

WHITE, JOHN (fl. 1613)
Well-willer to mathematics. Published almanacs for London for 1613–51.

WHITE, JOHN (fl. 1677)
Surveyor, author of an almanac for 1677 published by Capt. Seymour at Westminster. Probably a pseudonym devised to capture the market of *Thomas White*.

WHITE, ROBERT (1693–1773)
A teacher of mathematics at Grantham; by 1755 he had moved to Bingham, Notts., where he boarded pupils. Born June 1693 and died 3 June 1773 (Partridge, 1775, sig. C8v). Published *The Coelestial Atlas* from 1750, which he called a 'piece of astronomical drudgery'. Attacked by *Poor Robin* in 1742 (sig. C4v), so he presumably compiled others before the series published under his own name. It was continued into the nineteenth century by Olinthus Gregory and W. Woolhouse.

WHITE, THOMAS (fl. 1677)
Surveyor; published almanac from 1677 into the next century for Toddington, Beds., continuing *William White*'s series. They were stereotyped in form, and the author was probably pseudonymous.
Taylor, p. 275.

WHITE, THOMAS (fl. 1739)
Student in mathematics. Published an almanac for Winchester for 1739, jointly with *John James*.

WHITE, WILLIAM (fl. 1651–76)
Student in astronomy. Published almanacs for Toddington, Beds., for 1651–76. One of these names baptized there 1627, buried 1686; a grocer and nonconformist (*Toddington par. reg.*, ed. Emmison, pp. 10, 71; J. H. Blundell, *Toddington* (1925), p. 84; will, information from Beds. R.O.).

WHITING, JAMES (fl. 1669)
'Student in celestial sciences.' Published an almanac for London for 1669. One of these names matriculated at Oxford, 1649, minister in Somerset and Gloucs. (Foster, *Al. Oxon.*, iv, p. 1622), but a connection is unlikely.

WILDBORE, CHARLES (1737–1802)
Editor of *The Gentleman's Diary* after *Peat*'s death; was paid 18 guineas in 1802 (Blagden, 'Thomas Carnan', p. 42). A minister, and kept a school at Bingham, Notts., and Keyworth (*1766*, p. 42), where he trained youth for 'Army, Navy, counting-house and university'.

Taylor, *HP*, p. 250; *D.N.B.*, s.v. Peat; Venn, pt. ii, vi, p. 466.

WILKINSON, THOMAS (fl. 1643–63)
Mathematician of Northampton; published almanacs for 1643 and 1658–63. A Thos. Wilkinson was baptized at All Saints, Northampton, on 9 October 1597 (information from Northants. R.O.); or possibly he was the T.W., client of *Booker*, born at Chesham, Herts., in April 1622 (Ms Ash. 225, f. 274).

WILLIAMS, GEORGE (fl. 1558–67)
Published a number of almanacs for 1558–67, none of which have survived.

WILSON, — (fl. 1727)
Apparently a compiler of *Poor Robin*; his name appears in an acrostic in the 1727 edition, p. 16.

WILSON, JEFFREY (fl. 1625–34)
Mathematician and physician; published almanacs for London for 1625–34.

WING, JOHN (1643–1726)
A surveyor of N. Luffenham and later (from 1683) Pickworth, Rutland. He taught and practised all branches of mathematics, including navigation, and music. Apparently a nephew of Vincent, though Green's account of his parentage is clearly wrong. Published almanacs from 1680 till his death, for Stamford.

D.N.B.; Taylor, p. 272; E. Green, *Pedigree of the Family of Wing* (1886), p. 4.

WING, JOHN II (1723–80)
Surveyor, son of *Tycho*; lived at Glinton, Northants., and was agent to the Duke of Bedford. Advertised in Wing, 1748–9, and perhaps helped to compile it.

Green, *Pedigree*, p. 5; Taylor, *HP*, p. 221.

WING, TYCHO (1696–1750)
Surveyor of Pickworth, where he boarded pupils, teaching mathematics; coroner of Rutland 1727–42. Called himself son of *John* (Wing, 1732, sig. C4v; Taylor says grandson, *HP*, p. 150; Green says great-nephew). John and Tycho advertised jointly, e.g. in Andrews, 1724, Wing, 1725. Tycho edited Coley by 1730, and probably also Moore and Andrews, as well as Wing (which continued in John's name till 1736). Tycho's widow was selling medicines at Pickworth as late as 1770 (advertisement in Partridge, 1770). A later Tycho (fl. 1760–81) was a surveyor and instrument-maker with a shop in the Strand, but there is nothing to link him with the almanacs.
Green, *Pedigree*, p. 4; Taylor, *HP*, pp. 150, 195, 208.

WING, VINCENT (1619–68)
A self-taught but highly respected mathematician, astronomer and land-surveyor, of N. Luffenham, Rutland; son of a small landowner. Published almanacs from 1641 till his death for Stamford, and for N. Luffenham (1647, 1654), Belvoir Castle, where he was lodging (1648), and Uppingham (1651).
D.N.B.; Taylor, pp. 222–3; Gadbury, *Life of Wing*; Green, *Pedigree*, p. 3.

WING, VINCENT II (1656–78)
Son of the last; continued his surveying practice, and edited the almanacs for 1670–2.
Taylor, p. 258; Gadbury, *Life of Wing*, p. 36; Green, *Pedigree*, p. 3; *Registers of N. Luffenham*, ed. P. G. Dennis (1896), p. 74.

WING, VINCENT III (1727–76)
Surveyor of Pickworth; younger son of *Tycho*. He advertised in Wing from 1753 (the advertisements continued till 1781), and probably contributed to it. Collaborated with *Thomas Wright* (see e.g. Saunders, 1773, sig. C8v), who may have done most of the work; see also *W. Harvey*.
Green, *Pedigree*, p. 4.

WINSTANLEY, WILLIAM (1626–98)
Miscellaneous writer of biographies, pamphlets and satirical verse. Born and lived mostly at Quendon, Essex, though he was a freeman of Saffron Walden and probably lived for a time in London. Revealed his identity in *Poor Robin*, 1671 and 1677. Compiled that series from 1662 till his death (S.C., Journal Bk., *passim*), and also *The Protestant Almanack* (ibid., fos. 127v, 158 etc.), *The Episcopal Almanack* by W.W., and probably *Poor Robin. The Yea and Nay Almanack*.
D.N.B.

WINTER, FRIG. (fl. 1633–46)
Published almanacs for Cambridge, 1633–8, and Huntingdon, 1646; probably a pseudonym.

WINTON, ALEXANDER (fl. 1638)
Bagford reported an almanac by him for 1638 (Harl. 5937, f. 17) Not traced, and possibly a slip for *Winter.*

WOOD, ROBERT (1622–85)
Minister, mathematician, and licensed physician, educated at Oxford. One of the founders of Durham College, F.R.S., chancellor of Meath, in Ireland, and a master at Christ's Hospital. Published a perpetual sheet almanac in 1680.
D.N.B.; Taylor, p. 226; Foster, *Al. Oxon.*, iv, p. 1672.

WOODHOUSE, JOHN (fl. 1610)
Gentleman, mathematician. Published almanacs for Wolverhampton for 1610–13, and for Chichester from 1614 (except 1620, for King's Clere, Hants.); from the 1650s they were for London. Servant to *Richard Forster*, the physician (Josten, *Ashmole*, p. 1377n). The series continued into the eighteenth century, though by 1655 Woodhouse had been dead for many years (Wharton, 1655, sig. B3v).

WOODHOUSE, WILLIAM (fl. 1601–8)
Student in astronomy and clerk in the customs at London. Published almanacs for 1601–8, for London and (1606–8) Wolverhampton.

WOODWARD, DANIEL (fl. 1682–1700)
A Whig astrologer and physician, who lived at the sign of the Gun, in the Strand. Born near Bristol (*1683*, sig. A2). Published almanacs for London for 1682–1700.

WRIGHT, THOMAS (c. 1716–d. 1797)
Surveyor and mathematician of Eaton, near Melton, Leics. Boarded pupils and taught Latin, Greek, English and mathematics (Season, 1775). Described by *Poor Robin* as grazier, astronomer, mathematician and professor of astrology (1787, sig. A2). Compiled Moore and Partridge by 1768 (see epistles to both), and probably earlier, and Season after 1775. Friend of *Henry Andrews* and *Vincent Wing III.* In 1773 he advertised his school at Goadby, Leics. (Saunders, 1773, sig. C8v), but was back at Eaton by 1775. Died 23 November 1797 in his eighty-second year (Heywood, *Three Papers*, iii, pp. 17–18). Not to be confused with the better-known mathematician, Thomas Wright of Durham (for whom see *D.N.B.* and Taylor, *HP*, pp. 195–6).

WYBERD, JOHN (c. 1615–75)
Mathematician, astronomer, physician and surveyor. Matriculated at Oxford in 1639, aged twenty-four; D.Med., Franeker (Friesland) 1644, incorporated Oxford 1654. Published almanacs for London for 1635–7. Died 1675, leaving a widow, Elizabeth. He was then living at Woodford, Essex (admin., December 1675, Guildhall Ms 9168/22, f. 231v). Served as physician with the English army in Ulster, 1651.
Taylor, pp. 212–13; Foster, *Al. Oxon.*, iv, col. 1691; Munk, *Physicians*, p. 251; *C.S.P.D., 1651*, p. 558.

APPENDIX II

Index of Dedications

THE APPENDIX LISTS dedicatees and the editions in which they appeared. In most cases the dedication was accompanied by remarks on friendship or patronage, and the list provides information on the clients, contacts and patrons of astrologers, especially in the later seventeenth century when the practice was most widespread. The recipients include gentlemen, merchants, physicians and lawyers. The custom died away completely at the very end of the Stuart period.

I have not included dedications to such amorphous bodies as 'all lovers of truth', etc.

Sir Edward Acton, Bt., of Aldenham, Salop., M.P. for Bridgenorth	Moore, 1701
Whitmore Acton, Esq., son of the above	Moore, 1711
Lancelot Andrewes, Bishop of Ely	Bedwell, 1614
Queen Anne	Parker, 1703, 1707
Elias Ashmole, Esq.	Booker, 1667; Lilly, 1664
Sir Richard Atkins, Kt., of Much Hadham, Herts.	Saunders, 1662
Hugh Ayscough, gent., of Willoughby, Lincs.	Coley, 1676
William Bakehouse (Backhouse), Esq. (see Josten, *Ashmole*)	Wharton, 1653
John Barefoot, of London	Partridge, 1678
Sir Richard Barker, Kt., of the Barbican, London, physician	Gadbury, 1672
William Battine, Esq., of Ringwood, Hants.	Gadbury, 1658
William Beal	Culpeper, 1653
Francis Bennet, of the Inner Temple, and Merefield, Dorset	Partridge, 1709
Mrs. Dorothy Bickers	Gadbury, 1662
William Bishop, Esq., of South Warnborough, Hants.	Wharton, 1657
William Briggs, attorney at law	Coley, 1689
Sir Thomas Bromley, Lord Chancellor	Lloyd, 1582
Andrew Broughton, Esq., of Seaton, Rutland	J. Wing, 1687

Dedicatee	Author
John Brown, surgeon at St. Thomas's Hospital, and surgeon to Charles II	Coley, *M.A.J.*, 1688
John, 'late lord Carleton' (facetious dedication)	Adams, ?1664
Capt. Charles Carter, of Gt. Yarmouth	Woodward, 1684
Charles I	Wharton, 1649
Charles II	Wharton, 1661
Dr. Arthur Charlett, Master of University College, Oxford	Abendano, 1697
Tobias Clere, Mayor of Sandwich, Kent	Harflete, 1656
Fitzwilliam Conningsbie, of Herefordshire	Dauncy, 1615
William Coulson, gent., of Newcastle-on-Tyne	Coelson, 1675
Sir John Coventry, Kt., M.P.	Westley, 1669
William Crane, of Hales, Norfolk	Woodward, 1686
Edward Cresset, of Cound, Salop., M.P. for Shropshire	Moore, 1713
Richard Cresswell, physician	Browne, 1624
Richard Cresswell, of Rudge, Salop., M.P. for Bridgenorth	Moore, 1702
Luke Cropley, of Broad St., London, attorney of the King's Bench	Gadbury, 1674
Sir John Curson, Kt. (author's grandfather)	Gadbury, 1656
Thomas Curson, Esq., of Water Perry, Oxon.	Gadbury, 1657
Sir John Davies, Kt.	Wharton, 1654
Sir Edward Dering, Kt.	Partridge, 1697; Streete, 1682
Robert Dudley, Earl of Leicester	Forster, 1575
Thomas Eagle, one of H.M. officials in the Mews	Coley, 1691
Dr. Jonathan Edwards, Principal of Jesus College, Oxford	Abendano, 1698
George Ent, Esq., F.R.S.	Partridge, 1679
John Evans, of London	Coley, 1674
Timothy Featherstone-Haigh, Esq., J.P. of Kirkoswald, Cumberland	Cookson, 1700
Edward Fiennes, Lord Clinton (Earl of Lincoln)	Digges, 1564
Daniel Finch, Earl of Nottingham, Secretary of State	Whalley, 1690
Sir John Fleet, M.P., Lord Mayor of London	Parker, 1694

Dedicatee	Work
William Fleetwood, Recorder of London	Lloyd, 1585
Sir Richard Ford, ex-Lord Mayor of London	*London Almanack*, 1673
Sir John Forster, Kt., Warden of the Middle Marches	Carre, 1593
(Sir) John Friend, of Hackney, Middx., M.P.	Coelson, 1671, 1681, 1686
Thomas Gardiner, Esq., surgeon to the royal household	Partridge, 1696
George I	Partridge, 1715
William Glaseor, Esq., vice-chamberlain and deputy to Robert Dudley, Earl of Leicester	Mounslow, 1579, 1581
Sir William Hedges, Kt., alderman of London	Cookson, 1701
Henry VII	Parron, 1500, 1502, 1503
Fretswald (Sir Frescheville) Holles, M.P.	Gadbury, 1663; idem, *Ephemerides*, 1672
Sir John Hoskins, Master in Chancery, F.R.S.	Coley, 1677
John Hough, Bishop of Oxford	Abendano, 1696
William, Lord Howard of Effingham	Mathew, 1605
Sir Richard Howe, M.P., Sheriff of London	Coelson, 1680
M. Humfrey, B.D., Fellow of Trinity College, Cambridge, his tutor (i.e. Wm. Humphrey, d. 1626: Venn, ii. 431)	Dauncy, 1614
Sir John Hungerford, Kt.	Browne, 1622
J. B. Hunniades	Lilly, 1645
Francis Hyde, Esq., of Pangbourne, Berks.	Wharton, 1658
Sir Charles Izac, Kt.	Coley, 1698
Sir Jefferey Jeffreys, Kt., alderman of London	Cookson, 1702
Master George Keable, Esq.	Thomas Hill, 1560
Sir William Lane, Kt., J.P., of Gloucs.	Cole, 1705
Christopher Layer, of Bury St. Edmunds	Andrews, 1662
William Leigh, Esq., of the Middle Temple	Cookson, 1704
John Lewkener, Esq., of Hungerford Park	Wharton, 1660
Henry Ley, Lord Ley (2nd Earl of Marlborough, 1629)	Browne, 1627
William Lilly (facetious dedication)	'Rabelais', c. 1659
Pierce Lloyd, Esq., J.P., of Anglesey	Saunders, 1661
John, 6th Lord Lumley	Bomelius, 1567

Sir Thomas Lynch, Kt., Governor of Jamaica	Gadbury, *Jamaica Almanack*, 1673
John Machell, Jr., of Wendover, Bucks.	Coley, 1682
Dr. Roger Mander, Master of Balliol College, Oxford	Abendano, 1699
Thomas Marsh, Esq.	Searle, 1609
Mary II	Salmon, 1692, 1695; Parker, 1693
Robert Mason, Esq., of Moulford, Berks.	Wharton, 1659
Thomas Meade, of Saffron Walden, son of Justice Meade	Harvey, 1584
Thomas Mewtys, Esq., clerk of the Privy Council	Powell, 1627
Sir Thomas Middleton, Bt.	Evans, *Ephemeris*, 1633
John Mingey, Mayor of Norwich	Burton, 1618
Sir James Modyford, Bt., late Governor of Jamaica	Gadbury, *Jamaica Almanack*, 1673, *W. India Almanack*, 1674
Henry Morgan, Esq., Lt.-Governor of Jamaica (and buccaneer), for favours received	Gadbury, *W. India Almanack*, 1675
Thomas Neale, Esq., of London, M.P. for Ludgershall, Wilts.	Davis, 1687, 1688, 1689
Sir John Norwich, Bt., of Brampton, Northants.	Saunders, 1659; Wing, *Ephemeris*, 1658
Sir Robert Owen, Kt., of Porkington, Salop.	Gadbury, 1689
M(aster) W.P.	Porter, 1585
Sir W.P., Kt.	Wharton, 1650
Sir Jeffrey Palmer, Bt. (attorney-general)	Gadbury, 1661
Henry Parry, Bishop of Worcester (1610–16)	Evans, 1613
Francis Partley, Esq., chief commissioner of Excise	Davis, 1691
John Partridge, of Putney (author's father)	Partridge, 1686
William Paulet, Marquis of Winchester	Hartgill, 1581
Thomas Peck, Esq., of the Inner Temple	Gadbury, 1660
Sir John Peeter (Petre), of Thorndon, Essex (1st Lord Petre, 1603)	Pond, 1602
George Penruddock, Esq., of Broad-chalke, Wilts.	Coley, 1675; Gadbury, *Ephemerides*, 1680
Isaac Pereira	Abendano, 1695

John Pern, gent., of West Harnham, near Salisbury	Woodward, 1683
Sir John Peyton, Lieutenant of the Tower	Tapp, 1602
Robert Richardson, of London, merchant	Trigge, 1662
Samuel Rixon, of Yeovil, Somerset (presumably the girt-web-maker mentioned in the text)	Woodward, 1685
John Robinson, of London, merchant (Master of Clothworkers' Company, 1656)	Wharton, 1656
B.S., Esq.	*Protestant Almanack*, 1669
S.S.	Cookson, 1703
Miles Sandys, Esq., of Miserdon, Gloucs.	Gadbury, 1669
Robert Seaman, Esq., surgeon and alderman of Harwich, Essex	Coelson, 1678
Capt. John Seymour, gentleman of the Privy Chamber	Gadbury, 1675
Robert Smith, Esq.	*Calendarium Londinense*, 1686
Noah Starling, of Reading, Berks.	Gadbury, 1673
Samuel Starling, Esq., Sheriff of London	Neve, 1662
Thomas Thirlby, Bishop of Ely (1554–9)	Dacquet, 1556
Jacob Thysius, lover of mathematics and astrology	Felgenhauer, 1655
Joseph Tily, Esq., of Lincoln's Inn	Partridge, 1682
Francis Trenchard, Esq., of the Inner Temple	Partridge, 1681
Henry Vernon and his son George, of Farnham, Surrey	Desmus, 1654
Sir Thomas Waite, Kt., M.P.	Wing, *Ephemerides*, 1652
Richard Walter, of Rugby, attorney of the King's Bench	Crawford, 1677
Sir William Warren, Kt., of Wapping, Middx.	Coelson, 1674
Josias Westwood, surgeon, of London	Bird, 1661
Thomas Wharton, physician (relation of author)	Wharton, 1652
William Whitchurch, Esq., of Frome, Somerset	Kendall, 1700
William III	Parker, 1693; Salmon, 1691/4/6, 1700
Onslow Winch, Esq., of Lincoln's Inn, son of Sir Humphrey, late L.C.J. of Ireland	Wedhouse, 1619

Groups and Institutions

Bibliography of English Almanacs to 1700

THIS BIBLIOGRAPHY NATURALLY owes much to Bosanquet, *S.T.C.* (including a draft of volume one of the revised edition) and Wing. It lists many items not in the published *S.T.C.*, a considerable number of additions to and deletions from the second edition of Wing, and references to almanacs known to have been published but now lost. An introduction to the bibliography of the eighteenth century can be found in Appendix I, which lists compilers and titles represented in the British Library and Bodleian.

The year given in the following entries is that *for* which the work was compiled, not that in which it was published (usually in the preceding autumn, notwithstanding the date usually printed on the title-page). I have given the location of the copy used for all items up to 1640, and for later editions which are hitherto unrecorded or listed only outside England. Where I have been unable to consult a work directly, I have used the symbol † (mostly American editions too fragile to be reproduced, and collections misplaced). Additions to Wing's revised list are indicated by the symbol *. I have not indicated additions for the period 1475–1640, which are numerous but should all be listed in the second edition of *S.T.C.*, vol. 1.

Titles published in an extended series have been listed in chronological not alphabetical order. This departs from Wing's practice, which has given rise to many errors of duplication. I have not listed minor variant editions, nor the variants of 'sorts', such as *Fly* and *Pond*, published simultaneously in London and Cambridge, especially in the 1640s. Most almanacs were in book form, mostly 8vo. I have distinguished sheet almanacs (as 'brs.'), and all sizes where more than one edition was published by an author for the same year.

I have added *S.T.C.*, Wing and Bosanquet numbers where this seemed helpful. 'Bos. F2', etc., refers to Bosanquet's list of editions no longer extant. 'Bos. A2', etc., refers to his addenda, in *The Library*, 4th series, viii (1927–8). 'Bos. Aa2', etc., refers to his addenda, ibid., 4th series, xviii (1937–8). I have used Wing's symbols where possible, with some additions (see Abbreviations, pages 387–91).

Fragments

(Alm. for c. 1500) brs. L Bos. i; *S.T.C.* 386
(Alm. for 10 Years, 1517) Now lost: Bos. F2
(Prog. for 1523) C Bos. xii; *S.T.C.* 20417
(Prog. for 1524) Ushaw† (*Cambridge*)
(Prog. for ?1539) CE Bos. xxii; *S.T.C.* 20420
(Prog. for ?1539) O† (untraced) Bos. xxi; *S.T.C.* 20419
(Prog. for ?1541) C Bos. xxiv; *S.T.C.* 20421
(Alm. and Prog. for 1544) brs. L Bos. cxxxv; *S.T.C.* 394
(Alm. and Prog. for ?1546) brs. L Bos. cxxxvi; *S.T.C.* 395
(Alm. and Prog. for ?1546) brs. L Bos. cxxxvii; *S.T.C.* 396
(Prog. for ?1551) C Bos. lxii (suggests 1565); *S.T.C.* 20426
(Alm. and Prog. for ?1559) C brs. Bos. cli; *S.T.C.* 402 (gives date 1581)
(Alm. for ?1559) Brox.
(Prog. for 1561) C
A Pro(gno)stication of 1567, *see* Coxe
(Alm. and) A Prog., or Declaration for 1568 WF
(Alm. for 1568) EFB† Bos. Aa4
(Alm. for 20 Years, 1570/1) Now lost: Bos. F118
A Newe Alm. for 1572 brs. L *S.T.C.* 401a
(Prog. for ?1575) OCC Bos. lxxx; *S.T.C.* 20427
(Prog. for ?1576) C Bos. c (suggests c. 1590); *S.T.C.* 402
(Prog. for ?1599) West. Bos. cx*; *S.T.C.* 20428 (ascribed to c. 1594). Probably by Buckminster
(Alm. and Prog. for 1625) C (*Cambridge*) *S.T.C.* 405

Almanacs: Anonymous, with No Distinctive Title

Alm. for xii Yere (1508–19) (1508) O Bos. clvi; *S.T.C.* 387
Xylographic calendar, untitled (pre-1521) L C LLP Bos. iia; *S.T.C.* 388
Alm. for xv Yeres (1522–37) (1522) L Bos. clvii; *S.T.C.* 389
Alm. ab Orbis Origine . . . 1523 brs. L Bos. cxxx
Alm. for xv Yeres (1524–40) (1525) MH Bos. clviii; *S.T.C.* 390
An Alm. and Pronosticacion, 1539 Sotheby's, 1944† Bos. Aa2
Alm. Most Exactly Sette Forth for the Term of xiii Yeres (1544–57) (1544) L Bos. clxiv; *S.T.C.* 393
Alm. for 1549, *see* Vopell
An Alm. and Prog. (for ?1555) WF Bos. A9 (suggesting 1566 as an alternative date, and Low as perhaps the compiler)

Alm. and Prog. for 1559 brs. EFB Sotheby's, 1944† Bos. cxlvi; *S.T.C.* 400
Alm. for 1567 brs. *B.A.R.*, lxiii, p. 17†
A Newe Alm. for 1572 brs. L *S.T.C.* 401a
A Perpetuall Kalender (1577), *see* DAWSON
An Alm. and Prono(stication) for 1584 brs. L Bos. clii; *S.T.C.* 402
(Alm. engraved on copper, 1591; untitled)† Bos. iii; *S.T.C.* 403
(Al)m. for 1636 brs. C (*Cambridge*) (perhaps belongs to the series by M.F.)
An Alm. for the Yeare of our Lord 1648 brs.
An Alm. for (1675) brs.* L (Harl. 5937/246)
An Alm. but for One Day (1686)
(c. 1700) L
An Alm. for Two Days (c. 1680)
(n.d., c. 1669–97)* pr. for P. Brooksby O

A., J. A Perfyte Pronosticacion Perpetual (?1555) L

A., M. Merlinus Anglicus, or Englands Merlin 1650 (a pirated version of Lilly's alm.)

ABENDANO, ISAAC The Jewish Kalender. . . . The Oxford Alm. for 1692 (Oxford series) continued each year to 1699. The order of the two title-pages was reversed after the first edition

ABENEZRAH, KINKI An Everlasting Prog. of the Change of Weather (?1620) L (not astrological)

ADAMS, JACK Jack Adams his Perpetual Alm. (?1664) Wing gives two edns. and suggests 1662 and 1663. Mention in the text of *Hudibras*, the trial of the 'German princess' (1663) and the Conventicle Act (1664) show these are premature, and the likely date is 1664, which was Bagford's suggestion (Harl. 5937, f. 17v)

ADKIN, M. (prob. pseud., *see* KIDMAN) Adkin. An Alm. for 1640 (*Cambridge*) Y

ADRIAN, MASTER, *see* VELTHOVEN

ALLESTREE, RICHARD Allestree. 1617. A New Alm. and Prog. LLP

1618 LLP	1627 O	1636 O
1619 O	1628 O	1637 LLP
1620 O	1629 O	1638 LLP
1621 O	1630 L	1639 O
1622 O	1631 L	1640 C (frag.)
1623 O	1632 O	1641
1624 L	1633 O	1642
1625 LLP	1634 L	1643
1626 O	1635 O	1651

First published 1617 (*1617*, sig. B2)

ALLEYN, HENRY Alleyn. 1606. An Alm. and Prog. LLP
1607 O 1608 LLP†; not O, as in *S.T.C.*
An Alm., or a Double Diarie 1609 O
Alleyn 1610 LLP
Allens Alm., or a Diary 1612 L

ANDREWS, WILLIAM Andrewes. 1655. The Caelestial Observator
1656
The Caelestiall Observator 1657
De Rebus Caelestibus 1658
1659
Newes from the Stars 1660
1661
De Rebus Caelestibus 1662
1663 1664
News from the Stars 1665
1666 1667 1668
Coelestes Observationes 1669
1670 1671
News from the Stars 1672
continued annually to 1700 (and beyond)
Series first published 1655 (1656, sig. A3). Wing A1267, 1267A are errors, the correct titles being given in Wing A1250–1
Physical Observations for the Year 1671

APIAN, PETER (Alm. and Prog. for 1541. Now lost: Bos. F7)

ASHWELL, SAMUEL Ashwell. 1640. A New Alm. L
1641 1642 1643
Now lost: 1646 (*N. and Q.*, 1858, p. 134)

ASKHAM, ANTHONY (?An Alm. and) A Prog. for 1548 HH†; O (t.p.) Bos. xxxviii
An Alm. and Prog. made for 1551 O; (variant edn.) LLP
1552. An Alm. and Prog. IU
1553 IU 1555 IU 1557 IU
1554 IU 1556 IU
An Alm. and Prog. made for 1555 brs. L
1556 brs. L
Now lost: Alm. and Prog. 1550 (Bos. F9); prog. 1558 (Bos. F25); alm. 1559 (Arber, i, p. 32)

Astronomical Observations for 1691 (Wing A1302), *see* SILVESTER

ATKINSON, CHARLES Panterpe: or a Pleasant Alm. for 1670
1671 1673
1672 1674

First published 1670 (*1670*, sig. B8)
Now lost: 1676/7 (Blagden, Table iv); not published for 1675

ATLEE, RICHARD (Greek) sive Alm.: or a Diurnall for 1647

AXFORD, JOHN The Merchants Daily Companion: or the Shop-keepers Speculum for 1700* brs. L

B., G., *see* BEVERIDGE

BALLES, THOMAS Balles. 1631. A New Alm. and Prog. L

BARHAM, W. W. Barham. 1639. An Alm. O

BARNARDYN, MASTER (Alm. and Prog. for 1568. Now lost: Bos. F97)

BASTON, JAMES Mercurius Hermeticus Ephemeris 1657
Mercurii Hermetici Ephemeris 1659
First published 1657 (*1657*, sig. Av); not published 1658 (*1659*, sig. Av)

BEALE, WILLIAM Beale. 1631. An Alm. L

BEDWELL, WILLIAM Kalendarium Viatorium Generale. The Travellers Kalender (1614) L

BELL, GEORGE Bel. 1622. A New Alm. and Prog. LLP (O has t.p. only)

BELLERSON, PHILIP Bellerson. 1624. An Alm. L
First published 1624 (*1624*, sig. A2)

BERIDGE, FERDINANDO (Greek) or An Alm. for the Yeare 1654
Now lost: 1655 (S.C. Journal Book, f. 16)

BEVERIDGE, WILLIAM Kalendarium Julianum (1666)†

BILLINGSLEY, (ROBERT) (Alm. for 1650) (Now lost: Harl. 5937, f. 17v)

BILLY, HIMBERT DE Certaine Wonderful Predictions, for Seaven Yeares (1604) WF

BIRD, T. Speculum Anni. Or a Glasse of the Year 1661
1662
First published 1661 (*1661*, sig. A6, misprint for C6)

A Black Alm. or Prediction 1651

The Black Dutch Alm. or Prediction (for 1652) (*see also* The Dutch Bloudy Almanack)

BLAGRAVE, JOSEPH Blagrave's Ephemeris for 1659
1660 1665
Now lost: 1658 (*1659*, sig. A3)

A Blancke and Perpetuall Alm., Serving as a Memoriall (n.d., but clearly 1566) GU

The Bloody Alm. for 1666

The Bloody Alm. . . . for 1699, Wing A1319A, pr. by A. Vincent, must be the entry given below, with the date misprinted, and the symbol CT given in error for LT

The Bloody Alm.: or an Astrologicall Prediction for 1649 LT

The Bloudy Alm., or Englands Looking-glass . . . 1651 (*see also* NAPIER; New Bloudy Alm., for kindred works)

(BLOUNT, THOMAS) Calendarium Catholicum: or an Universall Alm. 1661
A New Alm. after the Old Fashion 1663
For the editions for 1686/9, ascribed by Wing to Blount (A1322–3), *see below* under Kalendarium; Calendarium

BLUNT, GABRIEL An Alm. for 1656
1657

BOGARDE, ARNOLD A Prog. for Divers Yeares. . . . trans. from French by John Coke (1553) Sotheby's, 24 January 1944†

BOGARDE, LODOWICK, *see under* S. HEURING

BOMELIUS, ELIS A New Alm. and Prog. for 1567 Lincoln Cathedral
Now lost: 1569 (Bos. F107)

BOOKER, JOHN Bowker. 1631. A New Alm. and Prog. O

1632 O	1633 Potter (lacks first sheet)	1634 O

Prognosticon Astrologicum Anni 1635* O (Ms frags. in Ms Ash. 333, fos. 47–54)
The Anatomie of the Yeare 1636 (*Cambridge*) O
Almanack: sive Prognosticon 1637 (*Oxford*) O
1638 LLP
1639. Alm. et Prognosticon LLP

1640 O	1641 DT (not L, as in Wing)	1642 1643

Mercurius Coelicus sive Alm. et Prognosticon 1644* Herts. R. O.

1645	1646	1647

Uranoscopia. No Wharton or Naworth: but an Alm. and Prog. 1648* E
Uranoscopia or an Alm. and Prog. 1649
Uranoscopia Britannica . . . 1650* C
Celestiall Observations 1651

1652	(Greek) 1654	1656
1653	1655	1657

An Old Alm. after a New Fashion 1658
Telescopium Uranicum 1659
continued with the same title to 1667
First published 1631. A Bloody Irish Alm. (Wing A1331) is not an alm., but a pamphlet attacking an Irish alm. Mercurius Coelicus; or a

Caveat (1644), Wing A1334A, is not an alm. For The New Bloudy Alm. (1644, 1645) Wing A1338–9, *see under* NAPIER

BORDE, ANDREW A Pronostycacyon or an Alm. for 1545 L (t.p.)

BOURNE, WILLIAM An Alm. and Prog. for Three Years 1571–3 (1567) OCC

An Alm. and Prog. for x Yeeres, Beginning 1581 (1581) OCC

Now lost: 1566 (Bos. F79)

BOWKER, JAMES Kalendarium . . . or an Alm. for 1668

1669	1671	1673
1670	1672	

Bowker, 1674. Kalendarium

Bowker, 1675. An Alm.

continued with the same title to 1684

Wing gives two editions for 1674 and 1675; the titles of Wing A1357 and A1374A are incorrect and should be as cited above

BRECKNOCK (Alm. and Prog. for 1618. Now lost: see Appendix I)

BRETNOR, EZEKIEL Bretnor. 1629. A New Alm. and Prog. L

1630 L

BRETNOR, THOMAS Bretnor. 1607. A New Alm. and Prog. L

1609 LLP	1613 O	1617 O
1610 LLP	1614 LLP	1618 O
1611 L	1615 O	1619 O
1612 L	1616 O	

BRISCOE, J. An Alm. for the Year 1695/6 (1696)†

BROTHYEL, MATHIAS A Pronostycacon Practysed by Master Mathias Brothyel 1545 L

BROWNE, DANIEL Browne. 1615. (A New Alm. and) Prog. O (Prog. only)

1616 LLP	1622 LLP	1628 O
1617 LLP	1623 O	1629 LLP
1618 LLP	1624 O	1630 L
1619 O	1625 O	1631 L
1620 O	1626 O	
1621 O	1627 L	

First published 1615 (1618: 4th edn.)

BRUNFELSIUS, OTTO A Very True Pronosticacion 1526 CE

BUCKMINSTER, THOMAS A New Alm. and Prog. for 1567 8vo IU

1568 IU	1582 L (t.p.)	1589 O
1571 WF	1584 O	

Buckminster 1590 WF
1595 C; (another edn.) LLP 1596 L 1598 (facsimile edn. ed. Bosanquet, 1935)
(Alm. and Prog. for 1591) 16mo C (frag.) Bos. civ
An Alm. and Prog. for 1593 brs. OWA†
1599 brs. MH
Now lost: Alm. and Prog. 1565/66/69 (Bos. F67, 73, 106); Spiritual Alm. for 1570 (Bos. F113); Prog. for 1570 (? part of same; F114); 1581 (Bos. F126)

BUCKNALL, JOHN The Shepherds Alm. 1675
(Hebrew) 1676
Calendarium Pastoris: or the Shepherds Alm. 1677
1678

BULLEINE, WILLIAM (Alm. and Prog. for 1564. Now lost: Bos. F60)

BURTON, GREGORY Burton. 1613. An Alm. or Kallendar O
1614 LLP
Burton. 1616. An Alm. and Prog. LLP
Burton. 1617. A New Alm. and Prog. LLP
1618 LLP 1620 LLP
1619 O 1621 O
First published 1613 (*1614*, sig. B7v); not published 1615 (*1616*, sig. B2v).

(BURTON, WILLIAM) (An Alm. for 1652)* brs. (*Oxford*) C
(—) An Alm. for the Year 1653 brs. (*Oxford*)
(—) An Alm. for the Year 1655 8vo (*Oxford*)
Now lost: brs. Alm. for 1656 (S.C. Journal Book, fos. 18v, 19)

BUTLER, ROBERT Butler. 1629. A New Alm. and Prog. LLP
1630 L 1631 (*Cambridge*) O 1632 (*Cambridge*) OB

BUTZLIN (BUTZLIUS), VALENTINE An Alm. and Pronostication 1552 brs. MR (two variant edns.)

Calendarium Catholicum. 1669

Calendarium Catholicum or, an Alm. for 1689

Calendarium Londinense, *see* RAVEN

CARRE, JAMES Carre. 1593. An Alm. and Prog. L

The Catholic Alm. for the Year 1687

A Catholic and Protestant Alm. for 1688

CATLETT, JOHN A Perpetual and Universal Alm. (1656)

CHAMBERLAINE (CHAMBERLIN), JOSEPH Chamberlin, 1627. A New Alm. and Prog. L

1628 O	1647	1649
1631 L	1648	

Chapman, *see* City

CHERRY, THOMAS Cherry. 1699. A New Alm. and Prog.

CHESICK, WILLIAM Chesick. 1661. A New Alm. and Prog.

CHILDREY, JOSHUA 1653. Syzygiasticon Instauratum, or an Ephemeris

The City and Country Chapmans Alm. 1685
continued with this title till 1692; then:
The Chapmans and Travellers Alm. 1693

1694	1695, continued as:

The English Chapmans Alm. for 1696
continued with this title to 1700

CLARK Clark 1633 LLP

1634 L	1637 L (t.p.)
1635 L (t.p.)	1638
1636 OB	

CLARKE, EUSTACE Clarke. 1628. A New Alm. and Prog. Leeds public library†

1629 O	1631 Swaffham parish church†

CLARKE, WILLIAM Synopsis Anni: or an Alm. for 1668 (*Cambridge*)

CLIFFORD, ABRAHAM Clifford. 1642. An Alm. and Prog.

COELSON, LANCELOT An Alm. for the Year 1671

1672	1673

Speculum Perspicuum Uranicum: or an Alm. for 1674
continued with the same title until 1687
First published 1671 (1687 = 17th edn.)

COLE, THOMAS Ephemeris, 1695 (Wing A1435; an error. The edition is for 1705, though the t.p. states that it was published in 1695)

COLEY, HENRY Hemerologium Astronomicum 1672
1673
Nuncius Coelestis 1674
continued with the same title until 1684
Nuncius Uranicus; or the Starry Messenger 1685
Nuncius Sydereus; or the Starry Messenger 1686
continued with the same title until 1690
The series was first published in 1672 (*1672*, sig. Av)

Merlini Anglici Ephemeris 1683 (compiled by Coley, though Lilly's name is on the t.p.)
1684 According to the Method of . . . Lilly
1685
Merlinus Anglicus Junior: or an Ephemeris 1686
continued with the same title until 1700

COLSON, NATHANIEL The Mariners Kalendar 1676†
The Mariners New Kalendar 1677
1679 1697† (6th edn.)
1696 1699

CONYERS, WILLIAM Hemerologium Astronomicum 1664 (The first edn.: sig. C2)

COOKSON, WILLIAM (Greek) An Ephemeris for 1699
1700
First published 1699 (*1699*, sig. A2)

CORNELIUS, GILBERT Cornelius 1647. A New Alm. and Prog.

CORONELLI, VINCENZO MARIO The Royal Alm. (2nd edn., 1696)

COULTON, JOHN Coulton. Theora Contingentium 1653
Coulton. 1654

The Country Almanack, *see* MARTINDALE

The Country-Mans Kalendar 1692 brs.

COWPER, THOMAS Cowper. 1637. An Alm. (*Oxford*) L (t.p.)

COXE, FRANCIS A Prog. made for 1566 C
(—) (—) 1567 L (B.L., Huth 50(49))
Now lost: Alm. for 1562/3/5 (Bos. F43, 49, 66, 72)

CRABTREE, *see* KRABTREE

CRAWFORD, HENRY Vox Uraniae, or Astrological Predictions for 1676
1677
First published 1676 (*1676*, sig. Av)

CROOKE, WILLIAM Crooke. 1652. An Alm. and Prog.
1653

CULPEPER, NICHOLAS An Ephemeris for 1651
continued with the same title until 1656
First published 1651 (*1651*, sig. G3)

CULPEPPER, NATHANIEL Culpepper Revived. Being an Alm. for 1680 (*Cambridge* series)
continued with the same title to 1700; the series lacks 1691
First published 1680 (*1680*, sig. C4v)

CUNNINGHAM (KENNINGHAM), WILLIAM A Newe Alm. and Prog. for 1558 IU

1564 CH | 1566 CH

Now lost: 1559, 1560/1/2/5 (Bos. F28, 33, 40, 46, 68)

CYPRIANO, JOHN A Most Strange and Wonderfull Prophesie (1595) L

DACQUETUS, PETRUS Alm. Novum et Perpetuum (1556) O

DADE, JOHN 1589. An Alm. and Prog. O

Dade 1591 C (t.p.)

1592 C (frag.)	1599 OCC	1608 L
1594 L (microfilm of Ms Cecil 333 in Dept. of Mss)	1600 L (t.p.)	1609 LLP
	1602 LLP	1610 LLP
	1604 L	1611 L
1595 LLP	1605 L	1612 L
1596 LLP†	1606 LLP	1613 O
1598 Potter	1607 O	1614 LLP

Now lost: 1603 (Harl. 5937, f. 17); the series was probably unbroken from 1589

A Triple Alm. for 1591 O

Dade 1600 16mo L (t.p.) Bos. cxxvi

DADE, WILLIAM Dade. 1615. A New Alm. and Prog. L

1616 LLP	1628 O	1638 LLP
1617 LLP	1629 LLP	1639 LLP
1618 LLP	1630 L	1640 L
1619 O	1631 L	1641
1620 LLP	1632 LLP	1642
1622 LLP	1633 LLP	1643
1623 LLP	1634 L	1647
1624 L	1635 LLP	1649
1625 LLP	1636 LLP	1651
1626 LLP	1637 LLP	1652* S.C.
1627 L		

and continued with the same title to 1700; the series now lacks 1656, 1662–3/5/8, 1674, 1691. Wing A1570A and B, and 1571 are clearly the detached second halves of the edns. for 1678/83/96

Gallen. 1692. A Compleat Pocket Alm., by William Dade

1694

DANIEL, HUMPHREY Daniel. 1651

1652	1654	1656

DAUNCY, GERVASE Dauncy. 1614. His President for the Stars LLP

Dauncy 1615. A New Reformed Kalender, or Alm. Against Alms. O

DAVIS, WILLIAM A New Alm. made in Wiltshire 1687
News out of the West from the Stars, or a New Ephemeris 1688
A New Ephemeris for 1689
A Compleat New Alm. made in Wiltshire for 1692

DAWE, JACK (pseud.) Voc Graculi, or Jack Dawes Prog. for 1623 O

DAWSON, THOMAS A Perpetuall Kalender (1577) LS

(DEKKER, THOMAS) The Ravens Alm. 1609 L

DERNYL, J. A Mery Prog. for 1567 (Now lost: Bos. F91) *See also*, A Mery Prognostication 1544, 1577, *and* W.W.

DESMUS, RAPHAEL (pseud., i.e. Sam. Sheppard) Merlinus Anonymous. An Alm. (between Jest and Earnest) for 1653
1654 1655
First published 1653 (*1654*, sig. A3v)

DIGGES, LEONARD A Prog. of Right Good Effecte . . . for Ever (1555) CH
A Prog. Everlasting (1556) L
(1564) O
(1567) L
ed. Thomas Digges (1576)†
(1578) L
and further edns. in 1584/5, 1592/6, 1605. First edn., now lost, in 1553 (*1555*, sig. *3)
(An Al)m. and Progn(ostication) for 1556 brs. O

A Directory to all Merchants for 1697* brs. L (Harl. 5937/386)

DOVE, JONATHAN Dove, 1627. A New Alm. and Prog. (*Cambridge* series) O
1631 WF
1633 Potter
1634 L
1635 L (t.p.)
1636
1637 OB
1638 WU†
1639 MH†
1640 OB
1641
Dove. Speculum Anni 1642
and continued with this title to 1700, as printed in Wing, adding 1652* O. The series lacks 1646 (mentioned in *N. and Q.*, 1858, p. 134) and 1650

DREKIN, *see* KINDER

DUNSTER, T. (Greek) An Alm. for Two Years, 1652 and 1653 brs.

The Dutch Bloudy Alm. 1653

EATON, NATHANIEL (Greek) A Treatise on Moneths and Years, with a Calendar for 1657

EDWARDS, CHARLES (Welsh Alm. for 1683–5, now lost; *see* Appendix I)

EINER, N. Einer. 1620. An Alm. LLP

1621 O	1623 LLP	1625 LLP
1622 O	1624 L	1626 L

First published 1620 (*1620*, sig. Av).

ELAND, WILLIAM Hemerologium Astronomicum . . . Alm. for 1656
A Tutor to Astrologie (with) an Ephemeris for 1657

ELLIS, JOHN Ellis. 1608. An Alm. and Prog. L

Endymion, 1663. Or the Man-in-the-Moon his Northern Weather Glass

England's Alm. 1700 brs. (Wing A1694B)=T.L., England's Alm. (Wing A1857A)

England's Monethly Observations for 1653 brs. (ballad based on Lilly and Culpeper)

English Chapman, *see* City

ERRA PATER The Prog. for Ever (?1536) L
and many subsequent edns.; *see S.T.C.* and Wing, adding 1657* Potter

EVANS, J. Evance. 1613. A New Alm. and Prog. O
Evans. 1625 LLP

1629 LLP	1630 L	1631 L

ed., An Ephemerides for Five Years (1633) L

F., M. An Alm. for the Year 1660 brs. (*Cambridge* series)

1661	1670* C	1677* C
1663	1671* C	1678* C
1664	1672* C	1679* C
1665	1673* C	1680* C
1666* C	1674	1681* C
1667* C	1675	1683* C
1668* C	1676* O, C	1694

Now lost: 1685–7 (Blagden, Table 1); the series probably also appeared in the other years now missing

A Faithfull and True Pronostication 1536, trans. M. Coverdale CCA†

1548 O	1549 WF

FAITHORNE, WILLIAM (A Perpetual Alm., 1678, now lost: Harl. 5937, f. 18)

FALLOWES, EDWARD Fallowes, 1636. A New Alm. and Prog. LLP

1637 LLP	1639 LLP	1640 L

FARMER, WILLIAM The Common Alm. or Kalender for 1587 O
Farmer. 1614. A Prognosticall Alm. LLP
Now lost: 1593 (Harl. 5937, f. 8v) and probably others (*1614*, sig. Av), though they may all have been issued in Dublin

FELGENHAUER, PAUL Postilion, or a New Alm. (1655)

FIELD, JOHN Ephemeris Anni 1557 O
Ephemerides Trium Annorum. 58, 59 et 60 (1558) L

FITZSMITH, RICHARD Syzygiasticon Instauratum or an Alm. and Ephemeris 1654

(FLATMAN, THOMAS) Montelion 1661
(—) (—) 1662
Wing A2110, 2111, where they are ascribed to Phillips; *see* Appendix I

Fly. 1657. An Alm.
continued with the same title to 1700; the series lacks only 1663

FORSTER, RICHARD Ephemerides Meteorographical 1575 O

FOSTER, WILLIAM An Ephemeris of the Celestial Motions 1662
First published 1662 (*1662*, sig. C3)

FOULEWEATHER, ADAM (pseud.) A Wonderfull, Strange and Miraculous Astrologicall Prog. for 1591 O
2nd edn., 1591 O

FOWLE, THOMAS Speculum Uranicum, or an Alm. and Prog. for 1680
continued with the same title to 1700, the series now lacking 1682/6, 1691. Wing wrongly ascribes 1686 and 1688 to Oxford, but a copy of 1688 does exist at E. First published 1680 (1699=20th edn.)

FRENDE, GABRIEL An Alm. and Prog. for 1585 Brox.: Ehrman
1587 Cant.
A New Alm. and Prog. for 1588 Cant.
1589 Cant.
Frende 1590. An Alm. and Prog. Cant.
1591 Cant. 1592 Cant. 1593 O
Frende 1594. A Double Alm. with a Prog. Hatfield, Ms Cecil 333 (Microfilm in L., Dept. of Mss)
1595 LLP
(—) 1596 C (t.p. of prog. only)
1597 An Alm. and Prog. L
1598 L; (variant edn.) Potter
1599 L
(An Alm. and Prog. for) 1589 16mo L (lacks t.p.)
(—) 1591 Shrewsbury School (impf.)
Friend. 1614. A New Alm. and Prog. 8vo series LLP

1615 O	1618 LLP	1621 O
1616 LLP	1619 O	1622 LLP
1617 LLP	1620 LLP	1623 LLP

First published 1584 (*1585*, sig. B2); also now lost: 1586 (1587=4th edn.)

FROST, WALTER Frost. 1627. A New Alm. and Prog. (*Cambridge*) L

FULKE, WILLIAM (Alm. for 1561, 1563, now lost: Bos. F39, 51; *see* Appendix I)

G., R. MDCLXVI A Prognostick on the Famous Year brs. (not astrological)

GADBURY, JOHN Speculum Astrologicum 1656

1657

(Greek) An Astrological Prediction for 1658

(Greek) A Diary of the Celestial Motions for 1659

continued annually with the same title to 1700; 1676 was published at Westminster

First published 1656 (1695=40th edn.)

(—) Merlinus Verax; or an Alm. for 1687 (*see* Blagden, Table 1) (Wing A1942)

The Jamaica Alm.: or an Astrological Diary for 1673

The West India or Jamaica Alm. for 1674

Diarium Astronomicum: or a West India Alm. for 1675 (Wing A1785 is an error, duplicating A1735)

Ephemerides of the Celestial Motions for x Years 1672–81 (1672)

for xx Years 1682–1701 (1680)

see also MISSONNE, F. (pseud., i.e. Gadbury)

GADBURY, TIMOTHY The Young Seaman's Guide: or the Mariner's Alm. (1659)

for 1661

GALE, THOMAS (Alm. and Prog. for 1566, 1567; now lost: Bos. F78, 82. A fragment from 1566 was noted as O during the preparation of the revised *S.T.C.*, but cannot be traced)

GALLEN, THOMAS Gallen. An Alm. and Prog. 1639 PHS†

1640 L

1642

1643

1647* OB

148 L (mislaid); Surrey R.O.†

1649

1652* Potter

1654* *B.A.R.*, 63, p. 17†

1658

1660* Potter

1661* Hatfield; Cornwall R.O.†

1662* OB

1663* OB

1664* L (in Ms Add. 41202B)

1667* Hatfield†

1668

1669* Potter; Essex R.O.

1670* C; Cornwall R.O.

1671* L (in Ms Add. 41202H)

1672

1673

1674 Cornwall R.O.†

1676* Cornwall R.O.†
1677* Cornwall R.O.†
1678* L
1680* Cornwall R.O.†
1681
1683* O (in Ms Lister 27)

Now lost: 1651 (*The Library*, 1928–9, p. 57); 1653/7/9 (S.C. Journal Bk.); 1665/6, 1675/9, 1682/4/5 (Blagden, Table 1), and no doubt the other missing years

GALLEN, WILLIAM Gallen. 1686. An Alm. and Prog. 1686

1688†
1689†

For editions for 1692 and 1694 *see under* WM. DADE. Lost edns. for 1687 (Blagden, Table 1) and 1693/6/7/9 (S.C. Journal Bk.) probably belong to that series

GARDNER, ROBERT Veterinarium Meteorologist Astrology: or the Farriers Alm. 1698

Now lost: 1697 (*1698*, sig. A2), and probably 1699 (ibid., sig. A8)

GASSER, ACHILLES A Prog. for 1546 O

GAYNSFORTH, BARNABY (An Alm. and Prog. for 1567. Now lost: Bos. F84)

GESNER, JACOB (An Alm. and Prog. for 1555) brs. C (frag.)

GIBBONS, WILLIAM (Alm. for 1655. Now lost: *N. and Q.*, 1858, p. 134)

GILBERT, SAMUEL A Sexennial Diary, or an Alm. for Six Years (1683)

GILDEN, G. Gilden. 1616. A New Alm. and Prog. L

1617 LLP
1618 LLP
1619 O
1620 LLP
1621 O
1622 LLP
1623 LLP
1624 L
1625 LLP
1626 LLP
1629 LLP
1630 L
1631 L
1632 LLP

First published 1616 (*1616*, sig. B2v)

GODFRIDUS Here Begynneth the Boke of Knowledge (with) The Husbandman's Practice, or a Prog. for Ever (1619) L

For later edns. see *S.T.C.*, Wing and Thomas, p. 296n

GOLDISBOROUGH, JOHN Goldisborough. 1662. An Alm. and Prog.

GOLDSMITH, JOHN Goldsmith 1656* Salop R.O.†

1660* Potter
1663†
1664
1665†
1668* Potter
1671* Cumbria R.O.†
1672* Essex R.O.†
1673* Shrewsbury School†
1674
1675†
1678* Northants. R.O.†

1679* L (in Ms Harl. 6452)　　1681* Dorset R.O.;　　Gloucester R.O.†

and thereafter as listed in Wing. adding 1691* L (in Ms Add. 22550)
Now lost: 1651 (*The Library*, 1928–9, p. 57), 1653/5/7/9. 1661 (S.C. Journal Bk.), 1666/7, 1669, 1670/6/7, 1680/3/4 (Blagden, Table 1), 1690/7/9 (S.C. Journal Bk.). It was no doubt annual from c. 1651

GOSSENNE, G. A Newe Alm. and Prog. for 1571 C

GRAMMAR, ABRAHAM Grammar. 1627. A New Alm. and Prog. L
1628 O

GRAPHAEUS, RUDOLPHUS Praedictio Astrologica. The Great and Wonderfull Prog.
1598 CE

GRAY, WALTER An Alm. and Prog. for 1588 O
1589 O
Gray. 1591. An Alm. and Prog. WF
1593 C (impf.)　　1604 O
1598 Potter　　1605 LLP

GREEN, CHRISTOPHER A New Perpetual Alm. Beginning 1691 brs. L

GREENWOOD, NICHOLAS Diarium Planetarum: or an Ephemeris for 1690

GRESHAM, EDWARD Gresham. 1603. An Alm. and Prog. OB
1604 L; (variant edn.) LLP　　1606 LLP
　　1607 O
First published 1603 (*1603*, sig. B2)

GUMDANTE, EDWIN Gumdante. 1621. A New Alm. and Prog. O

Gusmans Ephemeris: or The Merry Rogues Calendar 1662* O

H., G., *see* HORTON

(HALLEY, EDMUND) Ephemeris ad Annum 1686
(—) 1687
(—) 1688

HARFLETE, HENRY (Greek) An Ephemeris for 1651
(Greek) Coelorum Declaratio. An Ephemeris for 1652
1653　　1654　　1656

HARRISON, JOHN Syderum Secreta, or a . . . Diary for 1688†
1689

HARTGILL, GEORGE (Alm. and Prog. for 1581) L (2nd t.p. only)
Now lost: Alm. for 1594 (Bos. F133)

HARVEY, JOHN Leape Yeere. A Compendious Prog. for 1584 O
An Alm. or Annual Calender, with a Prog. for 1585 Brox: Ehrman
1589 O
First published 1584 (*1584*, sig. A2). Now lost: 1587 (Frende, 1588, sig. Av)

HARYCOCKE, DR. (i.e. Harcock, Edmund) (Alm. for 1563. Now lost: Bos. F52)

HAWKINS, GEORGE Hawkins. 1624. An Alm. and Prog. L
1625 LLP 1627 L

HEALY, RICHARD Healy. 1655. A New Alm. and Prog.
1658

HEATHCOTT, WILLIAM Speculum Anni 1664* O (survives in Ms only: Ms Ash. 347, fos. 106 ff)
Annus ab Incarnatione 1665. An Alm. and Prog.

HEATLEY,— (Alm. for 1665. Now lost: Blagden, Table 1)

HERBERT, THOMAS Herbert. 1651. Speculum Anni
1652 1653

HEURING, SIMON An Alm. and Prog. for 1551 brs. O
and BOGARD, LODOWICK An Alm. and Prog. for 1551 8vo (*Worcester*) IU
Now lost: Alm. for 1545 by Heuring (Bos. F8)

HEWIT, THOMAS Annus ab Incarnatione Domini. Hewit. 1654
1655
Now lost: 1653, and perhaps earlier edns. (1654, sig. A5)

HEWLETT, WILLIAM Hewlett. 1625. A New Alm. and Prog. LLP
1627 L 1628 O 1629 LLP

HEYMAN, JOHN An Alm. for 1660
First published 1660 (*1660*, sig. A2v)

HILL, (HENRY) Hill. 1603. A Prog. LLP (lacks the alm.)
A New Alm. and Prog. for 1609 LLP

HILL, HENRY (Greek) A Starry Lecture for 1684

HILL, THOMAS A Necessary Alm. and Kalender for 1560 OCC
An Alm. Published at Large for 1571 O
Alm. for the Yere 1572 brs. O
(An Alm. and) Prog. for 1572 O
Now lost: 1561/3/7, 1573 (Bos. F.42, 57, 94, 122)

HIPPOCRATES Prog. Drawen out of the Book of Ipocras (?1530) L

HOBBS, MATTHEW An Alm. for 1693
Chaldaeus Anglicanus being an Alm. for 1695
1696
First published 1693 (*1693*, sig. Av)

HOLDEN, MARY The Womans Alm. for 1688
1689

HOLMES, WALTER, SR. An Annuall Alm.: Showing how to Read the Chapters of the Whole Bible Once in the Yeare (1649)

HONIWAX, I. Honiwax. 1629. A New Alm. and Prog. LLP
1630 L

HOOKER, RICHARD Coelestis Legatus: or an Astrologicall Diarie 1668 (*Cambridge*)

HOPKINS, THOMAS (Alm. and Prog. for 1569. Now lost: Bos. F111)

HOPTON, ARTHUR Hopton. 1606. An Alm. and Prog. LLP

1607 O	1610 LLP	1613 O
1608 L	1611 L	1614 O

Now lost: 1605 (*1606*, sig. B2)

HORTON, GEORGE The Bloody Alm. for 1652 (Wing A1955, ascribed to Napier)
Merlinus Anglicus: or England's Merlin for 1653* LT (plagiarized from Lilly, Wharton, Booker, Culpeper)

HOWELL, HUMPHREY 1656. Duplus Annus
Duplex Annus 1657
Now lost: 1653 (Harl. 5937, f. 17v); 1655 (*1656*, sig. B7)

HUMPHREYS, THOMAS (A Perpetual Prog., late 16th century. Now lost: Harl. 5937, f. 8v)

JACKSON, THOMAS Speculum Perspicuum Uranicum 1653
1655

JEFFEREYS, THOMAS Jeffereys. 1623. A New Alm. and Prog. LLP
1635 LLP

JENKYNSON, THOMAS (Alm. and Prog. for 1568. Now lost: Bos. F102)

JESSEY, HENRY A Calculation of the Present Year 1645 According to the Word of God (ascribed by Wing to Henry Jessop following Thomason's speculative extension of the printed initials H.J. on the B.L. copy (E1189). The work is clearly the first edn. of the following series)
A Scripture Alm. 1646
1647 (3rd edn.)
1648 A Scripture Alm.
1649 The Scripture Calender
continued with the same title to 1662, and revived later by J.S., q.v.
Now lost: 1656–9 (1660=16th edn.), 1662 (1669, by J.S.=20th edn., and series was only resumed in 1668)

JINNER, SARAH (An Alm. and Prog. for 1658)
1659 1660†
An Alm. for the Year 1664
(spelt Ginner, ?pseud.) The Womans Alm.: or Prog. for Ever 1659

JOHNSON, G. 1659. An Account Astrological
1660

JOHNSON, JOHN Johnson. 1611. An Alm. and Prog. L
1612 L 1616 LLP 1622 LLP
1613 O 1617 LLP 1623 LLP
1614 LLP 1618 LLP 1624 L
1615 L 1621 O
First published 1611 (1613=3rd edn., sig. Bv)

JOHNSON, R. An Alm. for the Year 1683

JOHNSON, THOMAS Johnson. 1598. An Alm. and Prog. Potter
1602 LLP 1604 LLP
An Alm. for 1600 brs. MH
1604 brs. L

JOHNSON, WILLIAM An Alm. and Prog. for 1569 Potter
Now lost: 1568, 1570 (Bos. F103, 155)

JONES, THOMAS Alm. am y Flwyddyn 1681†
Y Mwyyat o'r Almanaccau 1691†
Y Lleiat o'r Almanaccau 1692
see further Appendix I

JONES, WILLIAM Joanes. 1626. A New Alm. LLP
1627 L

Kalendarium Catholicum for 1686 (*see also* Catholic; Calendarium)

The Kalender of Shepherds (1503) (for the many subsequent edns. *see S.T.C.* and Wing)

KAYE, RICHARD Kaye. 1608. An Alm. and Prog. L
1609 L
First published 1608 (*1608*, sig. B2)

KEENE, JOHN Keene, 1612. A New Alm. and Prog. L
1613 O 1615 L 1617 LLP
1614 LLP 1616 LLP
First published 1612 (*1612*, sig. B2)

KENDAL, ROGER Ephemeris Absoluta; or a Compleat Diary for 1700
First edition 1700 (*1700*, sig. A2v)

KIDMAN, THOMAS Kidman, 1631. A New Alm. and Prog. (*Cambridge* series) O

1633 LLP 1635 O 1637 L (t.p. only)
1634 O 1636 E† (missing) 1638 WU

KINDE, JOHN Kinde. 1625. A New Alm. and Prog. LLP

(KINDER, PHILIP) Drekin. 1619. A New Alm. and Prog. LLP
1620 'by Philip Kinder' LLP

KIRBY, RICHARD An Ephemeris for 1681
1682
Vates Astrologicus: or England's Astrological Prophecier 1683–1702 (1683)
A Diurnall Speculum for 1684

KNIGHT, RICHARD Knight. An Alm. for 1638 (*Cambridge*) OB

KNIGHT, WILLIAM Pleiades, Hoc est Septennium Prognosticon. Or an Alm. and Prog. for Seaven Years, Beginning the 1. of Jan. 1652 (1652)* Potter

KRABTREE, HENRY Merlinus Rusticus 1685. Or a Country Alm.

KYNNET,— (Alm. for 1581 and 1582. Now lost: Bos. F126–7)

L., T. Englands Alm. Shewing how the East India Trade is Prejudicial (1700) brs.

LAET, ALPHONSUS An Alm. and Prog. for 1548 brs. L

(LAET, JASPER, SR.) (A Prog., c. 1500) O (Bos. iv; *S.T.C.* 20415)
The Pronosticaciō of Iasper Late 1516, trans. N. Longwater CT (Bos. viii)
(Prog. for 1517) L (Bos. ix)
Prenostica Effectuum Celestium 1518 (*Oxford*) brs. C (Bos. cxxix)
Prenosticatio Mgrī Iasp. La(et) 1520 C; (variant edn.) MR (Bos. xa and b)
(Prog. for 1523) L (Bos. xi)
A Pronosticacyon of Master Iasper Laet 1524 L (t.p. only) (Bos. xiii)
Pronosticum Magistri Gasparis Laet pro 1529 O (Bos. xiv; *S.T.C.* 15127)
Pronosticum Magistri Gasparis Laet 1530 L (t.p. only) (Bos. xv)
Now lost: Prog. for 1493 by J. Laet (i.e. Johannes or Jasper), Bos. F1; 1521, by Johannes Laet (but perhaps should be Jasper), Bos. F3

LAET, JASPER, Jr. Almynack and Pronostication of 1530 brs. L (Bos. cxxxi)
The Pronosticacion by Magister Iasper Laet 1533 O (Bos. xix; *S.T.C.* 15129)
(Prog. for 1534) L (t.p. only) (Bos. xx)
(Prog. for 1539) OJ (frag.)†
Alm. and Pronostication of Iasper Laet for 1541 8vo O (Bos. xxiii)
An Alm. & Prog. of 1541 16mo L (two t.p.s only) (Bos. xxv, xxvi)
An Alm. & Pronostication of 154(3) 16mo L (frag.) (Bos. xxvii)

An Alm. and Pronosticacion of Iasper Laet 1543 brs. Hereford Cath. (Bos. cxxxiii)
Pronosticatiō of Ia. Laet 1544 4to L (t.p. only) (Bos. xxix)
Alm. and Pronostication of Iasper Laet 1544 16mo or 32mo L C (frags.) (Bos. xxxii)
An Alm. and Pronost(ica)tion of Iasper Laet 15(45) 16mo C (Bos. xxxv)
A Prog. for 1545 4to MH†
An Alm. & Pronostication of Jasper Laet 1546 16mo L (Bos. xxxvii)
Now lost: 1535, 1550 (Bos. F6, 11)

Lakes, Thomas Lakes. 1627. The Country-Mans Kalender (*Cambridge*) L
Now lost: 1628 (Ms Ash. 383, f. 1)

Langley, Thomas Langley. 1635. A New Alm. and Prog. LLP

1636 LLP	1640 L	1643
1637 LLP	1641	1647
1638 LLP	1642	1648* E
1639 LLP		

A Lasting Alm. (Wing A1862A), *see* T. Webb

The Last Protestant Alm. or a Prog. 1680

Lea, Philip London Alm. for xxx Years (1680) brs.

Lele, W., pseud. An English Ephemeris or General and Monethly Predictions for 1650 (plagiarized from Lilly) (Wing A1877, ascribed to Lilly)

The Levellers Alm.: for the Year of Wonders 1652

Leybourne, William Speculum Anni: or a Glasse 1648

1649	1651

Liby, W., pseud. (perhaps Sam. Sheppard) Merlinus Democritus; or the Merry-conceited Prognosticator 1655 (Wing L1971)

Lighterfoote, Richard Lighterfoote. 1607. A New Alm. and Prog. O
First edition (*1607*, sig. B4)

Lilly, William Merlinus Anglicus Junior 1644; 2nd edn., enlarged, 1644
Anglicus, Peace or No Peace 1645
Anglicus: or an Ephemeris for 1646
Merlini Anglici Ephemeris 1647
and continued with the same title to 1682. For the editions for 1683–5 (Wing A1916–18) *see* Coley, by whom they were compiled. For an English Ephemeris for 1650 (Wing A1877) *see*, probably, Lele. Wing A1878 is probably an error for Lilly's alm. for 1651

(Livie, J.) The Bloody Alm.; or Monethly Observations for 1654
(—)

1655	1659

LLOYD, EVANS 1582. An Alm. and Prog. L
An Alm. and Prog. for 1585 Brox.: Ehrman
Now lost: 1581 (Bos. F126); 1583 (Frende, 1585, sig. B2)

LLWYD, HUMFREY An Alm. and Kalender . . . for Ever (1563) (Now lost: Taylor, p. 319)

London Alm. for ye Year of our Lord 1679* brs. L
1686† | 1693* E. Sussex R.O.† | 1698* L
1690 | 1697* L | 1699* L
1692* Y† | | 1700* L

LORD, JOHN An Alm. and Prog. for 1678

LOVE, GEORGE Love. 1625. A New Alm. and Prog. LLP

LOW, HENRY An Alm. and Prog. for 1554 C
(An Alm. and) Prog. for 1560 IU
1563 HH† 1564 O
A New Alm. and Prog. for 1569 OP
1574. An Alm. and Prog. C
(Alm. and Prog. for ?1558) brs. O
(?1566) brs. (See *The Library*, 4th ser., viii (1927–8), p. 471)†
Now lost: 1558/9, 1565–8, 1570 (Bos. F23–4, 30, 64, 74, 80, 96, 112)

M., A. *see* MARTINDALE, ADAM

The Mad-merry Merlin: or the Black Alm. for 1654

MAGINI, ANTONIO The Italian Prophecier. That is, a Prog. made for 1622 L
A Strange and Wonderfull Prog. for 1624 L
Now lost: 1623 (*1624*, sig. A2)

MARKHAM, GEORGE An Alm. for 1656
1657

MARTIN, HENRY A Bloody Alm., and Prog. for 1662

M(ARTINDALE), A(DAM) The Country Alm. for the Year 1675
1676 1677
First published 1675 (*1675*, sig. Av)

MATHEW, WILLIAM Mathew. 1602. An Alm. and Prog. LLP
1604 L | 1608 LLP† | 1612 L
1605 LLP | 1609 LLP | 1613 O
1606 LLP | 1610 LLP | 1614 LLP
1607 O | 1611 L |

Mercurius Civicus The London Alm., or a Compendium of 1673 8vo (Wing A1926)
1674

Merlinus Verax, *see* GADBURY, J.

A Mery Pronostication 1544 CH
see also DERNYL, J.; W.W.

METCALFE, FRANCIS Hemerologeion ad Annum Secundum . . . A Revolutionall Description of 1654

MISSONNE, FR., pseud. (i.e. Gadbury, J.) Merlinus Gallicus: or a Prediction for 1660

MONIPENNIE, J. A Christian Alm. (1612) O (reissue of A Faithfull Pronostication; the compiler's name is given in Arber, iii, p. 208b)

Montelion, *see* PHILLIPS, J.; FLATMAN, T.

MONTULMO (MOTULIND), ANTONIUS DE A Ryghte Excellente Treatise of Astronomie for 1554 and 1555 O
An Alm. and Prog. for 1555 L

MOORE, FRANCIS Kalendarium Ecclesiasticum 1699

MOORE, PHILIP A Fourtie Yeres Alm., with a Prog. (1567) O
1570. An Alm. and Prog. for xxxvii Yeres Brox.: Ehrman
1571. An Alm. and Prog. for xxxvii Yeres OCC
An Alm. and Prog. for xxxiiii Yeres (1573) O
1580. An Alm. and Prog. for xxxiiii Yeres (1580) LUC† (all of these are modified reissues of the first work)

(MOORE, ROBERT) (An Alm. and) Prog. for 1570 Brox.: Ehrman

MORGAN, EINON Hysbys Ruwdd 1693†

MORTON, ROBERT An Ephemeris for 1662

MOUNSLOW, ALEXANDER An Alm. and Prog. for 1561 C
(An Alm. and) Prog. for 1576†
1579. An Alm. and Prog. O
1581 O
Now lost: 1571 (Bos. F121), 1577/8 (*1579*, sig. B2), 1580 (*1581*, sig. B2)

MUSSEMIUS, JOHANNES Prognosticon D. Ioannis Mussemii 1544 C

N., H., *see* WINSTANLEY

NAPIER, JOHN The Bloody Alm. by Mr. John Booker. Being a Perfect Abstract of the Prophecies made by Napier (1643) (Booker's name was added merely to boost sales)
with additions (1643)
A Bloody Alm. Foretelling many Predictions for 1647 . . . By Napier
A Bloody Alm. . . . for 1648

for 1654 (Wing A1956) Untraced; perhaps = (J. Livie), 1654, Wing A1921

See also Bloody Alm.; New Bloody Alm.; HORTON

NEVE, JEFFREY Neve. 1604. A New Alm. and Prog. LLP

1605 LLP	1612 L	1619 O
1606 LLP	1613 O	1620 LLP
1607 O	1614 LLP	1621 O
1608 O	1616 (Univ. microfilm)	1622 OB
1609 LLP		1623 LLP†
1610 LLP	1617 LLP	1624 L
1611 O	1618 LLP	1625 LLP

First published 1604 (*1604*, sig. Cv)

An Alm. for the Yeere 1607 brs. series L

1609 L

1612 L (in Ms Add. 27632)

1615 (reproduced in J. Lewis, *Printed Ephemera* (Ipswich, 1962), p. 58)

1618 L

1621 OP

NEVE, JOHN Neve. 1626. A New Alm. and Prog. LLP

1627 L	1632 LLP	1637 LLP
1628 O	1633 LLP	1638 LLP
1629 L	1634 LLP	1639 LLP
1630 L	1635 LLP	1640 Y†
1631 L	1636 O	

continued with the same title to 1661, the series lacking 1644–5 and 1650

NEVE, RICHARD Nox Britannica (1661) Wing A1972: an error: not an alm.

NEVE, ROBERT Neve. 1662. A New Alm. and Prog.* O

1664

continued with the same title to 1667

Merlinus Verax 1668

continued with the same title to 1672

The New Bloody Alm. for 1644 . . . with Observations from Booker

1645 (both ascribed to Booker by Wing)

A New Perpetuall Alm. for Ever (1690) brs. (perhaps another edn. of the work by C. Green)

The New Protestant Alm. for 1677 (perhaps by Winstanley)

NICOLSON, JAMES A Prog. for 1563 16mo C, OCC (frags.)

1563 ON†

NIGHTINGALE, ROBERT Mercurius Philastrogus or an Alm. for 1653

(NORTON, HUMPHREY) (1579. An Alm. and Prog.) OT (frag.)
1581. An Alm. and Prog. for Winchester L (frag.)

NOSTRADAMUS An Alm. for the Yeere 1559 8vo CN
The Prog. of Maister Michael Nostredamus 1559 ('*Antwerp*') L
An Alm. made by the Noble and Worthy Clerke Michel Nostredamus 1559 brs. LLP
An Excellent Treatise, Shewing such Infirmities as Shall Issue 1559, and 1560 O
A Prog. for the Yeare 1560 L (Royal Ms 17 Bxxxviii; in manuscript)
An Alm. for the Year 1562 WF†
An Alm. for the Year 1563 IU
1564 IU
An Alminacke and Prodigious Premonstration 1566 L (t.p. only)
(A Prog. for 1567) WF
(A Prog. for 1568) L (frag.)† (listed in revised *S.T.C.*, but not located)
Now lost: Alm. for 1561 (Bos. F38)

Now or Never: or the Princely Calendar. Being a Bloudy Almanack (for 1660) (Wing N1435)

NUNNES, THOMAS An Alm. or Ephemerides for 1661
continued with the same title to 1666, lacking 1663. First published 1661 (*1661*, sig. C6)

NYE, NATHANIEL Nye. 1642. A New Alm. and Prog.
1643 1645 1648
Wing A2000/1 are merely the second portions of the alms for those years

OSBORNE, GEORGE Osborne. 1622. A new Alm. and Prog. LLP
1625 L 1626 O 1628 O
First published 1622 (*1622*, sig. B2)

The Owles Alm. (1618) L

P., C. The Sheepherd's New Kalendar (1700) (Wing P11)

PARKER, GEORGE Mercurius Anglicanus, or the English Mercury 1690
continued with the same title to 1698. First published 1690 (*1692*, sig. A3v). Wing lists an edn. for 1699 which is ascribed wrongly to O (Wing A2014)
An Ephemeris of the Coelestial Motions 1695†
1696 1697† 1699
A Double Ephemeris, for 1700
Now lost from this series: 1691–4 (1696=6th edn.) and probably 1698

PARKHURST, FERDINANDO (Hebrew) or an Alm. for 1648

PARRON, WILLIAM (A Prog. for ?1498) O
Ad Henricū . . . de M.d. Pronosticon Libellus O
1502 C 1503 Brox.: Ehrman

PARTRIDGE, DOROTHY The Woman's Alm. for 1694

PARTRIDGE, JOHN (Hebrew) Calendarium Judaicum, or an Alm. for 1678
(Greek) Being an Alm. for 1679
1680
Mercurius Coelestis, being an Alm. for 1681
1682
Merlinus Redivivus being an Alm. for 1683
1684
1685
1686
1687 Wing A2047; in fact this is by 'S. Partridge', q.v.

(—) An Alm. for the Year of our Redemption 1687* O (8vo F131 Linc.)
Annus Mirabilis: being an Alm. for the Year of our Redemption 1688
Mene Mene Tekel Upharsin . . . Treating of the Year MDCLXXXIX (not an alm., but comprises a prog. for 1689) (Wing P619)
Merlinus Liberatus; being an Alm. for 1690
continued with the same title to 1700
The titles listed for 1679–86 in Wing (A2020–7) are inaccurate, and should be as above and in Wing A2028–31, 2043–6, which they duplicate. Annus Mirabilis 1689 (Wing A2018) is not an alm.

PARTRIDGE, S. (pseud.) Merlinus Redivivus for 1687
Ostensibly a continuation of John Partridge's series; the compiler was Rd. Saunder

PARTRIDGE, SETH Partridge. 1649. An Alm. and Prog.
1651 1652
A Survey of the Yeer 1653
1654 1655
Synopsis Anni 1656
continued with this title to 1660

PARTRIDGE, SILVESTER (pseud.) The Infallible Astrologer . . . What shall Happen Every Day of the Week (1700–1)* LG (a satire, in weekly parts)

PEMBROKE, SIMON (Alm. and prog. for 1568. Now lost: Bos. F99)

PEREGRINE, AN(THONY) Peregrine. 1636. A New Alm. and Prog. LLP
1637 LLP

PERKINS, FRANCIS Perkins. 1655. A New Alm. and Prog.

continued with the same title to 1700, as in Wing, adding the following:
1671–3, 1676, 1685–6, 1690, 1700* all in O

The series lacks 1656 (ascribed wrongly to O by Wing, A2071), 1661/3/5/8, 1691

PERKINS, SAMUEL Perkins. 1625. A New Alm. and Prog. LLP

1626 LLP	1632 LLP	1638 LLP
1627 L	1633 LLP	1639 LLP
1628 O	1634 L	1640 Y†
1629 LLP	1635 LLP	1641
1630 L	1636 LLP	1642
1631 L	1637 LLP	1643

First published 1625 (*1625*, sig. B3)

A Perpetual Alm. (c. 1670) brs.

PETER, JOHN The Astral Gazette: or an Alm. for 1678
The first edition (t.p.)

PETER OF MOORBECK (Prog. for 1550. Now lost: Bos. F10)

PHILLIPPES, HENRY An Alm. for 1654
continued with the same title to 1658
A Constant Calender or an Alm. for 300 Years (1656)
(1677)†
Now lost: Alm. for 1651 (S.C. Journal Bk., f. 4; *The Library*, 1928–9, p. 57); 1653 (*1654*, sig. b8v)

(PHILLIPS, JOHN) Montelion. 1660. Or the Prophetical Alm.
For the edns. for 1661–2 *see* FLATMAN, T.

(—), Mercurius Verax: or the Prisoners Prog. for 1676 (Wing P2093)

PIERCE (PIERS), MATTHEW Pierce. 1634. A New Alm. and Prog. L

1635 LLP	1638 LLP	1640 O
1637 LLP	1639 LLP	1641

PIGOT, FRANCIS Pigot. 1630. A New Alm. and Prog. L
1654. Speculum Anni
Pigot. 1655. The Country-mans Kalender
Pigot. 1657. An Alm.
continued with the same title to 1662
There is no edn. for 1656 at O, as given by Wing (A2118). Wing A2122–3 duplicates Wing A2114–15

POND, BEN. (pseud.) A New. Alm. for 1689 (Oxford) The only extant example of over twenty alms. for 1689 published illegally by the University. *See above*, p. 38 and n. 91.

POND, EDWARD Ponde. 1601. A New Alm. and Prog. L (t.p.)

1602 LLP	1603 C

Enchiridion: or Pond . . . 1604 L
Pond his Polymnos. 1605. A President for Prognosticators O
Ponde 1606. A President for Prognosticators LLP

1607 O	1609 L	1611 O
1608 L (t.p.)	1610 O	

Pond. 1612. An Alm. O
Pond. 1625. A New Prog. (*Cambridge*, as for most of the following) IU†
1626 O
Pond. 1627. A New Alm. L

1629 C	1633 LLP	1637 WC†
1630 OB	1634 L	1638 L
1631 O	1635 OB	1640 OB
1632 O	1636 E†	

continued yearly as in Wing, adding:

1644* Potter	1650* OB	1651* OB

Now lost: 1628 (Ms Ash. 383, f. 1), and probably the other missing years after the revival of the series in 1625. Wing gives an edn. for 1644, with locations at O and L, neither of which appear to exist; but see above. I have not set out the London/Cambridge variant edns.

PONT, J. A Register, or a Generall Alm. for Every Year (1646)

POOLE, JOHN Poole. 1642. A New Alm. and Prog.
Pool. 1655. An Alm. and Prog.
1656 1657

Poor Robin, *see* WINSTANLEY, W.

PORTER, THOMAS An Alm. or Prog. for 1585 Brox.: Ehrman

POWELL, THOMAS The Attornies Alm. (1627) O

P(RICE), L(AURENCE) The Shepherds Prog. (1652) (appears in Wing with the wrong title and date: Wing P3383)

PRINCE, VINCENT The Constables Calender: or an Alm. for 1660
Now lost: 1664 (S.C. Journal Bk., f. 36)

The Princely Alm. (Now lost: advertised in Harl. 5937/183. ?1678)

A Prognosticall Prediction of Admirable Events Within Lesse than a Yeare (1644) (Wing P3650)

Prog. & Alm. of Two Shepherdes (1556) CH

The Protestant Alm., *see* WINSTANLEY, W.

(PRYNNE, WILLIAM) An Old Parliamentary Prog. (for 1655)

PTOLEMY Here Begyneth the Compost of Ptolomeus (c. 1530)
For further editions see *S.T.C.*

(RABELAIS, F.) Pantagruel's Prog. (c. 1659; not c. 1644, as Wing suggests, Wing R106)

Now lost: Gargantua his Prophecie, 1591 (Bos. F132)

RAMESEY, WILLIAM Vox Stellarum. Or the Voice of the Starres 1652 (not an alm., but a prog. for the year)

RANGER, PHILIP Ranger. 1615. An Alm. L

1616 LLP	1622 LLP	1628 O
1617 LLP	1623 LLP	1629 O
1618 LLP	1624 L	1630 L
1619 O	1625 LLP	1631 L
1620 LLP	1626 LLP	
1621 O	1627 L	

RAVEN, (JOSEPH) Calendarium Londinense or Raven's Alm. for 1677* L brs. series

1678 (Wing A1387)	1689* L
1683* L	1693* Sussex R.O.†
1686 (Wing A1387A)	1699* L

First published 1676 (1686=11th edn.)

RAYNOLDS, RICHARD (Alm. and prog. for 1567. Now lost: Bos. F85)

READMAN, WILLIAM An Alm. and Prog. for 1680

The Rebels Alm.: Calculated for the Use of All Loyal Subjects (for 1660)

RED, WILLIAM Alm. Ephemerides MCVII L

RIDER, SCHARDANUS (or CARDANUS), pseud. (i.e. Rd. Saunders)

Mercurius Cambro-Britannicus 1654* WF†

Riders: 1656. Brittish Merlin

continued with the same title as listed in Wing, adding the following:

1665* Sotheby's 1944†
1666* WF†
1667* Potter; L (Add. Ms 41202C)
1669* L (Add. Ms 41202E)
1671* Potter; Cornwall R.O.
1676* *B.A.R.*, 66, p. 17†
1677* L (Add. Ms 41202M)
1691* Kent, Northants. and Lincs. R.O.
1692 L (Add. Ms 41202R); Essex R.O.
1695* L (Add. Ms 41202U)
1697* L (Add. Ms 41202V)
1699 Northants. R.O.†

Now lost: 1652 (*N. and Q.*, 1858, p. 134), 1657, 1662 (S.C. Journal Bk., fos. 23v, 130), and no doubt the other missing years

RIDERS, THOMAS The Black Remembrancer for 1661 brs.

RIVERS, PEREGRINE, Rivers. 1627. A new Alm. and Prog. (*Cambridge* series) L

1629 O	1633 LLP	1637 L (t.p.)
1630 C	1634 L	1638 O
1631†	1635 L (t.p.)	1640 L

First published 1626 (1629=4th edn.)

RIVERS, WILLIAM Rivers. 1628. A New Alm. and Prog. O

ROBERTS,—Roberts, 1639. Alm. for 1639 LLP

ROGEFORD (ROCHEFORT), HENRY An Alm. and Prog. for 1560 L
1561 C (frag.)
Now lost: Alm. and Prog. for the Years 1565–8 (Bos. F65, 69, 75, 86, 100)

ROSE, GEORGE Rose. 1656. A New Alm. and Prog.
continued with the same title to 1700, as in Wing, adding 1700* in O. The series lacks 1658 and 1663

ROWLEY, JOHN Speculum Perspicuum Uranicum 1651
1652
First published 1651 (*1651*, sig. B2)
The Royall Merlin: or Great Brittains Loyal Observator (for 1655)

RUDSTON, JOHN Rudston. 1615. A New Alm. and Prog. O

1616 O	1620 LLP	1627 L
1617 LLP	1624 L	1628 LLP
1618 LLP	1625 LLP	
1619 O	1626 LLP	

RUDSTON, THOMAS Rudston. 1606. A New Alm. and Prog. L (t.p.)
1607 O
Rudston. 1609. A Double Alm. and Prog. LLP
Rudston. 1610. A New Alm. and Prog. LLP

1611 L	1612 L	1613 O

RUSSE, WILLIAM (Prog. for 1560. Now lost: Bos. F32)

RUSSELL, JOHN A Coelestiall Prospect, or an Ephemeris for 1660†
1661

RY (RYFF), W. An Alm. and Prog. for 1544 brs. St. James, Garlick Hill† (now lost) (Bos. cxxxiv)

S., J. 1668. The Scripture Kalender Revived†
1669 (20th edn.)
A revival of the series by Jessey, under whom they are listed by Wing (A1841B, 1842). Revived in 1668 (*1669*, sig. Av)

SALMON, WILLIAM Salmon's Alm. for 1684
The London Alm. for 1691 (8vo series)
continued with the same title to 1700. First published 1684 (*1684*, sig. A2); not published in the intervening years

SALOMON A Wounderfull Prophecie or Prog. Begynnynge 1531 (1543) C

SAUNDER, RICHARD 1684. Apollo Anglicanus
continued with the same title to 1700; a continuation of the following series

SAUNDERS, RICHARD Saunders. 1654. Apollo Anglicanus
1656. Apollo Anglicanus
continued with the same title to 1683, and then taken over by Richard Saunder

SAUVAGE, JACOBUS (An Alm. and Prog. for 1547) brs. WF (Bos. cxxxviii)
(—1548) 16mo West.; Cartmel
A Prog. for 1551, trans. W. Harrys 8vo OBR

SAVAGE, WILLIAM Savage 1610. A New Alm. and Prog. LLP
1611 L
First published 1610 (*1610*, sig. C3v–4)

SCOURFYLDE (i.e. SCHÖNFELD), VICTORIUS (Progs. for 1564, 1565. Now lost: Bos. F61, 70)

SCUTE, CORNELIUS A Pronostication for the Yere 1544 L

SEAMAN, HENRY Kalendarium Nauticum: the Sea-mans Alm. for 1675
1676 1677
First published 1675 (*1675*, sig. C4v)

SEARLE, JOHN An Ephemeris for Nine Yeeres 1609–17 (1609) L

A Second Edition of a New Alm. for the Year 1656

SECURIS, JOHN (An Alm. and) Prog. for 1562 8vo L (Bos. lvi)
A Prog. for 1562 16mo O (Bos. lvii)
An Alm. and Prog. for 1562 brs. CS (frag.)
A Prog. for 1566 16mo? L (Bos. lviii)
A Newe Alm. for the Yere 1567 brs. O
A Newe Alm. and Prog. for 1568 8vo O
1569 8vo L
A New Prog. for 1570 Vicar's Library, Marlborough (missing†) (Bos. lxxii)
A New Alm. and Prog. for 1571 8vo WF
A Prog. made for 1573 ?8vo L (t.p.)
1574. An Alm. and Prog. 8vo L
A Prog. for 1576 16mo O (t.p.) (Bos. Aa5)
1578 8vo OP†

1579. An Alm. and Prog. 8vo O
1580 OC (frag.)
1581 Potter; Hatfield, Ms Cecil 333 (microfilm in L)
Now lost: 1561 (*1562*, sig. A2v), 1563, 1564, (Bos. F48, 58), 1565 (mentioned in *1566*), 1567 (?8vo) (Bos. F87), 1577 (Harl. 5937, f. 7v)

(SELLER, JOHN) L(ondon Alm. for 1678)* brs. O (Rawl. Prints a2(56))
An Alm. for xxx Years (1682)
An Alm. for an Age (1684)

SEYFRIDT, G. (An Alm. and Prog. for 1537) brs. O, West. (frags.)

SHAKERLEY, JEREMIAH Anni a Nato Christi, 1649 . . . or an Alm.* O (in Ms only: Ms Ash. 133, fos. 166 ff.)
Anni Aerae . . . 1651 . . . a Brief Description of 1651
Now lost: 1650 (Harl. 5937, f. 17v; Ms Ash. 423, f. 123)

SHINKIN-AP-SHONE (pseud.) Shinkin-ap-Shone her Prog. for 1654

SHON-AP-LEWIS (pseud.) The Welsh-mans New Alm. and Prog. for 1648

SILVESTER, JOHN 1681. Astrological Observations and Predictions

1682	1691

Astrological and Theological Observations and Predictions for 1700 (*Bristol*)
First published 1681 (*1681*, sig. A2–v)

SLITER, ROBERT A Celestial Glasse, or Ephemeris for 1652

SMITH,— (Alm. for 1665, 1666. Now lost: Blagden, Table iv)

SMITH, JOHN Smith. 1631. A New Alm. and Prog. L

SMITH, JOHN Smith. 1652. A New Alm. and Prog.
Hemerologium Hermeticum or, a Mercuriall Calender for 1653
continued with the same title to 1656

SMITH, JOHN Speculum Anni, or a Glass . . . 1673

1674	1675

SMITH, REYNOLD Smith. 1622. A New Alm. and Prog. LLP
1625 LLP
A Table, Containing an Alm. for 72 Years (1620) brs. LS

SOFFORD, ARTHUR Sofford. 1618. A New Alm. and Prog. LLP

1619 O	1625 LLP	1631 L
1620 LLP	1626 LLP	1632 LLP
1621 O	1627 L	1633 LLP
1622 LLP	1628 O	1634 LLP
1623 LLP	1629 O	1635 LLP
1624 L	1630 L	1637 LLP

1638 LLP 1640 L
1639 LLP 1641

SOLEMNE, ANTHONY DE Eenen Calendrier Historiael (Norwich, 1570; new edition, ed. E. M. Beloe, King's Lynn, 1915)

SPARKE, MICHAEL The Money-Monger. Or the Userer's Alm. (1626)
The Treasurers Alm., or the Money-Monger (1627) (another edn. of the preceding; further edns. in 1628, 1629, 1630, 1631, 1636 and '4th edn.', 1650 * in L (Harl. 5937/215))

A Spirituall Alm., Wherein Every Christian Man and Woman May See What They Ought Daylye to Do (?1546) C

STARTOPP, THOMAS (pseud.) (Alm. and Prog. for 1568. Now lost: Bos. F95)

The States-Mans Alm: Being an Excellent New Ballad (n.d., 1688. Wing dates it 1683, but it was ostensibly written from the imperial camp outside Belgrade, which must be early in 1688)

STATHNYNNGS, CHRISTOPHER (Alm. for 1563. Now lost: Bos. F50)

STAYNRED, PHILIP Staynred. An Alm. for 1635 (Cambridge) (L t.p.)
1648

STEPHENSON, N(ICHOLAS) The Royal Alm.: or a Diary for 1675 L (in Add. Ms 41202K)
1676 1677 1678* Potter

STEPHINS, THOMAS A Newe Alm. and Prog. for 1569 Potter

Strange Predictions: or a Prophecy for 1653 brs. (satirical ballad)

STREETE, THOMAS A Double Ephemeris for 1653
Angelus Solis . . . with Astrological Predictions for 1663
A Compleat Ephemeris for 1682
continued with the same title to 1685
Now lost: 1655 (Harl. 5937, f. 17v); 1656 (*N. and Q.*, 1858, p. 134)

STROF, WALTER Strof. 1626. A New Alm. and Prog. (Cambridge series) L
1627 L

STRUTT, THOMAS The Weaver's Alm. 1688
1690
Now lost: 1689 (1690, sig. A4)

SWALLOW, THOMAS Swallow. 1628. An Alm. and Prog. (*Cambridge* series) LU
1633 LLP 1636 E†
1634 L 1638 O 1640 L
1635 L (t.p.) 1639 O

continued with the same title to 1700 as in Wing, adding 1645* OB (pr. in London)
The series lacks 1644, 1650, 1656

SWAN, JOHN An Ephemeris, or Alm. for 1657 (*Cambridge* series)
continued with the same title to 1684

TANNER, JOHN Angelus Britannicus 1657
continued with the same title to 1700. First published 1657 (*1657*, sig. A3)

TANNER, ROBERT (Alm. for 1585. Now lost: Harl. 5937, f. 8)

TAPP, JOHN The Seamans Kalender, or an Ephemeris (1602)
and many later editions, by Tapp and others: see *S.T.C.* and Wing

TAYLOR, JOHN (Greek) An Alm. for 1696
1697†
First published 1696 (*1696*, sig. Av)

TEMPLE, CHARLES An Alm. for 1656
1657

THIBAULT, JOHANNES Pronosticacyon of Maister Thibault 1530 C
1533 L (frag.)

THOMAS, JOHN Thomas 1612. A Prog. for 1612 L

THURSTON, SAMUEL Angelus Anglicanus: or a Generall Judgement of 1652

TRIGGE, S(TEPHEN) (pseud?) Most Strange and Terrible Astrological Predictions for 1684 (a satire; Wing T2275)

TRIGGE, THOMAS Speculum Astrologicum, or an Astrologicall Glasse for 1659
Calendarium Astrologicum 1660†
continued with the same title to 1700; the series lacks 1663

TURNER, THOMAS Turner 1633. An Alm. (*Cambridge* series) LLP
1634 L

TURNER, WILLIAM An Alm. for 1687
continued with the same title to 1700 as in Wing, adding 1693* L

TWELLS, WILLIAM Twells. A New Alm. for 1637 (*Cambridge* series) L (t.p.)
1638 WU† 1639 WF

TWYNE, THOMAS (An Alm. for) 1579 brs. EFB (Bos. Aa16)†
(An Alm. and) Prog. for 1585 Brox.: Ehrman
Now lost: 1581 and 1582 (Bos. F126–7), 1584 (*1585*, sig. B3), and perhaps others (Harl. 5937, f. 8v)

UPCOTE, AUGUSTINE Upcot. 1614. A New Alm. and Prog. O

1615 L	1617 LLP	1619 O
1616 O	1618 LLP	

VAUGHAN, LEWES A Newe Alm. and Prog. for 1559 CH
An Alm. and Prog. for 1560 brs. Salisbury Cathedral
A Newe Alm. and Prog. for 1561 IU

VAUX, JOHN Vaux. 1621. A New Alm. and Prog. O

1622 LLP	1630 L	1638 LLP
1623 LLP	1631 L	1642
1624 L	1632 LLP	1643
1625 LLP	1633 LLP	1648* E
1626 LLP	1634 L	1649
1627 L	1635 LLP	1652
1628 O	1636 LLP	
1629 LLP	1637 LLP	

continued with the same title to 1666, the series lacking 1663. Now lost: editions for all the missing years (1635=15th edn., 1664=44th edn.)

(VELTHOVEN), ADRIAN The Prog. of Maister Adrian 1520 CH Bos. Aal

Verus Pater, or a Bundell of Truths (1622) O

VOPELL (VOPELIUS), KASPAR An Alm. and Prog. of 1549 brs. NEK (2 variant edns.)
(—) (—) 1549 8vo Herts. R.O. (another edn. of the same work in a different format)

W.W. A New, and Merie Prog. (1623) L

W.W. The Episcopal Alm., *see* WINSTANLEY

WALTER, M., *see* RY(ff)

WATERMAN, ANDREW (?pseud.) Waterman: the Sea-mans Alm. and Prog. for 1655 (Wing in error gives 1656)

WATERS, FR. Waters. 1627. A New Alm. and Prog. (*Cambridge*) L

WATSON, ROBERT Watson. 1595. A New Alm. and Prog. LLP

1598 O	1601 L	1605 L (t.p.s. only)
1599 O (frag.)	1602 LLP	
1600 C	1604 LLP	

WEBB, THOMAS A Lasting Alm. of the Reign of the Fifth Monarchy (1660) brs. L (Wing A1862A)

WEDHOUSE, JOHN Wedhouse. 1619. An Alm. and Prog. LLP

The Welsh Mans New Alm. and Prog. for 1643

WESTHAWE, ROBERT Westhawe. 1594. An Alm. and Prog. LLP
1595 LLP

WESTLEY, JAMES An Ephemeris for the Year 1669 (The only edn.: see Blagden, Table iv)

WHALLEY, JOHN Praecognita Astrologia: or Astrological Judgements on 1688 (Wing W1531)
England's Mercury, or, an Ephemeris for 1690
Mercurius Britannicus: or, an Alm. for 1691
England's Mercury 1691 (Wing A2644) appears to be an error duplicating Mercurius Britannicus

WHARTON, GEORGE Naworth. 1641. A New Alm. and Prog.
1642
1643
1644 (*Oxford*)
1645 (*Oxford*)
Wharton. 1645. An Alm. and Prog. (*Oxford*)
No Merline, nor Mercurie: but a New Alm. 1647
1648
Hemeroscopeion, or a New Alm. for 1649
:the Loyal Alm. 1650
:a Meterologicall Diary 1651
Anni Intercalaris 1652
1653
1654
Ephemeris, or a Diary Astronomicall 1655 (pr. for T. Vere and N. Brookes)
1655 (different edn., pr. by M.J.)
Hemerologium: or a Register 1656
Calendarium Ecclesiasticum 1657
continued with the same title to 1660
Calendarium Carolinum: or a New Alm. for 1661
continued with the same title to 1666
According to Wood, Wharton issued alms. from c. 1637, but there is no evidence to support this (note on Wood's copy of Wharton, 1648, in O). Wing gives a Cal. Carolinum for 1660 (Wing A2651); this is an error, the series changing its title only from 1661

(WHEELER, MAURICE) The Oxford Alm. 1673 8vo (*Oxford*) O OB
(—) (The Oxford) Alm. for the Year of Our Lord God 1673* brs. O (Ms Carte 114, f. 546) (perhaps=Wing A1247B)
(—) The Oxford Alm. for 1674 brs. (*Oxford* series)
(—) —1676
continued with the same title to 1700. Wing gives an edn. for 1675 (A2678), for which no alm. was published

WHITE, JOHN White. 1613. A New Alm. and Prog. O

1614 LLP	1623 LLP	1632 LLP
1615 O	1624 L	1633 LLP
1616 LLP	1625 LLP	1634 L
1617 LLP	1626 LLP	1636 LLP
1618 LLP	1627 L	1637 O
1619 O	1628 O	1638 LLP
1620 LLP	1629 O	1639 LLP
1621 O	1630 L	1640 L
1622 LLP	1631 L	

continued with the same title to 1651, lacking 1644, 1645, 1650. First published 1613 (*1613*, sig. C6v). The edn. for 1653 (Wing A2715) is by William White

WHITE, JOHN White. 1677. The Country-mans Kalender

WHITE, THOMAS White. 1677. A New Alm.
continued with the same title to 1700. Wing lists an edn. for 1670, at L, which must refer to William White

WHITE, WILLIAM A Brief and Easie Alm. (1650) brs.†
White. 1652. A New Alm.
continued with the same title to 1676, lacking 1663. Wing gives an alm. for 1651 (A2738) which is presumably that of John White

WHITING, JAMES An Ephemeris for the Year 1669 (*Cambridge*)

WILKINSON, THOMAS Wilkinson. 1643. A New Alm. and Prog.
Wilkinson, 1658. A Kalender and Prog.
1659. Apollo Northamptoniensis
Mercurius Northamptoniensis 1660†
Philosophia Coelestis: or an Alm. for 1663†
First published 1643 (*1643*, sig. B8v)

WILLIAMS, GEORGE (Alm. and Prog. for 1558, 1559, 1562, 1567. Now lost: Bos. F22, 29, 62, 81)

WILSON, JEFFREY Wilson 1625. A New Alm. and Prog. LLP

1626 O	1633 LLP	1634 L

WING, JOHN (Greek) An Alm. for 1680 (*Cambridge* series)
continued with the same title to 1699; lacks 1700, which is listed by Wing as at O

WING, VINCENT An Alm. and Prog. for 1641
Wing. 1642. An Alm. and Prog.

1643	1647
1646* Potter	1648

Speculum Uranicum 1649

(Greek) An Alm. and Prog. for 1651
(Greek) An Alm. and Prog. for 1652
(Greek) An Alm. and Prog. for 1653
continued with the same title to 1672
(—) Wing 1648. Alm. for the Year 1648* 8vo (*Cambridge*) OB
An Alm. for 1667 brs. series
1680* P.R.O. (see *C.S.P.D., 1679–80*, p. 364)
1682
1684†
1690* LG
1692
1693
An Ephemerides of the Coelestiall Motions for vii Years 1652–8 (1652)
An Ephemerides . . . for xiii Years (1659–71) (1658)
Wing's Ephemeris for Thirty Years (1669)

(WINSTANLEY, WILLIAM) An Episcopal Alm. for 1674
continued with the same title to 1678
(—) Poor Robin. 1664. An Alm. after a New Fashion
continued with the same title to 1700
(—) Poor Robin. Or a Yea and Nay Alm. 1677†
(—) A Yea and Nay Alm. 1678
(—) A Yea and Nay Alm. 1679, 'by H.N.'
(—) —1680 (4th edn.)
(—) The Protestant Alm. for 1668
(—) —1669
(—) —1680
continued with the same title to 1685, and revived 1689–1700

WINTER, FRIG. Winter. 1633. An Alm. for 1633 (*Cambridge* series) LLP
1634 O
1635 L (t.p.)
1638 O
1646

WINTON, ALEXANDER (Alm. for 1638. Now lost: Harl. 5937. f. 17. *See* Appendix I)

WITHER, GEORGE (pseud.) The Doubtful Alm. (1647) (Not a true alm. and disclaimed by Wither)

WOOD, ROBERT A New Al-moon-ac for Ever* brs. (1680?) L
A Specimen of a New Al-moon-ac for Ever (1680)
Novus Annus Luni-solaris (1680)

WOODHOUSE, JOHN Woodhouse. 1610. A Plaine Alm. and Prog. LLP
1611 L
1612 L
1613 O
1614 LLP
1615 L
1616 LLP
1617 LLP
1618 LLP
Woodhouse. 1619. An Alm. and Prog. O

1620 LLP	1627 L	1634 L
1621 O	1628 O	1635 LLP
1622 LLP	1629 LLP	1636 LLP
1623 LLP	1630 L	1637 LLP
1624 L	1631 L	1638 O
1625 LLP	1632 LLP	1639 O
1626 LLP	1633 LLP	1640 L

continued with the same title to 1700 as in Wing, adding 1652* LCS. The series lacks 1644–5, 1650–1, 1656, 1661, 1663, 1668

WOODHOUSE, WILLIAM Woodhouse. 1602. An Alm. and Prog. for 1602 LLP

1604 L	1607 O
1606 LLP	1608 L

Now lost: 1601 (*C.S.P.D.*, 1589–1601, p. 585)

WOODWARD, DANIEL Vox Uraniae or an Alm. for 1682
continued with the same title to 1688
Ephemeris Absoluta 1689
continued with the same title to 1700; the series lacks 1699

WYBERD, JOHN Wyberd. 1635. An Alm. and Prog. LLP
1636 LLP
Synopsis Anni Christi 1637 (*Oxford*) O

Abbreviations

*	Additions to Wing's revised list
†	Works not directly consulted
A.D.B.	*Allgemeine Deutsche Biographie*
Allen, *Star-Crossed Renaissance*	D. C. Allen, *The Star-Crossed Renaissance. The Quarrel about Astrology and its Influence in England* (1966)
Arber	E. Arber, ed., *A Transcript of the Registers of the Company of Stationers of London, 1554–1640 A.D.* (1875–94)
Armytage, *Obituary*	*Obituary prior to 1800*, ed. Sir G. J. Armytage (Harleian Soc., 1899–1901)
Aubrey, *Brief Lives*	J. Aubrey, *Brief Lives*, ed. A Clark (Oxford, 1898)
B.A.R.	*British Auction Records*
B.L.	British Library (formerly British Museum), London
Blagden	C. Blagden, *The Stationers' Company: a History, 1403–1959* (1960)
Blagden, 'Distribution'	C. Blagden, 'The Distribution of Almanacks in the Second Half of the Seventeenth Century', *Studies in Bibliography*, xi (1958)
Blagden, 'Thomas Carnan'	C. Blagden, 'Thomas Carnan and the Almanack Monopoly', *Studies in Bibliography*, xiv (1961)
Bodl.	Bodleian Library, Oxford
Bollème, *Almanachs populaires*	G. Bollème, *Les Almanachs populaires aux xvii*e *et xviii*e *siècles* (Paris, 1696)
Bosanquet	E. F. Bosanquet, *English Printed Almanacks and Prognostications. A Bibliographical History to the Year 1600* (1917)
Bosanquet, 'Further Addenda'	E. F. Bosanquet, 'Notes on Further Addenda to English Printed Almanacks and Prognostications to 1600', *The Library*, 4th ser., xviii (1937–8)
Bowden, 'Scientific Revolution'	M. E. Bowden, 'The Scientific Revolution in Astrology: The English Reformers, 1558–1686', Yale Ph.D. thesis, 1974

Brox.	The Broxbourne collection (partly housed in the Bodleian, partly in the possession of Mr. John Ehrman, Sloane House, 149 Old Church Street, London SW3)
brs.	broadsheet; almanac published in sheet form
C	Cambridge University
Cant.	Canterbury Cathedral
CCA	Gonville and Caius College, Cambridge
CE	Emmanuel College, Cambridge
CH	Huntington Library, San Marino, California
CN	Newberry Library, Chicago
Coley, *M.A.E./M.A.J.*	H. Coley, *Merlini Anglici Ephemeris/Merlinus Anglicus Junior*
CS	St. John's College, Cambridge
C.S.P.D.	*Calendar of State Papers, Domestic*
CT	Trinity College, Cambridge
D.N.B.	*Dictionary of National Biography*
DT	Trinity College, Dublin
E	Edinburgh University
EFB	The collection of E. F. Bosanquet, mostly sold at Sotheby's in January 1944; much is now in the Potter collection
E.H.R.	*English Historical Review*
Ellis, *Orig. Letters*	*Original Letters of Eminent Literary Men*, ed. Sir Henry Ellis (Camden Soc., xxiii, 1843)
Emden, *Register*	A. B. Emden, *A Biographical Register of the University of Oxford, A.D. 1501 to 1540* (Oxford, 1974)
ep. ded.	epistle dedicatory
Foster, *Al. Oxon.*	J. Foster, *Alumni Oxonienses: the Members of the University of Oxford, 1500–1714* (Oxford, 1891–2)
Frank, *English Newspaper*	J. Frank, *The Beginnings of the English Newspaper* (Cambridge, Mass., 1961)
Goodall	C. Goodall, *The Royal College of Physicians of London . . . and an Historical Account of the College's Proceedings against Empiricks and Unlicensed Practisers* (1684)
GU	University of Glasgow
Hellmann, *Versuch*	G. Hellmann, *Versuch einer Geschichte der Wettervorhersage im XVI Jahrhundert* (Abhandlungen der preussischen Akademie der Wissenschaften, Jahrgang 1924, I)

Heywood, *Three Papers*	A. Heywood, *Three Papers on English Printed Almanacks* (1904)
HH	Haigh Hall, Wigan
H.L.Q.	*Huntington Library Quarterly*
H.M.C.	Historical Manuscripts Commission
Hone, *Year Book*	W. Hone, *The Year Book* (1832)
IU	University of Illinois, Urbana
Jenkins, 'Welsh Books'	G. H. Jenkins, 'Welsh Books and Religion, 1660–1730', University of Wales, Aberystwyth, Ph.D., 1974
Josten, *Ashmole*	*Elias Ashmole (1617–92). His Autobiographical and Historical Notes. . . .*, ed. C. H. Josten (Oxford, 1966)
L	British Library, London
LG	Guildhall, London
Lilly, *Life and Times*	*William Lilly's History of his Life and Times from the Year 1602 to 1681, Written by Himself* (1715), edited by K. M. Briggs under the title *The Last of the Astrologers* (1794)
LLP	Lambeth Palace, London
Longstaffe, *High Commission*	*The Acts of the High Commission Court within the Diocese of Durham*, ed. W. H. D. Longstaffe (Surtees Soc., xxxiv, 1858)
LS	Society of Antiquaries, London
LT	British Library, Thomason collection
LU	London University
LUC	University College, London
McKerrow, *Dictionary, 1557–1640*	R. B. McKerrow, *A Dictionary of Printers and Booksellers . . . 1557–1640* (1910)
Matthews, *Calamy Revised*	A. G. Matthews, *Calamy Revised* (Oxford, 1934)
MH	Harvard University, Massachusetts
Morrison, *Index, 1641–1700*	P. G. Morrison, *Index of Printers, Publishers and Booksellers . . . 1641–1700* (Charlottesville, Virginia, 1955)
MR	John Rylands Library, Manchester
Munk, *Physicians*	W. Munk, *The Roll of the Royal College of Physicians of London* (1861)
N. and Q.	*Notes and Queries*
NEK	University of Newcastle
Nicolson, 'New Astronomy'	M. H. Nicolson, 'English Almanacs and the "New Astronomy"', *Annals of Science*, iv (1939–40)
O	Bodleian Library, Oxford

OB	Balliol College, Oxford
OBR	Brasenose College, Oxford
OC	Christ Church, Oxford
OCC	Corpus Christi College, Oxford
OJ	St. John's College, Oxford
ON	New College, Oxford
OP	Oxford University Press
OT	Trinity College, Oxford
OWA	Wadham College, Oxford
par. reg.	parish register
Phil. Trans.	*Philosophical Transactions of the Royal Society*
PHS	Historical Society of Pennsylvania, Philadelphia
Plomer, *Dictionary, 1641–67*	H. R. Plomer, *A Dictionary of Booksellers and Printers . . . 1641 to 1667* (1907)
Potter	Collection of Mrs. W. Potter, Lambley House, Woodborough, Notts.
PRO	Public Record Office
Raach, *Directory*	J. H. Raach, ed., *A Directory of English Country Physicians, 1603–1643* (1962)
R.O.	Record Office
S.C.	The Company of Stationers, London
Smyth, *Obituary*	*The Obituary of Richard Smyth*, ed. Sir Henry Ellis (Camden Soc., 1849)
Soc. Gen.	The Society of Genealogists, London
S.T.C.	A. W. Pollard and G. R. Redgrave, *A Short-title Catalogue of Books Printed in England . . . 1475–1640* (1926); 2nd edn., vol. ii, I–Z, ed. K. Pantzer (1976)
Taylor, *Hanoverian Practitioners* (*HP* in Appendix I)	E. G. R. Taylor, *The Mathematical Practitioners of Hanoverian England, 1714–1840* (Cambridge, 1966)
Taylor, *Practitioners* (Taylor in Appendix I)	E. G. R. Taylor, *The Mathematical Practitioners of Tudor and Stuart England* (Cambridge, 1954)
Thomas	K. V. Thomas, *Religion and the Decline of Magic* (1971)
Thorndike, *Magic*	L. Thorndike, *A History of Magic and Experimental Science* (New York, 1923–58)
t.p.	title-page
T.R.H.S.	*Transactions of the Royal Historical Society*
Ushaw	St. Cuthbert's College, Ushaw, Durham
V.C.H.	*Victoria County History*

Venn, *Al. Cant.*	J. and J. A. Venn, *Alumni Cantabrigienses . . . to 1751* (Cambridge, 1922–7)
WC	Wellesley College, Mass.
West.	Westminster Abbey
WF	Folger Library, Washington
Williams, *English Journalism*	J. B. Williams, *History of English Journalism* (1908)
Wing	D. Wing, *Short-title Catalogue of Books Printed in England . . . 1641–1700* (New York, 1945–51); 2nd edn., vol. i (New York, 1972)
Wood, *Ath. Oxon.*	A. Wood, *Athenae Oxonienses*, ed. P. Bliss (Oxford, 1813–20)
Wood, *Life and Times*	*The Life and Times of Anthony Wood, Antiquary, of Oxford, 1632–95*, ed. A. Clark (Oxford Hist. Soc., 1891–1900)
WU	University of Wisconsin, Madison
Y	Yale University, New Haven, Conn.
Zech-du Biez, *Almanachs*	G. Zech-du Biez, *Les Almanachs belges* (Braine-le-Comte, 1902–4)

Note I have generally modernized the spelling of quotations. Books cited were published in London, unless otherwise stated. I have abbreviated references in the notes to almanacs to the author and year, except where a compiler issued two or more editions for the same year. Full titles can be found in the Bibliography (or, for post-1700 almanacs, in Appendix I).

Notes

Chapter 1 Introduction (*pages* 15–22)

1. L. Thorndike, 'The True Place of Astrology in the History of Science', *Isis*, 46 (1955), pp. 273–8. There is a vast literature on astrology, including Thorndike, *Magic*; T. O. Wedel, *The Mediaeval Attitude toward Astrology* (Yale, 1920); Allen, *Star-Crossed Renaissance* and M. H. Nicolson, *The Breaking of the Circle* (New York, 1962). For some further titles see Thomas (pp. 283n–4n), chapters 10–12 of whose work provide an excellent account of the social and intellectual position of astrology in early modern England.
2. Booker, 1644, sig. B2 (2nd signature). Nicolson, op. cit., ch. 1, contains a good description of the micro/macrocosm theory and its place in literature.
3. Thorndike, *Magic*, vol. v.
4. For whom see Thorndike, *Magic*, iv, ch. xlii.
5. Ibid., ii, pp. 452, 672–3, 896–7, 953–4; iii, pp. 411; iv, pp. 105–6, 147, 249, 321, 416, 441, 452; v, p. 294; vi, pp. 108, 176, 201; J. Butler, *A Brief (but true) Account of the Certain Year, Moneth, Day and Minute of the Birth of Jesus Christ* (1671), p. 258; J. G(regory), *Notes and Observations upon Some Passages of Scripture* (1646), p. 152.
6. Thorndike, *Magic*, iv, pp. 141–2.
7. Ibid., iv, chs. xli, lvii, lviii; S. de Phares, *Recueil des plus célèbres Astrologues*, ed. E. Wickersheimer (Paris, 1929), *passim.*
8. Thorndike, *Magic*, iv, pp. 425, 560–1; v, ch. xiii, esp. pp. 256, 259; Phares, *Recueil*, pp. 260–1, 263.
9. E. Defrance, *Catherine de Médicis: ses astrologues et ses magiciens-envoûteurs* (Paris, 1911), *passim.*
10. Thorndike, *Magic*, vii, pp. 479; Allen, *Star-Crossed Renaissance*, p. 52.
11. *Calendar of State Papers, Venetian, 1555–6*, vi (i), p. 376; R. J. W. Evans, *Rudolf II and his World: a Study in Intellectual History* (Oxford, 1973).
12. Thorndike, *Magic*, vii, pp. 99–100; *Catastrophe Mundi: or Merlin Reviv'd* (1683), sig. A2.
13. Phares, *Recueil*, pp. 252, 257, 261. Phares spells the name as 'Wuelx'.
14. Thomas, pp. 289–90, 312–13; Taylor, *Practitioners*, pp. 165, 170–1; *D.N.B.*, Dee, Lambe, Robins; Goodall, p. 400; J. Gadbury, *The Novice-Astrologer* (1660), p. 3; *Mercurius Elencticus*, 3 (12–19 November, 1647), p. 22.
15. Thomas, p. 288; Thorndike, *Magic*, v, ch. xi. An apparent exception is a tract on 1524, possibly a prognostication, issued by John Siberch, the Cambridge printer, of which a fragment survives at Ushaw College.
16. P. French, *John Dee. The World of an Elizabethan Magus* (1972); Bowden, 'Scientific Revolution', pp. 62–78.
17. See below, Chapter 6.
18. For this section see Thomas, chs. 2, 3 and *passim.*
19. J. Selden, *Table-Talk*, ed. S. H. Reynolds (Oxford, 1892), p. 130.
20. Below, p. 143 and n. 74; Thomas, pp. 378–81.
21. Thomas, pp. 634–5.
22. Ibid., p. 632.
23. Below, pp. 79–80, 166.
24. Thomas, pp. 305–22; below, pp. 72–88.
25. W. Sprigge, *Philosophicall Essayes* (1657), pp. 40–2; below, pp. 204–8.

26. The point was made by the Restoration dramatist, John Wilson: *The Cheats*, ed. M. C. Nahm (Oxford, 1935), I, iii.
27. J. Securis, *A Detection and Querimonie* (1566), sig. C3v, 5v; W. Perkins, *Foure Great Lyers* (1585), sig. F6v–7v; *The Tatler*, ed. G. A. Aitken (1898–9), iv, p. 227; N. Ward, *The London Spy*, ed. A. L. Hayward (1927), pp. 101–4; T. Brown, *Amusements*, ed. A. L. Hayward (1927), pp. 80, 336–7. One Jones, a Restoration physician of Covent Garden, advertised himself as 'the English Physician' as a distinguishing characteristic: B.L. 546 d 44, nos. 3, 4.

Chapter 2 The Development of the Almanac (*pages* 23–66)

1. Allestree, 1622, sig. A8.
2. Blagden, 'Distribution', Table 1. J. C. Somerville in *The Library*, 5th ser. xxix (1974), pp. 221–5, suggests that though New Testaments and Bibles sold in smaller numbers they were kept longer and reached an equally wide market.
3. T. Brown, *Amusements Serious and Comical*, ed. A. L. Hayward (1927), p. 416. The Devil was said to prefer Coley's almanacs.
4. *Bishop Percy's Folio Manuscripts*, ii (1868), pp. 24–5; the almanacs are those of Booker, Pond, Rivers, Swallow, Dove and Dade. Cf. a similar and earlier set of puns in Booker, 1632, sig. B8.
5. e.g. Allestree in Jonson's *The Magnetic Lady*, Bretnor and Gresham in his *The Devil is an Asse*. Literary allusions to almanacs are discussed in Allen, *Star-Crossed Renaissance*, ch. 4 and T. Tomkis, *Albumazar*, ed. H. G. Dick (Berkeley and Los Angeles, 1944), introd.
6. John Gadbury, John Tanner and others also included portraits. The earlier compiler, William Cunningham, had done so in 1558.
7. J. Crow, 'Some Jacobean Catch-Phrases and some Light on Thomas Bretnor', in *Elizabethan and Jacobean Studies*, ed. H. Davis and H. Gardner (Oxford, 1959), p. 25; T. Nashe, *Works*, ed. R. B. McKerrow and F. P. Wilson (Oxford, 1958), iii, p. 64.
8. Chamberlaine, 1628, sig. Bv; E. Worsop, *A Discoverie of Sundrie Errours* (1582), sig. F2, 3. A newspaper editor in 1655 wondered whether the duration of the first Protectorate Parliament would be calculated by the 'almanac account' (calendar month) or lunar month: *Mercurius Politicus* (4–11 January 1655), p. 5046.
9. By Thomas Powell and Michael Sparke respectively.
10. Lilly, *Life and Times*, p. 42; R. Gell, *A Sermon Touching God's Government of the World by Angels* (1650), p. 37.
11. Gadbury, 1692, sig. C5.
12. R. Whitlock, *Observations on the Present Manners of the English* (1654), p. 250.
13. Coley, *Nuncius*, 1682, sig. C3v; Coley, *M.A.E.*, 1684, sig. C3v.
14. Saunders, 1673, sig. A8. The story originated from *Falcon* which reached Plymouth on 22 October 1671, and also appears in W. Andrews, *The Yearly Intelligencer* (1673), p. 6. For the mermaid, which predicted an English victory in the Anglo-Dutch war, see J.A., *An Almanac, 1666* (Aberdeen, 1666), sig. B4v.
15. Booker, 1664, sig. C3v. The origin of the story was perhaps Napier's charge that the pope received 40,000 ducats a year from papal brothels (Napier, *A Plaine Discovery of the Whole Revelation* (Edinburgh, 1593), p. 45; repeated in *The Popes Spectacles*, an appendix to the *Works of Thomas Brightman* (1644), p. 1080. The brothels later increased to 45,000 (*Protestant Almanack*, 1698, sig. B2).
16. See the almanacs of Pond, Keene, Bretnor, Dauncy, Allestree and Mathew in 1612 and subsequent years; the feuds of the 1640s are discussed by Rusche in *E.H.R.*, lxxx (1965), and below, pp. 72 ff. There were equally rancorous disputes among the early Scottish, Welsh and Irish compilers.
17. Partridge, 1692, sig. C8v, and 1699, sig. C7v. Parker made a qualified denial in his *Ephemeris*, 1699, esp. sig. B3–4v.
18. *The Last Wills and Testaments of J. Partridge* . . . (1716); see below, p. 244.

19. R. Plot, *The Natural History of Staffordshire* (Oxford, 1686), pp. 418–32 gives a full description.
20. *Gesamtkatalog der Wiegendrucke*, ii (Leipzig, 1926), pp. 15ff.; Thorndike, *Magic*, iv, ch. lviii.
21. Phares, *Recueil*, pp. 267, 268; *A.D.B.*, xvii, pp. 510–11; Bosanquet, pp. 17–19, 193; Laet, 1533 (cropped; no pagination).
22. Thorndike, *Magic*, iv, pp. 444ff.
23. C. A. J. Armstrong, 'An Italian Astrologer at the Court of Henry VII', in *Italian Renaissance Studies*, ed. E. F. Jacob, 1960, pp. 433–54. Parron mentioned a prognostication of 1473 concerning England (ibid., p. 438), but it was probably handwritten or printed abroad.
24. *S.T.C.*, 388 (of which 392 is another copy); described by Bosanquet, pp. 15–16, 77–8. The illuminated copy is B.L., Add. Ms 17367.
25. Robins, 'A New Calendar', in Kent R. O., U1121 Z1; he says that it was designed to be printed, but there is no evidence of publication. Bodl. Mss Ash. 384 (Forman) and 242 (Heydon); Ms Bodl. 671 (Lydiat), based on Lydiat's work on chronology (Ms Bodl. 662), which he had sought to have published (Ms Bodl. 313, fos. 25-v, 96). On Robins see Thorndike, *Magic*, v. pp. 320–1, and for Lydiat see *D.N.B.* See also the perpetual almanac of Oswald Whittington (1584), dedicated to his patron, Sir Thomas Fairfax: B.L. Ms Sloane 18602.
26. Frende, 1585, sig. B2; Silvester, 1681, sig. A2v.
27. Bomelius, 1567, t.p.; for him see *D.N.B.* and Appendix I; B.L. Ms Royal B17 xxxviii (Nostradamus).
28. P. Morgan, 'George Hartgill: an Elizabethan Parson-Astronomer and his Library', *Annals of Science*, 24 (1968).
29. Laet, 1533; 1520 (Bos. x[a]).
30. Thibault, 1533; Salomon, 1543; Brothyel, 1545.
31. For examples see Peter of Moorbeck, Scute, Heuring, Vopell, Apian, Schönfeld, Gasser, Gesner, Seyfridt and Adrian (Velthoven), from whose edition for 1520 the quotation is drawn.
32. H. O. Sommer's edition of *The Kalender of Shepherdes* (1892) reprints the editions of 1503 and 1506 and discusses the others; Hopton, op. cit., sig. A5.
33. For the Gospels see e.g. Vopell, 1549; for good and evil days see Thomas, pp. 615–16, 622–3, and below, p. 210
34. Gasser, 1546, sig. C7–D.
35. Brothyel, 1545, sig. Cv.
36. Laet, 1517 (frag.); Bosanquet, p. 87.
37. See on this subject Thomas, esp. ch. 13, and G. R. Elton, *Policy and Police* (Cambridge, 1972), ch. 2; for the buoyancy of the market, see 'The Day-Book of John Dorne, 1520', ed. F. Madan, *Collecteana*, i (Oxford Historical Society, 1885).
38. Bosanquet, 'Further Addenda', pp. 41–5, 56. This item was sold at Sotheby's in 1944; it passed into the collection of Mrs. W. Potter (see below, p. 348).
39. Borde, 1545, t.p.
40. Bosanquet, p. 5; for Askham see *D.N.B.* and Appendix I.
41. *The Rules and Ryght Ample Documentes Touching the Use and Practise of the Common Almanackes* (1558), trans. from French by H. Baker.
42. On control of the press see below, pp. 46–50; on the Company see Blagden, chs. 1–2.
43. W. Fulke, *Antiprognosticon* (1560), sig. A8; see S. V. Larkey, 'Astrology and Politics in the first Years of Elizabeth's Reign', *Bull. Inst. for the Hist. of Medicine*, iii (1935), pp. 171–86.
44. Nicolson, 1563, t.p.; Stephins, 1569, sig. A (2nd signature); for the injunctions see F. S. Siebert, *Freedom of the Press in England 1476–1776* (Urbana, 1952), p. 57; W. W. Greg, *London Publishing 1550 to 1650* (Oxford, 1956), pp. 44, 47.
45. Bosanquet, p. 195n; Larkey, art. cit., pp. 185–6.
46. Bomelius, 1567, sig. E3v–4v, and Appendix I; Stephins, 1569, used the same tactic.
47. Bosanquet, pp. 41–2, 197.
48. Bosanquet, pp. 9, 42; Blagden, pp. 75, 234–6.
49. On the history of the figure see H. Bober, 'The zodiacal miniature of the *Tres Riches Heures* of the Duke of Berry—its sources and meaning', *Journal of the Warburg and Courtauld Institute*, xi (1940); see also below, p. 231.

50. Title-page.
51. Graphaeus, 1598, sig. A4v; de Billy, 1604, p. 24 and *passim.*
52. A. Magini, *The Italian Prophecier* (1622), esp. pp. 16, 22. His *A Strange and Wonderfull Prognostication* appeared in 1624.
53. Abenezrah, *An Everlasting Prognostication* (?1620); see T. Percy, *Reliques of Ancient English Poetry* (1885), iii, pp. 291–6.
54. *The Pronostycacion for ever of Erra Pater* (?1535), sig. A4v–5; see Thomas, pp. 295–6, and details in the proofs of *S.T.C.*, 2nd edn., vol. i.
55. J. Melton, *Astrologaster* (1620), p. 12; J. Booker, *Mercurius Coelicus: or a Caveat* (1644), p. 1; G. Wharton, *Mercurius-Coelicus-Mastix* (1644), p. 3. The anonymous *Verus Pater* (1622) was of course a play on this mistranslation.
56. See *S.T.C.*, 2nd edn., and Wing for the numerous editions.
57. By one J.A.; t.p., sig. A2v and *passim.*
58. W. Oakeshott, 'Sir Walter Ralegh's Library', *The Library*, 5th ser., xxiii (1968), p. 326.
59. Bollème, *Almanachs populaires*, pp. 18–19; Laet, 1520, frag.; Scute, 1544, sig. A2 (replying to one Henry Swart). For the controversy over astrology see the works of Allen, Thomas and Kocher, and below, Chapter 5.
60. Fulke, *Antiprognosticon*, sig. B and *passim*; Coxe, *A Short Treatise* (1561), sig. A5v–6.
61. N. Allen, *The Astronomers Game* (?1569), sig. *4–v and *passim*; the victims appear to have been Buckminster, Securis, and Low. The work is not in *S.T.C.* but a copy exists at Corpus Christi College, Oxford.
62. E. Worsop, *A Discoverie of Sundries Errours* (1582), sig. F4v.
63. W. P(erkins), *Four Great Lyers* (1585), viz. the almanac-makers B(uckminster), F(rende), T(wyne) (or perhaps Tanner) and D(ade). For Perkins' authorship see H. G. Dick in *The Library*, 4th ser., xix (1938–9); it was generally known in the seventeenth century: see, e.g., Dauncy, 1615, sig. A2; W. Lilly, *Englands Propheticall Merline* (1644), sig. A4; Booker, 1648, sig. C; W. Ramesey, *A Reply to a Scandalous Pamphlet* (1650), p. 2; W. Rowland, *Judicial Astrology* (1652), pp. 244–85; G. Atwell, *An Apology* (1660), pp. 42–3.
64. See below, pp. 132, 140.
65. Fouleweather, 1591, sig. A4v; see further pp. 231–5, below.
66. R. Stewart-Brown, 'A Chester Bookseller's Lawsuit of 1653', *The Library*, 4th ser. ix (1928–9), pp. 57–8. The solitary work was by Nathaniel Homes.
67. Lloyd, 1585, sig. B5; see also below, p. 114.
68. The last, by Thomas Strutt, in fact contained no specialized information, and did not sell well (Strutt, 1690, sig. A4).
69. Excise rates given by N. Greenwood, 1690; the others were by Vincent Prince and Robert Gardner respectively.
70. See further below, pp. 126, 245–7.
71. Nashe, *Works*, i, p. 167; iii, p. 72; *Miscellaneous Works of Sir Thomas Overbury*, ed. E. F. Rimbault (1890), p. 93; Blagden, 'Distribution', Table 1; advertisement for *The Princely Almanack*, 1678, B. L. Harl. 5937 (183).
72. The last three titles were all probably by William Winstanley; quotation from *The Protestant Almanack*, 1682, sig. Av. See below, Chapter 5, part iii.
73. 1680, sig. Av.
74. Digges, 1556, brs.; Alleyn, 1607, sig. C6v–8; Tanner, 1683, sig. Av.
75. See Chapter 7, below.
76. Saunders, 1690 and 1700 for an example of each.
77. See Chapter 7, below.
78. Dauncy, 1614, sig. A5; S. Butler, *Hudibras*, ed. H. G. Bohn (1903), p. 227; Lilly, *Life and Times*, p. 26 ('Here lieth buried Sir Thomas Jay, Knight,/Who being dead, I upon his grave did shite.').
79. Fouleweather, sig. A4v; Securis, 1581, sig. C2v; Nunnes, 1662, sig. C2; Andrews, 1673, sig. A5.
80. Lilly, 1677, sig. B7 (Bodl. copy, Rawl. Alm. 51).
81. See below, Chapter 5, and Thomas, ch. 12.
82. Lilly, 1675, sig. B7; Andrews, 1675, sig. A6; Wing, 1682, sig. B5; Russell, 1661, A3.
83. Securis, 1569, sig. A2v (2nd signature); Booker, 1632, sig. B5 (in fact a vague prediction

of the death of kings and fall of kingdoms); *D.N.B.*, Booker; R. Edlin, *Prae-Nuncius Syderius* (1664), p. 42.

84. Wing, 1658, sig. B4; Gadbury, 1668, sig. C5; Andrews, 1667, sig. C2v.
85. Thomas, pp. 336–7; Booker, *A Bloody Irish Almanack* (1646), sig. A3; Baston, 1657, sig. B7; Lilly, 1677, sig. A2v; Gadbury, 1668, sig. A2v; many other examples could be cited.
86. Lilly, 1649, sig. A4; idem, 1660, sig. A2; 1661, sig. A2; 1668, sig. A2.
87. Gadbury, 1667, sig. A2; 1668, sig. A2v; 1670, sig. A3-v.
88. Coley, 1694, sig. C8; cf. Thomas, pp. 336–8.
89. Blagden, pp. 101–4, 145, 199–201; see also S. C. Roberts, *The Cambridge University Press, 1521–1921* (Cambridge, 1921).
90. Blagden, pp. 104, 195–9, 201–4; J. Johnson and S. Gibson, *Print and Privilege at Oxford to the Year 1700* (Oxford, 1946), *passim*; H. Carter, *A History of the Oxford University Press*, i (Oxford, 1975). An earlier breach was the series of almanacs by Wm. Burton at Oxford in the 1650s; see Bibliography, above, and Wood, *Ath. Oxon.*, iii, col. 440.
91. *Remarks and Collections of Thomas Hearne*, ed. C. Doble et al. (Oxford Hist. Soc., 1885–1921), iii, p. 96 (22 pseudonymous authors, e.g. 'Walter Lilly'); *Reliquiae Hearnianae*, ed. P. Bliss (1869), iii, p. 316 (I owe this latter reference to Mr. H. Carter.) Only 'Ben. Pond's' edition appears to survive.
92. *C.S.P.D., 1663–4*, p. 369; Blagden, pp. 193–5; Gadbury, 1676, t.p.; *English Reports*, 86, pp. 865–6 (cf. no. 84, p. 1015; 98, p. 254). For 1677 Seymour issued an almanac by 'John White' and *Poor Robin or a Yea and Nay Almanack*.
93. S. C., Court Book E, 1674–83, f. 97; 'Thomas Jones the Almanacer', *Journ. of the Welsh Bibl. Soc.*, i, ii (1915/18); *Dictionary of Welsh Biography*; Jenkins, 'Welsh Books', esp. pp. 527–9, 654–63. I would like to thank Dr. Jenkins for his help with early Welsh almanacs.
94. Bodl. Ms Rawl. D317, f. llv; Ellis, *Orig. Letters*, p. 187.
95. S.C., Court Book D, 1654–79, f. 151.
96. Ibid., f. 226v. The work was no doubt a first edition of *The Royal Almanack*, by Nicholas Stephenson, who acknowledges Moore's help on the title-page; issues survive for 1675–8, published by the Company. Cf. S.C., Journal Book, f. 57v.
97. W. W. Greg and E. Boswell, eds., *Records of the Court of the Stationers' Company 1576–1602* (1930), p. 56; W. A. Jackson, ed., *Records of the Court of the Stationers' Company 1602 to 1640* (1957), pp. 142, 293–4, 375, 379, 481; S.C., Liber A, f. 99; Court Book C, fos. 180, 273v, 286, 297v; ibid., D, fos. 87v, 189v, 190v; ibid., E, f. 153.
98. S.C., Court Book E, f. 251–v.
99. Ibid., F., f. 47v. (The prisoner was a John Gellibrand.)
100. Booker, 1644, sig. B8 (the perpetrator was John Aston, a sometime draper).
101. Andrews, 1683, sig. Av; ibid., 1684, sig. C8; Bowker, 1676, sig. C8v; Wing, 1649, sig. C8v; Partridge, 1691, sig. Av; cf. also S.C., Journal Book, f. 11 (counterfeit Culpeper 1653) and f. 75 (*Protestant Almanack*, 1676).
102. W. Lele, pseud., *An English Ephemeris* (1650), dated by Thomason 11 October 1649; Lilly, 1650, sig. Av (accusing 'the Boy-printer, J.R.' of responsibility).
103. e.g. R. Desmus (i.e. S. Sheppard), *Merlinus Anonymous*, 1653–5; *The Mad-merry Merlin*, 1654; *The Royall Merlin*, 1655.
104. S.C., Court Book D, fos. 67v, 68v; *Poor Robin*, 1676, sig. Av.
105. *Montelion*, 1662, sig. A4v; S.C., Court Book D, f. 68v.
106. S.C., Court Book D, f. 69; S.C., Journal Book, fos. 33v, 40v, 41 and *passim*; Blagden, 'Distribution', Table 1. For Winstanley's authorship see Appendix I. A mock chronology had earlier appeared in Desmus, *Merlinus Anonymous*.
107. S.C., Court Book F, f. 65v; Blagden, p. 172. For Hills' erratic career see *D.N.B.*, corrected by Plomer, *Dictionary 1641–1667*, pp. 98–9, and idem., *Dictionary 1668–1725*, pp. 154–5.
108. Blagden, 'Distribution', note to Table 1.
109. S.C., Journal Book, fos. 11, 75, 109, 183v, 184v; Court Book F, fos. 109v, 263, 270; Blagden, 173, 235. On the licensing laws see F. Siebert, *Freedom of the Press in England, pp. 1476–1776* (Urbana, 1952).
110. S.C., Court Book D, f. 123–v; Blagden, 'Distribution', pp. 111–12, 116 and Table 1.
111. S.C., Court Book F, f. 270.

112. S.C., Court Book D, f. 341v; Partridge, 1680, sig. C8; idem., 1681, sig. A3v. At the beginning of the century Pond completed his edition for 1605 on 20 May 1604 (1605, sig. C8v).
113. Gadbury, 1689, sig. A4v; idem., 1690, sig. Av. For a similar mistake see Andrews, 1689, 'To the Reader'.
114. Lists of prices exist in a collection of almanacs for 1659 in the Bodleian (Rawl. Alm. 11; cf. Thomas, p. 294n) and in *N. and Q.*, 2nd series, v (1858), pp. 134–5; Blagden, 'Distribution', p. 115. Many surviving copies have the price noted by the original owner, including most bought by Anthony Wood (*Life and Times, passim*). For price variations note Securis's statement that his almanacs cost 'only two poor pence, or three pence at the most' (1576, sig. B); Wood paid 6d and 4d for two copies of Wharton, 1658. *Poor Robin*, 1700, cost 3d, but 7d/8d if well bound and interleaved (sig. Av).
115. Gadbury, 1658, sig. C8v.
116. Parker, *Mercurius Anglicanus*, 1695, sig. Av.
117. Hewit, 1654, sig. C8v; Beridge, 1654, sig. C4v.
118. *Thurloe State Papers*, ed. T. Birch (1742), vii, p. 371.
119. Jackson, *Records of the Stationers' Company*, p. 224; S.C., Court Book D, fos. 89, 90v.
120. *C.S.P.D., 1635*, pp. 483–4; Lilly, 1667, sig. C; Pond, 1659, sig. A2.
121. Alleyn, 1609, sig. B8v; cf. a similar blunder in Healy, 1658.
122. e.g. Neve, 1639; Woodhouse, 1642; Blunt, 1656, Temple, 1657.
123. Perkins, 1643, sig. Av, B3–8v (the first is the northern chronology again).
124. e.g. J.A., *A New Prognostication 1668* (Edinburgh, 1668); L.D., *A New Prognostication for 1673* (Glasgow, 1673); *A New Prognostication for 1679* (Glasgow, 1679).
125. Blagden, 'Distribution', p. 116 and Table 1.
126. B.L. Ms Sloane 2281, fos. 51–9v. Booker earlier returned an almanac offered by William Salmon for 1665 (Bodl. Ms Ash. 428, f. 270v).
127. Atkinson, 1670, sig. B8 (but he was also responsible for the unauthorized almanac by 'Atkeson' published in 1666: Blagden, 'Distribution', p. llln; below, p. 46).
128. Ms Ash. 385, f. 7; Lilly, *Life and Times*, pp. 41–2.
129. S.C., Court Book D; f. 23 (Blagrave); Journal Book, f. 21 (Coulton); Blagden, 'Distribution', p. 111; Ellis, *Orig. Letters*, pp. 307–8. For two such expressions of hope, both misplaced, see Hill, 1684, sig. C8v, and Nightingale, 1653, sig. C8v.
130. *Entered at Stationers' Hall* (1871), p. 30.
131. The list is on the flyleaf of a Bodleian collection, Rawl. Alm. 123; S.C., Journal Book, f. 89; and see also fos. 49 (Gadbury,) 57v, 64 (Coley), etc.
132. Bird names were probably suggested by the earlier burlesque almanacs (e.g. *Owles*, *Raven's*); they were also used in unauthorized editions, e.g. Sparrow's and Pigeon's (Blagden, 'Distribution', p. llln). But curiously Bird, Swan, Wing, Partridge, Raven and Thomas Sparrow were genuine compilers of a later period.
133. *A Perpetuall Kalender*, 1577 (Dawson); Dunster, 1652; S.C., Court Book F, f. 94v, and G, fos. 113v–14 (Raven); Wharton, 1645, sig. C6v (Gallen).
134. See below, pp. 270, 275.
135. Nashe, *Works*, iii, p. 72; Blagden, 'Distribution', p. 114.
136. Ms Ash. 333, f. 55; R. D. Altick, *The English Common Reader* (1963), pp. 20–1; H. R. Plomer, 'A printer's bill in the seventeenth century', *The Library*, new ser., vii (1906), p. 35; J. Allen, *Several Cases of Conscience, concerning Astrologie* (1659), p. 19.
137. Blagden, 'Distribution', Table 1 and *passim*; Blagden, pp. 188, 203–4.
138. Martindale, 1677, sig. Av; Blagrave, 1660, sig. B2 (misprint for A2).
139. Heyman, 1660, sig. A2v–3.
140. Silvester, 1681, sig. A2.
141. Hopton, 1611, sig. B2; Pond, 1612, sig. A2; Wharton, 1642, sig. A2, C4; Gadbury, 1673, sig. B3–v; see also Holden, 1689, sig. B3v.
142. Ms Ash. 333, f. 162 (Booker's draft for 1640; the passage was deleted from the printed text); Ms Ash. 423, f. 222v; Tanner, 1660, sig. C6v; see also Wharton, 1655 (printed for Vere and Brookes), sig. B3v; *Poor Robin*, 1675, epistle.
143. Bosanquet, p. 10; Thomas, p. 300; Wharton, 1655 (printed for Vere and Brookes), sig. B4; S.C., Journal Book, fos. 175 (Fowle), 175v (Leybourne) and *passim.*
144. Pond, 1612, sig. Av; Coley, *Merlinus*, 1688, sig. A2; cf. Martindale, 1677, sig. Av.
145. Wharton, 1655 (Vere and Brookes edn.), sig. B–2v. No copies of the Company's version of 'Wharton' for 1654 appear to have survived.

146. Ms Ash, 190, f. 109.
147. Atkinson, 1670, sig. B8; Blagden, 'Distribution', p. llln.
148. Ms Ash. 423, f. 123; Josten, *Ashmole, passim.*
149. Whalley, 1688, p. 3 (an almanac he compiled to replace the one 'lost'; licensed 13 August, the Guildhall copy bears a Ms date 1 September); Whalley, 1690, sig. Av.
150. Allestree, 1617, sig. B2; Vaux, 1624, sig. Bv.
151. M. Adkin was however probably identical with Kidman, of which the name is an anagram. Simon Forman, the well-known astrologer, also lived at Salisbury.
152. Bosanquet, p. 9; Siebert, *Freedom of the Press*, esp. p. 144; Greg, *London Publishing*, pp. 49–50.
153. Beale, 1631; W. Prynne, *Canterburies Doome* (1646), p. 184; *The Works of William Laud*, ed. W. Scott and J. Bliss (Oxford, 1847–60), iv, pp. 261–6. On Gellibrand see *D.N.B.*, Hill, *Intellectual Origins*, and Taylor, *Practitioners*, pp. 205–6.
154. *C.S.P.D. 1634–5*, pp. 262, 266, 270, 378; Jackson, *Stationers' Company*, p. 260. Only a small part of Booker's edition for 1635 survives, in manuscript: Ms Ash. 333, fos. 47–54v.
155. Booker, *A Bloody Irish Almanack* (1646), sig. A3; idem, *Mercurius Coelicus: or a Caveat* (1644), pp. 1–2, giving a list of chaplains. For the many deletions from Booker's almanac for 1640 compare his draft (Ms Ash. 333, fos. 55ff.) with the published version.
156. C. H. Firth and R. S. Rait, *Acts and Ordinances of the Interregnum 1642–1660* (1911), i, p. 187.
157. Wharton, 1648, sig. Av; Ms Ash. 423, f. 222v.
158. Proclamation of 25 September 1660 (B.L. 669, f. 26).
159. Lilly, 1662, sig. A2v, F.
160. Tanner, 1662, sig. A5.
161. On L'Estrange see *D.N.B.* and G. L. Kitchen, *Sir Roger L'Estrange* (1913). The Company paid him ten guineas a year for licensing almanacs: S.C., Journal Book, fos. 55, 57 etc.; he was approved by the bishop of London (Bodl. Ms Rawl. C983, f. 18).
162. The drafts are in Mss Ash. 241 and 353. For the 1668 edn. see Ms Ash. 241, f. 70; Ms Ash. 353, fos. 72, 78, 94, 100; cf. Lilly, 1668, sig. A2, D, E.
163. Ms Ash. 241, esp. fos. 90v, 99, 104v–5v.
164. Lilly, 1671, sig. A2; Ms Ash. 241 fos. 123, 128v, 130, 131v–2; Ms Ash. 353, fos. 186, 190, 192, 196, 198, 204. For his comments in 1661 see Ms Ash. 241, f. 54.
165. Josten, *Ashmole*, pp. 1229, 1260.
166. Josten, *Ashmole*, pp. 1354 and n, 1377; Lilly, 1674, sig. B5v–6. The draft in Ms Ash. 241, fos. 155–6v, contains the mediaeval treatise not the offensive material.
167. Lilly, 1655, sig. E; 1677, sig. A2v; 1673, sig. B. He probably saw the Declaration of Indulgence and the outbreak of the third Anglo-Dutch war, both in 1672, as a vindication of his suppressed remarks.
168. Gadbury, *Magna Veritas* (1680), p. 10; cf. Partridge, 1692, sig. Av.
169. S.C., Wardens' Accounts 1663–1727, under the dates 18 December 1674, 19 December 1674, 19 December 1687, 10 December 1690. Other recipients included the archbishop of Canterbury, bishop of London, attorney- and solicitor-generals and the judges: ibid., *passim.*
170. See further Chapter 3, below.
171. S.C., Court Book E, fos. 43, 43v.
172. Gadbury, 1686, sig. Av, B2v; Harrison, 1689, sig. Av (licensed 28 July 1688, before William's invasion); Tanner, 1688, sig. C2v; idem, 1690, sig. A4v; Andrews, 1687, sig. A2; idem, 1688, sig. A2.
173. S.C., Court Book F, f. 43; for Midgeley see *D.N.B.*, and (also for his colleagues) J. Dunton, *Life and Errors* (1818), pp. 266ff.
174. The episode is recounted in G. Parker, *Double Ephemeris 1700*, sig. A5v–6.
175. Siebert, *Freedom of the Press*, pp. 261–3; Blagden, pp. 175–6; for vetting after the expiry see e.g. S.C., Journal Book, f. 182 (1697) and below, pp. 266 and n8.
176. Browne, 1618, sig. B2.
177. See below, p. 143.
178. J. Gadbury, *A Brief Relation of the Life and Death of . . . Vincent Wing* (1670), p. 11.
179. On Borde see *D.N.B.*; for Hill, see F. R. Johnson, 'Thomas Hill: an Elizabethan Huxley', *H.L.Q.*, vii (1943–4).

180. *Montelion*, 1660, sig. A4; *Poor Robin*, 1681, sig. Av; Bucknall, 1677, sig. A7. See also *Mrs. Sarah Bradmores Prophecy* (1686), p. 2.
181. T. Brown, *Amusements Serious and Comical*, ed. A. L. Hayward (1927), p. 415; S.C., Journal Book, fos. 91, 93, 96v, 97 etc.; Saunder also invested in the Company: ibid., fos. 106, 108v.
182. S.C., Journal Book, fos. 13, 18v, 20, 20v, 21v, 22v, 23v, 25v, 26 (Lilly); 17v, 161 (Andrews).
183. e.g., Securis, 1562; Stephins, 1569, Parkhurst, 1648 and very many others.
184. There are good collections in B.L., at 546 d 44, 551 a 32, C112 f 9; N. Ward, *The London Spy*, ed. A. L. Hayward (1927), p. 56; J. Alden, 'Pills and Publishing: some notes on the English Book Trade, 1660–1715', *The Library*, 5th ser., vii (1952). Most items are not in Wing.
185. Pond, 1612, sig. Av–2; Atkinson, 1670, sig. Av; Wing, 1699, sig. C8v; Keene, 1615, B2v.
186. e.g., Coelson, 1676, sig. C8v; Lilly, 1677, sig. A2 and 1678, sig. A2. It is just possible that Swift's 'assassination' of Partridge was suggested by similar rumours spread by rival astrologers about each other for commercial reasons.
187. Davis, 1689, sig. B8v; E. Weaver, *The British Telescope* (1725), sig. A3. On the role of inns, see A. Everitt, ed., *Perspectives in English Urban History* (1973), ch. 4.
188. Salmon, 1684, sig. A2; Woodward, 1685, sig. C8–v (Woodward also issued printed handbills). For attacks on quacks see e.g. Securis, 1588, sig. A4; Burton, 1619, sig. B8; Tanner, 1672, sig. C8.
189. The subject is discussed in E. F. Bosanquet, 'English Seventeenth-Century Almanacs', *The Library*, 4th ser., x (1929–30).
190. Gadbury, 1665, sig. Av; ibid., 1671, sig. A6; Salmon, *The London Almanack 1701*, sig. C8v.
191. e.g. J. Case, *Cure for a Clap* (n.d., B.L.C112 f 9(14); not in Wing); for Archer see e.g. White, 1687, sig. A2v; *Poor Robin*, 1690, sig. C8v.
192. Lilly, 1673, sig. F8. Andrews, 1704, sponsors a spectacle-maker patronized by the author.
193. Acted 1625; II, i, III. i.
194. *The Character of a Quack Astrologer* (1673), sig. C3.
195. Lilly, *Life and Times*, p. 21.
196. J. Gadbury, *The Novice Astrologer* (1660), p. 3; Josten, *Ashmole*, pp. 1219, 1479; Booker, 1636 (Bodl., Ash. 69).
197. Rowley, 1651, sig. B2; Shakerley, *The Anatomy of Urania Practica* (1649), p. 2; for the others see Appendix I and Taylor, *Practitioners*.
198. Gresham, 1603, 'To the Reader'; Keene, 1612, sig. B2–v; ibid., 1613, sig. B2–v. 'Simeatical' does not appear in the *O.E.D.*; for similar abuse see below, pp. 73, 75.
199. Booker, 1634, sig. C8; Wing, 1641, sig. B2. Shakerley later abused Wing in similar terms, and sparked off a major row.
200. Keene, 1612, sig. B2.
201. Thomas, pp. 230, 632 and chs. 11, 12 and 21 *passim*.
202. J. Pool, *Country Astrology* (1650), sig. A3; Thomas, p. 346.
203. Lloyd, 1585, sig. B2–3v.
204. Thomas, p. 305.
205. Lilly, *Life and Times*, pp. 67–9, 69–71, 85–6 (his lawyer was John Greene, later Recorder of London). For other astrologers protected by influential patrons see ibid., pp. 48, 49, 50.
206. Above, p. 47; Wharton, *Merlini Anglici Errata* (1647), p. 2.
207. Coxe: *D.N.B.*; Allen, *Star-Crossed Renaissance*, p. 112; Bomelius: Goodall, pp. 313–14; J. Strype, *The Life and Acts of Matthew Parker* (1711), pp. 293–5; Pembroke: *A Most Strange and Rare Example of the Just Judgement of God* (1577); Vaux: Longstaffe, *High Commission*, pp. 34–42; Evans: Goodall, op. cit., pp. 442–3.
208. Bowker, 1668, sig. C8v; Jeffereys, 1635, sig. B2–v.
209. Burton, 1613, sig. B; Gresham, 1607, sig. B2; see also Coelson, 1674, epistle.
210. Hopton, 1607, sig. Bv; ibid., 1613, sig. Av; ibid., 1611, sig. B2; Burton, 1616, sig. B2v.
211. Wharton, 1657, sig. G4; cf. ibid., 1658, sig. A2 and 1653, sig. A2v; Booker, *Mercurius Coelicus* (1644), p. 6; Lilly, *The Worlds Catastrophe* (1647), p. 59. The same verse, but

with mackerel in place of small-coal, was used by Francis Moore in his edition for 1703, p. 15.

212. See below, pp. 235–6.

213. J. Geree, *Astrologo-Mastix* (1646), p. 11; R. Head, *The English Rogue* (1665), pp. 23–4; Ward, *The London Spy*, pp. 260, 263–4; J. Melton, *Astrologaster* (1620), pp. 6, 8 and *passim*; Thomas, pp. 340–1.

214. *The Character of a Quack-Astrologer* (1673), sig. C3. The reference is to the Ottoman practice of fratricide at the accession of a new sultan.

215. Partridge, 1697, sig. C7; Parker, *Merlinus*, 1698, sig. A2v; idem, *Ephemeris*, 1699, sig. A3v.

216. Lilly, *Life and Times*, p. 42 (but cf. his generous assessment on pp. 27–8); *Diary of Samuel Pepys*, 24 October 1659.

217. Ms Ash. 180, f. 122.

218. Allestree, 1619, sig. B5v (similar comments in his other editions); Winter, 1633, sig. A2 (the same verse appeared in Swallow, 1633; Rivers, 1638 and other Cambridge editions).

219. Martindale, 1675, sig. Av–2, and 1676, sig. Bv–2; Partridge, 1656, sig. B4, and 1658, sig. C4v; Bellerson, 1624, sig. Av, B4; Gallen, 1640, sig. Av; Winter, 1646, sig. A; Frende, 1588, sig. C7v.

220. B.L. Ms Sloane 3856–7; *Christian Astrology* ends with an 11-page bibliography; *Life and Times*, p, 23.

221. Lilly, *Life and Times*, pp. 19–20, 31, 35.

222. Josten, *Ashmole*, p. 1050; Lilly, 1682, sig. E.

223. Lilly, *Life and Times*, pp. 38, 67–9, 73–4.

224. Lilly, 1677, sig. F.

225. Josten, *Ashmole*, p. 1210; above, pp. 48–9.

226. Ibid., p. 1209.

227. Lilly, 1677, sig. A2v; *Life and Times*, pp. 67–9.

228. Josten, *Ashmole*, pp. 1171, 1221, 1222, 1224, 1229, 1355, 1362, 1415, 1444, 1479. In 1650 Ashmole engagingly set figures to see if he would be prosecuted under the Rump's legislation against adultery, fornication and blasphemy (ibid., pp. 534–5).

229. Lilly, *Life and Times*, pp. 27–8; *Culpeper's School of Physick* (1659), sig. C2v–3.

230. Lilly, *Life and Times*, p. 21.

231. Blagden, p. 189 (reproducing a list of November 1691); B.L. Harl, 5937 (338), a list of twenty-seven titles available for collection on 27 November 1694; I. Massey, *Midsummer's Prognostication* (1642), p. 3; Brown, *Amusements*, p. 415.

232. See the stocklists of booksellers in London, Chester and Shrewsbury in *The Library* (1923–4, 1928–9, 1958); above, p. 33. Heuring's almanac for 1551, the only provincial edition in the Tudor period, was printed at Worcester, and sold there and in Shrewsbury (sig. B8v).

233. Jones, 'Welsh Books', pp. 656, 678; cf. D. T. Pottinger, *The French Book Trade in the Ancien Regime 1500–1791* (Cambridge, Mass., 1958), p. 139 for the sale of French almanacs by haberdashers.

234. See the advertisements in B.L. 546 d 44, nos. 5, 6, 13, etc; C112 f 9, no. 1; Woodward, 1685, sig. C8–v; below, pp. 115–16.

235. Above, pp. 33–4.

236. Fowle, 1693, sig. B4v (2nd signature); Tanner, 1658, sig. C8v; Wharton, 1657, sig. G4; L. Meriton, *Money Does Master all Things* (York, 1696), p. 86; W. L. Sachse, ed., *Minutes of the Norwich Court of Mayoralty 1623–1635* (Norfolk Rec. Soc., xxxvi), p. 119; L. B. Wright, *Middle-class Culture in Elizabethan England* (Chapel Hill, N. Carolina, 1935), p. 96.

237. Hopton, 1612, sig. B2.

238. C. Hindley, *A History of the Cries of London* (1884), p. 60; S. Rowland, *The Melancholy Knight* (1615), p. 36, in *Complete Works*, ed. S. J. H. Herrtage (Glasgow, 1880); Bodl. Ms Rawl. poet. 71, p. 5; Ellis, *Orig. Letters*, p. 310.

239. Longstaffe, *High Commission*, p. 40.

240. Charles's collection is now B.L. C28 a 3; Lilly, *Life and Times*, p. 59; *D.N.B.*, Wharton.

241. Frende, 1594, sig. B3v, 4ff. (the series is at Hatfield, but a microfilm is in the B.L., Cecil Papers, reel 333); cf. Thomas, p. 290; V. F. Snow, 'An Inventory of the Lord General's Library, 1646', *The Library*, 5th ser., xxi (1966), p. 122.

242. C. Wren, *Parentalia* (1750), p. 133; B.L. Add. Ms 22550 (Clarendon's annotated copy of Goldsmith, 1691).

243. W. C. Costin, 'The Inventory of John English', *Oxoniensia*, xi–xii (1946–7), p. 114; R. F. Overell, 'Brian Twyne's Library', *Oxford Bibl. Soc.*, N.S., iv (1950), *passim*; J. Harrison and P. Laslett, 'The Library of John Locke', *Oxford Bibl. Soc.*, N.S., xiii (1965), pp. 71, 140, 162, 175, 204, 206, 221, 265.

244. Wright, *Middle-class Culture*, p. 84.

245. 'The Journal of John Weale', in *Naval Miscellany*, iv, p. 127 (Navy Records Soc., xlii, 1952).

246. I owe this point to Mrs. Helen Forde's Leicester Ph.D. (in progress), 'Nottinghamshire and Derbyshire Quakers of the 17th and 18th Centuries'; the reference is Notts. C.R.O., Breach Monthly Meeting Minutes (Q59).

247. S. Rowland, *The Night-Raven* (1620), p. 4; Brown, *Amusements*, p. 194; Stephen Duck, *Poems on Several Occasions* (1736), p. 313. (I owe this reference to Dr. Margaret Spufford.)

248. Wood, *Life and Times*, ed. A. Clark (Oxford Hist. Soc., 1891–1900); 'Diary of Adam Winthrop' in *Winthrop Papers, i, 1498–1628* (Mass. Hist. Soc., 1925); 'The Diary of John Greene 1635–57', *E.H.R.*, xliii–iv (1928–9); *The Diary of Walter Powell*, ed. J. A. Bradney (Bristol, 1907); F. H. Stubbings, 'A Cambridge Pocket-Diary, 1587–92', *Trans. Cambridge Bibl. Soc.*, v (1971); 'Diary of Isabella Lady Twysden', *Arch. Cant.*, li (1939). See also D. G. Hoffman, 'Tylden's almanac', *Journ. of the Rutgers Univ. Lib.*, xvi (1953); 'Expense Book of James Masters Esq.', *Arch. Cant.*, xv (1883); G. Turner, 'Extracts from the Diary of Richard Stapley, Gent.', *Sussex Arch. Coll.*, ii (1849).

249. Nicholas: B.L. Add. Mss 41202 B-L; Higgs: Bodl., Wood Alm. A; for Patrick and Moore see almanacs by Abendano, Gallen and Goldsmith in C.U.L.; Sellcock: Bodl., Alm. g 1668. 1, and see also *Bodl. Quart. Rec.*, vi (1928–31); Hammond: Bodl., Rawl. Alm. 87, 91b, 96 (Riders, 1693/4/6). For Hammond see *D.N.B.*

250. *The Autobiography of the Rev. Henry Newcome*, ed. R. Parkinson (Chetham Soc., xxvi, xxvii, 1852), pp. 283, 288; *Oliver Heywood's Life of John Angier . . . also Samuel Angier's Diary*, ed. E. Axon (Chetham Soc., xcvii, 1937), p. 152; *Diaries and Letters of Philip Henry*, ed. M. H. Lee (1882), pp. vii–viii, 175–6. One of Henry's diaries, in a copy of Goldsmith, 1673, is now at Shrewsbury School, Ms James xxviii (I owe this reference to the librarian, Mr. J. B. Lawson). Dunton, *Life and Errors*, p. 174.

251. L. Clarkson, *The Lost Sheep Found* (1660), pp. 29–30; Wm. Salt Library, Stafford, Salt Ms 2016 (King's copy of Gadbury, 1696). On King and astrology see Thomas p. 320.

252. Goldsmith, 1694 (C.U.L., SSS 34.32); *The Journal of James Younge (1647–1721)*, ed. F. N. L. Poynter (1963), pp. 226–7.

253. Gallen, 1672 (Bodl., 8vo Rawl. 439); Aubrey, *Brief Lives*, ii, pp. 175–6.

254. Abendano, 1692 (Bodl., Alm. f 1692.1).

255. Gallen, 1672 (see n253, above); Bretnor, 1617, sig. B4 (Bodl., Alm. f. 1615); Hopton, 1613, sig. A3 (Bodl., Ash. 66)—the lost tooth; its owner was a Puritan minister, apparently minister of Saxthorp, Norfolk, and perhaps the Matthew Page whose name appears on the flyleaf, for whom see Venn, *Al. Cant.*

256. *Endymion*, 1663, sig. A5v, 6v and *passim*; cf. *Poor Robin*, 1671, sig. A7.

257. Chamberlaine, 1649, sig. B3v.

258. Buckminster, 1590, sig. A2–v; Pond, 1611, sig. A2; Wharton, 1648, sig. A5; M. Prynne, *Canterburies Doome* (1646), p. 516.

259. For criticism e.g. Ms Ash. 383; Perkins, *Four Great Lyers*; Allen, *The Astronomers Game*; for replies, Stephins, 1569, sig. Av; Vaughan, 1559, sig. Av; Gilden, 1616, sig. B3; ibid., 1624, sig. B2; Davis, 1689, sig. A2v; Frende, 1589 (16th edn.), sig. E6.

260. Frende, 1590, sig. C4 (Stubbings, art. cit., pp. 192–3).

261. Martindale, 1676, sig. Bv–2; Partridge, 1656, sig. B; *Poor Robin*, 1696, sig. Av.

262. B. Jonson, *Every Man out of his Humour*, I. i; Thomas, p. 298; Lilly, *Life and Times*, p. 59.

263. *A Fair Quarrel*, in *The Works of Thomas Middleton*, ed. A. H. Bullen (1886), iv, p. 263; *The Inner Temple Masque*, ibid., vii, p. 211; cf. a character who ignores an evil day to his cost, in *No Wit, No Help like a Woman's*, ibid., iv, pp. 295–7.

264. Ramesey, *Astrologia Restaurata* (1653), p. 11; Frende, 1587, sig. A3v; Swallow, 1640,

sig. B4; Gadbury, 1692, sig. Av; Whalley, 1691, p. 44; Ramesey, *Lux Veritatis* (1651), pp. 34–5; *Poor Robin*, 1664, sig. C8v; ibid., 1696, sig. Av; Hill, 1684, sig. A8; J. Gaule, *Mag-Astro-Mancer* (1652), p. 135; J. Butler, *The Most Sacred and Divine Science of Astrology* (1680), p. 77.

265. Partridge, 1755, sig. C3.
266. Coley, 1679, sig. C7v–8; Einer, 1622, sig. A2; Parker, *Mercurius Anglicanus*, 1695, sig. Av.
267. Above, p. 28; for Bretnor's lists see J. Crow, 'Some Jacobean Catch-Phrases', *passim*; see also below, pp. 229–30.
268. Below, pp. 289–90.
269. Perkins, *Four Great Lyers*, sig. B2v; Thomas, p. 341; Rogeford, 1560, sig. B4; Ben Jonson's Sordido is an example. See above, pp. 32.
270. J. Primrose, *Popular Errours* (1651), pp. 240–54; R. Whitlock, *Observations* (1654), p. 49. On astrological medicine see C. Camden, 'Elizabethan Astrological Medicine', *Annals of Medical Hist.*, N.S., ii (1930); H. G. Dick, 'Students of Physic and Astrology', *Journ. of the Hist. of Medicine*, v (1946); Thomas, esp. chs. 10, 11.
271. Frende, 1598, sig. A4.
272. Rivers, 1638, sig. A2 (similar verse in many Cambridge edns.); cf. *N. and Q.*, 2nd ser., iii (1857), p. 278. In 1654 Pigot agreed that if 'Johnny' finds the 'Monster' missing, 'He will cry pish, and say it's not the best,/And presently will frown and cast it by' (Pigot, 1654, sig. Av).
273. Primrose, op. cit., pp. 243, 252; N. Merry, *A Friendly and Seasonable Advertisement concerning the Dog-days*, n.d. (B.L. 551 a 32(20); not in Wing), p. 1; Thomas, pp. 333–4.
274. Gadbury, 1674, sig. D2; ibid, 1679, sig. Av.
275. Now in Balliol College Oxford, 670 a 5.
276. Collection now in the Bodleian, Alm. f. 1615; 'Winthrop Papers', i, p. 237.
277. B.L. Add. Mss 34169–72; the diary is printed in *Arch. Cantia*, li (1939). Lady Twysden may previously have found Wharton's illicit pieces unobtainable.
278. 'Diary of John Greene', *E.H.R.*, xliii, pp. 386, 390; xliv, p. 108.
279. S.C., Court Book D, f. 208v. In a stocklist of a Chester bookseller in 1650–1, the editions of Booker, Lilly, Wharton, Gallen, Goldsmith and Phillips were listed individually, the others being lumped together as blanks, sorts and sheets. The latter three named were very small, pocket-sized editions. R. Stewart-Brown, in *The Library*, 4th ser., ix (1928–9), pp. 57–8.
280. Fowle, 1693, sig. B4v (2nd signature); ibid., 1697, sig. Bv.
281. Booker, 1648, sig. C.
282. Gadbury, 1658, sig. C8v; Partridge, 1656, sig. B; Farmer, 1614, sig. Av; Pond, 1649, sig. A2.
283. Tanner, 1658, sig. C8v; *Poor Robin*, 1687, sig. A7; ibid., 1696, sig. Av; ibid., 1699, sig. A8; T. Tomkis, *Albumazar*, ed. H. G. Dick (Baltimore, 1944), introd., p. 40; cf. J. Tipper, *Great Britain's Diary*, 1711, sig. B2.

Chapter 3 Almanacs and Politics (*pages 67–101*)

1. Above, Chapter 2, and below, pp. 68ff.
2. Parron, 1498 (frag.); 1500, sig. Bff.; 1502, sig. a6v–b2v and *passim*.
3. Laet, 1516; 1520; 1529; 1534; 1543.
4. *Letters and Papers . . . of Henry VIII*, ed. J. S. Brewer et al. (1886–1932), viii, p. 2; Scute, 1544, sig. E3–F.
5. Above, p. 28.
6. See e.g. Swallow, Twells and Winter.
7. Rogeford, 1560, sig. B2v–3; see also e.g. Securis, 1562, sig. A7v (2nd signature); idem, 1566, sig. A5v; Neve, 1605, sig. C2; Gresham, 1606, sig. B7; Hopton, 1607, sig. B6v.
8. Stephins, 1569, sig. A2, A7v; anon., Prognostication, 1568 (frag.); Carre, 1593, sig. B5.

9. *Secret History of the Court of James the First* (Edinburgh, 1811), i, p. 393.
10. B. Porchnev, *Les soulèvements populaires en France de 1623 à 1648* (Paris, 1963), p. 50; Thomas, ch. 13.
11. *Letters and Papers of . . . Henry VIII*, ed. J. S. Brewer et al., viii, p. 131.
12. *C.S.P.D., 1598–1601*, p. 585; H.M.C., *Salisbury*, xvii, pp. 23, 25; B. L. Harl. 5937, f. 7v; *Observations upon . . . Mr. John Gadbury* (1680), p. 3; below, pp. 89, 92–3, 94.
13. Nostradamus, *Prognostication*, 1559 ('Antwerp'), sig. A4, B5, B7v–8, C5; idem, 1563, sig. A3v.
14. J. Strype, *The Life and Acts of Matthew Parker* (1711), pp. 37–8; Thomas, p. 290; L. Humfrey, *The Nobles: or, of Nobilitye* (1563), sig. y6v–7; S. V. Larkey, 'Astrology and Politics . . .', *Bull. Inst. for the Hist. of Medicine*, iii (1935).
15. Op. cit., sig. E4, v and *passim*.
16. J. Cypriano, op. cit., sig. A3, 4v, B, Bv, B3, B4 and *passim*; W. W. Greg and E. Boswell, eds., *Records of the Court of the Stationers' Company 1576 to 1602*, pp. xx and 42, 44 etc.; McKerrow, *Dictionary 1557–1640*, p. 156, on Cypriano, and the apocalyptic tradition, see below, p. 167.
17. Bourne, 1581, sig. A5; Allestree, 1624, sig. A7, B, Cv–2; Frende, 1594, sig. B5v; Bellerson, 1624, second t.p. and sig. B4; Dove, 1634, sig. C3–v; Johnson, 1621, sig. B4v.
18. Gresham, 1607, sig. B7.
19. Dauncy, 1615, sig. Av.
20. Booker, 1632, sig. A6, C8v; *D.N.B.*, Booker; Lilly, *Life and Times*, pp. 27–8; above, p. 47. Booker took some of these comments from Hopton, 1613, sig. C7v.
21. Harvey, 1589, sig. B7; Buckminster, 1589, sig. C7v; see also his almanac for 1595 for a similar verse which forms an acrostic on the word 'Elizabeth'.
22. Watson, 1604, sig. C8; Alleyn, 1606, sig. A5; Browne, 1624, sig. B4; Perkins, 1625, sig. A6v.
23. Pond, 1629, sig. A3; Hewlett, 1629, sig. B2v; Perkins, 1631, sig. B2.
24. White, 1626, sig. B4.
25. Ms Rawl. D 398, fos. 237v–8; Ms Rawl. poet. 71, p. 5; I. Massy, *Midsummer's Prognostication* (1642); *The Parliament's Kalender of Black Saints* (1644); *The Great Eclipse of the Sunne* (1644).
26. Booker, 1644, sig. B3, B7, 2nd signature, sig. B4v; Wharton, 1644, sig. A4v–5, C7v–8v. For Wharton see *D.N.B.*; Wood, *Ath. Oxon.*, iv, cols. 5–9; *The Works of Sir George Wharton*, ed. J. Gadbury (1683), introd.
27. Booker, *Mercurius Coelicus* (1644); Wharton, *Mercurio-Coelico-Mastix* (1644); J. Taylor, *No Mercurius Aulicus* (1644); S. Morgan, *Prognosticon Posthumum 1643/4* (1644); 'T. Philo-Bookerus', *Mercurius Vapulans, or Naworth Stript and Whipt*, (1644). The major contributions in the pamphlet war are discussed in H. G. Rusche, '*Merlini Anglici*: Astrology and Propaganda from 1644 to 1651', *E.H.R.*, lxxx (1965).
28. Booker, *Mercurius Coelicus*, p. 6; idem, *A Rope for a Parret* (1644), pp. 4, 6; idem, *No Mercurius Aquaticus* (1644), p. 4; Wharton, *Mercurio-Coelico-Mastix*, p. 14; Taylor, *No Mercurius Aulicus*, p. 4; 'Philo-Bookerus', *Mercurius Vapulans*, p. 8.
29. Lilly, *Life and Times*, pp. 41–2; Bodl. Ms Ash. 186, fos. 127–30, 132–43; Rusche, art. cit., pp. 324ff. *Lilli's Propheticall History of . . . 1642* (dated by Thomason 4 November 1641) suggests that Lilly's manuscript works may have been well known, though this tract is primarily a parody of the grammarian William Lily.
30. Dated by Thomason 13 July 1644.
31. Lilly, *Life and Times*, pp. 42–3; Ms Ash. 186, fos. 136, 142; Lilly, *Supernatural Sights* (1644), sig. Av; Lilly, *A Prophecy of the White King* (1644), p. 6; see also Rusche, art. cit., pp. 324ff.
32. Lilly, 1645, sig. A3v–4v, p. 17.
33. Ibid., sig. A3v, pp. 13, 20, 59, 71.
34. Lilly, 1646, sig. A4v, G2v–3v; Lilly, 1647, sig. A3–v; Lilly, 1648, sig. A3; Lilly, 1649, sig. A2v, 3.
35. Booker, 1646, sig. A7; Wing, 1648, sig. C7v; Nye, 1645, sig. B5v, 7v and *passim*.
36. Wharton, 1647, sig. B5v; 1648, sig. C5v; *Mercurius Elencticus*, 6 (29 December 1647–5, January, 1648), p. 43; I.B., *A Faire in Spittle Fields* (1652), pp. 6, 7. For Wharton's newspaper see Frank, *English Newspaper*.
37. *D.N.B.*, Wharton; Wharton, 1649, sig. C6v; 1651, sig. A4.

38. H. Johnsen, pseud., *Anti-Merlinus* (1648), pp. 23, 44, 50–1; Lilly, *Life and Times*, pp. 33–4, 63, identifying the author at p. 34; Wood, *Ath. Oxon.*, iv, cols. 747–9.
39. Ms Ash. 423, f. 197; see also f. 235.
40. Lilly, *Life and Times*, pp. 43, 63, 78; Thomas, p. 342; Rusche, art. cit., pp. 324–6.
41. Wharton, *Works*, p. 250.
42. Lilly, *Life and Times*, pp. 61, 77.
43. Ibid., p. 61; Williams, *English Journalism*, pp. 124, 132–3; J. Frank, *The Levellers* (Cambridge, Mass., 1955), pp. 148, 155; Frank, *English Newspaper*, pp. 200–1; J. Blackwell, *The Nativity of Mr. Will. Lilly* (1660), p. 5.
44. Harflete, *Vox Coelorum* (1645), sig. A2v, pp. 49ff.; Appendix I, below.
45. Lilly, *Life and Times*, pp. 41–2; Plomer, in *The Library*, N.S., vii (1906), p. 35; J. Allen, *Judicial Astrologers* (1659), p. 15; Frank, *English Newspaper*, pp. 172, 177, 212, 222, 223, 226, 227, 247, 259. *Merlinus Anglicus 1650*, by 'M.A.', was lifted from Lilly's almanac for the year. It appeared in May, and ran up to April 1651. The predictions for January–April 1651 were those of Lilly for January–April 1650.
46. Lilly, *Life and Times*, p. 68; Thomas, pp. 372–4; below, pp. 83, 100.
47. Wharton, 1644, sig. C7v; idem, 1647, sig. A5; Booker, pseud., *A Brief Judgement Astrologicall* (1649), repudiated in Booker, 1650, sig. C; W. Lele, pseud., *An English Ephemeris 1650*, repudiated in Lilly, 1650, sig. Av; J.C., *The Character of a Moderate Intelligencer* (1645), p. 4.
48. *The Late Storie of Mr William Lilly* (1648); *Mercurius Elencticus*, 11 (2–9 February 1648), pp. 77–8; *C.S.P.D., 1645–7*, p. 135; Lilly, *Life and Times*, p. 59.
49. Lilly, 1649, sig. A2ff.
50. Lilly, *Life and Times*, pp. 43–5; cf. the enmity of Bradshaw: ibid., p. 63.
51. Ibid., pp. 52–3; Lilly, 1645, pp. 63, 79; 1648, sig. A3v–4; 1649, sig. A3v; 1650, sig. A2v, A3v–4.
52. e.g. Booker, 1643, sig. Av; Lilly, 1648, sig. A2v, A4.
53. Lilly, 1645, sig. A4v; Booker, 1649, sig. C2v.
54. Lilly, 1650, sig. A3v.
55. Booker, *No Mercurius Aquaticus* (1644), p. 5; Booker, *A Bloody Irish Almanack* (1646); Booker, 1646, sig. B4v; 1650, sig. A8v; 1652, sig. C3; Lilly, 1644, p. 19; 1645, p. 26; 1648, sig. D5.
56. Lilly, 1657, sig. A6.
57. Ibid., 1651, sig. A2–v, B2–v, B8v, E; 1650, sig. F8–v; Lilly, *Annus Tenebrosus* (1652), p. 10.
58. Lilly, 1651, sig. B2, B4v; Wing, 1652, sig. C6.
59. Lilly, 1651, sig. A2v, B8v.
60. *A Black Almanack 1651*; *The Bloudy Almanack 1651*; G.H. (probably George Horton, the publisher), *The Bloody Almanack 1652* and *Merlinus Anglicanus 1653*. Horton also published *The Levellers Almanack 1652*. Another series of *Bloody Almanacks*, using Booker's name and based on the predictions of Napier, were probably the work of Henry Walker (Booker, 1649, sig. C7v); editions survive for 1643, 1647, 1648.
61. Lilly, 1651, sig. A4; 1648, sig. A4; 1650, sig. A2v, E3; *Levellers Almanack*, p. 6; on the Norman Yoke see C. Hill, *Puritanism and Revolution* (1962), pp. 50–122.
62. See Hill, op. cit., pp. 123–57.
63. G.H., *Bloody Almanack 1652*, p. 3; M.A., *Merlinus Anglicus 1650*, sig. A2; Thurston, 1652, sig. C3.
64. *Levellers Almanack*, p. 4; Culpeper, 1653, pp. 24, 28ff., sig. D7; Thurston, 1652, sig. A4v–7.
65. Booker, 1651, sig. C; Lilly, 1649, sig. F6; Culpeper, *Catastrophe Magnatum* (1652), p. 36.
66. On apocalyptic interest in the civil war see e.g. C. Hill, *Antichrist in Seventeenth-century England* (1971) and *The World Turned Upside Down* (1972); P. Toon, ed., *Puritan Eschatology* (1970); B. S. Capp, *The Fifth Monarchy Men* (1972); on the astrological connections, see below, pp. 170–3.
67. Lilly, *Annus Teneorosus* (1652), pp. 38–40 and *passim*; Booker, 1652, sig. A4v, C4v; Wing, 1652, sig. C3v–4; Culpeper, 1651, sig. E8; Culpeper, 1652, pp. 16–17; Wharton, 1652, t.p., and pp. 88–92; W. Ramesey, *A Short Discourse* (supplement to *Lux Veritatis*) (1652); Thurston, 1652, sig. A4v–7.

68. Thomas, pp. 299–300; *On Bugbear Black-Munday* (1652); *The Astrologers Bug-beare* (1652), sig. A4v–6; Wharton, 1653, sig. E8v–F.
69. e.g. J. Vicars, *Against William Li-Lie* and W. Brommerton, *Confidence Dismounted* (both 1652); see also n68, above. The astrologers defended their predictions, e.g. Lilly, 1653, sig. A2–3; Culpeper, 1654, p. 15; Gadbury, *Philastrogus Knavery* (1652).
70. On the elect nation see e.g. my *Fifth Monarchy Men*, pp. 33–4, 37–8, 151–2. Despite Haller, it is now accepted that Foxe did not invent or propagate the idea: see V. N. Olsen, *John Foxe and the Elizabethan Church* (1973), prologomena.
71. Lilly, 1647, sig. A2v; cf. *Bloody Almanack 1649*, p. 4; *Bloudy Almanack 1651*, p. 4.
72. Lilly, 1652, sig. A7v, D; Smith, 1653, sig. Cv; Booker, 1651, sig. C6.
73. J. E. Farnell, 'The Navigation Act of 1651, the First Dutch War, and the London Community', *Econ. Hist. Rev.*, xvi (1963–4); see also Capp, *Fifth Monarchy Men*, pp. 152–4.
74. Llly, 1651, sig. B3v–4 (quoting Jer. li:13); Lilly, *Life and Times*, p. 78.
75. Lilly, 1652, sig. A4v; the theme was taken up later by Gadbury, 1675, sig. E5.
76. Piublished 1651, 1653 respectively; Culpeper, 1654, p. 20.
77. Lilly, 1649, sig. F6; 1651, sig. B7; *Dutch Bloudy Almanack*, 1653, p. 4.
78. Lilly, 1651, sig. B6v; *Dutch Bloudy Almanack*, p. 6.
79. Lilly, 1649, sig. A2v; 1650, sig. A2–3v; 1651, sig. B8v; Lilly, *A Prophecy of the White King* (1644).
80. Lilly, 1650, sig. B2; 1651, sig. B5; 1652, sig. A3; 1653, sig. B3; Lilly, *Annus Tenebrosus*, p. 40.
81. Herbert, 1652, sig. B8v; 1653, sig. C.
82. Lilly, *Life and Times*, pp. 64–5; Lilly, *Annus Tenebrosus*, esp. pp. 54–5; Lilly, 1652, sig. A2–v, Bv, B3, C3; 1653, sig. B.
83. Lilly, *Life and Times*, pp. 67–9.
84. Lilly, 1654, sig. A4–v, F7v–8.
85. Lilly, *Life and Times*, pp. 68, 74; Blackwell, *Nativity of Lilly*, p. 8; *William Lilly . . . His Opinions touching Monarchy* (1660), p. 5 (probably by Gadbury); *A Declaration of the Several Treasons* [of] *William Lilly* (1660), p. 3; Lilly, 1654, sig. C3; 1655, sig. A6, A7v; 1657, sig. A6.
86. Lilly, 1658, sig. A7v; Saunders, 1656, sig. A6. On the relations between Lilly and Saunders see *William Lilly . . . touching Monarchy*, sig. Av.
87. Gadbury, 1657, sig. C5.
88. Lilly, 1658, sig. B4; Booker, 1658, sig. B3; Saunders, 1658, sig. A2, B2; *William Lilly . . . touching Monarchy*, sig. Av; Gadbury, 1659, sig. A3v; Wing, 1658, sig. A5.
89. See below, pp. 170–3.
90. Andrews, 1658, sig. B6v; 1659, sig. B8. The allusion to eighty-eight is of course to the defeat of the Armada in 1588.
91. Phillippes, 1657, sig. C5v–6; Saunders, 1656, sig. C4v; cf. Lilly, 1656, sig. A8.
92. Lilly, 1656, sig. C; 1658, sig. F; see also Tanner, 1659, sig. A7.
93. Lilly, 1659, sig. A3v.
94. Lilly, 1654, sig. A8–v; 1655, sig. A5v; 1657, sig. A8v–B8; 1658, sig. C, D5; 1659, slg. A2v, A3v, A5v.
95. Lilly, *Life and Times*, pp. 73–4; F. Dahl, *King Charles Gustavus of Sweden and the English Astrologers William Lilly and John Gadbury* (Uppsala, 1937, reprinted from the journal *Lychnos*), pp. 166–8, 171.
96. Lilly, *Life and Times*, pp. 73–4.
97. J. Gadbury, *Nuncius Astrologicus* (1660); *The Novice-Astrologer* (1660), p. 10; G.J. (i.e. Gadbury), *The Spurious Prognosticator* (1659), pp. 10–11; F. Missonne, pseud. (i.e. Gadbury), *Merlinus Gallicus 1660*, sig. A6v, B–5v; W. Kilburne, *A New Years Gift* (1659); Dahl, op. cit., *passim*; Gadbury, 1695, sig. A7.
98. Wharton, 1650, sig. A6, B4–C3, p. 20; 1651, sig. A3v–5; Lilly, *Life and Times*, p. 63; *D.N.B.*, Wharton.
99. Wharton, 1652, sig. A2v; 1653, sig. C2v.
100. *C.S.P.D.*, *1653–4*, p. 193; see above, p. 45.
101. Wharton, 1655 (M.J. edn.), sig. H8–14v; Josten, *Ashmole*, pp. 677–8; *C.S.P.D.*, *1654*, p. 354, ibid., *1655–6*, p. 121; *D.N.B.*, Wharton; Wharton, 1658, sig. B2, B3–5; 1659, sig. B2; 1660, sig. B4v.

102. *C.S.P.D., 1653–4*, p. 193; Fitzsmith, 1654, sig. A7v, B8, D3. Fitzsmith was a friend (or possibly pseudonym) of Childrey: Childrey, 1653, sig. A4v.
103. Thomas, p. 291; J. Merrifield, *Catastasis Mundi* (1684), sig. A2v; *C.S.P.D., 1657–8*, p. 304.
104. J. Heydon, *The Rosie Crucian Infallible Axiomata* (1660), sig. A3v; Thomas, p. 344.
105. R. Desmus, pseud., 1653, sig. C2v; 1654, sig. A6, B6 and *passim*. On Sheppard see Frank, *English Newspaper*, pp. 139, 144–5, 164–5, 234, 235; Williams, *English Journalism*, pp. 83, 85, 86, 114.
106. Culpeper, 1654, sig. C3 and *passim*; 1655, sig. A4v; 1656, sig. E; *Culpeper's School of Physick*, (1659), sig. C8.
107. Jinner, 1658, sig. C; 1659, sig. B2v, Cv, C3, C3v.
108. Blagrave, 1659, sig. D4.
109. Booker, 1660, sig. C5; Andrews, 1660, sig. A3, B; Tanner, 1659, sig. B4, B6, C7.
110. Lilly, 1659, sig. A3v, 8v, D7, E7; 1660, sig. A2, 3.
111. Dated 26 September by Thomason.
112. Wharton, 1661, sig. B4.
113. *The Rebels Almanack*; *A Declaration of the Several Treasons . . . by William Lilly*; *Lilly Lash't with his own Rod* (all 1660); *William Lilly . . . touching Monarchy*; Blackwel, *Nativity of Lilly*; T. Riders, *The Black Remembrancer* (1661). Lilly sought and obtained an official pardon: *Life and Times*, p. 86.
114. Lilly, 1661, sig. A2–3v; 1662, sig. A5, F; J. Allen, *Several Cases of Conscience* (1659) p. 18; Blagden, 'Distribution', Table 1; but cf. above, pp. 48–9..
115. Booker, 1661, sig. A8; *Booker Rebuk'd* (1665), p. 8 and *passim*. The author was Thomas Blount, allegedly piqued by the poor sales of his own almanac: A. Wood, *Ath. Oxon.*, iii, col. 149.
116. Tanner, 1661, sig. B8; 1662, sig. A5; 1663, sig. A4v.
117. *C.S.P.D., 1664–5*, p. 174; ibid., *1666–7*, p. 429; ibid., *1663–4*, p. 367; Capp, *Fifth Monarchy Men*, p. 211; Josten, *Ashmole*, pp. 1072–5; *London Gazette*, 48 (26–30 April 1666). Lilly was questioned by a parliamentary committee in 1660 over the identity of the king's executioner, and arrested briefly in January 1661 (for which his own date of 1662 seems to be an error): *Life and Times*, pp. 83–6.
118. Heydon had been released from an earlier imprisonment by Buckingham's intervention: *C.S.P.D., 1666–7*, pp. 428–9, 431, 490, 541; Heydon, *The Wise Man's Crown* (1664), sig. A6v; Thomas, pp. 344, 374.
119. Gadbury, 1663, sig. A2v (reprinted in Trigge, 1664, sig. A2); Vaux, 1662, sig. A2, B2–4.
120. Andrews, 1661, sig. A3v (an allusion to Isaiah); Bird, 1662, sig. B4v–5.
121. Wing, 1661, sig. C4v.
122. Vaux, 1664, sig. B8–Cv; Bird, 1662, sig. B5; *Calendarium Londinense, or Raven's Almanack 1678*.
123. Gadbury, 1662, sig. C5v–6, C7–8; 1663, sig. C3; Vaux, 1666, sig. A2; Saunders, 1675, sig. A2.
124. Trigge, 1666, sig. Cv; 1667, sig. A5, 6v; Andrews, 1665, sig. C3v; 1667, sig. A7, B3, C8v; Wharton, 1666, sig. B6v; Lilly's almanacs for 1665–7 and 1673–4, *passim*. The collections were *Astrological Predictions of Englands Happy Success* (1667), and *News from the Heavens* (1673); see also *The Dangerous Condition of the United Provinces Prognosticated . . . by Mr. William Lilly* (1672), based on his and other writings.
125. Trigge, *The Fiery Trigon* (1672), p. 10; Wharton, 1666, sig. B2v; Lilly, 1673, sig. A3ff; Saunders, 1667, sig. C2. Lilly regretted the assassination of the De Witt brothers, and by implication the fall of the republican regime: Lilly, 1673, sig. A2.
126. See generally J. P. Kenyon, *The Popish Plot* (1973); J. Miller, *Popery and Politics* (Cambridge, 1973); D. Ogg, *England in the Reign of Charles II* (Oxford, 1955); J. R. Jones, *The First Whigs* (1961); K. H. D. Haley, *The First Earl of Shaftesbury* (Oxford, 1968).
127. J.B., *Good and Joyful News for England* (1681), p. 7 and *passim*.
128. For Lilly: *Life and Times*, pp. 102–3; Josten, *Ashmole*, e.g. pp. 1433, 1440–1. For Coley: Parker, *Ephemeris*, 1699, sig. A3v; Bodl. Ms Add. B8, f. 70v.
129. Partridge, 1679, sig. C2, C6; idem, *Prodromus* (1680), pp. 15, 28–9.
130. Partridge, 1682, sig. Av, 3, 4, 5, B6, C8v; 1683, sig. B2–6, C6v–7.
131. Gadbury, 1679, sig. A5; Gadbury, 1680, sig. B8; Trigge, 1679, sig. A3v.

132. *C.S.P.D., 1679–80*, p. 291; ibid., *1680–1*, p. 520; Gadbury, 1681, sig. C8v; 1682, sig. Av–2; 1684, sig. Av–2; Gadbury, *Magna Veritas* (1680), pp. 6, 7 and *passim*; idem, *Cardines Coeli* (1684), p. 35; idem, *Merlinus Verax, 1687*, pp. 10–12, 19; Wharton, *Works*, sig. A3; *Observations upon the . . . Prophecies of Mr. John Gadbury* (1680); T. Dangerfield, *Animadversions upon Mr. John Gadbury's Almanack 1682* (1682); *The Case of Th. Dangerfield* (1680); Partridge, *A Short Answer to . . . John Gadbury* (1687), p. 3 and *passim*; idem, *Mene Tekel* (1688), p. 3; idem, *Opus Reformatum* (1693), p. 89; H.M.C., 36, *Ormonde*, N.S., v, p. 263; H.M.C., 6, *7th Report*, Appendix, p. 680; Thorndike, *Magic*, viii, p. 333; *A Complete Collection of State Trials*, vii, ed. W. Cobbett (1810), pp. 1044ff.

133. Gadbury, 1684, sig. Av; *Merlinus Verax 1687*, pp. 9, 18; *Observations*, p. 3.

134. Gadbury, 1681, sig. A3v, 5, v; *Autobiography and Anecdotes of William Taswell D.D.*, ed. G. P. Elliott, Camden Soc., lv (1853), pp. 29–31; Gadbury, 1682, sig. B6v, C6; 1683, sig. B2, B4, B7, v; 1684, sig. A2.

135. Gadbury, 1684, sig. A2, A3, A3v–4, B2; Gadbury, 1685, sig. Av; see also Culpepper, 1683, *passim*; Streete, 1684, sig. B8v; Trigge, 1685, sig. A3ff.

136. Gadbury, 1684, sig. A3. For the background see Ogg, op. cit.; J. R. Western, *Monarchy and Revolution* (1972).

137. Holwell, *Catastrophe Mundi* (1682); *Middlesex County Records*, ed. J. C. Jeaffreson (1886–92), iv, pp. 212–13.

138. T. Sprat, *A True Account . . . of the Horrid Conspiracy* (1685), pt. ii, pp. 60–1; *C.S.P.D., 1682*, p. 564; Gadbury, *A Reply to that Pernicious Libel* (1687), sig. Iv–2; Parker, 1699, sig. A3–5v; Parker, 1700, sig. A3–v.

139. Partridge, 1685, sig. B.

140. *D.N.B.*, Partridge; J. Dunton, *The Life and Errours* (1818), p. 246; above, p. 50. William Salmon, a violent Whig compiler in the 1690s, also sought refuge abroad, in the West Indies: Salmon, 1691, sig. B8v; Salmon, 1694, sig. A2v.

141. Coley, *Nuncius Syderius 1686*, sig. A3; ibid., 1688, sig. A3; Culpepper, 1688, sig. A2; Wing, 1686, sig. A2; Trigge, 1688, sig. C3.

142. Davis, 1688, sig. A5v.

143. Saunder, 1688, sig. A2 (reprinted in his edn. for 1689).

144. Gadbury, 1686, sig. A3v, A6, B2v; 1689, sig. A2.

145. Gadbury, 1688, sig. A5, 7, 8, B2, 3, 6, C3; 1689, sig. A2, v, B2, 3, 8, C3; *Merlinus Verax 1687*, *passim* (identified as Gadbury's by Partridge, *Nebulo Anglicanus* (1693), sig. A2; cf. Blagden, 'Distribution', Table 1; S.C., Journal Book, 1650–98, f. 115v). For the events described see Western, op. cit.

146. Woodward, 1689, sig. Av; Whalley, 1688, p. 5; Tanner, 1688, sig. C2v; above, p. 50.

147. Anonymous broadside; no date, but clearly belongs to 1688.

148. *D.N.B.*, Partridge; (Partridge), 1687, sig. Av, B4v and *passim*. Extracts from this and the 1688 edn., which appears not to have survived, were reproduced in *Annus Mirabilis* (1688/9); *Partridge's Advice to the Protestants of England* (?1689); *Mr. Partridge's Wonderful Predictions Pro Anno 1688*; *Mene Tekel* (1688); B.L. Ms Sloane 2281, fos. 83v–85v.

149. *A Reply*, sig. Av, 4v, Bv, pp. 3–4, 6–7, 25–7, sig. I2v. A variant edition appeared in September. Wing wrongly ascribes the work to G. Parker.

150. Partridge, *A Short Answer to . . . Gadbury* (suffix to *Mene Tekel*), *passim*; *Nebulo Anglicanus*, p. 8 and *passim*; Partridge, *Opus Reformatum*, p. 86; Coley, 1700, sig. Av.

151. *Mene Mene*, sig. A3–v and *passim*; see also n148 to p. 96, above. There are recent accounts of the Revolution by J. R. Jones and M. Ashley.

152. Gadbury, 1689, sig. A2, A4v; above, p. 41. Andrews made the same mistake in his edition for 1689. Partridge, *Mene Mene*, pp. 26–7; *Gadburies Prophetical Sayings* (1690), brs.

153. Gadbury, 1690, sig. Av; *C.S.P.D., 1689–90*, p. 241; ibid., *1690–1*, p. 30; Partridge, *Opus Reformatum*, p. 87; idem, *Nebulo Anglicanus*, pp. 9–10; H.M.C., 71, *Finch Mss*, iii, p. 379.

154. Coley, 1692, sig. A3; Cookson, 1699, sig. A3; Hobbs, 1693, sig. C2v; Hobbs, 1696, sig. C4v; Salmon, 1691, sig. A2; idem, 1694, sig. A4v; idem, 1697, sig. A5; Woodward, 1693, sig. B6v; Partridge, 1690, t.p. and sig. Av; Whalley, 1691, sig. A2v.

155. Tanner, 1698, sig. C; Hobbs, 1695, sig. C5v; Partridge, 1692, sig, A2, C2.

156. Partridge, 1690, sig. A4v; ibid., 1694, sig. C8v; ibid., 1698, sig. A3; Salmon, 1692. sig. A2.
157. *D.N.B.*, Parker; Parker, 1690, sig. A3; 1691, sig. D5; 1692, sig. B4.
158. Partridge, 1691, sig. Av; Whalley, 1691, sig. Av.
159. Partridge, 1692, sig. B; 1694, sig. A4; 1696, sig. B, B8; *Opus Reformatum*, pp. 22–40; see also the chronologies in his almanacs for 1692–4; (Gadbury), *Merlini Liberati Errata* (1692), sig. A2–v (author identified on t.p. of Bodl. copy, Ash. E39(6)).
160. Tanner, 1690, sig. A5v.
161. Gadbury, 1692, sig. C7v; Partridge, *Opus Reformatum*, p. 87; idem, *Nebulo Anglicanus*, pp. 9–10; Partridge, 1699, sig. C5.
162. Parker, *Mercurius Anglicanus 1698*, sig. Av–2v, C4v–7v; idem, *Ephemeris 1699*, sig. A4v–5v, B2vff.; 1700, sig. A3–7; (Gadbury), *Merlini Liberati Errata, passim*; Partridge, 1692, sig. Av, 2, C8v; 1693, sig. Av, C8v; 1695, sig. C7–v; 1699, sig. C5, 7v–8.
163. Partridge, 1693, sig. B4; 1697, sig. A7.
164. Partridge, 1691, sig. C8; Tanner, 1696, sig. C3; Woodward, 1694, sig. B2v.
165. Tanner, 1691, sig. C8; Partridge, 1695, sig. A4.
166. Partridge, 1681, sig. C2; 1682, sig. A5, 6v, B; idem, *The Nativity of . . . Lewis XIV* (1680) (ascribed by Wing to Gadbury, but Gadbury ascribed it to Partridge in his *Merlini Liberati Errata*, p. 18); Holwell, *Catastrophe Mundi;* Woodward, 1684, sig. B3.
167. Partridge, 1691, sig. C2; 1693, sig. A7; 1694, sig. A4; 1695, sig. B7; 1696, sig. C6v; Woodward, 1693, sig. A2; 1694, sig. B5, C6v; 1695, sig. B3v; 1696, sig. A4v, C6; Whalley, 1690, sig. C7; R. Godson, *Astrologia Reformata* (1696), p. 38; Salmon, 1692, sig. C6v; idem, 1695, sig. C6v; Coley, 1692, sig. C4–v; Tanner, 1690, sig. C4v; Holwell, *An Appendix* (1683), p. 39; Ms note on Partridge's *Nativity of Lewis XIV*, B.L. copy 718 g 12(6) at p. 29.
168. Kirby, *Catastrophe Galliae* (1690), p. 19.
169. Coley, 1692, sig. A3; Woodward, 1695, sig. Av. 5ff., C5v–6; idem, 1696, sig. Av, 4v, C; Salmon, 1692, sig. C6v; idem, 1696, sig. C5v; Hobbs, 1693, sig. A2, C2v; idem, 1696, sig. C8.
170. Below, pp. 177–8, 252.
171. Lilly, *Life and Times*, p. 67; *Perfect Occurrences* (24 September–1 October 1647), p. 601.
172. Lilly, *Life and Times*, p. 68; Thomas, pp. 313, 314, 321, 372–3.
173. Thomas, esp. pp. 291–2, 312–13, 349–57; *C.S.P.D., 1671–2*, p. 83; ibid., *1673*, p. 10; ibid., *1698*, p. 393; below, pp. 287–8.
174. A list of county and borough seats was printed by the astrologer Arthur Hopton in *A Concordancy of Years* (1612), pp. 199–203, and reprinted in e.g. Hawkins, 1625. Lilly's surveys sometimes included even the Tartars and Mongols, e.g. Lilly, 1676, sig. A5.
175. Gadbury, 1686, sig. Av; idem, 1694, sig. Av.

Chapter 4 Society (*pages* 102–30)

1. Gadbury, 1688, sig. A3; Eaton, 1657, pp. 94–6; Pigot, 1659, Sig. A2–5.
2. Alleyn, 1606, sig. A7; Frende, 1623, sig. A6v; Bucknall, 1676, sig. B.
3. Dade, 1666, sig. C3; Gray, 1591, sig. B7v; Hopton, 1607, sig. A8v; Evans, 1613, sig. A7v; Bowker, 1679, sig. B8; and many others.
4. Dove, 1672, sig. B4; *Poor Robin*, 1690, sig. B8.
5. Vaux, 1627, sig. B5.
6. Wing, 1685, sig. C5.
7. Vaux, 1627, sig. B5; Watson, 1604, sig. C2v; Ranger, 1621, sig. A6v; Hewlett, 1627, sig. B3; Securis, 1566, sig. A3v; Martindale, 1676, sig. B7.
8. Gadbury, 1676, sig. A3; Wharton, 1642, sig. B3 (citing Eccles. x:20).
9. Parker, 1690, sig. C7v; Brothyel, 1548, sig. Cv; Alleyn, 1606, sig. A5.
10. Riders, 1670, sig. C4; Watson, 1604, sig. C2v.

11. Hewit, 1654, sig. A7.
12. Gadbury, 1670, sig. B4; Gadbury, 1677, sig. B3; Booker, 1649, sig. B3–v; Securis, 1581, sig. C2v.
13. Coelson, 1687, sig. C3, v. For other examples see below, pp. 147–8, 255
14. Gadbury, 1665, sig. C6v; Vaux, 1664, sig. C2; Strutt, 1690, sig. C2; Bowker, 1670, sig. C5v; Lilly, 1661, sig. A5v.
15. Booker, 1658, sig. B8; see also e.g. Gardner, 1698, sig. C3.
16. Wing, 1685, sig. C5; Securis, 1566, sig. A8; Culpeper, 1653, sig. E3.
17. Harflete, 1656, sig. A7v–8; Gadbury, 1665, sig. C6v; Saunder, 1698, sig. B4; below pp. 112–13.
18. Pond, 1605, sig. C7; Carre, 1593, sig. B4v; Gresham, 1603, sig. B4v; Pond, 1610. sig. A8; Rogeford, 1560, sig. B4; Brothyel, 1545, sig. B4; Sucuris, 1581, sig. C4. See H. C. White, *Social Criticism in Popular Religious Literature in the Sixteenth Century* (1944, reissued 1965) for similar attacks.
19. Gadbury, 1665, sig. C6v; Trigge, 1682, sig. C2–v (cf. Carre, 1593, sig. B4v, approving the execution of Achan for covetousness: Joshua vii); Dove, 1672, sig. B4.
20. Securis, 1568, sig. A6; idem, 1574, sig. B2; Wing, sig. C3v; 1668, sig. C6v–7 (quoting Isaiah v:8); 1669, sig. C5. Many of these comments were repeated by John Wing, in e.g. Wing, 1685, sig. C5. The Wings lived in Rutland in the east midlands where continuing enclosure and engrossing provoked other criticism in the mid-century: see J. Thirsk, ed., *The Agrarian History of England and Wales*, iv (1970), p. 238. For the Wings' advertisements see e.g. Wing, 1649, sig. C8v; 1692, sig. C8v. See also Pond, 1610, sig. A8; Wharton, 1648, sig. C2; Lilly, 1657, sig. A6.
21. Ranger, 1628, sig. A3; Buckminster, 1587, sig. A7; Gresham, 1603, sig. B4v–5. See also Securis, 1574, sig. B2; Wharton, 164, sig. C2.
22. Vaux, 1631, sig. B8–C2; Coelson, 1677 sig. A3. Most almanacs were prompt in recording the reduction of interest from 10% to 8% (1624) and to 6% (1652). M. Sparke's *Usurer's Almanack* (1626) reached a '4th' edn. by 1650; see also R. Butler, *The Scale of Interest* (1633), sig. A2 and *passim*. On peasant indebtedness and bonds see M. Spufford, in *Land, Church and People*, ed. J. Thirsk (1970), pp. 143–4.
23. Harflete, 1656, sig. A8 (2nd signature).
24. Hewit, 1654, sig. A2; Gray, 1604, sig. A7v; Bowker, 1675, sig. A2 (2nd signature) (widely repeated, e.g. Partridge, 1731, sig. A3); Partridge, 1681, sig. A2v; *Owles Almanacke*, 1618, pp. 5–6.
25. H.N., *A Yea and Nay Almanack*, 1679, sig. A4; Pond, 1635, sig. A4.
26. Bretnor, 1617, sig. C7; Coelson, 1676, sig. Av; idem, 1677, sig. A2.
27. Culpeper, 1654, sig. D5; Booker, 1632, sig. A6; Saunders, 1659, sig. A2; Bretnor, 1617, sig. Cv; Booker, 1655, sig. C6; Culpepper, 1699, sig. Av; Gilbert, 1683, sig. Bv; Gadbury, 1681, sig. A4; *Poor Robin*, 1666, sig. A2; idem, 1675, sig. A5v; W. Ramesey, *The Gentlemans Companion* (1672), p. 224.
28. Culpeper, 1654, sig. D5; Andrews, 1658, sig. B2; Baston, 1656, sig. B5v; Booker, 1655, sig. C5v; Lilly, 1649, sig. D3. See generally D. Veall, *The Popular Movement for Law Reform 1640–1660* (1970); S. Prall, *The Agitation for Law Reform* . . . (The Hague, 1966).
29. Fitzsmith, 1654, sig. Dv; Desmus (i.e. Sheppard), 1655, sig. A3; Wharton, 1651, sig. Dv; idem, 1652, sig. A3v; 1653, sig. B3v; 1655, sig. B3; 1656, sig. B2; 1659, sig. B2v.
30. Saunders, 1654, sig. Av; Culpeper, 1654, sig. D.
31. Lilly, 1653, sig. C7; idem, 1651, sig. B5; 1655, sig. A6v; Gadbury, 1656, sig. A4.
32. Bodl. Ms Ash. B6, f. 126.
33. Coley, 1690, sig. A2; Culpepper, 1682, sig. Av; *Protestant Almanack*, 1694, sig. A2.
34. Wharton, 1663, sig. B; Saunders, 1661, sig. A (2nd signature); Gadbury, 1661, sig. A3.
35. Tanner, 1660, sig. A2; Tanner, 1659, sig. B6. On the Norman Yoke, see above, p. 78
36. Tanner, 1659, sig. A2; Jinner, 1659, sig. A2 (both printed by the political pamphleteer John Streater).
37. Ramesey, *Gentlemans Companion*, p. 223 (B.L. copy).
38. *Poor Robin*, 1666, sig. A2.
39. Culpeper, 1653, pp. 26–7, plagiarized in *The Dutch Bloudy Almanack 1653*, p. 4; Lilly, 1645, p. 79.
40. Napier, *Bloudy Almanack*, 1648, p. 8.
41. See below, Chapter 5.

42. Partridge, *Defectio Geniturarum* (1697), sig. b–2v; Partridge, 1697, sig. C7. The allusions are to Coley and probably Trotter: see *Dr. Trotter's Fortune-Book* (1708). See also above, pp. 54, 56.
43. Burton, 1613, sig. B5; idem, 1620, sig. B3; Bretnor, 1615, sig. B; Booker, 1660, sig. C2; cf. Ramesey, *De Veneris* (1663), sig. A8.
44. Langley, 1642, sig. B2; Gadbury, *London's Deliverance* (1665), sig. A3; Watson, 1601 (notes for April); Culpepper, 1696, sig. A6v.
45. Holden, 1689, sig. B3v.
46. Tanner, 1672, sig. C8; Vaux, 1658, sig. A8—B; Beridge, 1654, sig. B4.
47. *Poor Robin*, 1688, sig. B5.
48. Saunders, 1654, sig. B; on Culpeper see *D.N.B.*; F. N. L. Poynter, 'Nicholas Culpeper and his Books', *Journ. of Hist. of Medicine*, xvii (1962); Hill, *Intellectual Origins*.
49. Lilly, 1655, sig. A6; idem, 1656, sig. B7v. Lilly himself acquired 'fee-farm rents worth £120 a year which he lost at the Restoration: *Life and Times*, p. 83.
50. Tanner, 1659, sig. C7v; Ramesey, *Astrologia Restaurata* (1653), p. 20.
51. Wharton, 1652, sig. A3; Gadbury, 1658, sig. C3; idem., 1684, sig. B2; Lilly, 1676, sig. B; Parker, 1693, sig. C5; Booker, 1648, sig. C4; Culpepper, 1681, sig. A5. See C. Hill, 'The Many-Headed Monster . . .' in *From the Renaissance to the Counter-Reformation* ed. C. H. Carter (1968).
52. Gadbury, 1684, sig. B2.
53. Laet, 1520, sig. A4v; Lloyd, 1582, sig. C2; de Billy, *Certaine Wonderful Predictions* (1604), p. 3.
54. Ramesey, 1652, p. 122; Coley, *Nuncius Sydereus*, 1690, sig. C4v; see also e.g. Silvester, 1682, pp. 9 (i.e. 6), 7, 11 (i.e. 10).
55. Gadbury, *London's Deliverance*, p. 10. The mortality rate was known to be far higher among the poor.
56. See below, pp. 123–6.
57. Parron, 1498, frag.; Hopton, 1613, sig. C8; Securis, 1568, sig. A8v; idem, 1569, sig. A7; Lloyd, 1582, sig. C3v; Johnson, 1598, sig. B3; *Poor Robin*, 1688, sig. B7; Blagrave, 1665, sig. C3v.
58. Trigge, 1666, sig. A7.
59. Culpeper, *Catastrophe Magnatum* (1652), pp. 10–11; J.S., *The Starr-Prophet Anatomiz'd* (1675), p. 23.
60. Culpeper, 1654, sig. E5; cf. the almanacs of Jinner and Thurston, *passim*, and J. Livie, 1654, p. 4.
61. Culpeper, 1654, sig. F; Livie, 1654, p. 6.
62. Lilly, 1649, sig. F8; Livie, 1654, p. 5; Thurston, 1652, sig. E.
63. Culpeper, *Catastrophe*, pp. 6, 11; idem, 1654, sig. C7v; Lilly, 1650, sig. A3v; idem, 1660, sig. A3v.
64. e.g. Buckminster, 1598, sig. B8–C6; Alleyn 1607, sig. Cv; White, 1629; Beridge, 1654; Dade, 1666; Woodhouse, 1666. For the background see e.g. Thirsk, ed., *Agrarian History*, ch. 3.
65. Wing, 1649, sig. C8v; Wing, 1692, sig. C8v; Woodward, 1687, sig. B; Lilly, 1673, sig. F8v; on Ward see Taylor, *Practitioners*, p. 270.
66. Gardner, 1698; Bucknall, 1675–8; Dade, 1685, sig. B3.
67. e.g. *City and Country Chapmans*, 1685, sig. C4v; Riders, 1695, sig. C6v (corrections to be sent respectively to Mr. Leigh and Benj. Tooke at Stationers' Hall).
68. *Mr. Lilly's New Prophecy: or Certain Notable Passages* (1678), p. 5.
69. Booker, 1648, sig. C3v.
70. T. Dekker, *The Shoemaker's Holiday* (1600), III. iii.
71. Frende, 1585, sig. C8.
72. *Mercurius Civicus*, esp. 1674, sig. C2.
73. Pigot, 1630, sig. B3v; Peregrine, 1636, sig. C4–v.
74. See esp. *Fly* (from 1657), *Rose* (from 1659) and later Turner.
75. Tanner, 1659, sig. C7; Bucknall, 1676, sig. A2v.
76. Harflete, 1653, sig. C3v.
77. Woodward, 1685, sig. C8–v (repeated in 1686).
78. The author was T.L.
79. Lilly, 1652, sig. A4v; Gadbury, 1675, sig. E5; idem, 1677, sig. Av. Gadbury acknowledged Roger L'Estrange as the originator of his scheme.

80. Gadbury, *West India*, 1674, sig. A2, and 1675, sig. A2v; idem, 1671, sig. E8. See also Lilly, 1656, sig. A8. For Gadbury's interest in exploration and navigation see below, pp. 202–3.
81. Andrews, 1655, sig. B2 (Venetians); Lilly, 1653, sig. A6v (Dutch); see also above, pp. 77–8 and below, p. 234.
82. *Poor Robin*, 1679, sig. C2v–3; idem, 1690, sig. C8.
83. Booker, 1664, sig. C3v.
84. *Arcandam*, 1592, sig. M; Season, e.g. 1761, pp. 2–3; Gadbury, 1663, sig. C6v; Saunders, *Palmistry* (1663), 2nd part, p. 145; cf. B. Jonson, *The Devil is an Ass*, IV. i, for a discussion of the breeding of lap-dogs by astrological methods.
85. Askham, 1554, sig. A5v; Alleyn, 1609, sig. B7v.
86. Frende, 1588, sig. C4v; Securis, 1581, sig. C4ff.; Allestree, 1621, sig. B4.
87. Buckminster, 1598, sig. A3 (in a verse frequently reprinted in *Neve* and *Dade*); Browne, 1620, sig. B6v.
88. Hewlett, 1625, sig. A6.
89. Askham, 1554, sig. A4v; Buckminster, 1598, sig. A5v; Harvey, 1584, sig. B; Gray, 1589, sig. A8v; Wing, 1654, sig. B7v; Riders, 1670, sig. C4; Dade, 1666, sig. B7v.
90. Riders, 1670, sig. B6; Securis, 1581, sig. C4v; Bretnor, 1615, sig. B2; Browne, 1623, sig. B5v; Krabtree, 1685, sig. B6; Frende, 1589, sig. C5v.
91. *Prognostycation of Two Shepherdes*, 1556, sig. A2; Allestree, 1629, sig. A7, 8; White, 1630, sig. A6.
92. *Owles Almanack*, 1618, p. 49; Dove, 1670, sig. A4.
93. Securis, 1581, sig. C7v–8; *Poor Robin*, 1666, sig. C8. The occupation of 'coffee-man' was listed in a Ms note in a copy of Piers, 1640 (B.L. 58 k 25(2)).
94. S. Partridge, *The Infallible Astrologer* (1700), p. 2; *Owles Almanack*, p. 32; cf. E. P. Thompson, 'Time, Work-Discipline and Industrial Capitalism', *Past and Present*, 38 (1967); K. V. Thomas, 'Work and Leisure in Pre-Industrial Society', ibid., 29 (1964).
95. Vaux, 1665, sig. Cv–2; Ranger, 1615, sig. B5; Wing, 1670, sig. C5; Bretnor, 1615, sig. B4; Culpeper, 1654, p. 8; cf. T. Brown, *Amusements*, ed. A. L. Hayward (1927), p. 83.
96. Frende, 1589, sig. C3; Securis, 1581, sig. C5, 8–v; Dove, 1670, sig. A3.
97. Woodhouse, 1642, sig. B4v.
98. Buckminster, 1590, sig. C3v–4; Neve, 1649, sig. B4–v.
99. Neve, 1649, sig. A6; Riders, 1670, sig. B7; Woodhouse, 1647, sig. B8; Beridge, 1654, sig. B4.
100. Bodl. Ms Add. B8, f. 1.
101. Wing, 1669, sig. C4v (reprinted in Wing, 1685, sig. C5).
102. Harflete, 1654, sig. A5v; see also *Poor Robin*, 1690, sig. A7.
103. Pond, 1607, sig. C6. For other comments on dogs see *Prog. of Two Shepherdes*, 1556, sig. B–v.
104. Frende, 1589, sig. C3–v; Buckminster, 1589, sig. C8; Booker, 1631, sig. A7 (a verse adapted from Bretnor, 1618, sig. B6); idem, 1654, sig. B5v; Lilly, 1677, sig. C8.
105. *Vox Graculi, or Iack Dawes Prognostication*, 1623, p. 44; *Prog. of Two Shepherdes*, sig. A4; Desmus, 1654, sig. A3v.
106. Johnson, 1624, sig. A5v; *Poor Robin*, 1685, sig. A3; Ramesey, 1652, pp. 108–9.
107. Bell, 1622, sig. B3v; Culpeper, *A Directory for Midwives* (1651), pp. 140–1. On sexual behaviour in this period see esp. A. D. J. Macfarlane, 'The Regulation of Marital and Sexual Relationships in Seventeenth Century England' (London M.Phil. thesis, 1968).
108. Allestree, 1626, sig. B3–4; Hopton, 1613, sig. C8v; Browne, 1620, sig. A2v, B3v; Wharton, 1642, sig. A5v; Trigge, 1679, sig. A5, 6; D. Partridge, 1694, sig. A3; Hopton, 1613, sig. C8v (abstain where there is no 'r' in the month); L. Mascall, *The Country Man's Jewel* (1680), pp. 386–7.
109. Dauncy, 1615, sig. Cv; *Montelion*, 1662, sig. B6, 8; *Poor Robin*, 1697, sig. B3. See also 'The Parliament of Women' in R. Thompson (ed.), *Samuel Pepys's Penny Merriments* (1976), p. 259.
110. See the discussion by L. Bradley and others in *Local Population Studies*, 4–6, 8, 11 (1970–3); B. M. Berry and R. S. Schofield, 'Age at Baptism in Pre-Industrial England', *Population Studies*, xxv (1971). The low figures in August cannot be explained by astrology or by abstinence during harvest, but perhaps baptismal services were postponed because of the pressure of harvest.

111. Gray, 1589, sig. A5; Harvey, 1584, sig. B, B4.
112. D. Partridge, 1694, sig. Av, A2v; e.g. Burton, 1613, sig. B2v; Dade, 1647, sig. C4.
113. Culpeper, *Directory for Midwives*, pp. 30, 81–2.
114. D. Partridge, 1694, sig. B2v; N. Culpepper, *Physical Receipts* (1690), pp. 14–15; R. Turner, *The British Physician* (1664), p. 90; Thomas, pp. 233–4.
115. Culpeper, *A Physicall Directory* (1649), p. 32; idem, *Pharmacopoeia Londinensis* (1653), p. 15; Swan, 1658, sig. C2; J. Archer, *A Compendious Herbal* (1673), pp. 34, 36, 87; T. Hill, *The Art of Gardening* (1574), pp. 42, 45, 78, 79; idem, *A Profitable Instruction of the Perfite Ordering of Bees* (1586), pp. 60–1; Turner, op. cit., pp. 4, 156, 261; Allestree, 1626, sig. B; P. Moore, *The Hope of Health* (1565), sig. D8v, E2. See also Thomas, pp. 188–9 and n; Partridge, 1698, sig. C6v.
116. Jinner, 1664, sig. B6v, 7; Swan, 1659, sig. C2v.
117. See on this subject E. A. Wrigley, 'Family Limitation in Pre-industrial England', *E.H.R.*, xix (1966).
118. e.g. Swan, 1661, sig. C3; idem, *Speculum Mundi* (Cambridge, 1635), p. 262; Turner, op. cit., p. 314. Gerard and Du Bartas were often cited as authorities. On abortion see e.g. P. Hair, ed., *Before the Bawdy Court* (1972), pp. 81, 152, 172, 204.
119. Jinner, 1658, sig. B6; idem, 1659, sig. B8; idem, 1664, sig. B4; *Aristotle's Masterpiece* (1694), p. 9.
120. H.N., *Yea and Nay Almanack*, 1680, sig. A4.
121. Ramesey, 1652, pp. 22–3 (cf. his *Gentlemans Companion*, p. 92); Perkins, 1699, sig. A4. See generally C. Camden, *The Elizabethan Woman* (1952).
122. Tanner, 1659, sig. B; *Poor Robin*, 1688, sig. C3; Graphaeus, 1598, sig. A3; Metcalf, 1654, sig. Cv; Allestree, 1651, sig. A2; Lilly, 1664, sig. B3; Trigge, 1683, sig. A6v.
123. *Erra Pater* (n.d. 1610? pr. T. Snodham), sig. A7–v.
124. *Poor Robin*, 1686, sig. A6; idem, 1669, sig. B2v; idem, 1685, sig. A5v.
125. *Arcandam* (1592), sig. C4v, D2, E6v, G8, H6v and *passim*.
126. Gray, 1604, sig. A5v; Fowle, 1695, sig. B2v.
127. *Poor Robin*, 1666, sig. B2; idem, 1691, sig. A8.
128. Idem, 1666, sig. B8v; idem, 1667, sig. C2v; idem, 1681, sig. A7; idem, 1682, sig. A7; Tanner, 1659, sig. B.
129. Hopton, 1613, sig. C6v; Booker, 1649, sig. A7v; Jinner, 1664, sig. B6v–7.
130. *Poor Robin*, 1666, sig. A6, A6v, B, B4; idem, 1699, sig. A7v; Swan, *Speculum Mundi*, p. 256. The nine sorts of cuckolds may have been suggested by *Hey for Horn Fair . . . Nine Several Sorts of Cuckolds* (1674).
131. Trigge, 1666, sig. A6v; Gadbury, 1672, sig. E3; *Poor Robin*, 1694, sig. C6; Fowle, 1694, sig. B3v; Desmus, 1654, sig. A7v.
132. *Poor Robin*, 1692, sig. A8; idem, 1698, sig. A5; cf. *The Letters of Dorothy Osborne*, ed. G. C. Moore Smith (Oxford, 1928), pp. 47, 71, 110.
133. Desmus, 1653, sig. C5; Thurston, 1652, sig. E5; *Levellers Almanack*, 1652, p. 6 (misprint for p. 8); *Poor Robin*, 1694, sig. C6; see K. V. Thomas, 'Women and the Civil War Sects', *Past and Present*, 13 (1958); C. Hill, *The World Turned Upside Down*, ch. 15.
134. *Poor Robin*, 1666, sig. C2v.
135. (Dekker), *Ravens Almanacke*, 1609; *Poor Robin*, 1689, sig. C7v; *Montelion*, 1662, sig. A6; *Poor Robin*, 1667, sig. A2; Bucknall, 1676, sig. B6. On skimmingtons: *Poor Robin*, 1699, sig. A7v; and see E. P. Thompson, 'Rough Music: *Le Charivari Anglais*,' *Annales E.S.C.*, 27 (1972).
136. *Poor Robin*, 1665, sig. C3v–4; see also *Diary of Henry Machyn*, ed. J. G. Nichols (Camden Soc., 1848), p. 48; *H.L.Q.*, xxii (1958–9), p. 355; T. Dekker, *The Shoemaker's Holiday* (1600), V. ii.
137. *Poor Robin*, 1665, sig. C8; Beridge, 1654, sig. A5v; Tanner, 1683, sig. Av; Hewlett, 1634, sig. B4; Frende, 1585, sig. C8.
138. *Prog. of Two Shepherdes*, 1556, sig. A4; Allestree, 1632, sig. B6; idem, 1642, sig. B5.
139. *Poor Robin*, 1694, sig. B5; idem, 1692, sig. A3v; (Dekker), *Ravens Almanacke*, in *The Non-Dramatic Works*, ed. A. B. Grosart (1885), iv, pp. 243–65; Lloyd, 1582, sig. C3v; cf. K. V. Thomas, 'The Double Standard', *Journ. of the Hist. of Ideas*, xx (1959).
140. Ramesey, *Gentlemans Companion*, p. 11. *The Owles Almanacke*, 1618, p. 61, thought literate women were ridiculous.

141. Jinner, 1658, sig. B, v; idem, 1659, sig. B3v; cf. Lucy Hutchinson, *Memoirs of the Life of Colonel Hutchinson*, ed. J. Sutherland (1973), p. 48.
142. Alleyn, 1606, sig. A5v.
143. Gadbury, 1673, sig. B7v; Harflete, 1654, sig. A7, 8; Hooker, 1668, sig. C2v.
144. *Endymion*, 1665, sig. A4v–5; *Owles Almanacke*, 1618, p. 36; S. Partridge, *The Infallible Astrologer* (1700), p. 8; *Poor Robin*, 1666, sig. C2.
145. Culpeper, *Directory* (1651), pp. 213–14; *Culpepper's Directory for Midwives* (1662), pp. 230–1; N. Ward, *The London Spy*, ed. A. L. Hayward (1927), p. 132.
146. Culpeper, *Directory* (1651), p. 86; Ramesey, *Astrologia Restaurata* (1653), p. 11. P. Laslett, 'Age at menarche in Europe in the early 18th century . . .,' *Journ. of Interdisciplinary History*, 2 (1971–2), suggests an age of sixteen to seventeen; J. B. Post in *Population Studies*, xxv (1971), pp. 83–7 makes a case for the earlier teens. For other contemporary estimates, mostly endorsing the age of fourteen, see K. V. Thomas, *Age and Authority in Early Modern England* (British Academy, 1977), p. 23n.
147. *Poor Robin*, 1681, sig. A5; idem, 1691, sig. A6; Gadbury, 1696, sig. B8. See R. W. Malcolmson, *Popular Recreations in English Society 1700–1850* (Cambridge, 1973) and D. Brailsford, *Sport and Society: Elizabeth to Anne* (1969).
148. *Owles Almanacke*, pp. 43, 47, 56; *Poor Robin*, 1667, sig. C3v; idem, 1673, sig. A5v, B2v; idem, 1677, sig. Av. Spurn-point may be a form of hopscotch (*O.E.D.*).
149. *Poor Robin*, 1688, sig. A7v; idem, 1694, sig. B.
150. Idem, 1666, sig. B; idem, 1690, sig. B.
151. Idem, 1678, sig. B; idem, 1666, sig. A8v; Andrews, 1658, sig. B8v; Howell, 1656, sig. A8, B.
152. *Poor Robin*, 1666, sig. A8v; idem, 1690, sig. A8; idem, 1692, sig. Ev.
153. Idem, 1666, sig. B3v; idem, 1681, sig. B3v; idem, 1688, sig. A4; Desmus, 1654, sig. A3v; Woodward, 1685, sig. B4. Hewson, said to be a cobbler by origin, was a regicide and one of Cromwell's 'new lords'; Hoyle committed suicide on the anniversary of the king's execution, allegedly in remorse; Noll's (Cromwell's) nose was a popular target for satirists; the hog-faced lady was Tannakin Skinker, whose visit to England produced a crop of ballads in 1639; see H. E. Rollins, *An Analytical Index of the Ballad Entries* (Chapel Hill, N.C., 1924), and his *A Pepysian Garland* (Cambridge, 1922), pp. 449–54 (ballad and portrait). Other 'curiosities' were mentioned, e.g. Jeffrey, the dwarf kept by Charles I's queen (*Poor Robin*, 1684, sig. C2v); Henry Welby, a hermit for forty-four years (Gadbury, 1701, sig. Av) and—frequently—Old Parr and Haddock, the 'sleeping preacher'.
154. *Poor Robin*, 1667, sig. C3v; idem, 1690, sig. B6.
155. Idem, 1685, sig. B7.
156. Gadbury, 1679, sig. B3; idem, 1696, sig. A5, C7 (acknowledging as his source John Aubrey, an acquaintance); *Owles Almanacke*, 1618, p. 48.
157. Jack Adams, c. 1664, p. 3; *Poor Robin*, 1678, sig. A3. On Mary Carleton, the German princess, executed 1673, see *The Complete Newgate Calendar*, ed. J. L. Rayner and G. T. Crook (1926), i, pp. 249–67.
158. Jinner, 1659, sig. B3, v; Johnson, 1598, sig. B3; Allestree, 1623, sig. B3v; Vaux, 1633, sig. Bv; Street, 1653, sig. D5; Culpeper, 1654, p. 29; Jinner, 1664, sig. B6v; Blagrave, *Blagraves Astrological Practice* (1673), pp. 121–3, 140–1; see Thomas, esp. pp. 317, 362–3, 632–4, and below, pp. 213–14.
159. Burton, 1619, sig. B8; Blagrave, op. cit., p. 140; Pond, 1609, sig. C7; Swallow, 1672, sig. B6v; Gadbury, 1676, sig. C5.
160. Pond, 1609, sig. C6v–7; C.P., *The Shepherd's New Kalender*, 1700, pp. 73–4. See also Ward, *London Spy*, p. 260.
161. e.g. James Newton offered residential care for the 'distracted and melancholy' at Cumberland House, near Clerkenwell Green: Coley, *Nuncius*, 1675, sig. B6; see also a similar advertisement by John Archer in Coley, *Nuncius*, 1684, sig. C8.
162. See, besides Wharton, Gadbury, 1658, sig. A7; Saunders, 1659, sig. A5; *Poor Robin*, 1690, sig. A8; idem, 1672, sig. A8v; idem, 1688, sig. B7. On attitudes to suicide see S. E. Sprott, *The English Debate on Suicide* (La Salle, Ill., 1961).
163. *Poor Robin*, 1694, sig. A7v; cf. idem, 1666, sig. B2. There was of course a late-Tudor literature of roguery, but rather different in tone.

Chapert 5 Almanacs and Religion (*pages 131–79*)

1. For general discussions see Thorndike, *Magic*; Thomas, esp. ch. 12; Allen, *Star-Crossed Renaissance*; P. H. Kocher, *Science and Religion in Elizabethan England* (San Marino, 1953), ch. 10; T. Tomkis, *Albumazar*, ed. H. G. Dick (Berkeley and Los Angeles, 1944).
2. J. Gaule, *The Mag-Astro-Mancer* (1652), pp. 24–5, 171–3 (quotation at p. 173); J.S., *The Starr-Prophet Anatomiz'd* (1675), p. 1; J. Chamber, *A Treatise against Judicial Astrologie* (1601), p. 95; Dauncy, 1615, sig. C4; J. Melton, *Astrologaster* (1620), p. 16; J. Geree, *Astrologo-mastix* (1646), pp. 11–12; G. Fox, *Here are Several Queries* (1657), pp. 1–4; J. A(llen), *Judicial Astrologers Totally Routed* (1659), p. 6; Thomas, pp. 358–9, 362–3.
3. S. Butler, *Hudibras*, ed. H. G. Bohn (1903), II, iii, pp. 957–9; Allen, *Judicial Astrologers*, p. 13.
4. See above, p. 17.
5. Melton, *Astrologaster*, p. 37; J.S., *Starr-Prophet*, p. 24.
6. Coverdale (trans.), *A Faythfull and True Pronostication* (1548), sig. A7v and *passim* (first published in 1536; reissued in 1549 and by J. Monipennie in 1612).
7. Thomas, pp. 70–4, 368–9, 391; Geree, *Astrologo-Mastix*, p. 19. For the pill see J.B., *An Account of the Vatican Pill* (B.L. 546 d 44(13)); cf. the popular 'Jesuits' Powder'.
8. Saunders, 1667, sig. C3, citing T. Fuller, *A Pisgah-Sight of Palestine* (1662), p. 160; Booker, 1648, sig. B4v.
9. Lilly, *Englands Prophetic Merlin* (1644), sig. A4v.
10. Heydon, *A Defence of Iudiciall Astrologie* (1603), pp. 193–4; G. Atwell, *An Apology or Defence of Astrology* (1660), sig. A6v.
11. Lilly, 1645, sig. A3; Atwell, *Apology*, p. 54; *D.N.B.*; G.E.C., *The Complete Peerage*, x, pp. 12–14. Pembroke was born 8 April 1580, died 10 April 1630.
12. Heydon, *Defence*, *passim*; Rowley, 1652, sig. C4v; Gadbury, 1688, sig. Av; Pond, 1690, sig. B3.
13. Gadbury, 1669, sig. A3, C8; idem, *Britain's Royal Star* (1664), p. 17; Thomas, p. 378 and n4.
14. Partridge, 1755, sig. C5v.
15. Vaux, 1633, sig. B2 (quoting John, xiv:2).
16. J. Gregory, *Notes and Observations upon some Passages of Scripture* (Oxford, 1646), p. 150; Atwell, *Apology*, p. 5; Heydon, *Defence*, p. 122; Bodl. Ms Add. B8, f. 67v.
17. Josephus, *Jewish Antiquities*, in *Works* (Loeb edn.), iv, pp. 33, 83; Heydon, *Defence*, p. 74; Hill, 1684, sig. A2v; Holden, 1688, sig. A5.
18. Heydon, *Defence*, p. 305; Montulmo, 1555, sig. A2 (2nd signature); Coley, *Nuncius*, 1679, sig. C6v–7; Whalley, 1691, p. 42; Hill, 1684, sig. A2v; T. Swadlin, *Divinity No Enemy to Astrology* (1653), pp. 19–20; R. Godson, *Astrologia Restaurata* (1696), pp. 50–1 (citing Psalms 8 and 19); W. Ramesey, *Lux Veritatis* (1651), pp. 21–5.
19. Gregory, *Notes*, sig. *4; Bodl. Ms Add. B8, f. 36v; Kepar, *The Gardener's Almanack*, 1702, sig. B6–v. For Bonatus see Thorndike, *Magic*, ii, p. 831. Heydon: Ms Ash. 242, f. 63v; cf. Matt. xxiv: 29 and Josephus, *Works*, iii, pp. 461–7.
20. Vaux, 1649, sig. B8; Pond, 1604, sig. B7; Booker, 1651, sig. C.
21. Securis, 1568, sig. A2; Lilly, 1681, sig. A2v.
22. Browne, 1619, sig. Cv; Lilly, 1681, sig. A2v.
23. Beridge, 1654, sig. B; Wing, 1695, sig. C6; Frende, 1593, sig. C; Wharton, 1642, sig. C2v; Lilly, 1675, sig. A2v; Bowker, 1675, sig. C2v.
24. Vaughan, 1559, sig. A2v.
25. Lilly, 1675, sig. B6v–7; above, p. 35.
26. J. Gadbury, *Obsequium Rationabile* (1675), sig. A5; Vaux, 1642, sig. B2.
27. Buckminster, 1571, sig. C2; Hubrigh, 1569, sig. A2.
28. Blagrave, 1660, sig. A3; Frende, 1592 (16mo), sig. C7; Hopton, 1606, sig. B8; above, p. 112.
29. Below, p. 280.

30. Lloyd, 1585, sig. B2v; Vaux, 1648, sig. Cv; Pond, 1690, sig. B, B3.
31. Kirby, 1684, sig. A2v.
32. Securis, 1568, sig. B2v–4; Securis, 1576, sig. C6v; Vaux, 1649, sig. B8; Culpeper, 1653, p. 6; Gadbury, 1674, sig. Cv; Coley, *Merlinus,* 1696, sig. C2v.
33. e.g. Keene, 1612, sig. B8v; Wing, 1656, sig. Cv.
34. Crawford, 1676, sig. A2; Gadbury, 1687, sig. A3v; S. Partridge, 1687, sig. C7; Wing, 1656, sig. Cv; Swadlin, *Divinity No Enemy*, p. 20.
35. Woodward, 1690, sig. A6.
36. e.g. Neve, 1628, sig. B6.
37. Gadbury, 1671, sig. A4v; Partridge, 1708, sig. B8.
38. Ramesey, *Astrologia Restaurata* (1653), p. 21; Gadbury, 1661, sig. C3.
39. Booker, 1662, sig. A6; Allestree, 1618, sig. A3; E. Gresham, 'Astrostereon', Bodl. Ms Ash. 192, p. 45; W. Ramesey, *A Reply to a Scandalous Pamphlet* (1650), p. 5.
40. J. Butler, *The Most Sacred and Divine Science of Astrology* (1680), p. 22.
41. Fowle, 1700, sig. Bv; Conyers, 1664, sig. A2; Wing, 1680, sig. C5v; Tanner, 1657, sig. B; Atwell, *Apology*, p. 31.
42. Smith, 1653, sig. A2v; Wing, 1684, sig. C4; J. Swan, *Speculum Mundi* (Cambridge, 1635), p. 341; Coley, 1708, sig. A5v.
43. Melton, *Astrologaster*, p. 37 (quoting Maternus); Swan, *Speculum Mundi*, p. 352.
44. *Erra Pater* (?1536; pr. R. Wyer), sig. C3; Coley, *Merlini Anglici Ephemeris 1684*, sig. B3–v.
45. Moore, 1571, sig. E6; Fowle, 1696, sig. Bv; Tanner, 1667, sig. C3v; Culpeper, 1696, C2; Securis, 1576, sig. Bv.
46. Ramesey, *Astrologia Restaurata*, p. 38.
47. Hewlett, 1627, sig. B2–v; R. Gell, *Stella Nova* (1649), sig. A3v; Thomas, pp. 329–30, 361–2.
48. Coley, *Nuncius*, 1683, sig. A8; Ms Ash. 180, f. 87.
49. G. C. Moore Smith, ed., *Gabriel Harvey's 'Marginalia'* (Stratford, 1913), p. 163; J. Blagrave, *Blagraves Astrological Practice of Physick* (1671), ep. ded.; Gadbury, *Life of Wing* (1670), p. 29; Culpeper, 1652, p. 7; Fowle, 1700, sig. Bv; Bucknall, 1677, sig. C3v; Rowley, 1651, sig. B2v; Atwell, *Apology*, p. 25; Thomas, pp. 362–3.
50. Thomas, pp. 383–5; H. Warren, *Magick and Astrology Vindicated* (1651), p. 27.
51. Desmus (pseud.), 1653, sig. A2v.
52. Lilly, 1676, sig. B3; E5; Gadbury, 1688, sig. A6v; anon., *The Petitioning-Comet* (1681); J. Partridge, *Mene Tekel* (1688), p. 18.
53. Ms Ash. 242, f. 63v; Booker, 1643, sig. B6; J. Case, *A Prophesie of the Conjunction of Saturn and Jupiter* (1680), p. 4; Silvester, 1682, p. 5.
54. Pond, 1606, sig. C3v–4.
55. A. R. Wright and T. E. Lones, *British Calendar Customs*, i (1936), pp. 96–8; T. Harley, *Moon Lore* (1885), p. 32 and *passim*; S. Baring-Gould, *Curious Myths of the Middle Ages* (1892), ch. ix. Sir Thomas Browne disavowed the idea of the sun's dance, and criticized the practice of depicting the sun and moon with human faces: *Works*, ed. G. Keynes (1928–31), iii, pp. 148–9.
56. Heydon, *Defence*, p. 53; Gadbury, 1703, sig. A2; Thomas, p. 385; Askham, 1553, sig. A2; Hewlett, 1628, sig. C4; Ramesey, *Astrologia Restaurata*, p. 78; Case, *Prophesie*, p. 4. For 'elwande' (not in *O.E.D.*) see J. Wright, *The English Dialect Dictionary* (Oxford, 1898–1905), ii, pp. 248–9.
57. J. Howell, *Familiar Letters, or Epistolae Ho-Elianae* (1903), iii, pp. 117; Coverdale, 1548, sig. A7v and *passim*; above, p. 19. The sermon of 1652 was by F. Bellers.
58. Carre, 1593, sig. Bv.
59. R. Crab, *The English Hermit, or Wonder of His Age* (1655), in *Harleian Miscellany* (1744–6), iv, pp. 458.
60. Booker, 1632, sig. C5v.
61. J. Harvey, *A Discoursive Probleme concerning Prophesies* (1588), p. 99; Lilly, *The Worlds Catastrophe* (1647), pp. 19ff.; On Trithemius see Thorndike, *Magic*, vi, p. 441; D. P. Walker, *Spiritual and Demonic Magic* (1958), pp. 86–90; and (also on the Cabala and Hermeticism) F. A. Yates, *Giordano Bruno and the Hermetic Tradition* (1964); J. L. Blau, *The Christian Interpretation of the Cabala in the Renaissance* (Port Washington, N.Y., 1965).
62. Sir G. Wharton, *Workes*, ed. J. Gadbury (1683), pp. 644–70 (quotation at p. 649); on

Rothman see Thorndike, *Works*, vi, pp. 506–7; see also Wharton, 1653, sig. E; Lilly, 1658, sig. B4v; Lilly, 1660, sig. B8v–C.

63. Andrews, 1686, sig. Cv; Blagrave, 1659, sig. A3; Howell, 1657, sig. Av–2; R. Gell, *A Sermon concerning Gods Government of the World by Angels* (1650), p. 13 and *passim.* Gadbury attacked the angelology of Lilly and Blagrave (*The Spurious Prognosticator* (1659), p. 12) but was sympathetic to Hermeticism: below, p. 210.
64. e.g. J. Brayne, *Astrologie Proved to be the Old Doctrine of Demons* (1653).
65. Chamber, *Treatise*, pp. 117–18.
66. Thomas, chs. 10, 11.
67. Lilly, 1646, sig. A3v; *The Collected Poems of Joseph Hall*, ed. A. Davenport (Liverpool, 1949), p. 30; T.S., *A Yoke for the Roman-Bulls* (with) *A Telescope for the New Astrologers* (1666), p. 5.
68. Hewlett, 1630, sig. B4v; Allestree, 1629, sig. C5v; Wing, 1642, sig. A2; Culpeper, 1653, p. 5; Montulmo, 1555, sig. A2v; Dove, 1667, sig. C; Wing, 1706, sig. C8v.
69. Thomas, 1612, sig. B2v.
70. Hubrigh, 1565, t.p.
71. Booker, 1651, sig. C2v; Gadbury, *Britain's Royal Star*, p. 17; Lilly, 1677, sig. A3–v.
72. Atwell, *Apology*, p. 13.
73. Chamber, *Treatise*, p. 102, quoted by Thomas, p. 359; Booker, 1640, sig. B8. Cf. Leybourne, 1648, sig. B: 'The Heaven's a book, the stars are letters fair,/God is the writer, men the readers are' (repeated in V. Wing, 1682, brs.; Wing, 1788, p. 42; Partridge, 1792, p. 9).
74. See Appendix I. To the list can be added Bedwell, Beridge, Billingsley, Gilbert, Kaye, Pigot, Wheeler and perhaps Raynolds, Grammar and Osborne. See also the scriptural almanacs of Coverdale, Jessey and Holmes, and the works by Beveridge, Webb and Wood.
75. J. Primrose, *Popular Errours* (1651), pp. 13–14; T. Brian, *The Pisse-prophet* (1637), p. 73; Ms Rawl. D146, 'A Discourse of the Lawless intrusion of Parsons and Vicars upon the Profession of Physick'; Gadbury, *Coelestis Legatus* (1656), sig. cc2–v (a list of parson-astrologers); Thomas, pp. 378–81; Atwell, *Apology*, p. 26.
76. Harvey, *An Astrological Discourse* (1583), sig. ¶2, 3; the bishops were John Fletcher and John Young. For Squire, noted as a supporter of astrology, see Foster, *Al. Oxon.*, p. 1403; B.L. Ms Harl. 5211, f. 7; Gadbury, loc. cit., sig. cc2. The book was also shown in advance to Dr. William Lewyn, sometime M.P. for Canterbury, for whom see Foster, op. cit., p. 905; Venn, *Al. Cantab.*, iii, p. 80.
77. W. Laud, *Works* (Oxford, 1847–60), i, p. 169; iii, pp. 140, 152, 157, 207; Gadbury, 1688, sig. Av; idem, *A Reply to that Pernicious Libel* (1687), pp. 29–30; Atwell, *Apology*, p. 16.
78. Gadbury, 1671, sig. A3v (for Taylor, citing his *Ductor Dubitandum*: see his *Works*, ed. C. P. Eden and A. Tyler, 1847–56, x, p. 550); Gadbury, *Cardines Coeli* (1684), sig. Av; idem, *Magna Veritas* (1680), p. 7; Gadbury, 1694, sig. A7.
79. For Gregory see *D.N.B.*; Ms notes on J. G(urgony), *Gregorii Posthuma* (1650), sig. av (Bodl., 4to Rawl. 251).
80. Thomas, pp. 367–9; Atwell, *Apology*, p. 16 (Preston); Lilly, *England's Propheticall Merlin* (1644), p. 44 (Greenhill); Gadbury, *Collectio Geniturarum* (1662), sig. A2 (Caryl).
81. Perkins, *Foure Great Lyers* (1585), sig. C3–v; Calvin, *An Admonicion against Astrology Judiciall* (1561), sig. A6; J. Vicars, *Against William Li-Lie* (1652); Conyers, 1664, sig. Cv.
82. Below, pp. 279–80.
83. Gresham, 1607, sig. B2v (titles given by Thomas, p. 381); Ms Ash. 788, f. 136; Parkhurst, *Critica Divina* (1660); Gadbury, *Life of Wing*, p. 11.
84. Lilly, 1645, sig. A4; Lilly, *Life and Times*, p. 3; above, pp. 57-8.
85. A. L. Rowse, *Simon Forman* (1974); Ms Ash. 802, *passim.*
86. For the rogues see Lilly, *Life and Times*; J. Halle, *An Historicall Expostulation* (1565), ed. T. J. Pettigrew, Percy Soc., xi (1844); C. J. S. Thompson, *The Quacks of Old London* (1928).
87. e.g. Heuring, 1551; Low, 1554; Kidman, 1633, sig. C4.
88. Einer, 1621, t.p., sig. A5ff.

89. e.g. Bell, 1622, sig. B6–v; Vaux, 1632, sig. C4–v; Goldsmith, 1686 etc.
90. Booker, *Tractatus Paschalis* (1664), p. 13 and *passim*; a draft of his letter to the king is in his almanac for 1640 (Ash. 72(6), between sig. Av–2); Gadbury, *Festum Festorum* (1687).
91. *The Kalender of Shepherdes*, ed. H. O. Sommers (1892), pp. 73–99 (1506 edn.) and pp. 173–9 (1508 edn.).
92. *Almanacke for xv Yeres* (?1522), last page.
93. Vaux, 1638, sig. Av; Vaux, 1643, sig. A2v; Neve, 1671, *passim*; Crawford, 1676, sig. B–2.
94. Ranger, 1616, sig. B8v; repeated by Pond, 1692, sig. A6; *The Records of the Church of Christ in Bristol, 1640–1687*, ed. R. Hayden, Bristol Rec. Soc., xxvii (1974), p. 96. The verse may, of course, antedate Ranger's use of it.
95. e.g. by F. Adams (1581), sig. B–2, and R. Triplet (1604), sig. B–2v; below, p. 146.
96. Vaux, 1624, sig. B5–6v; Pond, 1611, sig. A5. Other examples in Buckminster, 1598, sig. B4; Smith, 1620, brs.; Allestree, 1624, sig. A3; Dove, 1639, sig. Av; Pond, 1641, sig. C3; Swan, 1666, sig. Av; Wheeler, 1674, brs.; Andrews, 1716, sig. Av. See further Thomas, pp. 620–1; L. Bradley in *Local Population Studies*, iv (1970), pp. 34–7; J. W. Legg, *English Church Life from the Restoration to the Tractarian Movement* (1914), pp. 260–1.
97. Fly, 1658, sig. B7v; Turner, 1687, sig. C3. The relevant phrase runs: 'I bequeath my Soule into the Hands of Almighty God my Maker, hoping that through the Meritorious Death and Passion of Jesus Christ my only Saviour and Redeemer to receive free pardon and forgiveness of all my sins.' See N.W. Alcock, *Stoneleigh Villagers 1597–1650* (Univ. of Warwick, 1975), pp. 15, 21n; M. Spufford, *Contrasting Communities* (Cambridge, 1972), ch. 13; Capp, in *Local Population Studies*, 14 (1975), pp. 49–50. There is another, closely-related formula in J. H(awkins), *The Young Clerks Tutor* (3rd edn., 1664), p. 142, and a much shorter one in J. Hill, *The Young Secretary's Guide* (7th edn., 1696), p. 118.
98. Wilkinson, 1658, 2nd t.p.; Booker, 1631, sig. A4v; Harflete, 1656, sig. A5. Coelson added a moral gloss even to a table of lunar phases: 'pray sirs be advised, and don't abuse/ Her light, to guide you to taverns and stews' (Coelson, 1679, sig. A4).
99. Hill, 1609, sig. A3; Neve, 1607, sig. A4v; Ranger, 1621, sig. A3; Buckminster, 1598, sig. B6; Evans, 1613, sig. A4v; Neve, 1616, sig. C3v; Askham, 1555, sig. A3v.
100. Buckminster, 1589, sig. B6v; Twyne, 1585, sig. B2v, 3v, 4v, 5v.
101. Fowle, 1685, sig. A7; cf. Vaux, 1642, sig. B2.
102. Evans, 1630, sig. A3, taken from his *The Sacrifice of a Contrite Heart* (1630), p. 1.
103. Vaux, 1633, sig. C3; Allestree, 1621, sig. B8; Alleyn, 1612, sig. A4.
104. Ranger, 1629, sig. A4v; Frende, 1598, sig. C2.
105. *Strange Neves* (*sic*) (1606), ed. Gresham, sig. A3 and *passim*.
106. No date; the B.L. copy of Wing A1246A has a manuscript date 1686. There were several editions around the turn of the century.
107. Vaux, 1654, sig. A2v; Coley, *Nuncius*, 1684, sig. Av; Coley, 1701, sig. Av; *The Woman Hater*, II, i, 259–61.
108. Hewlett, 1630, sig. A3v; Norton, 1581, t.p.; Ranger, 1616, sig. B8v; Ranger, 1628, sig. A6; above, p. 104.
109. Gadbury, 1697, sig. Cv.
110. Cunningham, 1564, sig. A5; Bretnor, 1614, sig. B2; Evans, 1630, sig. A5v; idem, *Sacrifice of a Contrite Heart*, t.p., pp. 2–3; the work ran to 354 pages, and contained prayers for personal and family use, including some 'for godly zeal' and for the fall of the 'Romish Beast', Antichrist.
111. Trigge, 1665, sig. A5v; Evans, 1625, sig. A4v.
112. Gadbury, *The Doctrine of Nativities* (1658), p. 262; Securis, 1569, sig. A3.
113. Dade, 1589, sig. C8; Balles, 1631, sig. A8v.
114. Frende, 1590, sig. C7; idem, 1588, sig. C4.
115. Buckminster, 1589, sig. B6; cf. Wing, 1668, sig. C6.
116. Above, pp. 102–3.
117. Bretnor, 1618, sig. B8, reprinted by Booker, 1631, sig. A8v; Culpeper, *Catastrophe Magnatum* (1652), p. 43.
118. For full discussions see Thomas, ch. 4; C. Hill, *God's Englishman: Oliver Cromwell and the English Revolution* (1970), ch. 9.

119. Wilson, 1626, sig. A5v–6; Browne, 1630, sig. C6; Booker, 1631, sig. A4v; Stephins, 1569, sig. B6.
120. Pigot, 1630, sig. B5v.
121. Lilly, 1654, sig. B2–v; cf. Wing, 1646, sig. C7, for sin as the cause of the civil war.
122. Smith, 1631, 'To the Reader'; Frende, 1615, sig. C3v.
123. Blagrave, 1660, sig. A3v; Bretnor, 1612, sig. Bv; Hill, 1603, sig. C3; Alleyn, 1606, sig. A8.
124. White, 1667, sig. A6v; above, p. 103.
125. Vaux, 1658, sig. A8v.
126. Askham, 1555, sig. A3v–B7. The author did not discuss papal supremacy or the suppression of the monasteries and chantries, except in the allusion to plunder.
127. Hopton, 1612, Sig. C2v; Hopton, 1614, sig. C7; Jeffereys, 1635, sig. C8–v, reprinted in Vaux, 1664 and 1666.
128. J. Swan, *Profano-Mastix* (1639); *A Sermon, pointing out the Chiefe Causes* (1639); *Loyalty's Speech* (1639); *Redde Debitum* (1640).
129. Gray, 1588, sig. A8v; idem, 1591, sig. B7v; *Poor Robin*, 1697, sig. C6.
130. Wing, 1654, sig. B7v; Vaux, 1658, sig. A8v.
131. Howell, 1656, sig. A3; Jessey, e.g. 1650, sig. B7v.
132. Vaux, 1648, sig. B2 (but probably meant ironically).
133. Jessey, e.g. 1660, sig. B6; Howell, 1656, sig. B6–v; *Montelion*, 1662, sig. B8v.
134. Atlee, 1647, sig. A6v–B2 (quotation at A6v); Dove, 1697, sig. A2.
135. Lloyd, 1585, sig. B5v.
136. Above, p. 47; for Udall, see Bodl., Ash. 66(1) at sig. B8, and *D.N.B.*, John Udall. For the owner of the almanac see below, p. 401, n255.
137. Booker, 1633, sig. C2; *Diary of John Rous*, ed. M. A. E. Green, Camden Soc., lxvi (1856), p. 102 (a verse representing the views of 'the Puritan'); above, p. 47.
138. Hopton, 1614, sig. Bv, B2v, C7; Ranger, 1621, sig. A7; idem, 1615, sig. B5v.
139. Sir C. Heydon, *An Astrological Discourse*, ed. N. Fiske (1650), sig. A4–5v; Booker, *Mercurius Coelicus* (1644), pp. 1–2.
140. Lilly, 1647, sig. A3; Lilly, 1652, sig. A3.
141. Lilly, 1653, sig. A2; idem, *Life and Times*, pp. 54, 67ff., 77–8; idem, *Annus Tenebrosus* (1652), sig. *4; Culpeper, 1651, sig. A3; idem, 1653, sig. D; Booker, 1652, sig. C6–v; Rowley, 1651, sig. B2v.
142. *Annotations upon all the Books of the Old and New Testaments* (1651), Jer. x: 2; Gataker, *His Vindication* (1653); idem, *A Discourse Apologetical* (1654), p. 103 and *passim*; Lilly, 1654, sig. A3–v, B2, B7v; idem, 1655, sig. F8v; idem, *Life and Times*, pp. 77–8; *The Last Will and Testament of Thomas Gataker* (1654); Gadbury, *Collectio Geniturarum* (1662), Bodl. copy, AA58 Art, note on p. 104; idem, *Animal Cornutum* (1654).
143. Lilly, 1647, sig. A3; Booker, 1651, sig. C (an allusion to papists, prelatists and presbyterians).
144. J. Pool, *Country Astrology* (1650), sig. A2; Healey, 1658, sig. A3; Wharton, 1653, sig. A3v, E5–v.
145. Culpeper, 1654, p. 12; idem, 1655, sig. A8v.
146. Lilly, 1647, sig. A3v; idem, *Annus Tenebrosus*, p. 16; *Life and Times*, pp. 54, 78; Josten, *Ashmole*, p. 1359.
147. Lilly, 1650, sig. C; *Annus Tenebrosus*, p. 11; Booker, 1652, sig. C6v.
148. Lilly, *Annus Tenebrosus*, p. 17; Lilly, 1651, sig. E.
149. Culpeper, *Catastrophe Magnatum*, p. 19; Culpeper, 1651, sig. G3–4; idem, 1653, sig. E5; idem, 1654, p. 12; idem, *A Directory for Midwives* (1651), pp. 112–13.
150. Lilly, 1651, sig. E; idem, 1653, sig. B2; idem, 1656, sig. F.
151. e.g. Andrews, 1658, sig. B2; Tanner, 1658, sig. A7; Healey, 1658, sig. A3; Thurston, 1652, sig. E.
152. Culpeper, *Catastrophe Magnatum*, p. 4; idem, 1654, sig. D5; idem, 1656, p. 12; Wharton, 1653, sig. A3v.
153. Lilly, 1650, sig. A3; idem, 1651, sig. B5; idem, 1654, sig. C3; Andrews, 1658, sig. B2; *The Levellers Almanack*, 1652, p. 5; Thurston, 1652, sig. A8v.
154. Woodward, 1684, sig. B5; Hill, 1684, sig. A6v, B8v.
155. *Mr. Partridge's Wonderfull Predictions pro Anno 1688*, p. 13; Partridge, *Opus Reformatum* (1693), p. 38.
156. Tanner, 1658, sig. C7; Wing, 1657, sig. C3v; Lilly, 1647, sig. A3v.

157. Gadbury, *The Novice Astrologer* (1660), sig. A2.
158. e.g. Wharton, 1656, sig. A4, p. 5; Fitzsmith, 1654, sig. A7v.
159. Gadbury, 1663, sig. A5; Trigge, 1666, sig. A3 (St. Paul's was of course destroyed by the Great Fire a few months later).
160. Quotation from the 1676 edn., sig. A3.
161. Cunningham, 1564, sig. A2v–3; F. Adams, *Writing Tables* (1581), sig. D7.
162. e.g. Browne, 1621, sig. B8; Ranger, 1615, sig. B5v.
163. *The New Bloody Almanack 1644*, sig. A4; Booker, 1643, sig. A5; above, Chapter 3, and especially below, section iv.
164. *Protestant Almanack*, 1682, sig. Av; ibid., 1669, sig. Cv, E4; ibid., 1668, sig. A3v, A4, C7–8.
165. Ibid., 1690, sig. B; Dove, 1696, sig. A5 (the later editions of Dove specialized in this material).
166. *Protestant Almanack*, 1669, sig. I4, K; ibid., 1690, sig. B8.
167. Ibid., 1669, sig. B3v–4, reprinted in 1682, sig. A3.
168. Partridge, 1687, sig. A3v, A6; *Annus Mirabilis 1688*, sig. Av, p. 29.
169. Whalley, 1691, sig. A6, p. 48.
171. Wharton, 1654, pp. 34–5; Desmus, 1654, sig. B4v. For Prynne see the good modern biography by W. M. Lamont (1960).
172. (Blount), 1663; for the other editions, in 1664 and 1688–9, see Bibliography, s.v. *Calendrium* and *Catholic*.
173. Andrews, 1668, sig. C2; idem, 1669, sig. Av; idem, 1671, sig. Av; below, p. 174.
174. (Gadbury), *A Reply to That Pernicious Libel* (1687), sig. B2, p. 43.
175. Lilly, *Supernaturall Sights* (1644), p. 11.
176. Booker, 1646, sig. A5, B2; idem, 1648, sig. A5v; 1660, sig. C4v.
177. Wing, 1648, sig. C7v; idem, 1653, sig. C6; idem, 1655, sig. C5.
178. Lilly, 1645, p. 71; idem, 1647, sig. A3; idem, 1651, sig. A7; idem, 1657, sig. A3; idem, 1658, sig. A7v, B4; idem, 1660, sig. C; idem, 1662, sig. B5v; idem, *Life and Times*, p. 64; for similar comments see Culpeper, 1651, sig. H.
179. Wharton, 1653, sig. E2; Jinner, 1659, sig. C5v; idem, 1658, sig. C3.
180. Webb, 1660, brs. For Webb see C. Hill, *The World Turned Upside Down* (1975 edn.), esp. pp. 226–7; on radicalism and feigned madness see the same work, ch. 13.
181. Bird, 1662, sig. A4; Wing, 1669, sig. C5.
182. Culpeper, 1651, sig. G3v.
183. Lilly, 1651, sig. B; idem, 1654, sig. B7–v; idem, 1655, sig. A4v.
184. Thomas, pp. 373–8; Heydon, *The Rosie Crucian Infallible Axiomata* (1660), sig. C2–3; idem, *The English Physitians Guide* (1662), sig. G3v–5; idem, *Theomagia* (1664), sig. G7v, 8. But he denounced Lilly, e.g. in *The Harmony of the World* (1662), sig. D4–5v. It should be remembered that Heydon sometimes pirated tributes composed for other authors: Aubrey, *Brief Lives*, i, p. 318.
185. Lilly, 1655, sig. A4v; idem, 1661, sig. Bv; idem, 1663, sig. B6v, C3; idem, 1671, sig. A2v; idem, *Life and Times*, pp. 53–4, 87; Josten, *Ashmole*, p. 1209; above, p. 48.
186. Woodward, 1685, sig. A2.
187. Gadbury, 1688, sig. C3; idem, *A Reply to That Pernicious Libel*, sig. B2; Trigge, 1689, sig. B.
188. Woodward, 1689, sig. B2v, B6v. The language seems to echo Butler's *Hudibras*.
189. Wharton, 1653, sig. A3v.
190. Saunder, 1696, sig. B2–3.
191. M. Eliade, *The Myth of the Eternal Return* (New York, 1954), esp. ch. 2; R. Patai, *Man and Temple* (1947), ch. 6.
192. e.g. references to the first Adam and second (Christ); first chosen people and second (English, Scots, New Englanders etc.); and the campaign to restore the Mosaic laws and the sanhedrin in the 1650s. John Rogers, the Fifth Monarchist, spoke of power passing in Israel from God to generals, to parliaments or sanhedrins and thence to kings, and now returning from King Charles to the Long Parliament, to General Cromwell and back to God: *To His Excellency the Lord Generall Cromwell. A Few Proposals* (1653), brs.
193. F. Cumont, 'La fin du monde selon les mages occidentaux', *Rev. de l'Histoire des Religions*, 103 (1931), esp. pp. 48–9; see also the papers of Eliade, Corbin and Puech in *Man and Time* (Papers from the Eranos Yearbooks, New York, 1957); C. A.

Patrides, *The Grand Design of God* (1972) and 'Renaissance Estimates of the Year of Creation', *H.L.Q.*, xxvi (1962–3), pp. 315–22.

194. Thorndike, *Magic*, iv, pp. 107–8, 147, 249–50, 265–6, 388, 443, 483.

195. Below, p. 168.

196. Matt. xxiv: 37; see e.g. A. Bogarde or Bogaert, *Prognosticon Futurorum Temporum* (Antwerp 1552), sig. B4; Securis, 1569, sig. A2; Ms Ash. 802, f. 120 (Forman's belief that Antichrist would reign at Jerusalem in 1656).

197. Mussemius, 1544, sig. D4.

198. See e.g. P. Toon, ed., *Puritans, the Millennium and the Future of Israel* (1970); L. E. Froom, *The Prophetic Faith of our Fathers* (Washington, 1946–54); W. Lamont, *Godly Rule* (1969), and the debates between Lamont and myself reprinted in C. Webster, ed., *The Intellectual Revolution of the Seventeenth Century* (1974).

199. Mussemius, 1544, t.p. and sig. D4. Bosanquet reproduces the cut and suggests that it might represent God: p. 36 and facsimile xi.

200. Salomon, 1543, esp. sig. B–8v; Brunfelsius, 1536, sig. D4, 6v and *passim* (licensed by John Hilsey, Bishop of Rochester).

201. e.g. Securis, 1569, sig. Avff.; Buckminster, 1589, sig. C8v; Gresham, 1603, sig. Av, B6v; Hopton, 1607, sig. B2v; Herbert, 1629, sig. B8; Vaux, 1633, sig. C3; see also J. Swan, *Speculum Mundi*, pp. 11–27.

202. *Propheceien und Weissagungen . . . Doctoris Paracelsi, Johan Lichtenbergers* (1549) f. 21; Bodl. Ms Rawl. D1349, f. 60v (early Elizabethan; n.d.); for Nostradamus see above, pp. 69–70. Cf. the number of doomsday ballads in the 1560s: H. E. Rollins, *An Analytical Index to the Ballad-Entries 1557–1709* (Chapel Hill, N. Carolina, 1924).

203. H. Baker, *The Wars of Truth* (1952), esp. pt. 2; V. Harris, *All Coherence Gone*, (Chicago, 1949).

204. Bretnor, 1615, sig. C8v; Booker, 1632, sig. B3; Securis, 1574, sig. B2v; idem, 1581, sig. Cv; Vaux, 1633, sig. C3. On the Chaucer prophecy see G. H. Campbell in *Modern Language Notes*, xxix (1914), pp. 195–6.

205. W. H. B. Stone, 'Shakespeare and the Sad Augurs', *Journ. of English and Germanic Philology*, 52 (1953); M. Aston, 'The Fiery Trigon Conjunction: an Elizabethan Astrological Prediction', *Isis*, 61 (1670); Securis, 1569, sig. Av–3 (2nd signature). On Leowitz see also Thorndike, *Magic*, vi, pp. 116–18; his work was the basis of Philip Moore's almanacs.

206. Stone, art. cit., pp. 461, 464, 465; J. Harvey, *A Discoursive Probleme concerning Prophecies* (1588), on which see Patrides, 'Renaissance Estimates', p. 322. Harvey's almanac for 1587 is lost, but is mentioned by Frende, 1588, sig. Av.

207. Frende, 1588, sig. Av, C7v; Farmer, 1587, sig. D4–v; T.R., *A Confutation of the tenne Great Plagues, Prognosticated by John Doleta* (?1587); Harvey, *Discoursive Probleme*, p. 99. There were still some doomsday ballads in the years after 1583: Rollins, op. cit.

208. Stone, art. cit., pp. 472–9; see also Lilly's comments in his copy of Harvey's *Probleme*, Bodl. Ash. 637 (1) at p. 133.

209. Securis, 1581, sig. Cv; Dade, 1589, sig. C8; Booker, 1633, sig. C2; quotation from Hewlett, 1629, sig. B8.

210. For an early example see Ms Rawl. D1349, composed in the 1560s.

211. N. Cohn, *The Pursuit of the Millennium* (1962); M. Reeves, *The Influence of Prophecy in the Later Middle Ages* (Oxford, 1969).

212. On Cypriano see also above, p. 70; on Torquatus see Reeves, *Prophecy*, pp. 299–300, 328, 364.

213. Ms Ash. 1490, f. 106v; *A Prophesie of the Judgment Day* (c. 1620) in Rollins, *A Pepysian Garland* (Cambridge, 1922), pp. 110–15; *Diary of Walter Yonge*, ed. G. Roberts, *Camden Soc.*, xi, (1848), p. 38; B.L. Add. Ms 38, 599, f. 58v (diary of Richard Shanne); Ms Rawl. C813, f. 165.

214. E. Gresham, 'Astrostereon' (1603) in Ms Ash. 192, f. 70; other Ms copies in Ms Ash. 1807, B.L. Mss Sloane 753, 3279, 3936. Gadbury published most of the work in his almanacs around 1700. See also Reeves, *Prophecy*, p. 507 and *passim*; the text is John x: 16.

215. *The New Starr of the North* (1632); *Learned Tico Brahe his Astronomicall Coniectur* (1632), a translation of part of his *Astronomiae Instauratae Progymnasmata* (1610); M. Roberts, *Gustavus Adolphus* (1953, 1958), i, pp. 522–6; Bainbridge, *An Astron-*

omicall Description (1619), pp. 31–3, 40. On Paracelsus see p. 420, n. 202 above, and Reeves, *Prophecy*, pp. 454–7.

216. On Grebner see Thomas, pp. 394–5; W. Lilly, *Monarchy or No Monarchy* (1651), pp. 20ff. For English interest in Gustavus see p. 420, n. 215, above, and J. Mede, *The Key of the Revelation* (1643), 2nd pagination, p. 117; *The Swedish Discipline*, (1632); *C.S.P.D., 1633–4*, pp. 204–5.
217. Heydon, 'A Recitall of the Celestial Apparitions', Ms Ash. 242 and 192; on Heydon see *D.N.B.*
218. Baker, *The Wars of Truth*; E. L. Tuveson, *Millennium and Utopia* (Berkeley and Los Angeles, 1949); J. H. Alsted, *The Beloved City* (1643), pp. 40–2.
219. Alsted *Thesaurus Chronologiae* (Herborn, 1624), following p. 324. (R. Le Wright), *Nuncius Propheticus* (1642) argued Alsted's debt to Tycho Brahe: p. 34.
220. Lilly, *Life and Times*, p. 98; *D.N.B.*, Napier (both were descendants of Sir Archibald Napier, 4th laird, d. 1522). George Atwell mistakenly thought they were brothers: *Apology*, p. 26.
221. Atwell, *Apology*, p. 26; *A Brief Description of the Future History of Europe* (1650), sig. Av.
222. J. Mede, *Works*, ed. J. Worthington (1664), i, p. viii, ii, 1077–8. Mede once strikingly described Daniel as 'the great almanac of prophecy': B. W. Ball, *A Great Expectation: Eschatological Thought in English Protestantism to 1660* (Leiden, 1975), p. 76.
223. *A New Bloody Almanack, 1645*, sig. A4v. The original *Calebbe Shillocke his Prophecie* (1607), in Rollins, *Pepysian Garland*, pp. 17–23, was a reissue of Doleta's prophecy (p. 166, above).
224. Lilly, *Monarchy or No Monarchy*, p. 26.
225. Brightman, *Works* (1644), pp. 1079–88; on Maxwell see *D.N.B.* and Reeves, *Prophecy*, pp. 499–500.
226. Ascribed by Wing to R. Le Wright, who provided a preface, but several contemporaries accepted as author the 'T.B.' whose initials appear at the end, and identified him as Thomas Boreman: e.g. Alsted, *Beloved City*, p. xviii; J. Gadbury, *Dies Novissimus* (1664), p. 31. Seth Ward, future bishop and F.R.S., provided an admiring verse.
227. Andrews, 1655, sig. B2; Booker, 1651, sig. C; idem, 1652, sig. B3v; Herbert, 1653, sig. Cv; Smith, 1654, sig. A6v; Street, 1653, sig. A7v, etc.; above, pp. 79–82.
228. Fitzsmith, 1654, sig. A3 and *passim*; Wharton, 1653, sig. E2v–F, and 1655 (pr. by M. J.), sig. Hff.
229. Harflete, 1654, sig. C7.
230. Vaux, 1654, sig. B3v.
231. Wing, 1643, sig. A6v–7v; idem, 1652, sig. C3v; idem, 1655, sig. C4v–6; idem, 1659 sig. C4v.
232. Saunders, 1658, sig. B8; idem, 1656, sig. C7v.
233. Phillippes, 1657, sig. Cv–7v.
234. e.g. Jessey, 1647, sig. B8v; idem, 1661, sig. B–v (citing Ezek. xxi. 27); similar prophecies in Howell, 1656, sig. C4; idem, 1657, sig. Av–2.
235. Felgenhauer, 1655, p. 2 and *passim*.
236. Coulton, 1655, sig. B5–6; Dove, 1654, sig. C3–v.
237. Culpeper, 1652, pp. 15, 21; 1653, pp. 24, 31; 1654, pp. 13, 21, 22–3; 1656, pp. 7, 31–2; idem, *Catastrophe Magnatum* (1652), pp. 15–16, 64, 67–72. Gadbury seems to have welcomed the failure of the bid to readmit the Jews: Gadbury, 1657, sig. A2v.
238. Lilly, *Life and Times*, p. 98; Lilly, 1656, sig. A3v; 1667, sig. A3, 4; idem, *The World's Catastrophe* (1647), sig. A3v; idem, *Monarchy or No Monarchy*, p. 26.
239. *A Brief Description*; *A Prophesie of Paulus Grebnerus* (1649); N. R., *Strange Newes of the Sad Effects* (1652), p. 3; see also *The Year of Wonders* (1652); A. Evans, *King Charls his Starr* (1654); *The Royall Health to the Rising Sun* (c. 1649); Thomas, p. 411.
240. Lilly, *Annus Tenebrosus* (1652), pp. 36–7; *Monarchy or No Monarchy*, p. 29 and *passim*.
241. Lilly, *Englands Prophetic Merlin* (1644), sig. b4, pp. 43–5, 57; *A Prophesie of the White King* (1644), pp. 5, 23–9; *World's Catastrophe*, pp. 20–1; Reeves, *Prophecy*, pp. 328, 392 and (on the Chastiser) p. 338.
242. *Monarchy or No Monarchy*, pp. 70–3.
243. Lilly, 1653, sig. B3v–4; idem, 1654, sig. B2–v, B8v; Reeves, *Prophecy*, pp. 299–301.
244. Lilly, 1657, sig. A8v–B6v; idem, 1658, sig. C; idem, 1659, sig. A2v, 3v, 5v.
245. Lilly, 1656, sig. A2v–4v; idem, 1657, sig. A2, 3. He noted sardonically that many

opposed the return of the Jews to England and yet expected their conversion, presumably 'by miracle, not admitting conversation with them'.

246. Saunders, 1656, sig. C3–v, C7–v.
247. Blagrave, 1659, t.p., sig. A3–6v; idem, 1660, sig. A5v–6v; idem, 1665, sig. C–8v.
248. P. Serarius, *An Awakening Warning* (Amsterdam, 1662), attacked by Lilly, 1664, sig. B6v–7v. R. Edlin, *Prae-Nuncius Syderius* (1663), expected upheavals to follow the conjunction of Saturn and Jupiter in that year.
249. Blagrave, 1665, sig. C–8v; *The Bloody Almanack*, 1666, p. 5. On 1666 and Charles II's prophetic role see now M. McKeon, *Politics and Popery in Restoration England. The Case of Dryden's 'Annus Mirabilis'* (1975), chs. 6–8.
250. Lilly, 1654, sig. B7–v; 1655, sig. A4v; see Reeves, *Prophecy, passim.*
251. Lilly, 1649, sig. A4v; 1655, sig. A4v; 1658, sig. B6; idem, *Annus Tenebrosus*, pp. 39–40.
252. Saunders, 1654, sig. C8v.
253. Lilly, 1664, sig. Bv; 1677, sig. A4–5.
254. Lilly, 1665, sig. A2–v; 1666, sig. A2; 1667, sig. A2–4v; 1668, sig. B7; 1669, sig. D5; 1674, sig. A5v.
255. Andrews, 1666, sig. Cv–2; 1668, sig. C2; 1669, sig. Av, Cv; 1671, sig. Av; Gadbury, 1668, sig. D4v–6.
256. Josten, *Ashmole*, p. 1040; Booker, 1663, sig. B6, C8; 1664, sig. C8; 1666, sig. C–v; Nunnes, 1666, sig. C8v; Tanner, 1666, sig. B2v–4, C4v, C8v; see also Blagrave, 1659, sig. A4; idem, 1660, sig. A6v; Thomas, p. 414; Capp, *The Fifth Monarchy Men* (1972), pp. 26, 213–14.
257. Wing, 1666, sig. C5–v.
258. R. G., *MDCLXVI. A Prognostick on this Famous Year* (1666), brs.
259. Gadbury, 1665, sig. C8; idem, 1666, sig. A3v; Trigge, 1666, sig. A5.
260. Gadbury, *Dies Novissimus* (1664), t.p.; idem, *A Brief Examination* (1661), p. 23, *Poor Robin*, 1666, sig. C6v; cf. Capp, *Fifth Monarchy*, p. 194.
261. Wharton, 1666, sig. Av.
262. The almanacs of Atkinson, an Anglican minister, contained however a regular discussion of the apocalypse: Atkinson, 1670, sig. B8v, and following years.
263. Gadbury, 1678, sig. C7v; 1681, sig. C4v–6; *John Gadbury . . . his Past and Present Opinion of the Ottoman or Turkish Power* (1683), esp. pp. 1–5; idem, *Fore-Warn'd, Fore-Arm'd* (1682), p. 4. Another Tory astrologer, John Merrifield, also sought to allay fears in his *Catastasis Mundi* (1684).
264. Holwell, op. cit., *passim*; *The Mystery of Ambras Merlin* (1683), p. 4.
265. Krabtree, 1685, *passim.* He remarked wistfully that millenarianism was 'so jovial a creed' that he wished it could be reconciled with the Bible (sig. A2).
266. Lilly, 1683, sig. A2, Bv–3v; see also e.g. *The Great and Wonderfull Predictions of . . . Lilly, Partridge, Coley . . . concerning 1683* (1683).
267. Coley, *Nuncius*, 1680, sig. C4v; 1682, sig. C3v; 1683, sig. Av.; Hill, 1684, sig. B3v, 4; Kirby, 1682, p. 11; Partridge, 1683, sig. C6v–7; *Mr. Partridge's New Prophecy* (1684); Woodward, 1685, sig. A6.
268. *Catastrophe Mundi: or Merlin Reviv'd* (1683), pp. 82–6 and *passim.*
269. Lilly, 1674, sig. A5v; *Mr. Lillies New Prophecies of a General Peace* (1674); *Mr. Lillies Astrological Predictions for the Year 1677*, p. 6.
270. Fowle, 1684, sig. B5–v; Nesse, *An Astrological and Theological Discourse upon the Present Great Conjunction* (1682); J. Case, *A Prophecy of the Conjunction of Saturn and Jupiter* (1682), p. 8 and *passim* (a Ms copy is in Ms Rawl. D 810).
271. Tongue, *The Northern Star* (1680).
272. R. Kirby, *Vates Astrologicus* (1683).
273. J. Howell, *Catastrophe Mundi; An Appendix to Holwell's Catastrophe Mundi* (1683). Holwell also published a pot-boiler, *Remarkable Observations on the Comet* (1682); Partridge, *Prodromus* (1680), pp. 30–1.
274. Gadbury, *A Reply to That Pernicious Libel* (1687), pp. 34–9.
275. Partridge, 1681, sig. C2; 1687, sig. Av; 1693, sig. C6 (the reference to Daniel, which was reprinted in *A Continuation of the History of the Plot* (1696), p. 5).
276. W. Atwood, *Wonderful Predictions* (1689). For Pareus's prophecy, in fact the conqueror of Telesphorus, see Reeves, *Prophecy*, pp. 391–2. This was the first English

translation of Torquatus, though extracts appeared in Maxwell's *Admirable and Notable Prophesies* (1615).

277. Tanner, 1690, sig. C3v; Partridge, 1697, sig. C6v; Woodward, 1698, sig. Av; Lilly, *Two Famous Prophecies* (?1681–5), p. 6.
278. Coley, *Merlinus*, 1691, sig. C3–v; 1692, sig. C4–v; 1696, sig. B5; 1700, sig. C5.
279. Hobbs, 1695, sig. C6v–7; Kirby, *Catastrophe Galliae* (1690), p. 20.
280. E. Labrousse, *L'Entrée de Saturne au Lion* (The Hague, 1974), pp. 6ff. and *passim* (apocalyptic speculation based on the solar eclipse of 1654. Labrousse points out that 'respectable' astrologers, e.g. Morin and Argol, did not take part, but a work on doomsday was fathered on Argol. For popular panics over doomsday see p. 35n (Germany) and p. 38 (France)). For the later period see J. H. Robinson, *The Great Comet of 1680. A Study in the History of Rationalism* (Northfield, Minnesota, 1916), esp. ch. 3.
281. See especially M. Jacob, 'Millenarianism and science in the late seventeenth century', *Journ. History of Ideas*, xxxvii (1976); idem, *The Newtonians and the English Revolution, 1689–1720* (1976); M. C. Jacob and W. A. Lockwood, 'Political Millenarianism and Burnet's *Sacred Theory*', *Science Studies*, 2 (1972).
282. Partridge, 1701, sig. C2ff.; for Pell see *D.N.B.* On eighteenth-century millenarianism see below, pp. 251–3, 266–7.

Chapter 6 Astrology, Science and Medicine (*pages* 180–214)

1. Nicolson, 'New Astronomy'; below, section ii.
2. Bowden, 'Scientific Revolution in Astrology', provides a valuable analysis of many of the proposals for reform, though she does not discuss the role of the almanac-makers.
3. E. Rosenberg, *Leicester, Patron of Letters* (New York, 1955), *passim*; Hill, *Intellectual Origins*, esp. pp. 29–30. Mounslow was patronized by Wm. Glaseor, Leicester's vice-chamberlain.
4. Cunningham, 1558, sig. A2v.
5. J. Evans, *An Ephemerides for Five Yeares to Come* (1633).
6. On Continental astrology see Thorndike, *Magic*, vols. iv–vi; C. Dariot, *A Brief and Most Easie Introduction to the Astrologicall Judgement of the Starres*, tr. F. Wither (1583, 1598). On Dariot see Thorndike, vi, pp. 105–6.
7. Bowden, 'Scientific Revolution in Astrology', ch. 1 and *passim*. Dr. Bowden discusses these various theories at length.
8. Sir C. Heydon, *An Astrological Discourse*, ed. N. Fiske (1650), sig. A4v, 5v.
9. Strof, 1627, sig. B8; Frost, 1627, sig. C4.
10. Frost, 1627, sig. C3v; Gresham, 1607, sig. B7; Allestree, 1618, sig. A3v; 1619, sig. B5–v; 1640, sig. Cv–2, 6–v; above, pp. 56–7.
11. Lilly, *Life and Times*, pp. 51–2, 61, the 2nd edition was 'sold at every stationer's' (Lilly, 1659, sig. F8v).
12. e.g. Gadbury, 1668, sig. E2v–7; Trigge, 1674, sig. Cff.
13. Booker, 1662, sig. A2v; Wharton, 1659, sig. F8v; Coley, 1672, sig. C6. For Morin see Thorndike, *Magic*, vii, ch. xvi.
14. Thorndike, *Magic*, viii, pp. 302–4; Partridge, *Opus Reformatum* (1693) and *An Astrological Vade-Mecum* (1679); Kirby, *Catastrophe Galliae* (1690), p. 30 (misprint for 38); Kirby and J. Bishop, *The Marrow of Astrology* (1687); Partridge, 1699, sig. Cff.; idem, 1702, sig. Av; Whalley, ed., *Ptolemy's Quadrapartite* (1701), sig. a3, v, and *passim*; Gadbury, 1698; Kepar, *The Gardener's Almanack 1702*, sig. B6–v; Gibson, *Flagellum Placidianum* (Gosport, 1711), esp. pp. 2, 6–7, 31; idem, *Astrologicum Britannicum 1712*, sig. C7–8v.
15. Thomas, pp. 351, 354; Smith, 1620, brs.
16. Childrey, *Indago Astrologica* (1652); idem, 1653; H.M.C., lv, *Var. Coll.*, viii, p. 61; Bowden, 'Scientific Revolution', ch. 4.
17. Coley, 1672, sig. C6v;
18. Gadbury, 1665, sig. C7; 1669, sig. A2; 1679, sig. Av; idem, *Nauticum Astrologicum* (1691), sig. A3; Thomas, pp. 309–10.

19. Culpeper, 1654, p. 15.
20. Coelson, 1687, sig. C4; Coley, *Merlini*, 1684, sig. B3; Gadbury, 1673, sig. B5v; Gadbury, *London's Deliverance* (1665), p. 22; J. H. (i.e. J. Heydon: see *D.N.B*); 'A New System of Astrology', B.L. Ms Sloane 2285, fos. 122v–3v.
21. Saunders, 1678, sig. B6.
22. Gadbury, 1665, sig. A2; 1666, sig. Av, A2; 1675, sig. D6.
23. Neve, 'Vindicta Astrologicae Judiciariae', Ms Ash. 418; Lilly, *Life and Times*, p. 26; *Lilly*, 1660, sig. F8v; Gadbury, *Obsequium Rationabile* (1675), pp. 129–32; idem, *Mr. Lilly's Envious . . . Postscript* (1676), p. 5.
24. Gadbury, 1664, sig. Av.
25. e.g. Gadbury, 1670, sig. C3–4; 1676, sig. C7–8.
26. Gadbury, 1677, sig. A2; idem, 1694, sig. B6; idem, 1699, sig. Av; J. Goad, *Astro-Meteorologia* (1686); Ms Ash. 368 (Goad's reports to Ashmole); Thomas, p. 327; Bowden, 'Scientific Revolution', pp. 176–87.
27. W. Cock, *Meteorologia* (1671); Ms Ash. 423, fos. 1–25 (Napier); T. Birch, *The History of the Royal Society of London* (1756–7), i. pp. 345, 372; *Phil. Trans.*, 116 (1675), p. 358 (Childrey).
28. Gadbury, 1692, sig. C–4; 1702, sig. Av–2.
29. Gadbury, 1675, sig. Ev–3v; 1680, sig. B2; 1703, sig. A2v; see also e.g. J. Tipper, *Great Britain's Diary 1710*, sig. B2; Bacon, *Works*, ed. Spedding, Ellis and Heath (1857–9), vi, pp. 513–14; cf. below, p. 224.
30. Gadbury, 1692, sig. Av; idem, 1674, sig. B4; Lilly, 1683, sig. Bv–3v; Saunders, 1678, sig. B5v–7v; Wharton, 1655, sig. H.
31. Gadbury, *Nauticum Astrologicum*, sig. R4v; Thorndike, *Magic*, v, p. 379; Thomas, pp. 327–8; Gadbury, 1672, sig. E5v, 6. For the Jamaican nativity (3 p.m., 10 May 1655): Gadbury, 1671, sig. E7–8; idem, *Jamaica Almanack, 1673*, sig. C5vff.
32. Gadbury, 1664, sig. Av; 1671, sig. A5–v.
33. On the Society see Thomas, p. 304 and n5; Josten, *Ashmole*, iv, pp. 1705, 1712; Ms Ash. 423, f. 168–v.
34. e.g. Thomas, pp. 353–4.
35. Lilly, *Life and Times*, p. 70; Ms Ash. 423, f. 173 (cf. f. 273 for an admiring letter to Saunders). On Whelock see Venn, *Al. Cantab.*, iv, p. 381 and *D.N.B.*
36. Taylor, *Practitioners*, pp. 199, 360, 364; and for Frost Appendix I, above.
37. e.g. Ms Ash. 423, fos. 152 (R. Billingsley of St. John's, later mathematician and minister: Taylor, op. cit., p. 235) and 165 (Rd. Hurst of King's); Josten, *Ashmole*, iv, p. 1857. See Venn, *Al. Cantab.*, and (for Barnes) *D.N.B.*
38. Ms Ash. 387, f. 229; Ms Ash. 418, fos. 4, 5.
39. Gadbury, *Ephemerides 1672* had tributes by Rd. Howard (Caius), Sam. Snowden (Corpus); Wing (1659) by Ed. Gardiner (Corpus), John Audley, M.A., Lively Moody (St. Catharine's). Howard, Snowden and Moody (later a D.D.) were or became clerics: Venn, op. cit.
40. Above, p. 182; J. Aubrey, *Brief Lives*, ii, pp. 108–9; Ms Ash. 423, f. 216.
41. Shakerley's letters in Ms Ash. 423; Shakerley, *The Anatomy of Urania Practica* (1649), p. 3; Taylor, *Practitioners*, p. 235; for the Towneley circle: C. Webster, 'Richard Towneley, . . .', *Trans. Hist. Soc. of Lancashire and Cheshire*, 118 (1966).
42. Josten, *Ashmole*, i, pp. 397; Wharton, 1647, sig. A3v; idem, *Merlini Anglici Errata* (1647), p. 58; Gadbury, 1695, sig. A6; idem, 1698, sig. A2v; idem, *Magna Veritas* (1680), p. 15. For Holland see Taylor, *Practitioners*, p. 205; for Scarburgh, J. J. Keevil, 'Sir Charles Scarburgh, 1615–1694', *Annals of Science*, 8 (1952).
43. Wharton, 1656, p. 9; C. Webster, *The Great Instauration* (1975), pp. 155, 168.
44. *The Correspondence of Henry Oldenburg*, ed. A. R. and M. B. Hall (Madison, Milwaukee, 1965–), ii, pp. 523, 648 (but cf. Thomas, p. 292); Gadbury, 1669, sig. D6–v; idem, *Nauticum Astrologicum*, sig. A2v.
45. Josten, *Ashmole*, *passim*; *The Diary of Robert Hooke 1672–1680*, ed. H. W. Robinson and W. Adams (1925), *passim*; Gadbury, 1694, sig. B. Gadbury was a friend of Aubrey for thirty years: Bodl. Ms Tanner 22, f. 126.
46. Taylor, *Practitioners*, pp. 221, 233; *Reliquiae Hearnianae*, ed. P. Bliss (1869), ii, p. 26; Gadbury, 1705, sig. B7; *D.N.B.*, Sherburne; Bowden, 'Scientific Revolution', pp. 54, 60–1. Sherburne's niece married Wharton's son.
47. Childrey: *Correspondence of Oldenburg*, vols. v, vi, *passim*; *Phil. Trans.*, 50, 64; Birch,

History, i, pp. 345, 372; Taylor, op. cit., pp. 226–7. Streete: L. Mulligan in *Past and Present*, 59 (1973), p. 115, and private correspondence; Birch, *History*, ii, p. 108; Taylor, op. cit., pp. 225–6; there are numerous respectful references in *Phil. Trans.*

48. Birch, *History*, ii, pp. 264, 449; *Oldenburg*, iv, pp. 426–7, 428; Saunders, 1680, sig. C5v–6v; Ms Sloane 2285, f. 98v; Taylor, op. cit., pp. 208, 227, 234; *Phil. Trans.*, 143 (1683), pp. 12–14.
49. Coley, *Nuncius*, 1677, sig. Av; Gadbury, *Collectio Geniturarum*, p. 186.
50. W. Ramesey, *Mans Dignity* (1661), ep. ded. (Wylde); Partridge, 1679, sig. Av; Gadbury, 1697, sig. B. (both Ent, son of Sir George); Gadbury, 1667, sig. B (Holles).
51. Josten, *Ashmole*, iv, pp. 1434, 1611–12, 1615–16; Ms Ash. 423, f. 147.
52. Ms Aubrey 23, f. 54v; Gadbury, 1668, sig. Ev; cf. Evelyn, *Kalendarium Hortense* (1666), p. 5.
53. Gadbury, 1694, sig. B5, 8; W. P(etty), *The Advice of W.P. to Mr. Samuel Hartlib* (1648), p. 12.
54. R. Kirby and J. Bishop, *The Marrow of Astrology* (1687), pt. ii, dedication; Boyle, *Tracts containing i. Suspicions about some Hidden Qualities in the Air* . . . (1674), esp. pp. 4, 24, 59. Boyle's favourable comments were reprinted by Coley, 1731, sig. C5–v. Boyle's theories are discussed in Bowden, 'Scientific Revolution', pp. 202–10.
55. *Correspondence of Oldenburg*, ii, pp. 224–5.
56. Thorndike, *Magic*, viii, p. 333; Taylor, *Practitioners*, p. 235; *Sale Catalogues of Libraries of Eminent Persons*; vol. 11, *Scientists* (1975), p. 187.
57. *Phil. Trans.*, 116 (1675), pp. 358–9; Gadbury, 1679, sig. Av. See Hanoverian editions of *The Ladies Diary* and a little later of Moore's *Vox Stellarum*. Cf. the suggestion in *Phil. Trans.*, 90 (1673), pp. 5140–2 that the *London Calendar* should record data of the weather, commodity prices and demographic material as well as astrological information.
58. Hooke, *Diary 1672–1680*, pp. 86, 102, 204, 248, 386, 400 and *passim*; *The Diary of Robert Hooke 1688–93* in *Early Science in Oxford*, ed. R. T. Gunther, x (Oxford, 1935), pp. 72, 73, 76, 141, 166, 206, 233, 236.
59. Thomas, p. 352; for other sympathetic scientists see ibid., pp. 292, 320 and n7. Bowden lays more stress on attacks by scientists, but her overall picture is similar; for burlesque almanacs by Flamsteed, now lost, see Bowden, op. cit., pp. 54, 60–1. On the decline of astrology, see below, pp. 276–83.
60. Thomas, p. 320; T. Dangerfield, *Animadversions* (1682), p. 6.
61. Gadbury, 1695, sig. A5, 8, B6; Thomas, p. 344 and n7; Hunt, *Demonstration of Astrology* p. iii.
62. B.L. Ms Egerton 2378 (Partridge); Mss Sloane 1683, 1684 (Fr. and Ch. Bernard).
63. See Appendix II; for Coventry and Friend see *D.N.B.*
64. Nicolson, 'New Astronomy'; F. R. Johnson, *Astronomical Thought in Renaissance England* (Baltimore, 1937), pp. 249–57.
65. Johnson, op. cit.; Johnson and S. V. Larkey, 'Thomas Digges, the Copernican System, and the Idea of the Infinity of the Universe in 1576', *Huntington Lib. Bull.*, v (1934); E. Gresham, 'Astrostereon', Ms Ash. 192, pp. 24ff., 59–60 (other copies at Ash. 1807; B.L. Mss Sloane 753, 3279, 3936).
66. Booker, 1634, sig. C8; above, pp. 180–1.
67. Gresham, 'Astrostereon', pp. 59–60; Gresham, 1603, sig. B2v; Taylor, *Practitioners*, pp. 181, 182–3, 208, 212, 221, 227, 231, 235.
68. Shakerley, 1651, sig. B7vff.; Taylor, op. cit., p. 235.
69. Taylor, op. cit., pp. 86, 223, 225–6.
70. E. G. Forbes, 'The Library of the Rev. John Flamsteed . . .', *Notes and Records of the Royal Society of London*, 28 (1973), pp. 137–8.
71. Parker, 1690, sig. A2v; Kepar (i.e. Parker), 1703, sig. B.
72. Rudston, 1624, sig. B3v–4v.
73. Clarke, 1629, sig. B6; Nye, 1643, sig. C2v; Shakerley, 1649 (survives in Ms only: Ms Ash. 133, fos. 185–v); Wing, 1686, sig. C7v–8.
74. J. Partridge, *Opus Reformatum* (1693), p. vi; see also J. Butler, *The Most Sacred and Divine Science of Astrology* (1680), p. 58; Gadbury, 1695, sig. C7–v; Thomas, p. 349.
75. Hopton, 1608, sig. B2–3; Hopton, *A Concordancy of Yeares* (1612), p. 46; Ranger, 1621, sig. B3v; Nicolson, 'New Astronomy', pp. 14–16; Johnson, op. cit. pp. 523–4.
76. Daniel Browne was a committed Ptolemaic, as was Allestree, whose attitude was determined by religious considerations.

77. Booker, 1634, sig. C8v; Dove, 1636, sig. C6; Ranger, 1621, sig. B3v; W. Rivers, 1628, sig. C3–4; Rudston, 1624, sig. B4; Strof, 1627; Nicolson, 'New Astronomy', p. 16 and n; Johnson, op. cit., pp. 255–6.
78. Dove, 1636, sig. C6 refers the reader to Swan's new book; it is quite possible that Dove was a pseudonym of Swan.
79. Wing, 1648, sig. C2–4v (Tychonic); Wing, 1651, sig. C5–6 (Copernican); see also his strongly Copernican *Harmonicon Coeleste* (1651) and *Astronomia Britannica* (1669).
80. Partridge, 1656, sig. B4; Coley, *Nuncius*, 1683, sig. A2; Nicholson, 'New Astronomy', pp. 24–6; Holden, 1689, sig. A8–v; *Poor Robin*, 1693, sig. C8v; see also e.g. Pond, 1679; Dade, 1690; Swallow, 1690.
81. Coley, *Nuncius*, 1690, sig. Bv.
82. Fowle, 1680, sig. B7v–Cv; Coley, *Merlinus*, 1691, sig. A3ff.; Wing, 1698, sig. C8v; Wing, 1712, sig. Cv; Dove, 1636, sig. C6.
83. Wing, 1690, sig. C8v.
84. Hill, *Intellectual Origins*, p. 118 (drawing on Nicolson).
85. e.g. Lilly, *England's Prophetical Merlin*, sig. b; Nye, 1643, sig. C2v; *Mr. Culpeper's Treatise of Aurum Potabile* (1656), p. 90; for Wing see above, p. 193.
86. Booker, 1657, sig. B5–v; 1658, sig. C; 1659, sig. Cv; 1661, sig. A8v; and Booker's epistles to Gadbury, *The Doctrine of Nativities* (1658) and Swan, *Calamans Mensurans* (1653).
87. e.g. Wharton, 1656, sig. F4; S. Morgan, *Prognosticon Posthumum 1643/4* (1644), p. 7.
88. Childrey, *Indago Astrologicum.*
89. J. Partridge, *Flagitiosus Mercurius Flagellatus* (1697), pp. 11, 20 (attacking George Parker, who published heliocentric tables).
90. Allestree, 1620, sig. C3v; idem, 1640 (frag.).
91. Browne, 1622, sig. B2, B5v, 6 (the patron was Sir John Hungerford). Browne cited Aristotle, Ptolemy and Sacrobosco.
92. Frost, 1627, sig. C3–v, repeated by Vaux, 1664, sig. B7.
93. Bowker, 1678, sig. C7–8v.
94. Gresham, 'Astrostereon', p. 24; Fowle, 1680, sig. C2–v; Saunder, 1700, sig. A6ff., B8.
95. Nicolson, 'New Astronomy', pp. 9–10.
96. Rudston, 1624, sig. B4, v; Sofford, 1624, sig. B6; Strof, 1627; Nye, 1643, sig. C2v; Nicolson, 'New Astronomy', pp. 11–13.
97. Rudston, 1624, sig. B4; Lilly, 1668, sig. A5–v; idem, 1673 sig. B4; idem, 1678, sig. A4; Nicolson, art. cit., pp. 12–13.
98. Andrews, 1682, sig. C2–3v; Wing, 1712, sig. C7v; Partridge, 1715, sig. C2v; Nicolson, art. cit., pp. 12–13.
99. Wharton, 1648, sig. A2.
100. Nye, 1643, sig. C2v; Phillippes, 1658, sig. C; Bowker, 1678, sig. C6.
101. Gray, 1604, sig. B3v; Pond, 1610, sig. C3; Ranger, 1616, sig. B4; Clarke, 1629, sig. B6v; Phillippes, 1658, sig. C3–4; Pond, 1671, sig. B8v; Saunder, 1700, sig. A5; *D.N.B.*, Muggleton; see also Thomas, p. 378 and n2; R. Whitlocke, *Observations on the Present Manners of the English* (1654), p. 215.
102. Lloyd, 1582, sig. A3; Gray, 1604, sig. B3v.
103. Digges, 1555, sig. Dv, 2; Ranger, 1631, sig. B5v, 6; Hopton, 1606, sig. B4 (his figure is in fact ninety miles an hour, clearly a misprint); Strof, 1627, sig. B7. See Johnson, *Astronomical Thought*, for Alfraganus and the expansion of the universe.
104. Saunder, 1700, sig. B8; Saunders, 1675, sig. A6.
105. Rogeford, 1560, sig. B2–v.
106. Hewlett, 1628, sig. B3v; Fowle, 1696, sig. B8–C.
107. Hopton, 1610, sig. B6.
108. Season, 1763, sig. A7.
109. M. Nicholson, *A World in the Moon* (Northampton, Mass., 1936); G. McColley, 'The Seventeenth-Century Doctrine of a Plurality of Worlds', *Annals of Science*, i (1936).
110. Gresham, 'Astrostereon', pp. 8–9.
111. Wing, 1698, sig. C6v, C8v.
112. Andrews, 1688, sig. Av., taken from G. Jones, *The Future State* (1683), p. 56; Howell, *Familiar Letters*, iii, p. 24; *Diary of Robert Hooke, 1672–1680*, p. 400; G.L. Kittredge, *The Old Farmer and his Almanack* (Boston, 1904), p. 252.

113. Nunnes, 1665, sig. C4v.
114. Hawkins, 1624, sig. B (his figure was based on the 1,028 stars in Ptolemy's star catalogue. Most contemporary astrologers took note of 1,022 or 1,025 stars, while accepting that others existed).
115. Lilly, *England's Prophetical Merlin*, sig. b; Coley, *Nuncius*, 1685, sig. A5; Coley, *Merlinus*, 1691, sig. C3v.
116. Edlin, *Prae-Nuncius Sydereus* (1664), p. 5; Shakerley, 1649 (Ms Ash. 133, fos. 183v, 185); Gadbury, 1694, sig. B5v; Culpepper, 1688, sig. A4v; Shakerley, *The Anatomy of Urania Practica* (1649), sig. A4.
117. e.g. H. Kearney, *Scholars and Gentlemen* (1970), pp. 123–4.
118. For this section see Taylor, *Practitioners*, *passim*; Hill, *Intellectual Origins*, esp. pp. 48–51.
119. Taylor, op. cit., p.4.
120. Taylor, *Practitioners*, pp. 181, 183, 196, 197, 199, 200, 203, 204–5, 343; Thomas, p. 292.
121. A. W. Richeson, *English Land Measuring to 1800: Instruments and Practices* (Cambridge, Mass., and London, 1966), chs 4, 5; Taylor, op. cit., pp. 230–1; C. E. Cenney, 'William Leybourne 1626–1716,' *The Library*, 5th ser., v (1950); J. W. Gough, *Sir Hugh Myddelton: Entrepreneur and Engineer* (Oxford, 1964), pp. 50–1.
122. Taylor, op. cit., pp. 175, 176, 208, 221–2, 258, 321, 381; Hill, *Intellectual Origins*, p.19, n4; H. J. Webb, 'The Science of Gunnery in Elizabethan England', *Isis*, 45 (1954); Nye, *The Art of Gunnery* (1648), *passim*; for Walgrave as astrologer see H. Coley (his friend), *Clavis Astrologiae* (1669), pp. 209–10.
123. Gilden, 1616, sig. B2ff; idem, 1624, sig. B2v; Bretnor, 1615, sig. Av; idem, 1616, A3v; idem, 1617 (on Napier); Browne, 1628, sig. B8v; White, 1619, sig. Av; Taylor, *Practitioners*, *passim*; Nicolson, 'New Astronomy', pp. 3ff.
124. Taylor, op. cit., pp. 209 (Partridge), 200 (Hopton), 203 (Browne), 209–10 (Osborne) etc.
125. Taylor, op. cit., p. 23; Askham, 1556, sig. B2–C5v, C–2 (notation erratic); Allestree, 1641, sig. C7–v; Wilkinson, 1643 (described by Taylor, p. 226); Wing, 1648, sig. Cv, White, 1688, sig. Bv–2.
126. *A Blank and Perpetual Almanack* (1566), sig. B6; Daniel, 1652, sig. B8v–C.
127. Browne, 1631, sig. Bv; Chamberlaine, 1631, sig. C; Vaux, 1648, sig. B8; D. W. Waters, *The Art of Navigation in England in Elizabethan and Early Stuart Times* (1958), pp. 94, 244–5.
128. Pond, 1607, sig. Cv; Hill, 1609, sig. B2.
129. See below, pp. 246–7.
130. Laet, 1541, sig. B2–v; *Blank and Perpetual Almanack*, sig. B7–8; Hubrigh, 1569, sig. B2v–5v (Hubrigh was from Middelburg in Zeeland; his almanacs were adapted for use in England); Osborne, 1625, sig. Bv. See generally Waters, op. cit., and E. G. R. Taylor, *The Haven-Finding Art* (1956).
131. W. Bourne, *A Regiment for the Sea, and Other Writings on Navigation*, ed. E. G. R. Taylor (Cambridge, 1963) contains two of his almanacs, with an assessment of his career.
132. Waters, op. cit., pp. 239–42; Taylor, *Practitioners*, pp. 56–7, 193, 207–8, 234; Birch, *History*, ii, p. 264; iii, p. 449; *Correspondence of Oldenburg*, iv, p. 426–7.
133. In 1659, 1661 (Gadbury); 1676, 1696 (Colson); 1675–7 (Seaman); 1655 (Waterman).
134. Bourne, *An Almanack for x Yeeres* (1581), sig. A5. But Phillippes was an exception.
135. Gadbury, *Nauticum Astrologicum*, *passim*; Thomas, pp. 310, 373.
136. Gadbury, 1703, sig. C4–8v; cf. J. Moxon, *A Brief Discussion of a Passage by the North Pole* (1674), which aroused considerable interest.
137. Gadbury, 1705, sig. Avff. Campanella, a prophet of universal monarchy, had suggested sending missionaries and astrologers to the New World: F. Yates, *Giordano Bruno and the Hermetic Tradition* (1964), ch. xx, esp. pp. 388, 394–5.
138. Fallowes, 1640, sig. B7–8; Askham, 1555, sig. A3; Dade, 1589, sig. C5v; Bretnor, 1615, sig. A2v.
139. Frost, 1627, sig. B7v; Nye, 1642, sig. B3v; Wing, 1654, sig. A2–v; Smith, 1654, sig. Cv–2; Woodhouse, 1666, sig. A2; see also Smith, 1625; Dade, 1658; Swan, 1677 and many others. Differences over Quinzay reflected uncertainty as to its modern identification.

140. Stephenson, 1676, sig. E5; see also above, p. 185; Saunder, 1687, sig. A8v.
141. e.g. Digges, 1564, fos. 5ff.; Evans, 1631, sig. B7ff.; Lakes, 1627, sig. C3v; see Thomas, ch. 20.
142. e.g. Wyberd, 1637, sig. C4v, C6v; Frende, 1585, sig. Cv, C4v; Vaux, 1637, sig. B2; Martindale, 1676, *passim*.
143. e.g. Dove, 1667, sig. C5; Digges, 1564, fos. 6v–7.
144. Allestree, 1634, sig. C6; see also Coverdale's scriptural almanacs.
145. Dove, 1653, sig. C6.
146. See on this subject W.S.C. Copeman, *Doctors and Diseases in Tudor Times* (1960); C. Camden, 'Elizabethan astrological medicine', *Annals of Medical History*, N.S., ii (1930); H. G. Dick, 'Students of Physic and Astrology', *Journ. of Hist. of Medicine*, i (1946); Thomas, ch. 10.
147. Munk, *Physicians*, p. 69; Goodall, pp. 337–9.
148. Frende, 1598, sig. A4; Pond, 1607, sig. C2; Pond, 1649, sig. C5v; Bretnor, 1613, sig. B2; Gadbury, 1692, sig. Av, C5v; *Blagrave's Astrological Practice of Physick* (1671), sig. Bv.
149. J. Primrose, *Popular Errours*, trans. R. Wittie (1651), pp. 240–2.
150. Quotation from title-page; see also above, p. 111 and n 48; Hill, *Intellectual Origins*, esp. pp. 81-2.
151. Salmon, *Iatrica seu Praxis Medendi* (1681); for the others see Wing.
152. *Kalender*, ed. Sommers (1892), pp. 115–17 (1506 edn.); for later examples see e.g. Porter, 1585, sig. B5; White, 1621, sig. C2; Swallow, 1647, sig. B5.
153. Securis, 1562, sig. A4–8; Vaux, 1627, sig. B2; Swan, e.g. 1657, sig. Cff.
154. Gadbury, *London's Deliverance Predicted* (1665), pp. 11, 18ff., 23–5 and *passim*. He refuted Booker's assertion that the plague *was* infectious in *Vox Solis* (1667), pp. 24–5. Gadbury's efforts were ridiculed by Oldenburg: *Correspondence*, ii, pp. 523, 526–7.
155. Allestree, 1626, sig. B3; *Diary of the Rev. John Ward*, ed. C. Severn (1839), p. 257.
156. Beridge, 1654, sig. B4; Pool, 1656, sig. B2–4v; Pond, 1667, sig. Cv.
157. Culpeper, *A Physicall Directory* (1649), p. 163.
158. Sir G. Keynes, *The Life of Dr. William Harvey* (Oxford, 1966), p. 439; Thomas, p. 292.
159. Gadbury, 1673, sig. B6; C. Webster, *The Great Instauration* (1975), p. 271. On Daniel Sennert see Thorndike, *Magic*, vii, chap. vii, esp. p. 215; La Rivière was professor at Montpellier. The works of both were frequently reprinted in England.
160. Ramesey, *Some Physical Considerations of ... Wormes* (1668), t.p.; Gadbury, *Ephemerides* (1672), t.p.; Partridge, *Opus Reformatum*, t.p. On the emptiness of many such titles see J. Young, *Observations in Chyrurgery and Anatomy* (1692), esp. sig. A7; Young attacked the 'royal' surgeon, John Brown (for whom see below), an admirer of Gadbury.
161. Ms Ash. 423, fos. 166, 167v, 197; Gadbury, 1663, sig. C7; idem, 1677, sig. C7v; Thomas, p. 351.
162. Barker: Gadbury, 1672, sig. B3; Salmon, *Horae Mathematicae, seu Urania* (1679), sig. A3; Scarburgh: above, p. 188; Prujean: Gadbury, 1702, sig. C8v.
163. Coley, *Merlinus*, 1688, sig. Av; Partridge, sig. Av.
164. Drs. John Betts, Thos. Shirley, Rd. Lawford, Thos. Harrington, Thos. Wharton: Gadbury, 1697, *passim*; Josten, *Ashmole*, ii, p. 559. Gadbury and Bird were friends of the surgeon, Josias Westwood (Bird, 1661, sig. Av; Gadbury, *London's Deliverance*, p. 19), and Gadbury of Ed. Bolnest (ibid., p. 39). For most of these see Munk, *Physicians*. Gadbury listed more enthusiasts in his *Coelestus Legatus* (1656), sig. CC2–v and *Collectio Geniturarum*.
165. Ms Sloane 1683; Ms Ash. 242, fos. 85v, 87v.
166. *The Life and Work of Robert Hooke*, ed. R. T. Gunther (Oxford, 1930), p. 326; Thomas, pp. 354–5. The eighteenth-century almanac-makers Moore, Weaver and Season possessed licences. For later survivals see T. Harley, *Moon Lore* (1885), *N. and Q.*, *passim*, and the volumes of the *County Folk-Lore* series.
167. A. G. Debus, *The English Paracelsians* (1965); Webster, *Great Instauration*.
168. J. Primrose, *The Antimonial Cup* (1640), p. 20; idem, *Popular Errours*, p. 35.
169. Debus, *English Paracelsians*, pp. 56, 147; Parkhurst, *Medicina Diastatica* (1653) sig. a.
170. Lilly, *Life and Times*, p. 21; Evans, *The Universall Medicine* (1634), sig. A and *passim*; Primrose, *Antimonial Cup*; Debus, op. cit., p. 170; Goodall, pp. 442–3.

171. Lilly, 1645, sig. A2; F. Sherwood Taylor and C. H. Josten, 'Johannes Banfi Hunyades', *Ambix*, v (1953), pp. 44–52; Lilly, *Life and Times*, p. 28.
172. Desmus, 1655, sig. C3; Culpeper, 1655, sig. B5v–6; see further F. N. L. Poynter, 'Nicholas Culpeper and the Paracelsians' in *Science, Medicine and Society*, ed. A. G. Debus (1972).
173. Gadbury, *Natura Prodigorum* (1660), sig. A6v; *London's Deliverance*, sig. A3; *Thesaurus Astrologiae*, ed. Gadbury (1674), sig. A3v; Baston, 1659, t.p., sig. B6v; Coelson, 1677, sig. C8v; idem, *Philosophia Maturata* (1668); Pool, 1656, t.p.; Salmon, *Doron Medicum* (1683), *passim*.
174. See for example M. H. Nicolson, *The Breaking of the Circle* (1960).
175. Booker, 1637, sig. B7; Hill, 1684, sig. B5 (the same passage is in *Mr. Lillies New Prophecie of a General Peace* (1674), p. 8).
176. Coelson, 1687, sig. C4; Swallow, 1690, sig. B4–v.
177. Ms Ash. 182, f. 201v–2; Harvey, 1585, sig. C4v; Hopton, 1606, sig. C8v (plagiarized belatedly by Leadbetter in Partridge, 1739, sig. C4).
178. Lilly, *Life and Times*, p. 32; see also ibid., pp. 93–7.
179. Salmon, 1696, sig. C2; Neve, 1668, sig. B2v–4v; *Blagrave's Astrological Practice*, p. 131.
180. Nye, 1648, sig. B4; Saunders, *Physiognomie and Chiromancie* (1653) and *Palmistry*, (1663); J. Rothman, *Chiromancy*, trans. Wharton (1652); Gadbury, *The Just and Pious Scorpionist* (1677), p. 12; Booker, 1666, sig. C–2; Tanner, 1667, sig. B5v; Blagrave, 1660, sig. A4v; see also Lilly, *Life and Times*, p. 93.
181. Wing, 1698, sig. C7v.
182. Digges, 1564, f. 6v; Vaux, 1624, sig. B6v–7v; C.P., *The Sheepherd's New Kalender 1700*, p. 30. On this subject see Thomas, ch. 20.
183. Dade, 1598, sig. C–4; de Billy, 1604, p. 27; J. Wilson, *The Cheats*, ed. M. C. Nahm (Oxford, 1935), IV, ii (p. 194), written in 1662. See also above, pp. 28, 57.
184. Allestree, 1651, sig. A4; Langley, 1648, sig. B7.
185. Langley, 1641, sig. B4v; Pont, 1646, p. 67; Swallow, 1649, sig. A5.
186. C.P., *Sheepherd's New Kalender*, *passim*.
187. *Pharmacopoeia Londinensis*, trans. Culpeper (1653), p. 31; Hooke, *Diary 1672–80*, pp. 263, 307.
188. e.g. Booker, 1665, sig. C8v; Pigot, 1630, sig. C3v; above, pp. 56–7.
189. Gadbury, 1666, sig. A3v, A8v; 1668, sig. C6v; 1669, sig. D8; 1673, sig. B5v; 1676, sig. C5; 1677, sig. C7v; Missonne (i.e. Gadbury), 1660, sig. A3v; *Nuncius Astrologicus* (1660), p. 21; *Dies Novissimus* (1664), p. 42 and *passim*; *Natura Prodigorum*, pp. 187, 190.
190. Vaux, 1629, sig. B8–v; *Blagrave's Astrological Practice*, p. 119; Langley, 1648, sig. C3v.
191. Bickerstaff, 1710, sig. C4.
192. Gadbury, *Natura Prodigorum* ('A book of prodigies is fit/In times prodigious to be writ': sig. A5); see also his almanac for 1681, sig. C4v–5v.
193. Culpepper, 1687, sig. A6; Trigge, 1677, sig. C2v–3; Langley, 1647, sig. C2–v; Coley, *Nuncius*, 1682, sig. C3v.
194. Andrews, 1696, sig. C6.
195. Hopton, 1610, sig. B8.
196. Langley, 1648, sig. C2v, 3.
197. Above, pp. 128–9; Thomas, pp. 362–3, 368, 632–4.
198. Gadbury reiterated the point: Gadbury, 1677, sig. C7v; 1679, sig. C7v–8v; *Natura Prodigorum*, p. 164; *Britain's Royal Star* (1661), epistle. Bomelius promised a separate work on witchcraft: Bomelius, 1567, sig. E2.
199. Gadbury, 1664, sig. C7; idem, 1677, sig. C8; *Thesaurus*, ed. Gadbury, postscript (citing Ady's sceptical tract on witchcraft.)
200. Coley, *Merlini*, 1684, sig. B3.
201. Ramesey, *Some Physicall Considerations of . . . Wormes*, pp. 70–5.
202. Partridge, 1706, sig. C5–6v; Moore, *Vox Stellarum, 1720*, pp. 11–20.
203. J. Glanvill, *Saducismus Triumphatus* (1681).

Chapter 7 History and Literature (*pages* 215–37)

1. *Almanac for the Year 1386* (1812), pp. 18–19 (listing e.g. expulsion of the Jews, murder of Becket, battle of Crecy, plagues and the peasants' revolt); xylographic almanac (*S.T.C.* 388; Bosanquet IIa; see Bosanquet, pp. 14–16); Porter, 1585, sig. A2. For Brute see below, pp. 216–17.
2. For the first examples see Gresham, 1603 and 1604; Pond, 1605; Neve, 1606; Dade, 1607, etc.
3. Aubrey, *Brief Lives*, ed. O. L. Dick (1972), p. 29.
4. For example, L. B. Wright, *Middle-Class Culture in Elizabethan England* (Chapel Hill, N. Carolina, 1935), esp. ch. 9; Winter, 1628, sig. B2; Trigge, 1679, sig. C2.
5. e.g. Allestree, 1629, sig. C2; Gresham, 1604, sig. A2; Wilson, 1626, sig. Av; Bowker, 1684, sig. A2v; Dove, 1641, sig. C6; Rose, 1685, sig. B8v. On the Brute legend see T. D. Kendrick, *British Antiquity* (1950).
6. e.g. Swan, 1673, sig. A2–v; Sellers, *Almanack for an Age*, 1685(?).
7. e.g. Wilson, 1626, sig. Av.
8. Perkins, 1628, sig. B4–5; Beridge, 1654, sig. C3v; Crooke, 1652, sig. B5; Swan, 1661, sig. A2; Swallow, 1666, sig. Av; Perkins, 1685, sig. B3v.
9. Bowker, 1684, sig. A2v.
10. Riders, 1675, sig. A3v.
11. Wing, 1647, sig. Cv; 1667, t.p.; the claim was also made by Readman, 1680, t.p.
12. e.g. Fallowes, 1640, sig. B3v; Woodhouse, 1621, sig. A2; Trigge, 1679, sig. C2; Riders, 1675, sig. A3v.
13. Joseph: Fallowes, 1640, sig. B3v; Perkins, 1628, sig. B5, and 1682, sig. B5; Rose, 1659, sig. B8v; Lucius: Browne, 1628, sig. A3v; Perkins, 1628, sig. B5v; Swan, 1661, sig. A2v; Trigge, 1679, sig. C2; Bowker, 1684, sig. A2v.
14. Dawson, 1577, brs. (no doubt taken from Holinshed's chronicle of the same year, which drew on Bale, who in turn based it on the forgeries of Annius of Viterbo: see Kendrick, *British Antiquity*, pp. 69–76.)
15. Pigot, 1630, sig. B5v.
16. e.g. Bretnor, 1615, sig. A3v; Browne, 1628, sig. A3v; Fallowes, 1640, sig. B4; *Poor Robin*, 1668, sig. A3; Bowker, 1673, sig. A3v; Fowle, 1698, sig. B2.
17. S. Rowlands, *A Fooles Bolt* (1614), p. 28, reprinted in *Complete Works*, (Glasgow, 1880), vol. ii. The expedition had been on an unprecedented scale. Henry took 48,000 troops, equivalent to two-thirds of the population of London.
18. e.g. Browne, 1628, sig. A3v (Athelstan); Woodhouse, 1613, sig. A2; Fowle, 1692, sig. A2 (Henry); Woodhouse, loc. cit.; Browne, loc. cit. (French); Bretnor, 1615, sig. A3v; Dove, 1649, sig. Cv; Bowker, 1681, sig. A3v (Drake).
19. Bowker, 1684, sig. A3v; Fowle, 1698, sig. B2.
20. May-Day: Neve, 1607; Perkins, 1628; Chamberlain, 1631; Bowker, 1681; see M. Holmes, 'Evil May-Day 1517: the Story of a Riot', *History Today*, xv (1965); Hacket: Perkins, 1628, sig. B6v; Coulton, 1653, sig. C2v; Culpepper, 1683, sig. B; Dove, 1686, sig. A3.
21. Heyman, 1660, sig. A4v.
22. Wharton, 1658, sig. D7.
23. e.g. Neve, 1651; Swan, 1661; Pond, 1675; Fowle, 1680; Riders, 1691.
24. Above, p. 78; see also e.g. Gadbury, 1656, sig. A2.
25. Porter, 1585, sig. A2.
26. e.g. Wharton, 1655 (Vere and Brookes edn.), sig. A3; Wheeler, 1674, brs.; Bowker, 1681, sig. A3v; B. Pond, 1689, sig. C5v. The regal table continued in this form throughout the next century: see e.g. Moore, 1800, p. 30.
27. Saunders, 1658, sig. A7.
28. White 1632, sig. B6v (and many subsequent years).
29. Trigge, 1665, sig. B2–3; idem, 1679, sig. C2, 3 (Trigge's details of Saxon society were derived from Thomas Blount; similar information appeared earlier in A. Hopton, *A Concordancy of Yeares* (1612), pp. 190–1).

30. Partridge, 1692, sig. A3v; Parker, 1690, sig. C4.
31. Rudston, 1624, sig. A8. See on this subject C. A. Patrides, 'Renaissance Estimates of the Year of Creation', *H.L.Q.*, xxvi (1962–3.)
32. e.g. Swallow, 1633, sig. B.
33. e.g. Perkins, 1628, sig. B3ff.; Clarke, 1629, sig. Bv; Beridge, 1654, sig. C2v.
34. Strof, 1627, sig. B; Bell, 1622, sig. Av.
35. Swan, 1661, sig. A2; Sofford, 1634, sig. B4; Dove, 1641, sig. C7v, 8.
36. Bowker, 1681, sig. A3v; Bird, 1662, sig. A2.
37. Ranger, 1624, sig. Av; Einer, 1624, sig. B2; Fallowes, 1640, sig. B2; Bird, 1662, sig. A2.
38. Pont, 1646, p. 75 (Jesuits); Pond, 1633, sig. A4 (Magdeburg); Gadbury, 1656, sig. A2v (Piedmont); St. Bartholomew was almost universal.
39. Browne, 1631, sig. A3; White, 1633, sig. Av; Swan, 1681, sig. C8v; Dove, 1686, sig. A3v; see Thomas, pp. 104–5 and n.
40. Ranger, 1624, sig. Av; Jessey, 1649, sig. A7.
41. Wharton, 1656, sig. Av (repeated by Fowle, 1692, sig. Av); (Blount), 1663, sig. A2–v; *Kalendarium Catholicum*, 1686, sig. C2–v; ibid., 1689, sig. A2–v.
42. Perkins, 1628, sig. B5v, 6; Grammar, 1628, sig. B2v; Ranger, 1628, sig. Av; Sofford, 1629, sig. B4–v; Pond, 1630 sig. C; Langley, 1640, sig. B8v; S. Partridge, 1653, sig. C4v–5; Coulton, 1654, sig. C4v; Goldsmith, 1662, sig. B8; Gadbury, 1668, sig. E8; Gallen, 1673, sig. A2v; Rose, 1685, sig. C–2; Dove, 1686, sig. A3.
43. Perkins, Ranger, Sofford, Bowker, Coulton and Gadbury, as in p. 221, n38, above; many other references. Bretnor and Wharton saw coaches as a sign of degeneracy (Bretnor, 1618, sig. B6; Wharton, 1656, sig. A3) but usually conform to the pattern.
44. Grammar, 1628, sig. B2v; Perkins, 1628, sig. B6; Sofford, 1629, sig. B3v; Fallowes, 1640, sig. B4; Langley, 1640, sig. B8v; Chamberlaine, 1649, sig. B2; Perkins, 1666, sig. B5v; Bell, 1622, sig. Av; Wing, *Ephemeris* (1669), sig. D2, also mentioned the Chinese precedence.
45. Fallowes, 1640, sig. B4; Blunt, 1656, sig. B6v; Partridge, 1653, sig. C4v–5; Chesick, 1661, sig. A2v; Goldisborough, 1662, sig. B8; Gadbury, 1668, sig. E8v; Rose, 1685, sig. Cv–2; Dove, 1686, sig. A3.
46. See also above, pp. 198–9.
47. Woodhouse, 1666, sig. A2v; Perkins, 1666, sig. B7; Dove 1690, sig. A3v; Swallow, 1649, sig. B2; on Parr see J. Taylor, *The Old, Old, Very Old Man* (1635).
48. Trigge, 1679, sig. C3.
49. Hopton, *Concordancy*, pp. 213–29; Winter, 1634, sig. B2ff.
50. Wharton, 1657–66; Saunders, 1670–3. On the *Gesta* see Bosanquet, 'English Seventeenth Century Almanacks', *The Library*, 4th ser., x (1930), pp. 372-4.
51. e.g. Swan, 1681, sig. C7–8 (from 1558); Dove, 1673–85 offered the period from 1640, but thereafter from 1558.
52. (Gadbury), *Merlinus Verax*, 1687 (the 'Plot Almanack'); C. Doble, ed., *Remarks and Collections of Thomas Hearne* (Oxford Hist. Soc.), iii, pp. 104, 105–6, 107; Gadbury, 1694, sig. A6. See also Bodl. Ms Tanner 22, f. 126 (Gadbury to Thomas Tanner).
53. Hearne, *Remarks*, vol. iv (ed. D. W. Rannie), p. 401. On Pointer see Foster, *Al. Oxon* iii, 1175. Hearne derided the book which seems nevertheless to have been popular. Aubrey also noted historical events recorded in his almanacs: *Brief Lives*, ii, pp. 181, 320, 323.
54. P. V. Coronelli, *The Royal Almanack* (2nd edn., 1696).
55. See also Browne, 1620 (Ireland); Kinder (Notts.); Piers (Durham); *Mercurius Civicus* (London).
56. e.g. Forster, 1576, sig. A5v; Sofford, 1634, sig. B2v–3; Jessey, 1649, sig. B8v; Goldsmith, 1686, sig. Bv.
57. e.g. Hopton, 1606, sig. B7.
58. See Chapter 5, above.
59. Piers, 1640, sig. B2v; Coley, 1673, sig. C.
60. Booker, 1632, sig. B5; Woodward, 1684, sig. B3; Coley, 1702, sig. C7v; idem, 1704.
61. Wing, 1682, brs.; repeated in Moore, 1785, p. 17. See also G. N. Clark, *The Cycle of War and Peace in Modern History* (Cambridge, 1949), esp. pp. 9–10, 16, 18; S. C. Chew, *The Virtues Reconciled: An Iconographical Study* (Toronto, 1947), pp. 125–6; H. Peter, *A Word for the Army* (1647), in *Harleian Miscellany*, v, p. 571.

62. Lilly, *The Worlds Catastrophe* (1647), pp. 42–56 (a translation of Trithemius); Wharton, 1653, sig. Eff. (derived from Bodin and Richter).
63. Edlin, *Prae-Nuncius Sydereus* (1664), p. 42; cf. Kendal, 1701, sig. C4v; Wharton, 1655 (printed by M. J.), sig. H.
64. Lilly, 1658, sig. B3v. The theory was denounced by John Graunt (*Natural and Political Observations* (5th edn., 1666, pp. 55–6), whose own efforts to explain the periodicity of plagues were scrutinized critically by Gadbury (Gadbury, 1702, sig. C3). See also Thomas, p. 328.
65. Bacon, *Works*, ed. Spedding Ellis and Heath (1857–9), vi, pp. 513–14; Gadbury, 1675, sig. Ev–3v; 1680, sig. B2; above, p. 185.
66. Allestree, 1622, sig. A8; see above, p. 23.
67. White, 1648, sig. C3v.
68. Trigge, 1659, sig. A3; cf. Hewit, 1654, sig. B8.
69. Booker, 1667, sig. A8; Dove, 1688, sig. B; Dade, 1594, sig. B2.
70. Buckminster, 1589, sig. C8.
71. Keene, 1615, sig. B2; cf. L. Reynolds, *Spiritual Intervals* (1641), p. 35: 'every man is as a urinal in the hand of the great physician of heaven and earth.'
72. *Some Further Remarks upon Mr. Gadbury's Defence of Scorpio* (1676), p. 27; the proverb is not listed in the standard collections.
73. *Miscellaneous Works of Sir Thomas Overbury*, ed. E. C. Rimbault (1890), p. 93 (also attributed to J. Cocke); Wright, *Middle-Class Culture*, p. 99; Jonson, *Works*, ed. F. Cunningham (1903–4), ii, p. 437 (the critic was Alexander Gill); 'Rabelais,' c. 1659, sig. A4v.
74. Coelson, 1674, sig. A5; Cookson, 1711, sig. Av; J. Partridge, *Flagitiosus Mercurius Flagellatus* (1697), p. 11.
75. Peter, 1678, sig. C8v; *The Spectator*, ed. D. F. Bond (Oxford, 1965), ii, pp. 356–7.
76. Allen, *Star-Crossed Renaissance*, pp. 204, 208–9.
77. H.M.C., *10th Report, Appendix iv*, pp. 441–2; B.L. Ms Add. 38599, fos. 59ff. (perhaps transcribed for their utilitarian content); Bodl. Ms Rawl. poet. 212: J. Davis, 'English epigrams' (1594), fos. 66vff.
78. Trigge, 1685, sig. A3.
79. *D.N.B.*, Gadbury and Wharton.
80. Henry Care, 'An Answer to a scandalous sheet Intituled, A poetical observacon [*sic*] on Lillies Almanacke', B.L. Ms Sloane 2285, fos. 141v, 142; for Care see *D.N.B.*
81. Desmus, 1653, sig. A3.
82. Culpeper, *Catastrophe Magnatum*, p. 48 (for May see *D.N.B.*); Gadbury, 1698, *passim*. His friends were Thomas Pecke (b. 1637), and Dr. Henry Birkhead (1617-96).
83. Evans, 1613 (the plagiarism was spotted by the owner of the Bodleian copy); for other examples see e.g. Culpepper, 1693, sig. C; Swan, 1666, sig. C3.
84. Swan, 1670, sig. B8v (Quarles); Neve, 1670, t.p. (Cowley); Perkins, 1699, sig. A5 (Butler); Bodl. Ms Add. B8, f. 67 (Dryden quoted by Coley); Saunder, 1688, sig. A2 (imitation of Dryden).
85. For Parkhurst see *D.N.B.*; Harflete, *A Banquet of Essayes* (1653); P. K.(inder), *Surfeit*, pp. 17, 27, 31, 32, 56, 57, 65. Kinder reveals his authorship in Ms Ash. 788.
86. Saunder, e.g. 1690, sig. A5ff. (the notes were taken, he said, from Dr. Hood).
87. Gray, 1589, sig. A8v; Vaux, 1665, sig. C2.
88. Nye, 1648, sig. B4; Coley, *Merlinus*, 1691, sig. C6v; Wing, 1684, sig. C8v; Taylor, *Practitioners*, p. 287 (Hobbs); J. Tipper, *Ladies Diary*, 1706, sig. Av; Pont, 1646, p. 68.
89. Securis, 1581, sig. C3; Vaux, 1665, sig. Cv.
90. See H. M. Petter, *The Oxford Almanack 1674–1946* (New York, 1946).
91. G. H. Jenkins, 'Welsh Books and Religion, 1660–1730', Univ. of Wales, Aberystwyth Ph.D., 1974, esp. pp. 527–42, 605–6, 654–63.
92. e.g. Trigge, 1661, sig. A3 (slabby); Coelson, 1673, sig. B3 (cray); Jeffereys, 1635, sig. D2 (lobcock, lollard); Gibson, 1708, sig. Av, C6 (lerry); Gadbury, 1681, sig. A5v (vafrous).
93. Porter, 1585, sig. B5v (*O.E.D.* gives 'irritable'); Pearse, 1758, sig. B6 (the only recorded use was by Bastwick in 1637); Fowle, 1696, sig. Bv.
94. Pond, 1664, sig. C2; Smith, 1631, sig. B6v; Jack Adams, 1662, p. 17; Hewlett, 1625, sig. A3.

95. *Poor Robin*, 1690, sig. C4 (the last three words remain in fairly common use, despite the transient nature of most slang).
96. Smith, 1631, 'To the Reader'; cf. M.P. Tilley, *Proverbs in England* (Ann Arbor, 1950), p. 26.
97. Booker, 1648, sig. C4; Tilley, p. 262 and cf. p. 125.
98. Culpeper, 1653, sig. C5; Tilley, p. 384.
99. *Poor Robin*, 1710, sig. A4; Tilley, p. 169.
100. Pond, 1612, sig. A5v; *The Oxford Dictionary of English Proverbs*, ed. F. P. Wilson (3rd edn., Oxford, 1970), p. 451.
101. Beridge, 1654, sig. C8; Felgenhauer, 1656, p. 2; cf. Tilley, pp. 125, 333.
102. e.g. 'When Bristleton doth wear a cap,/The neighbours near it fear a clap', referring to Bristleton Hill in Durham (Vaux, 1623, sig. C).
103. Bretnor, 1616, sig. C5, 6; Gresham, 1603; Wing, 1648, sig. A5v; above, p. 63. For a general discussion see J. Crow, 'Some Jacobean Catch Phrases and Some Light on Thomas Bretnor', in *Elizabethan and Jacobean Studies*, ed. H. Davies and H. Gardner (Oxford, 1959), pp. 250–78.
104. See especially Allen, *Star-Crossed Renaissance*, chs. iv, v.
105. Tilley, pp. 123, 438; Partridge, 1755, sig. C2v; Howell, *Familiar Letters*, ii, pp. 201–2.
106. Howell, *Familiar Letters*, i, p. 216; iii, p. 122; Allen, op. cit., p. 193; J. Canne, *A Voice from the Temple* (1653), quoted in Tai Liu, *Discord in Zion* (The Hague, 1973), p. 84; see also Lord Keeper Williams, cited by P. Zagorin, *The Court and the Country* (1969), p. 45; N. Church, *Cheap Riches* (1654), p. 31.
107. T. Middleton, *No Wit, No Help like a Woman's*, V. i, in *Works*, ed. A. H. Bullen (1886), iv, p. 418; see also S. Rowlands, *Humour's Looking Glasse* (1608), p. 26; Dekker, *The Non-Dramatic Works*, ed. A. B. Grosart (1884–6), ii, p. 283. Dryden is said to have expressed the same wish to his own wife: J. Sutherland, ed., *The Oxford Book of Literary Anecdotes* (1975), p. 38. See also F. Peck, *Desiderata Curiosa* (1732), viii, p. 49, on Sir Henry Savile and his wife.
108. *An Almanack-Husband; or a Wife a Month* (1708); for the proberb see Tilley, p. 706.
109. R. Whitelock, *Observations on the Present Manners of the English* (1654), p. 298.
110. Allen, *Star-Crossed Renaissance*, pp. 230–1; W. Hone, *The Year Book* (1832), pp. 683–4; T. J. Pettigrew, *On Superstitions connected with the History of . . . Medicine* (1844), p. 31. Another author, in a reference that has strayed, was reminded by the figure, with its arrows pointing to the sections of the body, of the martyrdom of St. Sebastian.
111. There are discussions by C. Camden in *The Library* (1931–2), F. P. Wilson, ibid. (1939), and Allen, op. cit., ch. v. All focus on the Elizabethan/Jacobean period, so in what follows I have used mainly later works.
112. Fouleweather, 1591, t.p., sig. A3v, C4.
113. Rabelais, c. 1659, pp. 4–5; Fouleweather, 1591, sig. B3; *Poor Robin*, 1687, sig. A7; ibid., 1690, sig. B.
114. *Poor Robin*, 1668, sig. C6v.
115. Ibid., 1665, sig. C7.
116. Fouleweather, 1591, sig. C3v, D3; *Poor Robin*, 1667, sig. C6. Cf. 'Alderman Hoyle's remedy for ague', i.e. hanging oneself: ibid., 1666, sig. C8.
117. *The Owles Almanack*, p. 30 and *passim*; there is a good modern edition by D.C. Allen (Baltimore, 1943).
118. *Poor Robin*, 1691, sig. A3v, 4. See also *Montelion*, Desmus, Guzman, and above, p. 40.
119. Desmus, 1654, sig. B6; repeated in Liby, 1656, p. 3.
120. *Poor Robin*, 1673, *passim*; for other examples see p. 62, above.
121. Adams, c. 1664, appendix, p. 1.
122. *Montelion*, 1662, sig. A3v.
123. *Poor Robin*, 1667, sig. C5.
124. Eyesore: *Poor Robin*, 1666, sig. C2; heraldry: ibid., 1669, sig. C5v; ibid., 1690, sig. C4; *1680. A Yea and Nay Almanack*, sig. B7.
125. *Poor Robin*, 1685, sig. C7.
126. Shinkin-ap-Shone, 1654, pp. 3, 5 and *passim*; cf. *The Welsh Mans New Almanack 1643*; Shone-ap Lewis, *The Welsh-Mans New Almanacke 1648*.
127. H.N., *1678. A Yea and Nay Almanack*, sig. A8, C, 2.

128. (Philipps), *Montelion*, 1660, sig. C3; *Montelion*, 1662, sig. A4v.
129. *Lillys Lamentations* (1652), p. 7; Desmus, 1655, sig. A4v; Liby, 1655, p. 4; *Montelion*, 1660, sig. A6.
130. Keene, 1615, sig. B2v; Bretnor, 1615, sig. A2; Evans, 1625, sig. C4; Lilly, *Life and Times*, p. 21.
131. For Partridge see Aubrey, *Brief Lives*, ii, p. 120.
132. Booker, 1648, sig. C, C7.
133. Frende, 1585, sig. B2v; Gadbury, 1673, sig. A4; Kirby, *Vates Astrologicus* (1683), 'To the Reader'; Lilly, *Life and Times*, pp. 4, 7.
134. Above, p. 217.
135. Lilly, 1655, sig. C; Andrews, 1656, sig. A3; Bell, 1622, sig. B4v–5v; Abendana, 1693, pt. ii, *passim.*
136. Gadbury, *Natura Prodigorum* (1660), sig. A6; Gadbury, 1670, sig. B5; Culpeper, *Mr. Culpepper's Treatise of Aurum Potabile* (1656), p. 26; cf. Culpeper, *Catastrophe Magnatum* (1652), pp. 36, 43.
137. Thomas, pp. 353–4; but see also above, p. 187.
138. C. Webster, *The Great Instauration* (1975), p. 218.
139. A. G. Debus, *Science and Education in the Seventeenth Century: the Webster-Ward Debate* (1970); J. Webster, *Academiarum Examen* (1654), p. 51; S. W(ard), *Vindiciae Academiarum* (Oxford, 1654), pp. 30, 31; Webster, *Great Instauration*, pp. 200, 204–5.
140. R. Godson, *Astrologia Reformata* (1696), pp. 4–5 (he also attacked contemporary natural philosophy as "foolish Foolosophy . . . blind guesses', p. 12); B.L. Ms Egerton 2378, f. 31.

Chapter 8 The Eighteenth Century (*pages* 238–69)

1. On the decline of astrology see below, pp. 276–83.
2. For a late example see R. Ball, *Astrology Improv'd* (1723). The author, an astrological physician and friend of George Parker, claimed to have studied the weather for forty years. The first edition of the work appeared in 1697.
3. Sparrow, 1726, sig. Av. (For the titles of eighteenth-century almanacs see Appendix I.)
4. See especially Partridge, 1739, largely devoted to the praise of Leadbetter. It contained Swift's verse, and plagiarisms from Hopton, Booker etc. For attacks see Wing, 1740, sig. C8; *Poor Robin*, 1741, sig. C8.
5. Saunder, 1705, sig. C2v; 1712, sig. C5v; 1714, sig. B3; 1715, sig. C4–v.
6. *Ladies' Diary*, 1723, sig. Av; White, 1750, sig. Av; idem, 1752, sig. Av.
7. C. Blagden, 'Thomas Carnan and the Almanack Monopoly', *Studies in Bibliography*, xiv (1961), p. 24n. (I am excluding here the sales of sheet almanacs.)
8. Partridge, 1708, sig. A3v–4, A5v; Gibson, 1712, sig. B3v. Among the episcopal licensers named (on Wing and other editions) were Benjamin Ibbot, F(ifield) Allen T(homas) Cartwright, J. Clapman, G. C., J. W., E. B., and W. G.
9. Blagden, pp. 203–4.
10. Parker, *Royal Speculum*, 1705, sig. A2 (2nd signature); *Parker's Ephemeris*, 1707, p. 4.
11. Parker, *Ephemeris*, pp. 4–6, 7; and later editions, *passim*, for attacks on Wing, Partridge and the Whigs; on Moore see also *A Double Ephemeris*, 1703, sig. A8v. On the dispute see also *D.N.B.*, s.v. Parker, and below, pp. 249–50
12. Blagden, 'Thomas Carnan', p. 26 and *passim;* for Heath see Taylor, *Hanoverian Practitioners*, pp. 180–1; *N. and Q.*, 1st ser., xi (1855), p. 441; below, p. 243
13. Blagden, pp. 234–5.
14. On the exploits of Harris see R. P. Bond, 'John Partridge and the Company of Stationers' *Studies in Bibliography*, xvi (1963), pp. 70–5.
15. e.g. in Coley, Gadbury, and *The Gentleman's Diary.*
16. The episode is discussed fully in Bond's article, cited above.
17. A Mr. Gadbury of Bristol, presumably a distant descendant, claimed in the mid-nine-

teenth century to hold the office of King's Astrologer: *N. and Q.*, 1st ser., v (1852), pp. 370–1.

18. See Appendix I for all these; on the Wing family see Everard Green, *Pedigree of the Family of Wing* (1886) and on Vincent Wing, senior, V. Wing, *Astronomia Britannica* (1669), p. 343. The successive editors of Moore are listed (with some mistakes) in W. Hone, *The Year Book* (1832), pp. 684–5, as John Wing, Tycho Wing, Wm. Harvey for Vincent Wing, Thomas Wright, Henry Andrews. Season referred to 'Mr. Moore alias Wright' (Season, 1772, sig. A6). Cf. also the astronomer Thomas Willson of N. Luffenham, Rutland (Pearse, 1764, sig. C8).
19. Appendix I; Taylor, *Hanoverian Practitioners*, pp. 110, 191–2, 339–40.
20. Ellis, *Orig. Letters*, pp. 307–8; *N. and Q.*, 1st ser., xi (1855), p. 441.
21. Season, 1733, sig. A3v; 1751, sig. A2; 1759, p. 3.
22. *N. and Q.*, 1st ser., xi (1855), p. 441; *The Mirror of Literature*, iv (1824), p. 403; *N. and Q.*, 1st ser., iv (1851), p. 162. On profits see further below, p. 263.
23. Weaver, 1725, sig. A3 (for details see above, p. 52); *Parker's Ephemeris*, 1730, sig. B.
24. See Partridge's and Parker's editions, *passim*, and the series they edited under the pseudonyms of J. Parrot (Partridge) and G. Kepar (Parker); also, e.g., Cookson, 1701, sig. C7v–8; Wing, 1702, sig. C7v–8.
25. Weaver, 1731, sig. C3; Partridge, 1739, introduction; Wing, 1740, sig. C8.
26. *Poor Robin*, 1741, sig. C8. The verse abused all the Company's editions.
27. Swift, *Predictions, passim*; for a full discussion see R. P. Bond, 'Isaac Bickerstaff, Esq.', in *Restoration and Eighteenth-Century Literature: Essays in Honor of Alan Dugald McKillop*, ed. C. Camden (Chicago, 1963), pp. 103–24; Bond, 'John Partridge', pp. 75–7.
28. e.g. *Great Britain's Diary for 1718*.
29. Season, 1750, sig. Av.
30. Anon., *Entered at Stationers' Hall* (1871), p. 23; *N. and Q.*, 5th ser., ix (1876), pp. 66–7.
31. 1736 edn., *passim*.
32. *Old Poor Robin, 1781–6* ('The Witch'); 'The Life and Adventures of Solomon Snip' followed in 1786–9. In similar vein the editor, John Pearson, published the 'Observations of Random Shandy' in Season's *Speculum* (e.g. 1786). For the catches: *Old Poor Robin*, 1787, sig. A3; 1790, p. 7.
33. Tipper, *Ladies' Diary*, e.g. 1706, 1710. The edition for 1707 carried the text of an interlude performed by the boys of Bablake Hospital in the mayor's parlour in Coventry on 27 June 1706, a day of thanksgiving for English victories, and listed the boys taking part: sig. B8v–C2v.
34. *Ladies' Diary*, 1717, pp. 15, 16.
35. Ibid., 1731, sig. Av.
36. Ibid., 1711, ep. ded; 1713, sig. Av. The magazine appeared in 1711 as *Delights for the Ingenious. Great Britain's Diary*, 1710, sig. Av., pp. 26–45. (*Parker's Ephemeris* was in many ways similar.)
37. *Ladies' Diary*, 1723, sig. Av (the editor was then Henry Beighton, but the sentiment was also Tipper's); ibid., 1747, sig. Av. *The Gentleman's Diary* was published from 1741.
38. e.g. *Ladies' Diary*, 1710, sig. A2–4; ibid., 1736, *passim*; see also Nicolson, 'New Astronomy', p. 31.
39. *N. and Q.*, 1st ser., xi (1855), p. 441.
40. Compilers are listed by Ellis, *Orig. Letters*, pp. 304–5, and discussed by Taylor, *Hanoverian Practitioners*; *Ladies' Diary*, 1759, sig. Av; Ellis, op. cit., p. 304; *The Mirror*, iv (1824), p. 404.
41. Blagden, 'Thomas Carnan', p. 24n (excluding sales of sheets).
42. Gadbury, 1703, sig. Av.
43. Salmon, 1705, sig. C8; Moore, 1705, sig. Av; see also Partridge, 1701, sig. A3v–4.
44. Partridge, 1706, sig. A5; Moore, 1707, sig. A8v; idem, 1708, sig. Av; Coley, 1707, sig. B3.
45. The phrase is by Gibson, 1707, sig. A4v (misprint for C4v).
46. Gadbury, 1707, sig. Av (the phrase was used earlier by Parker, *The Royal Speculum*, 1705, sig. A8).
47. Moore, 1707, pp. 4–7; Tanner, 1710, sig. C3; Partridge, 1705, sig. C6.

48. Gibson, 1711, sig. A8v, B7v; Cookson, 1711, pp. 44–8; for Parker see above, pp. 240–1, and below, pp. 249–50; Parker, 1711, sig. A2.
49. Partridge, 1706, sig. A4 (note the echo of Defoe in line 2); see generally G. S. Holmes, *British Politics in the Age of Anne* (1967) and the same author's *The Trial of Dr. Sacheverell* (1973).
50. Partridge, 1707, sig. A4; Tanner, 1707, sig. Bv, B6v–7.
51. Moore, 1708, sig. A4v, p. 13; Tipper, *Great Britain's Diary*, 1711, sig. B2.
52. Partridge, 1709, sig. A3v–4.
53. Dove, 1708, sig. A5, 6; Partridge, 1707, sig. B8; Moore, 1711, p. 14.
54. Canner, 1709, sig. C; Moore, 1710, sig. Av; Partridge, 1708, sig. C3.
55. Parker, 1707, p. 7; 1711, sig. A2, 3–4, v, 7, B6v–8, C4–8v.
56. Gibson, 1712, sig. B2v, 3v, 4v, 5v.
57. *Remarks and Collections of Thomas Hearne*, ed. Doble et al., Oxford Hist. Soc. (1885–1921), i, pp. 56, 177, 205; H. M. Petter, *The Oxford Almanack 1674–1946* (New York, 1946), pp. 10, 26–8.
58. Parker, 1715, sig. A2 and *passim.*
59. Partridge, 1716, sig. A4, B4.
60. Ibid., sig. B4.
61. Moore, 1717, sig. Av; Moore, 1730, sig. Av.
62. Partridge, e.g. 1715, sig. B5v; Moore, 1730, pp. 10–11.
63. Moore, 1731, pp. 10–11.
64. See above, Chapter 5; M. C. Jacob, *The Newtonians and the English Revolution, 1689–1720* (Hassocks, Sussex, 1976), ch. 3, an excellent account of Anglican millenarianism in that period.
65. e.g. Parrot, 1702, sig. B3; Fisher, 1704, sig. C6v–7v.
66. Moore, 1701, sig. C3v–4; 1703, pp. 7–10; 1706, p. 15; 1709, pp. 7–8; 1711, pp. 7–9, 1715, p. 7; 1717, p. 15; 1718, pp. 14–18.
67. Partridge, 1702, sig. C5–6v.
68. Tanner, 1702, sig. C3ff.; Kendal, 1701, sig. C6; Salmon, 1705, sig. C8; J. Corderoy, *The Key of Future Events* (1705), *passim.*
69. Andrews, 1702, sig. Av; 1704, sig. B4v–5; 1706, sig. Av; 1707, sig. C8; 1710, sig. C8v; 1711, sig. C7v; Coley, 1704, sig. C7v.
70. e.g. Wing, 1702, sig. C7; Wing, 1743, sig. C4v–5; 1745, sig. C8v; 1746, sig. C7v–8; Moore, 1734, pp. 9–10; 1736, p. 10; 1741, pp. 5–9; Andrews, 1750, sig. C6–7; Pearse, 1734, sig. A4v. For Floyer and Whiston see *D.N.B.*
71. Moore, 1750, sig. B6–8; 1757, pp. 7–8, 11–12.
72. Moore, 1763, pp. 7–12. The astrological dimension of millenarianism is not mentioned by the authorities on it in the eighteenth century, e.g. W. H. G. Armytage, *Heavens Below: Utopian Experiments in England, 1560–1960* (1960); E. P. Thompson, *The Making of the English Working Class* (Harmondsworth, 1968); see also below, pp. 266–7.
73. Partridge, 1730, sig. A2.
74. Moore, 1737, sig. Av.
75. Pearse, 1756–9, *passim;* the poem appears in the calendar. Pearse was presumably dead long since, and the poet declined to reveal his identity (1759, sig. B3). Quotations from, in order: 1758, sig. A7; 1756, sig. A5; 1757, sig. B6; 1758, sig. A7.
76. Moore, 1716, sig. Av (the poet was John Norris); Gadbury, 1736, sig. C8v.
77. Partridge, 1769, sig. C6, v.
78. For Poor Fred: Moore, 1731, sig. Av.
79. Pearse, 1770, sig. C5–8v.
80. There were several harsh references to early Methodists, e.g. Pearse, 1741, sig. C3v; Season, 1765, sig. B6ff.; *Poor Robin*, 1776, sig. Av. Season's account of a lecherous Methodist quack fused several of his obsessions.
81. Coley, 1701, sig. Av; Pearse, 1737, sig. A4v–5; Lane, 1730, sig. Cv.
82. Moore, 1775, sig. A2.
83. Andrews, 1723, sig. C7; Season, 1775–6 (Season was dead by this time).
84. Cf. Jacob, *The Newtonians and the English Revolution, 1689–1720,* and J. Redwood, *Reason, Ridicule and Religion: the Age of Enlightenment in England, 1660–1750* (1976).
85. Gadbury, 1708, sig. Av; cf. Jacob, op. cit., pp. 63, 197–8.
86. Saunder, 1716, sig. B4, 7, 8.
87. Pearse, 1768, sig. B3.

88. On the history (real and imaginary) of the society see D. Knoop and G. P. Jones, *The Genesis of Freemasonry* (Manchester, 1949), which does not, however, mention the almanacs. The compiler may have been Ebenezer Sibly (1751–1800), whose *A Complete Illustration of the Celestial Science of Astrology* (1788) was dedicated to the Freemasons by the author, 'your accepted Brother.'
89. Moore, 1708, sig. A3v–4; ibid., 1714, p. 15; Parker, 1716, sig. B; Partridge, 1731, sig. A3. The chronologies remained traditional in form, though with greater emphasis on military and political events. Pearse continued the old practice of recording new bridges over the Thames, e.g. Fulham, Putney, Wesminster, Kew, Blackfriars (1765, sig. C2v–4v). Andrews, 1765, offered a 'summary of English chronicles' on early history, in prose form (sig. C6–8v); Pearse supplied a history of translations of the Bible into English (1761, sig. C5–6v).
90. Tobacco: Andrews, 1770, sig. B6.
91. Moore, 1768, p. 9; see above, pp, 105–6.
92. Culpepper, 1702, sig. C2–3v; Wing, 1712, sig. C7v; Andrews, 1723, sig. C4–5.
93. Saunder, 1716, sig. A5ff.; 1717, C3–v; Wing, 1720, sig. C7v–8; Pearse, 1768, sig. C6; Season, 1770, sig. C3v–4.
94. Andrews, 1705, sig. Av, C–v; Partridge, 1708, sig. C2–v; Moore, 1758, p. 11; Season, 1773, sig. C6v.
95. Jacob, *The Newtonians*, pp. 61–2 and *passim;* D. Kubrin, 'Newton and the cyclical cosmos: providence and the mechanical philosophy', *Journ. of the Hist. of Ideas*, xxviii (1967), esp. pp. 325–6, 342; Moore, 1790, p. 44 (citing Whiston's *Six Discourses*).
96. Above, pp. 238–9; Saunder, 1712, sig. C3, 4v; 1714, sig. B3.
97. Wing, 1743, sig. C4v; 1744, sig. C7.
98. Hartley, 1734, sig. C8–v; Parker, 1741, sig. B.
99. Coley, 1731, sig. C5–v, quoted from J. Harris, *Lexicon Technicum* (1st edn., 1704, 1710); Moore, 1790, p. 44.
100. Gadbury, 1703, sig. Av.
101. See e.g. Partridge, 1768, sig. Av; Moore, 1788, p. 7.
102. Coley, 1723, sig. C7v; S. Penseyre, *A New Guide to Astrology* (1726), pp. 155–6. Penseyre was a native of Lausanne; his handbook on horary astrology is notable for its discussion of clients' fears about female sexual 'wickedness', including Lesbianism (pp. 184–6). For examples of flippant clients see e.g. *The Letters of Dorothy Osborne*, ed. G. C. Moore Smith (Oxford, 1928), p. 175; *The Diary of Dudley Ryder, 1715–16*, ed. W. Matthews (1939), pp. 336–7.
103. Gadbury, 1710, p. 14; Andrews, 1712, sig. C–3.
104. Season, 1733, sig. A3v; 1761, sig. A8; 1769, sig. Av; 1770, sig. C4v; 1772, sig. C4v; 1774, sig. C3.
105. Lane, 1731, sig. C8; Season, 1734, sig. A2–3, 4; Season, 1739, t.p., sig. A7; Season, 1750, t.p., sig. C8; *Poor Robin*, 1756, sig. C7–v.
106. Sir William Musgrave, *Obituary prior to 1800* (Harleian Soc.), vol. v (1903), p. 239; Blagden, 'Thomas Carnan', p. 24n; Season, e.g. 1750, sig. A2; 1751, sig. A2v; 1763, pp. 2–3; 1772, pp. 2, 4; *Poor Robin*, 1756, sig. C7–v.
107. Season, 1774, p. 2; cf. Season, 1763, p. 2.
108. See e.g. Season, 1755, sig. A4v; 1768, p. 8; 1771, p. 8; 1774, pp. 6–7 for approving references in the chronologies to Raleigh, Monmouth, Sacheverell, George I, Flamsteed, Newton, Wilkes and Beckford; abusive comments on Cromwell, the Old Pretender, snuff and tobacco; and notes on the capture of Gibraltar, the execution of Byng (which Season claimed to have foretold) and a famine in 1766 caused allegedly by profiteers.
109. Season, 1774, sig. C–v; 1762, p. 7. On the episode see C. Roth, *A History of the Jews in England* (3rd edn., Oxford, 1964), pp. 212–23.
110. Season, 1770, sig. C3v–4.
111. Season, 1762, sig. B3–C2 ('treatise on stout'), p. 7; 1763, sig. B4; 1770, sig. B4; 1774, sig. A6–B4. Tea was acceptable, but taken twice a day 'is bordering upon luxury': 1771, sig. B7.
112. Season, 1768, sig. A2; 1770, sig. B4.
113. e.g. Season, 1768, sig. C6; 1772, sig. A6, 7.
114. Season, 1768, sig. A8; 1769, pp. 8–9; 1764, sig. B7; 1756, sig. B4.
115. Season, 1769, p. 3; 1771, p. 4.; c.f. 1751, sig. A2v; 1762, sig. A6ff. A Mr. Rolt was

rector of Broomham (1772, sig. A8). Shelburne's house was at Bowood, Wilts.
116. Season, 1739, sig. A4 (repeated on subsequent occasions); 1762, p. 7.
117. Season, 1771, sig. C7v, C6.
118. Season, 1772, sig. C6v (and cf. sig. C7); 1774, sig. C6. On Wilkes see e.g. G. Rudé, *Wilkes and Liberty* (1962).
119. Season, 1763, sig. B4; 1768, sig. C. Season's opinion on the true date of Easter, 1761 (a vexed issue among the learned) was sought by 'an eminent lord at court', probably Shelburne, and published in London and Salisbury newspapers: 1762, sig. A6–B3.
120. Season, 1761, pp. 2–3.
121. Season, 1769, sig. B8–Cv.
122. Blagden, 'Thomas Carnan', *passim;* the figures dropped from 544,000 (1775) to 268,000 (art. cit., p. 40).
123. Anon., *Entered at Stationers' Hall* (1871), pp. 22–4.
124. E. Howe, *Urania's Children* (1967), p. 22; Blagden, 'Thomas Carnan', pp. 24n, 33, 40, 42; *The Mirror of Literature*, iv (1824), p. 403.
125. Season, 1787–9; quotations from 1787, pp. 36–7; 1789, p. 39.
126. Moore, 1789, p. 43; 1790, pp. 6–7; 1796, p. 40; 1797, pp. 38ff.; 1800, pp. 40–2. The rainfall data was first supplied for Royston (e.g. 1790), later for London.
127. *Old Poor Robin*, 1792, p. 34.
128. Hone, *Year Book*, p. 59; Moore, 1793, p. 45; 1788, p. 47.
129. *N. and Q.*, 1st ser., iv (1851), p. 162; Moore, 1789, p. 43.
130. Moore, 1788, p. 29.
131. Moore, 1789, pp. 21, 23, 25, 29; 1795, p. 2.
132. Ibid., 1792, p. 15 and *passim*; 1793, p. 19. The edition for 1792 was the first to discuss the Revolution. By contrast *Old Poor Robin* abandoned wit and denounced the revolutionaries, Tom Paine and English democrats such as Horne, Tooke, and Godwin as the fanatical successors of the Fifth Monarchy Men: 1793, pp. 37–47; 1794, pp. 38ff.
133. Ibid., 1794, pp. 42, 43, 45.
134. On popular English support for the Revolution, and on Paine, see E. P. Thompson, *The Making of the English Working Class* (Harmondsworth, 1968).
135. Moore, 1795, p. 47.
136. Moore, 1795, p. 42; 1796, p. 43; 1797, pp. 42–4; 1798, p. 44. For millenarianism in the 1790s see Thompson, op. cit.; C. Garrett, *Respectable Folly: Millenarianism and the French Revolution in France and England* (1975); Armytage, *Heavens Below.*
137. Moore, 1804, p. 24.
138. *The Mirror*, iv (1824), p. 403; Heywood, *Three Papers*, pt. iii, p. 17; G. Eliot, *Adam Bede* (1859), ch. xviii.
139. Hone, *Year Book*, p. 59.
140. Ibid., pp. 59, 685; *The Mirror*, iv (1824), p. 403; *The London Magazine*, 3rd ser., ii (1828), esp. pp. 600, 606.
141. *The London Magazine*, pp. 591, 601, 606; see also Heywood, *Three Papers*, pt. iii, pp. 17ff.; L. James, *Print and the People 1819–1851* (1976), pp. 53–9.
142. Bladgen, p. 266; Hone, *Year Book*, p. 684.
143. Blagden, pp. 271, 281; Heywood, *Three Papers*, pt. iii, pp. 11, 14, 16.
144. Heywood, *Three Papers*, iii, pp. 11, 28 (the impression for 1898 ran to 1,054,248 copies); E. Russell, *Astrology and Prediction* (1972), chs. 7, 8.
145. Heywood, op. cit., iii, pp. 16, 29; Blagden, 'Thomas Carnan', p. 38.
146. Mrs. Gaskell, *Cranford* (1853), chap. viii.
147. E. Howe, *Urania's Children* (1967); Russell, op. cit.; figures for *Old Moore* from *The Times*, 4 January 1975, p. 12, referring to the Foulsham edition; there is also an edition by Walker's.

Chapter 9 Conclusion (*pages* 270–92)

1. Thorndike, *Magic*, *passim*; Hellmann, *Wettervorhersage*; above, pp. 25–6.
2. Thorndike, vi, p. 165ff.; vii, p. 131; Cervantes, *Don Quixote* (Everyman edn.), i, p. 69. No study appears to exist of the Spanish almanac; several editions survive in the B.L.

3. See esp. J. H. Robinson, *The Great Comet of 1680* (Northfield, Minnesota, 1916), ch. 3.
4. Bollème, *Almanachs populaires*, pp. 24–6 and *passim*; R. Mandrou, *De la Culture populaire aux xviie et xviiie siècles* (Paris, 1964), pp. 56–9. See also J. Grand-Carteret, *Les Almanachs Français 1600–1895* (Geneva, 1968, first pub. 1896); E. Socard, *Etudes sur les Almanachs* (Troyes, 1882).
5. Bollèmè, *Almanachs populaires;* idem, *La Bible bleue* (Paris, 1975), pp. 22 and *passim* (see also the review by T. Zeldin in *Times Literary Supplement*, 17.9.1976, p. 1171); D. T. Pottinger, *The French Book Trade in the Ancien Regime 1500–1791* (Cambridge, Mass., 1958), esp. pp. 57, 59, 139–40.
6. Bollème, *Almanachs populaires*, pp. 20, 40–6; idem, *La Bible bleue, passim*; Zeldin, loc. cit.
7. See Bollème, *Almanachs populaires*, pt. iii.
8. There were some exceptions, e.g. Jean Petit who printed his address (in Paris) and advertised his services as astrologer and physician; Grand-Carteret, op. cit., p. 95.
9. English chap-books, a neglected field, are now being studied by Dr. Margaret Spufford of Keele.
10. See especially E. Defrance, *Catherine de Médicis: ses Astrologues et ses Magiciens-envoûteurs* (Paris, 1911).
11. Defrance, op. cit., *passim*; Thorndike, *Magic*, vii, pp. 94–106 and ch. xvi; E. Labrousse, *L'Entrée de Saturne au Lion* (The Hague, 1974), pp. 47n, 47–9.
12. Thorndike, *Magic*, vii, pp. 98–9; Grand-Carteret, op. cit., p. 4.
13. H. de Billy, *Certaine Wonderful Predictions* (1604), p. 7.
14. Grand-Carteret, op. cit., p. 2; Defrance, *Catherine de Médicis*, pp. 201ff., 216ff.; Thorndike, *Magic*, vii, p. 99 and n, and ch. v, *passim.*
15. For the significance of the 1650s see Labrousse, *L'Entrée de Saturne.*
16. B.L. Catalogue, under 'Ephemerides'; F. Dahl, *King Charles Gustavus of Sweden and the English Astrologers William Lilly and John Gadbury* (Uppsala, 1937), pp. 168, 171.
17. On this topic see W. R. McDonald, 'Scottish Seventeenth-Century Almanacs', *The Bibliotheck*, 4 (1963–6), pp. 257–322.
18. *Partridge's Observations for the Year 1691* (Edinburgh, repr. 1691); *1692.*
19. E. Evans, *Historical and Bibliographical Account of Almanacks . . . published in Ireland* (Dublin, 1897), *passim.* I am grateful for further information to Mr. M. Pollard of Trinity College Library, Dublin, who is working on the control of the Irish book trade.
20. For what follows see M. B. Stowell, *Early American Almanacs* (New York, 1977); H. Leventhal, *In the Shadow of the Enlightenment* (New York, 1976), ch. 2; G.L. Kittredge, *The Old Farmer and his Almanack* (Boston, 1904).
21. For the status and practice of astrology in America, see Leventhal, op. cit., ch. 2. My comments need revising in part in the light of A. R. Raymond's recent article, 'To Reach Men's Minds: Almanacs and the American Revolution', *New England Quarterly*, 51 (1978).
22. For a recent account of the English debate: N. H. Nelson, 'Astrology, *Hudibras*, and the Puritans', *Journ. of the Hist. of Ideas*, xxxvii (1976). For the French: Labrousse, *L'Entrée de Saturne.*
23. Webster, *Great Instauration, passim.*
24. *Bickerstaff's Almanack for 1710*, sig. C4; *Reliquiae Hearnianae*, ed. P. Bliss (1869), ii, p. 166; Foster, *Al. Oxon.*, iv, p. 1485; D. C. Douglas, *English Scholars* (1943), pp. 78–81. Hearne was also an old acquaintance of Parker.
25. J. Nichols, *Literary Anecdotes of the Eighteenth Century*, vi (1828), p. 228; for the club and its rules see R. Bowes, 'The Zodiac Club', *Cambridge Antiq. Soc.*, xiii (1908–9).
26. Above, p. 258; Thomas, p. 355; Whiston, *Six Dissertations* (1734), p. 234 (and see pp. 254, 262); Season, 1768, sig. A2; Moore, 1790, p. 44. On Mead's astrology see Bowden, 'Scientific Revolution', pp. 210–12.
27. Sibly, *A Complete Illustration of . . . Astrology* (1788), pp. 366, 618–19, 807ff. For Witchell see Taylor, *Hanoverian Practitioners*, p. 221.
28. For discussions see M. Graubard, 'Astrology's Demise and its Bearing on the Decline and Death of Beliefs', *Osiris*, xiii (1958); Thomas, esp. pp. 349–57 and ch. 22; Bowden, 'Scientific Revolution', conclusion.
29. Season, 1770, sig. C4v.
30. Wing, 1732, sig. C8 (citing Huygens); above, pp. 196-7.

31. I fully accept Dr. Bowden's thesis of an abortive scientific revolution in astrology. But this seems to explain its surprising longevity, in various forms, rather than its decline, as she suggests.
32. Thomas, esp. pp. 647–63.
33. Thomas, pp. 45, 277–8; the point was emphasized by John Bossy in his review, in *History*, lvii (1972), p. 402.
34. Cervantes, *Don Quixote* (Everyman edn.), i, 253. 'Thou talkest sometimes with so much sense', replies Don Quixote, 'that one would imagine thee to be something of a scholar.'
35. J. Calvin, *An Admonicion against Astrology Iudiciall*, trans. G. C. (1561), sig. A6ff. P(erkins), *Four Great Lyers*, sig. C2vff.
36. *Blagraves Astrological Practice of Physick*, epistle.
37. Jacob, *The Newtonians and the English Revolution*, *passim.*
38. P. Bayle, *Miscellaneous Reflections Occasion'd by the Comet which Appear'd in December 1680* (1708), i, pp. 27, 33 and *passim.*
39. For the early stages see Nelson, 'Astrology, *Hudibras* and the Puritans'.
40. (J. Younge), *Sidrophel Vapulans: or the Quack-Astrologer Toss'd in a Blanket* (1699), sig. A3v–4, p. 28 and *passim.*
41. Despite the fact that Partridge was ostentatiously loyal to the English crown after 1689.
42. Season, 1768, sig. C8. 'For such, alas! is their unhappy lot,' he continued, 'As soon as heard they are almost forgot.'
43. Act IV, sc. ii. For an exception see Penseyre's guide of 1726 (above, p. 437, n102)—written, significantly, by a foreign-born astrologer.
44. (New Wessex edn., 1975), ch. 26. The 'prophet' uses a combination of astrological and other lore. He is also mentioned, with others, in *Tess*, ch. 21.
45. Partridge, 1755, sig. C3; Season, 1762, p. 3.
46. Hardy, *The Return* (New Wessex edn., 1974), ch. 3.
47. Culpepper, 1749, sig. B; *Old Poor Robin*, 1782, p. 5; Season, 1769, p. 7
48. L. B. Wright, *Middle-Class Culture in Elizabethan England.*
49. For Continental manuals see Thorndike, *Magic*. The contribution of printing to the dissemination of astrology was recognized by Sebastian Brant: *The Ship of Fools*, ch. 65. (I owe this reference to Dr. Henry Cohn.)
50. Some references are collected in C. Clark, *Shakespeare and Science* (Birmingham, 1929), pp. 105, 137.
51. Thomas, p. 618; Heywood, *Autobiography, Diaries . . .*, ed. J. Horsfall Turner (Brighouse, 1882), iii, p. 125; above, p. 24.
52. *N. and Q.*, 6th ser., ix (1884), pp. 299, 316–17; G. Fox, *Journal*, ed. J. L. Nickalls (Cambridge, 1952), pp. 478–9.
53. W. L. Cross, *The History of Henry Fielding* (New York, 1963), ii, pp. 189–91. For Emily Brontë and R. L. Stevenson see A. C. Daley, 'The Moon and Almanacs of *Wuthering Heights*', *H.L.Q.*, xxxvii (1974). I am told that Jane Austen did likewise.
54. Above, pp. 144, 438.
55. Above, p. 54; Season, 1767, sig. Av.
56. Above, p. 147; cf p. 146 for links between changing time and calls for repentance.
57. Gadbury, *John Gadbury (Student in Astrology) his Past and Present Opinion of the Ottoman or Turkish Power* (1683), p. 6; *Autobiography and Anecdotes of William Taswell D.D.*, ed. G. P. Elliott, Camden Misc., ii (1853) pp. 29–31.
58. Sir T. Overbury, *Miscellaneous Works*, ed. E. F. Rimbault (1890), p. 93; Season, 1772, p. 3; above, p. 24.
59. Sir L. Namier, *Personalities and Powers* (1955), p. 54.
60. e.g. H.M.C., 1, *Appendix to 1st Rep.*, p. 33; *App. to 2nd Rep.*, p. 2.
61. See above, pp. 196–8.
62. D. Hirst, *The Representative of the People?* (Cambridge, 1975). Dr. Hirst suggests that on the eve of the civil war up to 40% of the adult male population had the right to vote (p. 105).
63. e.g. R. M., *Micrologia, Characters in Essayes* (1629), sig. C8v.
64. *The Letters of John Chamberlain*, ed. N. M. McClure (Philadelphia, 1939), ii, p. 185; (Birch), *The Court and Times of James the I* (1848), ii, p. 110; L. Aikin, *Memoirs of the Court of King James the First* (1822), ii, pp. 113–14; *C.S.P.D., 1611–18*, p. 597; *The*

Poems of Richard Corbett, ed. Bennett and Trevor-Roper (Oxford, 1955), pp. 63–5, 135–6. For an opposite reaction later ascribed to James see Thomas, p. 299.

65. *The Journal of John Aston, 1639*, ed. J. C. Hodgson, Surtees Soc., cxviii (1910), p. 12.
66. Above, pp. 72–7, 100; Lilly, *Life and Times*, pp. 88–90.
67. Thomas, pp. 313–14, 373–4.
68. *The Diary of Ralph Josselin 1616–1683*, ed. A Macfarlane (1976), pp. 234, 255, 294, 327, 334, 515; see also p. 15. His view that the White King was Charles, King of Scots, matched Lilly's current interpretation: Lilly, 1651, sig. A2v.
69. Josselin, *Diary*, p. 330.
70. *Diary of the Rev. John Ward*, ed. C. Severn (1839), p. 94.
71. *C.S.P.D., 1671–2*, p. 83.
72. Above, pp. 79–80; Thomas, pp. 299–300.
73. G. H. Jenkins, 'Welsh Books and Religion 1660–1730', Univ. of Wales, Aberystwyth, Ph.D., 1974, p. 538.
74. Labrousse, *L'Entrée de Saturne*, pp. 35n, 38; Thorndike, *Magic*, viii, p. 309.
75. Above, esp. pp. 63–5; Thomas, pp. 297–8.
76. Above, pp. 64–5, 205–8; Thomas, p. 297, n2; see also for the later part of the period L. Meager, *The New Art of Gardening* (1683 and other edns.); L. Mascall, *The Country Man's Jewel*, ed. R. Ruscam (1680), p. 307 (Mascall had been chief farrier to James I); J. Bell, *A Book of Cookery . . . with Certaine Points of Husbandry* (1605) p. 100; J. Archer, *A Compendious Herbal* (1673), sig. K2v; S. Gilbert, *The Florists Vade-Mecum* (1670 and other edns.); J. W(orlidge), *Systema Agriculturae* (4th edn., 1687), pp. 97, 307; but cf. his criticism in ch. xiv.
77. *N. and Q.*, 10th ser. iv (1905), p. 234; *A Seventeenth-Century Doctor and his Patients: John Symcotts*, ed. F. N. L. Poynter and W. J. Bishop (Beds. Hist. Rec. Soc., 1951), pp. 25, 38.
78. *Diary of the Rev. John Ward*, pp. 104–5.
79. Josselin, *Diary*, pp. 472, 477, 506, 515–16, 599, 615, 629, 638.
80. Ms note in Frende, 1587, sig. A3v (Canterbury Cathedral, V.2.17); B.L. Add. Ms 38, 599, fos. 59ff.
81. J. Evelyn, *Diary*, ed. E. S. de Beer (Oxford, 1955), iii, p. 81 and n, iv, p. 200; idem, *Kalendarium Hortense, or the Gardners Almanac* (1666), p. 5.
82. *Rural Economy in Yorkshire in 1641. Being the Farming and Account Books of Henry Best*, ed. C. B. Robinson (Surtees Soc., xxxiii, 1857), pp. 23, 97.
83. Leventhal, *Shadow of the Enlightenment*, pp. 39–44 and n; Kittredge, *Old Farmer and his Almanack*, pp. 309–12.
84. Thomas, *passim*; A. D. J. Macfarlane, *Witchcraft in Tudor and Stuart England* (1970), esp. pp. 30, 120.
85. Thomas, esp. pp. 314–15.
86. Evans, 1630, sig. B5.
87. T. Harley, *Moon Lore* (1885), p. 176 (and seq. for specific instances).
88. Above, p. 269; Lincolnshire, ed, Mrs. Gutch and M. Peacock (County Folk-lore Society, 1908), pp. 15–16; *The Folk-lore of Herefordshire*, ed. E. M. Leather (1912), p. 15; G. E. Evans, *The Pattern under the Plough* (1966), pp. 142–4; *N. and Q.*, 1st ser., iii, (1851), p. 381; ibid., 5th ser., x (1878), p. 55.
89. Bod. Ms Add. B8, f. 81v; in 1677 Coley wrote that he was visited by so many 'scholars and querents' that only at night was he able to work on his almanac (Ms Ash. 240, f. 213).

Index

The index does not include the Appendices. Peers are indexed under their titles, and biblical persons, except Christ, under *Bible.*

INDEX

Printed and bound by CPI Group (UK) Ltd, Croydon, CR0 4YY

19/06/2025

01903785-0001